AN IMAM IN PARIS

AN IMAM IN PARIS

Account of a Stay in France by an Egyptian Cleric (1826–1831)

(Takhlīṣ al-Ibrīz fī Talkhīṣ Bārīz aw al-Dīwān al-Nafīs bi-Īwān Bārīs)

By

Rifāʿa Rāfiʿ al-Ṭahṭāwī

Introduced and translated by

Daniel L. Newman

SAQI

ISBN: 978-0-86356-407-9

First published in hardback in 2004 by Saqi Books

This new edition published by Saqi Books, London, in 2011

A full cip record for this book is available from the British Library.
A full cip record for this book is available from the Library of Congress.

Printed and bound by CPI Group (UK) Ltd, Croydon, CR0 4YY

SAQI
26 Westbourne Grove, London W2 5RH
www.saqibooks.com

Contents

Note on Transcription

The transcription of Arabic words in this book is that of the *Encyclopaedia of Islam* (2nd edn), with the following deviations: k͟h = kh; d͟j = j; s͟h = sh; ḳ = q. The transcription does not reflect the regressive assimilation (*idghām*) of the lateral in the definite article *al* with the so-called 'sun letters' (t, th, d, r, z, s, sh, ṣ, ṭ, ḍ, ẓ, n): e.g. al-Ṭahṭāwī (and not aṭ-Ṭahṭāwī). In line with common usage, *hamza* is not transcribed in word-initial positions, whereas the so-called 'nunation' (*tanwīn*) – regular indefinite inflectional noun endings – is dropped throughout (except in some cases for the accusative singular *-an*), as are the anaptyctic vowels of catenated speech. Place names appear in their common historical English forms – e.g. Aleppo (instead of Ḥalab) – or in transliteration, usually followed by an English equivalent in brackets, when it involves little-known towns or areas for which no established English form is available, e.g. Ṭahṭā (Tahta). Arabic technical terms are transliterated and italicized, except for words such as 'Islam', 'Muslim' or 'sultan' where common sense has been allowed to prevail. Save for such familiar forms as *'ulamā'* (sing. *'ālim*), plurals of isolated Arabic words appear in the singular with the English regular plural *-s* marker, e.g. *sharīfs* (instead of *shurafā'*). The *tā' marbūṭa* noun end-marker is not rendered in transcription when it appears in pre-pausal positions, only when it is affixed to the head-noun in a genitive construction (*status constructus*), in which case it is transliterated as *t*, e.g. *madrasa*, but *madrasat al-alsun*.

Finally, a word about the dates. On the whole, only the Georgian dates are given, with the dates of the Muslim (lunar) *Hijra* calendar (which starts in 622 A.D., the year in which the Prophet Muḥammad emigrated from Mekka to Medina) added in the event of overlaps or ambiguity, in which case the *Hijra* calendar year comes first, e.g. 1236/1820–21.

Preface to the Second Edition

It is gratifying to note that the first edition of the book was very well received. In addition to its appeal to a wider audience interested in the early modern history of the Middle East and Alterist discourse, the book has enjoyed success as a text in university courses in the fields of Arabic literature, history, sociology and cultural anthropology.

If anything, the interest in Rifāʿa Rāfiʿ al-Ṭahṭāwī has increased in the English-speaking world, if references to him are a measure to go by. This is perhaps not as surprising as it seems in view of the fact that our protagonist has withstood the test of time and his views are as relevant now as they were over 150 years ago.

When faced with the prospect of a second edition, the question that arises is, of course, the extent to which the 'old one' needs to be revised and 'updated' lest it be out of step with contemporary scholarship. Whilst there is always room for improvement, change should not be an aim in itself, and it became clear that the second edition only required relatively minor amendments, additions and corrections.

Durham, August 2010

Preface

In more ways than one, the current work may be said to be an extension of my doctoral research into 19th-century Tunisian travellers to Europe. Time and again, I was struck by the huge importance of al-Ṭahṭāwī's book to modern Arabic literature and the development of modern Arab political and social thought, as well as its essential value as a source for any historical study in the field of Muslim Alterist discourse. Furthermore, the author is inextricably linked with the cultural Renaissance (*nahḍa*) of Egypt, in which he was one of its driving forces, and has rightly been called the father of Egyptian nationalism and of modern Islamic educational thought, as well as being one of the forerunners of modern Arab historiography. In spite of this, it took until the last quarter of the 20th century before the book was translated into a European language, first into French by Anouar Louca, then into German by Karl Stowasser.[1] Neither translation, however, was quite complete. The English-speaking reader, on the other hand, had to make do with a mere five and a half pages in a survey of modern Arabic literature.[2] It is indeed extraordinary that in what must be called a veritable wave of translations of modern Arabic literature into English from the mid–1970s onwards, the 19th century is conspicuous by its absence. Naturally, to a large extent this may be ascribed to changes in literary tastes as well as other factors, among which one may cite the political situation in the Middle East, whereas the award of the Nobel Prize for literature to the Egyptian author Nagīb Maḥfūẓ whetted the appetite of Western audiences for contemporary Arabic fiction. To be sure, most of the translations are aimed at the general public, yet the situation is not that different in the academic world, where research on Arabic literature seems to be split

1. Though respectively completed in 1957 and 1966, both translations were published in 1988: A. Louca, *Tahṭāwī. L'Or de Paris. Relation de voyage, 1826–1831*, Paris (Sindbad), 342pp. (based on the 1849 edn); K. Stowasser, *Rifāʿa al-Ṭahṭāwī. Ein Muslim entdeckt Europa. Die Reise eines Ägypters im 19. Jahrhundert nach Paris*, Munich (C. Beck), 339 pp. (based on the 1834 edn).
2. J. Haywood, 1971: 72–7.

between that of the modern age (the 20th century or, more precisely, the latter half thereof) and that of the Middle Ages (the so-called 'Classical' or 'Golden Age' of Arabic literature), while the literary output of the 19th century is exploited predominantly by historians, political and social scientists, linguists, etc.

Despite a firm intention to produce an English translation of the book, circumstances – both academic and personal – for a long time precluded me from devoting the necessary time to the project. At the same time, it may be said to be both fortuitous and fitting that the translation should have been completed in the year marking the 200th anniversary of the author's birth.

The introduction to the translation attempts to place both the book and its author in the appropriate historical context. However, it must be stressed that it has no pretensions to being a general study of the life and works of Rifāʿa al-Ṭahṭāwī. For while such an endeavour is long overdue in English (or in any other European language), the scope of the introduction is clearly delimited by the work in question.

I should like to take this opportunity to thank a number of people whose feedback has greatly contributed to this work. First and foremost, my thanks must go to Pierre Cachia (Columbia University) and Jacques Thiry (University of Brussels) who read early drafts of the work and provided many valuable and helpful comments and recommendations, which were subsequently incorporated into the definitive version. It stands to reason that I alone remain responsible for any remaining faults and errors. I should also like to extend my gratitude to Hossam El-Khadem (University of Brussels) and Robin Ostle (St John's College, Oxford) for their encouraging feedback on my translation. I am also pleased to be able to thank Nieves Paradela Alonso and María Luisa Ortega from the Universidad Autonóma in Madrid. Heartfelt thanks are equally due to the head of my college, Frans De Laet, for providing both logistical support and encouragement for my research. Finally, I owe a word of thanks to Saqi Books, and especially Sarah Al-Hamad, for their support and what sometimes seemed boundless patience.

PART ONE

INTRODUCTION

ONE

The 'Egyptian' Mission to Europe

Background

After destroying the power of the former rulers of Egypt, the slave-soldier dynasty of the Mamlūks,[1] Muḥammad ʿAlī (1770–1849) – a former Albanian mercenary who had been part of the Ottoman force sent to oust the French from Egypt (with the help of the British) – found himself in total control of the country. In 1805, he was appointed *walī* (governor) by the Ottoman Sultan, to whose empire Egypt belonged, and received the honorary title of *Pasha*. It was clear from the start that the new ruler was not going to allow his dominion to continue its slumber of times past. Nothing if not ambitious, Muḥammad ʿAlī Pasha set about building a

1. The Arabic *mamlūk* (pl. *mamālīk*), which as the passive participle of the verb *malaka*, 'to own', literally means 'one who is owned', was used for slaves of non-Muslim origin, especially those hailing from the European provinces of the Ottoman Empire, with a clear preference for Circassians (*Jarākisa, Sharākisa*). They were destined for duties at the court, for which they received special training. It was common for *mamlūks* who distinguished themselves to be granted their freedom, and many were to be found in the highest echelons of power. From 1250 to the Ottoman conquest of 1517, Egypt was ruled by several Mamlūk dynasties, which included such famous 'slave-soldier' sultans as Baybars (1260–77) and Qalā'ūn 'al-Alfī' (1278–90). In the mid–17th century, the Mamlūk Beys regained control over Egypt, albeit technically as vassals of the Ottoman Sultan. The Beys were organized in various 'Houses' (*bayt*), which were almost constantly involved in factional struggles for supremacy. It was not until Muḥammad ʿAlī's reign that the hold by the Mamlūk oligarchy over Egypt was finally broken. In Tunisia, too, many Mamlūks rose to high office within the Beylical administration; the most famous of them was undoubtedly the statesman and reformer Khayr al-Dīn al-Tūnisī, who after having held several ministerial posts in Tunisia ended his official career as Grand Vizier to the Ottoman Sultan. See ʿA. al-Jabartī, 1997: *passim*; *EI1*, s.vv. "Egypt" (C. Becker), "Mamlūks" (M. Sobernheim/J. H. Kramers); *EI2*, s.v. "Mamlūks" (D. Ayalon); A. Raymond [A. Ibn Abī 'l-Ḍiyāf], 1994: II, 38–40; D. Ayalon, 1949; U. Haarmann, 1988; H. Laurens, 1997: 66ff.

regional superpower (as well as a dynasty), which would on more than one occasion bring him into conflict with his liege lord in Constantinople. Having witnessed modern European warfare capability, Muḥammad ʿAlī realized that in order to further his ambition, he would require outside help in the guise of military aid from the West. It is not as if this approach was entirely new; indeed, the core of the Ottoman contingent sent to Egypt had been trained by German officers and constituted the first companies within the so-called 'New Army' (*niẓām-i jedīd*), set up by the 'modernizing' Sultan Selīm III (1789–1807).[1] Europeans had been involved in the modernization of Ottoman education since the first half of the 18th century, Count Claude-Alexandre de Bonneval (d. 1747) having founded the first school of geometry (*hendesehane*) in Constantinople in 1734,[2] whereas the famous Franco-Hungarian engineer Baron de Tott (d. 1793) set up a technical college.[3] These were followed by other institutes such as the Imperial Naval School (*Mühendishane-i bahri-i hümayun*, 1773) and the Military Engineering School (*Mühendishane-i hümayun*, 1784). The latter establishment marked the first milestone in the introduction of European-style education as its staff consisted for the most part of French military engineers.[4] This school also gave a new impetus to the translation movement started under Muṣṭafā III (d. 1774), shifting its focus to military manuals, especially French ones.[5] It was not until the reign of Selīm III that European experts and army personnel were brought in to build and train a European-style army, whereas it is interesting to note that the young Napoleon Bonaparte was at one time put forward as the head of a military mission to Turkey.[6] It was also in the same period of what can be called the Ottoman *perestroika* that for the first time permanent embassies were established in various European capitals: London (1793), Vienna (1794), Berlin (1795) and Paris (1796).[7]

Although at first Muḥammad ʿAlī's primary concern lay with all matters military, i.e. the formation of his own *Niẓām al-jadīd*,[8] he soon began to hatch far more ambitious plans, aimed at modernizing the entire

1. See S. J. Shaw, 1971; B. Lewis, 1969: 56ff. *et passim*.
2. Cf. G. Goodwin, 1994: 193, 195; de Tott, 1784: II, 78; S. Gorceix, 1953.
3. See G. Goodwin, *ibid.*, 92, 107; F. Hitzel in D. Panzac, 1985: 814; B. Lewis, 1994: 235ff.
4. Cf. F. Hitzel, *ibid.*, 815, 816–17; M. Göcek, 1986.
5. F. Hitzel, *ibid.*, 820–22.
6. F. Masson, 1897–1919: II, 96–7, 120–24; H. Laurens, 1997: 29–30.
7. After the Sultan's fall (1807) the system was suspended until the 1830s when it was restored by Maḥmūd II. Interestingly enough, the Vienna legation remained open for business throughout the entire period; see R. Davison, 1985.
8. On Egypt's 'New Army', see D. Nicolle, 1978.

country through the introduction of European sciences. The key to the project was, of course, education. And so, in addition to recruiting foreign military advisers and trainers, he chose the revolutionary path of sending people to the very places where these sciences had been developed.

The first to be sent was a Turk by the name of ʿUthmān Nūr al-Dīn (1797–1834), whose beginnings could hardly have been more humble as his father was a water carrier at Muḥammad ʿAlī's court. Nevertheless, for reasons still unclear, his name was put forward by Joseph Bokty, the consul-general of Sweden, who had been entrusted with selecting some boys for training in the European sciences in Italy. Although the initial idea was to send a group of students, ʿUthmān was the only one chosen, and in 1809 he left for Europe, returning to his native land only eight years later.[1] After a brief spell in Switzerland and Germany, he proceeded to Italy, where he stayed for several years and studied engineering and military and naval sciences (in Livorno, Milan and Rome), and finally ended up in Paris, where he remained for a little over a year to study French, English and mathematics. In addition to educating himself, ʿUthmān was also charged with acquiring as many books as he could, as Muḥammad ʿAlī, though illiterate himself until his late forties, was interested in any and all books dealing with the modern sciences and technologies or any other subjects that could be useful in the training of officials and the advancement of the country.[2]

Naturally, these works would have to be translated as well as printed, and so in addition to purchasing presses in France and Italy, he in 1815 sent the 15-year-old Syrian-born Niqūlā Massābikī (d. 1830) to Milan to learn the art of printing.[3] He was accompanied by at least two other Syrian Christian students, Rafāʾīl Massābikī and Ilyās Ṣabbāgh, who after a short and, it would seem, inauspicious stay in Milan went on to Turin where they took classes in, respectively, mathematics and chemistry.[4]

That the first students were sent to Italy was not exactly a coincidence. First of all, there were long-standing trading links between the two countries, and Italian city-states were the first to have diplomatic representation in

1. See J. Tagher, 1951; A. Louca, 1970: 34–5; J. Heyworth-Dunne, 1940: 328; A. Silvera, 1980: 7; F. Charles-Roux, 1955: 33–4.
2. Cf. J. Heyworth-Dunne, 1940: 328ff.
3. K. Ṣābāṭ, 1958: 148–51; J. Heyworth-Dunne, 1940: 331; A. Louca, 1970: 34; A. Silvera, 1980: 7.
4. A. Louca, 1970: 34. A total of some 28 students were sent abroad over a period stretching between 1809 and 1818; unfortunately, as a result of the fire that ravaged Citadel records in 1820, no records are available on any of them; Y. Artin, 1890: Annexe E.

Egypt (as well as in other Muslim lands). Second, it had the advantage of geographical proximity. Third, Italians made up more than two-thirds of the European expatriate community; predominantly traders, many also served as doctors or as officers in the Egyptian army. Finally, the presence of large Italian trading communities all along the Islamic shores of the Mediterranean meant that Italian was the most widely understood European language in both the Near East and North Africa. Indeed, at least one Muslim ruler, the Tunisian Aḥmad Bey (1837–55) actually spoke it and conversed in it with the French King Louis-Philippe during a state visit to France in December 1846.[1] The preferential linguistic relationship with Italy was reinforced through the *lingua franca*, the Romance-based commercial link language in use in the eastern and southern Mediterranean Basin since the Middle Ages. Within this creole, which was a mixture of several languages (both Eastern and Western), Italic dialects constituted the dominant Romance substratum.[2]

It is worth noting that none of these students was in fact a native Egyptian. The main reason for this was the fact that there were hardly any native Egyptian officials, nearly all being of foreign (Turkish, Georgian, Albanian) extraction, as indeed Muḥammad ʿAlī himself was. The Syrian Christian connection, on the other hand, went back to the French occupation of Egypt. Many of the Syrian expatriates, who had themselves escaped religious persecution at home or were descendants of refugees, established close links with the French administration, and because of their language skills (developed through long-standing trading contacts with Europeans) served as interpreters and liaison officers with the local population. In the face of Muslim opposition, Bonaparte very early on availed himself of the services of the local religious minorities (Syrian Christians, Copts) as they were most inclined towards the French cause. Minorities were also recruited into the French forces, a policy that would later become standard practice in the French military and was to be used with great success in other campaigns, notably in Algeria (e.g. the Zouaves). This led to the creation of a Greek legion, led by Colonel Papas Oglou, a Mamlūk renegade from Chios, who played a part in the suppression of the first Cairo insurgence of October 1798.[3] By far the most significant creation, however, was an independent Coptic legion placed under the command of Muʿallim Yaʿqūb (1745–1801). From an ill-trained ragtag band, the legion

1. A. Ibn Abī ʾl-Diyāf, 1963–65: IV, 100.
2. Cf. H. Schuchardt, 1909; H. and R. Kahane and A. Tietze, 1958.
3. G. Guémard, 1927.

grew into a disciplined fighting unit, which, by 1801, counted a staggering 24,000 men.[1] In addition, French policy included the appointment of minorities to local government structures, which were dominated by Copts, who had the additional advantage of being wholly Egyptian and of having administrative experience, though they had never been allowed officially to hold public office.[2] Bonaparte even appointed two Syrian Christians to his council of local dignitaries (*Dīwān*). Unsurprisingly, these types of collaboration with the foreign infidel, combined with rumours of plans for a semi-independent Egyptian state run by Copts,[3] caused a great deal of bad blood among the Muslim population, which feelings were exacerbated by accounts of maltreatment of Muslims by their Christian compatriots, while, one may suspect, the privileged economic status of many Syrian Christians (and to a lesser extent Copts) did not help matters much either.[4] As a result, many of them (though far fewer than one might expect), fearful of an anti-Christian backlash, accompanied the French expedition force home in self-imposed exile.[5] Some would continue to play a role as intermediaries between the East and their adoptive France. Notable examples were the Syrians Michel Sabbag (Mīkhā'īl al-Ṣabbāgh),[6] Joanny Pharaon (see below) and Bāsīl Fakhr (Basile Fackr),[7] and the Copt

1. See al-Jabartī, 1997: IV, 336, 647, 670; G. Delanoue, 1982: I, 86–90; H. Laurens, 1997: 222–3, 385 *et passim*; J. Savant, 1949; G. Homsy, 1921; Sh. Ghurbāl, 1932 (= ʿA. al-Jabartī 1997: 788–809); G. Douin, 1924; G. Guémard, 1927.
2. See ʿA. al-Jabartī, 1997: 1082–8; A. Raymond, 1998: 306ff.; H. Laurens, 1997: 68ff., 228ff., 421ff.; T. Philipp, 1985; A. Bittar, 1992; M. Motzki, 1979.
3. The famous Chevalier Théodore de Lascaris, a sometime knight of Malta who had joined the French forces, had indeed worked out such a scheme; cf. G. Douin, 1924; G. Haddad, 1970.
4. Cf. A. Raymond, 1998: 214–15, 270, 324ff.
5. According to contemporary sources, the expatriate contingent (excluding women and children) consisted of 438 Copts and 221 Greeks, as well as 93 Mamlūks; A. Raymond, 1998: 271.
6. The ʿAkka-born Christian Mīkhā'īl b. Niqūlā b. Ibrāhīm Ṣabbāgh (1784-1816) went on to work with the famous French orientalist Silvestre de Sacy (see Translation, note no. 2, p. 160), and wrote a number of works, among which a grammar of colloquial Arabic (Syrian/Egyptian), entitled *al-Risāla al-tāmma fī kalām al-ʿāmma wa 'l-manāhij fī aḥwāl al-kalām al-dārij* ('Treatise on the Speech of the Common People and Insight into the Features of the Vernacular'), which was published by H. Thorbecke in 1886 (*Mīhā'īl Sabbāg's Grammatik der arabischen Umgangssprache in Syrien und Aegypten,* Strasbourg, Karl J. Trübner Verlag, x/80pp.) is still a major source in the field of diachronic dialectology. See L. Shaykhū, 1991: 22-3, 34-5; G. Graf, 1944–53: III, 249–51; J. Aumer, 1866: 400ff.; Michaud, 1854: XXXIX, 427; Y. Sarkīs, 1928: 1192–4; J. Humbert, 1819: 291ff.; *GAL*, II, 479, *GALS*, II, 728; ʿA. al-Jabartī, 1997: IV, 1083.
7. A rich merchant, Fakhr (d. 1830) returned to Egypt, where he became the French consul in Damietta (under the consul-general Mathieu de Lesseps) and was put in charge of promoting trade with France. Fakhr's palatial Damietta dwelling became an obligatory

Ellious Bocthor (Ilyās Buqṭur al-Asyūṭī),[1] all of whom made substantial contributions to Arabic studies in France and played a significant role as cultural intermediaries.

In Egypt, certain Christian orders (especially the Franciscans) had already in the 18th century actively pursued the idea of sending young Copts (and later Syrian Christian refugees) to Europe in order to train as missionaries.[2] Though the policy was not as successful as it was in Syria and Lebanon, there is a record of at least one such student, a Coptic convert to Catholicism by the name of Rafā'īl Ṭūkhī (Raphael Tuki). Originally sent to Rome as a child to be trained as a priest, he stayed on and compiled the very first printed book to be used in Egypt, the *Missale Copto-Arabicum* (1734), which, tellingly, was published by the Vatican Propaganda College.[3] At about the same time, there also seems to have been an Egyptian-born Greek by the name of Constantin undergoing training as a *Jeune de langue* at the Paris-based Louis-le-Grand college.[4] Initially, the *Jeunes de langue* were young Levantine boys, who were recruited by the Capuchins for missionary training and/or to serve as dragomen at French diplomatic postings in the Levant. In the 1720s, however, the Levantines were replaced by French students (often the offspring of French diplomatic staff in the East), as the former were deemed incapable of meeting the required standards to complete the extremely demanding and rigorous linguistic training.[5]

---

stop for visiting French officials, aristocrats, etc. See J.-M. Carré, 1956: I, 197–8, 257; Auriant, 1923; *idem* 1933: 70–104; A. Silvera, 1980: 11.

1. On E. Bocthor (1784–1821), who briefly held the chair in colloquial Arabic at the prestigious Ecole des Langues Orientales (the precursor to the present-day Institut National des Langues Orientales), and was the century's first Arab lexicographer, see: A. Louca, 1958; Michaud, 1854: LVIII *Sup.* 408; F. Hoeffer, 1862–77: VI, 314; Y. Sarkīs, 1928: 574–5; 'U. Kaḥḥāla [n.d.]: II, 312; A. Messaoudi 2008: 72ff.; F. Pouillon 2008 (A. Messaoudi): 115.
2. Cf. J. Heyworth-Dunne, 1938.
3. J. Heyworth-Dunne, 1940: 326.
4. G. Dupont-Ferrier, 1921–5: III, 419.
5. The history of this institution went back as far as 1669, with the establishment of an *Ecole des Enfants de Langues* by Colbert in response to a shift in focus of French commercial policy towards the Mediterranean Basin and the creation of trading posts (*comptoirs*) in the main ports (*échelles*). In addition, French traders had lodged several complaints to the Marseilles Chamber of Commerce regarding the lack of interpreters and the detrimental effect this was having on commercial dealings. Though the prestigious *Collège de Clermont* (renamed *Collège de Louis le Grand* in 1682) was its official seat, classes were actually taught at the Capuchin monasteries in Pera (Constantinople) and Smyrna until 1700. This *Ecole des Enfants de Langues* produced such famous graduates as the Ruffins (father and son), Pétis de la Croix, Caussin de Perceval and Venture de Paradis (Bonaparte's chief interpreter in Egypt). In addition to the classics (Latin, Greek) and French, the boys received intensive training in Turkish, Persian and Arabic, alongside so-called *sciences accessoires* such as physics, history, geography, law, commerce

However, Ṭūkhī may not have been the first native Egyptian to receive instruction in Rome as records reveal the presence in France in the early 17th century of another Copt, a certain Yūsuf Ibn Abū Dhaqn (Josephus Abudacnus), who served as the main linguistic informant to the Dutch Arabist Thomas Erpenius (1584–1624) during the latter's stay there (1609–11).[1] Unfortunately, little is known about Abū Dhaqn, whose educational attainment seems to have been quite poor, since according to Erpenius he 'could not read classical Arabic' and was thus able to help the Arabist develop his conversational skills only.

Christians (and Jews) had always had more contacts with Europeans, and none more so than those of the Levant. Indeed, many Syro-Lebanese clerics received religious training in Europe, especially Rome. Arguably one of the first Levantines to spend a long period there was the Maronite Jibrā'īl al-Qilāʿī, who had been 'recruited' by a Franciscan passing through his village around 1468. Three years later, he left for Italy where he was to stay for 23 years, after which he returned to his native Lebanon as a missionary.[2] In 1583, the Papal authorities in Rome set up a Maronite seminary (Collegium Maronitarum), which produced a number of famous scholars, some of whom even settled in Europe,[3] e.g. Jibrā'īl al-Ṣahyūnī (Sionita),[4] Ibrāhīm al-Ḥāqilī (Abraham Ecchellensis),[5] Yuḥannā al-Ḥaṣrūnī (Hesronita),[6] Yūsuf Simʿān al-Simʿānī (Assemanus).[7] In addition to boosting Oriental studies in

and drawing. See AN AJ62 12 (anon. Report on the history of the Ecole des Langues Orientales Vivantes); F. Masson, 1881: 905–30; G. Dupont-Ferrier, 1921–5: III, 360–98.

1. See A. Hamilton 1994; M. Houtsma, 1888: 6–12.
2. Al-Qilāʿī left a huge number of letters (written in the Syriac script, the so-called *Garshūnī*), which are a primary source regarding the Maronite and Syriac Jacobite communities in the Mamlūk period. See R. Jabre Mouawad, 2001.
3. See P. Raphael, 1950.
4. This scholar (d. 1648) went on to teach Arabic and Syriac at the Sapienza College, and was later invited by the French King Louis XIII to lecture at the Collège Royale (the future Collège de France). Together with al-Ḥāqilī, he produced the first polyglot Bible to include Syriac and Arabic (1628–42); moreover, he collaborated with al-Ḥaṣrūnī on the famous 'Maronite Grammar' (*Grammatica Arabica Maronitarum*) and the Latin translation (1619) of an (anonymous) abridgement of Sharīf al-Idrīsī's *Kitāb nuzhat al-mushtāq fī ikhtirāq al-āfāq* ('The Pleasure Excursion of One Who Wishes to Travel through the Horizons') – also known as 'The Book of Roger' (*Kitāb Rūjar, al-Kitāb al-Rūjarī*), in reference to the author's patron, Roger II, the Norman ruler of Sicily. The abridgement, which had been printed by the Rome-based Medici press in 1592, was the very first Arab geographical work to receive attention in Europe. See G. Graf, 1944–53: III, 351–3; L. Shaykhū, 1924: 137 (no. 507); J. Fück, 1955: 73–4.
5. See G. Graf, 1944–53: III, 355–9; L. Shaykhū, 1924: 88 (no. 312).
6. See G. Graf, 1944–53: III, 354–5; L. Shaykhū, 1924: 91 (no. 323); J. Fück, 1955: 74–5.
7. This was undoubtedly the most famous of these Maronite expatriate scholars. As curator of the Arabic and Syriac manuscripts at the Vatican library, he compiled a monumental

Europe through translations and research into Arabic language, literature and culture, these clerics were also the first native carriers of European culture in their homeland. Those who returned home played a crucial role as intermediaries between East and West because of their linguistic skills and intimate knowledge of European culture. These contacts between Syrian Christians and the West were also instrumental in the introduction of printing in the Near East, the St Antony monastery in Qazḥayyā (Lebanon) obtaining its first (Syriac) press in 1610. The first Arabic press was set up in Aleppo in 1702, and others followed in al-Shuwayr (1734) and Beirut (1751).[1] The missionary schools set up in the Near East by various orders (mainly Jesuits) formed another important avenue of contact with Europe; the most famous were the establishments at ʿAyn Ṭūra (1734) and ʿAyn Waraqa (1789).

Massābikī's mission, which lasted four years, directly resulted in the creation in 1821 of the Official Government Press in the Cairo suburb of Būlāq.[2] Though officially headed by ʿUthmān Nūr al-Dīn, Massābikī was in charge of the day-to-day running of the press that he had brought back from Italy. Interestingly enough, the very first book to roll off the press was an Italian-Arabic dictionary by the Syrian Melchite priest Rafā'īl Anṭūn Zakhūr (1759–1831), who had been one of the official interpreters to the French occupation force.[3] In the same year, the press started printing

catalogue, entitled *Bibliotheca Orientalis Clementino-Vaticana*, dedicated to Pope Clement XI. Assemanus also played an important official role as the Pope's envoy to the most important religious gathering of the 18th century, i.e. the synod at the al-Luwayza monastery in Lebanon (1736). This, the second such meeting after that in Qannūbīn in 1596, consolidated the close relationship between Rome and the Maronites (who had accepted Papal authority in 1180), and brought the latter's liturgy more in line with that of the Roman Catholic Church. See G. Graf, 1944–53: III, 444–55; L. Shaykhū, 1924: 118–19 (no. 421).

1. See J. Nasrallah, 1958; Kh. Ṣābāt, 1958; *EI2*, s.vv. "maṭbaʿa" (G. Oman/Günay Alpay Kut), "djarīda" (B. Lewis-Ch. Pellat/P. Holt/P. Hitti).
2. See *EI2*, s.v. "Būlāḳ" (J. Jomier); A. Riḍwān, 1953. For a detailed catalogue of the early output of the press, see J. T. Reinaud, 1831; T.. Bianchi, 1843.
3. *Qāmūs Iṭālyānī wa ʿArabī. Dizionario italiano e arabo, che contiene in succinto tutti vocaboli che sono più in uso e più necessari per imparar a parlare le due lingue correttamente*, 266/6pp. This cleric, whose family had emigrated to Cairo from Aleppo in the early 18th century, received his religious instruction in Rome, where he studied at the St Athanasius college (1775–79), after which he stayed on for another two years to perfect his Italian. In France, he became known as Don Raphaël de Monachis. The only native Egyptian member of the Institut d'Egypte (in the *Littérature et Beaux-arts* class), he was the chief interpreter to the *Dīwān* set up by General Menou in November 1800. In recompense for his services to the French army, Don Raphaël in 1803 became the first incumbent of the chair in dialectal Arabic (created especially for him) at the prestigious Ecole des Langues Orientales, where Champollion was among his first pupils. He held the chair until

a Turkish-Arabic court bulletin for official use only, which was little more than a record of reports from the various government departments. This register was entitled *Jurnāl al-Khidiw* ('The Khedivial Journal'), which thus became the world's first printed Arabic periodical.[1] Six years later, this was succeeded by a veritable official gazette, the *Waqā'i' Miṣriyya* ('Egyptian Events'), with Shaykh Ḥasan al-ʿAṭṭār (see below) as its first editor. The first issue of this bilingual Turkish-Arabic publication, which later became *al-Waqā'i' al-Miṣriyya*, saw the light on 3 December 1828 (25 Jumādā I 1244).[2]

The second stage in Muḥammad ʿAlī's grand educational designs was, of course, the provision of schooling at home. At the time, the Egyptian educational system, like that in other Islamic countries, consisted of religious schools (*kuttābs*), usually attached to mosques, where Muslim children received rudimentary religious instruction and were taught basic reading and writing skills. As for the country's famous university-mosque,

---

1816 when he was succeeded by another Egyptian expatriate, Ellious Bocthor, though it took until 1821 for the latter to be officially appointed, whereupon he became the second (and last) non-European to hold the rank of professor. On his return to Egypt, Don Raphaël started working as an interpreter, and was among the first teachers at the school set up by ʿUthmān Nūr al-Dīn. The Egyptian government press also published his translation of Pierre-Joseph Macquer's manual of silk printing, *Art de la teinture en soie* (Paris, Desaint, 1763, ix/86pp.), under the title *Ṣinā'at ṣabāghat al-ḥarīr* (1238/1823, 12/118pp.). See ʿĀ. Nuṣayr, 1990: 163 (no. 1061), 192 (no. 6/441); Y. Sarkīs, 1928: 895–6; C. Bachtaly, 1934–35; ʿA. al-Jabartī, 1997: 1084ff.; A. Silvera, 1980: 7; L. Shaykhū, 1924: 109–10 (no. 387); G. Graf, 1944–53: III, 255–6; J. Heyworth-Dunne, 1940: 337–8; A. Lọuca, 1970: 34 (note 4); A. Raymond, 1998: 300; L. de la Brière, 1897: 59.

1. At first handwritten and then lithographed, the 'journal' appeared very irregularly before becoming a weekly and finally a daily publication. See A. Ayalon, 1995: 14–15; I. ʿAbduh, 1983: 29–34. It should be pointed out, however, that many scholars (P. di Ṭarrāzī, 1913–4: IV, 214–15; I. ʿAbduh, 1951: 23–5; A. Muruwwah, 1961: 73, 142, 148–9; P. Vatikiotis, 1991: 182, note no.6 [p. 516]; *EI2*, s.v. "djarīda" [B. Lewis *et al.*]) bestowed this honour on another periodical, *al-Tanbīh* ('Notification'), which was allegedly published in Alexandria from early December 1800 onwards by order of the French General Menou, who indeed on 25 November 1800 announced the creation of a 'journal arabe' of that name, whose aim should be to spread '*dans toute l'Egypte la connaissance des actes du gouvernement français, à prémunir les habitants contre les préventions et les inquiétudes qu'on pouvait chercher à leur inspirer, enfin à entretenir la confiance et l'union qui s'établissent de plus en plus entre ces peuples et les Français*' (quoted in A. Raymond, 1998: 233). Some (P. di Ṭarrāzī, 1913–14: I, 48–9; J. Zaydān, 1957: IV, 48) have given precedence to another publication, entitled 'The Daily Events' (*al-ḥawādith al-yawmiyya*), based on the account by al-Jabartī that Ismāʿīl al-Khashshāb (d. 1814), the Secretary of Bonaparte's *Dīwān*, was entrusted with preparing accounts of daily developments within the French administration which would then be translated into French for the benefit of the troops. However, even al-Jabartī does not state that the Arabic versions were also printed. In an attempt to solve the problem, P. di Ṭarrāzī took it one step further and stated that *al-Ḥawādith al-Yawmiyya* and *al-Tanbīh* were one and the same publication. Whatever the case may be, there are no records to suggest that either was ever printed, nor has a single copy survived.
2. For a history of this publication, see I. ʿAbduh, 1983. Also see A. Ayalon, 1995: 13ff.

al-Azhar, this provided little general education, concentrating on religious sciences and the Arabic language, whereas the job opportunities of its graduates were limited to preaching or scribal duties.[1] Things were not much different for the Coptic minority, whose children also received little more than basic instruction, and for whom no higher education was available at all. The first step towards the creation of a specialized school system intended to provide both present and future officials in his administration with the necessary skills came in 1816, when Muḥammad ʿAlī set up a school at the Citadel where the palace Mamlūks were taught calligraphy and arithmetic. Soon afterwards, the curriculum was expanded to include Turkish, Persian and Italian, as well as basic military training.[2] In 1820, a geometry school was also set up, which was primarily aimed at training land surveyors. At the request of ʿUthmān Nūr al-Dīn, this school was in May 1821 relocated to Būlāq, where he had set up a library at the palace of Ibrāhīm Pasha, the viceroy's son and heir apparent, with the books he had purchased in Europe.[3] One of the teachers at this school was the French architect Pascal Coste, who would later make a name for himself with his research on Arab and Islamic architecture.[4] In 1825, the school was again moved, this time to Qaṣr al-ʿAynī, and was renamed *Madrasa jihādiyya* ('Military School').[5] ʿUthmān, who had been put in charge of the Būlāq school, retained his position and moved with it to its new premises. Like the earlier avatars, the Military School was not accessible to Egyptians, allowing only Turkish, Georgian, Armenian, Greek and Kurdish students.[6] Indeed, the viceroy's intention was to train an *Ottoman* aristocracy to form the backbone of his power, for which purpose he ordered the purchase of white slaves in Constantinople.[7] Muḥammad ʿAlī realized, however, that despite the presence of foreign teachers (predominantly Italians, Italian also being the chief medium of instruction), the school would not be able to deliver either the level or the diversity of education he wanted, whereas he

1. For a contemporary account, see E. Lane, 1923: 60ff. (early education), 215ff. (on al-Azhar). Literally meaning 'the radiant (one)', the mosque took its name from the Prophet's daughter Fāṭima, who was known as 'Fāṭima al-Zahrā'', i.e. 'the brilliant/ radiant one'. This, the oldest Muslim university in the world, was built in Cairo 970–72, immediately after the Fāṭimid dynasty took control of Egypt; see "al-Azhar", *EI1* (A. Wensinck), *EI2* (J. Jomier).
2. A. Louca, 1970: 36.
3. J. Tagher, 1951: 393; G. Brocchi, 1841: I, 159–61.
4. J. Heyworth-Dunne, 1938; 108; A. Louca, 1970: 36; J.-M. Carré, 1956: I, 287.
5. For more details on this school, see A. ʿAbd al-Karīm, 1938: 221ff.
6. Y. Artin, 1890: 70; A. Silvera, 1980: 6–7.
7. A. Louca, 1970: 41.

was also mindful of the inherent dangers of teaching through interpreters.[1] He therefore instructed his adviser on foreign matters, Boghos Bey Yūsuf, to arrange a study stay in Europe for a group of students. In January 1826, the latter contacted Drovetti,[2] the French consul-general, and asked him to which country the contingent should be sent. Though himself of Italian extraction, Drovetti strongly argued in favour of France, claiming that religious prejudice in Italy, combined with anti-Egyptian feeling over the country's war with Greece, would make life difficult for the students.[3] At the same time, it should be said that as early as 1811, the French, in the guise of Edme-François Jomard[4] – the editor of the monumental *Description d'Egypte* – had already submitted a '*plan pour la civilisation de l'Egypte par l'instruction*' (via Drovetti), under which Egyptian students would go to France for training in the modern sciences.[5] In fact, it went back even further than that. Bonaparte, himself, saw education, especially French education, as a means of conquering the minds of people and of spreading

1. Cf. A. Silvera, 1971.
2. Born in Barbania, Bernardino Drovetti (1776–1852) was a lawyer in Livorno before enlisting in the French army after the first Italian campaign in 1796, and later accompanied the French troops to Egypt as ADC to General Murat. In 1802, at his own request, he was appointed vice-consul to Egypt, serving under Mathieu de Lesseps, whom he replaced in 1807. He actively curried favour with Muḥammad 'Alī and in September 1807 organized the defence of Cairo against the British. Thanks to his privileged contacts with the ruler, Drovetti had obtained permission to look for Egyptian antiquities, aided and abetted by the French Colonel Boutin and with the connivance of the French government. In 1811–12, he organized a number of digs in Memphis and Thebes (the Valley of the Kings). In 1814, Louis XVIII's government replaced him as he was considered a Bonapartist. However, he did not leave Egypt, choosing instead to continue his archaeological researches, entering in direct competition with the English consul, the famous Arabist Henry Salt. In March 1820, he persuaded Muḥammad 'Alī to send an expedition to the Siwa oasis in his relentless quest for archaeological treasure. The account of this journey was shortly afterwards edited by E. Jomard (*Voyage à l'Oasis de Syouah*, Paris, 1823). In 1821, Drovetti again became consul-general of France. In 1829, he returned to his native Italy and settled in Turin, where he died. The vast collection of antiquities he had amassed during his stay in Egypt ended up in the museum of Turin (though he had first offered it to French museums). For a detailed study of his life, see R. Ridley 1998.
3. R. Ridley 1998: 206–7; A. Louca, 1970: 37; A. Silvera, 1980: 8.
4. A graduate from the prestigious *Ecole Polytechnique*, the engineer, geographer and archaeologist Edme-François Jomard (1777–1862) was one of the 67-strong contingent of scholars that accompanied the French troops to Egypt. A member of the *Institut d'Egypte*, he was officially inducted into the *Institut de France* in 1818, and ten years later founded the Cartography Department (*Département des Cartes et Plans*) at the French National Library. In March 1828, Jomard, together with Laplace, Humboldt, Cuvier, Walckenaër and Malte-Brun, founded the Société de Géographie. See J.-M. Carré, 1956: *passim*; A. Louca, 1970: *passim*; C. du Bres, 1931.
5. F. Charles-Roux, 1955: 34; A. Louca, 1970: 33, 253–4; A. Silvera, 1980: 5–6.

the ideas and principles of the French Revolution and civilization. As such, it was just another propaganda tool – albeit a very powerful one – like the celebration of Islamic festivals and Bonaparte's expressions of admiration of Islam, or the incorporation of locals into the French army. Shortly after taking Malta (on the way to Egypt), he ordered that a group of some 60 Maltese boys from the island's most prominent families be sent to France for education, with a view to creating a local élite imbued with French ideas and the French Cause. Unfortunately, he soon discovered that this policy would not work with Muslim notables in Egypt; at the same time, his attention was needed for more pressing practical matters, such as fighting battles and controlling a generally hostile population.[1]

Shortly before ʿUthmān Nūr al-Dīn left Paris at the end of his study stay, Jomard entrusted him with another copy of the proposal to give to the viceroy.[2] However, ʿUthmān's loyalties lay with Italy, and he did not press the issue with Muḥammad ʿAlī, who decided to postpone things.[3]

Despite intensive lobbying by both the pro-Italian faction within the highest echelons of his administration (led by Boghos and ʿUthmān) and British diplomats, the viceroy in the end decided the tug of war in favour of Drovetti. One may speculate that the arrival shortly before of a group of French officers (led by General Boyer) to train the Egyptian military was a factor that strongly pleaded in favour of France.[4] Furthermore, to one such as Muḥammad ʿAlī, most of whose modernization projects were aimed at increasing his military capability, the military superpower status of France (and the advantages to be drawn from this) must have been a powerful element of persuasion as well. Indeed, at the very moment the viceroy took his decision, construction work on two frigates was going on at the Marseilles shipyards.[5] In addition to motive, there came also opportunity with the arrival of a French ship, *La Truite*, in Alexandria in March 1826. After being received at the court by the viceroy, the captain of the vessel, a certain Robillard, went on to pay an official visit to General Boyer's training camp at Abū Zaʿbal. Nothing if not mercurial, Muḥammad ʿAlī decided to strike while the iron was hot and ordered the formation of the student contingent so that they could sail to France on *La Truite*.

1. Cf. A. Silvera, 1980: 4–5.
2. A. Louca, 1970: 35.
3. G. Douin, 1923: 110.
4. See G. Douin, 1923.
5. See G. Douin, 1926.

The Students

Initially, the group consisted of forty-four members, chosen (as was the case for most court appointments) mainly for reasons of favouritism rather than on merit or ability, many of them hailing from leading Cairene families.[1] Only eighteen of the students had been born in Egypt; the others were Circassians, Greeks, Georgians, Armenians (the most prominent among them being the Artīn brothers)[2] and Turks, whereas two (Muṣṭafā Mukhtār Efendi and Aḥmad Efendi) came from Muḥammad ʿAlī's hometown of Kavalla. As a result, the majority were Turkish-speaking, though some of the Turkish-speakers could also converse in Arabic, while others had some Italian. None of them knew any French. All of them were Muslims, except for the four Armenian Christians.

The educational background of the students was quite poor: eleven of them had had no education whatsoever and few could boast more than an elementary knowledge of arithmetic. Twenty-five of them had spent some time at the Būlāq and/or Qaṣr al-ʿAynī schools, while three (Rifāʿa, Aḥmad al-ʿAṭṭār, and Muḥammad al-Dashṭūṭī) had studied at al-Azhar.

In terms of age, the students also made up a motley crew, the youngest (the Cairo-born Muḥammad Asʿad) being barely fifteen (the other six below the age of eighteen were also born in Egypt), whereas the eldest, the Turk Ḥasan al-Iskandaranī (one of the leaders) was thirty-seven. The average age was twenty-one (nineteen of the students were below that age), which meant that, at twenty-four, al-Ṭahṭāwī was only slightly older than the others.

The group was led by three high officials, ʿAbdī Efendi and the aforementioned Muṣṭafā Mukhtār Efendi and Ḥasan al-Iskandarānī, who were destined for training in, respectively, civil administration, military organization, and naval engineering and administration.[3]

The 'second-class' status of the students of native Egyptian stock became clear from the studies for which they were destined. While the Turks, Circassians and Armenians were slated for military and administration-related courses, naval, and political sciences – i.e. all leading directly to high

1. For a full list of the participants, see E. Jomard, 1828: 109ff.; J. Zaydān, 1957: IV, 21–2; J. Heyworth-Dunne, 1938: 163. Also see A. Silvera, 1980: 8ff. In the first year of the mission, five students (among them the Egyptian shaykhs Muḥammad al-Ruqayqa and al-ʿAlawī) returned home, while another two Egyptians (Ḥusayn Efendi and Qāsim al-Jundī) were added.
2. See Translation, note no. 4, p. 359.
3. On these three men, see Translation, notes, pp. 131–2.

office within government – the Egyptians dominated in more 'practical' fields such as natural history, metal founding, mechanics, engraving and typography, and chemistry, all of which were held in relatively low esteem by the ruler, who did not set great store by what he considered to be purely academic pursuits of no immediate use to him or his government.

The students left Cairo on 18 March and set sail for Alexandria on board small boats. The journey, which involved several stops at villages along the way, took four days. They were put up at the viceroy's sumptuous Alexandria palace to await their departure for France some twenty-three days later. On 13 April, the party boarded the ship, which sailed the following day.

From Alexandria, they went towards Crete, then to Sicily, where they dropped anchor off Messina and stayed for five days (28 April–3 May), without, however, being allowed on shore because of quarantine regulations. Then they continued their journey towards Naples, thence sailing on to Corsica (12 May) and Marseilles. After a sea journey lasting thirty-two days, the ship finally docked in Marseilles on 15 May 1826. The adventure was about to begin. But before recounting their experiences in Europe, it is time to take a closer look at the most famous member of the mission and the author of the only account of it.

TWO

Life of al-Ṭahṭāwī

Auspicious Beginnings[1]

The small market town of Ṭahṭā (Tahta) lies on the west bank of the Nile in Upper Egypt (al-Ṣaʿīd), some 430 km south of Cairo, midway between the district capitals Asyūṭ (Asyut) and Ṣuhāj (Sohag). Once the site of a temple dedicated to the god Horus, the town never occupied a prominent place in history. However, it was here that on 14 October 1801, as the last French soldiers were leaving Egyptian soil in defeat, a young baby boy was born into a noble and wealthy family of *sharīfs*,[2] whose branches could be found all over Upper Egypt.

On his father's side, his lineage went all the way back to the Prophet Muḥammad via his daughter Fāṭima, and his ancestors included the famous mystic saint (*walī*) Sīdī Jalāl al-Dīn Abū 'l-Qāsim (d. 1361), who

1. We are fortunate to have two contemporary biographical accounts of al-Ṭahṭāwī's life – one full-length study written by his disciple Ṣ. Majdī (1958), and a short sketch by his long-standing rival ʿA. Mubārak (1886–8: XIII, 53–6). Also see G. Delanoue, 1982: II, 383–487; A. Badawī, 1959; Ḥ. F. al-Najjār [n.d.]; M. al-Ḥijāzī, 1975: 3–135; M. ʿImāra [al-Ṭahṭāwī], 1973–80: I, 9–241; ʿA. Al-Rāfiʿī, 1930: 498–543; J. Heyworth-Dunne, 1937–42; Y. Sarkīs, 1928: 942–7; Y. Dāghir, 1972–83: II, 552–5; *EI1*, s.v. "Rifāʿa Bey" (Maurice Chemoul); J. Zaydān, 1910: II, 19–24; *GAL*, II, 481; *GALS*, II, 731; ʿA. Ḥamza, 1950: I, 88–138. For al-Ṭahṭāwī's role in the Egyptian translation movement, also see J. al-Shayyāl 1951: *passim*; J. Heyworth-Dunne, 1938: *passim*. Aspects of his political and social thought are discussed in I. Altman, 1976; G. Delanoue, 1982: II, 462ff.; E. Orany, 1983; J. Cole, 1980; L. ʿAwaḍ, 1962–6: II, 175–246; A. Hourani, 1989: 69–83; L. Zolondek, 1964. For al-Ṭahṭāwī the educationist, see S. Ali, 1994; J. Livingston, 1996; J. Heyworth-Dunne, 1938; L. ʿAwaḍ, 1962–6: I, 7–19. His historical and work and thought are examined in J. Crabbs, 1984: 67–86 *et passim*; Y. Choueiri, 1989: 3–24. For an overview of al-Ṭahṭāwī's works, see G. Delanoue, 1982: 618–30; A. Badawī *et al.*, 1958; Y. Sarkīs, 1928: 1996–8.
2. *sharīf* (pl. *shurafāʾ*) denotes a freeborn man who occupies an eminent position in society because of his noble and illustrious ancestry; *EI1*, s.v. "sharīf" (C. Van Arendonk); S. Elatri, 1974: 403–4.

gave his name to the mosque and Qur'ān school (*madrasa*) in the town. The boy's mother, Fāṭima, was the daughter of Aḥmad al-Farghalī al-Anṣārī, whose ancestry went back to the Medinese Khazraj tribe, who are commonly designated as *al-Anṣār*, i.e. 'Helpers' (of the Prophet), in recognition of their assistance to the Prophet after his flight from Mekka (622 A.D.). The boy's proud parents named their only child Rifāʿa, after one of his mother's ancestors, Rifāʿa b. ʿAbd al-Salām al-Khaṭīb ('the Preacher') al-Anṣārī, whose tomb is still today a popular pilgrimage site.[1] The family enjoyed great respect and standing within the community, several members being judges (*qāḍīs*) and scholars (*ʿulamāʾ*); his maternal uncles, for instance, included the grammarian and poet Abū ʾl-Ḥasan ʿAbd al-Azīz al-Anṣārī, the *Ḥadīth* (religious traditions) expert ʿAbd al-Ṣamad al-Anṣārī, and the Shāfʿī *faqīh* (legal scholar) Farrāj al-Anṣārī. In traditional Muslim society, great kudos was conferred upon families of such pious ancestry, and throughout his life Rifāʿa would remain extremely proud of his noble descent, referring to it on several occasions.[2]

Like so many rural families, the Abū ʾl-Qāsim witnessed a dramatic reversal of fortunes with the introduction of Muḥammad ʿAlī's land reforms, which included the abolition of the *iltizām* (tax farming) system.[3] Rifāʿa's father was one of those tax farmers (*multazim*) whose property was expropriated, as a result of which he was reduced to poverty overnight. So, after a relatively carefree childhood, during which Rifāʿa got much of his early education from his uncles, he left Ṭahṭā with his parents in 1813, as his father desperately sought means to provide for his family. After staying with relatives from the Abū Quṭna family at Mansha't al-Nīda (near the district capital of Jirjā), they went on to Qinā (Qena) and thence to Farshūṭ

1. His full name was Abū ʾl-ʿAzm Rifāʿa Rāfiʿ Ibn Badawī al-Ḥusaynī al-Qāsimī al-Shāfiʿī (Ṣ. Majdī, 1958: 17; Translation: Preface).
2. See Translation: Preface, Second Essay (First Section); al-Ṭahṭāwī, 1973–80: I, 537ff. (*Manāhij*).
3. The principle of the *iltizām* involved the sale at auction (*muzāyada*) – usually held in September – of the right to collect taxes (*mīrī*) in a district, village, urban property, etc. In return, the concession holder (*multazim*) – usually a local official or notable – was granted part of the *iltizām* for his own use (the so-called *ūsya* land). Though originally granted for one or several years, *iltizāms* in Egypt had on the eve of Muḥammad ʿAlī's reign become hereditary properties, held by members of the ruling caste; for instance, in the late 18th century, all of Egypt's agricultural revenues were controlled by a mere 1,600 Mamlūks and army officers (especially janissaries). As a result, the state was deprived of part of the agricultural income. Furthermore, yields were systematically reported below their actual levels in order to limit the tax attachment. In 1812, Muḥammad ʿAlī confiscated all Upper Egyptian *iltizāms* without compensation; Lower Egyptian *multazims*, on the other hand, were compensated (1814). See *EI2*, s.vv. "iltizām" (G. Baer), "mültezim" (F. Müge-Göçek); G. Baer, 1962; R. Owen, 1993: 12ff.; A. Raymond, 1998: 9.

(east of Nagʿ Ḥammādī), before returning to their native town, where they moved in with the mother's family. Rifāʿa's father died soon afterwards. It was during those three years on the road that Rifāʿa, whose intellectual ability had already manifested itself, learned the entire Qur'ān by heart under the supervision of his father. He had also started studying some of the texts in use at the al-Azhar mosque with the help of his uncles.

The First Exile

In 1817, after a two-week boat voyage on the Nile, mother and son arrived in Cairo, where Rifāʿa enrolled at al-Azhar, the undisputed centre of learning in the Near East. Here, he received a classical training in the religious sciences and Arabic (grammar and rhetoric) from some of the most eminent scholars of his day, among them Ibrāhīm al-Bājūrī (grammar and Qur'ān exegesis),[1] Ḥasan al-Burhān al-Quwīsnī,[2] Muḥammad al-Damanhūrī,[3] and Muḥammad Ibn Shāfiʿī al-Faḍālī (*Ḥadīth*),[4] whose attention he attracted

1. As his name indicates, Ibrāhīm Ibn Muḥammad al-Bājūrī (1783–1860) was born in the village of Bājūr (Manūfiyya province). Undoubtedly one of the most famous *'ulamā'* of his day, he in 1847 became *shaykh al-Azhar*, a post he held until his death. He wrote a huge number of commentaries and glosses on works of Islamic law, theology, grammar, rhetoric, etc. Under this scholar, al-Ṭahṭāwī also studied the comprehensive treatise on syntax, entitled *Mughnī al-labīb 'an kitāb al-a'ārīb* ('The Intelligent Person's Guide to Desinential Inflections') by the 14th-century Egyptian grammarian Jamāl al-Dīn Ibn Hishām al-Anṣārī (see below). See M. `Abd al-Raziq, 1922: 760; G. Delanoue, 1982: I, 109–18; "al-Bādjūrī", *EI1* (T. Juynboll), *EI2*; Y. Sarkīs, 1928: 507–10; ʿA. Mubārak, 1886–8: IX, 2–3; *GAL*, II, 487; *GALS*, II, 741.
2. This blind *shaykh* (d. 1838), who became rector of al-Azhar in 1834, was a specialist in inheritance law, on which he wrote an authoritative text, *Risāla fī 'l-mawārīth* ('Treatise on Inheritances'); see ʿU. Kaḥḥāla [n.d.]: III, 43. With him al-Ṭahṭāwī read the *hadīth* collections *Jamʿ al-Jawāmiʿ* by the polymath Jalāl al-Dīn al-Suyūṭī (d. 1505) and the *Mashāriq al-anwār al-nabawiyya min ṣiḥāḥ al-akhbār al-Muṣṭafawiyya* by Ḥasan b. Muḥammad (al-ʿAdawī al-Ḥamzāwī) al-Ṣaghānī (1181–1252), who is perhaps best known for his lexicographical endeavours such as the supplements to al-Jawharī's uncompleted dictionary, *al-Ṣiḥāḥ*, and his own *al-ʿUbāb* ('The Floods'); see Y. Sarkīs, 1928: 1208–9; ʿU. Kaḥḥāla [n.d.]: III, 279.
3. With this *shaykh* (d. 1284/1868–9) al-Ṭahṭāwī studied the often published commentary (*sharḥ*) by the Egyptian Ibn ʿAqīl (d. 1367) of Ibn Mālik's famous grammar manual *al-Alfiyya*. Al-Damanhūrī would later on join the faculty of the School for Translation until becoming tutor to Muḥammad ʿAlī's sons. See Ṣ. Majdī, 1958: 56; Y. Sarkīs, 1928: 883–4. On Ibn ʿAqīl see ʿU. Kaḥḥāla [n.d.]: VI, 70; *GAL*, II, 88; *GALS*, II, 104; Y. Sarkīs 1928: 187–8.
4. Very little is known of the life of this scholar (d. 1821), who had also been one of al-Bājūrī's teachers. Al-Faḍālī wrote two works: *Risāla fī lā ilāha illā 'llāh* ('Treatise on "There is no God Except God"') and *Kifāyat al-ʿawāmm fīmā yajibu alayhim min ʿilm al-kalām* ('What Is Sufficient for the Common People to Acquaint Them with the Things They Must Know about Scholastic Theology'). Both of these works were commented by al-Bājūrī. Al-Ṭahṭāwī studied the famous *ḥadīth* collection by the 9th-century scholar

by writing an *urjūza* (a poem in the *rajaz* metre) on the unity of God (*tawḥīd*).[1] However, the one who would have the greatest influence on the young *ʿālim* was Shaykh Ḥasan al-ʿAṭṭār (see below), who instilled in his protégé a love of learning and a passion for poetry, while arousing his interest in medicine, astronomy, history and geography, as well as in the new European sciences that he had witnessed first-hand during his visits at the Institut d'Egypte. At al-Azhar, al-Ṭahṭāwī also studied several works of ṣūfism (*taṣawwuf*), and under Shaykh al-Bukhārī he read the famous *Kitāb al-Ḥikam* ('Book of Maxims') by the ṣūfī Ibn ʿAṭā' Allāh al-Iskandārī (d. 1309), a member of the Shādhilī brotherhood.[2] He also received instruction from Aḥmad b. ʿAlī al-Damhūjī (d. 1848), who would become *shaykh al-Azhar*, i.e. Rector, in 1838. A member of the Khalwatiyya order (*ṭarīqa*),[3] he was a *khalīfa* (official representative) of the famous Shaykh ʿAbd Allāh al-Sharqāwī[4], a contemporary of the historian al-Jabartī.

While still a student, al-Ṭahṭāwī regularly returned to the south, where he did some teaching at the Yūsufī mosque in the west-bank town of Mallawī (*c.* 50km south of al-Minyā) and that named after his ancestor in his native Ṭahṭā. During his first classes, at the end of his first year at al-Azhar, he already impressed scholars with his lectures on *Ṣughrā al-Ṣughrā*, a famous theological work by the Moroccan-born Muḥammad Abū ʿAbd Allāh al-Sanūsī (d. 1490).[5] After four years at al-Azhar, al-Ṭahṭāwī received several *ijāzas*, i.e. permissions from *shaykhs* to teach their courses, and as from 1821 he, too, became a lecturer at al-Azhar. It seems that he had a natural talent for teaching and soon made a name for himself, specializing in *ḥadīth*, logic, rhetoric, poetry and prosody. Besides the already-mentioned *urjūza*,

---

Muḥammad b. Ismāʿīl al-Bukhārī (*al-Jāmiʿ al-Ṣaḥīḥ*) with al-Faḍālī. See G. Delanoue, 1982: I, 104–9; Y. Sarkīs, 1928: 1453–4; *GAL*, II, 489; *GALS*, II, 744.

1. According to Ṣ. Majdī (1958: 25), al-Faḍālī was so impressed with the work that he promised to write a commentary on it. Unfortunately, it is not known whether he actually did so.
2. q.v. *EI1*, s.v. "Ibn ʿAtā' Allāh" (Brockelmann); *GAL*, II, 117–18; ʿA. Mubārak, 1886–88: VII, 70; Y. Sarkīs, 1928: 184–5.
3. On this *ṣūfī* society, which spread to Egypt (from the Caucasus via Anatolia) in the late 15th century, see B. G. Martin, in N. Keddie, 1972: 275–305; E. Bannerth, 1964–66; E. Lane, 1923: 251.
4. Appointed *shaykh al-Azhar* in 1793, al-Sharqāwī (1737–1812) was later put at the head of the *dīwān* set up by Napoleon (25 July 1798) as part of his Islamist appeasement policy. Al-Sharqāwī continued to hold this office until the withdrawal of the French forces. On this scholar, who wrote several works on Shāfiʿī law and commentaries, see G. Delanoue, 1982: I, 84ff.; Y. Sarkīs, 1928: 1115–17; *GAL*, II, 479–80, *GALS*, II, 729; ʿU. Kaḥḥāla [n.d.]: VI, 41–2, XIII, 400.
5. Y. Sarkīs, 1928: 1058–9; ʿA. Ibn Sūda, 1950: 292; *GAL*, II, 250, *GALS*, II, 352–3; ʿU. Kaḥḥāla [n.d.]: XII, 132.

al-Ṭahṭāwī during his student days also composed a *khātima* ('conclusion') to the famous treatise of syntax entitled *Qaṭr al-nadā wa ball al-sadā* ('The Dripping of Moisture and the Beneficent Wetness') by Ibn Hishām al-Anṣārī (1309–60).[1] In his early teaching career at al-Azhar, he is known to have composed at least two other didactic poems; one on geometry (no doubt under the influence of al-ʿAṭṭār) – of which two verses have been preserved in the *Takhlīṣ* (see Sixth Essay, Seventh Section) – and one on the methodology (*muṣṭalaḥ*) of *ḥadīth*.

However, life for a young scholar like Shaykh Rifāʿa, as he was now known, was not exactly a bed of roses, not least because of the paltry salary. In order to supplement his meagre income and support his mother, he was compelled, like so many of his colleagues, to seek remunerated employment elsewhere. It is worth pointing out that even established *shaykhs* had a number of sidelines and were not, provided the price was right, averse to teaching private classes or performing religious ceremonies for private individuals. No lesser man than the above-mentioned al-Sharqāwī – the *shaykh al-Azhar* – made a start on what would eventually become quite a fortune through gifts received for the performance of *dhikrs* (*ṣūfī* rituals involving the repetition of specific formulae in glorification of God) at the houses of wealthy patrons.[2] In al-Ṭahṭāwī's case, the obvious thing was, of course, teaching, and in addition to private classes to the sons of the Turkish elite of Cairo, he also taught a few hours a week at a private school for Mamlūks, which had been set up by Muḥammad Lāzughlī. It was his former mentor al-ʿAṭṭār who came to the rescue and intervened on his behalf to secure a post as a preacher (*wāʿiẓ*) in one of the units of Muḥammad ʿAlī's newly founded *niẓām jadīd* (1824). This marked a milestone in the young man's life as it brought him for the first time into close contact with Europeans (mostly Frenchmen), who had been employed by the viceroy to train his army. Second, it was while in the military that al-Ṭahṭāwī was able to see first-hand some of the effects of

1. The Egyptian scholar Jamāl al-Dīn Abū Muḥammad b. Hishām al-Anṣārī studied with the leading grammarians of his day and may be considered the last of the great classical Arabic grammarians in the tradition of Sībawayh and Ibn Jinnī. The depth and range of his scholarship were already praised by Ibn Khaldūn, who referred to him as 'one of the rare wonders of the world'. Ibn Hishām wrote numerous works on various aspects of grammar, but is best known for *Shudhūr al-dhahab fī maʿrifat kalām al-ʿArab* ('Gold Extracts Regarding the Knowledge of the Speech of the Arabs'), on which he also wrote an extensive commentary, and *Mughnī 'l-labīb ʿan kutub al-aʿārib* (see Translation, note no. 3, p. 190). Al-Ṭahṭāwī also edited Ibn Hishām's commentary of the *Shudhūr* (Būlāq, 1837, vi/194pp.). See *EI1*, s.v. "Ibn His̲h̲ām" (M. Ben Cheneb); *GAL*, II, 23–5; *GALS*, II, 16; Y. Sarkīs, 1928: 273–6; Ibn Khaldūn [F. Rosenthal], 1986: II, 289–90 *et passim*.
2. Also see A. Marsot, 1977.

Muḥammad ʿAlī's modernization programme. And when, two years later, it was decided to send a student contingent to France, al-ʿAṭṭār quite naturally thought this would be a great opportunity for his former pupil and had him appointed *imām* to provide the group with religious guidance during their stay in the heathen Europe. In the end, al-Ṭahṭāwī stayed in Paris for five years and the experiences, know-how and skills acquired during his Paris days, which will be discussed in the next chapter, were to have a decisive and lasting impact on the cultural and scientific development of his native country.

Ḥasan al-ʿAṭṭār: An Early Reformist ʿĀlim

Although initially Muḥammad ʿAlī had relied strongly on the *ʿulamā'*, his modernization of the state quickly gave rise to bad blood among *ʿulama'*.[1] A notable exception was Ḥasan al-ʿAṭṭār (1766–1835), who, as we have seen, was to play an important role in the life of al-Ṭahṭāwī, and thanks to whom the latter was included in the student mission to France.[2]

The son of a small perfume merchant (*ʿaṭṭār*) of Moroccan extraction, al-ʿAṭṭār seems to have been endowed with an exceptional mind, and despite his rather irregular attendance of classes at al-Azhar, combined with work in his father's business, he qualified at a very early age as a teacher and eventually (1830–34) became *shaykh al-Azhar*, in which position he quickly gained a reputation for his wide interests, which extended beyond the traditional sciences of Arabic and religious exegesis.[3]

When the French invaded Egypt, al-ʿAṭṭār, like so many of his fellow *ʿulamā'*, fled to Upper Egypt, where he stayed for some eighteen months. Upon his return to Cairo, he was one of the few *ʿulamā'* to establish contact with members of the Institut d'Egypte, and was invited to witness their experiments; he even taught Arabic to several of them.[4] His visits to the

1. For an excellent discussion, see D. Crecelius, 'Non-ideological responses of the Egyptian Ulama to modernization', in N. Keddie, 1972: 167–209; A. Marsot, 'The beginnings of modernization among the Rectors of al-Azhar (1798–1879)', in W. Polk and R. Chambers, 1968: pp. 267–80; *idem*, 'The role of the *ʿulamā'* in Egypt during the early nineteenth century', in P. Holt, 1968: pp. 264–80; *idem*, 'The *ʿulamā'* of Cairo in the eighteenth and nineteenth centuries', in N. Keddie, 1972: 149–65.
2. See *EI1* & *EI2*, s.v. "al-ʿAṭṭār" (H. Gibb); F. De Jong, 1983; G. Delanoue, 1982: II, 344-57; M. ʿA. Ḥasan, 1968; ʿA. Mubārak, 1886–88: IV, 38–40; P. Gran, 1979: *passim* (esp. chap. 4); ʿA. Ramaḍān, 1948; Y. Sarkīs, 1928: 1335–7; A. Taymūr, 1967: 19–38; ʿA. al-Jabartī 1958–67: VII, 334–41; *GAL*, II, 473; *GALS*, II, 720.
3. Cf. al-Ṭahṭāwī, 1973–80: I, 536 [*Manāhij*].
4. E.g. the hot-air balloon, electricity, gases; ʿA. al-Jabartī, 1997: IV, 148ff., 156–60; P. Gran, 1979; A. Raymond, 1998: 349–51.

Institut at the sumptuous Ḥasan Kāshif palace,[1] and his close intercourse with French scholars aroused his interest in the modern European sciences and raised the awareness of their importance to the development of his own country. It seems he was particularly impressed with the printing press, the large numbers of books the French had at their disposal and the fact that they had been designed to facilitate the acquisition of knowledge.[2] In al-ʿAṭṭār's personal account of his relations with the French, he refers to them as 'peaceful people', who 'are violent only towards those that make war on them'. He even reports that the French scholars invited him to stay with them, but after some hesitation the *shaykh* wisely declined the offer as he realized it would have made him an outcast in his native society.[3] For all of the above, it would be stretching a point to call al-ʿAṭṭār a reformer or modernizer, let alone a Westernizer, as there is no question of a coherent ideological construct of any shape or form. Yet, his views of the ways in which Islamic society should advance clearly prefigured the ideas formulated by such people as Khayr al-Dīn al-Tūnisī, Muḥammad ʿAbduh or indeed Rifāʿa al-Ṭahṭāwī. Like them, he believed that the answers lay not in blindly copying Europe, but rather in taking those things that could benefit their native societies and by rediscovering the wealth of Islamic culture and sciences, many of which were at the basis of modern European technology and inventions. He was very much part of a traditional Islamic scholarly tradition, as his literary output clearly shows, and it is therefore difficult to see that he could have conceived of 'progress' as being rooted in anything other than Divine Law.

While he was impressed by French technology and progress, he was far less so by the general frivolous behaviour of the French troops, who squandered all their money 'between the muleteer and the wine-merchant' (*bayna ḥammār wa khammār*), a reference to the popular donkey races organized in the streets of Cairo.[4]

1. The scientists' private quarters, however, were located at the mansion of Ibrāhīm Katkhudā al-Sinnārī. See J. Goby, 1953.
2. ʿA. Mubārak, 1886–88: IV: 38. Al-ʿAṭṭār's fellow *ʿulamā'* were equally taken in by the French scholars' activities and books; indeed, the number of Egyptian visitors to the library must have been quite substantial since the French even hired a librarian, Ibrāhīm Ṣabbāḥ; cf. A. Raymond, 1998: 291–4; ʿA. al-Jabartī, 1997: IV, 154–6; P. Gran, 1979: 189–90.
3. This is further borne out by the account by the French diplomatist Baron Boislecomte of his visit to al-ʿAṭṭār in 1833, during which the latter apparently told him: 'I enjoy receiving Europeans, but I invite them to come at an hour I am not accustomed to receiving visitors since I would not be doing myself any good as far as the *ʿulamā'* are concerned.' (G. Douin, *La mission du baron Boislecomte. L'Egypte et la Syrie en 1833*, Cairo, IFAO, 1927, pp. 142–3, quoted in G. Delanoue,1982: 347).
4. A. Raymond, 1998: 301. It was indeed the moral behaviour of the French that most

This 'modernist' *shaykh* also stood out from his fellow Islamic scholars by his *Wanderlust*, which took him all over the Ottoman Empire. He left Egypt in March 1803, with the intention of travelling to the European provinces of the Ottoman Empire.[1] Sailing first to Istanbul, he subsequently made his way (for reasons still unknown) to the town of Shkodër – then also known as *Iskandariyyat al-Arna'ūd* ('Alexandria of the Albanians') or *Iskandariyyat al-Rūm* ('Alexandria of the Byzantines') – where he taught, and had a wife and child, both of whom died.[2] By the middle of 1808, al-ʿAṭṭār had returned to Istanbul, where he met with the highest religious authority in the Ottoman Empire, the *shaykh al-Islām* (Grand Mufti), ʿArab-Zādeh Meḥmed. Al-ʿAṭṭār presented him with one of the works he had written during his stay in Shkodër, entitled *Tuḥfat gharīb al-waṭan fī taḥqīq nuṣrat al-shaykh Abī 'l-Ḥasan* ('The Foreigner's Gift in the Report on the Victory of Shaykh Abū 'l-Ḥasan'),[3] on which ʿArab-Zādeh wrote a glowing eulogy.

After a brief residence near or in the town of Üsküdar (Scutari), al-ʿAṭṭār slowly embarked on his homeward journey, with stops in Izmir, Damascus (where he arrived in April 1810) and Jerusalem, after which he toured Palestine. He subsequently returned to Damascus (May 1811) and resumed his teaching at a city *madrasa* (religious school) until leaving for Mekka to perform the pilgrimage. And so, in 1813, after a sojourn abroad of a decade, al-ʿAṭṭār found himself once again on his native soil. It seems he almost immediately took up his teaching post at al-Azhar, where, just a few years later, he would have the young al-Ṭahṭāwī as one of his pupils. Despite the age difference, a close friendship quickly developed between them, and the *shaykh* imparted his wide erudition in non-traditional sciences such as medicine, geometry, astronomy, geography and history, as well as in Qur'ān and *ḥadīth* exegesis, logic and Arabic grammar and rhetoric, on all of which he is known to have written treatises.[4]

Meanwhile, al-ʿAṭṭār's intellectual standing continued to grow and did not remain unnoticed at the court, where he was held in high esteem by the ruler himself. Muḥammad ʿAlī's respect for al-ʿAṭṭār was, one may

offended observers like al-Jabartī, who expressed disgust at their burial practices, alcohol consumption, food and acts of public indecency (ʿA. al-Jabartī, 1969: 32–5, 65; *idem*, 1975: 12/43, 29/57).

1. On al-ʿAṭṭār's wanderings, see the excellent study by F. De Jong, 1983.
2. ʿA. Mubārak, 1886–88: IV, 40.
3. For the other works he wrote during his expatriation, see F. De Jong, 1983: 112ff.; P. Gran, 1979: 197–208.
4. For a list of al-ʿAṭṭār's works (very few of which were actually printed), see F. De Jong, 1983: 112–26.

suspect, further increased by the obvious endorsement by the latter of his modernization policies, which apparently brought him in conflict with his long-time friend, the historian ʿAbd al-Raḥmān al-Jabartī (1753–1826),[1] who fiercely opposed both the introduction of European (infidel) sciences and practices and the ruler's absolutist governance.

It was thanks to the favour al-ʿAṭṭār enjoyed with Muḥammad ʿAlī that he was able to have his favourite disciple, Rifāʿa al-Ṭahṭāwī – one of the few native Egyptians – appointed to the student mission, albeit primarily as *imām*.

1. This scholar produced the single most important contemporary source for the French occupation of Egypt, on which he wrote no fewer than three versions. The first, *Tārīkh muddat al-Faransīs bi-Miṣr* ('History of the French Presence in Egypt'), deals with the first months of the campaign (July-December 1798). This was first edited (and translated) by S. Moreh (*Al-Jabartī's chronicle of the first seven months of the French occupation of Egypt, Muḥarram-Rajab 1213/15 June-December 1798*, Leiden, E. J. Brill, 1975), the translation part of which was reprinted in 1997 in a collection of related texts under the title *Napoleon in Egypt. Al-Jabartī's chronicle of the French occupation, 1798* (Princeton, NJ: Markus Wierner Publishers). The second, *Maẓhar al-taqdīs bi-dhahāb dawlat al-Faransīs* ('Act of Grace for the Departure of the French Nation'), was compiled in December 1801, after the liberation of the Grand Vizier Yūsuf, to whom it is also dedicated. In addition to the one used here (1969), the following editions of the text were made: Muḥammad ʿAṭā *ed.*, *Yawmiyyāt al-Jabartī* ('Al-Jabartī's Memoirs'), 2 vols, [n.d.]; Cairo (Dār al-Maʿārif); ed. ʿAbd al-Raḥmān ʿAbd al-Raḥīm, 1998, Cairo (Matbaʿat Dār al-Kutub al-Miṣriyya); ed. ʿAbd al-Rāziq ʿĪsā & ʿImād Hilāl, 1998, 2 vols, Cairo (al-ʿArabī li'l-Nashr wa'l-Tawzīʿ). *Ajā'ib al-āthār fī 'l-tarājim wa 'l-akhbār* ('Biographical and Historical Wonders') deals with the whole of Egyptian history from 1517 to 1821. This was first published in 1297/1879–80 (4 vols, Būlāq). Since then, it has been re-edited a number of times: e.g. 1322/1904–05 (4 vols, Cairo: Maṭbaʿat al-Ashrafiyya); 1958–67 (7 vols, ed. Ḥasan Muḥammad Jawhar, ʿAbd al-Fattāḥ al-Sarnajāwī, ʿUmar al-Dasūqī and Ibrāhīm Sālim, Cairo: Lajnat al-Bayān al-ʿArabī); 1997 (4 vols, ed. ʿAbd al-ʿAzīz Jamāl al-Dīn, Cairo: Maktabat Madbūlī), 1997–98 (4 vols, ed. ʿAbd al-Raḥmān ʿAbd al-Raḥīm, Cairo: Maṭbaʿat Dār al-Kutub al-Miṣriyya). A French translation (by Alexandre Cardin) of the part dealing with the French expedition appeared as early as 1838 and was accompanied by excerpts from the only other contemporary source, i.e. Niqūlā al-Turk's chronicle [which was later edited and translated in its entirety by Gaston Wiet as *Chronique d'Egypte (1798–1804)*, 1950, Cairo: IFAO]; *Journal d'Abdurrahman Gabarti pendant l'occupation française en Egypte; suivi d'un précis de la même campagne par Mou'Allem Nicolas al-Turki* (Paris). A (bad) French translation of the entire *'Ajā'ib* was published in 1888–96 (9 vols, Cairo: Imprimerie Nationale) by Chefik Mansour Bey, Abdulaziz Kahil Bey, Gabriel Nicolas Kahil Bey and Iskender Ammoun Efendi. The first (abridged) English translation appeared in 1994 (Thomas Philipp and Moshe Perlmann, *'Abd al-Raḥmān al-Jabartī's History of Egypt*, 2 vols, Stuttgart: Franz Steiner). The parts on the French occupation were translated into German by Arnold Hottinger: *Bonaparte in Ägypten: aus der Chronik des Abdarrahman al-Gabarti (1754–1829)*, 1983, Zurich: Artemis. On al-Jabartī (of whom E. Lane spoke very highly), see G. Delanoue, 1982: I, 3–83 (by far the most perceptive and in-depth study of al-Jabartī and his ideas); A. ʿAbd al-Karīm, 1976; K. Shaybūb, 1948; ʿA. Mubārak, 1886–88: VIII, 7–13; M. al-Sharqāwī, 1955–6: I, 3–24; D. Ayalon, 1960; *idem* in B. Lewis and P. M. Holt, 1962: 391–402 ("The historian al-Jabartī"); "al-Djabartī"; *EI1* (D. B. MacDonald), *EI2* (D. Ayalon); J. al-Shayyāl, 1958: 10–27; H. Pérès, 1957: 122–9; T. Philipp and G. Schwald, 1994: 1–13; M. Cuoq, 1979: 13–7; E. Lane, 1923: 222.

The next stage in al-ʿAṭṭār's official career came with his appointment as editor of the official gazette, *Waqāʾiʿ Miṣriyya*, in 1828, and he reached the pinnacle of his career in 1831 when he rose to the rank of *shaykh al-Azhar*, and thus became the highest religious authority in the land. He remained in this post until his death four years later (April 1835).

Return of the Prodigal Son

In late spring of 1831, al-Ṭahṭāwī returned to his native land, secure in the belief that his benefactor was pleased with him and that great things lay ahead. However, things did not immediately pan out as one would have expected. To be sure, his mentor was duly impressed with his pupil's account of his stay in Europe, as al-Ṭahṭāwī himself explained in a letter written to Jomard shortly after his arrival back home:

> *Le Cheykh el-Islam lui-même, qui a lu mon voyage, en a été très satisfait, et m'a promis d'écrire à son Altesse pour l'engager à le faire imprimer, regardant cette publication comme le moyen le plus efficace d'engager les musulmans à aller chercher les lumières à l'étranger, et venir ensuite les propager et les naturaliser dans leur pays.*[1]

In the same letter, al-Ṭahṭāwī also pointed out the favour he received from his fellow Azhar *ʿulamāʾ*:

> *Comme mon oncle, qui est devenu mon beau-père, se trouve être le mouphti du Cheikh el-Islam, j'ai été généralement bien accueilli des oulémas; et ce qui prouve en faveur de la civilisation de l'Egypte c'est que plusieurs d'entre eux sont venus me trouver de leur propre mouvement, en me priant de leur enseigner la langue française.*[2]

And although it was encouraging that he was at least given a chance to work in his chosen profession, his first position, as a translator and French teacher at the School of Medicine (*madrasat al-ṭibb*) at Abū Zaʿbal,[3] was not exactly abrim with career opportunities. His colleagues

1. E.-F. Jomard, 1831.
2. E.-F. Jomard, 1831.
3. This village to the north-east of Cairo, which today is in the district of Shibīn al-Qanāṭir (Qalyūbiyya governorate), was also the site for Egypt's first modern European-style hospital as well as being a major military training ground. Both the hospital and the school had been set up by the French physician Antoine-Barthélémy Clot-Bey (founder

at the school included the Tunisian-born Shaykh Muḥammad b. ʿUmar al-Tūnisī (1789–1857), the Syrian émigré Yūḥannā (Ḥannā) ʿAnḥūrī – not to be confused with the author (and Paris-trained physician) Ḥannā ʿAnḥūrī (1836–1890) – and Yūsuf Firʿawn, all of whom played an important role in the early translation movement of European scientific works. The early career of al-Tūnisī, who was in charge of revising medical manuals, in many ways resembled that of al-Ṭahṭāwī in that he too was an Azhar graduate and a former preacher in the Egyptian army.[1] ʿAnḥūrī, for his part, was the chief translator at the medical school, and translated a great many French works (often via an Italian version) on medicine, anatomy and the natural sciences (physics, botany),[2] while Firʿawn[3] – a relative of the French interpreter 'Joanny (or Jean) Pharaon'

and head of the Egyptian health service) in 1827. See J.-M. Carré, 1956: I, 286–90 *et passim*; D. Panzac, 1989; J. Zaydān, 1957: IV, 32ff..

1. Al-Tūnisī, who had spent many years in Darfur and travelled all over North and Black Africa, also gained wider fame for the travelogues that dealt with his African peregrinations. The first was *Riḥla tashḥīdh al-idhhān bi-sīrat bilād al-ʿArab wa ʾl-Sūdān* ('Journey to Sharpen the Minds Regarding the Way of Life in Arab Lands and Those of the Blacks'), which was published in Paris in 1850 at the encouragement of his friend, the French chemistry teacher Dr Perron (who headed the Qaṣr al-ʿAynī medical college between 1839 and 1847), with the French title *Voyage au Darfour ou L'aiguisement de l'esprit par le voyage au Soudan et parmi les Arabes du centre de l'Afrique*. A French translation (by Perron) had already appeared in 1845 (*Voyage au Darfour par le cheikh Mohammed Ebn Omar el Tounsy*). In 1851, Perron published his translation of al-Tūnisī's other travel account, *Riḥlat Wādāy*, under the title *Voyage au Ouaday*. See *EI1*, *EI2* s.v. "al-Tūnisī" (M. Streck); ʿA. Ḥamīda 1984: 660ff.; ʿU. Kaḥḥāla [n.d.]: XI, 82–3; Y. Sarkīs, 1928: 1683–4; L. Shaykhū, 1991: 104; J. Zaydān 1957: IV, 206; *GAL*: II, 491; *GALS*, II, 748–9; ʿĀ. Nuṣayr 1990: 175 (Nos. 5/360, 5/364), 177 (no. 5/419), 182 (no. 6/135), 185 (no. 6/237), 186 (no. 6/279); J.-M. Carré, 1956: I, 274.
2. ʿAnḥūrī's translation of a French medical manual was the first ever printed. Entitled *al-Qawl al-ṣarīḥ fī ʿilm al-tashrīḥ* ('Clear Exposition of the Science of Anatomy'), it was published in Būlāq in 1248/1832 (28/46pp.), and based on Antoine Laurent Bayle's *Manuel d'anatomie descriptive, ou description succincte des organes de l'homme* (3rd edn, Paris, Gabon, 568pp., 1826). ʿAnḥūrī may also have been responsible for the very first modern medical treatise in Arabic, *Qawāʿid al-uṣūl al-ṭibbiyya al-maḥrura ʿan al-tajārib li-maʿrifa kayfiyya ʿilāj al-amrāḍ al-khāṣṣa bi-badan al-insān* (2 vols, Būlāq, 1242/1826), a translation of Francesco Vaccà Berlinghieri's *Codice elementare di medicina pratica sanzionato dall'esperienza per conoscere e curare i mali particulari del corpo umano* (2 vols, Pisa, 1794). See J. Zaydān, 1957: 170; Y. Sarkīs, 1928: 1389–90; E. Van Dyke, 1896: 440–1; T. Bianchi, 1843: 40 (no. 73), 42 (Nos. 87, 92), 51 (no. 160); ʿĀ. Nuṣayr, 1990: 174 (no. 5/333), 175 (no. 5/370), 177 (no. 5/420), 181 (no. 6/95), 182 (Nos. 6/157–8), 183 (Nos. 6/159–60), 184 (no. 6/218), 187 (Nos. 6/298, 6/314).
3. Būlāq, iv/210/4pp. Later editions of the book appeared in: 1849 (2nd revised edn, by the author, Būlāq); 1905 (Cairo, Dār al-Taqaddum); 1958 (Cairo, Muṣṭafā al-Bābī al-Ḥalabī); 1973 (in M. ʿImāra, *Aʿmāl al-kāmila li-Rifāʿa al-Ṭahṭāwī*, II, pp. 7–266); 1975 (in M. al-Ḥijāzī 1975: 139–413); [1982] (Cairo, Maktabat al-Kulliyyat al-Azhariyya/Beirut, Dār Ibn Zaydūn); 1993 (Cairo, GEBO); 2001 (Cairo, Dār al-Hilāl), 2001 (Sousse, Dar al-Maʿārif li

(Yūḥannā Firʿawn), whose son Florian became the first Arab editor of the French newspaper *Le Figaro*[1] – produced a number of translations in the areas of anatomy, veterinary science and pharmacology. One of al-Ṭahṭāwī's first students at the school was Muḥammad ʿAlī Bāshā al-Baqlī (1813–76), who was a member of the twelve-strong contingent of medical students sent to Paris for further study by Clot-Bey. He later became one of Egypt's first modern surgeons – which earned him the sobriquet al-Ḥakīm ('the Physician') – as well as a driving force in the modernization of the country's healthcare system.[2] Al-Ṭahṭāwī's literary output during this early period consisted of a translation of Cyprien-Prosper Brard's *Minéralogie Populaire* (1832) and of Georges-Bernard Depping's *Aperçu Historique sur les Moeurs et Coutumes des Nations* (1833), both of which had been completed during his Paris stay. In addition, he revised a translation by Yūsuf Firʿawn (with corrections by Muṣṭafā Ḥasan Kassāb) of a French veterinary manual, *al-Tawḍīḥ li-alfāẓ al-tashrīḥ al-bayṭarī* ('The Clarification of Terms Related to Veterinary Anatomy')[3]. Besides his teaching and translation duties, al-Ṭahṭāwī also

'l-Ṭibāʿa wa 'l-Nashr); 2002 (Cairo, Maktabat al-Usra); 2002 (Abu Dhabi, Dār al-Suwaydī li 'l-Nashr wa'l-Tawziʿ); 2003 (Cairo, Dar al-Anwar li 'l-Tibaʿa wa 'l-Nashr wa 'l-Tawziʿ); 2006 (ed. Yunān Labīb Rizq, Cairo, Dār al-Kutub wa 'l-Watha'iq al-Qawmiyya). The present translation is based on the 1834 edition.

1. One of the Egyptian refugees who had left the country after the withdrawal of the French troops, Joanny Pharaon (1802–46) served as interpreter to the Egyptian student mission when they arrived in France, in which capacity he also acccompanied the French invasion force in Algeria. A sometime teacher of Latin (!) at the prestigious Saint-Barbe Lycée in Paris, he wrote the very first manual of Algerian Arabic, *Grammaire Elémentaire d'Arabe Vulgaire ou Algérien, à l'usage des Français* (Paris, Didot, 1832, 96pp.), as well as two works dealing with the 1830 revolution, which one may suspect provided a useful source for al-Ṭahṭāwī's discussion of it (see Fifth Essay): *Histoire de la Revolution de 1830 et les Nouvelles Barricades* (with F. Rossignol), Paris (Ch. Vimont), iv/384pp.; *Biographie des Ex-ministres de Charles X, mis en accusation par le peuple*, Paris (Les marchands du nouveautés), 47pp. See A. Massé, 1933: 210–11; A. Louca, 1970: 39 (note); A. Silvera, 1980: 11; Y. Sarkīs, 1928: 1445; Bibliothèque Nationale, 1897–1981: CXXXV, 879–80. A. Messaoudi 2008: 594–5.
2. q.v. Y. Sarkīs, 1928: 575–6; ʿU. Kaḥḥāla [n.d.]: XI, 44–5; L. Shaykhū, 1991: 229; J. Zaydān, 1957: IV, 31, 174–5; ʿĀ. Nuṣayr, 1990: 182 (Nos. 135–6).
3. Būlāq, 1833, 2 vols in 1; J. Shayyāl, 1951: 132; ʿĀ. Nuṣayr, 1990: 177 (no. 5/435); Y. Sarkīs, 1928: 1446; E. Van Dyke 1896: 439. This was a translation of *Traité d'Anatomie Vétérinaire, ou histoire abrégée de l'anatomie et de la physiologie des principaux animaux domestiques* (2nd edn, Paris, Mme Huzard, 1819–20, 2 vols; 3rd edn, 1830) by the anatomist Jean Girard, the then head of the Veterinarian College of Alfort. A decade later, two more of his works were translated by Muḥammad Efendi ʿAbd al-Fattāḥ (with corrections by Muṣṭafā Ḥasan Kassāb): the first, *Traité du Pied Considéré dans les Animaux Domestiques, contenant son anatomie, ses difformités, ses maladies* (Paris, Mme Huzard, 1813, 288pp.; 2nd edn, 1828, xxxix/383pp.; 3rd edn, 1836, 446pp.), appeared as *Tuḥfat al-qalam fī amrāḍ al-qadam* (Būlāq, 1258/1842, 7/219pp.); ʿĀ. Nuṣayr, 1990: 186 (no. 6/264); Y. Sarkīs, 1928: 1752. The second,

headed the 'preparatory' school (*madrasa tajhīziyya*) attached to the Medical School. Finally, one may also presume that much of his time in this early period was taken up by the revisions of the *Ṭakhlīṣ*, to which he added a number of chapters (see below).

His new career and the increased financial security[1] also allowed him to start thinking about starting a family. He married one of the daughters of his uncle, Shaykh Muḥammad al-Anṣārī, who at the time occupied the position of *amīn al-fatwā*, i.e. deputy to the Rector of al-Azhar. The couple would have several children, including two sons, 'Alī Fahmī and Badawī Bey, the former of whom followed in his father's footsteps and rose to high office in the civil service (see below).[2]

In 1833, al-Ṭahṭāwī was transferred to the military school (*madrasat al-ṭobjiyya*) at Ṭura, a few miles south of Cairo, where he replaced the French Orientalist Koenig Bey[3] as chief translator. His duties included the translation as well as the supervision and revision of translations of works related to geometry and military science. It seems that his stay at the school was far from a happy one, owing in no small measure to the animosity on the part of the principal of the school, the Spaniard Don Antonio de Seguerra Bey, a former member of the short-lived liberal parliament of

---

al-Bahja al-sanniyya fī a'mār al-ḥayawānāt al-ahliyya (Būlāq, 1260/1844, 4/111pp.), was based on Girard's *Traité de l'Age du Cheval, augmentée de l'âge du boeuf, du mouton, du chien et du cochon* (3rd edn, Paris, Béchet jeune, 1834, 202pp.); 'Ā. Nuṣayr, 1990: 190 (no. 6/386); Y. Sarkīs, 1928: 1676.

1. Al-Ṭahṭāwī's salary at the Medical School amounted to what must to him have appeared the kingly sum of 1,322 piastres (excluding clothing and other allowances), which was more than five times the average monthly wages of a *shaykh* at al-Azhar. It is worth noting here that throughout his career al-Ṭahṭāwī would amass a huge fortune, both in money (during his stint at the Military School of the Citadel in 1856–61, for instance, he earned a staggering EPt 13,000 a month) and in real estate – according to 'Alī Mubārak (1886–88: XIII, 56), al-Ṭahṭāwī left a total of 1,600 feddans (*c.* 1,600 acres), 700 of which had been gifts from rulers (250 from Muḥammad 'Alī; 200 from Sa'īd; and 250 from Ismā'īl) in exchange for services rendered to the country. In addition, he owned numerous houses and properties in Cairo, as well as in his native Ṭahṭā. For a salary history, see Ṣ. Majdī, 1958: 42.
2. Very little is known about the younger son, Badawī, who spent most of his adult life in Ṭahṭā, managing the family's estate. See 'A. Mubārak, 1886–88: XIII: 56; A. Badawī, 1959: 86ff.
3. Mathieu Auguste Koenig (1802–65) left his native France for Egypt in 1820 and embarked on a five-year tour, which also took him to neighbouring territories (e.g. Syria). He settled in Cairo in 1827 and after being a French teacher he was appointed tutor to Muḥammad 'Alī's children (1834). Soon afterwards, he was awarded the title of Bey and was put in charge of the Translation Office of the Ministry of Foreign Affairs. He translated a number of French works on a variety of subjects (mathematics, physics, military affairs) into Arabic. See J. Balteau *et al.*, 1933-: XVIII, 1245; G. Vapereau, 1893: 877.

Cádiz.[1] According to J. Heyworth-Dunne,[2] this should be viewed against the ideological struggle between the Saint-Simonians and those opposed to their ideas. The leading figure of the former group was Barthélémy Prosper Enfantin (1796–1864), who had been a close associate of Saint-Simon's, and was known by his adepts as 'Le Père' (Father) Enfantin (in reference to his status as high priest within the movement which early on asserted itself as a 'church'). He had arrived in Egypt in October 1833, together with a group of supporters, and immediately set about realizing his master's dream of constructing a canal linking the Red Sea with the Mediterranean.[3] In Egypt, the Saint-Simonian ideas of the omnipotence of modern science and technology held great appeal for such prominent members of the French expatriate community as Sulaymān Pasha al-Faransāwī (Colonel Joseph Sève), Muḥammad ʿAlī's chief foreign military adviser, Ferdinand de Lesseps, who was then vice-consul of France in Egypt, and the brilliant engineers Linant de Bellefonds and Charles Lambert, all of whom would acquire huge fame in their chosen fields. Egypt, in fact, occupied a crucial place within the Saint-Simonian Christian Socialist ideology as it was seen as the stepping stone in their mission to bring Africa into the global fold. The country was considered to be at the crossroads of the past in all its glory and splendour and the modern dream of a brotherhood uniting all men, European technology and science being the cure for all ills. The Suez canal symbolized this union and 'brotherhood' between the different continents separated by the Mediterranean. However, while there was indeed serious opposition to the Saint-Simonians in Egypt, J. Heyworth-Dunne's claim that this was responsible for souring relations between al-Ṭahṭāwī and Seguerra does not really stand up to scrutiny. For one thing, there was the timing; al-Ṭahṭāwī's arrival at the school predated the start of the Saint-Simonians' Egyptian 'crusade'. And while Seguerra was indeed hostile to Saint-Simonian ideology, there is no indication that at that time al-Ṭahṭāwī had any contacts with the people around Enfantin or that he embraced their ideas. And even though one may conjecture that he would have agreed with several of their proposals, there is nothing to suggest that he ever became an adept of the Saint-Simonian ideology. Indeed, there is no clear proof to support the view that Seguerra Bey disliked al-Ṭahṭāwī because he suspected the latter of being sympathetic to the Saint-Simonian

1. Cf. P. Hamont, 1843: II, 163.
2. 1937–39: 965.
3. For a discussion of Saint-Simonian activities in Egypt, see J.-M. Carré, 1956: I, 261–77; P. Régnier & A. Abdelnour, 1989.

ideals as a result of his study stay in France, or because he resented French control over and influence on educational policy. One cannot rule out more mundane personal reasons either.

His second year at the school marked a turning point in his career, with the release of the *Takhlīṣ*.[1] The same year (1834) also saw the publication of his revision of Yūsuf Firʿawn's translation of a geographical treatise, entitled *Kanz al-mukhtār fī kashf al-arāḍī wa 'l-biḥār* ('Selected Treasure in the Discovery of Regions and Seas').[2] His interest in geography also resulted in a geographical manual, *al-Taʿrībāt al-shāfiyya li murīd al-jughrāfiyya* ('Healing Translations for the Student of Geography'), which was based on the works of Humboldt, Maissas and Michelot;[3] further, Muḥammad ʿAlī's conquest of Syria was more than coincidental to the writing of the (unpublished) *Risāla fī jughrāfiyā bilād al-Shām* ('Geography of Syria').[4]

In early autumn of the same year (1834), Egypt was once again struck by the plague, which entered the country by sea (allegedly through a Greek vessel), just as it had done during the first epidemic of the century (1813–25), and Alexandria was the first victim. Despite frantic attempts by the authorities to confine the deadly disease to the port, it quickly spread inland. In February 1835, it reached Cairo, whence it continued to Upper Egypt, where Luxor and the Fayum oasis recorded their first casualties as early as May.[5] Shortly after the first deaths were reported in Cairo, al-Ṭahṭāwī left his post and returned to his native Ṭahṭā, where he stayed for six months in an attempt to protect himself against the disease, though the difficult working conditions at the school may have played a role as well. It was during this unauthorized 'sabbatical' that he completed

1. Būlāq, iv/210/4pp. Later editions of the book appeared in: 1849 (2nd revised edn, by the author, Būlāq, 236pp.); 1905 (Cairo, Dār al-Taqaddum); 1958 (= 2nd edn; ed. Mahdī ʿAllām, Aḥmad Aḥmad Badawī, Anwar Lūqā, Cairo, Muṣṭafā al-Bābī al-Ḥalabī); 1973 (= 2nd edn; ed. M. ʿImāra, Aʿmāl al-kāmila li-Rifāʿa al-Ṭahṭāwī, II, pp. 7–266); 1975 (= 2nd edn; M. al-Ḥijāzī 1975: 139–413); [1982] (= 1st edn; Cairo, Maktabat al-Kulliyyat al-Azhariyya/ Beirut, Dār Ibn Zaydūn, 335pp.); 1993 (= 2nd edn; Cairo, al-Hay'a al-Miṣriyya al-ʿĀmma li 'l-Kutub/General Egyptian Book Organization); 2001 (ed. Muṣṭafā Nabīl, Cairo, Dār al-Hilāl). The present translation is based on the 1834 edition.
2. Maṭbaʿat Maktab al-Ṭōbjiyya, 1250/1834, 250pp. Cf. J. Shayyāl, 1951: 132; ʿĀ. Nuṣayr, 1990: 241 (no. 9/115). According to J. Livingston (1996: 562, note no. 11), this was the astronomical treatise al-Ṭahṭāwī composed in Paris.
3. Cairo, al-Maṭbaʿa al-Amīriyya, 1250/1834; 2nd edn, 1254/1838). The book also includes a glossary of technical terms related to geography. See Y. Sarkīs, 1928: 944; G. Delanoue, 1982: 622; J. Shayyāl, 1951: 132–4.
4. G. Delanoue, 1982: 623.
5. It would take until 1844 before the disease was finally vanquished. See D. Panzac, 1985: 128–132, 162–3 *et passim*.

the translation of the first volume of Conrad Malte-Brun's *Précis de Géographie Universelle*, which he had started towards the end of his Paris stay. Upon his return to Cairo, he presented it to Muḥammad ʿAlī, who was clearly impressed with the endeavour as the young translator received a generous financial emolument, alongside a promotion to the military rank of *ṣāghaqūl aghāsī*.[1] Al-Ṭahṭāwī's travelogue, to which his mentor al-ʿAṭṭār had written the preface, had also found much favour with the ruler (though less so with the average population),[2] who ordered a translation into Turkish, the mother tongue of the overwhelming majority of government officials. The task was entrusted to Rustam Efendi Bāsim (Rüstem Besim). It was published in 1839 by the government press (*al-maṭbaʿa al-amīriyya*) in Būlāq under the title *Sefārat nāme-ye Rifāʿat Bey*. Muḥammad ʿAlī was so taken with the book that he had it distributed to all of his high officials and students at the new schools, and even sent copies to Constantinople, where it attracted much interest from the Sublime Porte.[3] The timing of the publication is quite interesting as it came amidst extensive reforms in Turkey with the promulgation of the so-called 'Noble Rescript' (*hatt-i şerif*) at Gülhane, which marked the beginning of the *tanẓīmāt* (constitutional reform laws) period.[4] It is not difficult to imagine that the political chapters in al-Ṭahṭāwī's text would have struck a chord with the reformers in Istanbul.

Upon hearing of the strained working relationship between al-Ṭahṭāwī and the head of the school, Muḥammad ʿAlī relieved him from his post, and appointed him librarian at the Qaṣr al-ʿAynī school. As it happened, shortly afterwards, de Seguerra himself was ousted as a result of intensive French lobbying. It was during al-Ṭahṭāwī's time at Qaṣr al-ʿAynī that he put some of his ideas regarding education on paper in the form of a report, which he submitted to the ruler and in which he called for the creation of a school for translators. The proposal was accepted and al-Ṭahṭāwī was put in charge of carrying it out. Translating and the training of translators thenceforth became his main activity in a career that was to span four decades.

---

1. This is a Turkish borrowing (*sağkol agası*), and denoted a rank between captain and major (corresponding to the modern term *rāʾid*). See S. Spiro, 1895 ('Adjutant-Major').
2. Cf. the scene witnessed by Edward Lane at a Cairo bookseller's, where a local described the book as the account of a journey to France, during which its author indulged in drinking, womanizing and the eating of pork; S. Lane-Poole, 1877: 70–1.
3. Ṣ. Majdī 1958: 62; Cf. *EI2*, s.v. "dustūr" (B. Lewis); J. Heyworth-Dunne, 1938: 166–7, 265–6, 297.
4. For background, see B. Lewis, 1969.

Teacher, Trainer, Translator, Editor (1835–49)

The venue of the Language School (*madrasat al-alsun*),[1] which is the direct precursor to the modern Faculty of Languages of the University of ʿAyn Shams in Cairo (ʿAbbāsiyya), was the splendid palace once owned by the Mamlūk ruler Muḥammad al-Alfī Bey in the sophisticated Azbakiyya (Ezbekiyya) quarter.[2] Al-Ṭahṭāwī wasted no time in shaping the establishment to his own ideas and aspirations. The set-up was in many ways exceptional for the time. First, there was the fact that al-Ṭahṭāwī was the only native Egyptian director within the 'modern' Egyptian educational system; other schools (at least those preparing students for a career in government or the military) were headed by Turks, who were often seconded by Europeans. Second, and more important, all of the students at the school were native Egyptians, as opposed to Turks (or Circassians, etc.) who made up the student population in other government schools. Initially, the number of students was limited to 50 and later on to 150, and the course of study was set at four years, after which time graduates were automatically awarded the rank of army lieutenant. Although the original idea seems to have been to select an equal number from both Lower and Upper Egypt, the composition reveals that most of them came, like their principal, from the Ṣaʿīd region.[3] The students were recruited from the 'preparatory' schools. Their ages varied between fourteen and eighteen. Among the first student contingent we find al-Ṭahṭāwī's future biographer, Ṣāliḥ Majdī (d. 1881), who would become a famous author and educator in his own right.[4] Al-Ṭahṭāwī was determined to provide a broad education and in addition to languages (French, English, Italian, Turkish, Arabic), the curriculum contained subjects like geography, mathematics and history, as well as French and Islamic law. As a result, it was the only school at that time that offered a truly general education, without a direct link with military affairs. Naturally, all depended on the quality of the teaching and al-Ṭahṭāwī took great pains in putting together a faculty that was up to the task. Most of them were Azharīs, among them al-Ṭahṭāwī's former

1. See A. ʿAbd al-Karīm, 1938: 221ff.; J. Heyworth-Dunne, 1938: 264–71; Ṣ. Majdī, 1958: 36–8; J. Shayyāl, 1951: 38–44; J. Tājir [n.d.]: 29–36, 52–6; al-Ṭahṭāwī, 1973–80: I, 438 [*Manāhij*] (*'madrasa li 'l-alsun al-ahliyya wa 'l-ajnabiyya'*).
2. According to J. Heyworth-Dunne (1937–39: 965), the Language School was the continuation of a *Madrasat al-Tarjama* ('School for Translation'), set up in June 1836 under the directorship of the Turk Ibrāhim Adham (see below), whom Rifāʿa replaced in January 1837 (when the school changed its name).
3. Cf. Ṣ. Majdī, 1958: 37; J. Tājir [n.d.]: 29.
4. See Y. Sarkīs, 1928: 1187–8.

teacher al-Damanhūrī (see above).[1] Originally, there were also three French teachers, who were replaced by graduates from the school as from 1839.

Al-Ṭahṭāwī displayed the same zeal and unflagging commitment and enthusiasm in his new task as he had done during his Paris student days. In addition to his duties as director (*nāẓir*) and as a member (together with such leading representatives from the expatriate French community as Clot-Bey, Lambert and Hamont) of the newly created (1836) Schools Council (*dīwān al-madāris*), which was led by one of the former leaders of the Egyptian student mission in Paris, Muṣṭafā Mukhtār Bey, he launched himself headlong into his teaching, giving classes that could last three or even four hours and sometimes teaching late in the evening or before dawn.[2] His other line of activity centred on translation, his own and the revision of those of others, while the responsibility of producing manuals for the school also fell on his shoulders.[3] In 1841, a translation adjunct (*qalam al-tarjama*) was added to the school, which was naturally also headed by al-Ṭahṭāwī, and its fifty-strong faculty consisted mainly of graduates from the Language School.[4] His enthusiasm and the overall quality of the teaching at the Language School meant that, very soon after its foundation, students began publishing their translations, albeit under the careful supervision of al-Ṭahṭāwī. In total, the school would produce 2,000 translations of foreign (European and Turkish) works.[5] The choice of books clearly reflected both al-Ṭahṭāwī's predilections (with a clear dominance of historical works) and French training inasmuch as it involved works he had read in Paris. Among them one may cite *Tārīkh al-falāsifa al-Yūnāniyyīn* ('History of Greek Philosophers') by ʿAbd Allāh Ḥusayn al-Miṣrī;[6] *Tanwīr al-mashriq bi-ʿilm al-manṭiq* ('Light of the East on the Science of Logic') by Khalīfa Maḥmūd;[7] *al-Dirāsa al-awwaliyya fi 'l-jughrāfiyā al-ṭabīʿiyya* ('Basic Study of

1. For a list of ten of them (including succinct biographies), see Ṣ. Majdī, 1958: 55–8.
2. Cf. ʿA. Mubārak, 1886–89: XIII, 54–5.
3. For instance, he wrote a commentary on the famous *Lāmiyyat al-ʿArab* by the pre-Islamic poet Shanfarā and an abridgement of the *Maʿāhid al-tanṣīṣ ʿalā shawāhid al-Talkhīṣ*. The latter work is a commentary by ʿAbd al-Raḥīm al-ʿAbbāsī (d. 1556) of *Talkhīṣ al-Miftāḥ*, a work of rhetoric by Jalāl al-Dīn al-Qazwīnī (d. 1338), which is itself an abridgement of part of al-Sakkākī's encyclopaedic *Miftāḥ al-ʿulūm* (see Translation, note no. 1, p. 188). S. Majdī, 1958: 26.
4. On the translation section, see J. al-Shayyāl, 1951; J. Tājir [n.d.]: 33–8.
5. ʿA. al-Rāfiʿī, 1930.
6. Būlāq, 1252/1836, 2/186pp. (Istanbul 1302/1885; Cairo 1328/1910); this is sometimes also referred to as *Tārīkh falāsifat al-Yūnān*. See G. Delanoue, 1982: 623; ʿĀ. Nuṣayr, 1990: 246 (no. 9/271); T. Bianchi, 1843: 47 (no. 124); Y. Sarkīs, 1928: 1294 ('*Tārīkh al-falāsifa*').
7. Būlāq, 1254/1838, 7/60pp.; see ʿĀ. Nuṣayr, 1990: 9 (no. 1/145); Y. Sarkīs, 1928: 834; . This was a translation of *La Logique* by the French philosopher and grammarian César

Natural Geography'), by Aḥmad Ḥusayn al-Rashīdī;[1] *Bidāyat al-qudamā' wa hidāyat al-ḥukamā'* ('Beginnings of the Ancients, and Gift from the Wise'), a history of Creation and the Prophets consisting of a compilation of several French and Arabic works, by Muṣṭafā Sayyid Aḥmad al-Zarābī, ʿAbd Allāh Abū 'l-Suʿūd and Muḥammad ʿAbd al-Rāziq;[2] *Qarrat al-nufūs wa 'l-ʿuyūn bi-siyar mā tawassaṭa min al-qurūn* ('Delight of the Soul and the Eyes in the Journeys of What Lies between the Centuries'), a history of the Middle Ages, based on French and Arabic works, with translations by Muṣṭafā Sayyid Aḥmad al-Zarābī;[3] *Maṭāliʿ shumūs al-siyar fī waqāʾiʿ Karulūs al-thānī ʿashar* ('The Rising Suns in the Life and Times of Charles XII'), a translation of Voltaire's history of Charles XII of Sweden, by Muḥammad Muṣṭafā al-Bayyāʿ;[4] *Naẓm al-la'ālī fī sulūk fī-man ḥakama Firansā wa min qābilihim ʿalā Miṣr min al-mulūk* ('Pearls of Wisdom Regarding Those Who Have Ruled France and a Comparison with Egyptian Kings'), a history of the kings of France by ʿAbd Allāh Abū 'l-Suʿūd,[5] and *Itḥāf al-mulūk*

Chesneau Dumarsais (1676–1756), which was reprinted in the year of al-Ṭahṭāwī's arrival in France. On Dumarsais, see Michaud, 1854: XI, 504–07; J. Balteau, 1933-: XII, 106–07.

1. Būlāq, 1838, 8/236pp. (2nd edn, Cairo, n. p., 1893, 236pp.); Y. Sarkīs, 1928: 937; E. Van Dyke, 1896: 413, 451; ʿĀ. Nuṣayr, 1990: 176 (Nos.5/380–01). This was a translation of *Résumé d'un Cours Elémentaire de Géographie Physique* (2nd edn, 1829, Paris, Verdière, 397pp.) by the botanist and natural historian Jean Vincent Félix Lamouroux (1779–1825); q.v. J. Balteau, 1933-: CXI, 637–9; Michaud, 1854: XXIII, 107–10.
2. Būlāq, 1254/1838, 28/16/7/271pp. (2nd edn, 1272/1855, 181pp.; 1282/1865, 280pp.); cf. ʿĀ. Nuṣayr, 1990: 251 (Nos. 426–8); Y. Sarkīs, 1928: 943; E. Van Dyke, 1896: 409; Bibliothèque Nationale, 1897–1981: CLI, 1058. Al-Ṭahṭāwī wrote the introduction to this work, and one may speculate he also had quite a hand in the establishment of the glossary of foreign words that precedes the text.
3. Būlāq, 1260/1844, 2 vols (268/359pp.); ʿĀ. Nuṣayr, 1990: 253 (no. 9/475); Y. Sarkīs, 1928: 965; E. Van Dyke, 1896: 425; A. Badawī, 1959: 214. Al-Ṭahṭāwī also wrote an introduction to the translation.
4. Būlāq, 1258/1841, 6/278pp.; T. Bianchi, 1843: 58 (no. 222); ʿĀ. Nuṣayr, 1990: 250 (no. 9/382); Y. Sarkīs, 1928: 1696; E. Van Dyke, 1896: 408, 424. Later on, al-Ṭahṭāwī also had Voltaire's *Histoire de l'Empire de Russie sous Pierre-le-Grand* (of which there were no fewer than three editions during al-Ṭahṭāwī's stay in Paris: F.-G. Levrault, 1826, xxiv/468pp.; Lecointe, 230/180pp.; A. Hiard, 1831, 242/262pp.) translated by Aḥmad ʿUbayd al-Ṭahṭāwī, with revisions by himself and Quṭṭa al-ʿAdawī (d. 1864), who was a teacher at the language and translation schools, and later became a reviser at the official printing press (*al-maṭbaʿa al-amīriyya*) in Būlāq. The translation was entitled *al-Rawḍ al-azhar fī tārīkh Buṭrus al-akbar* ('The Brilliant Gardens Regarding the History of Peter the Great') and appeared in 1266/1850 (Būlāq, 348pp.); Y. Sarkīs, 1928:1247; ʿĀ. Nuṣayr, 1990: 253 (Nos. 9/484–86).
5. Būlāq, 1257/1841, 24/351pp.; ʿĀ. Nuṣayr, 1990: 253 (no. 9/480); T. Bianchi, 1843: 58 (no. 221); A. Badawī, 1959: 214. This work also contains al-Ṭahṭāwī's translation of the *Marseillaise* and *La Parisienne* (a revolutionary song composed during the July uprising of 1830); ʿA. Abū 'l-Suʿūd, 1841: 212–20 (also see M. ʿAllām *et al.*, 1958: 219–22 (*Marseillaise*), 223–5 (*Parisienne*).

al-alibbā' bi taqaddum al-jam'iyyāt fī bilād Ūrubbā ('Presents of the Wise Regarding the Progress of Societies in European Countries'), a translation of Robertson's history of the reign of Charles V, by Khalīfa Maḥmūd.[1] As the topics moved away from the purely scientific (and military), Egypt witnessed the emergence of a veritable translation movement – the second in Arab history (the first being that of mediaeval Greek translations) – encompassing all arts and sciences and in which al-Ṭahṭāwī was both the formidable driving force and one of the principal contributors.[2]

Naturally, his exacting schedule at the school left little time for his own translations in the early period. Between 1837 and 1841, his output in this field was restricted to the publication of his translation of Malte-Brun's geography (see above) and of Legendre's *Eléments de Géométrie* – which he had also started in Paris.[3]

Judging by the high-flying careers of the alumni of the Language School and the Translation Section, the school was clearly a success.[4] Besides the already-mentioned Ṣ. Majdī, the graduates included people such as Muḥammad Qadrī Pasha (d. 1888), who played a pioneering role in Egypt's legal reforms and eventually became Justice Minister;[5] Muḥammad 'Uthmān Bey Jalāl (1829–94), who translated many French literary classics (including plays by Racine and Molière, and La Fontaine's fables) and is often credited with being one of the precursors of the modern Arabic novel and theatre;[6] and 'Abd Allāh Abū 'l-Su'ūd (1821–78) – the founder of

1. Būlāq, 1258/1842, 269pp.; T. Bianchi, 1843: 58 (no. 223). This was the first part of a translation of the French version of William Robertson's history (*The History of the Reign of Emperor Charles V, with a view of the progress of society in Europe from the subversion of the Roman Empire to the beginning of the sixteenth century*, London, W. Strahan & T. Cadelle, 1769), entitled *L'Histoire du Règne de l'Empereur Charles Quint, précédé d'un tableau des progrès de la société en Europe depuis la destruction de l'empire romain, jusqu'au commencement du XVIe siècle* (2 vols, Paris, Janet et Cotelle, 1817). The second and third volumes of the Arabic translation followed in 1844 and 1849, under the title *Itḥāf mulūk al-zamān bi-tārīkh al-imbirāṭūr Sharlkān*. Cf. 'Ā. Nuṣayr, 1990: 253 (Nos. 9/469–71).
2. For a general overview of the Egyptian translation movement in the first half of the 19th century, see: J. al-Shayyāl, 1951; J. Tājir [n.d.]; J. Zaydān, 1957: IV *passim*; L. Zaytūnī, 1994.
3. See Translation, note no. 5, p. 295.
4. Cf. the impressive list of 72 names given by Ṣ. Majdī, 1958: 43–51. Also see J. Heyworth-Dunne, 1938: 269–71.
5. In addition to works of jurisprudence such as *al-Aḥkām al-shar'iyya fī 'l-aḥwāl al-shakhṣiyya* (1875), Qadrī translated the French criminal code (which served as a basis for that of Egypt) and also published a trilingual language manual, entitled *al-Durr al-muntakhab min lughāt al-Fransīs wa 'l-'Uthmāniyyīn wa 'l-'Arab* (1875). See Y. Sarkīs, 1928: 1495–6; J. Zaydān, 1957: IV, 274; 'Ā. Nuṣayr, 1990: 81 (Nos. 2/1830, 2/1840), 95 (no. 2/2254), 109 (Nos. 3/143, 3/144), 130 (no. 4/3).
6. 'Uthmān Jalāl also had a successful career in government, and in addition to being an official translator and judge he briefly held a post in the Cabinet (under Khedive

Egypt's first private newspaper, *Wādī 'l-Nīl* (1866) – who went on to make a name for himself as a poet, journalist and author.[1] The long-term vision of al-Ṭahṭāwī also manifested itself in the fact that many of the graduates tended to join the faculty, before setting off on their careers in the country's administration. Muḥammad ʿAlī also seemed to be favourably impressed with the work at the Language School and, in recognition for services rendered, its *nāẓir* was promoted to the rank of major in the infantry (*binbāshī biyāda mulkiyya*).

There is little doubt that the organization and curriculum of the Language School were a direct result of al-Ṭahṭāwī's stay in France and constituted the first attempt at realizing his vision of an education that would combine (local Muslim) tradition and a modern European approach, even though it would take a few more decades before he would express these views within the framework of a more comprehensive cultural reformist thought.

The reputation of the school soon extended across the borders of Egypt and attracted the attention of the Tunisian ruler Aḥmad Bey, who also shared Muḥammad ʿAlī's dream of creating a modern (Europeanized) industrialized state. In March 1840, the Bey set up a military school (*maktab ḥarbī*).[2] It was first located within the walls of the beylical Bardo palace before moving to its own premises in former army barracks. It was the Regency's very first government-run secular school, and as such its foundation marked the first step towards the creation of a European-style educational system. The Bardo school was organized on the principle of a French *Ecole Polytechnique* and modelled on the Istanbul School of Military Sciences and Muḥammad ʿAlī's Artillery School. Like the Egyptian schools, the Bardo Military school was headed by Europeans, who also made up the teaching staff.[3] Its first director was a former

---

Ismāʿīl). M. Badawī, 1992: 28–9, 63–4, 183, 421–3 *et passim*; Y. Sarkīs, 1928: 1306–07; ʿĀ. Nuṣayr, 1990: 101 (no. 2/2453), 109 (no. 3/132), 124 (Nos. 3/633, 3/643, 3/657), 201 (no. 8/263), 217 (Nos. 8/769–72), 218 (Nos. 8/809–10), 235 (no. 8/1385), 236 (Nos. 8/1390–01), 244 (no. 9/204).

1. See ʿU. Kaḥḥāla [n.d.]: VI, 78–9; Y. Sarkīs, 1928: 314–15; P. dī Ṭarrāzī, 1913–14: I, 130–31 II, 162; L. Shaykhū, 1991: 146–7; I. ʿAbduh, 1948: 114–18.
2. On this institute, see: A. Chenoufi, 1976; M. Qābādū, 1984: II, 32, 46; M. ʿAbd al-Mawlay, 1977; Ibn Abī 'l-Ḍiyāf, 1963: IV, 36; B. Tlili, 1974: 446ff; L. Brown, 1974: 292-5; P. Marty, 1935: 317-38; M. Kraïem, 1973: II, 173-81; M. Ibn ʿĀshūr, 1972: 28ff; M. Smida, 1970: 290–93; S. Binbilghīth, 1995: 56–7 *et passim*; C. Monchicour 1929: 298–301. L. Brown (1974: 292), J. Ganiage (1959: 116), P. Marty (1935: 315–17), B. Tlili (1974: 447) and N. Sraïeb (1992: 203; 1995: 14) give 1838 as the creation date. However, there is no evidence to support that the school was operational before 1840.
3. Cf. P. Marty, 1935: 316–17, 331–2; B. Tlili, 1974: 446; R. Drevet, 1922: 22; N. Sraïeb, 1995:

instructor of the Ottoman army and sometime member of its general staff, the Piedmontese captain Luigi Calligaris.[1] The curriculum was patterned on that of contemporary European military academies (particularly St Cyr), and included engineering, mathematics and surveying; French was a core subject and, like in Egypt and Constantinople, 'became not only the symbol, but virtually the content of cultural modernity'.[2] Apart from instruction, the school had to provide translations (especially of European military manuals) and, of course, train students for this purpose. In this movement, the poet Maḥmūd Qābādū played a crucial role.[3] In total, some forty translations were made, either directly from French or indirectly via Turkish.[4] A great many of these military translations were made before the advent of printing, and it is interesting to find that the official government press would print only two! This may be explained by the fact that, as from the 1860s, the Bey's military efforts were severely curtailed because of financial difficulties. Furthermore, it is useful to point out that, unlike in Egypt, where the translation movement started with 'practical' sciences but then developed in other areas, Tunisia never went beyond the first stage. At the same time, al-Ṭahṭāwī may have influenced the educational policy of the statesman Khayr al-Dīn al-Tūnisī, who also had an unwavering belief in the 'civilizing' role of education and had been equally impressed with European education. Indeed, though the two men never met, they clearly admired each other.[5]

In the 1840s, al-Ṭahṭāwī's career continued to soar, several other adjuncts being added to the Language School, among them a 'preparatory' school (1841), a Faculty of Islamic Law (*Madrasat al-sharīʿa al-Islāmiyya*, 1847), a Faculty of Accountancy (1845) and a Faculty of Land Management (1846). And if this was not enough, Muḥammad ʿAlī in 1841 put his brightest star in charge of the European library (*kutubkhāna*) of Qaṣr al-ʿAynī, and in the following year, al-Ṭahṭāwī was appointed editor-in-chief of the official Gazette, *al-Waqāʾiʿ al-Miṣriyya*, in order to modernize what was essentially a poorly edited rag.[6] And so, once more, al-Ṭahṭāwī followed in the footsteps

54; F. Arnoulet, 1994: 26; H. Dunant, 1858: 81.

1. See C. Monchicour, 1929: 295-307; B. Tlili, 1974: 447-8; J. Ganiage, 1959: 116; A. Demeerseman, 1956: 281ff.; ʿA. al-Mawlay, 1977: 18–19; H. Hugon, 1913: 95-6; P. Marty, 1935: 317-18; Y. Sarkīs, 1928: 1042-3; M. Ibn ʿĀshūr, 1972: 29.
2. C. Findley, 1989: 144.
3. See M. Qābādū, 1984: II, 46–7.
4. Cf. lists in M. Chenoufi, 1974: 57–62; A. Chenoufi, 1976: 81–5; S. Binbilgīth, 1995: 20ff. On the translation movement and its protagonists, see Binbilgīth, 1995: 99ff.
5. See, for instance, al-Ṭahṭāwī, 1973–80: II, 440 (*Manāhij*).
6. See R. al-Jayyid, 1985: 46–55; A. Muruwwah, 1961: 145; A. Badawī, 1959: 61–6; J. al-Shayyāl,

of his mentor, al-ʿAṭṭār, who had been the first editor. Although al-Ṭahṭāwī managed to introduce a number of changes – the first of which was the use of Arabic rather than Turkish (up until then all articles were written in this language and then translated into Arabic) – it seems that his benefactor was not ready for the kind of overhaul his protégé had in mind. Indeed, after about a year, in which al-Ṭahṭāwī published a number of articles dealing with general political issues – both European and Muslim – the content of the Gazette slowly but surely drifted back to its earlier staid format of government announcements and panegyrics on the ruler. One may speculate that the change of tack was the result of pressure from Muḥammad ʿAlī, who had perhaps obtained more than he had bargained for. Indeed, it is difficult to imagine that he would have welcomed any kind of political commentary (even if it was laudatory) inspired by novel European ideas, lest it should burgeon and become a source of political criticism that might be difficult to quell afterwards.

Nevertheless, al-Ṭahṭāwī continued to enjoy Muḥammad ʿAlī's favour; in 1844 he was promoted to lieutenant-colonel and two years later, after submitting the third and final part of his translation of Malte-Brun's *Universal Geography*, he rose to the rank of colonel (*amīr alāy al-rafīʿa*) and was thenceforth entitled to add the honorific 'Bey' to his name.

As the reign of Muḥammad ʿAlī drew to a close, dire times lay ahead of Rifāʿa Bey, who would fall victim to the vicissitudes of political life. In the last years of his rule, Muḥammad ʿAlī's increasingly failing physical and mental health caused him to withdraw from the day-to-day business of government and in 1848, his son Ibrāhīm Pasha took over the reins of power, but unfortunately died in November of that year – nine months before the demise of his father. The great viceroy was succeeded by his grandson (the son of the late Ṭūsūn), ʿAbbās I, who would hold the throne until 1854. The irony of history is such that the last endeavour in this most fertile period of al-Ṭahṭāwī's life was the revision of the *Takhlīṣ*, the book that had brought him fame and recognition. The second edition appeared in 1849, just a few months before the death of his benefactor.

The Second Exile (1850–54)

The new *vali* – as the rulers of Egypt were known in the Ottoman hierarchical nomenclature – did not share his grandfather's interest and belief in European inventions and his reign has traditionally been associated with a

1951: 139ff.; ʿA. Ḥamza, 1950: 109ff.

reversal of his predecessor's policies, driven by a profound anti-European sentiment. However, it would seem that many of his decisions were rooted in pragmatism, rather than xenophobia. To be sure, ʿAbbās resented the foreign influence, especially by the French, on Egypt, yet to extrapolate this to a hatred of all things European is, at best, an exaggeration. At need, he was not averse to calling upon European expertise, as was the case for the railway (Cairo-Alexandria), which was built by a British company.[1] Furthermore, although he closed down the *Ecole Militaire Egyptienne* in Paris, he continued to send students to Europe – albeit in smaller numbers – for further education, with missions to France,[2] as well as to England, Italy, Austria and Prussia.[3]

That a new wind was blowing at the court became clear almost from the start of ʿAbbās' rule, with the closure (as was the case for al-Ṭahṭāwī's Language School) or merger of the modern schools set up by his grandfather. Unfortunately, for al-Ṭahṭāwī this was only the beginning. Indeed, there seem to have been darker forces at work in his fall from grace since he himself in no uncertain terms held the action by a certain 'prince' (*baʿḍ al-umarāʾ*)[4] responsible for his being sent to the Sudan, ostensibly to set up and head a primary school in Khartoum for the offspring of Egyptian officials resident in the region. At the same time, one may suspect that the publication of the second edition of the *Takhlīṣ* may also have played a part, as its author's attention to the French parliamentary system must have left a less than favourable impression on the Khedive.

Al-Tahṭāwī arrived in the Sudan in 1850 for a stay that was to last for four years.[5] The Sudan was Egypt's equivalent of the Gulag and many a dissenter found himself struggling to survive in the disease-infested swamp that was Khartoum. The death toll tended to be astronomical and al-Ṭahṭāwī himself reported that half of the Egyptians that shared his exile died as a result of some epidemic or other.[6] One of them was his long-time

1. See H. Rivlin, 1961; E. Toledano, 1990: *passim* (see index).
2. One of three students to be sent to Paris (1850) was the astronomer and future Minister for Education, Ismāʿīl b. Muṣṭafā b. Sulaymān al-Falakī (1825–1900). Upon his return, Ismāʿīl, who was of Turkish extraction, was put in charge of the Cairo Observatory and of the Engineering School. See A. Louca, 1970: 100; Y. Sarkīs, 1928: 444–5; J. Zaydān, 1957: IV, 214; E. Van Dyke, 1896: 461; ʿU. Kaḥḥāla [n.d.]: II, 296.
3. In total, 41 students were sent to study scientific subjects (medicine, engineering). See J. Heyworth-Dunne, 1938: 296–9, 301–07.
4. al-Ṭahṭāwī, 1973–80: I, 453 [*Manāhij*].
5. On this period in al-Ṭahṭāwī's life, see al-Ṭahṭāwī, 1973–80: I, 453ff. [*Manāhij*]; A. Sayyid Aḥmad, 1973.
6. al-Ṭahṭāwī, 1973–80: I, 453 [*Manāhij*].

friend and fellow student in Paris, Muḥammad Bayyūmī, who succumbed to illness in 1852.[1] It was also here that the French author Charles Didier (the founder of the homonymous publishing house) met al-Ṭahṭāwī, whom he likened to 'Denis in Corinth', as he taught children how to read in order to make a living, adding however that '*notre magister prenait assez bien son parti et se résignait, en bon musulman, aux décrets d'Allah*'.[2]

During his exile, he translated Fénelon's *Les Aventures de Télémaque*, under the title of *Mawāqiʿ al-aflāk fī waqāʾiʿ Tilīmāk* ('The Orbits of the Celestial Bodies in the Adventures of Telemachus').[3] This was the very first story of Greek mythology to be translated into Arabic.[4] However, in view of the circumstances one may speculate that it was not this aspect that attracted al-Ṭahṭāwī to this classic of French literature (1699). Originally written by the French archbishop and theologian François de Salignac de la Mothe-Fénelon (1651–1715) for his pupil, the grandson (and heir-apparent) of Louis XIV, the book is much more than a mere account of the adventures of Odysseus' son Telemachus. Composed in the then popular tradition of 'Mirrors for Princes', *Les Aventures de Télémaque* was above all intended to serve as a guide for good – i.e. just and wise – government for the future king. One should hasten to add, however, that this literary genre was by no means unknown in Arabic literature, with its long tradition of 'wisdom' literature. The earliest 'Mirrors for Princes' were translations from Pahlavi or Indian tales, the most famous of which is undoubtedly *Kalīla wa Dimna*, adapted by the Persian-born Ibn Muqaffaʿ (d. 757).[5] In his book, Fénelon expressed the core of his political ideas, criticizing despotism and praising rulers who encourage justice, education and trade.[6] Indeed, it is not difficult to see how Fénelon's admonitions struck a chord with one who was the victim of an absolutist decision. Fénelon's thought

1. At 17, Bayyūmī had been one of the youngest members of the student contingent. After a nine-year stay in Paris, where he had studied engineering (specializing in hydraulics) at the Paris Ecole Polytechnique, Bayyūmī became a teacher (in chemistry, though) at the Cairo Engineering College (*muhandiskhāna*), while joining al-Ṭahṭāwī at the Translation School. He is particularly known for his translations of mathematical works, Y. Sarkīs, 1928: 622; Ṣ. Majdī, 1958: 39; ʿU. Kaḥḥāla [n.d.]: IX, 124; ʿA. Mubārak, 1886–88: XI, 68; J. Shayyāl, 1951: 110–12; J. Zaydān, 1957: 188–9; A. Louca, 1970: 50.
2. C. Didier, 1856: 37–8.
3. al-Ṭahṭāwī, 1973–80: I, 462, 570 [*Manāhij*]; Y. Sarkīs, 1928: 946. For a discussion, see, for instance, M. Peled, 1979: 139–46; A. Hourani, 1989: 73–5.
4. It would take another 70 years before the second attempt appeared, i.e. Sulaymān al-Bustānī's translation (from the original Greek) of Homer's *Iliad* (1904).
5. See *EI1*, s.vv. "Ibn Muqaffaʿ" (Cl. Huart), "Kalīla wa Dimna" (C. Brockelmann); *EI2*, s.v. "Ibn Muqaffaʿ" (F. Gabrieli); J. Ashtiany *et al.*, 1990: 48–77 (J. Latham).
6. e.g. Fénelon, 1995: 226ff.

left a lasting impact on al-Ṭahṭāwī, in whose later, more philosophical, works many of the ideas and recommendations of the 17th-century French theologian resurfaced. Finally, one may point to the fact that Fénelon's other major work, *Traité de l'Education des Filles* (1687), may have been a direct inspiration for al-Ṭahṭāwī's own *al-Murshid al-amīn li 'l-banāt wa 'l-banīn* ('The Trustworthy Guide for Girls and Boys').[1]

The humiliation of exile was clearly heavy to bear, and al-Ṭahṭāwī on several occasions requested that he be allowed to return to Cairo, and even wrote an 84-verse eulogy (*wāfir* metre) for Ḥasan Pasha, the Katkhudā (Interior Minister), imploring him to intercede on his behalf.[2] All his entreaties were in vain, however, and he states that his prayers were answered only after composing a long laudatory poem on the Prophet Muḥammad (*qaṣīda nabawiyya*), which was a *takhmīs* (five-fold amplification) of an ode by the 11th-century Yemeni poet ʿAbd al-Raḥmān Ibn Aḥmad al-Buraʿī.[3]

For obvious reasons, al-Ṭahṭāwī thought it politic to shelve his *Tilimāq*, at least for the time being, and it took until 1867 before the book was finally published (in Beirut!),[4] but even then it caused quite a stir at the court.

As far as al-Ṭahṭāwī's reversal of fortunes is concerned, there is, however, still one mystery to be resolved: who was this 'prince' (namely, a high official) who brought about his downfall? Although his name is not given, it was more than likely a man who had become his arch-rival and with whom he would on several other occasions come into conflict. It was, of course, none other than ʿAlī Mubārak (1824–93), who also played a hugely important role in the history of modern Arabic education and culture.

ʿAlī Mubārak: 'The Father of Education' (Abū 'l-Taʿlīm)

Twenty-three years al-Ṭahṭāwī's junior, ʿAlī Mubārak was born in the small Delta village of Birinbāl al-Jadīda (Daqahliyya province), where his father was the local *imām*.[5] His early life held little promise of a career of any

1. 1279/1872–3, Cairo, Maṭbaʿat al-Madāris al-Malakiyya, 4/395pp; 2nd edn, Cairo, Maṭbaʿat al-Madāris al-Malakiyya, 1295/1875; 3rd edn, in al-Ṭahṭāwī, 1973–80: 269–767.
2. al-Ṭahṭāwī, 1973–80: I, 453–6 [*Manāhij*].
3. al-Ṭahṭāwī, 1973–80: I, 456–62 [*Manāhij*]. The poem counts 208 verses (*basīṭ* metre). On al-Buraʿī, see *GAL*, I, 259; *GALS*, I, 459; Y. Sarkīs, 1928: 550–51; ʿU. Kaḥḥāla [n.d.]: V, 202; M. de Slane, 1883–95: I, 550.
4. Al-Maṭbaʿa al-Sūriyya, 792pp. (2nd edn, 1885, revised by Shāhīn ʿAṭiyya, Beirut, al-Maṭbaʿa al-Lubnāniyya, 1885, 439pp.). Interestingly enough, a Turkish translation of the book (by no less a man than the Ottoman Grand Vizier Yūsuf Kāmil Pasha) already appeared in 1862.
5. The basic source for ʿA. Mubārak's life is the autobiography in his own chronicle (ʿA. Mubārak, 1886–88: IX, 37–61), a German translation and study of which was made by S.

sort. In line with tradition, he received his early education in the village Qur'ānic school (*kuttāb*), but the young boy found it hard to adjust to the severe discipline of the classroom and ran away. After surviving a bout of cholera, he was tracked down by his father, who took him home. Unable to convince his son to return to the classroom and the sadistic and venal teacher, he decided that a trade would be the next best thing, and so ʿAlī became an apprentice to a carpenter. It did not take long, however, before relations between the fractious youth and his master were soured to such an extent that the latter terminated the apprenticeship agreement. It seems the argument centred on the *bakshīsh* (kickbacks) received by the carpenter, though the young boy himself was not averse to accepting bribes. In fact, this combination of envy, greed and ambition was to remain the dominant feature in ʿAlī Mubārak's life and career.

Increasingly desperate, ʿAlī's father sent his wayward son to a tax collector, hoping that this trade would appeal to him. But when one day the boy helped himself to his salary that had not been paid for three months, the clerk filed charges and the young boy was put into prison. It was only through an extraordinary case of luck that his father was able to obtain a pardon from Muḥammad ʿAlī, himself, who happened to be visiting the region. Already well versed in the ways of the world, young ʿAlī curried favour with his gaoler, who took pity on the child convict, and when a high official was looking for an assistant the guard suggested him. A sample of his scribal skills, accompanied by a suitable *bakshīsh,* resulted in his being hired. This was to mark a turning point in ʿAlī's career. When meeting his new master, ʿAnbar Efendi, for the first time, he was shocked to find that he was a former Abyssinian slave. In his autobiography, he expressed his wonder and surprise at finding a Negro occupying a government position, nearly all of which were, of course, pre-empted for Turks.[1] Eventually, he found out that the reason for the slave's ascension to government office lay with his training at the Qaṣr al-ʿAynī school, at which he had been among the first batch of students. Spurred on by ambition and single-mindedness, ʿAlī from then on had only one goal in mind – to be enrolled at that

Fliedner (1990). Other full-length studies on ʿA. Mubārak include: M. ʿAbd al-Karīm [n.d.]; M. Khalaf Allāh, 1957; Ḥ. al-Najjār, 1987; M. al-Sharqāwī, 1962; S. Zāyid, 1958; M. ʿImāra, 1988; S. Abū Hamdān 1993. Also see: G. Delanoue, 1982: 488–559, 654–7 (by far the best and most perceptive study of Mubārak's life and work); Y. Sarkīs, 1928: 1367–9; *EI1*, s.v. "ʿAlī Pāshā Mubārak" (K. Vollers); *EI2*, s.v. "ʿAlī Pāshā Mubārak" (K. Vollers); A. Rāfiʿī, 1987: I, 212–55; J. Zaydān, 1910: II, 33–9; J. Crabbs, 1984: 109–29; A. Amīn, 1949:184–201; L. Kenny, 1967; J. Heyworth-Dunne, 1938: *passim*; *GAL*, II, 482; *GALS*, II, 733.

1. ʿA. Mubārak, 1886–88: IX, 39.

school. The first step towards achieving his ambition was to get into the government education system through one of its elementary schools, where the most promising students were selected to continue at Qaṣr al-ʿAynī. So, the former school dropout, jailbird and general troublemaker applied for, and was accepted at a school in the town of Minyat al-ʿIzz. Soon after, he got what he wanted as he was selected to leave for Cairo. He was all of twelve years old.

Though he had finally achieved what he had so desperately wished for, reality hit hard. His time at Qaṣr al-ʿAynī was not a happy one; the level of teaching was quite poor and living conditions were almost unbearable. As a result of the draconian regime of strenuous physical exercise, military drills and undernourishment, the young boy ended up in hospital. Yet, in spite of admonitions from his father, who even made arrangements to 'spring' his son from the sick ward, Mubārak continued. Three years later, he was admitted to the Būlāq-based Engineering School (*muhandiskhāna*), which had been founded in 1834 and was led by Lambert Bey.

When, in early 1844, Sulaymān Pasha al-Faransāwī was putting together a contingent of students for training in Paris at what was to become the *Ecole Militaire Egyptienne*, ʿAlī Mubārak did not fail to make himself noticed. As the mission, which eventually comprised thirty-seven students, was also to include Muḥammad ʿAlī's sons Ḥusayn and Ḥalīm, as well as Ibrāhīm's sons Ismā'īl (the future Khedive) and Aḥmad – for which reason it subsequently became known as the *ba'that al-anjāl* ('the Mission of the Descendants') – the ambitious Mubārak realized the benefits to be drawn from an association with the princes, and training in the modern sciences, which would secure his future.[1] The school, which was located at the rue du Regard (off the fashionable rue du Chèrche Midi, near the Boulevard Raspail), was led by one of al-Ṭahtāwī's fellow students in Paris, the Armenian Iṣṭifān Bey (see below).[2] Furthermore, al-Ṭahṭāwī's son, ʿAlī Fahmī, was also among the first batch of students! The school curriculum, drawn up by another veteran of the first mission, E. Jomard, was intended to prepare the students for the French military academies. In view of the royal connections of some of the students, the school was often the venue of grand receptions and galas (with visits by the heir apparent to the French throne and other members of the royal family). In May 1846, the school was inspected by Ibrāhīm Pasha, who was then on an official visit to

1. ʿA. Mubārak, 1886–88: IX, 41–2.
2. On this establishment (which between 1844 and 1849 received seventy students), see A. Louca, 1970: 75ff.; ʿA. Mubārak, 1886–88: IX, 42–3.

France, and the students formed an honorary guard when he was officially received by Louis-Philippe.[1] While the young Beys and princes enjoyed the high life of the capital,[2] the more humble-born students applied themselves diligently to their work, and ʿAlī Mubārak and his two friends Ḥammād ʿAbd al-ʿAṭī and ʿAlī ʿIbrāhīm, in particular, consistently ranked highest in their class. It was also during Mubārak's Paris studies that he, like al-Ṭahṭāwī, displayed a particular interest in history.

In January 1847, the three friends were admitted to the Artillery and Engineers' School in Metz, where they attended classes for two years. A few months into their practical training in an Engineering unit, upon the accession to the throne of ʿAbbās Pasha, the European adventure suddenly came to an end as all students were recalled to Egypt.

Upon his return to his homeland, ʿAlī Mubārak set about building a career that would cover all fields, from education to government, the military and trade. Promoted to the rank of captain, he took up his first professional appointment as a teacher at the artillery school (*maktab al-ṭōbjiyya*) of Ṭura. Shortly afterwards, however, he began his ascendance to power, when he and his two Paris schoolfriends were invited to act as the Khedive's personal advisers, ʿAlī Ibrāhīm becoming tutor to ʿAbbās' son, Ilhāmī. With disarming honesty, Mubārak later reminisces that this call to the corridors of power filled him with great apprehension as he was quite aware of the drawbacks to a close association with the Khedive and his entourage.[3] One of the projects in which he threw himself with his usual gusto was the reorganization of the government schools – many of which had been closed by ʿAbbās (including, as we have seen, al-Ṭahṭāwī's Language School), who had also considerably reduced the government budget for education – into one single establishment with Mubārak, of course, at its head (1850–54). The picture of this period that emerges from his memoirs is that of a tireless organizer, administrator, and manager, who even found time to teach classes (especially physics and architecture), write schoolbooks, draw up curricula, and inspect literally every aspect of the educational experience (including the clothing, food, and indeed general welfare of the students).[4] As a student, he had frequently lamented the lack of textbooks at Egyptian establishments, a hiatus he now set about

1. See G. Wiet, 1948.
2. Two of the students apparently indulged a bit too much in the good life as they were recalled and sent direct to the galleys in Alexandria for committing 'reprehensible acts'; *al-Waqāʾiʿ al-Miṣriyya*, 16 Shaʿbān 1264/18 July 1848.
3. ʿA. Mubārak, 1886–88: IX, 43–4.
4. ʿA. Mubārak 1886–8: IX, 44–5.

remedying with a vengeance. With the help of his teachers, he continued the work of the defunct Language School and its Translation adjunct, and produced a number of textbooks. In order to meet distribution demand, he set up movable type and lithograph presses at the Engineering College, where sixty thousand (!) copies of schoolbooks were printed for various government schools, while atlases and other illustrated materials were lithographed. The teaching methods, too, were subject to radical changes. He introduced some of the methods he himself had been able to try and test in France, whereas his ordeal of the first year at Qaṣr al-ʿAynī may also have had something to do with his strong opposition to corporal punishment in his classrooms.

Though there is no proof that Mubārak actively plotted against other stars in the Egyptian educational firmament, it is, to say the least, significant that two days after gaining control over the new programme, Ibrāhīm Adham Pasha[1] was dismissed as head of the Department of Education, whereas his protégé al-Ṭahṭāwī was banished to the Sudan a few months later. It is unclear when the rivalry between Mubārak and al-Ṭahṭāwī started, and whether it was simply a matter of conflicting personalities, political rivalry, or resentment at the favour al-Ṭahṭāwī had enjoyed with Muḥammad ʿAlī. Whatever the case may be, there is little doubt that Mubārak did not have a great deal of personal liking for al-Ṭahṭāwī.

Mubārak's fortunes changed abruptly with the arrival of the new Khedive, Saʿīd, when he, as a result of court intrigues, found himself dispatched to the Crimea to join the Egyptian forces who were fighting the Russians on the side of the Ottomans. Nothing if not resilient, the mercurial Mubārak took the entire experience into his stride and even learned Turkish during a four-month stay in Istanbul. There was no real improvement in his situation when he returned from his travels in 1857, and for a while it seemed as if his bright career had just been a damp squib. At one point, he even contemplated retiring to the country and continuing his existence as a farmer.[2] The rest of Saʿīd's reign brought little solace for

1. A former officer in the Ottoman army, Adham (Edhem) had been attracted by Muḥammad ʿAlī's army modernization scheme. He also became a friend of Colonel Sève, and like him was a staunch supporter of the Saint-Simonian ideology. After having risen in the hierarchy (becoming a general, and Minister for Education) and enjoying the favour of subsequent Egyptian rulers, he fell from grace when Ismāʿīl rose to the throne. Adham Bey left Egypt and settled in his native Istanbul, where he died soon after (1869). See ʿA. Mubārak 1886–8: XII, 5–6; J.-M. Carré 1956: I, 272.
2. ʿA. Mubārak 1886–8: IX, 47.

Mubārak, with brief stints in lowly positions in government departments alternating with periods of viceregally imposed unemployment. Teaching remained in his blood, however, and when Ibrāhīm Adham Pasha was in search of someone to teach the three Rs to Egyptian officers and NCOs, Mubārak jumped at the opportunity 'of sharing the benefits of knowledge' with his compatriots.[1] By all accounts, it was somewhat of a back-to-basics approach, with the great educator being reduced to teaching his students 'on the hop' as it were, sometimes teaching the alphabet by writing the letters in the sand with his students sitting around in makeshift tents doubling as classrooms. His experiences later culminated in textbooks on geometry,[2] mathematics and engineering,[3] biology,[4] and the teaching of Arabic reading and writing.[5]

During the last months of Saʿīd's reign, Mubārak's life was at a particularly low ebb, both professionally and personally. But then, in 1863 the Khedive died and was succeeded by Mubārak's former schoolmate from the *Ecole Militaire Egyptienne*, Ismāʿīl, whose ambition it was to turn Egypt into the continent's superpower, within which the adoption of European culture was a key component. Suddenly, Mubārak's future looked a great deal brighter again. After nine long lean years, the reign of the westernizing Khedive would coincide with the most productive and rewarding period in Mubārak's life.[6] Appointed as a member of Ismāʿīl's cabinet (*maʿiyya*), he was put in charge of the Nile Barrages (*al-qanāṭir al-khayriyya*) and

1. ʿA. Mubārak 1886–8: IX, 48.
2. *Taqrīb al-handasa li istiʿmāl al-ʿaskariyya al-Miṣriyya* ('Guide to Geometry for Use by the Egyptian Military') 1873, Cairo, Maṭbaʿat Wādī'l-Nīl, 95/4pp. ʿĀ. Nuṣayr 1990: 168 (no. 5/145).
3. *Tadhkirat al-muhandisīn wa tabṣirat al-rāghibīn* ('Treatise for Engineers and Enlightenment for Those Wishing to Acquire Knowledge'), 1873 (1876), Cairo, Maṭbaʿat al-Madāris al-Malikiyya, 419pp. ʿĀ. Nuṣayr 1990: 168 (no. 5/142–4).
4. *Tanwīr al-afhām fī taghadhdhī al-ajsām* ('Enlightenment of the Mind Regarding the Nourishment of the Body'), 1872, Cairo, Maṭbaʿat al-Madāris al-Malakiyya, 72pp. ʿĀ. Nuṣayr 1990: 181 (no. 6/111).
5. *Ṭarīq al-hijā wa 'l-tamrīn ʿalā 'l-qirāʾa fī 'l-lugha al-ʿArabiyya* ('The Road Towards the Alphabet and Arabic Reading Exercises'). This book, which was direcly inspired by the French language manuals Mubārak had studied during his Paris stay, was published in 1285/1868 (Maṭbaʿat Wādī 'l-Nīl), and reprinted no fewer than eleven times in the last quarter of the century; cf. ʿĀ. Nuṣayr 1990: 162 (nos. 4/1027–44), 163 (no. 4/1050). The first volume (20/88pp.) consisted of writing samples, whereas the second (144pp.) was made up of reading texts chosen by Rifāʿa al-Ṭahṭāwī's former disciple Ṣāliḥ Majdī (who at the time was working at the *Qalam al-Tarjama*). The often moralizing texts were very similar to those used in French manuals, whereas several texts were clearly translations from French originals.
6. The definitive study of Ismāʿīl's reign is ʿA. al-Rāfiʿī 1987. For a discussion of his modernization schemes, also see L. Kenny 1965.

the works involving the redirection of the Nile waters away from the Rosetta tributary. In 1865, Mubārak represented Egypt in the international commission charged with negotiating land rights between Egypt and the Suez Canal Company. With diplomatic flair, he was able to satisfy both his ruler and the French Emperor Napoleon III, both of whom showed their gratitude: the Khedive bestowed upon him the rank of *mutamāyiz* and awarded him the prestigious *nīshān majīdī* (3rd class) medal, whereas the French made him an officer of the *Légion d'Honneur*.[1] In October 1867, Mubārak became Deputy Minister (*wakīl*) for Education (under Sharīf Pasha), and then, one year later, Minister for Education (*wazīr al-ma'ārif*), as well as Minister for Public Works (*wazīr al-ashghāl*), thus becoming the first native Egyptian in modern times to head a government department. In the Ministry of Public Works, his duties included the supervision and execution of the monumental project for the modernization of Cairo – part of Ismā'īl's dream of creating his own Paris at home – as well as the expansion of the railways, and, of course, the preparations for the opening of the Suez Canal. In 1867, he was sent to Paris to negotiate a loan on behalf of the Khedive. He took advantage of his stay to gather material on public education, and to examine first-hand a key component of modern town planning, the sewers, to which he devotes almost an entire page in his autobiography.[2] In the same year, inspired by the French educational system, he unified the educational system, and introduced a three-tier system, within which the *kuttāb* were to be elevated to primary schools, which would directly improve the chances of educational attainment for the population at large.[3] It is this project which earned him the honorific of 'Father of Education'.

His reforms even gained currency beyond Egypt's frontiers, and there is little doubt that it helped shape the Tunisian statesman Khayr al-Dīn's ideas for the famous Ṣādiqī college (*al-madrasa al-Ṣādiqiyya*), although ultimately its roots, like those of the Egyptian schools, went back to the French *collèges* for which Mubārak and Khayr al-Dīn alike had great admiration.[4] Founded in 1875, the *Collège Sadiki*, whose faculty also consisted almost entirely of

---

1. 'A. Mubārak 1886–8: IX, 49; 'A. al-Rāfi'ī 1987: I, 230–1.
2. 'A. Mubārak 1886–8: IX, 49–50.
3. On these and other educational reforms in Ismā'īl's reign, see G. Delanoue 1982: 507ff.; J. Crabbs 1984: 93ff.; A. 'Abd al-Karīm 1945: II; E. Dor 1872.
4. For a detailed discussion on this establishment, see D. Newman 1998: 317ff.; N. Sraïeb 1995; A. Abdesselam 1975. Also see M. Smida 1970: 301–320, 401–404; G. Van Krieken 1976: 192–198; M. Kraïem 1973: II, 195–201; F. Arnoulet 1954: 160–167; M. Chenoufi 1974: 747–766; M. Bayram 1884–93: II, 66ff., 126.

native teachers, aimed to provide three-tier education to Muslim students – regardless of background – with a combination of both modern and traditional instruction, with the new being integrated into, rather than superimposed on, the traditional. Or, to put it in the words of one of the school's historians, the Ṣādiqī was to provide

> <*une*> *culture toute à la fois profondément enracinée dans la tradition musulmane et largement ouverte sur les civilisations étrangères et les sciences modernes.*[1]

Naturally, Mubārak's success was the source of much envy at the court, with many equally ambitious – though not necessarily equally competent – men standing in the wings, poised to sweep down on him at the right moment. This came in 1870, when he refused to turn over the railways revenues to the Finance Minister Ismāʿīl Pasha Ṣiddīq unless the latter was prepared to take on the maintenance and servicing. Less than six months later, however, the competent Mubārak was again recalled to government, and was put in charge of the non-governmental schools (*al-madāris al-ahliyya*). Shortly afterwards, he was reinvested as Minister for Education, while the *Awqāf* (pious foundations) Ministry was added to his already impressive collection. In order to be able to manage his affairs, he turned the Muṣṭafā Fāḍil palace in Darb al-Jamāmīz into a central headquarters for all his activities. Incredible though it may seem, this also included all the government schools of Cairo, with Mubārak continuing to make spot inspections in the course of the day to apprise himself of student activities and progress. When both ministries were handed to the Khedive's son, Ḥusayn Kāmil, Mubārak stayed on as his adviser.

As we have seen, Mubārak considered the availability of books a key factor in education. This resulted in the creation in 1870 of the first national library, the *Dār al-Kutub* ('House of Books'), patterned on the French National Library that had so impressed him during his study stay in Paris. He also added a laboratory which contained all the necessary equipment to conduct experiments in a variety of sciences (physics, chemistry, mathematics).[2] In the same year, Mubārak also set up a journal, *Rawḍat al-Madāris* ('The Garden of Schools'), which contained articles on a very wide range of scientific subjects as well as educational methods and to which he himself contributed, as did other famous educators, scholars, and

---

1. A. Abdesselam 1975: 25.
2. ʿA. Mubārak 1886–8: IX, 51; J. Zaydān 1957: IV, 100–102; ʿA. al-Rāfiʿī 1987: I, 236–7.

authors like al-Ṭahṭāwī, ʿAbd Allāh Fikrī, or Ismāʿīl al-Falakī. Whatever the feelings between al-Ṭahṭāwī and Mubārak, there is little doubt that the latter recognized his former rival's abilities as it was al-Ṭahṭāwī who was put in charge of the journal, with his son ʿAlī Fahmī Bey as the editorial secretary.[1]

Another European-inspired facility was the conference hall at Darb al-Jamāmīz for lectures by both foreign and Egyptian teachers, where for instance the Dutch Orientalist Brugsch delivered a famous series of talks on pharaonic Egypt.[2] It was officially inaugurated in July 1871, and baptized *Dār al-ʿUlūm* ('House of Sciences'), the name which would the following year be given to the teacher training college. This college constituted the coping stone in Mubārak's vision for a modern educational system for Egypt. It was set up to train the staff for the new schools, and provided courses (taught by both native and European lecturers) in religious subjects (Qur'ān, Islamic law) as well as modern sciences like history, physics, architecture, mechanics, etc.[3] This was in fact his way of introducing Azharīs to the modern sciences. Realizing that he would never be able to overcome *ʿulamāʾ* opposition to the inclusion of these subjects into the Azhar curriculum, Mubārak came up with an idea that was as brilliant as it was simple: rather than attempting an outright reform of the highly conservative mosque-university, he set out to introduce its students to the new sciences within the framework of a separate entity. It is worth adding that this institution has endured to this day and has retained its prominent position within the Egyptian educational system.[4] Al-Ṭahṭāwī's name would live on in the Dār al-ʿUlūm after his death with the appointment of his son ʿAlī Fahmī in 1878 as director. Clearly endowed with his father's organizational skills, he one year later was put in charge (*wakīl*) of the *makātib ahliyya*, and in 1882 rose to the rank of deputy Minister for Education, under ʿAbd Allāh Fikrī.

In October 1873, Ismāʿīl Ṣiddīq dealt another harsh blow to Mubārak's standing at the court when he accused him of being critical of the government in his book *Nukhbat al-fikr fī tadbīr al-Nīl Miṣr* ('The Best Plan

1. This journal appeared every fortnight as from 15 Muḥarram 1287/17 April 1870. Its last issue was published in September 1877. See M. Ḥasan & ʿA. al-Dasūqī 1975.
2. J. Heyworth-Dunne 1938: 353–4.
3. Today, the Dār al-ʿUlūm is a faculty of the University of Cairo and specializes in Arabic language and religious sciences. It is located near the famous Dome (*qubba*) of Cairo University in Giza.
4. ʿA. Mubārak 1886–8: IX, 51; ʿA. al-Rāfiʿī 1987: I, 235–6. Also see M. Reimer 1997 for a discussion of Mubārak's views on al-Azhar.

for the Regulation of the Nile'). The fact that these accusations were based on a manuscript version of the text (the book was not published until 1298/1880)[1] reveals the level of intrigue and skulduggery at the Egyptian court. And so, his empire began inexorably to crumble as he lost post after post.

It would take until 1878 before Mubārak was able to return to government, with the appointment to his old departments of Education and the Awqāf in Nūbār Pasha's highly unpopular cabinet (1878–79).

Under Ismāʿīl's successor, Tawfīq (1879–92), Mubārak was again put in charge of the Ministry of Public Works in the Riyāḍ Pasha cabinet (1879–81). It is interesting to note that it was his old friend ʿAlī Ibrāhīm who became Minister for Education when Tawfīq acceded to the throne. Ibrāhīm, who had also dabbled in a number of fields, ranging from the law to engineering (he designed the famous Muḥammad ʿAlī street), made quite a mark as he founded the first school for the blind and the deaf and dumb, whereas he is also credited with introducing the award of final certificates.

The final stages of Mubārak's political life were dominated by ill-chosen affiliations and alliances, a case in point being his attitude towards the events surrounding the ʿUrābī rebellion and the British occupation (1882).[2] His final major political appointment came in September 1882, as Minister for Public Works in the fourth Sharīf Pasha cabinet. When the government fell in 1884, the by then 60-year-old Mubārak apparently had had enough and decided to return to his birthplace to manage his country estate, only to return for one last time as Minister for Education in another Riyāḍ Pasha cabinet, in 1888. In a curious quirk of history, Mubārak, who had introduced so many foreign elements into Egyptian education and been an outspoken critic of ʿŪrābī Pasha and his supporters, began a crusade against foreign schools in Egypt, which he felt had become too numerous and disregarded national and religious elements in education. He also recommended that the government impose a uniform compulsory primary school curriculum. When he once more returned to the country in 1891, he was not able to enjoy his retirement much as his ailing health forced him to return to the capital, where he died on 14 November 1893.

---

1. Maṭbaʿat Wādī 'l-Nīl, 206pp. (ʿĀ. Nuṣayr 1990: 188, no. 6/241) For a discussion, see M. Khalaf Allah, 1957: 208ff. The book was reprinted in ʿAlī Mubārak's collected works (ed. M. ʿImāra, 1979–80: III, 5–220).
2. For this period, see G. Delanoue, 1982: 516–23. For background, see, for instance, Donald Malcolm Reid, 'The `Urabi revolution and the British conquest', in M. Daly, 1998: 217–38; D. Daly, 'British Occupation, 1882–1922', in *ibid.*, 239–51.

In addition to his staggering range of political and administrative activities, Mubārak was also a prolific writer and translator. Besides the already mentioned school manuals, one should cite three works. The first is an abridged translation of Sédillot's famous *Histoire des Arabes* (1854), under the title *Khulāṣat tārīkh al-ʿArab*.[1] The choice of this book was no coincidence inasmuch as Sédillot's book on the grandeur of Arab culture had become a favourite reference work for Muslims, keen on stressing the Arab origins of European modern civilization, and a source from which other travellers, such as the Tunisians Khayr al-Dīn[2] and Muḥammad b. al-Khūja,[3] quoted extensively.

The second is the monumental *al-Khiṭaṭ al-tawfīqiyya al-jadīda li-miṣr al-qāhira wa mudunihā wa bilādihā al-qadīma wa 'l-shahīra* ('The New *Khiṭaṭ* for Tawfīq, Regarding Cairo, its Famous Ancient Cities and Towns'), the first part of which appeared in 1886. Dedicated to Tawfīq, this twenty-volume treasure trove on Egyptian history, geography and topography was patterned on the *Khiṭaṭ* by the 15th-century Cairo-born historian Taqī 'l-Dīn al-Maqrīzī (1364–1442). Revealing Mubarak's penchant for history, the work is based on both Arab and European records, as well as inscriptions, maps, etc, and includes numerous biographies. It was very well received in European scholarly circles, as witnessed by Ignaz Goldziher's review in the *Wiener Zeitschrift für die Kunde des Morgenlandes* of 1890,[4] even though the German Arabist Karl Vollers expressed a slightly less favourable view in Mubārak's obituary notice.[5]

Finally, Mubārak, like al-Ṭahṭāwī, also wrote a book on his experiences in Europe. Unlike al-Ṭahṭāwī's, however, Mubārak's account is a fictional travelogue. The four-volume book (running to a total of 1,490 pages), entitled *ʿAlam al-Dīn* (1888), stands out from other 19th-century works on European visits both by its structure and pedagogic intent, and has been called 'one of the earliest critiques of European Orientalism'.[6] The story is that of the imaginary journey of an Azhar *shaykh*, ʿAlam al-Dīn, and his

1. Būlāq, 1311/1893, 256pp.; 1309/1891, Cairo, Maṭbaʿat Muḥammad Muṣṭafā, 16/298pp.; ʿĀ. Nuṣayr, 1990: 254 (Nos. 9/511–12). According to the contemporary M. Durrī (1894: 60–61), Mubārak did not do the translation himself, but commissioned it.
2. 1867: 28–31 (cf. L. Sédillot, 1854: i-v, 332ff.).
3. 1900: 47–8 (cf. L. Sédillot, 1854: 183, 364), 49–50 (cf. L. Sédillot, 1854: 367–9, 439).
4. Vol. 4, 347–52. On the work, see, e.g., G. Baer in P. Holt, 1968: 13–27; J. Crabbs, 1984: 116ff.
5. K. Vollers, 1893: 721.
6. P. Vatikiotis, 1991: 110. For a discussion of this work, see A. Louca, 1970: 88–100; G. Delanoue, 1982: 526ff.; W. al-Qadi, 1981. The book was reprinted in ʿA. Mubārak's collected works (ed. M. ʿImāra, 1979–80: I, 316–685).

young son Burhān al-Dīn. They are accompanied by an English Orientalist who invited ʿAlam al-Dīn to help him with the translation of the *Lisān al-ʿArab*, the famous Arabic dictionary. The relationship between the Egyptian and the European was more than likely inspired by the friendship between the Egyptian scholar Ibrāhīm al-Dasūqī and the English Arabist Edward William Lane. The former was indeed of great help (notably in copying out all twenty-four volumes of another Arabic dictionary, the *Tāj al-ʿArūs*) during Lane's stay in Cairo,[1] and in his *Khiṭaṭ*, Mubārak included al-Dasūqī's account of his contact with Lane.[2]

At the outset, the author made clear that he intended to write an educational work, whose basic aim was to provide as much information as possible about mankind and the sciences, to compare the past and the present and to compare East and West through two contrasting characters.[3] Unfortunately, his other objective, to do so in a way that was attractive to read, is never actually attained. Poorly structured and uneven in style, the book never really succeeds in capturing the reader's imagination and despite the dialogue format, Mubārak – ever the history teacher – delivers what is a rather uninspiring kind of primer on European society and culture. The journey to Paris (via Marseilles) and the stay there are a pretext for a series of philosophical dialogues (*musāmarāt*) – 125 in all – between the central characters on an incongruously mixed bag of subjects related to various aspects of European civilization and society, Arab and Egyptian history and religious issues or more prosaic questions such as 'storms' and 'loneliness'. It is worth noting that Mubārak's work may have inspired another fictional jaunt, i.e. that by the protagonists in Muḥammad al-Muwayliḥī's *al-Riḥla al-Thāniyya* ('The Second Journey'),[4] which first appeared in the 1927 edition of that author's *Ḥadīth ʿĪsā b. Hishām*, commonly considered the first Arabic 'novel'. Here, the eponymous narrator, ʿĪsā b. Hishām, and a Pasha who has awakened from the dead, travel to the 1900 Paris Exposition Universelle (which al-Muwayliḥī also visited) together with a French Orientalist. For another thing, the narrative of *Hadīth ʿĪsā b. Hishām* is also developed through dialogues, just as in *ʿAlam al-Dīn*, where it was used

1. Cf. G. Alleaume, 1982; G. Roper, 'Texts from Nineteenth-Century Egypt. The role of E. W. Lane', in P. and J. Starkey, 1998: 248.
2. ʿA. Mubārak, 1882: XI,10.
3. ʿA. Mubārak, 1882: I, 7.
4. Interestingly enough, in his study of Muwayliḥī's *Ḥadīth ʿĪsā b. Hishām* that precedes the English translation (1992), R. Allen does not comment upon the similarities between *ʿAlam al-Dīn* and the 'Second Journey' (which, it must be added, is not included in the translation).

for the first time in modern Arabic literature. *'Alam al-Dīn* is probably the first example in modern Arabic literature of the *Erziehungsroman* (*al-riwāya al-ta'līmiyya*).[1]

Finally, *'Alam al-Dīn* also contains an interesting clue regarding the relationship between Mubārak and al-Ṭahṭāwī as the former could not resist sneering at the author of the *Takhlīṣ*, claiming that he talked about things he had not experienced first-hand.[2]

al-Ṭahṭāwī the Reformer (1854–73)

On 14 July 1854, ʿAbbās I was assassinated by two of his eunuchs. His successor was his uncle, Saʿīd (I) Pasha, the last surviving son of the great Muḥammad ʿAlī. Unlike his nephew, the new ruler was an enthusiastic Francophile, who immediately surrounded himself with European advisers like Linant de Bellefonds, Clot Bey and Ferdinand de Lesseps (who had even briefly been his tutor). And so al-Ṭahṭāwī once again entered upon the scene, while, as we have seen, it was Mubārak's turn to recede into the wings for a while.

His first appointment was as Director of the European Department of the Cairo Governorate, after which he went on to Ṣalība to become deputy head (under Sulaymān Pasha) of the Military School (*madrasat al-rijāl*). At the same time, al-Ṭahṭāwī and his associate Adham Pasha, who was then inspector of the Schools Council (*dīwān al-madāris*) and governor of Cairo, started working on a project for the establishment of government schools, thereby continuing the efforts started by Muḥammad ʿAlī.[3] The proposal provided for the creation of, initially, ten schools – eight in Cairo, one in Būlāq and one in Old Cairo – accessible to all inhabitants, regardless of background, age or educational attainment. These *makātib ahliyya* ('national' or 'people's schools') were to fill the gap that existed between, on the one hand, the *kuttābs* and, on the other, the viceregal (i.e. government) schools (*makātib amīriyya*). They thus constituted the very first attempt at introducing general basic education for all Egyptians, with a curriculum and structure clearly patterned on European institutions. Unfortunately, the timing was not right and al-Ṭahṭāwī's project failed to convince the Khedive; as we have seen it would take many more years and the drive of ʿAlī Mubārak before these 'people's schools' saw the light of

1. ʿA. Badr, 1963: 63–4.
2. ʿA. Mubārak, 1882: IV, 1334.
3. Cf. A. ʿAbd al-Karīm, 1945: II, 176ff.; *ibid.*, III, Annexe I, 1–14.

day. In the 1850s, al-Ṭahṭāwī was also at the basis of a new literary genre, the patriotic poem (*waṭaniyyāt*), of which he published five in 1856, and which were patterned on French models he had encountered during his stay in Paris.[1] Later on, patriotism would appear as a key factor for progress and prosperity in a country.[2] It is this view that later earned him the title of 'the Father of Arab Nationalism',[3] though, as one observer pointed out, a more apt sobriquet would be 'the Father of Egyptian Nationalism'.[4]

In the same year, in yet another example of Khedivial whim, al-Ṭahṭāwī's lack of military training did not prevent him from being put in charge of the newly founded military school (*madrasat al-ḥarbiyya*) at the Citadel, to which a translation section was added, led by his protégé, Ṣāliḥ Majdī. Thanks to the former *imām*'s educationalist and administrative skills, the school's popularity soared; al-Ṭahṭāwī's son, Badawī Fatḥī Bey, was later to be one of its students. In addition to his directorial duties at the Military School, al-Ṭahṭāwī was also responsible for three other establishments (Accounting, Civil Engineering and Architecture), which were subsequently annexed. An even more incongruous appointment came in the shape of an inspectorship in the Cairo Building and Construction Department.[5] In 1861, the momentum of al-Ṭahṭāwī's career was again broken when the ruler pulled the plug on the entire college, and a depressing two years of inactivity followed.

The reign of Ismāʿīl ushered in a period of tremendous activity for al-Ṭahṭāwī.[6] Once again, he was allowed to ply his translation trade as head of a new translation office, specializing in European legal texts. It was during this period that he translated the *Code Napoléon* (together with his former pupils ʿAbd Allāh Bey al-Sayyid, Aḥmad Ḥilmī and ʿAbd al-Salām), which appeared in 1866.[7] Two years later, he also published his translation of the French commercial codex, *Qānūn al-tijāra*.[8] In the field of education, he was as busy as ever, as a member of the *dīwān al-madāris* and as the author in 1869 of what has subsequently been called the first modern Arabic grammar schoolbook, *al-Tuḥfa al-maktabiyya li-taqrīb al-lugha al-ʿArabiyya* ('Present

1. G. Delanoue, 1982: 626–7; J.Heyworth-Dunne, 1940–42: 399–400; ʿA. al-Rāfiʿī, 1954: 8–12; W. Braune, 1933: 119–23.
2. al-Ṭahṭāwī, 1973–80 [*Manāhij*]: I, 251ff. Cf. K. Al-Husry, 1966: 29ff.
3. M. ʿImāra [al-Ṭahṭāwī], 1973–80: I, 132.
4. J. Crabbs, 1984: 78.
5. Ṣ. Majdī, 1958: 42.
6. Cf. Ṣ. Majdī, 1958: 42–3; J. al-Shayyāl, 1958b: 46–50.
7. 2 vols, Būlāq; ʿĀ. Nuṣayr, 1990: 111 (no. 3/205), 114 (Nos. 310–13); Y. Sarkīs, 1928: 944.
8. Būlāq, 8/224pp. (2nd edn, 1896) ʿĀ. Nuṣayr, 1990: 112 (Nos. 3/243–5); Y. Sarkīs, 1928: 944.

for Schools for the Clarification of the Arabic Language'),[1] which he wrote at the request of ʿAlī Mubārak (then the head of the Schools Council). The layout and structure of the work, with its explanations couched in simple language and easy-reference tables, are clearly reminiscent of the practical approach to grammar the author had so admired in the manuals he studied in France.

The following year, at the age of seventy, al-Ṭahṭāwī even picked up his journalistic pen as the editor-in-chief of *Rawḍat al-Madāris* (see above).

The late 1860s were also the most prolific in terms of literary output, with major 'philosophical' works like *Manāhij al-albāb al-Miṣriyya fī mabāhij al-ādāb al-ʿaṣriyya* ('The Roads of Egyptian Hearts in the Joys of the Contemporary Arts')[2] and the already mentioned *al-Murshid al-amīn li 'l-banāt wa 'l-banīn* (which was completed not long before his death). These must be considered the culmination of, respectively, al-Ṭahṭāwī's social, political and educational thought. The latter book addresses all aspects of education, and thanks to its emphasis on equal education for boys and girls its author has been called a pioneer of women's emancipation.[3] The *Manāhij*, on the other hand, provides a unique insight into the development of his views of politics and government. In the field of history, he embarked upon a monumental history of Egypt, finishing the first two volumes, of which unfortunately only one was published during his lifetime, i.e. *Anwār tawfīq al-jalīl fī akhbār Miṣr wa tawthīq banī Ismāʿīl* ('The Lights of the Great Success in Events about Egypt and the Strengthening of Ismāʿīl's Dynasty').[4] The book deals with pharaonic Egypt up to the Muslim conquest and may indeed have been the very first book on the country's ancient past to be written by an Egyptian.[5] Equally noteworthy is the fact that the author used both Arabic and European sources. The second volume, a biography of the Prophet entitled *Nihāyat al-ījāz fī sīrat sākin al-Ḥijāz* ('Ultimate Abridgement of the Life of an Inhabitant from the Ḥijāz'),[6] was published posthumously, edited by the author's son ʿAlī Fahmī.

1. Cairo, Maṭbaʿat al-Madāris, 180pp. (= M. Imara, 1973–80: III, 7–262). ʿĀ. Nuṣayr, 1990: 162 (Nos. 4/1019–20); Y. Sarkīs, 1928: 943; A. Badawī, 1959: 111–12; J. Heyworth-Dunne, 1940–42: 404–06.
2. 1286/1869, Būlāq, 18/269pp.; 2nd edn, 1330/1920, Cairo, Maṭbaʿat Sharikat al-Raghā'ib, 20/450pp. (ed. by the author's grandson, Muḥammad Rifāʿa); al-Ṭahṭāwī, 1973–80: I, 243–591. For a discussion, see A. Hourani, 1989: 72ff.; G. Delanoue, 1982: esp. 451–81; J. Crabbs, 1984: 74ff.; K. Al-Husry, 1966; J. Cole, 1980; 1966: 23ff.; I. Altman, 1976.
3. See S. Ali, 1994: 13ff.; G. Delanoue, 1982: 481ff.
4. 1285/1868, Maṭbaʿat al-Madāris, 553pp. (= al-Ṭahṭāwī, 1973–80: III, 7–262).
5. Y. Choueiri, 1989: 6ff.
6. 1291/1874, Maṭbaʿat al-Madāris al-Malakiyya, 332/8pp. (= al-Ṭahṭāwī, 1973–80: IV).

Rifāʿa Bey died on 1 Rabīʿ I 1290/27 May 1873, and was buried the following day, with the *shaykh al-Azhar*, Muḥammad al-Mahdī al-ʿAbbāsī, leading the prayers. His body was committed to the soil in the Cairo cemetery al-Qarāfa al-Kubrā, at the foot of the Muqaṭṭam hills, in the 'Scholars' Garden' (*Bustān al-ʿUlamāʾ*). In January of that year, the very first Muslim girls' school had opened its doors in Cairo.

It is difficult to overestimate the importance of the contribution made by al-Ṭahṭāwī and, for that matter, ʿAlī Mubārak to Egyptian society in the century and the impact they had on the further development of the modern nation. They symbolized the best of the syncretism between East and West, tradition and modernity. To this day, the results of their achievements and reforms live on.

THREE

al-Ṭahṭāwī in Europe

No sooner had the Egyptian students set foot on French soil than they were led to the lazaret at the rather misleadingly named *Nouvelles Infirmeries* in the north of the city to spend their quarantine. After eighteen days their confinement was lifted on 4 June 1826, and they were taken to their lodgings, the Château de Bonneveine, on the outskirts of town, to begin their education. And so, for the next thirty days (June-July), they devoted themselves to learning the French sounds and alphabet.[1] However, it was not all toil since the students were occasionally allowed to do some sightseeing in Marseilles. Among the things that attracted their attention were the *bistros*, the beautiful shops and, of course, the elegantly dressed (and unveiled!) French women.

The reaction of the local population to the Egyptians was somewhat less enthusiastic than had been expected, though. The media whipped up latent pro-Greek feelings and a more radical element seized upon the mission to attack Prime Minister Villèle for his pro-Ottoman stance.[2]

During their pleasure outings, they also established contacts with the Egyptian refugees (the remnants of Muʿallim Yaʿqūb's Coptic legion), nearly all of whom had been settled in Marseilles and were still drawing a pension from the War Ministry. Marseilles was also the first town outside Paris to have a course (sponsored by the *Ecole des Langues Orientales* in Paris) in *arabe vulgaire*, which had been set up at the recommendation of de Sacy and the Syrian priest Gabriel Taouil (Jibrā'īl al-Ṭawīl), who taught

1. In addition to the information provided by al-Ṭahṭāwī himself, the following sources provide a discussion of the author's stay in France: A. Louca, 1970: 33–74; G. Delanoue, 1982: II, 386–97; J. Heyworth-Dunne, 1938: 159–70; M. ʿAllām, Aḥmad A. Badawī, A. Lūqā eds., *Takhlīṣ al-Ibrīz fī talkhīṣ Bārīz*, Cairo (Muṣṭafā al-Bābī al-Ḥalabī), 1378/1958, pp. 3–51. For general details on the Egyptian student missions, see J. Heyworth-Dunne, 1938; A. Silvera, 1980; ʿU. Ṭūsūn, 1934.
2. A. Louca, 1970: 37–8; A. Silvera, 1980: 9.

it between 1807 and 1835 (when he was succeeded by the famous Eusèbe de Salles).[1]

Contacts between the new arrivals from the motherland and their expatriate brethren were not always smooth, and though al-Ṭahṭāwī expressed his joy at encountering someone from his native Ṣaʿīd – a distant relative to boot! – he was also shocked to find that many of his former coreligionists had converted to Christianity, and some could not even speak Arabic any more.

In order to make their first contact with Europe as pleasant as possible, Jomard had also enlisted the help of a number of interpreters, recruited from among the 'Orientals' in Marseilles. These were the already mentioned Joanny Pharaon, Michel Halabi (Mikhā'īl al-Ḥalabī), Eid Bajali (ʿAyd Bajalī), Joseph Awad (Yūsuf ʿAwaḍ) and Joseph-Elie Agoub (Yaʿqūb). The last of these was by far the most famous and would also remain with the Egyptian mission during most of their stay in France; he even taught them French-Arabic translation at the Collège Louis-le-Grand. Born in Cairo in 1795 to an Armenian father and a Syrian mother, Agoub had left Egypt with his parents in the wake of the withdrawal of the French troops and settled in Marseilles. He was already a celebrated author and his poetry, much of it painting a highly romanticized picture of Egypt and its history, successfully tapped into the Egyptomania that had taken hold of France ever since the Egyptian campaign. His main claim to fame was a collection of poems entitled *La Lyre Brisée* (1824), which was translated by al-Ṭahṭāwī not long after his arrival in France (1827) and was printed by the same publishing house as the original (Dondey-Dupré). This was also the first Arabic translation of any European literary work.[2] In the book, Agoub also included poems in praise of Muḥammad ʿAlī,[3] which did not fail to achieve the desired result of bringing the author to the attention of the Egyptian court. Boghos Bey even had the poems translated into Turkish, presumably at Jomard's instigation, and its author was appointed Jomard's personal assistant (which post also carried a generous allowance).

Of greater scholarly interest were Agoub's translations of Egyptian folk songs, the so-called *mawwāls*,[4] in which he made a good fist of rendering

1. It is worth adding that already in the 1840s some French secondary schools (*lycées*) were offering Arabic classes; for instance, in Montpellier, an Algerian by the name of Yūsuf (Youssouf) was teaching Arabic (as well as '*rhétorique française*'). See AN F17 4097, 4099. *L'Orient des Provençaux dans l'Histoire*, 105–26 (A. Louca/P. Santoni).
2. On the translation, see *Revue Encyclopédique*, XXXVI, Nov. 1831, pp. 208–09.
3. E.g. J. Agoub, 1824: 6.
4. See Translation, note no. 3, p. 294.

Egyptian colloquial into very polished and readable French. Agoub's version of the *mawwāls* found much favour with leading French literati of the day such as the celebrated poet de Lamartine, and they inspired Gustave Flaubert, who had also heard the real thing during his journey to Egypt with Maxime du Camp, to write a pastiche entitled *Chant de la Courtisane*.[1]

These endorsements, combined with the appeal of the exotic, made Agoub, for a while at least, a rising star within Parisian literary circles, enjoying much acclaim at the salon hosted by the flamboyant Madame Dufrénoy. Unfortunately, his fortunes quickly dwindled, and he died completely destitute in his adopted home town of Marseilles. He was only thirty-seven years old.[2]

On 24 July, Agoub accompanied the three leaders of the mission to Paris, where Jomard organized a banquet in their honour in the presence of other surviving members of the Egyptian expedition such as General Belliard, who had commanded the French division in Upper Egypt (together with Desaix). The rest of the group followed a few days later. They made only one brief stopover in Lyon, and by 5 August, the entire group assembled at what was to be their new home, a beautiful town residence (*Hôtel*) at no. 33 Rue de Clichy, in the Trinité quarter (9th *arrondissement*), just a few houses down from Victor Hugo's future residence (no. 21). Four days later, classes started in what must have been a gruelling schedule for the Egyptians: the school day started at seven o'clock in the morning and ended at six in the evening. In addition to technical drawing, they were instructed in French, history, arithmetic, engineering and geography. Meanwhile, Jomard's propaganda machine was running at full steam to satisfy heightened popular demand for information and gossip about these 'Turks', the goals of the mission, their activities, progress, etc.

As might be expected, the appallingly poor preparation of most of the students meant that progress was slow and difficult, particularly in the area of French. As a result, Jomard had to put his plans for specialized training on hold until his pupils had acquired sufficient knowledge of the language to be able to follow classes. The main obstacle to progress in this area was a familiar one in language education, both past and present, i.e. the fact that as the students all lived together, they lacked *immersion* in the target language and still spent most of their time talking in their native language(s). Except in addressing their teachers, they had little or no opportunity to

1. J.-M. Carré, 1956: I, 288, II, 121–3.
2. On Agoub, see A. Louca, 1958; *idem*, 1970: 26 *et passim*; A. Silvera, 1980: 10–11; J.-M. Carré, 1956: I, 288, II, 122; A. Messaoudi 2008: 72ff., 692-3; F. Pouillon 2008 (A. Messaoudi): 8.

speak French. Indeed, it seems that the students themselves did not feel they were making much progress either, as al-Ṭahṭāwī's comments make clear.[1] In order to solve the language issue, it was decided to divide the students into small groups and to send some to different *pensions* (boarding schools), while others boarded with a private teacher.[2] Al-Ṭahṭāwī was sent to the house of a military engineer by the name of Chevalier, a graduate of the Ecole Polytechnique, who also provided language instruction. In addition to full board, educational materials (books, pens, etc.), clothing and medical expenses, the students also received a monthly stipend (the scales of which had been carefully determined in Cairo). The size of the allowance varied greatly; al-Ṭahṭāwī, for instance, received 250 piastres (= *c.* FF80), whereas the head of the mission, ʿAbdī Efendi Shukrī, got 2,500 piastres, which was doubled as from late 1828. At the bottom end, there was Aḥmad al-ʿAṭṭār, who was paid a paltry 80 piastres. By comparison, an ordinary factory worker or soldier in Egypt earned between 10 and 15 piastres a month and al-Ṭahṭāwī's *Takhlīṣ* would go on sale in 1834 at EPt15.[3] In addition to the leadership, several students, among them al-Ṭahṭāwī, also had Egyptian servants.[4]

Initially the students were kept on a tight rein by Jomard (who as *directeur d'études* was in charge of the students' curriculum) and their leaders, who would take command in turns, at first daily, then monthly. After about a year, ʿAbdī Efendi became the sole leader. After his return to Egypt in October 1831, he was replaced by one of the other Turks, Amīn Efendi. When the students were all still staying at the mission residence at the Rue de Clichy, they were not allowed to leave it by day or night, except on Sundays, and then only if they had a permit issued by one of the leaders. Once they were staying in the *pensions*, they were allowed to go out with their French schoolfriends and teachers in the evenings if they did not have homework or classes, and on Sundays, Thursday afternoons and on public holidays. Naturally, this did not apply to the three leaders as the teachers had received specific instructions to the effect that they should not be given any homework. All student movements were strictly regulated,[5] and violations were punishable by confinement to quarters or, in case of repeated misbehaviour, expulsion to Egypt. In addition, the viceroy kept close tabs on his subjects, who, like their leaders, had to

1. See Translation, p. 278.
2. *Revue Encyclopédique*, XXXII, December 1826, 837.
3. J. Heyworth-Dunne, 1938: 159ff.; T. Bianchi, 1843: 42 (no. 90).
4. See Translation, p. 223.
5. See Translation, pp. 281–3.

submit detailed monthly reports on their progress. That their ruler was a hard and demanding taskmaster becomes clear, for instance, from the letters that would arrive frequently in Paris, exhorting students to perform better or voicing disapproval about poor past performance.[1] It is also in this light that one should view the inclusion in the *Takhlīṣ* of detailed lists of books studied by the author. Jomard, in particular, carefully monitored his protégés' progress and assiduity, offering encouragement and praise when necessary.[2] The students were also regularly reminded of how much their education was costing their ruler and how they should repay him by applying themselves to their work with the utmost zeal and diligence.

In July 1827, at the end of their first academic year, the students sat their first exam, which was devoted almost entirely to testing their knowledge of French. Though the results were not brilliant, they did sufficiently impress the Egyptian ruler to continue the experiment and, in gratitude for his efforts, Jomard was granted an annual salary of 10,000 francs.[3] Those students who performed well at the exam were rewarded with presents. In the case of al-Ṭahṭāwī this was a luxury edition of Barthelémy's *Voyage du Jeune Anacharsis en Grèce*, accompanied by a highly praising letter from Jomard.[4]

In the same month, Egyptomania reached new heights with the arrival in Marseilles of a giraffe sent by Muḥammad ʿAlī as a present to King Charles X.[5] This also renewed interest in the Egyptian students, who, together with the giraffe, were the protagonists in a vaudeville show, entitled *La Girafe, ou une journée au Jardin du Roi* (in reference to the *Jardin des Plantes*, which housed the animal).[6] The poets Barthélemy and Méry also included references to both the giraffe and the students in their mock-heroic epic poem, *La Bacriade, ou la guerre d'Alger* (1827), in which the members of the mission featured as pawns in an intricate international plot and had allegedly been sent by the Egyptian viceroy at the request of the Algerian ruler (*Dey*) to recover funds embezzled by a Jewish Algerian trader by the name of Nathan Bacri (Bakrī), the protagonist in the eponymous 'Bacriana'. Not only do the students fail to fulfil their mission, but their actions also provoke the French government into attacking Algeria. The

1. See Translation, pp. 282ff.
2. See Translation, pp. 283-4 and 301.
3. A. Louca, 1970: 43.
4. See Translation, p. 301.
5. See G. Dardaud, "L'extraordinaire aventure de la girafe du Pacha d'Egypte", *Revue des Conférences françaises en Orient*, 1951, 13, pp. 1–72.
6. Cf. A. Louca, 1970: 255.

story was actually based on a highly complex and shady affair that went back as far as the Directoire (1795–99) and involved unpaid Algerian wheat, which had been supplied to France between 1793 and 1798 by two Jewish merchant families (Bakrī and Bushnaq), in collusion with Talleyrand. The Algerian Bey Ḥasan (1790–98) had in 1796 given the French government an interest-free loan to buy wheat in Bône and Constantine, additional loans being granted over the next two years. Although initially the wheat had been destined for France's southern provinces, it soon became vital to Napoleon's armies in Italy and Egypt. In fact, it was as the result of the increasingly insistent demands for repayment by the new Bey, Muṣṭafā (1798–1805), that Napoleon briefly contemplated attacking the Regency. The total amount of the debt was put at FF7.9m in 1800 and FF24m in 1815. However, this sum was, subsequent to a deal (28 October 1819) between the Jewish traders and the French government, slashed to FF7m, much to the horror of creditors (among whom the Dey) of the Bakrī-Bushnaq house. A watershed in the affair came with accusations of the alleged humiliation suffered by the French consul in Algiers, Pierre Deval, at the hands of the Algerian ruler, Dey Ḥusayn. On 29 April 1827 an argument erupted between the two men during which the Dey accused the consul of withholding official letters from the French government pertaining to the debt issue and of embezzling consular funds. Deval, for his part, demanded the return of two papal vessels and wanted assurances from the Dey that his corsairs would refrain from attacking ships sailing under Church State flag, which enjoyed the protection of the French as the Pope did not pay any tribute. During this undoubtedly heated exchange, the Dey allegedly slapped Deval in the face with a fly-whisk.[1] This affair received a great deal of attention in France, and the government did not waste time in imposing a blockade on the port of Algiers, while for his part the Dey had the *comptoirs* in Bône and La Calle destroyed. At the time, there was, however, no question of France actually embarking on an expedition, the blockade being little more than just another instance of gunboat diplomacy. Furthermore, public interest quickly waned and neither party relished the prospect of a costly war. Yet, in a dramatic case of life imitating art, the Bakrī affair would indeed serve as a pretext for an all-out attack on Algiers in 1830, as part of an ingenious scheme by the Polignac ministry to solve the particularly intractable debt problem, and in the process exact more preferential trade tariffs and divert the attention of the population from Charles X's

1. See E. Plantet, 1930; K. Chater, 1984; C.-A. Julien, 1986: 21–63.

disastrous domestic policies. Finally, it is worth adding that there was also an Egyptian connection in this entire affair. The quick-witted Drovetti had for a long time harboured a dream for his adoptive Egypt as the sucessor to the Ottoman Empire. Within this vision, he saw Egypt expanding its territory westward as well as eastward. Realizing that there was capital to be made out of the Algerian issue, he approached Polignac in 1829 regarding a joint Franco-Egyptian attack on all three Regencies (Algeria, Tunisia, Libya), France providing naval support for the Egyptian land forces led by Ibrāhīm Pasha. Eventually, it was Muḥammad ʿAlī's refusal to accede to the demand by the French government that it should gain control over Algeria that scuppered the plan.[1] At the same time, one may wonder whether things would ever have gone that far, as it is difficult to see how either the Ottomans or other European powers (especially Britain) would have stood idly by as France and Egypt effectively dismembered the Empire and radically changed the existing balance of power.

On 28 February and 1 March 1828, the students had to sit another exam marking the end of their preparatory training. Presided over by the MP Count de Chabrol, a veteran of the Egyptian expedition and at the time Prefect of the Seine department, it was a highly solemn and dignified affair, attended by a host of luminaries such as the Orientalists Amédée Jaubert (professor of Turkish at the *Ecole des Langues Orientales*), T. Bianchi and Garcin de Tassy, Academicians, generals (including the already mentioned Belliard) and other notables. Even more significant was the presence of the British admiral Sir Sidney Smith and His Majesty's consul, David Morier. The exam consisted of a written and an oral. For the former, which was held on 28 February, students were allocated one hour to compose a French essay and one hour and a quarter to solve their mathematics questions (arithmetic, algebra and geometry), while their mark for drawing would be based on recent samples.[2] It becomes clear from the content of the mathematics questions that demands were quite low: for instance, one of the geometry questions involved completing a triangle for which two lines and the angle opposite one of the two lines had already been given. Another question, more arithmetical in nature, involved calculating the portions of water to be given to 42 men on board a ship for 25 days if current rations of half a litre a head will last for only 15 days.[3] For the French assignment students were asked to write a letter to a friend in

1. Cf. C.-A. Julien, 1986: 33ff.
2. E. Jomard, 1828.
3. *ibid.*, 98.

Egypt and describe what had most impressed them during their stay in France. The oral exam was intended to test their general knowledge and the ability to express their views in French cogently and correctly. Al-Ṭahṭāwī's question, for instance, was, 'What is an exam?' (*Qu'est-ce qu'un examen?*'), though his rather succinct reply, 'After the exam, a man is respected or despised' ('*Après l'examen, on estime un homme ou on le méprise*'), seemed to impress the jury far less than the eloquence displayed by a Khalīl Maḥmūd.[1] The star of the show, however, was one of the youngest members of the mission, the Cairo-born Turk, Maẓhar, who, together with the Armenian Iṣṭifān and the native Egyptians ʿAlī Haybah and Khalīl Maḥmūd, won the prize for French composition and parsing and came out first in algebra and geometry as well. Maẓhar, whose essay was the only one to be published in Jomard's official report in the scholarly *Journal Asiatique*,[2] had already been attending classes at the Collège Royal de Bourbon, where he had come in sixth out of seventy, and was among the first seven students allowed to sit for the elementary geometry exam at university. Muṣṭafa Mahramji and Muḥammad Bayyūmī, too, showed a singular aptitude for geometry and the latter was even preparing for the admission exam at the prestigious Ecole Royale Polytechnique.[3]

Though al-Ṭahṭāwī received special praise from Jomard, who even mentioned the former's translation of his *Almanac de l'Egypte et de la Syrie* and Cyprien-Prosper Brard's mineralogy manual, the young *imām*, like five of his fellow students, only qualified for a consolation prize ('*prix d'encouragement*') for progress made, which took the form of Silvestre de Sacy's Arabic poetry chrestomathy.[4] Jomard was manifestly pleased to note that the native Egyptians performed just as well as the Egypt-born 'Osmanlis', eight of the former group (out of a total of seventeen) and six of the second batch (also out of a total of seventeen) obtaining prizes. The Turks not born in Egypt were the least successful. Far more determining in Jomard's mind was the age factor and he did not fail to add that all three of the most promising students (Maẓhar, Bayyūmī and Maḥramjī) were also among the youngest of the group (seventeen years upon arrival), adding that '*on doit regretter que le Gouvernement d'Egypte n'ait pas envoyé des sujets plus jeunes encore*'![5]

1. *Ibid.*, 99. One should hasten to add that al-Ṭahṭāwī's oral command of French remained below his written ability and, according to his biographer Ṣ. Majdī, he never really learned to speak it fluently.
2. *Ibid.*, 102–03.
3. *Ibid.*, 105.
4. *Ibid.*, 100, 104; see Translation, p. 301.
5. E. Jomard, 1828: 101.

And so, the students were finally ready to embark on their specialist training. Fifteen subject areas were decided upon, the students being allocated, to use Jomard's words, '*selon leurs goûts et leurs facultés*', though one may suspect that it was Jomard himself (no doubt in close consultation with the group leadership and in compliance with viceregal instructions) who made the final choice.[1] The first course, that of military administration, started on 10 April and was attended by one of the leaders of the mission, Muḥammad Mukhtār, and his compatriot, Rashīd Efendi. ʿAbdī Efendi, Artīn, his brother Muḥammad Khusrū and the Georgian Salīm, for their part, attended classes in civil administration (or diplomatic affairs). The other subjects included artillery, chemistry, medicine (including surgery and anatomy), military engineering, naval affairs, government, mechanics and hydraulics, technical drawing and engraving, agriculture, natural history and translation.[2] The training took the form of tutorials and selected classes at university. The students destined for naval training left for the French naval academy in Brest, whereas those specializing in agriculture continued their education at the experimental farm in Roville. In 1829, two of the Egyptian students were accepted at the Faculty of Medicine. Maẓhar, Bayyūmī and Mahramjī even attended mathematics classes with the famous Auguste Comte, on whom they left a very favourable impression as, some years later, he even provided Maẓhar with a glowing letter of introduction to John Stuart Mill, calling him '*le plus intelligent et le plus affectueux des jeunes Egyptiens*'.[3]

Al-Ṭahṭāwī, who had been singled out by Jomard for translation training almost upon arrival in France, now began to concentrate all his efforts on this art. His main teachers were the above-mentioned Chevalier, as well as a certain Laumonerie, with whom he went through an impressive list of books on a wide variety of subjects, ranging from geography and history, to logic, philosophy, literature and geometry.[4] In addition, he also devoured newspapers and magazines, displaying a keen interest in articles related to the Ottoman Empire and his native country,[5] and he also composed a treatise on astronomy.[6] His work schedule was such that he even endangered his health, and at one point the long nights spent poring

1. *Ibid.*, 105; P. Hamont, 1943: II, 192.
2. For course content, see E. Jomard, 1828: 105–08.
3. A. Louca, 1970: 260–2.
4. See pp. 293ff.
5. See pp. 299ff.
6. R. al-Tahṭawī, 1872–3: 24.

over his books caused a serious eye complaint.[1] His final exam (19 October 1831) just before his return to Egypt reveals the astounding number and range of topics of the translations he did in the space of one year.[2] The *Takhlīṣ* also contains a number of translations from French (the French Constitutional Charter, a medical treatise and a newspaper article), which probably started out as exercises.

The importance of the graduation of the first translator who was to be instrumental in '*faire jouir l'Egypte de nos ouvrages scientifiques, et la faire participer un jour aux avantages de nos institutions*', as Jomard had put it three years earlier,[3] was such that the scholarly *Revue Encyclopédique* published the full transcript of the proceedings in its November issue.

In view of the encouraging results of the members of this first mission, it was not difficult for Jomard to convince the viceroy to turn the venture into something more permanent and to supply more students. In August 1828, in the wake of the destruction of the Egyptian fleet at Navarino, six Egyptian artisans arrived at the port of Toulon to study naval construction, and others followed in what seemed to become a steady stream in the course of that same year. In May 1829, another thirty-four were dispatched to Paris for training in a variety of fields. These and other students that were sent to the capital tended to be better prepared for what lay ahead, and most were graduates of the Qaṣr al-ʿAynī school which was in full operation by then. The 1829 mission also included six African slave boys (aged between eight and twelve), whose freedom had been bought by the French consul Drovetti as part of another of the latter's grand schemes, i.e. to bring civilization and education to the African interior.[4] Unfortunately, this mission was marred by the fact that one of the African boys died of tuberculosis in Paris within the same year. But it was not just to France that the viceroy looked for education, and in October 1829, fifteen to twenty students were sent to England.[5]

In 1832, Paris played host to twelve medical students, selected by Clot-Bey to work as teachers at his School of Medicine in Abū Zaʿbal, which had originally been set up to meet Muḥammad ʿAlī's demands for doctors for his armed forces. The aim was to train native teachers in order to bypass the cumbersome and ineffective system of foreign-language lectures being

1. See p. 305.
2. See p. 302.
3. E. Jomard, 1828: 104.
4. A. Louca, 1970: 255–6.
5. ʿU. Ṭūsūn, 1934: 104–18.

simultaneously translated for the students.[1] Naturally, as always, there was also a clear political prize to be gained at what was a particularly sensitive time in East-West relations. Equally interesting is the fact that probably for the first time students were selected on ability, rather than connections, and all except one in Clot's group were native Egyptians. All were Azhar graduates who had completed the five-year training at the Abū Zaʿbal college. Upon arrival in Paris in November 1832, they took the Royal Medical Academy entrance exam, which they all passed, and were then broken up into groups for study at some of the most prestigious Paris hospitals such as the Hôtel-Dieu and La Charité. This mission also stands out for another more mundane reason in that three of the medical students married French girls.

Most of the members of the first contingent stayed for an average of four to five years, some for up to eight years.[2] Exceptional in this regard is the case of Aḥmad Efendi. A cousin of Mukhtār (one of the leaders) and treasurer to the mission, Aḥmad was supposed to study natural history and metal founding but was called back to Egypt eight years later for getting into debt without obtaining the slightest qualification.[3] In total, five students of the first mission were repatriated for health reasons or general academic ineptitude.

At its height, the Egyptian school in Paris counted 115 students, whereas according to the self-appointed historian of the Egyptian educational missions, Prince ʿUmar Ṭūsūn, some 311 students were sent to Europe (France, Italy, Austria, England) between 1813 and 1849.[4] Other observers even put the number as high as 360.[5]

But then, disaster and disappointment struck in December 1835, with the arrival of a letter from Cairo destined for Jomard in which he was advised that, for reasons still unknown, the viceroy was recalling all students.

The results of the first mission, in particular, also merit some attention. As we have seen in the case of al-Ṭahṭāwī, his training led to a flourishing if at times unstable career in his chosen speciality. Maẓhar, too, was able to put his engineering skills into practice and assisted Moungel in the construction of the Delta barrage and the Alexandria lighthouse, and later became Director (*nāẓir*) of the Department of Public Works. Ḥasan al-Iskandarānī, who had studied naval engineering, was first put in charge of the Alexandria dockyards

1. J. Zaydān, 1957: IV, 31; A. Louca, 1970: 46–7; A. Clot-Bey, 1833: 219ff.; *idem*, 1840: II, 414; *idem*, 1949: 174–5; P. Hamont, 1943: II, 107.
2. A. Silvera, 1980: 16; A. Louca, 1970: 48.
3. ʿU. Ṭūsūn, 1934.
4. ʿU. Ṭūsūn, 1934: 414ff.
5. R. Wielandt, 1980: 38.

before becoming Minister for Naval Affairs, while the Artīn brothers rose to high office under successive rulers. Many others, however, were not so lucky, and their careers were driven by their ruler's whimsical view of where they were needed. So, we find Iṣṭifān's diplomatic training being put to use in the Department of Education. Bayyūmī, who had specialized in hydraulics and whose academic ability was held in great esteem by Jomard, was appointed as a chemistry teacher, while the metal founder Amīn Efendi became the head of a gunpowder factory. The Circassian Maḥmūd, who had studied naval engineering in Brest and Toulon, was assigned to the Treasury Department. One of the saddest examples of this policy was Khalīl Maḥmūd, who after becoming a bookbinder was reduced to selling his services as a tourist guide to visiting Europeans.[1] At the same time, the story by Artīn's son, Yaʿqūb, that, in view of the need for translations, returning students were effectively confined at the Citadel for a period of three months and released only after having produced a Turkish translation of a book in their speciality should be taken with more than just a pinch of salt.[2]

One should, however, resist temptation to dismiss the entire educational venture as insignificant simply because its objectives were not met. To be sure, the small number of individuals involved, the uneven level of education and the subsequent misuse of their training, combined with (or engendered by) a suspicious and hostile bureaucracy meant that very little remained of the viceroy's dream of creating a nucleus of 'super officials' that would be the driving force behind the reorganization and modernization of the country. At the same time, their poor educational background and, in many cases, age and inadaptibility to their new environment meant that, for the most part, they did not draw as much benefit from their modern education as they could have done.[3] Of course, there were some who did not take their task very seriously (like the already mentioned Aḥmad Efendi) and were perhaps dazzled by the more frivolous aspects of European civilization, as witness the words of the French scholar Prisse d'Avennes, who despondently made the following comment about some of the members of the first Egyptian mission:

> '*chaque conversation les* [étudiants] *ramenait au souvenir de nos charmantes grisettes, à nos danses, à nos yeux, à nos spectacles*'.[4]

1. A. Louca, 1970: 48ff.; A. Silvera, 1980: 14, 17–19; P. Hamont, 1843: II, 192ff.
2. Y. Artin, 1890: 73.
3. Also see J. Heyworth-Dunne, 1938: 157ff., 243ff.; 'U. Ṭūsūn, 1934; R. Wielandt, 1980: 34ff.
4. Quoted in A. Louca, 1970: 52.

Another contemporary observer was even more cynical when it came to the results of the missions, stating:

> *'la plupart n'apprenaient à Paris que trois choses: à parler assez bien le français, à boire du vin et à rire du Mahomet'.*[1]

In fact, many individual members of the first mission, not least al-Ṭahṭāwī himself, made valuable contributions to the country's intellectual, cultural and political life. A case in point in this respect is the translation movement, which was a vital component in the development of a modern educational system. Furthermore, one should not underestimate the returnees' role as cultural intermediaries between Europe (France) and Egypt. Several of them provided information to European travellers, al-Ṭahṭāwī, for instance, playing host to the French authors Jean-Jacques Ampère[2] and Charles Didier (see above) and the British historian Paton,[3] whereas Flaubert and his long-suffering companion Maxime du Camp availed themselves of the services of Khalīl Maḥmūd.[4]

The story of the Egyptian educational missions did not, however, end in 1835. Indeed, as we have seen, less than ten years later, Muḥammad ʿAlī's French military adviser, Sulaymān Pasha, persuaded his master to set up the Ecole Militaire Egyptienne, which would remain in operation until 1849. The viceroy's successors continued his policy, France remaining the main recipient. For instance, of the fifty-odd students receiving instruction in Europe in the early 1870s, twenty-four were in France, which figure was to rise to thirty-eight on the eve of the British occupation of Egypt in 1882.[5] Other Muslim rulers too followed suit. Foremost among them was the Ottoman Sultan. Not to be outdone by his liege subject, he sent, despite a great deal of opposition, an even larger group of 150 students to Europe (four of whom arrived in Paris) the next year. These were for the most part military and naval cadets and future teachers for the new schools that were going to be set up. The first of these was a medical school, which opened in Istanbul a mere month after Muḥammad ʿAlī's *madrasat al-ṭibb* of Abū Zaʿbal.[6]

1. E. Dor, 1872: 343.
2. J. Ampère, 1881: 258–9.
3. A. Paton, 1863: II, 271.
4. See Translation, note no. 1, p. 360.
5. A. Louca, 1970: 103.
6. B. Lewis, 1969: 83–4; *idem*, 1982: 133; *idem*, 1964: 39. It is interesting to note that the next two schools to be set up in Constantinople were also directly inspired by Egyptian

Another of the Ottoman Sultan's vassals, Aḥmad Bey of Tunis, who had also hired huge numbers of European (mainly French) craftsmen and technicians to assist his grand modernization plans, sent several of his soldiers to the military training academy at Saint-Cyr,[1] while the first non-military student mission – all of whose eight members were graduates from *al-madrasa al-Ṣādiqiyya* – arrived in Paris in October 1880 and enrolled at the Lycée Saint-Louis. Unfortunately, the mission came to an abrupt end a few months later with the start of the French Protectorate.[2]

Iran had also sent small groups of students to Europe as early as 1811 and 1815, and at least one of the Persian trainees, Mirzā Muḥammad Ṣāliḥ Shīrāzī, also wrote an account of his travels.[3]

Until the latter half of the 19th century Egypt remained the main provider of Arab students in Europe, and in the 300-strong Muslim student population reported by the Tunisian émigré Sulaymān al-Ḥarā'irī in 1862 the Egyptians formed the single largest Arab group.[4]

In the second half of the century, the Ottoman Sultan once again followed his vassal's lead by setting up his own school in Paris. The Ecole Impériale Ottomane (*Mekteb-i Osmani*) was located on the premises of the Ottoman embassy in the Rue Violet of what was then the leafy suburb of Grenelle (which in 1860 was annexed by the metropolis to form the 15th *arrondissement*) and was in operation between 1857 and 1864. The curriculum was a bit more varied than in its Egyptian counterpart and comprised French, (Ottoman and French) history, mathematics, physics, chemistry, geography and drawing, as well as general military training. The classes were organized by the French Ministry of Education, though some of the teachers were Turks, as was the head of the school.[5] Like their Egyptian

---

establishments, the Imperial Music School (1831), where a brother of the Italian composer Donizetti was one of the teachers, and the School for Military Sciences (1834). The Egyptian precursor to the former was the 'Military Music School' (*madrasat al-mūsīqā al-'askariyya*), founded in 1824, whereas the idea behind the latter was undoubtedly inspired by the Cairo Military School, even though by the time it opened it was clearly modelled on the French Military Academy of St Cyr. Cf. B. Lewis, 1969: 84.

1. Originally, the Bey had asked for the admission of six Tunisian officers but in the end only two were accepted: Muḥammad al-Mūrālī (artillery) and 'Alī Qādirī (infantry) spent a little under two years (Oct. 1862–July 1864) at Saint-Cyr. See P. Marty, 1935: 329–30.
2. See N. Sraïeb, 1995: 59, 92; G. Van Krieken, 1976: 196; A. Abdesselam, 1975: 33–4.
3. See Hafez Farman Farmayan, 'The forces of modernization in nineteenth century Iran: a historical survey', in W. Polk and R. Chambers, 1968: 122ff.; B. Lewis, 1962: 133: C. Storey, 1939–97: I:2, 1148–50.
4. S. al-Ḥarā'irī, 1862: 1.
5. D. Newman, 2002a; K. Kreiser, 1995: 843–4.

predecessors, some Turks also attended classes at Parisian *collèges* such as Sainte-Barbe, Louis-le-Grand and Charlemagne, whereas several went on to study at universities in France, Germany, Italy and Belgium.[1]

As a postscript, it is worth mentioning that in some cases the European student missions yielded an unexpected and, as far as the rulers were concerned, unwelcome return in that it later on in the century proved to be one of the main channels for new political ideas. As a place of exile, Paris became a centre for dissidents and activists of various plumage for organizing resistance to the regimes in Constantinople and Cairo, among them people like the Egyptians James Sanua (Yaʿqūb Ṣanūʿ) – also known by his sobriquet Abū Naẓẓāra Zarqāʾ ('the man with the blue glasses') – and Muḥammad ʿAbduh and the latter's mentor, the Persian mystic Jamāl al-Dīn al-Afghānī, or the Young Ottoman group around Namik Kemal.[2] It was also in Paris that several of them set up periodicals to publicize their views. The most famous of these was undoubtedly Muḥammad ʿAbduh and al-Afghānī's *al-ʿUrwa al-Wuthqā* ('The Unbreakable Handle'), which gained wide popularity in the East.[3]

1. C. Findley, 1989: 159–60.
2. B. Lewis, 1969: 136ff.
3. This magazine, whose French title was '*Le Lien Dissoluble*', first appeared weekly and then bimonthly, and took its name from Qur. II:257 and XXXI:21. In all, 18 issues were published (13 March 1884–16 October 1884).

FOUR

The Book

Genesis and Themes

As we have seen, al-Ṭahṭāwī was not the first Egyptian or, indeed, Arab to set foot on European soil. Nor was he the first to write an account of his journey there. That honour goes to an Andalusian Jew, Yaʿqūb al-Ṭurṭūshī, who visited large parts of western Europe in the middle of the 10th century. Unfortunately, only fragments of his travelogue have survived in later works. The first full-fledged accounts of visits to Europe were those by 17th/18th-century Moroccan ambassadors, whose main destination was Spain, though one of them, a Morisco by the name of Aḥmad b. Qāsim al-Ḥajarī (d. 1645), travelled as far north as the Low Countries.[1] These works, however, remained largely unknown to the outside world and their scope was very limited. Indeed, al-Ṭahṭāwī was the first to set out to write a comprehensive account of European society and culture. In addition, he expanded his compatriots' vision of the physical world and it is in the *Takhlīṣ* that many countries outside Europe were mentioned for the first time and thus became part of the Arab consciousness. Though some forty travellers from both eastern and western Muslim lands would follow in his footsteps, the pre-eminence of the *Takhlīṣ* in terms of content and stylistic innovation endured, as did its author's fame.[2] The Tunisian Muḥammad b. al-Khūja even paid his own special tribute by naming his own travelogue to France in 1900 *Sulūk al-ibrīz fī masālik Bārīz*, which may be translated as 'The Behaviour of Pure Gold in the Streets of Paris'. The importance of the

1. For a detailed discussion, see D. Newman, 2001.
2. Many later travellers would in fact refer to the book; Khayr al-Dīn, 1867: 69; A. Ibn Abī 'l-Ḍiyāf, 1963: III, 169 , IV, 99 (1971: 139); F. al-Shidyāq, 1882: 222, 272, 289; M. Ibn. al-Khūja, 1900: 6; *idem*, 1913 (intro); M. al-Ṣaffār [S. Gilson Miller], 1992: 123; M. al-Sanūsī, 1891–92: 236; *idem*, 1976–80: I, 82–3.

Takhlīṣ also lies in the invaluable insight it offers into the preconceptions and prior knowledge of Europe by Muslims of the day by the things its author included, such as the fact that people in France eat with knife and fork and sit on chairs. In addition to the perception of the Other, the book also lifts the veil on the perception of the Self (Europe) as conveyed to the Other (the Muslim).

As al-Ṭahṭāwī himself reports, it was at the suggestion of his mentor Ḥasan al-ʿAṭṭār that he decided to keep a detailed journal of his experiences in the new continent. This brings us to the next feature that differentiates the *Takhlīṣ* from previous attempts in the genre, i.e. its didactic intent. From the outset, it was clear that it was to serve to educate his compatriots about the West.

From the moment al-Ṭahṭāwī left Egypt, he started taking notes of each stage of the journey and his stay and activities in Paris, eagerly availing himself of the French sources that became available to him. One European source even had an influence on the structure of the book as it can hardly be called a coincidence that the fourth, fifth, and sixth chapters on Paris – on housing, food and clothing, respectively – clearly mirror the first three chapters of Depping's *Aperçu Historique sur les Moeurs et Coutumes des Nations*, of which al-Ṭahṭāwī finished the translation in 1829.

The *Takhlīṣ* is divided into two broad parts: an introductory section (preface and introduction) and the 'core'. The first sets out the aim of the visit, while providing some details on the leaders of the mission and a geographical overview of the modern world with special emphasis on the location of Europe. The body of the book (*maqṣid*) is divided into Essays (*maqālāt*), each subdivided into sections (*fuṣūl*). Of widely varying length, the Essays group a number of related topics. The first involves the sea journey from Alexandria to Marseilles, whereas the second deals with the stay in the latter city. The third Essay offers a detailed survey of various aspects of life in the French capital, within which the comprehensive account of the organization of the French state, education and entertainments are key components. The Fourth Essay is devoted entirely to the author's studies, the mission, etc. The Fifth Essay focuses on the 1830 revolution, which al-Ṭahṭāwī witnessed first-hand, and includes details on the background of the events as well as the the final outcome, i.e. the ousting of the king. In the Sixth and final Essay, there is a discussion of various sciences, though it deals mostly with language (including an account of French), arithmetic and logic.

It is clear that there were several versions of the book. The first draft was completed not long before the author's departure for Paris. The outline of this version included in the *Takhlīṣ*[1] shows that the core of the book was expanded by about a third, as it originally contained only four Essays. The single most important addition were the chapters on the French Revolution, which the author probably included at the behest of one of his Parisian friends.[2] At the same time, al-Ṭahṭāwī inserted an entire essay devoted to the day-to-day running of the study activities (including the books he read and a full report on the final exam), the mission regulations, etc. The 'new' Fourth Essay also contains a number of letters from leading French scholars in praise of the author and his book. The inclusion of such eulogies (*taqārīẓ*), though strange today, was common practice in Arabic literature. Usually, of course, these were written by *'ulamā'* and other leading personalities who thus gave their imprimatur to the work.[3] The final addition is al-Ṭahṭāwi's already mentioned translation of a medical treatise, which appears as an appendix to the section on the medical sciences in Paris (Third Essay, Ninth Section). It is not clear when this was written, but one may speculate that its purpose was to serve as a textbook for the Abū Zaʿbal medical school. There are also other clues regarding the time of writing of certain parts. In fact, it would seem that the last revisions/additions were made in 1832. These include historical references such as a poem on ʿAkka, presumably inserted to honour Muḥammad ʿAlī's capture of the town in 1832, or the mention in a letter by the famous French Orientalist Joseph-Toussaint Reinaud of a revised edition of Malte-Brun's *Géographie Universelle* (which al-Ṭahṭāwī had started translating in Paris), the first volume of which was published only in 1832. Naturally, there were also omissions. The first was a passage relating to Ḥasan al-Iskandarānī's devoutness, which originally rounded off the fourth Chapter of the Introduction.[4] The second is of more interest as it involves a passage on the turning of the earth, which was more than likely omitted as it might have left the author open to accusations of unreligiousness.[5] The third and final known omission – a lengthy philosophical discussion on the virtues of round shapes – was apparently decided for reasons of readability, at the suggestion of de Sacy.[6]

The title, too, changed somewhat; in the *Takhlīṣ* itself,[7] it is given as *Takhlīṣ al-ibrīz* fī *talkhīṣ Bārīz*, i.e. 'The Extraction of Pure Gold *in* the

1. See Translation, note no. 1, p. 135.
2. See Translation, pp. 289–290.
3. Cf. Khayr al-Dīn, 1867.
4. See A. Louca, 1970: 64, note no.3.
5. See Translation, note no. 2, p. 354.
6. See Translation, pp. 285–6.
7. See Translation, p. 106.

Abridgement of Paris', whereas on the cover of the first edition (as well as all subsequent ones), it appeared as *Takhlīṣ al-ibrīz* ilā *talkhīṣ Bārīz*. The change in preposition may be more significant than one might be led to believe in that it changed the meaning to 'the extraction of pure gold [*on the road*] *towards* the abridgement of Paris.'

Any discussion of the *Takhlīṣ* defies easy inferences and rash interpretations, and the inclusion of certain features of European society does not automatically presuppose a favourable view by the author. It is rare, for instance, for the author explicitly to advocate the adoption of European innovations (notable exceptions being European sciences and taxation). In some cases, such as the French political system, the opposite is true. Though it is introduced here as an example, al-Ṭahṭāwī's later work clearly shows that he was not in favour of a European-style parliamentary democracy for his own country. Much is implicit and one would therefore be wrong to expect the *Takhlīṣ* to offer some kind of convenient philosophical or ideological construct addressing the inherent conflicting nature of interaction between the two cultures. This would come only some three decades later in his other works. Unfortunately, researchers examining the author's later works have often sought corroborative theories in the *Takhlīṣ*, which is essentially a descriptive work. Not only did al-Ṭahṭāwī not have the wherewithal to incorporate his experiences and views within a broader ideological framework, but the historical context also did not yet demand it. The fact that al-Ṭahṭāwī does not address the complex religious issues attendant upon the adoption of Western sciences is not proof of naivety but of the fact that there was no need yet to do so; the impact of the West in this field had barely begun. We are a long way away from his call, three decades later, that modern sciences should be taught at al-Azhar.[1] Hence, to qualify his admiration for European sciences and the fact that he feels they should be introduced into Muslim states as the manifestation of some *avant la lettre* reformism between the axes of tension of Westernization (progressive modernism) and conservatism (traditionalism) or revivalism[2] is, at best, anachronistic.

Another controversial example is the mention of European philosophers like Montesquieu, Condillac, Humboldt, Rousseau and Voltaire, all of whom were part of al-Ṭahṭāwī's reading list. Naturally, one is tempted to associate him with one school or another. However, a closer

1. al-Ṭahṭāwī, 1973–80 [*Manāhij*]: I, 534.
2. M. Zaki Badawi, 1978: 13ff.; H. Sharabi, 1970: 6ff. (who calls this middle ground simply 'the reformist position').

look reveals a number of intractable contradictions. While it is easy to imagine that he would have agreed with Voltaire's view that absolute monarchy is the best type of government or with the philsopher's anti-clericalism and criticism of Christian intolerance of other religions (cf. *Traité sur l'Intolérance*), it is impossible to square Montesquieu's natural determinism with Voltaire's rigorous empiricism and hostility to any organized guiding principle. It is equally far-fetched to imagine the young *imām* agreeing with Voltaire's thesis that history is driven only by human will and passion. As for Rousseau's philosophy, this is in many ways diametrically opposite to Voltaire's. Prompted by a belief in the superior unbreakable laws of man, the former advocated absolute democracy, in which the sovereign and his subjects are part of the same citizenry; together they constitute the indivisible body politic. At the same time, this point precludes any mention of Montesquieu in the same breath, since in his view the two powers were *independent*; for Rousseau, they were anything but that. Moreover, how would al-Ṭahṭāwī have got round Rousseau's fierce condemnation of the influence of religion on people's daily lives, which runs counter to the very foundations of Islamic society? And while Condillac's Christian-inspired belief in the reality of the soul undoubtedly struck a chord with the Azharite, one can easily guess at his perception of the French philosopher's brand of empirical naturalism (sensationalism) in which all human knowledge is based on observations made by the senses (without any divine intervention). Finally, the fact that two of the philosophers mentioned – Montesquieu[1] and Voltaire[2] – did not hide their anti-Islamic feelings must also rule out any real association with their thought. More importantly, however, in view of al-Ṭahṭāwī's background, it seems unlikely that any European rational philosophy could have held any real attraction for him.

True to his initial objective, al-Ṭahṭāwī discusses literally every aspect of European society, and the *Takhlīṣ* reveals his deep admiration for European culture and civilization, which can still be seen in his later works such as the *Manāhij*. Before discussing the major themes of the book, it is important to look at the concept of 'Europe' that emerges. In more ways than one, it is appropriate to talk of a 'multi-Europe' or multi-layered Europe. The first that emerges is a (semi-)mythical construct predicated on progress, industry and science. This is inextricably bound up with the Europe of Generality – a unidimensional continent, in

1. See A. Gunny, 1978.
2. See I. Netton, 1996: 12–16.

which the specific is elevated to the universal. It is possible to adumbrate two synecdochic levels. On a supranational level, Europe as a continent appears as a macrocosm of France, with 'French' and 'Franks' being used interchangeably at times. On a lower, national level, France blends in with Paris, which emerges as the only realization of the nation, which in turn is almost reduced to an abstract. Interestingly enough, it is this approach and ensuing generalizations that constituted one of de Sacy's main criticisms of the *Takhlīṣ*.[1] The vision of Europe also fits into a dichotomic or, to be more precise, Manicheic framework in which the differences between the traveller's native land and his new environment appear through a set of opposites: e.g. advanced/backward, unreligious/devout.

This Franco-centrist approach also means that certain political events that were taking place during or near al-Ṭahṭāwī's stay in Paris do not get any mention at all; for instance, in spite of a detailed discussion of the popular uprising against Charles X, the author does not draw any parallels with revolutions in other parts of the world, whether in Latin America or closer to 'home' (Belgium). The other single most bizarre omission is the French invasion of Algeria – a fellow Muslim state! – which took place while al-Ṭahṭāwī was still in Paris. The sparsity of the information on this event is all the more surprising since he is known to have written a treatise on the attack.[2]

One of the main themes of the *Takhlīṣ* centres on the sciences and technologies of Europe and the need to introduce them into Islamic lands so that they, too, can enjoy their benefits and regain their former glory. It is here for the first time that we find the argument that would later be used by several people, i.e. the fact that many of those sciences have their origins in Islamic/Arab science. Equally interesting is the fact that on more than one occasion the author emotionally and convincingly defends the viceroy's policy of hiring foreign advisers and seeking training in the European sciences, even though it is not always clear against whom.[3] He both admired and reprimanded Europeans' total reliance on reason, which he recognized as being at the heart of European progress. As a result, his view was close to that held by Egyptian *'ulamā'* at the beginning of the century, who saw in it proof of the French denial of divine law and, thus, their irredeemable irreligiousness. In this connection, one can only be dumbfounded by the nature of the attack on al-Ṭahṭāwī by Renan half a century later. In his (in)

1. See Translation, p. 285.
2. *Nabdha 'an dukhūl al-Faransīs li 'l-Jazā'ir*; cf. A. Badawī, 1958: 25.
3. See Translation, pp. 114–5 and p. 118.

famous speech on '*l'Islamisme et la Science*' of 29 March 1883,[1] in which he referred to the religion as '*la chaîne la plus lourde que l'humanité ait jamais portée,*'[2] adding that it had always persecuted science and philosophy,[3] he arrived at the conclusion that '*ce qui distingue ... essentiellement le musulman, c'est la haine de la science, c'est la persuasion que la recherche est inutile, frivole, presque impie: la science de la nature, parce qu'elle est une concurrence faite à Dieu; la science historique, parce que, s'appliquant à des temps antérieurs à l'Islam, elle pourrait raviver d'anciennes erreurs.*'[4] It was in regard to the last statement that he referred to al-Ṭahṭāwī, stating that '*un des témoignages les plus curieux ... est celui du cheik Rifaa, qui avait résidé plusieurs années à Paris comme aumônier de l'Ecole égyptienne, et qui, après son retour en Egypte, fit un ouvrage plein des observations les plus curieuses sur la société française. Son idée fixe est que la science européenne, surtout par son principe de permanence des lois de la nature, est d'un bout à l'autre une hérésie; et, il faut le dire, au point de vue de l'islam, il n'a pas tout à fait tort.*'[5]

In the area of government, al-Ṭahṭāwī was particularly impressed with the freedom enjoyed by the population – a concept for which he introduced the Arabic term, and which he considered a prerequisite, together with justice, for prosperity. This may be set against his later political thought, in which these two components are replaced by the general (public) good (*al-manāfiʿ al'umūmiyya*) and religion (or moral behaviour rooted in the true religion).[6]

However, in the *Takhlīṣ*, we are not dealing with a liberal, as 'freedom' is explained as that 'which we call justice and equity', two cornerstones in Islamic political theory, rather than the way in which he saw it in practice in France. Furthermore, at no point does he even attempt to address the fundamental incompatibility between the concept of 'freedom' and slavery, which was still very much alive in his home country.

The French justice system also finds much favour, especially the security that compliance with the law provides to the inhabitants, though one may wonder what his benefactor thought of the comment that 'not even the king is immune from prosecution'!

His views in the sphere of economics are even harder to tease out in that there seems to be only one actor and source of wealth, i.e. industry; labour and agriculture are almost entirely ignored.

---

1. *Journal des Débats*, 30 March 1883 (= E. Renan, 1947: I, 944–65).
2. E. Renan, 1947: I, 956.
3. *Ibid.*: I, 955.
4. *Ibid.*: I, 957.
5. *Loc. cit.*
6. Al-Ṭahṭāwī [*Manāhij*], 1973–80: I, 249–50. Also see L. Zolondek, 1964.

One should hasten to add that al-Ṭahṭāwī was not uncricitically admiring of all things French/European. This comes out mainly in his views on the people's general character, morals, etc. The French and, by extension, the Europeans, are miserly, self-indulgent, frivolous, unreligious, etc., which traits are consistently contrasted with those of the Arabs, who thus gain the upper hand in the human arena. As a result, this view, which is just as one-sided as that of the 'Europe of modernity', may be considered a way of compensating for the feelings of inferiority regarding the technologically and scientifically advanced Europe. However, when discussing the charities in Paris, al-Ṭahṭāwī did find himself in a bit of bind, since this is, of course, related to generosity, which he identifies as a peculiarly Arab trait. As a way out, he introduces a distinction between 'collective' (societal) and 'individual' (personal) generosity. The latter is, he feels, totally lacking in France, where people are driven by their unrelenting pursuit of individual wealth and prosperity.

Related to this is the aspect of religion or, to be more precise, Christianity, which is also discussed at great length. This was of course a delicate issue, as such close interaction with the 'obstinate infidel' made the author vulnerable to all manner of accusations. It is interesting that at no time does the author feel that there is a contradiction in the 'Europe of technology' and 'the Europe of infidelity' (or for that matter immorality). On several occasions, al-Ṭahṭāwī distinguishes between the European Christians and the Egyptian Christians, the Copts, thus successfully removing any link (whether suggested or inferred) between Christianity and technological and scientific advances.

Format and Style

In addition to content, the *Takhlīṣ* stands out in style as well from other literary works of the period in its use of simple language – in conformity with its author's intent to provide a book for as wide a readership as possible – and its departure from the trammels of rhymed prose (*saj'*) and lexical ornateness that dominated Arabic literature. At the same time, al-Ṭahṭāwī's work is firmly rooted in the mediaeval genre of the *riḥla*, or travelogue, as he himself indicates in the introduction.

In addition to a linear narrative continuity, the *Takhlīṣ* is based on identifiably personal observation, in the course of which the traveller intervenes as an individual who acts upon his environment.[1] A second

1. See D. Newman, 2001.

crucial element within the *riḥla* genre are the clearly marked stages. The first is the introduction with its statement of purpose and mention of fellow travellers; as in other *riḥlāt* concerning journeys to the lands of the infidel, the author starts by justifying the undertaking. Carefully explaining the reasons behind his journey, al-Ṭahṭawī adduces relevant religious texts proving the lawfulness of travel – the most important being the well-known *ḥadīth* (religious tradition), according to which the Prophet is said to have enjoined the believer 'to seek knowledge, even as far as China' – lest his laudatory comments on European society should raise suspicions of having gone 'native', i.e. *tafarnuj*. This is further corroborated by al-Ṭahṭāwī's declaration that he will 'approve only that which does not run counter to Islamic precepts'. His French mentor, Jomard, was also keenly aware of the problem, and when he suggested the young *imam* translate Depping's book, he allegedly added that 'those things that were derogatory or defamatory to Islamic customs' should be left out.[1]

It is also in this light that one should interpret the use in the introduction of the classical device of rhyming prose, which bears out the author's solid Muslim and *'ālim* credentials. In other words, both *signifiant* and *signifié* in this case manifest his allegiance to his native culture. The same applies to the very traditional content of the prefatory and introductory sections and the multitude of poetic quotes. In addition to bringing out the 'Arabness' of the author, the fact that they predominantly date back to the Golden Age of Arabic literature associates both the author and his reader with the glorious past of Arab/Muslim civilization. It is interesting to note that these elements would be largely absent from his successors' works, who concentrated instead on the historical *scientific* achievements of Muslim civilization, and the debt European culture owed to them.

The second stage in the *riḥla* is the actual journey, the first leg being described in great detail, in which, as in the past, water plays a crucial role and the traveller's resolve and faith are tested from the very start. The third component involves arrival at the destination and a description of the stay there. Finally, there is the journey home.

This three-stage process may be contrasted with the graduated stages in the inner journey, or alienation of the traveller, which starts the minute the author steps on to the French vessel that will take him to his destination. Indeed, it was the first time al-Ṭahṭāwī or his fellow travellers

1. al-Ṭahṭāwī, 1833: 3.

had spent any length of time in the close company of Christians, let alone Europeans. During the stay, the traveller straddles two worlds: his own and that of the new environment, the most prominent feature being that the traveller, to use R. Barthes's words, '*fait du pays résidentiel ... espace composite où se condense la substance de plusieures grandes villes, un élément dans lequel le sujet peut plonger.*'[1] In this respect, one can even say that the 'traditionalist' chapters at the beginning of the *Takhlīṣ* are a way of delaying engagement with the new world and thus the alienation.

In spite of the author's good intentions, the text itself is not always easy, and the *littérateur* sometimes gains the upper hand and lets himself be carried away with polysemic word play, rhymes and pregnant homographic double-entendres. Similarly, the connection between the poems and the text to which they are supposed to refer is usually tenuous and always contrived; moreover, occasionally one gets the impression the author had a quota of quotes for every given chapter. Naturally, this is a contemporary judgement, which disregards literary tastes of the time.

Generally though, the register of language betrays a European influence, and one may imagine that al-Ṭahṭawī attempted to provide a syncretism between the Arabic and French literary styles, which he discusses at some length.[2] It is the often incongruous mix of high classical and informative styles, sprinkled with some colloquialisms, that reveals that this was still an experiment.

Vocabulary, too, merits some attention as the *Takhlīṣ* is the first modern Arabic literary work to make extensive use of loanwords (*ta'rīb*), with some seventy examples of French borrowings (as well as some from Turkish), several of which have endured until the present day, e.g. *nimra* ('number'), *ūbira* ('opera'), *aghusṭus* ('August'), *akadima* ('academy'), *bārūn* ('baron'), *būlītīqa* ('politics'), *bulwār* ('boulevard'), *busṭa* ('post'), *jinrāl* ('general'), *dūk* ('duke'), *fabrīqa* ('factory'), *kāẓīṭa* ('newspaper'), *marshāl* ('marshall'), *santimitr* ('centimetre'), *mitr* ('metre'), *tilighrāf* ('telegraph'), *tiyātir* ('theatre').[3] Equally interesting are the loan translations (calques), which, one may assume, must have thrown the readership somewhat: *al-zaman* ('time') for weather (cf. French *le temps*), *mawāḍi'* ('places') for squares (Fr. *places*). One should point out that, like the *taqārīẓ* by European scholars, the use of loans is significant in that it constituted a sign of modernity, marking the author's inclusion in, and association with, the modern world and its sciences.

1. R. Barthes, 1972: 183.
2. See Translation, p. 186ff.
3. Cf. D. Newman, 2002b; M. Sawā'ī 1999; M. Sawaie 2000.

Unsurprisingly, the new concepts and ideas also led to a large number of lexical inconsistencies. One case in point is the translation of such political concepts as 'nation', 'state', and 'community' or even 'the people' in the sense of 'the body politic' (*le peuple*), al-Ṭahṭāwī being seemingly unable to make up his mind, wavering between a variety of words from Islamic political thought.

Translation to a lesser or greater extent always involves a trade-off, and this is particularly true for 'classical' texts. My aim throughout has been to provide a translation that would render the feel of the original as much as possible, without sacrificing readability, and thus give the non-Arabic-speaking reader some idea of the style of a 19th-century Arabic text.

PART TWO

Takhlīṣ al-Ibrīz fī Talkhīṣ Bārīz

Preface

In the name of God, the merciful, the compassionate.

Praise be to Him who guides the footsteps of mankind towards that which has taken place in His prescience, He who makes it possible for people to fulfil His decree and judgement. Whether strong or weak, lowly or noble, none is able to escape that which was set forth in the essence of the Book.[1] Whether one is rich or poor, important or wretched, one can but approach the folds of this veil. I praise Him, God the Almighty, in the way of one who, tested by Him, has shown steadfastness and, enriched by Him, has given thanks.[2] I thank Him with the gratitude of one who, having taken his heart along the path to His satisfaction, has been allowed to stroll in the gardens of the chosen.

I pray and salute the One the mounts of whose ardent love rode to the Disposer of things, and the goodness of whose nature bears out the nobility of his ancestry – our Master Muḥammad who, in the company of his faithful Gabriel, travelled to Syria,[3] fled to Medina[4] and went from the Holy Mosque[5] to Jerusalem.[6]

1. Cf. Qur. XIII:39 (trans. A. Arberry, 1983: 244).
2. This is a clear reference to the vicissitudes of the author's family, from the ruin of his father to his current situation of one enjoying the favour of the ruler.
3. *al-Shām* or *bilād al-Shām* (also *Sha'm*), 'the land of Shām', is today synonymous with the Republic of Syria (as well as its capital, Damascus). However, in previous times, it covered an area stretching across the modern states of Syria, Lebanon, Jordan and Israel, and should thus be more appropriately equated with what was formerly known as 'Greater Syria'. In al-Ṭahṭāwī's day, the geopolitical construct *al-Sha'm* was an Ottoman province, composed of four *pashaliks* (each subdivided into a number of *sanjaqs*) – Damascus (including Jerusalem and Beirut), Tripoli, Aleppo and Acre (previously Sidon). It is of course in the wider sense that 'Syria' will be used in this translation. See *EI1*, s.v. "al-S͟ha'm" (H. Lammens).
4. The Arabic reads 'the hijra to Medina'. After spreading the message of Islam in his native Mekka, the Prophet was chased by its inhabitants in 622 A.D. and fled to Medina, a city originally called *Yathrib*, but which subsequently became known as *Madīnat al-Nabī* ('City of the Prophet') or, simply, *al-Madīna* (The City).
5. This refers to that of Mekka.
6. The Arabic text uses the *pars pro toto* of *al-masjid al-aqṣā* ('the Further Mosque'). This entire passage bears a close relation to the opening of Qur. XVII ('The Night Journey'):

My prayers and blessings also go out to his people, his companions, his relatives and his loved ones.

I address myself to his Highness, in the name of our Lord Muḥammad,[1] to unfold the banners of might and justice and to spread the greatest standing and benefit across the regions of Egypt, the Ḥijāz, the Sudan and Syria through to the radiant star of the admirable governance and extraordinary construction of the most exalted minister – the honoured and magnificent lordship, the rarest and most exceptional among princes of all times; he whose efforts have rejuvenated the sciences, and who has re-established the marks of Islam[2] through war and exertion; he who holds outstanding wisdom; the conqueror of the holy sites, his Excellency, the Benefactor,[3] endowed with eminent qualities, Ḥājj[4] Muḥammad ʿAlī. May God the Exalted bring him what he wishes and has wished. Amen.

In goodness our Lord keeps him
in glory and happiness
By bringing him the blessing of creation
and his dynasty the people who rule

Thus speaks the humble servant in need of the helping hand of his Lord, who goes where He sends him, who relies on Him, the Generous Benefactor – Rifāʿa, the son of the late Sayyid Badawī Rāfiʿ, al-Ṭahṭāwī after the name

---

'Glory be to Him, who carried His servant by night from the Holy Mosque to the Further Mosque ...' (trans. A. Arberry, 1983: 274).

1. The Arabic phrase provides a play of words on Muḥammad ʿAlī: *al-ḥaḍrat al-ʿaliyya, bi 'l-ḥaḍrat al-Muḥammadiyya.*
2. This is a reference to Muḥammad ʿAlī's fight against the Wahhābīs (vide post). After the death of Muḥammad b. ʿAbd al-Wahhāb (1792) – the eponymous founder of the movement – the Wahhābīs embarked on a series of raids from their capital, Dariya, and expanded their territory, taking control of most of the Ḥijāz (1804–06) – including the Holy Cities – as well as launching attacks on Baghdad and Damascus. The growing threat of the Wahhābī empire caused considerable concern to the Ottoman Sultan, who called upon Muḥammad ʿAlī to wage a counteroffensive (September 1811). In 1812, his son, Ṭūsūn, captured Mekka. Six years later, following the death of Ṭūsūn, Muḥammad ʿAlī's other son, Ibrāhīm Pasha, took the Wahhābī capital; the movement's leader, ʿAbd Allāh, was sent to Constantinople and beheaded. However, shortly after Ibrāhīm's departure, the Wahhābīs again revolted (this time in the Najd), establishing their control along the coast of the Persian Gulf. See *EI1*, s.vv. "al-Wahhābīya" (D. S. Margoliouth), "Muḥammad ʿAlī Pasha" (J. H. Kramers).
3. *walī al-naʿim* (also *walī al-niʿma*), 'bestower of beneficences'.
4. This word denotes one who has performed the pilgrimage (*ḥajj*), after which it is used as an honorific.

of his 'native' town, al-Ḥusaynī al-Qāsimī after his lineage, al-Shāfiʿī[1] after his legal school:

When God – Praise the Lord the Exalted – bestowed upon me the blessing of study at the university of al-Azhar, the place of enlightenment, which is a paradise of science with low-hanging fruit, a garden of knowledge filled with full blooms, or, to use the words of my teacher, the most erudite al-ʿAṭṭār:

Attend with perseverance, if you seek the virtues, a mosque
illuminated by the sun of varied sciences
It holds the gardens of science with flowers in bloom
And that is why it is called al-Azhar[2]

Somebody else put it well in two verses in which reference is made to scholars from the holy cities of Mekka and Medina:

Let he who is in foreign lands, far away from the flowers of wisdom, lament[3]
the distance that separates him from the home of science and scholars
Where there are great men with knowledge like that of overflowing seas,
whereas elsewhere there are only seas with scantily washed shores[4]

And I have indeed acquired that which the Opener[5] granted me and which allows man to leave obscurity and distinguish himself from among the

1. This refers to the *madhhab* (theological school), named after the Mekka-born Abū ʿAbd Allāh Muḥammad b. Idrīs al-Imām Shāfiʿī (d. 820). A member of the Quraysh (the tribe of the Prophet Muḥammad), he was also a Hāshimī, and thus related to the Prophet. He studied under Mālik b. Anas (see note no. 4, p. 124) in Medina, and afterwards went to Egypt and Baghdad. He died in Cairo, where his tomb is still a popular pilgrimage site. The Shāfiʿī *madhhab* is especially popular in Egypt, some of the Gulf states, as well as in parts of Central and South-East Asia. See "al-Shāfiʿī", *EI1* (Henning), *EI2* (E. Chaumont); *EI2* s.v. "al-Shāfiʿiyya" (E. Chaumont); J. Schacht, 1975; *idem*, 1966: 45ff., 58ff.
2. The verse plays on the homonym '*zahr*', meaning 'flower', and the verb '*zahara*' ('to blossom' or 'to bloom').
3. Here, the poet plays on the homograph (in the absence of vowel markings) '*azhar*' ('radiant', 'brilliant') and '*azhur*' ('flowers').
4. The Arabic relies on the intricacies resulting from the polysemy of the word '*baḥr*', which can mean 'sea', 'wise man with knowledge as vast as the sea' (*baḥr al-ʿilm*), and 'metre (poetry)'. In the last line, there is also a possible play on the homographs *ʿarūḍ* ('shore', 'beach') and *ʿurūḍ* (sing. *ʿarḍ*, 'cloud at the horizon'), which would change the translation to 'clouds that do not provide water'.
5. i.e. of the gates of sustenance; this is one of the attributes of God and one of the so-called '99 beautiful names' (*al-asmāʾ al-ḥusnā*) of God.

ranks of the common people.[1] Hailing from a family[2] that time oppressed, after having showered abundance on its households, and whose travails have been borne out by the years after they had erected the markers of comfort on their noble home.[3] It is established in what one hears both in past and present, and there is consensus among religious authorities that next to the Book and Ḥadīth,[4] science is the best and the most important of all things. Its fruit in this life and the next benefits those who possess it and its merit is borne out in all times and places. Thus, it was easy for me to enter the service of His Excellency, first as a preacher (*wā'iẓ*) in the army, and then to be elevated to the rank of envoy to Paris to accompany the Efendis[5] who were sent to study the sciences and arts present in that magnificent city.

When my name was entered among those of the travellers, and I made preparations to go, some relatives and well-wishers, especially our Shaykh al-ʿAṭṭār[6] – who is passionately fond of listening to wondrous stories and of knowing exceptional works – told me to observe in great detail everything that would take place on this trip, everything I saw and encountered that was strange and wondrous, and to write it down so that it could be useful to discover the face of this region, of which it is said that it is the bride

1. *'awāmm*, sing. *'āmma*; derived from a root meaning 'to be spread out, cover entirely', both the singular and plural – though the former is the more common – denote the 'masses' in opposition with the notables, *al-khāṣṣa* ('the exceptional ones'). See *EI2*, s.v. "al-k͟hāṣṣa wa 'l-ʿāmma" (M. A. J. Beg).
2. *ma'shar*; in the second edition this was changed into *ma'shar ashrāf*, i.e. 'a family of *sharīfs*'.
3. The Arabic *mazār* (pl. *mazārāt*) means 'place one visits' and, by extension, a pilgrimage site, especially the tomb of a Muslim saint, and is thus a clear allusion to that of the author's ancestor (see Translator's Introduction). This reinforces the religious connotation of the earlier *naṣab* ('marker', 'signpost'), whose plural *anṣāb* denotes the perimeter of the sacred enclosure of the mosque at Mekka. The entire passage is, of course, a lament for the material decline of the Ṭahṭāwī family.
4. Here, the author includes three of the *uṣūl al-fiqh*, i.e. 'pillars of religious law' – the agreement on religious matters by qualified legal scholars (*ijmā'*), the Qur'ān and Ḥadīth (the corpus of the sayings and actions of the Prophet Muḥammad and his Companions). See *EI2*, s.v. "uṣūl al-fiqh" (N. Calder); *EI1*, s.v. "id͟jmāʿ" (D. B. MacDonald); N. Coulson, 1978: 76–81 *et passim*.
5. *Afandiyya* (sing. *Afandī*), an Ottoman title, whose origins can be traced to the (Byzantine) Greek ἀφέντης (cf. αὐθέντης, 'lord, master'). It was an honorific used for various dignitaries, the sultan himself being known as *Efendimiz* ('our Master'); in Egypt, the Arabic equivalent *Efendīnā* was used for Muḥammad ʿAlī and his successors. The chief secretaries of the *dīwān* were also known as 'Efendi', as indeed were all high functionaries as well as members of the ruling house. In practice, 'Efendi' soon became a term/reference of address used for all persons with a certain standard of literacy. See "Efendi", *EI1* (Cl. Huart), *EI2* (B. Lewis); ʿA. al-Jabartī, 1997: IV, 83 (Note).
6. See Translator's Introduction.

among all regions,[1] and in order for it to remain a guide for would-be travellers wishing to go there. This is especially apt since, as far as I know, nothing has appeared in Arabic up until now on the history of the city of Paris, the seat of the Kingdom of the French, nor is there any information on its condition or of the condition of its people. Praise be to God, who has made this possible through our Benefactor, in his reign, and because of his concern for and encouragement of the sciences and arts.

I did not fail to record a brief account of my journey, which I have kept free from faults related to indulgence and prejudice. I have also eschewed errors related to sloth and rivalry for precedence. I have adorned it with some useful digressions and convincing corroborations, and phrased it so as to urge Islamic countries to examine the foreign sciences, the arts and the crafts. To be sure, the perfection of this is to be found in the lands of the Franks,[2] and it behoves one to follow the truth.[3] By God, during my stay in this country, I was grieved by the fact that it had enjoyed all those things that are lacking in Islamic kingdoms.

But beware of finding that which I have to tell you as being against your customs and thus difficult to believe. Nor should you consider it prattle and fables, or within the realm of exaggeration and hyperbole. When all is said and done, '*some suppositions are a sin*', and '*an eyewitness can see that which one who is absent cannot.*' Also, '*if you have not seen the new moon, rely on those who have seen it with their own eyes.*'

I take God – praise be to Him the Exalted – as my witness that in all that I will say I will not stray from the path of truth and that, as much as my mind allows it, I shall express a favourable judgement of the many things and customs of that country when circumstances require it. Naturally, I shall approve only that which does not run counter to the prescriptions of

1. This is a reference to Egyptian parlance, in which Alexandria is known as 'the Bride of the Mediterranean' (*'arūs al-baḥr al-abyaḍ*) or Asyūṭ as 'the Bride of Upper Egypt' (*'arūs al-ṣa'īd*). It is interesting to compare this passage to Edward Lane's words upon catching sight of Egypt (in 1825): 'As I approached the shore, I felt like an Eastern bridegroom about to lift the veil of his bride.' (Quoted in L. Ahmed, 1978:1.)

2. *Ifranj* (also *Firanj*, *Ifranjiyyūn*, φράγγοι) goes back to the Middle Ages, and already appears in Ibn Khurdādhbih's *Kitāb al-Masālik wa 'l-Mamālik* ('The book of itineraries and kingdoms'), which dates back to the 9th century and is the oldest surviving Arabic geographical manual (Ibn Khurdādhbih, 1889: *passim*). For more details on this term and the people and regions it denoted, see D. Newman, 2001: 10–12; I. Guidi, 1909; E. Ashtor, 1969; Y. al-Khuri, 1967; *EI2*, s.v. "Ifrandj" (B. Lewis); A. Miquel, 1967–80: II, 342ff., 354–62; B. Lewis, 1994; I. Krachkovskij, 1963: I, 272ff.; A. El-Hajji, 1970: 119–24; H. Eisenstein, 1994. In the course of the translation, it will usually be rendered as 'Franks' or, more rarely, as 'Europeans'.

3. Cf. Qur. X:35.

Muḥammadan law[1] – the best of prayers and noblest greetings to Him who proclaimed it. This short *riḥla* is not just an account of the journey and its events; rather, it also includes its fruits and goals. It also contains a short exposé on the sought-after sciences and skills, presented in the way that the Franks use to record, conceive, and establish them. This is why I usually trace the origins of things that give rise to consideration or dispute to their origins, thus bearing out that my sole intention is to give an account of them. I have called this *riḥla* '*Takhlīṣ al-ibrīz fī talkhīṣ Bārīz aw al-dīwān al-nafīs bi-īwān Bārīs*' ('The Extraction of Pure Gold in the Abridgement of Paris, or the precious *dīwān* in the *īwān* of Paris').[2] It includes an introduction, with several chapters; the core of the book, which contains several essays, each of which is subdivided into sections – or, if you will, books composed of chapters – and an epilogue. The reader is referred to the table of contents at the beginning of the book.

In the writing of this book I have tried to follow the path of terseness, while pursuing simplicity of expression so as to enable all people to arrive at its water basins and to visit its gardens.[3] Even though it is not thick or voluminous, it is full of innumerable precious benefits and impenetrable unbored pearls.

When it appears, do not think little of its size
On your life, it contains much good

I implore God – praise to Him the Exalted – that this book be favourably received by his Excellency, the Benefactor, the source of virtue and generosity, and that with it He will arouse all Islamic nations – both Arab and non-Arab – from their sleep of indifference. For He is the All-hearing, the Granter of wishes; whoever addresses himself to Him will not be disappointed.

---

1. *naṣṣ al-sharīʿa al-muḥammadiyya*. The avoidance of the use of the word *sharīʿa* in English is justified here since it would have inappropriately narrowed the concept to which the author refers.
2. The Arabic *īwān* (pl. *īwānāt*, *awāwīn*) denotes an estrade in a large room (in Egypt also called *līwān*), on which a mattress and cushions were placed. In traditional Arab architecture, *dīwān* (pl. *dawāwīn*) refers to the reception room. However, it also had several other meanings: 'ledger', 'poetry collection', '(state) council', as well as a type of caravanserai. Also see E. Lane, 1923: 12; "dīwān", *EI1* (Cl. Huart), *EI2* (A. A. Durri – H. L. Gottschalk); *EI2*, s.v. "īwān" (O. Grabar).
3. This rather convoluted phrasing is, of course, more euphonic in Arabic: *al-wurūd ʿalā ḥiyāḍihi wa 'l-wufūd ʿalā riyāḍihi*.

Introduction

First Chapter. Regarding what seemed to me to be the reason behind our departure for this Land of Infidelity and Obstinacy, which lies far away from us and where there are great expenses because of the high cost of living

I can say that this requires some kind of introduction. Originally, man was simple and devoid of adornments; he existed in a purely natural state, and knew only instincts. Then, some people acquired some knowledge that they had not previously had. This was uncovered to them by chance, accident, inspiration or revelation. The divine law or the intellect judged that this knowledge was useful and thus it was applied and preserved. For instance, in earliest times, some people were completely ignorant of how to cook food by means of fire, since the latter was completely unknown among them. As a result, their diet was restricted to fruit, things ripened in the sun, or raw foodstuffs, as is still the case in some countries today. Then one of them by chance saw a spark coming from a flint as it was hit with a piece of iron or something like that. When he did the same thing, he managed to extract the fire and learned about its properties. There were also people who, for instance, did not know how to dye clothes purple, until, that is, one of them saw a dog take a shell from the sea, open it and eat its contents, after which his palate turned red, coloured by what was inside. And thus they began to make use of it and learned the art of dyeing things in this colour. A similar story is recounted about the people of Tyre in Syria. Initially, they had no idea how to sail the sea. Then, through divine inspiration or human coincidence, they found out that one of the characteristics of wood is that it floats on the surface of the water, so they started building boats. Afterwards, they boarded the ships and took to sea. Then, they also started loading the ships, and they built many different types. At first, these were small vessels destined for trade, but then they worked their way up to those suited for war (*jihād*) and combat. The same can be said of battles, which were first fought with arrows and spears, then with swords and later on with cannons and mortars. From the beginning of time, people worshipped the sun, the moon, the stars and other such things and then, through inspiration from God the Exalted, and through the Messengers sent by Him, they started to worship only one God.

And so, the more we go back in time, the more you can see the backwardness of people in terms of human skills and civil sciences. Conversely, as you descend and observe the slope of time [to the present], you generally see the elevation and progress of these. By measuring the degree of this advancement and calculating the distance from and proximity to the primitive state, creation as a whole can be divided into a number of categories. The first category is that of wild savages,[1] the second of the uncivilized barbarians, whereas the third comprises people who are cultured, refined, sedentarized (*taḥaḍḍur*), civilized (*tamaddun*) and have attained the highest degree of urbanization (*tamaṣṣur*).[2]

The first group is exemplified by the savages of the lands of the Blacks,[3] who are always like roaming animals and who do not distinguish between what is lawful and unlawful;[4] they are unable to read or write and they do not know anything about things that facilitate this life or the hereafter. They are like animals in that they are [solely] driven by the urge to satisfy their desires. They sow only a few things or hunt a little in order to provide

1. *hamal*, which refers to people living in nature without any cultural, political and legal organization or fixed social structure.
2. In many ways, *taḥaḍḍur*, *tamaddun*, and *tamaṣṣur* can be – and often are – used interchangeably to denote 'civilization'. However, there are subtle differences between them. The first (*taḥaḍḍara*, 'to settle among sedentary people') stresses the settling of people in fixed dwellings, the cognate *ḥaḍāra* being a common Modern Standard Arabic (henceforth 'MSA') word for 'civilization'. The second is derived from a root meaning 'to settle down (in a city)', and is closely related to the concept of the πόλις, i.e. of life in civil society (cf. Khayr al-Dīn, 1867: 5, 19, 27, 44 *et passim*). In one of his later writings, al-Ṭahṭāwī describes *tamaddun*, which he contrasts with *takhashshun* ('coarseness'), as follows: '[it] expresses the fact that [a country] has acquired all that is required for civilized people (*ahl al-'umrān*) in terms of the necessary tools for the improvement of their condition', and leads to 'perfection in upbringing, a propensity for praiseworthy qualities (...) and the elevation of the quality of life' (1973–80: II, 469 [*al-Murshid al-amīn*]). Closely related to *tamaddun* is *tamaṣṣur* ('to build large cities'), which may thus, in a way, be considered the necessary adjunct of the first two.
3. *bilād al-Sūdān*. Arab geographers used this term to denote the regions inhabited by the black peoples south of Egypt, as well as Islamicized Sub-Saharan Africa (stretching roughly from the Senegal basin to the Upper Nile basin). See "Sūdān", *EI1* (Maurice Delafosse), *EI2* (A. S. Kaye); M. Cuoq, 1975; S. Kaplan, 'Arab geographers, the Nile, and the history of the Bilād al- Sūdān', in H. Erlich and I. Gershoni (eds), 2000.
4. It is clear that by using *ḥarām* and *ḥalāl*, respectively, both of which have an exclusively religious connotation, the author viewed these peoples primarily in terms of their 'heathenness'.

for themselves. They build a few huts or tents to protect themselves from the heat of the sun and the other natural elements.[1]

An example of the second category are the Arabs of the desert, who have a type of human society, sociability and harmony since they know how to distinguish what is lawful from what is unlawful. They can read and write as well as other things, and understand matters related to religion. Nevertheless, the degree of elevation of their living standard, civilization,[2] human skills and rational and traditional sciences[3] is not perfect either, despite the fact that they are familiar with construction, agriculture, animal husbandry and things like that.

The third category includes Egypt, Syria, Yemen, the lands of the Rūm,[4]

1. This derogatory view of blacks can, in fact, be traced to the Middle Ages, with geographers expressing almost identical views; cf. B. Lewis, 1971 (which offers an in-depth historical overview of Muslim perceptions of black people).
2. *'umrān*; derived from a root meaning 'to build' or 'to cultivate', it denotes 'any settlement above the level of individual savagery' (F. Rosenthal [Ibn Khaldūn], 1986: I, lxxvff.). It was a core concept in the social thought of Ibn Khaldūn, where it acquired the meaning of 'population' inasmuch as he posited an inextricable link between *'umrān* and cooperation among people. In practice, it can be translated in a variety of ways, varying from 'culture' to 'civilization', 'prosperity' and 'populousness'. Also see Khayr al-Dīn, 1867: e.g. 4, 8, 10, 21, 22, 27 *et passim*; B. Tlili, 1972a; V. Monteil, 1960: 215ff.; L. Brown [Khayr al-Dīn], 1967: 138 (note 189).
3. *'ulūm 'aqliyya wa naqliyya*, which literally translates as 'sciences of the mind and those related to transmission' (of religious traditions). The 'intellectual' sciences (*'ilm*, pl. *'ulūm*) consist of seven branches: *manṭiq* (logic), *handasa* (geometry), *hay'a* (astronomy), musicology, *ṭabī'yāt* (physics, also including *filāḥa*, 'agriculture'), *ilāhiyat* (metaphysics), *ṭibb* (medicine). As for the religious sciences, these Ibn Khaldūn (1986: II, 436ff.) identified as *tafsīr* (Qur'ānic commentary) and *qirā'āt* (Qur'ān readings), *ḥadīth*, *fiqh* (jurisprudence), *uṣūl al-fiqh* (pillars of Islamic law), *kalām* (theology), *taṣawwuf* (mysticism), *ta'ābīr al-ru'yā* (oneiromancy). Traditionally, *'ilm* has often been contrasted with *ma'rifa*, the latter meaning 'coming to know by experience or reflection', as opposed to 'knowledge (of a definite thing)'. The 14th-century theologian al-Jurjānī (1339-1413), for instance, explained the difference between the two types of 'knowledge' as follows: '*ma'rifa* also means knowledge of something as is, which is preceded by ignorance, as opposed to *'ilm*; this is why God is called *al-'ālim* and not *al-'ārif*.' (1983: 382). In Muslim Neo-Platonist thought, on the other hand, *'ilm* is used to refer to 'knowledge of a superordinate, that is, anything of a composite nature, anything with a hyperonym, while *ma'rifa* is used for meronyms or primes; that is why the latter is used in referring to any kind of knowledge of God, never the former.' (I. Netton 1984.) It must be said that this distinction no longer holds today, *ma'rifa* being most often used in humanities, in the sense of 'epistemology', or 'cognition'; indeed, 'cognitive' (or sometimes 'epistemological') is rendered in Arabic by the neologism *ma'rifī*. MSA *'ilm*, on the other hand, is used mainly in the exact and natural sciences, with the adjective *'ilmī* denoting 'scientific'. See *EI1*, s.v. "'ilm" (D. B. Macdonald); F. Rosenthal, 1970; M. Enani 2000: 20ff.
4. This collective ('Ρωμαιο; *nomen unitatis*: *Rūmī*) first appeared in the Qur'ān, where it denoted the Byzantines, which were also sometimes known as the *Banū ('l-) Aṣfar* ('the tribe of Aṣfar ['the Yellow One']'). *Rūm* would retain this meaning throughout history,

Persia, the Franks, the Maghrib,[1] Sennār,[2] most of the lands of America (*Amrīkā*), and many of the islands of the Encircling Sea[3] [Oceania]. All of these nations have civilization and political institutions, sciences and industries, laws and trade. They are proficient at technical equipment, possess the skills to carry heavy loads through light means and are familiar with seafaring and things like it.

In this third category there are discrepancies between these countries in terms of the sciences and arts, the standard of living, compliance with a given system of laws and progress in craftsmanship. For instance, Frankish lands have attained the highest degree of proficiency in mathematics, natural sciences and metaphysics, in regard to both their theoretical foundations and the various branches. Some Franks possess knowledge of some Arabic sciences and have gained access to their intricacies and secrets,

---

though it often appears as a synonym of 'Christian'. Mediaeval Arabic geographers generally distinguished the Byzantines/*Rūm* from the (ancient) Romans (*Rūmāniyyūn*) and the ancient Greeks (*al-Yūnāniyyūn, al-Ighrīqiyyūn*), though not always (e.g. al-Masʿūdī, 1894: 129; al-Dimashqī, 1866: 258). Some authors, like al-Dimashqī (1866: 260) and Abū 'l-Fidā' (1840: 213) even had another term for the inhabitants of the early Eastern Roman Empire, i.e. *al-Kharā'iṭa*, which the second author traced to *kharaṭa* (Abū 'l-Fidā', 1840: *ibid.*; also see trans., II/1, 313 note 2). The etymology of this word is far from clear, but one may conjecture a link with *Karaite* (followers of the 8th-century Jewish sect), or the New Testament Greek P VD4Jg4< ('to bless'). Spanish Christians were variously referred to as *Ifranj* or *Rūm* (cf. e.g. Ibn al-Khaṭīb, 1956: II, 11–12, 23). Interestingly enough, 17th/18th-century Moroccan travellers would use *Rūm* only for 'Romans' (e.g. al-Miknāsī, 1965: 35). Later on, the Turks employed *bilād al-Rūm* to denote the European provinces of the Ottoman Empire. At the same time, the Ottomans used the term *Rūm* to designate the modern Greeks (also *Urūm*) and, more rarely, Turkey in general. Later on in the text, al-Ṭahṭāwī uses *arwām* (pl. of *Rūmī*) for the modern Greeks; it is in this sense that this term is still used today in colloquial Egyptian Arabic, whereas in MSA it is applied to adherents of the Greek Orthodox Church. See "Rūm", *EI1* (F. Babinger), *EI2* (Nadia El Cheikh/C. E. Bosworth); *EI1*, *EI2*, s.v. "Aṣfar" (Goldziher); A. Miquel, 1967–80: II, 381–481; S. Elatri, 1974: 361.

1. Strictly speaking, this word denotes 'the place where the sun sets', i.e. the West (as opposed to *al-Mashriq*, 'the place where the sun rises' – the East), and denoted the Islamic lands to the west of Egypt (the Europeans' *Barbary* or *Africa Minor*), sometimes including al-Andalus. Today, 'al-Maghrib' is the name for Morocco. See "Maghrib" *EI1*, *EI2* (G. Yver).
2. This former Christian Nubian kingdom was situated between the White Nile and the Blue Nile, in the eastern Sudan. The homonymous town in the Sudan is about 270km south of the capital, Khartoum. See *EI1*, s.v. "Sennār" (S. Hillelson).
3. *al-baḥr al-muḥīṭ* (the Greeks' Ωκεανός). This sea, which mediaeval Arabic geographers also referred to as *baḥr Ūqiyānūs al-muḥīṭ, al-Muḥīṭ, Ūqiyānūs* (or *Uqiyānus*) – as well as *al-Baḥr al-Akhḍar* ('The Green Sea') – derives its name from the fact that they conceived of the ocean as a circular water mass enclosing the entire habitable world (and the source of all other seas). In many cases, it corresponded to the Atlantic Ocean (though the part adjacent to al-Andalus and the Maghrib was often considered part of the *Baḥr al-Maghrib*, 'The Western Sea'). See "Baḥr muḥīṭ", *EI1* (Carra de Vaux), *EI2* (D. M. Dunlop).

as we shall see later. Nevertheless, they have not pursued the straight path,[1] or entered upon the road towards salvation.

Islamic countries, for their part, distinguished themselves in the legal sciences and their application, and in the rational sciences, but neglected all of the philosophical branches,[2] and so they needed Western countries to acquire what they did not know. This is why the Franks held that the scholars of Islam knew nothing except their law and their tongue, i.e. matters related to the Arabic language. However, they do acknowledge that we were their teachers in all sciences and that we had an advance on them. Intellect and observation have established that credit goes to the precursor. Is it not so that the one who comes later delves into what has been left [by his predecessor], and is guided by his directions? This has been put admirably in the following words by the poet:

What moved me was that I was asleep
Assuaging thereby excessive languor
Until the dove wept in the branches of the thicket
Its lament ringing out in a sweet chant
If before its lament I had wept with fervent longing
my soul was healed by my happiness prior to remorse
But then his weeping was there before me, and moved me to tears
And I said: merit is due to the one who came first

Equally pleasing are similar words in regard to recompense:

I am the brave one who was there, thirsty
in the midday heat, on the sun-baked soil in the wadi
You gave water – out of your grace it sprang
unstintingly, and it healed the suffering of the parched
This is your reward; not a boon we bestow, but
credit goes to the one who took the first step

---

1. '(*lam yathdadū*) *al-ṭarīq al-mustaqīm*', which is a paraphrase of a frequently encountered Qur'ānic expression '*al-ṣirāṭ al-mustaqīm*', which already appears in the opening *sūra* (I:6), and of course refers to 'the True Faith', which usually denotes Islam (e.g. II:142, III:101, IV:68), but is also used for the preaching of Moses (XXXVII:118), and Jesus (III:51), and even applies to a generally religious way of living (VII:16). The exact phrase *al-ṭarīq al-mustaqīm* occurs only once (XLVI:30), out of the mouth of a converted *jinn*.
2. *al-'ulūm al-ḥikmiyya*, which can also be translated as 'positive sciences'.

Indeed, in the time of the caliphs[1] we were the most perfect of all countries. The reason for this is that the caliphs helped scholars, artists and others like them. Some of the caliphs even got personally involved in these pursuits. Take for instance al-Ma'mūn,[2] the son of Hārūn al-Rashīd,[3] who in addition to his support of the timekeepers[4] in his realm, was himself engaged in astronomy. And look at how he determined the angle between the zodiac and the equator, finding, after examination, that it amounted to 23 degrees, 35 minutes.[5] The 'Abbāsid Ja'far al-Mutawakkil[6] encouraged

1. The word *khalīfa* (pl. *khulafā'*) literally means 'one who follows (someone else)'; it was first used for the immediate successors of the Prophet Muḥammad, who were subsequently known as the 'Rightly guided caliphs' (*al-khulafā' al-rāshidūn*). The time to which al-Ṭahṭāwī refers here, however, is the so-called Golden Age of Islam, i.e. the era of the 'Abbāsid rulers, during which the Islamic empire reached its zenith.
2. Abū 'l-'Abbās 'Abd Allāh b. Hārūn al-Rashīd, known as al-Ma'mūn, was the seventh 'Abbāsid caliph (786–833); in 813, he succeeded his brother al-Amīn (809–13) after the latter's assassination. In addition to being a great warrior, he was also an avid patron of the arts and sciences, which reached an apogee during his reign, culminating in the creation of the *Bayt al-Ḥikma* ('House of Wisdom') in 830. Al-Ma'mūn also ordered the building of an observatory in Baghdad (as well as in Damascus), where his scholars set about establishing the coordinates of the towns and cities of the known world, as well as compiling catalogues of fixed stars, and revising astronomical tables. Undoubtedly the most famous astronomical exploit in al-Ma'mūn's reign was the field experiment conducted with a view to measuring the meridian degree, with two parties moving in opposite directions in the desert, measuring the distance covered in one degree latitude by taking sightings of the Pole Star. Based on the two sets of findings, the caliph himself fixed the length of a one-degree meridian arc at 56 2/3 miles, i.e. 111.8 kilometres (a mere 0.7 km off today's accepted value!). In a later work, al-Ṭahṭāwī offers more praise for al-Ma'mūn's achievements, calling him a 'renewer' (*mujaddid*) for his concern for the secular sciences, while chastising him for his religious policy (al-Ṭahṭāwī, 1871: 17–8). See "al-Ma'mūn", *EI1* (K. V.Zetterstéen), *EI2* (M. Rekaya); *EI2* s.v. "bayt al-ḥikma" (D. Sourdel); C. Nallino, 1944: 301ff.; A. Sayili, 1960: 50ff.; P. G. Donini, 1991: 21, 36ff.; A. Zeki Validi Togan, 1937–8: 65ff.
3. al-Rashīd (763–809) is undoubtedly the most famous of all the 'Abbāsid caliphs. With the translation of the Arabian Nights, in which he makes a number of appearances, Hārūn's fame spread to Europe, where he became a figure of fascination and mystery, and 'the personification of Oriental power and splendour' [K. V. Zetterstéen, *EI1*, III, p. 272). While his court was a centre for learning, scholarship and art, he was also an extremely adroit politician and warrior and waged a number of successful campaigns, which strengthened the Empire. See "Hārūn" *EI1* (K. V. Zetterstéen), *EI2* (F. Omar).
4. The author uses the Egyptian colloquial Arabic *mīqātiyya* (sing. *mīqātī*).
5. In fact, the scholars set it at 23° 23' (today considered to be 23° 27'). One should hasten to add that there are no records that corroborate al-Ṭahṭāwī's claim that al-Ma'mūn was personally involved in these experiments. See P. G. Donini, 1991: 36.
6. Abū 'l-Faḍl Ja'far b. Muḥammad, al-Mutawakkil 'alā 'llāh (822–61) was the son of the 'Abbāsid caliph al-Mu'taṣim. During his reign he gave a powerful impetus to the translation movement, with the setting up of a school around his physician Ḥunayn b. Isḥāq (d. 873), while a new school of philsosophy and medicine blossomed in Ḥarrān, thanks to the work of the famous mathematician Thābit b. Qurrah (836–901) and his

Stephen (*Iṣṭifān*) to translate Greek books like that of Dioscorides on medicines,[1] while the ruler of al-Andalus,[2] ʿAbd al-Raḥmān al-Nāṣir,[3] asked the King of Constantinople, Armanius (*Armāniyūs*),[4] to send him a man who could speak Greek and Latin to train his slaves as translators, after which a monk by the name of Nicolas was sent.[5] However, there were many other instances of this kind.

From this you can understand that in any period the sciences do not spread except through the support extended by the ruler to his people. One proverb says that '*people follow the religion of their kings*'.

The might of the caliphs dissolved and their possessions were broken up, as witnessed by al-Andalus, which has been in the hands of the Spanish Christians (*al-Naṣārā al-Isbānyūl*) for some 350 years now, while the might of the Franks was strengthened because of their skills, organization, justice, technical know-how, versatility and inventiveness in matters of warfare. If Islam had not been protected by the might of God – praise be to Him the Exalted – it would have been nothing in relation to the Franks' power, multitude, wealth, proficient skills, etc. There is a famous saying that states the following: '*the most intelligent kings are those who are more mindful of the consequences of things*'. This is why the Benefactor – may God the

disciples. See M. Young, 1990: 486, 487, 495; *EI2*, s.v. "al-Mutawakkil ʿalā ʻllāh" (H. Kennedy).

1. =*De Materia medica* by the Greek physician Pedanius Dioscorides (d. *c.* 90). The reference is to Iṣṭifān Ibn Bāsīl (Stephanus, son of Basilius), a pupil of Ḥunayn Ibn Isḥāq, who himself translated many Greek medical works into Arabic and supervised the translation of the pharmacopoeia. Stephen is particularly known for translating some of Galen's works; cf. *GAL*, I, 255; *GALS*, I, 370. M. Young, 1990: 362, 487–91.
2. Al-Andalus is the name the Arabs gave to the Muslim-occupied part of the Iberian Peninsula. Christian Spain as well as modern Spain is referred to as *Isbāniyā* (cf. Chap. III of the Introduction), the inhabitants often being *Isbānyūl*, alongside *Isbān*. The latter is already mentioned by Ibn Khurdādhbih, who explained the origin of the name as follows: 'During the conquest of al-Andalus, it [Isbān] was ruled by a king called Roderick [*Lūdhrīq*], from Iṣbahān (Isfahan), which is why the people from Cordoba are called *al-Isbān*.' (1889: 89).
3. ʿAbd al-Raḥmān III b. Muḥammad b. ʿAbd Allāh (912–61) was the eighth Umayyad caliph of Cordoba, and the first to take the title of *al-khalīfa al-Nāṣir* ('the Saviour Caliph'). He is best known for his magnificent palace, al-Zahrā', near Cordoba. In addition to bringing peace to the Peninsula and establishing his supremacy over the west of the Mediterranean and North Africa, he was also a great patron of the arts.
4. =Romanos I (ruled 922–44).
5. This Byzantine monk assisted the Cordoban Jewish doctor (as well as vizier, linguist and diplomat) Ḥasday b. Shaprūṭ (905–75), who oversaw the Arabic translation of Dioscorides' *Materia medica*, which was finished in 951. A copy of this manual had been sent to al-Nāṣir by the famous Byzantine emperor-scholar Constantine VII Porphyrogenitus (905–59) as a present. See M. Young, 1990: 494–5; E. Lévi-Provençal, 1953: IV, 508; E. Meyerhof, 1935.

Exalted protect him – since he was made the ruler of the land of Egypt the victorious by God – praise be to Him the Exalted – has made it his goal to restore its former youth and revive its faded splendour. Since the start of his reign – may he enjoy the protection of the Almighty God – he has concentrated on the treatment of an illness, which, without him, would have remained incurable, and on the remedy of its decay, whose termination had almost become inconceivable. The masters of outstanding arts and useful skills among the Franks come to him and he showers them with his abundant munificence to the extent that the masses in Egypt and even elsewhere – out of ignorance – inwardly rebuke him for receiving the Franks, welcoming them and bestowing his favours upon them. What those people do not know is that he – may God protect him – does this only because of their human qualities and because of their sciences – not because they are Christians.[6] Indeed, necessity calls for it, and how excellent is the one who said:

Both the teacher and the doctor alike
provide counsel only if they are honoured
So bear your ailment if you treat the doctor harshly
And endure your ignorance if you treat the teacher harshly

Nobody can deny that the arts and skills are thriving today in Egypt, nay, that they prosper, whereas previously they did not exist. What our ruler has spent on that was entirely appropriate. One need only look at the workshops,[7] factories, schools and other similar things. Look at the organization of the military, which is indeed among the best things the ruler has done and among those most worthy of entering history as beneficences. The necessity of such a reorganization can be understood only by one who has seen the lands of the Franks or who has actually witnessed the developments. The long and short of it is that the hopes of our Benefactor are always related to constructing things. As the well-known saying goes: '*building is like life, and ruin is like death*', and '*each king builds*

6. These and other comments in fact serve a double purpose: on the one hand, they are the customary eulogy to the patron of the author, while they also provide justification for the author's own journey to these infidel lands and his extolling of their virtues – albeit solely in material areas.
7. *wirash*, sing. *warsha*; though this word is often traced back to the English 'workshop', the fact that it already existed at the beginning of the 19th century, when the linguistic impact of English was nil, makes it seem more prudent to concur with K. Vollers in saying that the origins of the word are '*unklar*' (1887–97: 636).

in accordance with the extent of his ambition'. The Benefactor – may God the Exalted protect him – hastened to improve his country. He brought in as many Frankish scholars as he could, and sent as many people as he could from Egypt to those countries, since their scholars exceed all others in the area of the philosophical sciences. According to a *ḥadīth*, '*knowledge is the stray sheep of the believer, he looks for it, even among the polytheists*'.[1] Ptolemy (*Baṭlīmūs*) the Second[2] said: '*take the pearls from the sea and the musk from the rat [that provides it], gold from the stone and wisdom from him who speaks it.*' Another *ḥadīth* states: '*seek knowledge, even if it is in China*'.[3] And it is well known that the people of China are pagans. The meaning of this *ḥadīth* is that one should travel to acquire knowledge. In short, there is no harm in travelling to a place where a person's faith is not in danger, particularly if it involves an advantage of this kind. Maybe this was the aspiration the ruler had in mind when sending this mission.[4]

The fruit of this journey will – God willing – be obtained with the dissemination and widespread distribution of the sciences and arts that will be discussed in the second chapter, and after the translations of the books related to it have been printed at the Benefactor's press. The scholars must encourage all people to devote themselves to the sciences, arts and useful skills. Our time will not allow that it will be said what Bahā' al-Dīn Ḥusayn al-ʿAmilī[5] said in a poem about spending one's life collecting, amassing and reading science books:

---

1. The Arabic *ahl al-shirk* (lit. 'people who associate [another with God]') or its cognate *mushrik* (pl. *mushrikūn*), was commonly used interchangeably with '*kāfir*' (lit. 'covering, concealing [God's benefits, blessings]'), i.e. 'unbeliever'. See "kāfir", *EI1*, *EI1* (W. Björkman), "shirk" *EI1* (W. Björkman), *EI2* (D. Gimaret); B. Lewis, 1994. This *ḥadīth* – or its variants '*al-ḥikma ḍāllat al-mu'min ya'khudhuhā ḥaythu wajadahā, al-ḥikma ḍāllat al-mu'min aynamā wajadahā qayyadahā* ('wisdom is the stray sheep of the believer who must seize it wherever he finds it') – was often quoted in relation to Muslim nations adopting European inventions, as witnessed by its use by, for instance, the 19th-century Tunisian statesman Khayr al-Dīn (1867: 6) and the early reformist *shaykh* Maḥmūd Qābādū (1984: II, 44).
2. = Claudius Ptolemy, with the addition 'Second' going back to the Middle Ages, when it was popularly held that the geographer was the son of Emperor Claudius; see *EI2*, s.v. "Baṭlamiyūs" (M. Plessner).
3. This *ḥadīth* was often adduced to support the lawfulness of travel in general and to non-Muslim lands (namely Europe!) in particular; cf. S. al-Ḥarā'irī, 1861: xi-xiv; S. Gellens, 1990.
4. In the second edition 'and those that followed' was added.
5 A native of Jabal ʿĀmilī in Syria, the Shīʿī polymath and poet Bahā' al-Dīn ('Ornament of Religion') Muḥammad b. Ḥusayn al-ʿĀmilī (1547–1622) wrote on such varied subjects as mathematics, astronomy and rhetoric, as well as gaining fame as both an Arabic and a Persian poet. He is best known for an anthology, entitled *al-Kashkūl* ('The Beggar's Bowl'). See *EI1*, s.v. "al-ʿĀmilī"; Y. Sarkis, 1928: 1262–4; E. Van Dyke, 1896: 240–1, 350; *GAL, II*, 415; *GALS, II*, 595.

On science books, your money you have spent
while wearying yourself with their correction
Day and night you have spent
on that which is of no use in the hereafter
All through the night till dawn you remain
poring over them, whilst your heart is not awake
In the morning, you are filled with passion – to no avail
in the composing of resolutions and arguments,
the clarification of things hidden in each chapter
and the presentation of questions and answers
By my life – you are straying from the right path
There will never be an end to your straying
and regret will be the harvest that you will reap
Privation will be yours until the day of resurrection
Your stopping and observation
will block the doors to your goals
Salvation does not come from straying
nor healing from ignorance
And guidance will not give you reason
Explanation will not make clear the proper thing to do
Elucidation obscures perception
as the lamp darkens the roads
Allusion does not make the indication appear
nor does elucidation clarify the road ahead
You spent the best part of dear life
on the brief revision of research
In doing so, life is spent in ignorance
So get up and exert yourself, for time is moving
Say goodbye to commentaries accompanied by marginal glosses[1]
for they are like veils over your eyes

He also said:

You who are in school
all you have acquired is murmurings [of the devil]
Your thought if it is with any other but the Loved One

1. *al-shurūḥ ma'a al-ḥawāshī*. This is a reference to the habit of classical Arab scholars of spending their time writing profuse text commentaries and supercommentaries (*ḥāshiya*) on commentaries (*sharḥ*).

will not have a share in the other life
So wash away with wine from the table of the heart
every science that does not bring salvation in the hereafter[1]

Second Chapter. Regarding the required sciences and desirable skills and crafts

Let us mention here the required skills so that you may know their importance and necessity in every state. In Egypt these arts are either underdeveloped or non-existent.

They may be subdivided into two categories: a general category for all pupils – arithmetic, geometry, geography, history, drawing; and a special category that contains several sciences that are divided among the pupils. The sciences in question are:

1. The science of civil organization. This is subdivided into several parts: the three branches of law pursued by the Franks – Natural law, Human law and Positive law; the study of countries, their interests and what concerns them; the science of economics;[2] the science of organizing financial transactions, accounting, treasury affairs and tax administration.[3]

2. The science of military organization.

3. The science of navigation and maritime affairs.

4. The art of knowing about the interests of states, by which is meant the science related to embassies, which includes delegations,[4] i.e. missions representing countries. It, in turn, comprises the following branches: knowledge of languages, law and technical vocabulary.

---

1. In the second edition, al-Ṭahṭāwī added a little conclusion to this chapter: 'Indeed, these are the words of someone who has freed (*tajarrada*) himself from the world, and has wholeheartedly abandoned himself (*inhamaka*) to the hereafter, or of someone who bought the sciences at the highest price, the value being reduced by the vicissitudes of time.' (M. 'Imāra (ed.): 19).
2. *'ilm al-iqtiṣād fī 'l-maṣārīf*, 'the science of moderation in expenditure'. In former times, this expression was used for bookkeeping. The MSA word for 'economics', *iqtiṣād*, was initially linked exclusively to 'economizing', and thus 19th-century Arabic lexicographical works only list the word in connection with 'savings' (i.e. as a synonym of *tawfīr*); K. Vollers (1897:322) states that it '*entspricht Oeconomie im Sinne von Sparsamkeit, wird aber erweitert zu den Begriffen von Staats- und Volkswirtschaft*'. In terms of the Classical Arabic use of the word, it is interesting to find that neither the *Lisān al-'Arab* nor E. Lane has a separate entry for this infinitive form (*maṣdar*). Cf. F. al-Shidyāq, 1881: 39; J. Habeisch, 1896: 237; G. Badger, 1895: 280; A. Kazimirski, 1860: II, 749.
3. *al-khāzāndāriyya*, which ECA term denotes 'what is related to the office of the *khazandār*' (see note no. 1, p. 196).
4. *īljiyya* (sing. *īljī*), which is, in fact, a Turkish word (cf. Mod. Turkish *elçi*) meaning 'ambassador', 'envoy'.

5. Hydrology,[1] i.e. the building of bridges, dams, quays, wells, etc.

6. Mechanics (*al-mīkānīqā*), i.e. the science dealing with engineering equipment and weight traction.

7. Military engineering.

8. The art of gunnery and its organization, i.e. the science of artillery.

9. The art of metal founding to produce cannon and weapons.

10. Chemistry and the production of paper. The term '*chemistry*' (*al-kīmiyā*) denotes the knowledge of the analysis and the composition of particles.[2] It comprises a number of things such as the production of powder and sugar. Chemistry does not refer to the 'philosopher's stone', as so many people believe, since this is not known to the Franks and they do not believe in it at all.

11. The art of medicine and its branches – anatomy, surgery and hygiene;[3] the art of diagnostics; the veterinarian art, i.e. the treatment of horses and other animals.

12. Agronomy and its branches: the knowledge of the species of plants, land management through the construction of appropriate buildings, etc., the knowledge of economical farming tools.

13. The science of natural history and its branches related to the study of animals, plants and minerals.

14. The art of engraving, with its branches: typography, lithography,[4] etc.

15. The art of translation, i.e. the translation of books. This is among the most difficult arts, particularly the translation of scientific books, which requires knowledge of the terminology used for the basic principles of the science to be translated. A truthful observer will remark that all these sciences, which are well known among these Franks, are insufficiently, if at all, known in our country. Those who do not know something need someone who has mastered that subject, whereas someone who does not deign to learn will surely die regretting it! May God be praised for having sent us our Benefactor to save us from the darkness of ignorance about the things that exist among other peoples. I believe that everybody of good taste and sound character will agree with me.

At the end of the book I shall return to some of these sciences if it pleases God the Almighty, to whom we pray for succour.

---

1. *fann al-miyāh*; 'the art of water'.
2. *ajzā'*, sing. *juz'*, 'part'.
3. *tadbīr al-ṣiḥḥa*, 'the organization/maintenance of health'.
4. *fann naqash al-aḥjār*, 'the art of engraving stones'.

Third Chapter. On the position of the Lands of the Franks in comparison with other countries, on the advantage the French nation has over all other Franks, and the reason why His Excellency decided to send us there and not to any of the other Frank kingdoms

The geographers among the Franks divided the world from the north to the south and from the east to the west into five parts: the lands of Europe (*Urubbā*), the lands of Asia (*Asiyā*), the lands of Africa (*Afrīqiya*), the lands of America and the lands of the Encircling Sea.[1]

In the north, the land of Europe borders on the Frozen Sea (*al-baḥr al-mutajammid*), which is called the Northern Ice Sea (*baḥr al-thalj al-shimālī*).[2] In the west it lies on the Sea of Darkness,[3] known as the Dark Sea and the Western Sea.[4] In the south, it borders on the Sea of the *Rūm*, which is known as the Middle Sea (*al-baḥr al-mutawassiṭ*) or the White Sea (*al-baḥr al-abyaḍ*),[5] and on the lands of Asia. Its eastern border is formed by the Sea of

1. Mediaeval Arabic geographers divided the inhabited world (*al-arḍ al-ma῾mūra*) into four parts (patterned on Claudius Ptolemy's); for instance, according to the 9th-century Ibn Khurdādhbih (1889: 154) the division was as follows: 'Europe (*Urūfā*), which contains al-Andalus, the Slavs, Byzantines, Franks and Tangier, until the border of Egypt; Libya (*Lūbiyyah*), with Egypt, Abyssinia, the Berbers and what lies beyond them, as well as the Southern Sea (...); Ethiopia (*Ītiyūfiyā*), including Tahama, Yemen, the Sind, Hind and China; and Scythia (*Isqūtiyā*), which also comprises Armenia, Khorasan, the Turks and the Khazars.'
2. Whereas the first term is clearly a reference to the Polar Sea (cf. Fr. 'Océan glacial'), the second would actually seem to denote the Arctic Ocean.
3. *Baḥr al-Ẓulamāt* (also *Baḥr al-Ẓulma/al-Muẓlim*). Classical Arabic geographers sometimes used this term as a synonym of Baḥr al-Muḥīṭ and it denoted the northern Atlantic. See *EI2*, "Baḥr al-Muḥīṭ" (D. M. Dunlop).
4. This is a rather confusing choice of terminology since this *Baḥr Gharbī* might quite easily be confused with *Baḥr al-Maghrib*, ('Sea of the West'), which was synonymous with the *Baḥr al-Rūm*. Interestingly enough, the same association had already been made by the 10th-century geographer-traveller Ibn Rustah (1892: 83, 85). Also see *EI1*, s.v. "Baḥr al-Maghrib" (C. F. Seybold); *EI2*, s.v. "Baḥr al-Rūm" (ed.).
5. In MSA, only *al-baḥr al-mutawassiṭ* is used, whereas *al-baḥr al-abyaḍ* was a calque from the Turkish *Aq Deniz* [see *EI1*, s.v. "Aq Deniz" (K. Süssheim)]. On these synonymous terms, see *EI2*, s.v. "Baḥr al-Rūm" (D. M. Dunlop); *EI1*, s.v. "Baḥr al-Maghrib" (C. F. Seybold). It should be added that in classical Arabic geographical literature, seas, or parts of them, were commonly named after peoples whose territory bordered them; for instance, the 10th-century traveller al-Mas῾ūdī refers to the Mediterranean as *al-baḥr al-Rūmī, huwa baḥr al-Shām wa Miṣr wa 'l-Maghrib wa 'l-Andalus wa 'l-Ifranj wa 'l-Ifranja wa 'l-Ṣaqāliba wa Rūmiyya wa ghayrihim* ('The sea of the Rūm, Shām, Egypt, North Africa, al-Andalus, the Franks, Slavs, Rome, as well as other nations'); al-Mas῾ūdī 1894: 56. The fact of associating a sea with a certain region or nation meant that the name could refer either to a part of it or to the whole; e.g. *Baḥr al-Shām* and *Baḥr al-Maghrib* could apply, respectively, to the eastern and western parts of the Mediterranean, or to the entire Sea. The resultant plethora of names was further confused by authors like Ibn Rustah

the Khazars,[1] which is also called the Sea of Jurjān or the Sea of Ṭabaristān, and the lands of Asia. Europe (*Ūrūbā*), then, is also used to denote the lands of the Franks and those of the Greeks, Constantinople, the Khazars, the Bulgarians, Wallachia (*al-Aflāq*), the lands of the Serbs, as well as other countries. It comprises about thirteen core territories, i.e. provinces,[2] four of which are in the north. These are England,[3] Denmark (*Danīmarq*), Sweden (*Aswij*) and Muscovy (*Mūsqū*). Six are in the centre, i.e. Holland,[4] the land of the French, Switzerland, Austria,[5] Prussia,[6] and the German Confederation.[7] There are three in the south – Spain, Portugal and Italy (*Ūṭāliyā*).

The Ottoman states that are part of Europe are: the lands of the Greeks (*al-Arwām*), the Albanians (*al-Arnā'ūṭ*), the Bosnians (*al-Bushnāq*),[8] the Serbs (*al-ḥarb*),[9] the Bulgarians, Wallachians and Moldavians (*al-Bughdān*).[10] From

making a distinction between *Baḥr al-Rūm wa Ifrīqiyya wa 'l-Shām* (1892: 83) and *Baḥr al-Rūm wa Ifrīqiyya wa Miṣr* (*ibid.*, 85, 86, 96), as well as between the *baḥr al-Shām* (which contains the islands of Cyprus and Rhodes), and *al-baḥr al-Shāmī* (*ibid.*, 97, 98).

1. = the Caspian Sea; see "Baḥr al-Khazar" *EI1*, *EI2* (D. M. Dunlop), where the author gives the rather unusual pronunciation *Khuzur* for this Caucasian tribe, originally hailing from the lower Volga and Daghestan, who in the 8th–10th centuries built an empire, which was even able to assert itself against the two superpowers of the age, i.e. the 'Abbāsid Caliphate and the Byzantine Empire.
2. *iyāla* ('management', 'exercise of power') was imported into Turkish as *eyālet*; in the Ottoman Empire, it denoted the largest administrative division, headed by a *beglerbeg* ('Bey of Beys', i.e. governor-general). In European sources, it is commonly translated as 'Regency'. Up until the French conquest, Algeria, for instance, was an *iyāla*, as was Egypt. In 1864, the *eyālet* system was officially replaced by that of the *wilāyets*. See *EI2*, s.v. "eyālet" (Halil Inalcik).
3. *bilād al-Inklīz* ('the land of the English'); curiously, al-Ṭahṭāwī at no point uses *barīṭāniyā* (or its variants), even though this is already found in mediaeval Arabic geographical literature; see D. Dunlop, 1957.
4. *bilād al-Falamank*, 'Flemish'. The modern *Hūlandī* to denote 'Dutch' was coined much later. The Dutch/Flemish first made their appearance in Arabic literature in the travelogue by the Moroccan Aḥmad b. Qāsim al-Ḥajarī (d. 1645), who provided detailed information about the Low Countries, which he called *Flanḍas*. See al-Ḥajarī, 1987: 105ff. *et passim*.
5. *al-Nimsa* (also *al-Nimsā*). This word was a borrowing from the Turkish *nem...e* ('mute'), which was, in turn, borrowed from Slavonic and used to denote the Germans, as well as the Holy Roman Empire or the territories under Habsburg rule. See *EI2*, s.v. "Nem...e" (M. Köhbach).
6. *bilād al-Brūs*. This is the very first mention in Arabic of Prussia. Cf. Khayr al-Dīn, 1867: 286–311 (*al-Brūsiyya, al-mamlaka al-Brūsiyāniyya*).
7. *Jarmāniyā al-muta'āhada*, which paraphrase literally means 'Germany bound by a covenant/alliance'. Cf. Khayr al-Dīn, 1867: 312ff. (*al-mu'āhada*).
8. Despite the fact that this was an Ottoman territory, the author provides the vowelling, which may be explained by the fact that his term is a transcription of the French *Bosniaque*, the usual Arabic form being *Būsna*.
9. The author adds that it can be spelt 'with a *b* or an *f* (namely *ḥarf*)'.
10. This is the Arabic form of the Turkish name for this country (Boghdān), after its founder Boghdan I Dragosh (1352). See *EI1*, s.v. "Boghdān" (Cl. Huart).

this, you learn that the interpretation by some translators of Europe as being the lands of the Franks is inadequate, unless, by God, the lands of the Franks also encompass the territories of the Ottoman State. However, this is gainsaid by the fact that the Ottomans restrict the term *Ifranjistān* to mean Europe without the territories held by them, which they refer to as 'the lands of the *Rūm*'.[1] Nevertheless, they also generalize the term *Rūm* inasmuch as they use it to mean the lands of the Franks as well as some Asian countries under their rule.

Asia is also delimited in the north by the Northern Frozen Sea; in the west by the lands of Europe and Africa; in the south by the Indian Ocean[2] and the Sea of China; and in the east by the Southern Encircling Sea [namely the Pacific Ocean] and the Bering Sea.[3] This [continent], too, is divided into ten core territories. The first, in the north, is Siberia (*Sībir*), whereas in the middle, there are seven: the lands of the Ottoman Empire – i.e. Syria, Armenia, Kurdistan, Baghdad, Basra, Cyprus, as well as others – along with Persia, Baluchistan, Kabulistan (*Qābūlistān*) and Afghanistan,[4] the land of the Great Tartar, China, and Japan.[5] In the south, there are two, i.e. the lands of the Arabs [Arabia] and the Hind.[6] The Ḥijāz and the

1. *bilād al-Rūm* (also *al-bilād al-Rūmiyya, bilād Rūmīlī*). This is Rumelia ('Land of the Rhomaeans'), which province covered the old territories of Thrace, Bulgaria, Macedonia, Serbia and Albania, as well as part of the ancient Hellas. See *EI1*, s.v. "Rumeli, Rumelia" (Franz Babinger).
2. *Baḥr al-Hind*, 'Sea of the Hind', which in classical Arabic geographical literature was also known as *Baḥr al-Zanj* ('The Sea of the Zanj'), *al-Baḥr al-Ḥabashī* ('the Abyssinian Sea'). See "Baḥr al-Hind", *EI1* (R. Hartmann), *EI2* (R. Hartmann – [D. Dunlop]).
3. *Bihrangh* (in addition to remarks on the vowelling, the author states that the final sound, *r*, can also be replaced by *k*). This is one of several examples in which spelling of a European language (usu. French) impinged on what was after all intended to be a phonemic transcription, the silent *h* being added simply because of the spelling of the proper name *Behring*.
4. The Arabic *Afghhānistān* is again a clear transliteration of the European spelling, which is further borne out by the fact that in his vowelling of the grapheme, al-Ṭahṭāwī ignores the *h* after the *gh* completely, which results in a phonologically disallowed triconsonantal cluster.
5. The author uses *Yābūn* (with remarks on vowelling); it has often been suggested that the *Wāqwāq* in mediaeval Arabic geographical literature in fact denoted Japan. See *EI1*, s.v. "Wāḳwāḳ" (Gabriel Ferrand); A. Miquel, 1967–80: II, 511–13 *et passim*.
6. This was the usual name in Arabic literature for the Indian Subcontinent (excluding the northern plain of the Ganges and Jamna, which was known as Hindūstān). In mediaeval Muslim geographical literature it denoted those parts of India that had not been conquered by Islam and was generally distinguished from the Sind (*al-Sind*) – the Muslim-controlled territories in the lower valley of the Indus (Miḥrān) and the delta (i.e. Baluchistan and the Indus valley up to Aror). See "Hind", *EI1* (M. Longworth Dames), *EI2* (S. Maqbul Ahmad); "Sind", *EI1* (T. Haig), *EI2* (T. Haig –[C. Bosworth]); "Miḥrān", *EI1* (T. Haig), *EI2* (C. Bosworth); A. Miquel, 1967–80: II, 82–97, *et passim*.; V. Minorsky:

territory of the Wahhābīs[1] are ruled by the Ottomans, the Yemen is under its protection, while Oman is independent – all of these are regions of the Arabian Peninsula. Those are the territories of Asia.

And now for Africa. In the north it borders on the Sea of the Rūm; in the west on the Atlantic Ocean (*al-baḥr al-Aṭlanṭīqī*), which is also called the Sea of Darkness; in the south, on the Southern Encircling Sea; in the east on the Indian Ocean, the isthmus of *Bāb al-Mandab*,[2] the Sea of Qulzum – also known as the Red Sea[3] – and Arabia. Africa can be divided into eight core territories. Two of these are in the north, i.e. the land of the Maghribīs and the land of Egypt. There are four in the middle – Senegambia (*Sīnighayniya*), Nigeria,[4] Nubia and Ethiopia – and two in the south – Guinea (*bilād Ghīnā*) and Kaffraria (*Kafarīrba*). This is what the Franks today call Africa, even though the term *Ifrīqiya* orignally denoted a well-known locality near Tunis, as well as its surrounding territory.

To Europe have been added the islands that are near it. The same is true for Asia and Africa. These three parts, i.e. Europe, Asia, and Africa, are called the 'Old World' or the 'Old Territory',[5] i.e. lands known to the Ancients. As for the territories of America,[6] these are called the 'New World'. In Arabic, 'America' is also called the West Indies[7] and *'Ajā'ib al-makhlūqāt*

235–54 ('India'), 371–3. ('Sind'). Also see J. Sauvaget, 1948; al-Mas'ūdī, 1960–79: I, 201 (par. 422ff.); *idem*, 1894: *passim*; Ibn Ḥawqal, 1938: 316–23 *et passim*; Yāqūt, 1866–73: III, 167, 497–8 *et passim*; Ibn Khurdādhbih, 1889: 54–7, 62ff. *et passim*; Abū 'l-Fidā', 1840: 353ff., 346ff.; Ibn Rustah, 1892: 124ff.; al-Qazwīnī, 1848: 62–3, 84–7 *et passim*.; al-Dimashqī, 1866: 170–76 *et passim*; al-Muqaddasī, 1906: 474; Ibn al-Faqih, 1885: 11–16 *passim*, 257 *et passim*; al-Iṣṭakhrī, 1927: 170–80.

1. The Islamic community of the *Wahhābiyya* was founded by Muḥammad Ibn 'Abd al-Wahhāb (1703–87), and adheres to a particularly stringent brand of Islam, allied to the school of Aḥmad b. Muḥammad b. Ḥanbal. The Wahhābīs consider all innovations after the third century of Islam as heresy, and are particularly opposed to the cult of saints. Today, it is the predominant school in the Kingdom of Saudi Arabia. See *EI1*, s.v. "Wahhābīya" (D. Margoliouth).
2. In Arabic geography this term ('the Gate of Wailing') denoted the strait between the Red Sea and the Gulf of Aden; See *EI1*, s.v. "Bāb al-Mandab"; Yāqūt, 1866–73: IV, 650ff.; Abū 'l-Fidā', 1840: 24, 154; al-Hamdānī, 1968: 53, 98, 127.
3. The former term of course derived from the town of Qulzum (the ancient Klysma), near Suez. This Sea was also commonly known as *Baḥr al-Ḥijāz* ('Sea of the Ḥijāz'). See "baḥr al-Qulzum", *EI1* (C. Becker), *EI2* (C. Becker – [C. Beckingham]).
4. *bilād al-Zanj* ('the country of the Zanj'), which usually denoted to the black peoples of the east coast of Africa. In Arabic history, however, *Zanj* usually refers to the rebel slaves who rose against their Arab masters (694, 868–83). See *EI1*, s.v. "Zandj" (L. Massignon); V. Minorsky, 1982: 471–2.
5. *al-arḍ al-qadīma*, a calque of the French '*la veille terre*'.
6. *bilād al-Amrīka aw Amrīkiyya*, the author adding that these terms were pronounced with either *k* or *q*.
7. *al-Hind al-gharbī*. The 17th-century traveller-priest Ilyās al-Mawṣulī – arguably the first

('the wonders of creation'). It first became known to the Franks after the Christians conquered al-Andalus and drove the Arabs from it.[1]

America lies on six seas. In the north it borders on the Frozen Encircling Sea and the Baffin Sea [Baffin Bay]; in the east on the Sea of Darkness and the Sea containing the Antilles (*al-Antīla*) islands [the Caribbean]; in the west on the Great Encircling Sea, called 'Ocean' (*Ūqiyānūs*) and the Bering Sea. It consists of two parts, viz. North and South America. The former comprises six core territories: Russian America (*al-Amrīka al-Rūsiyya*), i.e. the part of America ruled by Muscovy;[2] Greenland (*Ughruwan*); New England;[3] the land of *Ītāzūniyā*,[4] i.e. the 'United Provinces'; Mexico (*al-Maksīk*); and Guatemala (*Ghuwātīmalā*).

Southern America, on the other hand, is also divided into nine territories: Colombia (*Kulunbiyā*), Guyana (*Ghiyāna*), Brazil (*Ibrīzīla*), Peru (*Biruh*), Bolivia (*Buwluwiyya*) – which is known as 'Upper Peru',[5] Paraguay (*Barāghiya*), La Plata (*Balāta*),[6] Chile (*Shillī*) and Patagonia (*Batāghūniyā*).

As for the islands of the Encircling Sea [Oceania], they lie to the west of America and to the south-east of Asia. They border on the Encircling Sea on all sides and consist of three core territories: Indonesia (*al-Nūtāziyya*), Australia (*al-Ustūrāliya*) and Polynesia (*al-Būlīniziya*).

In Europe, there are four major cities, famous for their trade:

Oriental to travel to the Americas – used the similar *bilād Hind al-gharb* ('the land of the Hind of the West') to refer to the American continent (notably the Central and Southern parts); see D. Newman, 2001: 48. Also see A. Ayalon, 1984.

1. In the second edition, al-Ṭahṭāwī added a page on the age of discoveries, the role played by the new modes of transport, etc., which are also prominent in many other Muslim travellers' accounts (e.g. M. al-Sanūsī, 1891–2; 19 *et passim*; *idem* 1976–81: I, 51, 197; Khayr al-Dīn, 1867: 76; M. Bayram, V 1884–93: II, 133, 134, III, 4, 7, 48, 67, 87, IV 79). Al-Ṭahṭāwī would also return to this theme in his later works, as witness, for instance, his eulogy on the steam engine (al-Ṭahṭāwī, 1869: 123–8). The addition sticks out in terms of style and language since it is in rhymed prose, while the rest of this chapter is not.
2. = Alaska and the north-western coast of the United States.
3. *Ibriṭāniya al-jadīda*, which should not be confused with the modern New England, an area in the modern United States. Here it refers, of course, to Canada (or a part thereof).
4. cf. French '*Etats-Unis*'.
5. *Bīrū al-ʿulyā*; cf. Spanish *Alto Perú*.
6. This is a reference to the United Provinces of the Río de La Plata (today's Argentina), which entity was created in 1816. Formerly, the territory had been part of the Spanish Viceroyalty of Río de La Plata (*Virreinato del Río de La Plata*), one of the four Viceroyalties – the others being those of New Spain, Peru and New Granada – created by Spain to administer its colonies of Central and South America. Established in 1776, it included the territory of what is today Argentina, Uruguay, Paraguay and Bolivia, all of which had previously been controlled by the Viceroyalty of Peru (1543). The Viceroyalty ceased in effect to exist in 1810.

Istanbul,[1] the seat of government of the Ottoman State; London (*Lūndra*) the capital of England; Paris (*Bārīz*) the capital of France; and Naples (*Nābulī*) in Italy. There are also four main cities in Asia: Beijing (*Bikīn*), the capital of China; Calcutta (*Qalqūṭā*), the capital of the Hind, which is currently under English rule; Surat (*Ṣūra*), which is also in the Hind, and, so it is said, used to be called al-Manṣūra; and Miyako (*Miyāqū*) in Japan,[2] i.e. the land of porcelain. There are four major cities in Africa: Cairo, the seat of the ruler of Egypt; Sennār, the seat of the ruler of the land of Nubia; and Algiers and Tunis in the land of the Maghribīs. The main cities in North America are: Mexico (*Maksīkū*) in Mexico; New York (*Nūyūrk*), Philadelphia (*Fīlādilfiyā*) and Washington[3] in the United States. There are four main cities in South America: Rio de Janeiro (*Riyū Jānīr*) in Brazil; Buenos Aires (*Banūsiris*) in La Plata; Lima (*Līma*) in Peru; and Quito (*Qīṭū*) in New Granada.[4] In the lands of the Encircling Sea (Oceania), there are two famous centres: Batavia (*Batāwiyā*) – the capital of the island of Java (*Jāwā*) – and Manilla (*Mānīla*).

The lands of the Franks are predominantly inhabited by Christians or unbelievers;[5] the territories belonging to the Ottoman Empire are the only Islamic lands in this part of the world. As for Asia, it is the cradle of Islam – indeed of all religions. It is the native land of prophets and messengers, and it is there that all divine books were revealed. It contains the noblest places, the blessed land and the mosques that are the sole destination of

1. *Islāmbūl*, which also has the variants *Isṭānbūl* and *Isṭānbul*, all of which go back to the Turkish *Istānbūl*, which was, in turn, derived from the Greek εις την πόλιν ('this is the city'). In addition, the city was also referred to in Arabic as *Qusṭanṭīniya* or *al-Āsitāna* (an ellipsis of the Turkish *āsitāna-i-sa'ādat*, 'the Gate of Bliss'). See *EI1*, s.v. "Constantinople" (J. Mordtmann).
2. This is another example of inconsistency on the part of the author, due, no doubt to a shaky knowledge of the geography of the world: the *Yābūn* of earlier on is transformed here into *bilād jazā'ir Yābūniyā* ('the land of the Japan Islands').
3. The Arabic transliteration '*Was-hinghitūn*' reflects the Latin spelling, the author giving a graphemic transcription.
4. Established temporarily between 1717 and 1724 and permanently in 1743, the Spanish Viceroyalty of New Granada (*Virreinato de Nueva Granada*), which had its capital in Santa Fé (today Bogotá), included present-day Colombia, Panama (after 1751), Ecuador and Venezuela, all of which had also previously been under the control of the Viceroyalty of Peru. In 1810, Spanish officials were driven out in the various territories – thus terminating the existence of the Viceroyalty – but Spain reconquered what had become the United Provinces of New Granada in 1814–16. It would take until 1823 before the Spanish yoke was completely thrown off. Between 1830 and 1858, Colombia was known as *Estado de Nueva Granada* ('State of New Granada'). It is also interesting to note that al-Ṭahṭāwī provides the dialectal pronunciation *Ghurnāta* (*al-jadīda*), instead of the traditional *Gharnāṭa*, well known because of the Spanish eponym.
5. The 'or unbelievers' (*aw kafara*) would be omitted in the second edition.

all travellers. It is also the birthplace and last resting place of the remains of the *'lord of those that have preceded and those that will come'*[6] and of his Companions. It is also the birthplace of the four *imāms* – may God the Almighty be pleased with them. The imām al-Shāfiʿī was born in Gaza; the imām Mālik[7] – may God be pleased with him – in Medina; the most outstanding imām Abū Ḥanīfa al-Nuʿmān[8] in Kufa; and the imām Aḥmad b. Ḥanbal[9] in Baghdad, which, as was said in the days of the caliphs, is to other cities what a master is to his servants. All of these places are in Asia. In the lands of the Asian continent there are also the Arabs, who are the noblest of tribes and whose language is generally held to be the purest and most eloquent. Among them we find the descendants of Hāshim,[10] who are the salt of the earth, the paragons of glory, the shield of honour. The predominance of Asia is borne out by the fact that it contains the favoured places such as the *Qibla*,[11] towards which everybody must turn five times

6. *'(sayyid) al-awwalīn wa 'l-ākhirīn'*; cf. Qur. LVI:49.
7. Born into a family of well-known traditionists, Abū ʿAbd Allāh Mālik b. Anas (d. 796) is one of the most famous Ḥadīth collectors and transmitters and the imām of the *madhhab* that bears his name (*al-mālikiyya*), i.e. the Mālikites. He spent most of his life teaching in Medina and is best known for his *magnum opus*, the *Kitāb al-Muwaṭṭa'* ('The Levelled Path'), which is the oldest surviving Muslim law book. The Mālikī *madhhab* is the most popular school in the Maghrib and Central and West Africa, and it also predominated in Muslim Spain. See *EI1*, s.v. 'Mālik b. Anas' (J. Schacht); *EI2*, s.v. "mālikiyya" (N. Cottart).
8. The jurist and Ḥadīth collector Abū Ḥanīfa (d. 767), whose name literally means 'Father of the True (religion)' is the founder of the homonymous *madhhab*. The body of Ḥanafite literature is based solely on accounts transmitted by his followers since he himself never seems to have written anything. The Ḥanafī *madhhab* is very popular in Syria and Iraq and was the Ottoman state *madhhab*. In Egypt, it is the *madhhab* applied in tribunals. See *EI1*, s.v. 'Abū Ḥanīfa' (T. Juynboll), 'Ḥanafīs', 'Ḥanīf' (F. Bruhl); *EI2*, s.vv. "Ḥanafiyya" (W. Heffening – [J. Schacht]), "Abū Ḥanīfa al-Nuʿmān" (J. Schacht); J. Schacht, 1975: 294ff. *et passim*; *idem*, 1966: 40ff., 65 *et passim*; N. Coulson, 1978: 50–2.
9. The theologian and founder of the *madhhab* that bears his name, Aḥmad b. Muḥammad b. Ḥanbal (780–855), known as Ibn Ḥanbal, was born in Baghdad, where he also died. He is most famous for a collection of *ḥādīth*, entitled *al-Musnad*, which were recorded (and expanded) by his son ʿAbd Allāh. The Ḥanbalī *madhhab* is the official school in Saudi Arabia. See *EI1*, s.v. "Aḥmed b. Muḥammad b. Ḥanbal" (Goldziher); *EI2*, s.vv. "Ḥanābila" (H. Laoust), "Aḥmad b. Ḥanbal" (E. Laoust); N. Coulson, 1978: 71–3 *et passim*.; J. Schacht, 1966: 63ff., 66ff.
10. According to Muslim tradition, Hāshim b. ʿAbd al-Manāf was the Prophet's grandfather, and allegedly got his name after he had broken (*hashama*) bread for the starving during a famine. Though many of the stories about him are no doubt apocryphal, it is certain that the Prophet was a member of his family. A family that is able to trace its lineage to that of Hāshim is entitled to bear the honorific 'al-Hāshimī'. This is the case, for instance, for the royal house of the modern state of Jordan, whose official name is, in fact, 'the Hashemite kingdom of Jordan' (*al-mamlaka al-Hāshimiyya al-Urduniyya*). See *EI1*, s.v. "Hāshim" (F. Buhl).
11. This is the direction of the Kaʿba in Mekka to which Muslims pray. In mosques, this is

a day and night, as well as the two cities in which the glorious Qur'ān was revealed. Hence, its merits are innumerable and the achievements of its people unfathomable. One of its inhabitants said the following:

Your attention, you who are protégés of the mountain
O people of goodness and generosity
We are the neighbours of this sanctuary
The sanctuary is devoted to man and goodness
We are a people living near it
And who feel protected against their fears
Who are concerned about the verses of the Books
So act with care towards us, weakling,
We know the plain (of Mekka) and it has made itself known to us
We have grown accustomed to al-Ṣafā[1] *and the House*[2]
al-Muʿallā and the slope of Minā[3] *are familiar to us*
Take cognizance of this and live accordingly
The best of mankind is our ancestor
And in ʿAlī the favoured we have found merit
And to the two tribes[4] *our lineage goes*
A lineage is free from blemish

indicated by the *miḥrāb*, i.e. prayer niche. See "Qibla", *EI1* (C. Schoy), *EI2* (A. Wensinck – D. King).

1. The name of a mound at Mekka, opposite al-Marwa; between these two places believers perform the so-called saʿy ritual, or 'run', during the annual pilgrimage. See "al-Ṣafā", *EI1*(B. Joel), *EI2* (F. Braemer and M. MacDonald); "ḥadjdj" *EI1* (A. Wensinck), *EI2* (A. Wensinck – [J. Jomier] – B. Lewis).
2. *bayt* ('house'), which refers to the Kaʿba here.
3. This is a place in the hills to the east of Mekka, on the road to ʿArafāt. At the end of the annual pilgrimage (*ḥajj*), it is the scene of several rituals, the most important of which is the apotropaic stone-throwing performed at the end of the ceremonies on the 10th day of the month of Dhū 'l-ḥijja – known as 'the Day of the Sacrifice' (*yawm al-aḍḥā*). The stones are thrown at three heaps of stones in the valley of Minā, which are known as *jamra* – *al-jamra al-ūlā* ('Upper Jamra', in the east, near the al-Khayf mosque), *al-jamra al-wusṭā* ('Middle Jamra', in the centre), and *jamrat al-ʿAqaba* (near the western exit of the valley). See *EI1*, s.vv. "Minā" (F. Buhl), "al-djamra" (F. Buhl), "ʿArafāt" (A. Wensinck), "al-Ṣafā" (B. Joel), "ḥadjdj" (A. Wensinck); *EI2*, s.v.), "ʿArafāt" (A. Wensinck – [H. Gibb]).
4. The Arabic dual *sibṭayn* (sing. *sibṭ*, 'tribe') is significant since the plural *asbāṭ* appears several times in the Qur'ān (II:136, II:140, III:84, IV:163, VII:160) but only in relation to biblical tribes of the Israelites. Here, however, it seems to refer to the mythical pre-Islamic tribes of the ʿĀd and the Thamūd, both of which had disappeared before the advent of the Prophet. Both are mentioned several times in the Qur'ān, most notably the story of their destruction. In early classical Arabic literature, they are often adduced as examples of the transitoriness of wordly glory. See *EI1*, s. vv. "Thamūd" (H. Bräu), "ʿĀd" (F. Buhl); al-Masʿūdī, 1960–71: II, 156ff. (chap. XXXVIII).

Although Islam was born there and spread from there to other places, a large part of Asia remains subject to unbelief – this is the case for China and parts of the Hind – whereas another part, though Islamic, follows the path of those who err, as is the case for the Persian 'defectors'.[1]

As for Africa, it contains the most glorious countries like Egypt, which is one of the greatest and richest countries. It is also the breeding ground for saints,[2] virtuous men and religious scholars. Such also are the inhabitants of the Maghrib, who are people of virtue, piety, knowledge and diligence. And, God willing, Islam will also spread in it to the Negro unbelievers thanks to the efforts of the Benefactor – may God the Almighty protect him![3]

As for America (*Amrīkiya*), this is a land of infidels. Originally, it was inhabited by idol-worshipping nomads, after which it was conquered by the Franks as their military power had increased. They brought people from their countries there, and sent priests, as a result of which many of the inhabitants of the Americas converted to Christianity. At present, most of America (*Amrīka*) is Christian, except for the nomads, among whom there are still idolaters. Islam does not exist there because of the strength of the Franks in the science of seafaring, their knowledge of astronomy and geography, their yearning for business and commerce and their love of travel.

As the poet said:

I was told by a greatness – and there was truth
in that which was uttered – glory and might lie in travel
If it were possible, from home, to reach one's desire
the sun would never leave the halo of the Ram

Another one said:

Guide your mount towards open country

1. *rawāfiḍ* (sing. *rāfiḍ*, 'defector'), which term denotes a section of Shīʿīs and, by extension, heretics. It is particularly used to refer to the Persian Shīʿīs.
2. *awliyā'* (sing. *walīy*), which is short for *awliyā' Allāh* ('friends of God, God's elect'). The traditional translation of this term as 'saints' or 'holy men' must be qualified in that it does not refer to the 'sanctified' (or beatified) humans of the Christian religion (for whom Arab Christians use the word *qiddīs*/pl. *qiddīsūn*) as this notion is alien to Islam. Similarly, the Muslim saints' superhuman deeds are never referred to as *muʿjizāt* (sing. *muʿjiza*) – a term reserved for Christian saints' miracles – but as *karāmāt* (sing. *karāma*), which may be rendered as 'venerable deeds', *āyāt* (sing. *āya*) being restricted to superhuman acts performed by prophets. Cf. *EI1*, s.v. "walī" (B. Carra de Vaux).
3. This refers to Muḥammad ʿAlī's conquest of the Sudan (1819); cf. P. Holt and M. Daly, 1994: 47ff.

Say goodbye to beautiful women and palaces
Those who do not leave their native lands
Are like those who reside in graves
Only separation from one's native country raises
pearls of the seas to the necks

Al-Ḥarīrī[1] said:

Traversing other countries – even in destitution –
is preferable for me to high rank

Still another one said:

Rise up and distance yourself from your homeland with diligence
He who settles in his land becomes despicable
like a pawn, continuously despised,
until – when it moves – it becomes a queen!

He also said:

Expend [the resources of] *your worthy patience and forbearance – indeed*[2]
he who gives from his patience need not fear poverty
and the man who stays on his own soil does not vanquish anything
just as the falcon does not hunt anything while he is in his nest

It is well known that pearls and musk become precious only when they have left their native land and place of origin. However, none of this belies the fact that the love of one's native land is an article of faith.[3] What is

1. The grammarian and poet Abū Muḥammad al-Qāsim b. ʿAlī al-Ḥarīrī (1054–1122) is particularly known for his collection of 50 *Maqāmāt* (lit. 'Standings', though often translated as 'Assemblies'), a narrative genre relying heavily on the use of *sajʿ* (rhyming prose) and the display of linguistic virtuosity. Each *maqāma* recounts the adventures of a single protagonist, usually transmitted by a narrator (in the case of al-Ḥarīrī these were, respectively, Abū Zayd al-Sarūjī and al-Ḥārith b. Hammām). The genre was invented by the Persian-born Aḥmad b. al-Ḥusayn al-Hamadhānī (968–1008), who in honour of his literary achievement and prowess had been endowed with the sobriquet of *Badīʿ al-Zamān* ('Marvel of the Age'). See J. Ashtiany *et al*,. 1990: 125–45; "maḳāma" *EI1* (C. Brockelmann), *EI2* (C. Brockelmann – [C. Pellat]); "al-Ḥarīrī", *EI1* (D. Margoliouth), *EI2* (D. Margoliouth – [C. Pellat]); "Hamadhānī" *EI1* (D. Margoliouth), *EI2* (R. Blachère).
2. Cf. Qur. XII:18.
3. *ḥubb al-waṭan min shaʿb al-īmān*; this is a famous *ḥadīth*, which has remained popular to this day.

intended is travel in the pursuit of discovery or earning a living, which does not exclude the fact that a human being is attached to his native land and birthplace, since this is instinctive.

As the poet said:

He who lives far from his native land
weeps for his sorrow alone
The more exacting the journey
the greater his suffering within

Another one said:

The pain in my heart is heightened
by a bird weeping on its branch
The thoughts he expressed were mine, and so
together we cried, each for his homeland

It is not irreconcilable with trusting in God and relying on one's Lord, as becomes clear from the following words by the poet:

I knew – and intemperance is not part of my being –
that my allotted sustenance shall come to me
I strive for it, and the effort exhausts me
If I sat still it would come to me without wearying me

Another one said:

Content yourself with the smallest measure of sustenance you receive
and beware not to chase wishes
The sea is clear only when it draws back
and is turbid only when it rises

The above are a consolation to those who do not like to travel, and may dissuade people from travelling out of greed.

As for the islands of the Encircling Sea, they have for the most part been conquered by Islam. On Java, for instance, the population is Muslim. Indonesia is predominantly Muslim, the Christian religion being a rarity.

In light of the above one has to recognize that five parts of the inhabited world may be arranged according to the degree of esteem some enjoy over others. That is to say, the merit of one part in its entirety can have precedence over another as regards its superiority in Islam and its attachment to it. Viewed from this angle, Asia is the best of all. Then comes Africa because it is inhabited by Muslims, holy men and pious people, and especially because it contains Egypt the Victorious.[1] This is followed by Europe because of the strength of Islam there and the presence of the greatest imam, i.e. the one of the two holy cities, the Sultan of Islam. Next, it is Oceania[2] as it is also inhabited by Islam – even though it appears that it is not far advanced in the sciences. The lowest rank is occupied by the lands of America, where Islam is absent; at least that is how it appears to me, but God knows better what is right. The above has been established from the point of view of Islam, the revealed law and inherent dignity. 'Dignity' (*sharaf*) is used here to mean that which is covered by the divine law as well as other things. One cannot say that most of this relies on superiority, since by itself it does not lead to excellence and virtue.

No fair man will deny that the lands of the Franks have today attained the highest degree of proficiency in the intellectual sciences. The most advanced in this respect are England, France and Austria. Their sages have surpassed the ancient scholars like Aristotle (*Arisṭāṭālīs*), Plato (*Iflāṭūn*), Hippocrates and others like them, and have achieved the utmost proficiency in mathematics, the natural sciences, religious sciences and metaphysics. Their philosophy is purer than that of the ancients since they construct proofs of the existence of the Almighty God, of the immortality of the souls and of (divine) reward and punishment.

The greatest city of the Franks is London, which is the capital of the English. Then comes Paris, which is the seat of the king of France. According to what people say, Paris has the advantage over London because of its healthy air, the character of its people and the lower cost of living. If you saw how it is managed,[3] you would understand the perfect

1. The Arabic *Miṣr al-Qāhira* is in fact a word play. Although it is the name for Cairo – *Miṣr* being used both for the country and the capital (as well as being a noun meaning 'city', 'capital'; pl. *amṣār, muṣūr*) – the author harks back to the etymology of *qāhira*, as the active participle of the verb 'to conquer', 'to be victorious'. The city owes its name to the fact that at the time it was founded, the planet Mars, which is also known as *Qāhir al-falak* ('the conqueror of planets'), was in ascendance.
2. *al-jazā'ir al-baḥriyya*, 'the Sea Islands'!
3. *kayfiyyat siyāsatihā*; derived from a root meaning 'to manage', the word *siyāsa* initially meant 'statecraft', 'management of the affairs of state' and, by extension 'politics', as it still does in MSA. Al-Ṭahṭāwī variously uses it to refer to 'political institutions', 'policies' or even 'law' (e.g. art. 46 of the translation of the French Constitution). In a later work, *Kitāb manāhij al-albāb al-Miṣriyya fī mabāhij al-ādāb al-'aṣriyya* (1869), he gives

sense of tranquillity enjoyed by strangers when they are there and the joy they experience when among the inhabitants. Most of the time the latter are friendly and pleasant towards strangers, even if they do not share the same religion. This is because most of the people of this city are Christians in name only and do not adhere to the precepts of their religion, nor do they display any zeal for it. Here, religion is the preserve of groups who use reason to distinguish between what is good and bad or of a group of libertarians (*ibāḥiyyūn*) who state that all actions allowed by reason are right. If you mention Islam to a Frenchman and contrast it with other religions, he will praise all of them as they enjoin people to do what is good and prohibit the reprehensible.[1] And if you mention it and contrast it with the natural sciences, he will tell you that he does not believe anything that is included in the holy books[2] since it falls outside the natural laws. On the whole, all religions may be practised in France. One does not oppose a Muslim building a mosque or a Jew building a synagogue, etc. All of this will be explained in the discussion of French politics.

The above may explain why the Benefactor chose to send more than forty people[3] there in order to study these sciences that we lack. Indeed, Christian kingdoms also send subjects there, with people coming from America, as well as other distant kingdoms. He – may God protect him – has also sent a small number of students to study the sciences in England.[4]

On the whole, all nations seek and strive towards glory, as al-Sharīf al-Raḍī[5] said: *Seek glory, for glory is not expensive.*

And what could be more glorious than that sciences and arts be sought by kings! The more powerful the king is, the more accurate his vision should be.

---

a detailed discussion of this concept, distinguishing five types (al-Ṭahṭāwī, 1973–80: I, 511ff., 517ff.). Also see *EI2*, s.v. "siyāsa" (C. Bosworth – F. Vogel).

1. This is a key concept within Islamic law and occurs several times in the Qur'ān (e.g. III: 104, 110, 114; VII: 157; IX: 67, 71, 112), and was also used by other Muslim travellers (e.g. al-Sanūsī, 1891–92: 201). Later on, al-Ṭahṭāwī will use it to 'legitimize' the theatre. For a discussion, see M. Cook, 2000.
2. *kutub ahl al-kitāb* ('books of the People of the Book'), i.e. the sacred books of the three revealed faiths: Islam, Christianity and Judaism. The phrase *ahl al-kitāb* occurs numerous times in the Qur'ān (e.g. II: 105, 109; III: 64–5, 70–72, 75). See "Ahl al-Kitāb", *EI1* (Goldziher), *EI2* (G. Vajda).
3. In the second edition 'this first time' was added.
4. See Translator's Introduction. In the second edition, the author added 'and to Austria'.
5. The Baghad-born poet Abū 'l-Ḥasan Muḥammad b. Abī Ṭāhir al-Sharīf al-Raḍī (970–1016) was a direct descendant of al-Ḥusayn, the son of ʿAlī – the Prophet's son-in-law and the fourth 'Rightly Guided' caliph – and the brother of the equally famous author Abū 'l-Qāsim ʿAlī b. al-Ṭāhir al-Murtaḍā al-Sharīf (966–1044), whose works reveal his Shīʿī beliefs. See *EI1*, s.vv. "al-Sharīf al-Raḍī" (F. Krenkow), "al-Murtaḍā al-Sharīf" (C. Brockelmann).

Fourth Chapter. On the leaders of this mission

Our ruler sent three notables from his state council (*dīwān*) with those going to France and appointed them general supervisors of the group of travellers. The dignitaries concerned were the following, in hierarchic order. The first leader is one in possession of perfect insight, knowledge, judgement and the two virtues of the pen and the sword, one who knows the decrees of Arabs and non-Arabs alike – the Honourable ʿAbdī Efendi,[1] the Keeper of the Seal.[2] The second is one who has righteousness of spirit and was born under an auspicious star, while in his love of glory he has thrown off all restraint – the esteemed Muṣṭafā Mukhtār Efendi,[3] the Master of Records.[4] The third is one who has combined science and action, the nib and the spear, the esteemed Ḥājj Ḥasan Efendi al-Iskandarānī[5]– may God grant him his wishes both here and in the hereafter. Amen.

---

1. Born in Constantinople, ʿAbdī Efendi Shukrī (d. 1854) was the son of Muḥammad ʿAlī's *katkhudā*, Ḥabīb Efendi. After studying Civil Law and Political Sciences (*administration civile*), Shukrī returned to Egypt in 1831. Three years later, he became a member of the Supreme Council (*al-majlis al-aʿlā*). After a stint as police chief, ʿAbdī Efendi was appointed head of the country's educational system (*mudīr al-madāris*) by ʿAbbās I (1850). See E. Jomard, 1828: 106; ʿU. Ṭusūn, 1934: 34–5; A. Louca, 1970: 41–51.
2. *Muhrdār* (Arabic *muhr*, 'signet ring', 'seal'/Persian '*dār*', 'holder'). This was originally a Turkish title (*mühürdār*) of an official who acted as private secretary to the high state functionaries. In Egypt (until 1848), the *Muhrdār* was the private secretary to the ruler. See *EI1*, s.v. "muhr" (J. Deny); "k̲h̲ātam" *EI1* (J. Allen), *EI1* (J. Allan – Ed.); R. Dozy, 1967: II, 621.
3. Mūṣṭafā Mukhtār Efendi (1802–39) was born in the same village as Muḥammad ʿAlī, viz. Kavalla, in north-east Macedonia. After studying military sciences (*administration militaire*) in Paris (with classes at the prestigious Ecole des Mines), he returned to Egypt in 1832, and in the same year received the title of Bey. As Ibrāhīm Pasha's ADC, he was then dispatched to Syria. M. Mukhtār's later appointments included president of the Council for Education (*dīwān al-madāris*) and president of the High Council (*al-majlis al-ʿalī*). See E. Jomard, 1828: 105; ʿU. Ṭūsūn, 1934: 36; A. Louca, 1970: 52; A. Silvera, 1980: 15; M. Ḥasan, 1949: 5–15.
4. *Dawīdār*, lit. 'he who holds the inkwell' (*dawā*). This Arabic-Persian blend (also *dawātdar, dawādār, duwaydār*) was an Egyptian Mamlūk title of an official who, together with the *jāndār* (the sultan's bodyguard) and the private secretary, received the correspondence for the sultan from the couriers and ensured the signing by the sultan of his letters. The position of 'Grand Dawādār' (*amīr dawādār al-kabīr*) steadily grew in power and prestige during the Mamlūk dynasties, and often combined several other responsibilities. See *EI1*, s.v. "d̲j̲āndār" (M. Sobernheim), "dawātdār" (M. Sobernheim).
5. After studying marine sciences in Brest, the Turkish-born Ḥasan al-Iskandarānī – who was held in great esteem by al-Ṭahṭāwī – was part of a small mission of students that was sent on to England for a year. Upon his return to Egypt in 1833, he was put in charge of the Alexandria shipyards, and later became Commander of the Navy (*nāẓir al-baḥriyya*). In 1855, he was killed when his ship was sunk in battle during the Crimean war. See E. Jomard, 1828: 107; ʿU. Ṭūsūn, 1934: 37–8; J. Heyworth-Dunne, 1938: 159; A. Louca, 1970: 51, 64.

These three honourable men also follow[1] classes like the rest of the group; the esteemed Keeper of the Seal concentrated on the science of civil administration, the esteemed Master of Records on military organization and the esteemed Ḥājj Ḥasan Efendi on the science of navigation and marine engineering. All three display the utmost zeal and the greatest desire for the acquisition of knowledge – even though this is commonly scorned by the powers that be.

The three men took command in turns, initially from day to day and later each month, until eventually the Keeper of the Seal became the only one in command. However, the three Efendis also had with them someone to organize the courses, Monsieur Jomard (*Mūsiyū Jūmār*),[2] whom our ruler had appointed to oversee the course of studies. He is one of the scholars of the Institut *(al-Anstitūt)*, i.e. the Council of Sciences,[3] of which he is a leading member. His behaviour and character reveal the love he has for our ruler and his willingness to serve him through his counsel. Time and again one can see in him a profound concern for the interests of Egypt when it comes to spreading knowledge and the sciences there – or indeed to other African countries. This becomes evident from his personality and conduct, as well as from the views expressed in the introduction to his *Almanac*, which he composed in 1244 ah.[4]

The fame of Monsieur Jomard's erudition and organizational expertise from the start impose on the human mind a preference for the pen over the sword, since he can get things done with his pen a thousand times better than others can with their swords. It is hardly surprising, therefore, that it is the pens that rule the regions. His scientific zeal results in a high output in terms of books and research activities. At the same time, this is a quality that can no doubt be found in all European scholars. An author is like a machine; when it stops, it is broken. Or like an iron key, which becomes rusty if it is not used. Monsieur Jomard devotes himself to the sciences day and night. We shall have occasion to talk of him many times

1. In the second edition, this verb and those that follow are in the past tense rather than the present.
2. See Translator's Introduction.
3. This is, of course, the *Institut de France*; cf. Khayr al-Dīn, 1867: 67 (*maktab Faransā*); M. Ibn al-Khūja, 1900 (*mashyakha li 'l-'ulūm*); M. al-Sanūsī, 1891–9: 145 (*majma'*).
4. = July 1828–June 1829 A.D. The work in question is *Almanac de l'Egypte et de la Syrie pour l'année 1244 de l'hégire* (Paris, 1830). The word used by al-Ṭahṭāwī is the Turkish *ruznāma* (Pers. *rūznāmce*), which was often used to denote these types of publications (though it originally meant 'ledger' or 'register'); cf. the Tunisian M. Ibn al-Khūja *al-Ruznāma al-Tūnisiyya* (see J. Quémeneur, 1967, 1968). See *EI2*, s.vv. "ruznāma" (C. Bosworth), "Taḳwīm" (D. Varisco), "daftar" (B. Lewis).

more in these pages, and, God willing, we shall include several letters I received from him.[1]

This concludes the introduction.

1. See Fourth Essay, Sections 3 and 6.

Core of the Book

This will deal with the journey from Cairo to Paris, the amazing things we saw on the way, the stay in the latter city, which is filled with all intellectual sciences and arts, as well as astounding justice and remarkable equity that must once again find a home in the lands of Islam and the territories subject to the law of the Prophet – God bless him and grant him salvation!

The core of this book comprises a number of Essays (*maqālāt*), which are, in turn, subdivided into Sections (*fuṣūl*).

The First Essay deals with the time from our departure from Cairo until our arrival in the city of Marseilles, a French seaport. This contains several Sections.

The Second Essay discusses the events from our entry into Marseilles until our arrival in the city of Paris. This contains two Sections.

The Third Essay focuses on our arrival in Paris and everything we saw there and learned about it. This Essay constitutes the primary aim behind the writing of this *riḥla*, which is why we have striven to provide as much detail as possible. Even so, all of this cannot do justice to this city; rather, it can only be an approximation of its actual contents. This will surprise only those who have not witnessed the wonders of travel. Someone once said:

He who has not seen Rome or its inhabitants
does not know anything of the world, or its people

This is even more true for the land of the Franks.

The Fourth Essay consists of brief surveys of the sciences and skills discussed in the second Chapter of the Introduction.[1]

1. Cf. 'Translator's Introduction on the genesis of the *Takhlīṣ*'.

First Essay

First Section. From the departure from Cairo to the arrival at the port of Alexandria

We left Cairo in the afternoon of Friday 8 Shaʿbān of the year 1241 A.H.[1] I regarded it as a good omen that this separation would be followed by reunion and that instead of goodbyes there would come salutations. We boarded small boats and headed for Alexandria. We spent four days on the blessed Nile, but there is no point in mentioning the towns and villages where we dropped anchor.

We entered Alexandria on Wednesday, the 13th day of the month of Shaʿbān,[2] and spent twenty-three days at the palace of the Benefactor.[3] We rarely went into the city and so it is difficult for me to say anything about it. Nevertheless, it seemed to me that in terms of both its geographical location and its general condition it closely resembles Frankish cities, even though I had obviously not seen anything of the latter at the time. I got this impression from the things I saw there and which do not exist anywhere else in Egypt. There are many Franks there, and the majority of the common people speak some kind of Italian or some other foreign language.[4] I was strengthened in my view when we arrived in Marseilles; Alexandria is both a sample and a model of Marseilles.[5]

Second Section. Treatise on this city, which is an abridgement of several Arabic and French books, from which we have retained that which appeared to be accurate

The name 'Alexandria' goes back to Alexander, the son of the Philosopher [namely Alexander the Great],[6] i.e. the one who killed Darius (*Dārā*) and

1. 18 March 1826.
2. 23 March 1826.
3. The Ra's al-Tīn ('Fig head') palace was built by Muḥammad ʿAlī in 1818 as part of his massive redevelopment programme for the city, which was at the heart of his Mediterranean expansionist policy. Though located on the same site (on the south-western end of the island of Pharos), the current Ra's al-Tīn palace was built in 1925.
4. This is of course a reference to the *lingua franca*; see Translator's Introduction.
5. In the second edition the following addition was made to this passage: '*When I went there in [12]62 [1846], I found a part of Europe there.*'
6. *Askandar Ibn al-Faylasūf*, the Arabic '*faylasūf*' presumably being a corruption (or hypercorrection) of Philippos, which appeared as *Filibus, Filifus, Filifūs* (cf. al-Masʿūdī, 1960–79: II, 7, par. 668). Also see *EI1*, s.vv. "al-Iskandar", "Iskandar-nāma", "Dhu 'l-qarnain"; *EI2* s.vv. "al-Iskandar" (W. Montgomery Watt), "Iskandar Nāma" (A. Abel – Ed.).

became king of the country. Alexandria is the name of sixteen towns that are called after him; among them there is a town in the Hind, one in Babylonia, one on the shores of the Great River, one in Soghd of Samarcand,[1] and one near Merw. It is also the name of the city of Balkh; of the greatest port of Egypt; of a village between Hamā (Hama) and Aleppo; of a village on the Tigris, near Wāsiṭ, where the man of letters Aḥmad b. al-Mukhtār b. Mubashshir[2] was born; of a village between Mekka and Medina; of a town on the streams of the Hind; and of five other cities.[3]

Merw is a town near Khorasan in Persia; the adjective related to it is either *Marwī* or *Marwazī*. Let us look at what is meant by 'the Great River' (*al-nahr al-a'ẓam*). In the book entitled *Taqwīm al-Buldān* ('The Survey of Countries') by 'Imād al-Dīn Abū 'l-Fidā' Ismā'īl b. Nāṣir, the ruler of Ḥamā,[4] I read that there is a river in al-Andalus that is called the 'Great River' and is, in fact, the river of Seville.[5] The exact text runs as follows: '*and among them the river of Seville in the land of al-Andalus; it is called the Great River by the Andalusians*'.[6] Maybe it was called the Great River by people because it distinguishes itself through the phenomenon of ebb and

1. *Ṣughd Samarqand* (al-Ṣoghd/al-ṣoghd), the ancient Sogdiane, which was a district in Central Asia. In mediaeval Arabic geographical literature, it corresponded to the lands east of Bukhara, with Samarcand as its capital. The ancient Samarcand, the almost mythical city of Transoxania (*mā warā' al-nahr*), was famous for its fertile land thanks to its river, *al-Sughd* (today's Zarafshān). See *EI1*, s.v. "Soghd" (W. Barthold); al-Dimashqī, 1866: 95, 178 *et passim*; Ibn al-Faqīh, 1885: 78; al-Ya'qūbī, 1892: 110ff.; al-Muqaddasī, 1906: 322 *et passim*.
2. A descendant of the 'Abbāsid caliph al-Hādī (ruled 785–56), Aḥmad b. al-Mukhtār b. Mubashshir Abū Bakr al al-Askandarānī (12th c.) spent most of his life in Baghdad. See Yāqūt, 1866–73: I, 256.
3. This entire passage is a quote from al-Fīrūzābādī's *Qāmūs al-Muḥīṭ* (n.d.: II:52). Cf. M. al-Zabīdī, 1888–90: III, 276.
4. Ismā'īl b. 'Alī al-Ayyūbī (1273–1331) was appointed ruler of the principality of Hama by his master, the Sultan al-Malik al-Nāṣir (whence he got the 'Nāṣir' in his own name), in 1310; ten years later, he obtained the hereditary rank of sultan, taking on the title of al-Malik al-Mu'ayyad. He derives his literary fame from the *Taqwīm* (an edition and translation of which would be edited by J. Reinaud as from 1840) as well as from a history of the world, entitled *Mukhtaṣar tārīkh al-bashar* ('Abridgement of the History of Mankind'). It is interesting to note that shortly after al-Ṭahṭāwī's return to Egypt, his mentor, Ḥasan al-'Aṭṭār, wrote a commentary on Abū 'l-Fidā''s *Taqwīm* (F. De Jong, 1983: 115, no. 38; P. Gran, 1979: 208, no. 60). See *EI1*, s.v. "Abū 'l-Fidā'" (Brockelmann).
5. This is, of course, the Guadalquivir, whose name is derived from the Arabic *al-wādī al-kabīr* ('the big riverbed'). See *EI1*, s.v."Guadalquivir" (C. Seybold).
6. Abū 'l-Fidā', 1840: 46. The text, however, differs slightly: '*wa minhā nahr Ishbīliyya min bilād al-Andalus wa yusammā 'ind ahl al-Andalus al-nahr al-a'ẓam*' (al-Ṭahṭāwī); '*nahr Ishbīliyya min al-Andalus [qāla Ibn Sa'īd wa huwa fī qadr dijla] wa huwa a'ẓam nahr bi 'l-Andalus wa tusammīhi ahl al-Andalus al-nahr al-a'ẓam*' ('According to Ibn Sa'īd, the river of Seville is of the size of the Tigris; it is the largest river of al-Andalus, whose inhabitants call it 'the Great River').

flow, to which Abū 'Fidā' draws attention, when he says: '*Flood and ebb become apparent in this river near a place called al-Arḥā, where ships go down at ebb, and rise with the flood'*. One of them once said about the rise and fall of the water level:

My beloved one, hasten with me to the river early in the morning
and stop where the flood doubles back on itself
Do not go beyond al-Arḥā – on the other side of it
lies a wilderness my eye cannot bear to look at![1]

And so, Alexandria was the name of a town in al-Andalus. Maybe Alexander settled a town in the Iberian Peninsula when he crossed it. The author of the book *Nashq al-azhār fī 'ajā'ib al-aqṭār*[2] ('The Inspiration of Flowers in the Wonders of the Regions') mentions that Alexander *Dhū 'l-Qarnayn* ('the one with two horns') crossed al-Andalus and opened the Strait of Gibraltar,[3] called *Baḥr al-zuqāq* ('the Sea Strait'), and that this isthmus was once solid land between Tangier and al-Andalus. Although he does not actually mention that Alexander built a town in this peninsula, this does not prove that there is no such town there either. From all that has been said it seems that there are two people who were called Alexander; one of them named '*Iskandar* the son of the Philosopher', and another '*Askander*' – with an *a* as the first vowel – who is the one who killed Darius. Elsewhere in the *Qāmūs* the following is stated: '*The one with two horns is Alexander the*

1. In fact, this entire passage – including the poem – is also taken from Abū 'l-Fidā' (1840: 47): '*wa yadkhuluhu al-madd wa 'l-jazr 'inda makān yusammā al-Arḥā, lā tazālu fīhi al-marākib munḥadira ma'a al-jazr ṣā'ida ma'a al-madd*' (al-Ṭahṭāwī); '*yablughu fīhi al-madd wa 'l-jazr saba'īn mīlan wa dhālika fawqa Ishbīliyya 'inda makān yu'rafu bi 'l-Arḥā ... wa 'l-marākib lā tazālu fīhi munḥadira ma'a al-jazr ṣā'ida ma'a al-madd*' ('It is subject to ebb and flow across a stretch of 70 miles, above Seville, at a place called al-Arḥā'). Interestingly enough, al-Ṭahṭāwī omits the middle section of the original, which states: 'In spite of the flow, the waters are not salty near Seville; rather, they remain fresh. The mouth of the river at Seville is 50 miles. So, the flow rises 20 miles above Seville. Ebb and flow never cease to alternate, day and night. And when the moon casts more light, the flow rises ... [ships go down at ebb ...]. The large Frankish vessels coming from the Ocean enter the river with their cargo, and cast anchor at the foot of the walls of Seville.'
2. This is the famous Egyptian historian Muḥammad b. Aḥmad Ibn al-Iyās (1448–1524), who is best known for his detailed chronicle of Egypt, entitled *Badā'i' al-zuhūr fī waqā'i' al-duhūr*, ('The Marvels of Flowers in the Events of the Times'); *EI1*, s.v. "Ibn Iyās" (M. Sobernheim); *GAL*, II, 295; *GALS*, II, 405–06; Y. Sarkīs, 1928: 42–3.
3. *jabal al-Ṭāriq*, which spurious term would translate as 'mountain of the knocking'. The actual name for Gibraltar in Arabic is *jabal Ṭāriq*, named after Ṭāriq b. Ziyād b. 'Abd Allāh, the Berber general who led the Muslim forces in the conquest of the Iberian Peninsula, as it was here that he first landed.

Greek because, as he called on them to worship God the Almighty, they struck him on his horn, but God the Almighty brought him back to life again. Then he called on them again and they hit him on his other horn, after which he died. However, God again brought him back to life. Either he had reached both hemispheres or he had two plaits.'[1] From these words it appears that 'Alexander *Dhū 'l-Qarnayn*' and Alexander the Greek are one and the same.

Oriental scholars hold that the *Dhū 'l-Qarnayn* mentioned in the holy verses[2] is not Alexander the Greek, as the former came before the latter.[3] It is the former of whom it is said that he was a prophet, that he built the dam of Gog and Magog and searched for the water of life, which was found by *al-Khaḍir*[4] – peace be upon him! – who is still alive as a result of this. As for the second Alexander, this is *Iskandar al-Rūmī* or *al-Yūnānī* – i.e. 'the Greek' (*al-Ighrīqī*) – since the ancient Greeks were called *al-Yūnān*,[5] while today's Greeks are known by the name of *Arwām*.

As far as the Franks are concerned, they do not speak about anybody else except Alexander the Great, the son of Philippos (*Fīlibush*, *Fīlibūsh*) the Macedonian. They associate him with what is said in Arabic historical works about Alexander *Dhū 'l-Qarnayn*, and ascribe to him all the wonderful things that are told about him, like the dam of Gog and Magog, and other such things. Yet they do not believe in the supernatural. In any case, both our scholars and the wise men of the Franks agree on the fact that Alexandria goes back to Alexander the Greek (*Iskandar al-Rūmī*).[6]

The names of the towns that are called Alexandria were mentioned in

1. al-Fīrūzābādī [n.d.]: IV, 260.
2. See Qur. XVIII: 83–98 (recounting how Alexander constructed a copper-covered wall or dam to hold back the mythical peoples of the Yājūj and Mājūj – the Biblical 'Gog' and 'Magog'). Also see *EI1*, "Yād̲jūd̲j wa-Mād̲jūd̲j" (A. Wensinck); A. Miquel, 1967–80: II, 503ff.; al-Qazwīnī, 1848: 400–02.
3. Cf. Al-Mas'udi, 1960–79: II, 8.
4. This legendary figure, whose name literally means 'the green man' (with the alternative form *al-Khiḍr*), is commonly identified with the (unnamed) servant (*al-fatā*) of Moses in the account of their quest for the 'union of the two seas' (*majma' al-baḥrayn*) in the Qur'ān (XVIII: 59–81). Important here is the fact that this figure also appears in the Alexander romance, one episode of which recounts a journey by Alexander and his cook Andreas (*Idrīs*), in the course of which the latter jumped into the well of life (thus gaining immortality), but was unfortunately unable to lead Alexander to it again. See *EI1*, s.v. "al-K̲h̲aḍir" (A. Wensinck).
5. The Arabic is a transcription of 'Ionia(n)' (Gr. Ἴων<ες>, 'Ionians'; Ἰωνία/Ἰαονία, 'Ionia').
6. In the second edition the following short paragraph is omitted in favour of a long exposé in which the author outlines his own views on Alexander. Identifying him with Hercules, he attempts to explain the latter's demigod status as the offspring of Jupiter (*al-mushtarī*) and the human Alkomene by relating it to a Muslim historical figure being born out of a marriage between an angel and a woman and to the sexual intercourse that can take place between *jinns* and human beings as revealed in Qur'ān LV: 56.

the excerpts from the *Qāmūs*. One town that does not go back to the famous Alexander the Greek is the Albanian town of *Iskenderyāsī*, i.e. Alexandria, which can, in fact, be traced to Iskander Bey.[1]

Some people have said that the city of Alexandria in Egypt was named *Qaysūn* before it was founded by Alexander in around 302 before the appearance of Jesus – Peace be upon Him.

The Franks say that it was called *Nū*. Before it fell to Islam, it was variously under Roman, Byzantine and Greek rule. It was conquered by ʿAmr b. al-ʿĀṣ[2] by order of ʿUmar b. al-Khaṭṭāb.[3] And when ʿAmr b. al-ʿĀṣ had conquered it, he wrote to ʿUmar – May God be pleased with both of them! – to say that he found 4,000 palaces there, 4,000 baths, 40,000 Jews paying the poll tax,[4] 400 squares, 12,000 grocers and greengrocers. These figures are probably an exaggeration by historians, who also exaggerated when talking about other places, like the city of Baghdad.

Among the wonders to be found there was the library which ʿAmr b. al-ʿĀṣ – may the Almighty God be pleased with him! – burned down. It contained 700,000 volumes.[5]

---

1. This is the Turkish name for the Albanian freedom fighter and national hero George Kastriota (1405–68), better known in Europe as Skanderbeg, who (briefly) drove the Turks from Albania. See *EI1*, s.v. "Skanderbeg" (J. Kramers); *EI2* s.v. "Iskender Beg" (H. Inalcik).
2. A member of the Prophet's tribe, ʿAmr b. al-ʿĀṣ(ī) al-Sahmī (d. *c.* 663) derived his fame from his conquest of Egypt (640). His name lives on in the large ʿAmr mosque, which is located north-east of the Coptic Museum in Cairo. It was erected by ʿAmr in 642 and is thus the oldest mosque of Cairo. Unfortunately, it was destroyed during the Crusades and most of the current structure in fact dates back to the 18th century. See *EI1*, s.vv. "Amr b. al-ʿĀṣ' (A. Wensinck); A. Butler, 1978; H. Kennedy, 1986: *passim*; P. Hitti, 1991: 160–8.
3. The second caliph (634–44) after the death of the Prophet, and thus one of the so-called 'Rightly Guided' ones. One of the most famous heroes of early Islam, ʿUmar Ibn al-Khaṭṭāb was the founder of the Arab empire (through which the religion spread across the then known world), and he also endowed it with most of the political institutions. In Muslim historical tradition, ʿUmar emerges as the archetypal severe but just and incorruptible ruler See *EI1*, s.v. "ʿOmar Ibn al-Khaṭṭāb" (G. Levi Della Vida); *EI2*, s.v. "ʿUmar Ibn al-Khaṭṭāb" (G. Levi Della Vida – [M. Bonner]); H. Kennedy, 1986: 57–69 *et passim*; P. Holt *et al.*, 1988: 57–103.
4. *jizya*. This tax was levied on the so-called *ahl al-dhimma* ('people of the covenant'), i.e. non-Muslims residing in Muslim-controlled territories. See "djizya", *EI1* (C. Becker), *EI2* (C. Cahen-Halik Inalcik); 'dhimma', *EI1* (D. MacDonald), *EI2* (C. Cahen); S. Elatri, 1974: 316.
5. The chief authority of this story seems to have been the 13th-century historian Gregorius Abū 'l-Faraj, better known as Bar-Hebraeus (Ibn al-ʿIbrī, 'son of the Jew'), who mentions it in the Arabic translation of his universal history, *Mukhtaṣar tārīkh al-duwal* ('Abridgement of the History of Nations'). Though clearly apocryphal, the story of the wilful destruction of the great library was subsequently taken over by other Arab historians and very soon became part of Western (Christian) historical tradition as well.

In earlier times, this city counted approximately 300,000 souls, but today this number is much lower.[1] It was conquered by the French, who were driven out by the English, after which it was returned to Islam. Today, the lights of the buildings shine over it thanks to the efforts of the Benefactor. Its trade has regained the splendour of previous times, when it was a centre for commerce. This place has become the residence of our ruler, who spends most of his time there. In its location and buildings it resembles Frankish ports. It is situated about 50 leagues[2] to the north-west of Cairo, 31 degrees and 13 minutes latitude, by which is meant the degree of distance from the Equator. Mention will be made later about the distance between it and Paris.

Third Section. On the voyage on the sea on which the port of Alexandria lies

In Arabic geographical works this sea is called *Baḥr al-Rūm* (Byzantine Sea), as on one side it touches their lands, or *Baḥr al-Shām* (Syrian Sea), since it lies next to Syria. The Franks call it the 'Middle Sea' or the 'Inner Sea'.[3] It derives its name from the fact that it lies in the middle of dry land. The Encircling Sea, on the other hand, surrounds all land, and so some have said that the latter continues to flow underneath solid land, which lies above the surface of its water. Others claim the converse based on the existence of dry land underneath the surface of the water, as is the case for instance for some parts of Muscovy. In Turkish, this Inner Sea is called

1. In 1828, Alexandria was said to have 12,528 inhabitants (against *c.* 4.6 million for the entire country and *c.* 264,000 for Cairo), which figure more than tripled in one decade, mainly as a result of the influx of workers for Muḥammad 'Alī's modernization programme, which included the building of the Maḥmūdiyya canal (1819) and the Arsenal (1829), which in the late 1830s employed no fewer than 4,000 staff. By the start of the British occupation (1882), the city counted 231,396 inhabitants; the population of Cairo, on the other hand, had only risen to 374,838, while that of the country numbered 6,831,131. See J. McCarthy, 1976; *EI1*, s.v. "al-Iskandarīya" (Rhuvon Guest); R. Owen, 1993: 216–17; M. Fahmy, 1954: 39ff.
2. *farsakh* (pl. *farāsikh*), 'parasang'. In classical times, this unit of measure of Persian origin, which initially denoted 'the distance covered in an hour by a horse walking', corresponded to three miles (*mīl*, pl. *amyāl*), one of which equalled 4,000 'official' cubits (*dhirā' shar'ī*) of about 50cm each, i.e. 1 1/4 English miles (*c.* 2 kilometres). As a result, the parasang must be set at 6km. However, later on in the book the author usually specifies that it involves French parasangs (*farsakh faransāwī*), which indicates that he was in fact expressing distances in French *lieues*, one *lieue* being about 4 km, which corresponds neatly to the three miles of the English 'league'. See W. Hinz, 1970: 61, 62, 63; *EI1*, s.v. "farsakh" (C. Huart); Ibn Khaldūn [F. Rosenthal] 1986: I, 96.
3. *al-Baḥr al-juwwānī*, the latter term being the Egyptian colloquial Arabic for the classical Arabic (CA) '*dākhilī*'.

baḥr Ṣafīd and the 'White Sea'[1] in order to distinguish it from the Sea of Pontos,[2] or Black Sea. However, there is another sea called 'White Sea' in Muscovy, and it is to this one that the [European] geographers' terms refer.[3]

We sailed on this sea (the Mediterranean) in the afternoon of Wednesday, the fifth day of Ramaḍān.[4] We boarded a French man-of-war,[5] which does not strike fear in the hearts of men. The seriousness of its craftsmanship so captivates the heart of the traveller that he becomes a child when he is on board this vessel. It contained every piece of equipment required for all manner of crafts and professions. It also included weaponry as well as soldiers,[6] and was fitted with eighteen guns.

The ship raised anchor on Thursday, the sixth day of the blessed month of Ramaḍān. At the time, there was a gentle breeze so that we were sailing without being aware of it and without suffering the slightest inconvenience from it. Prior to embarking, I had drunk large handfuls of salty seawater in compliance with what I had been told by one of my fellow *'ulamā'* who had travelled to Istanbul.[7] He said that it would ward off seasickness. As it happens, I did not get sick. However, at the time that I boarded the vessel I was gripped with fever, from which I was freed only as a result of the voyage and the movement of the ship. Sometimes, the body heals through illness! We continued to sail without any violent movement or buffeting for about four days, after which a storm rose and the sea began to surge and swell, playing with the bodies and souls of those on board. Most of us held on fast to the ground, and we all besought help from Him who mediates on the Day of Judgement. The words of a certain wit also came

1. Turkish *Baḥr-i safīd* (cf. Persian) and *Aq Deniz* ('White Sea'), which, as we have seen (see note no. 1, p. 119), denoted the Mediterranean.
2. '*baḥr Bunṭush*' (Lat. 'Pontus (Euxinus)'; cf. Turkish *Qara Deniz*), which is a strange amalgam of the correct *Bunṭus* and the frequent erroneous spelling variant *Nīṭash* (the result of graphemic confusion between pointing and vowelling). In classical geographical literature it was also often named after contiguous peoples (e.g. *Baḥr al-Rūs*, *Baḥr al-Bulghār*, etc.) or localities (e.g. *Baḥr al-Ṭarābazunda*, 'Sea of Trebizond'), and the earliest extant geographical manual even identifies it with *Baḥr al-Khazar* (e.g. Ibn Khurdādhbih, 1889: 105) – as does al-Mas'ūdī, 1894: 138ff. (cf. *idem*, 1960–79: I, 146: '*baḥr bunṭus*'!) – though this usually denoted the Caspian Sea (see note no. 2, p. 119). In MSA, only *Baḥr al-Aswad* is used. See *EI2*, s. vv. "Baḥr Bunṭus" (D. Dunlop), "Baḥr al-Khazar" (D. Dunlop); *EI1*, s.vv. "Qara deniz" (J. Mordtmann); "Baḥr al-Khazar"; "Baḥr al-Maghrib" (C. Seybold).
3. This would then refer to (part of) the Barents Sea.
4. = 13 April (1826).
5. = *La Truite*; see Translator's Introduction.
6. *harbajiyya*, sing. *harbajī*, i.e. 'someone carrying the *ḥarba* ('lance', 'pike'), with the agentive suffix '*-jī*' betraying its Turkish origin (*harbejī*).
7. This is another reference to Ḥasan al-'Aṭṭār.

to us: '*Danger befalls him who sails the sea; but more dangerous is he who sits in the company of kings without knowledge and wisdom.*' It confirmed to us that which our erudite friend al-Ṣaftī[1] inserted in a humorous poem written by Abū Nuwās:[2]

I saw all fears surrounded
by coitus as you – my servant girl of the sea – were pregnant
I swore on my life that I would no longer board a ship
only on the backs of animals would I travel for evermore

Yet he who puts his trust in the Most Generous need not fear any great mishap. And how true are the following words of the poet:

Why did we sail the sea
when we all but perished from fear
On the Most Generous we relied
He will surely not leave us

The storm subsided after about three days, and from then on it visited us from time to time only. Among the laudable qualities of the Franks that distinguish them from other Christians is their love of external cleanliness. Indeed, all the dirt and filth with which God – may He be praised and exalted – has cursed the Copts of Egypt he gave to the Franks as cleanliness, even when they are on the high seas.[3] The crew of the ship that we were on took great care cleaning it, removing the dirt as much as possible; they washed the sitting area every day, whereas the sleeping cabins were swept every two days. They also beat, aired and removed the dirt from the

1. 'Abd al-Raḥmān al-Ṣaftī al-Sharqāwī (d. 1848) was a famous poet, best known for his collection entitled *Talāqī al-arab fī marāqī al-adab* ('The Encounter of Desire in the Stairs of Refinement'); 'U. Kaḥḥāla [n.d.]: V, 142; *GALS*, II, 721.
2. al-Ḥasan b. Hāni' al-Ḥakamī Abū Nuwās (747–814) is generally considered one of the greatest and most versatile Arabic poets of the classical age. A favourite of the legendary 'Abbāsid caliph Hārūn al-Rashīd, he is especially known for his love poetry (*ghazal*), drinking songs (*khamriyyāt*) and acerbic satires (*hijā'*). See *GAL*, I, 15; "Abū Nuwās", *EI1* (C. Brockelmann), *EI2* (Ewald Wagner); *EI2*, s.v. "k͟hamriyya" (J. Bencheikh); J. Ashtiany *et al.*, 1990: 290–99 *et passim*.
3. It is important to add that the author's home town counted a sizeable Coptic community, in which connection it is interesting to compare these comments with those found in the entry for Ṭahṭā in Wallis Budge's guide book (1895: 264): '...[it] is the home of a large number of Copts, in consequence of which, probably, the town is kept clean'.

mattresses, etc., despite the fact that 'cleanliness is part of [the true] faith',[1] of which not an ounce can be found among them!

Despite the high degree of cleanliness of the French as compared with our countries, they do not count themselves among those who care greatly about it. This becomes clear from the following excerpt from the translation of the book on habits and customs, which was originally written in French:[2]

The people who devote most attention to the cleanliness of their houses are the Dutch. In their cities, most of the streets are paved with white stones, which are sedulously cleaned. Their houses are also embellished on the outside, whereas their windows – yes, even the outside walls – are regularly washed. There is also cleanliness in parts of England and in the United States of America.[3] *It is, however, rare in France, Austria and other countries. There are nations who are very dirty and lice-ridden; indeed, some of these peoples are actually being eaten by lice, and they are not bothered by it! Leprosy was in fact conquered by the widespread use of white sheets, which are washed and changed once or several times a week. White clothes have on the whole resulted in cleanliness and wholesomeness overcoming disgusting filth.*[4]

Fourth Section. On the mountains, countries and islands we saw

On the seventh day of our journey (20 April), we sailed past the island of Crete.[5] From afar, we saw its towering mountain, which the Greeks call 'Ida'

1. *al-naẓāfa min al-īmān*, which is a famous *ḥadīth*.
2. This is a reference to the *Aperçu historique sur les mœurs et coutumes des nations* (Paris, aux Bureaux de l'Encyclopédie portative, 1826, xii/256pp.), by the German-born historian and geographer Georges-Bernard Depping (1784–1853), who is also known for his *Histoire de commerce entre le Levant et l'Europe* (2 vols, Paris, 1830). It was at the suggestion of Jomard that al-Ṭahṭāwī translated *Aperçu*... The translation was completed on 2 Jumādā II 1245/29 November 1829 and published under the title *Qalā'id al-mafākhir fī gharīb al-awā'il wa 'l-awākhir* ('Exquisite Poetry of the Glorious Qualities of the Strange Customs of Those that Come First and Those that Come Last') in Cairo (Būlāq) in 1249/1833 (105/112pp.). The book also includes a long list of French technical terms with explanations by the translator.
3. *bilād al-aqālīm al-mujtama'a min Amrīka* ('the land of the assembled provinces of America') – cf. Fr. 'le pays des Etats-Unis' – as opposed to the earlier *al-aqālīm al-mujtama'a*. The use of the *aqālīm* (sing. *iqlīm*) is quite interesting since besides 'climate' (Gr. κλίμα) its basic meaning in geographical literature was 'region' as well as 'province', for which political entity al-Tahṭāwī usually uses *'imāla* (cf. French *départements*) or *iyāla*. Also see M. de Goeje, 1879: 180.
4. The sentence 'Leprosy ...' is, in fact, an addition of al-Ṭahṭāwī's and was not included in Depping's original.
5. *Krīd*, which is clearly a transcription of the French *Crète*. The usual Arabic form of this island was *Iqrīṭi/ush*, which is also how it appears in mediaeval Arabic geographical

(*Īdā*), and which is famous for the strange things that are recounted about it in their chronicles. On the 13th day of our journey we saw the island of Sicily (*Sīsīliyā*), which is famous in Arabic under the name of *Ṣaqāliyya* or *Ṣiqilliyya*. This island is located to the south of Italy and is separated from it by an isthmus called the Straits of Messina (*Massīna*). This is one of the biggest and most fertile islands of the Mediterranean Sea, and because of this it used to be known in former times as the granary of Rome. In past eras, it was the cause of war between the Romans and the people of Carthage, i.e. the inhabitants of the West. This ended when it came under Roman rule. Then, it was transferred to the kings of Greece, after which it was conquered by the Muslims, who were, in turn, vanquished by the Norman Christians (*al-Naṣārā al-Nurmandiyya*),[1] a French tribe. Then, some Spanish and Austrian kings ruled it. In the end, it became part of the Kingdom of Naples (*Nābulī al-Kattān*),[2] which is called Puglia (*Būliya*),[3] so that together with Naples the Franks today often refer to it as 'the Two Sicilies', Sicily being granted precedence over Naples. In geographical manuals, it is stated that the population of this island amounts to 100,000, whereas its cities are situated on mountain tops.

On the 14th day (27 April), we saw from a distance the mountain called Mount Etna (*Mantithnā*). This name consists of two words, one of which is *mant* – which means mountain – and the other *Ithnā*. So, it is best written [separately in Arabic] as *Mant Ithnā*. This mountain is today known as *Jubayl*.[4] However, it seems to me that this word is a corruption of *jabal*,

literature. See *EI2*, s.v. "Iqrīṭish" (M. Canard); al-Dimashqī, 1866: 142; Abū 'l-Fidā', 1840: 194; al-Mas'ūdī, 1894: 58; *idem*, 1960–79: I, 112 (par. 215), 139 (par. 276); Ibn Ḥawqal, 1938: 63, 203; al-Iṣṭakhrī, 1927: 70; Ibn Khurdādhbih, 1889: 112, 231; Ibn Rustah, 1892: 85 (*Iqrīṭiya*); Yāqūt, 1866–73: I, 326; Ibn Sa'īd, 1958: 103.

1. Mediaeval Arabic historians from the Maghrib and al-Andalus used the term *Majūs* to refer to both the Normans and the Scandinavian Norsemen, both of whom regularly attempted incursions into western Muslim territories. In the East, the term denoted the Zoroastrians. *EI1*, s.vv. "al-Madjūs" (E. Lévi-Provençal), " Madjūs" (V. Büchner); *EI2*, s. v. "al-Madjūs" (A. Melvinger).
2. See below.
3. First mentioned in Arabic literature as early as the 13th century (Ibn Sa'īd, 1958: 103), this region (the ancient Apulia), which is situated in the south-east of Italy, was actually part of the Kingdom of Naples. The title of 'Two Sicilies', which had been in use during the Spanish and Bourbon rule of the island of Sicily and the Kingdom of Naples between the 16th and 19th centuries, became official in 1815. In 1860, both areas were subsumed into the newly founded kingdom of Italy. The modern Puglia extends from the Fortore River in the north-west to the tip of the Salentine Peninsula (the 'heel' of Italy) and comprises the Provinces of Foggia, Bari, Taranto (also the capital of the region), Brindisi and Lecce.
4. Unfortunately, the author does not, for once, provide the vowelling of this word and so it can be read either as a spurious *Jabīl* or as *Jubayl*, i.e. the diminutive of the word *jabal*

an Arabic word, which the Muslims introduced to this island to denote this mountain. Even after their expulsion, the word was retained, albeit modified as a result of the mispronunciation of it by the inhabitants of this island. This mountain is a fire mountain (*jabal nār*), which spews fire, smoke and – at night – flames. Sometimes, it throws up burning stones. In the Frankish tongue fire mountains are called 'volcanic mountains' (*jibāl bulkāniyya*), and a single one is called a 'volcano' (*bulkān*). This word was mispronounced in Arabic as *burkān* – with an *r* – which is perhaps a direct loan from the language of the Andalusian people, who called it *Ṭahmah*, as does al-Masʿūdī[1] in his book entitled *Murūj al-dhahab* ('The Golden Meadows').[2] The mouth of the volcano is called *cratère* (*krātīra*) in French.

Volcanoes are usually found only on islands. According to people who have measured this mountain, its height above the level of the Encircling Sea amounts to 1,903 feet,[3] while its circumference at the foot is said to be about 55 French leagues, and that of its crater one quarter of a league.

In general, a fire mountain alternates between eruption and calm. Sometimes, it remains dormant for such a long time that people think that it has extinguished completely, only to erupt again several centuries later. Mount Etna has erupted thirty-one times, including the eruption in the year 1809 of the Frankish calendar. The biggest eruption was in 739, when it destroyed the city of *Kābān* and killed 18,000 people.[4] Signs that a volcano is

('mountain'). Arab geographers and chroniclers referred to it simply as (*al-*)*jabal*, (cf. e.g. Ibn Ḥawqal, 1938: 256), which later gave rise to the (Sicilian) Italian *Mongibello* (*monte-jabal*).

1. The historian, geographer and compulsive traveller Abū 'l-Ḥasan b. ʿAlī b. al-Ḥusayn al-Masʿūdī (d. 956) was born in Baghdad, which he left at a very early age, travelling all over the Islamic world and beyond. Of his enormous output, only two works have come down to us: *Murūj al-dhahab wa maʿādin al-jawāhir* ('The Golden Meadows and Sources of Gems') – an encyclopaedic geographical-cum-historical survey of the then known world – and its abridgement, *Kitāb al-tanbīh wa 'il-ishrāf* ('The Book of Warning and Revision'). The former, in particular, is of enormous importance as it is the single most important mediaeval source on Arab knowledge of non-Muslim peoples (cf. the excellent study by A. Shboul, 1979). Also see I. Krachkovskij, 1963: I, 177–85; *EI1*, s.v. "al-Masʿūdī" (C. Brockelmann); R. Blachère, 1957: 201–04; Yāqūt, 1936–38: XIII, 90–94; *GAL*, I, 150–02; *GALS*, I, 220–21.
2. Cf. al-Masʿūdī, 1960–79: II, 146, par. 912 (*'Aṭma'*! – also see I, 139, 222). Also see al-Masʿūdī, 1894: 59–60. Cf. Ibn Ḥawqal, 1938: 255–6 (*burkān*). Curiously, al-Ṭahṭāwī does not mention the Stromboli volcano, which is also mentioned by Ibn Ḥawqal as *Siranjulū* (*ibid.*: 255).
3. This number is, of course, a gross underevaluation as the actual height is more than 10,000ft (*c.* 3,200m).
4. There are a number of things that merit attention here. First, Mount Etna is known to have erupted 57 times between the start of the Christian era and 1825. Second, there is no trace of an eruption in 739 A.D. The extent of the disaster and the number of casualties

about to erupt are a violent roaring, rumbling and thundering underneath the surface of the earth and the build-up of smoke. Some physicists have claimed that if we compare earthquakes and volcanic activity it becomes clear that these two phenomena have the same underlying cause, viz. fires that rage underneath the earth['s surface], or are congested in its interior. Nevertheless, the effects of earthquakes are more extensive than those of volcanoes. The impact of earthquakes can be seen to cover a wide area of the earth, whereas that of volcanoes is restricted to the immediate vicinity. Generally speaking, an earthquake also becomes more violent the farther it is from a volcano. This has led someone to state that the fire beneath the surface of the earth is looking for a way out; if there is a volcano, then it will leave through it. As a result, the fire loses its strength and thus the earthquake does not take place. Conversely, if the surface of land does not have volcanoes, the fires fail to find a way of escape, and so the earth trembles. Another scholar also held that both the volcanic and seismic phenomena ensue from friction-based magnetism, which in French is called *électricité* (*al-iliktrīsitah*) – [in Arabic] this is known as *rasīs*, which is a property of yellow amber (*kahrabā*) when it is rubbed.[1] In reply to this theory, others have stated that this is incompatible with the views of another scientist regarding the make-up of the earth and the arrangement of its geological strata. One hard and fast rule is that the higher the volcano is, the less frequent the eruptions are. This is what usually happens, and God – may He be praised and exalted – knows best.

---

would seem to point to that of 1669 (March-July), during which half of the town of Catania was submerged by the lava flow. This is made even more plausible by the fact that the Arabic *kābān* would then simply be a misprint for *Kātān* (even though earlier on the town appears as *al-Kanān*). The question of the date remains unresolved, and matters do not become any easier if one presumes the author was, in fact, talking about 793 of the Islamic era, i.e. 1391 A.D., since there is no record of an eruption taking place in that year (though there was a big one in 1381). Finally, the possibility that the date is 1793 is also scuppered by the fact that the town of Catania did not suffer any large-scale damage because of Etna between 1669 and al-Ṭahṭāwī's visit.

1. Later on, the word appears in its proper spelling, i.e. with final *hamza* – *kahrabā'* (cf. Persian *kahrobā*, 'attracting straw'). It is presumably on the grounds of this that W. Braune (1933) credited al-Ṭahtawī with being the inventor of the modern word for 'electricity', *kahrabā'iyya*. It seems that Bayram V (1884–93: III, 26) was one of the first to use *kahrabā'* in the sense of electricity (cf. al-Sanūsī, 1976–81: I, 86). The timing is interesting inasmuch as it was in the same period that the word first made its entry into dictionaries (E. Gasselin, 1880–86: I, 599). Up until then, it was only used in the sense of 'amber' (cf. F. al-Shidyāq, 1919: 284; Khayr al-Dīn, 1867: e.g. 297). It is also interesting that the lexicographer Kazimirski gives *rasīs* (1860: I, 858) for 'electricity' – which Freytag explains as '*initium amoris; prudens, intelligens*' (1830–37: II, 147) and in MSA means 'covered with verdigris' – as well as *jādhibiya muḥāka* (A. Kazimirski, 1860: I, 469). Also see V. Monteil, 1960: 134–5; K. Vollers, 1887–97: 648 (1896).

On the 15th day (28 April), we dropped anchor at the city of Messina but we did not leave the ship at any time since the people there do not allow people from Eastern countries to enter their territory, unless they go into quarantine (*karantīna*), which involves a stay of several days in order to expel the smell of the plague. However, they do bring people all they require in return for payment; [afterwards, they put the money] in a container filled with vinegar, or something of that kind, with the utmost caution. (The reader is referred to the first Section of the second Essay.) We took the necessary provisions of fruit, vegetables, drinking water, etc from this city.

We spent five days in its port. From the distance, we saw its towering castles and tall and lofty temples. We looked on as, just before sunset, the lamps and lights, which would continue to burn until after daybreak, were lit. During the whole of our stay we heard the sound of bells. The way they strike the bells is truly delightful. On one of these nights, while talking with some wits, I composed an amusing *maqāma*,[1] which comprised three thoughts. The first contains the argument that nothing prevents a healthy disposition from admiring something that is beautiful with chastity. I composed a number of pleasant variants on this, among which the following words:

I have deep desire for every being filled with beauty
without fearing my youthful passion
Doubts about love I have none
Yet chastity is my nature

The second is that the lover is drunk on the finest wine in the eyes of the beloved, and does not need real wine for his recreation.[2] I composed the following words on this theme:

As he appeared, a goblet in his hand, I declared
while the essence of the wine resembles his jaws
the purity of his beauty my eye beheld was enough for me
as was my drunkenness on the enthralling fascination of his eyes

The third one dealt with the influence the sound of the bell ringing has on the soul when he who rings is someone with taste and is proficient at it. On this theme I recited the words of the poet:

1. Vide ante.
2. The Arabic plays on *rāḥ* ('wine') and *rāḥa* ('rest', 'repose').

No sooner had he come while ringing the bell than I said to him
Who taught the gazelle to ring the bells?
And I said to my soul: 'What are the blows that grieve you?'
Is it the striking of the bells or the blow of the distance that separates me?

To the above I appended some ornamented verses, an examination of their meanings and the types of embellishments, answers to some grammatical problems, etc. However, this is not the place to talk about this.

On the 20th day of our journey (3 May), we left this city and continued until we were alongside the fire mountain and then beyond it.

On the 24th day (7 May), we passed the city of Naples, which in Turkish is known as *Puliya*. We were some 90 miles past it when the wind turned completely around and blew straight into the front of the ship, which was thrown off course and was no longer heading towards its desired goal, since this was where the wind was coming from. I am pleased to remember the words of a certain poet:

A slender one turned away from me, not turning
towards me one day – out of my pain born from being distant, I spoke
Why, oh branch of purity, will you not bend towards me?
It answered: how can I when you are standing with the wind in your back?

As a result of the turning of the wind, we returned to the city of Naples and dropped anchor near it. However, we could not enter the city for the same reason as before. It is one of the great cities of Europe and its king [also] rules over the above-mentioned island of Sicily. The city of Naples is the seat of this king. In Arabic it is known as *Nābul al-Kattān* – perhaps because of the fine quality of its flax (*kattān*).[1] The kingdom of Naples remained in the hands of the Muslims for about 200 years, after which it was conquered, together with the kingdom of Sicily, by the Norman Christians. To this day, it has remained in the hands of the Italian Christians, which is why it is called 'southern Italy'. As we have already said above, the city of Naples is one of the major trading centres of Europe.

On the 29th day (12 May), we saw the island of Corsica (*Qursuqa*), which is ruled by the French, and is today called *l'île de Corse* (*jazīrat al-Qurs*). It was conquered by the Muslims, but it did not remain in their possession

1. Though this is a tempting etymology, the origin of the name, which also serves to distinguish it from the homonymous Tunisian town of *Nābul* (Nabeul), is related to the proximity of the city to Catania.

for long. It is the homeland[1] of Napoleon, who has become famous by the name of Bonaparte (*Būnabarta*), who conquered Egypt during the French campaign, and then ruled France, despite the fact that his father was only an artillery captain.

On the 33rd day (15 May), we dropped anchor in the port of Marseilles (*Marsīliyā*). So, in total we had been at sea for 33 days, including the five days we spent off Messina and about one day off Naples. If it had not been for the delays caused by the wind, we would have arrived after a much shorter period of time.

Second Essay

First Section. On our stay in the city of Marseilles

We dropped anchor at the quay of Marseilles, which is one of the ports of France. We disembarked from the ship on which we had voyaged into small launches, and arrived at a house outside the city. This was used for quarantine (*karantīna*) as, following their custom, anyone coming from foreign lands must go through quarantine before being allowed to enter the city.[2]

1. *waṭan* (pl. *awṭān*); this is arguably the first use of this word in its MSA meaning of 'homeland' (A. al-Rāfiʿī, 1930: 410). At the same time, however, one should be careful not to attribute to it any of the emotional connotations usually associated with 'fatherland'; indeed, the very notion of 'patriotism' or 'nationalism' (MSA *waṭaniyya*, *qawmiyya*) was, at the time at least, alien to al-Ṭahṭāwī's thought as his first allegiance lay with the broader Islamic community, i.e. the *umma*. Moreover, elsewhere in the text he also uses the word to denote 'region' (cf. *iqlīm*). In his later writings, however, we can see a clear shift in stress towards the native land, on which he would compose a number of odes and eulogies. For instance, in *al-Murshid al-Amīn li 'l-banāt wa 'l-banīn* (1872), he describes *waṭan* in a decidedly modern way: 'it is a person's nest (*ʿushsh*), from which he departs; it is the place where his family is; the place where his umbilicus has been cut; the country in which he came into existence, grew up, and which has fed and loved him, gave him the air to breathe and where the protective amulets of childhood have been taken off (i.e. where he reached the age of reason).' Stressing the emotional, visceral bond between a person and his homeland, he adds: 'people have an ardent desire for their native countries without knowing why' (ed. M. ʿImāra, 1973–80: II, 429). Also see S. Ali, 1994: 10ff.; D. Newman, 1998: 299ff. In contemporary Arab societies, the terms *umma* and *waṭan* seem occasionally to merge, *umma* being used for *umma waṭaniyya*, i.e. 'nation-state'. See A. Amor, 1983; Sylvia G. Haim, 'Islam and the theory of Arab nationalism', in W. Laqueur, 1958; *EI2*, s.v. "ḳawm" (A. J. Wensinck); R. Dozy, 1967: II, 324–5.
2. Marseilles and Toulon were the French ports where ships from the Levant and North Africa could dock. Although, true to its etymology, quarantine (It. *quarantina*, 'set of 40') originally did last 40 days (allegedly in reference to the time Christ spent in the

Let us mention here what has been said on the subject of quarantine by Maghribī *'ulamā'*, as it was recounted to me by a trustworthy eminent scholar from Morocco. He said that a dispute arose over the lawfulness of quarantine between the esteemed Shaykh Muḥammad al-Mannāʿī al-Tūnisī al-Mālikī,[1] a teacher at the Zaytūna mosque,[2] and the Ḥanafī *muftī*,[3] the

Wilderness), the periods actually varied considerably over time and between individual countries (and cities). In France, the minimum was five days (the period in isolation for the plague and yellow fever ran between, respectively, five and seven and ten and 15 days). In 1822, France had further tightened quarantine regulations after the yellow fever epidemic of 1821. Shortly before al-Ṭahṭāwī's arrival, the French government had added a 300-metre-long dyke between the islands of Pomègue (where the ships had to dock) and Ratonneau (where work was still going on to complete the Caroline hospital) in order to increase the capacity of the quarantine facilities in Marseilles. The lazaret was situated some 300m north of the city, and covered an area of *c.* 18 hectares. It should be added that in the first half of the century, quarantine was only rarely applied in Britain and northern European countries; the former even officially abolished it in the early 1850s – some 40 years before the French (1894). Muslim countries, too, had their own quarantine regulations. The first ruler to impose it was Muḥammad ʿAlī (1813), the first Egyptian lazaret being built in April 1832, in Alexandria. However, it is worth pointing out that it had already been used as early as 1722 by the Tunisian Bey Ḥusayn on ships coming from Marseilles, which at the time was in the throes of the plague. The Ottomans first used quarantine in 1838, and over the next decade set up lazarets in some 29 Mediterranean ports. See D. Panzac, 1986; *idem*, 1985: 449, 466, 484ff., 495ff.; N. Gallagher, 1983; M. Berthelot, 1886–1902: s.v. "police sanitaire"; P. Larousse, 1866–77: s.v. "quarantine". Cf. Bayram V, 1884–93: I, 135, II, 60 (*karantīna* alongside *muddat al-ḥimya* – 'protection period'); A. Ibn Abī 'l-Ḍiyāf, 1963–65: III, 165–7, IV, 97; F. al-Shidyāq, 1881: 45; al-Salāwī, 1956: V, 183–4. The first Arabic author to use the borrowing was the 18th-century Moroccan envoy to Spain, Muḥammad b. ʿUthmān al-Miknāsī, in whose *riḥla* it appears as *kuranṭīna* (cf. al-Kardūdi, 1885: [19]). Other variants in the 19th century included *kūrantīna* (J. Habeisch, 1896: 662; K. Vollers, 1887–97: 320, 621), *kārantīna* (E. Bocthor, 1881: 658) and *qarantīna* (S. Spiro, 1895: 515). Also see H. Kahane *et al.*, 1958: 365–6 (no. 529); A. Jal, 1848: 1244.

1. Official scribe (*kātib*) to the Tunisian Bey Ḥusayn (1824–35), Abū ʿAbd Allāh Muḥammad b. Sulaymān al-Mannāʿī (d. 1831) studied at al-Zaytūna in Tunis and later completed his education at Fès, where he fell in with Aḥmad al-Tījānī (1737–1815), the eponymous founder of the Tījāniyya *ṣūfī* order (*ṭarīqa*), which he joined. He is also the author of a little-known treatise entitled *Tuḥfat al-muwqinin wa murshidat al-ḍāllīn* ('Gift of the Pigeon Hunters and Guide for Those who Have Strayed'). A. Raymond [A. Ibn Abī 'l-Ḍiyāf], 1994: II, 150–51 *et passim*; ʿU. Kaḥḥāla [n.d.]: XII, 50; A. Ibn Abī 'l-Ḍiyāf, 1963–65: III, 130, 145.
2. Located in the centre of Tunis, the Zaytūna mosque (also known as the Great Mosque) was founded as early as 734 and under the Ḥafṣid dynasty (1207–1534) became one of the great religious (teaching) centres of the Muslim world, often cited on a par with al-Azhar, many of its graduates pursuing careers in Eastern Islamic lands. For a survey of this institution and its importance, see, for instance, M. Abdel Moula, 1971.
3. This term denotes someone who is entitled to hand down *fatwās* (formal legal opinions). In the 18th and 19th centuries, the Tunisian *majlis al-sharʿī* (the supreme religious court) counted three Mālikī and three Ḥanafī *muftīs*, and was presided over by a Ḥanafī *muftī*. The senior *muftī*, known as the *bāsh muftī* ('Grand Mufti'), enjoyed greater authority than his Mālikī counterpart since he represented the (Ottoman) state *madhhab*, and was

esteemed Shaykh Muḥammad Bayram, who wrote a number of books on the traditional religious and rational sciences, as well as a history of the Ottoman state since its beginnings up until the rule of the current Sultan Maḥmūd.[1] According to the former it was forbidden, whereas the latter said that it was lawful, adding that it was, in fact, a duty. He wrote a treatise on the subject guided by the Holy Book and the *sunna*.[2] His opponent, for his part, adduced proof of its prohibition and wrote a treatise in which his reasoning was based on the fact that quarantine constitutes a flight from divine providence.[3]

A similar dispute also arose between both scholars over the roundness or

---

sometimes referred to as *ra'īs al-fatwā*, or *shaykh al-fatwā*. In official Tunisian parlance, the holder of the office of *bāsh muftī* was also referred to as *shaykh al-Islām*, even though, strictly speaking, there was only one official *shaykh al-Islām* in the entire Ottoman Empire, i.e. the one in Constantinople, who was the ultimate religious authority, whereas the Provinces had only *muftīs*. In 1847, however, the Tunisian ruler Aḥmad Bey made the title official. Nevertheless, it remained a highly delicate issue, and the official investiture documents would continue to refer exclusively to *bāsh muftī*. See "shaykh al-Islām", *EI1* (J. Kramers), *EI2* (J. Kramers – [R. Bulliet] – R. Repp); A. Demeerseman, 1978; A. Raymond [A. Ibn Abī 'l-Ḍiyāf], 1994: II, 30–32, 35–6; R. Brunschvig, 1965; M. Bayram V, 1884–93: II, 3, 6, 67, 124ff. *et passim*.

1. The reference is to the famous Muḥammad Bayram II (1749–1831) – the great-grandfather of the traveller and reformer Bayram V (1839–90) – who in 1801 had been appointed *shaykh al-Islām*. The quarantine treatise was entitled *Ḥusn al-anbā' fī jawāz al-taḥaffuẓ min al-wabā'* (Cairo, al-Maṭba'a al-I'lāmiyya, 1302/1884–85); one should add that in his views on the subject, he was driven by more than legalistic ratiocination since he had lost his wife and five children to the disease when it struck Tunisia in 1785. As for the historical work, this was in fact a long poem consisting of an enumeration of the Ottoman Sultans, entitled *'Iqd al-durr wa 'l-marjān fī salāṭīn 'āl 'Uthmān* ('The Pearl and Coral Necklace Regarding the Sultans of the House of Osman'). See A. Abdesselem, 1973: 288–95; Y. Sarkīs, 1928: 613; A. Raymond [A. Ibn Abī 'l-Ḍiyāf], 1994: II, 132.
2. This word, which originally means 'beaten path', 'custom', 'habit', is generally used in Islamic jurisprudence to denote the authoritative deeds, utterances and unspoken approval of the Prophet Muḥammad (passed down directly or indirectly through his Companions). See *EI1*, s.v. "sunna" (A. Wensinck); N. Coulson, 1978: 39ff. *et passim*; J. Schacht, 1975: 58–81.
3. On the controversy, see N. Gallagher, 1977: 71ff.; *idem*, 1983: 31–2. The group around al-Mannā'ī referred to Abū 'Ubayda 'Amr b. al-Jarāḥ, who had opposed the caliph 'Umar b. al-Khaṭṭāb when the latter decided against sending his troops into plague-ridden Syria, claiming that an invocation was the best defence against the disease. Bayram, for his part, referred to the *ḥadīths* '*lā 'adwā wa lā ṭayra*' ('no contagion and no evil omen') and '*firra min al-majdhūm fararaka min al-asad*' ('flee the leper as you do the lion'), the chronicler Ibn Abī 'l-Ḍiyāf explaining the first as 'deny its effect and the substance remains' ('*nafī ta'thīruhā fa baqiya aṣluhā*'). For more details on the religious attitude towards epidemics, see D. Panzac, 1985: 280ff. (chap. 11); J. Sublet, 1971; A. Ibn Abī 'l-Ḍiyāf, 1963–65: III, 127–32; A. J. Wensinck, 1992: IV, 91. It is interesting to add that al-Ṭahṭāwī would appear to have been an adherent of the Bayram school, since he himself, when a cholera epidemic struck Cairo in 1834, fled to his native Ṭahṭā, where he stayed for six months.

flatness of the earth; as far as al-Mannāʿī was concerned, it was flat, whereas Bayram claimed it was round. Among the Maghribī *ʿulamā'* who claimed that the earth was round, we find the eminent Shaykh Mukhtār al-Kintāwī,[1] who comes from Azawāt, near Timbuktu, and is the author of an abridgement of Mālikī law, which he patterned on the text of Khalīl,[2] as he had also done with Ibn Mālik's grammar manual, *Alfiyya*.[3] He also wrote other works on the exoteric and esoteric sciences, such as chants and prayers[4] like those of al-Shādhilī.[5] He also wrote a book called *al-Nuzha* ('The Excursion'), in which he collected all sciences and on occasion talks about astronomy. He discusses the roundness of the earth and its rotation, explaining everything. Summarizing his exposé, we can say that the earth is a sphere and that there is nothing wrong with thinking that it moves or remains still.[6] This *shaykh* died in the year 1226 A.H. (1811) – may the best prayers and purest greeting be upon him. His grandson, who bears the same name, succeeded him.

---

1. This is presumably Mukhtār b. Būna al-Shinqīṭī, whose work on the *Alfiyya* was called *al-Alfiyya wa 'l-iḥmirār*. See Y. Sarkīs, 1928: 1148; ʿU. Kaḥḥāla: XII, 210.
2. The Egyptian jurist Khalīl b. Isḥāq Abū 'l-Mawada Ḍiyā' al-Dīn, commonly known as (Ibn) al-Jundī (d. 1374), was one of the greatest Mālikī scholars of his day. The work to which reference is made here is *al-Mukhtaṣar (fī 'l-fiqh)*. See *EI1*, s.v. "Khalīl" (M. Ben Cheneb); *GAL*, II, 83.
3. The Jaén-born Jamāl al-Dīn Abū ʿAbd Allāh Muḥammad b. ʿAbd Allāh b. Mālik (1203–74) is one of the most celebrated Arabic grammarians in history. A number of his works have survived, among which the famous *Kitāb al-khulāṣa al-alfiyya* ('The 1,000-Verse Summary'), an abridgement of his own *al-Kāfiya al-shāfiyya*. The former, which is usually abbreviated to *al-Alfiyya*, derives its title from the fact that it comprises 1,000 (Arabic *'alf'*) verses (in the *rajaz* metre). Ibn Mālik's works were (and still are) compulsory reading at al-Azhar, and Ḥasan al-ʿAṭṭar wrote a commentary (*Ḥāshiya ʿalā Lāmiyyat al-afʿāl li Ibn Mālik*) on Ibn Mālik's *Lāmiyyat al-afʿāl* (also known as *Kitāb miftāḥ fī abniyāt al-afʿāl*, 'Key to the Construction of Verbs'), a poem in verses (*basīṭ* metre) rhyming in '(the letter) l' (Arabic *lām*) on the subject of syntax. See "Ibn Mālik", *EI1* (M. Ben Cheneb), *EI2* (H. Fleisch).
4. *aḥzāb wa awrād*. A *ḥizb* (sing. of *aḥzāb*) denotes a 60th part of the Qur'ān (used during prayers), whereas a *wird* (sing. of *awrād*) refers to a set portion of the Qur'ān to be read as part of the devotions. However, both are also used in Ṣūfī orders, where they are special prayers composed by saints (*awliyā'*) and to be recited or chanted regularly (or at need), especially during Ṣūfī ceremonies. *EI1*, s.vv. "ḥizb" (D. MacDonald); "dhikr", *EI1* (D. MacDonald), *EI2* (L. Gardet); E. Lane, 1923: 251.
5. The Moroccan-born Abū 'l-Ḥasan ʿAlī b. ʿAbd Allāh al-Sharīf al-Zarwīlī (d. 1258) was a celebrated mystic, and founder of the religious (Ṣūfī) brotherhood (*ṭarīqa, ṭā'ifa*) that bears his name, i.e. al-Shādhiliyya, which, in turn, spawned a great many other brotherhoods. It was (and still is) particularly popular in the Maghrib. Al-Shādhilī left a number of works, most of which are *ḥizb* collections. See *EI1*, s. vv. "al-Shādhilī" (A. Cour), "Shādhiliyya" (D. Margoliouth); "taṣawwuf", *EI1* (Louis Massignon), *EI2* (W. Chittick – F. De Jong).
6. It is clear that al-Ṭahṭāwī had to tread very carefully here so as not to offend the Azharites; also see below (note No. 3, p. 354) on the passage he dropped on the turning of the earth.

The lazaret where we stayed during the quarantine was very spacious and solidly built, and contained large buildings and gardens. It was there that we became aware of the high-quality construction of this country's buildings, which are filled with gardens, fountains, etc. The first day, almost without our being aware of it, we experienced things that were for the most part strange. They brought a number of French servants to us although we did not know their language. We also received about 100 chairs to sit on, since in this country it is considered strange for people to sit on a kind of rug spread out on the floor – indeed, the very fact of sitting on the floor amazes them. Then, they laid the table for breakfast for which they brought high round tables,[1] on which they placed white earthenware plates. In front of every plate they put a glass goblet, a knife, fork and spoon, and on each table there were about two bottles filled with water, a small container with salt and another with pepper. Around the table they then arranged chairs, one for each person. Afterwards, they brought the food in. On each table they placed one or two large dishes from which one of the people at the table ladled and distributed the food to all the others. Each person received something in his plate which he was supposed to cut with the knife that was before him, and then to bring it to his mouth with the fork – not the hand. People here do not eat with their hands and they never eat with someone else's knife or fork or drink from someone else's glass. They claim that this is cleaner and healthier. From what one can see among the Franks, they never eat from copper plates or receptacles – not even if they have been tinplated, as these are used for cooking only. However, they do always use enamel plates.

With them, meals consist of several set stages, each of which may be multiple. The meal starts with soup, which is followed by meat, various types of dishes such as vegetables and pastries, followed by salad (*salaṭa*). Sometimes, the enamel plates are in the same colour as the food served, salad dishes, for instance, being painted green, the colour of the salad. They end their meal with fruit, followed by an alcoholic beverage,[2] although they drink little of it. Then it is time for tea or coffee. The above holds true for both the rich and the poor, each in accordance with his means. Every time somebody has eaten food from his plate, it is changed, whereupon another, unused plate is brought in for the next course. Then they brought

1. *ṭabliyyāt*, sing. *ṭabliyya* (< Italian) are large low round tables, resembling salvers, around which in the East diners sat on the floor. It is interesting that al-Ṭahṭāwī used this ECA term, rather than the Classical *khuwwān*/pl. *akhwina* (MSA: *minḍada*/pl. *manāḍid*; *mā'ida*/pl. *mā'idāt, mawā'id*; *ṭāwila*/pl. *ṭāwilāt*; *sufra*/pl. *sufar*).

2. *mukhaddir*, i.e. 'anaesthetic', 'drug'.

us bedding, and in accordance with their custom one must sleep on something raised, like a bed. They brought us all that.

We stayed in this place for eighteen days without ever leaving it. However, it is very spacious and there are large gardens and vast areas for walking and to relax in.

Afterwards, we boarded beautifully decked-out carriages, which continue to trundle along night and day, and journeyed to a building in the city or, to be more precise, on the edge of it. It was a palace, built outside the city, with gardens and other facilities.[1] We stayed there awaiting our departure for Paris. During our sojourn in this place, we sometimes went out for a couple of hours to amuse ourselves in the town, and we visited a few coffee houses. However, the coffee houses in this country are not the meeting places of riff-raff, but of decent people.[2] Indeed, these places are decorated with such beautiful and precious things that they are suited only for the

1. This was the Château de Bonneveine (currently the Château Boréli).
2. Very soon after its introduction into Arab countries and Turkey in the 16th century from the Yemen, coffee (originally a great luxury) quickly gained wide popularity. However, very early on religious objections were raised because of its intoxicating properties, resulting in the prohibition of the beverage. Most often, though, the anti-coffee regulations were not enforced until the reign of Murād IV, who in 1632 applied the most stringent restrictions. At the same time, there were also practical considerations and coffee houses were temporarily closed in Egypt in the 17th century because soldiers were spending too much time there and neglecting their duties. In the 17th–18th centuries, coffee played a huge role in the economy of Egypt (particularly in its Red Sea commerce), Cairo being the redistribution hub for Yemenite 'mocha'; in the period 1690–1750, for instance, coffee accounted for one-third of Egypt's imports and one-fourth of its exports. At the end of the 18th century, there were said to be 1,200 coffee houses in Cairo (excluding Būlāq and Old Cairo), many of which also served as entertainment venues, with performances put on by professional narrators, musicians and shadow players. Despite the ubiquitous use of the beverage, coffee houses were often considered haunts of the lower classes (even though coffee was served at gatherings of all classes) in both North African and Near Eastern countries. At the same time, one should point out that the issue of the lawfulness of coffee remained a problem well into the 19th century – witness the treatise on the subject by the Tunisian Shaykh Sulaymān al-Ḥarā'irī (himself an expatriate in France) entitled *Risāla fī 'l-qahwa sammāhā al-qawl al-muḥaqqaq fī taḥrīm al-bunn al-muḥarraq aw tanbīh al-ghāfilīn 'ammā irtakabūhu in tanāwul al-bunn al-muḥarraq fī hādhihi 'l-sinīn* ('A Treatise on Coffee, entitled the true saying on the unlawfulness of roast coffee, or a warning to those who are unaware of the sins they have committed when partaking of roast coffee in recent years', Paris, 1860). See A. Raymond, 1973: I, 108–64; *idem*, 1995: 55ff.; S. Faroqhi, 1986; "ḳahwa", *EI1*, *EI2* (C. Van Arendonk – K. Chaudhuri); E. Lane, 1923: 339–41; N. Hanna, in M. Daly, 1998: 107ff.; A. Abdesselem, 1973: 94. In November 1798, the French expedition forces opened a French bistro in Cairo (in Ghayṭ al-Nūbī, next to Azbakiyya), which 'A. al-Jabartī described as follows (1997: IV, 151): 'they [the French] built a place for entertainment (*manzaha*) where women and men gather for entertainment and debauchery (*khalā'a*) at specific times. Only people who have paid a certain sum or who have received authorization and hold a ticket (*waraqa*) can gain entry.' Cf. A. Raymond, 1998: 342ff.

very rich. The prices there are very high, so only wealthy people can go there. As for the poor, they go to some seedy coffee houses, taverns or hashish dens.

I have already stated that the city of Alexandria resembles Marseilles. I should like to add here that the difference between them is the spaciousness of the streets and roads [in the latter], enabling several carriages to move along the same thoroughfare.[1] Furthermore, on the inner walls of all halls, galleries and grand reception parlours, there are large magnificent mirrors. In many halls, there are glass mirrors on every side, so that they appear even more splendid.

The first time we went out to visit the town, we passed superb shops, whose shop windows consisted of these mirrors, and which were filled with beautiful women.[2] This was at noon time. The women of this country are used to revealing their face, head, the throat as well as what lies beneath it, the nape of the neck and what lies beneath it, and their arms almost up to the shoulders.[3] It is also the custom that the shopping is strictly for women, whereas labour is the preserve of men. And so, we took pleasure in looking at them [the women] in these shops, coffee houses, etc., and at what went on inside them.

The first wonderful thing on which our gazes rested was a magnificent coffee house. We went in and saw that it was extraordinary both in terms of appearance and arrangement. The owner[4] was a woman who sat at a large raised desk. In front of her, there were inkwells, pens and a list. The coffee was actually made in a room far away from the patrons and young waiters moved between the public sitting area and the coffee room. The room where people sit is fitted with chairs upholstered with flower-print fabrics, and the tables[5] are made out of superior mahogany wood. Each table is covered with a black or coloured marble slab. In this type of coffee house they sell all

1. In the second edition the following sentence was added: 'However, thanks to the ruler's efforts, Alexandria has almost reached the same level.'
2. The book palpably lurches here as the author for the first time truly engages with his new surroundings – it is highly significant that he does so through the subject of women!
3. The chronicler ʿA. al-Jabartī's comments on the appearance of French women who accompanied the soldiers of the Expedition d'Egypte were far more judgemental, and he strongly condemned their lack of chastity and modesty, likening their behaviour to that of the women among the riff-raff; ʿA. al-Jabartī, 1997: IV, 579ff. (1994: III, 161–2/252–3; trans., 1979: 320–01).
4. *qahwajiyya*, which ECA word is both the plural and feminine form of *qahwajī* ('coffee house owner/attendant'). Naturally, in Egypt only the male variant existed!
5. *ṭāwu/ilāt* (sing. *ṭāwu/ila*, It. *tavola*); cf. M. al-Sanūsī 1891–92: 65, 266; E. Bocthor, 1882: 792; E. Gasselin, 1880–86: II, 731–2; S. Spiro, 1895: 358; J. Habeisch, 1896: 615; G. Badger, 1895: 1071; J. Heyworth-Dunne, 1940–42: 408; K. Vollers, 1887–97: 314, 320.

types of beverages and pastries. When one of the customers orders something from a waiter, he submits it to the owner, who orders that it be brought to him. She writes it down in her ledger and tears off a small piece of paper on which the price is put. The waiter gives this to the customer when the latter wishes to pay. Normally, when someone wants to drink coffee, it is brought together with sugar, so that the customer can mix it in his coffee where it dissolves before drinking. We did all this in accordance with their custom.[1] Their coffee-cups are quite large – on the whole about the size of four cups used in Egypt. In fact, it is a goblet, rather than a cup. In these types of coffee houses, there are daily newspapers[2] for patrons to read.

When I entered this coffee house and sat down there, it felt like being in a huge bazaar because of the huge numbers of people there. When a group of people appeared both inside and outside, their faces appeared on all sides in the mirrors, and one could see the multiplicity of people walking around, sitting and standing. One thus got the impression that this coffee house was a street, and I realized that it was an enclosed coffee house only because I saw our multiple images [reflected] in the mirrors. I became aware that all of this was due to the peculiar properties of the glass. In our country, the mirror usually duplicates the image of one person, as someone said on the subject:

I veil the view of the mirror from him
for fear it should double before my eyes
I suffer what is my unique suffering
but what if two stars should reveal themselves ?

Because of the great number and size of mirrors on the walls in Frankish dwellings, they tend to multiply a single image from all sides and corners. As I once wrote:

1. The historian al-Jabartī was equally interested in French restaurant arrangements and customs: 1997: III, 12/19, 44/69.
2. *awrāq al-waqā'i'* ('news events papers'). Later on in the text, al-Ṭahṭāwī also uses *awrāq al-waqā'i' al-yawmiyya* ('daily event sheets'), *al-waqā'i' al-yawmiyya* ('daily events'), *al-tadhākir al-yawmiyya* ('daily tickets'), or, simply, *al-waqā'i'*, as well as the borrowings *jurnāl* and *kāẓīṭa* (vide post). Interestingly, only the foreign borrowings would be taken up by future travellers, F. al-Shidyāq (1881: 81) being probably the first author to use the MSA *ṣaḥīfa* (pl. *ṣaḥā'if*, *ṣuḥuf*), alongside *ṣaḥīfa akhbāriyya* (1855: *passim*). The other MSA term, *jarīda* (*jarā'id*), also dates back to the 19th century; Khayr al-Dīn, 1867: 19 *et passim*; M. al-Sanūsī, 1891–92: *passim*. It should be added that the two MSA words quickly crowded out the borrowings, and in the last quarter of the century, an author like M. al-Muwaylīḥī used *ghāẓītah* only to stress the medium's foreign origin, preferring *jarīda* in general contexts.

He disappeared from me, and not a trace of him has remained
except in my heart, and no news is heard from him
And when he appears, the mirror shows his appearance
in which houses full of images become visible

Our Shaykh al-ʿAṭṭār once said: '*I have never seen anything more imaginative regarding this topic than the words of Ibn Sahl:*'[1]

In the mirror of my thought he cast the sun of his image
Its reflection kindled the flames of my insides

Al-Ḥarīrī said with regard to a beautiful youth holding a mirror in his hand:

He saw the beauty of his image in the mirror
and his ardent love for it afflicted him with a grave and drawn-out illness
His worn garment sent Jacob as messenger
to indicate that he had seen Joseph

The conclusion of all of the above will come in the treatment of the city of Paris.

The period of our stay in Marseilles after quarantine was spent studying the individual sounds, i.e. the spelling of the French language.

In the city of Marseilles, there are many Christians from Egypt and Syria, who accompanied the French during their retreat from Egypt.[2] All of them wear French clothes. It is rare to find a Muslim among those who left with the French: some of them have died, whereas others have converted to Christianity – may God protect us from that! This is especially true for the Georgian and Circassian Mamlūks and women who were taken by the French when they were still very young. I came across an old woman who had remained with her religion. Among those who converted to Christianity, there was a certain ʿAbd al-ʿĀl, of whom it is said that the French had made him Agha of the Janissaries[3] during their time [in Egypt].

1. This is the Andalusian-born poet Abū Isḥāq Ibrāhīm b. Sahl al-Ishbīlī al-Isrā'īlī (d. 1251). It is interesting to note that the first printed edition of his *Dīwān* (lith. 1279/1862) was that by Ḥasan al-ʿAṭṭār. See *GAL*, I, 273; *GALS*, I, 483; Y. Sarkīs, 1928: 123; *EI2*, s.v. "Ibn Sahl" (H. Monés).
2. See Translator's Introduction.
3. *inkishārīya* (sing. *inkishārī*), Tu. *yeni-çeri* ('new troops'). This was the name for the regular infantry troops created by the Ottomans in the 14th century. The members of this corps (*ojaq*), which was commanded by an *agha* ('elder brother' – Ar. *āgha*), were originally recruited through the so-called *dewshirme*, a levy imposed on Christian peoples within

When they left, he followed them, and remained a Muslim for about fifteen years, after which he converted to Christianity – may God protect us from that! – because of his marriage to a Christian woman. Shortly afterwards, he died.[1] However, I saw two of his sons and one daughter, who came to Egypt and who were all Christians. One of them is currently a teacher at the School of Abū Zaʿbal.[2]

I was told a similar story about another one of them, i.e. the French commander-in-chief [in Egypt], whose name was Menou,[3] who took control of Egypt after the death of general (*al-jinrāl*) Kléber (*Klaybar*)[4] and embraced

the Empire, the tribute consisting of children who were subsequently converted to Islam and educated as slaves to the sovereign. With the expansion of the Ottoman Empire, Janissary corps were set up in each occupied territory. The mode of recruitment, however, did not remain the same. In Egypt, for instance, the corps consisted mostly of Turks, though native freeborn Egyptians were also allowed to join. On the whole, the Janissaries (whether at home or abroad) had a very bad reputation, owing to their general undisciplined, corrupt and thuggish behaviour, added to which they were not averse to mutinying against the rulers. Although the Ottoman 'mother' corps was suppressed by Sultan Mahmud II in 1826, the militias in the dominions continued to exist for many years (in Tunisia, for instance, they were abolished only in 1856). In Cairo, the Janissaries performed police duties (alongside their many commercial interests!). See *EI1*, s. vv. "Janissaries" (C. Huart), "Dewshirme" (C. Huart), "Agha" (C. Huart); *EI2*, s.vv. "devshirme" (V. Ménage); "Bāb-i Serʿaskerī" (B. Lewis); B. Lewis, 1969: *passim*; A. Raymond [Ibn Abī 'l-Ḍiyāf], 1994: II, 14–16; *idem*, 1995; G. Goodwin, 1994.

1. In the second edition, the following addition was made: 'It is said that on his deathbed, he was heard crying out: come to my aid, O Prophet of God. He was probably granted a peaceful end as he had returned to his faith. He is reported to have said: praise be to God! My school is that of the Ḥanafīs, God is my Lord and the son of Āmina is Prophet.'
2. This is, of course, a reference to the medical school (*madrasat al-ṭibb*), where al-Ṭahṭāwī himself started his professional career upon his return from Europe. See Translator's Introduction.
3. Jacques Menou (d. 1810) embraced Islam in 1799. His marriage to Zubayda took place on 17 Ramadan 1213 A.H./23 February 1799 A.D. She bore him one son, called al-Saʿīd Sulaymān Murād Jacques Menou (born in Rosetta, 8 December 1800); cf. ʿA. al-Jabartī, 1997: IV, 512ff.; H. Laurens, 1997: 283ff.; R. Khoury, 1978; A. Bahgat, 1898; *idem*, 1900; A. Raymond, 1998: 238, 305. Later on, Zubayda's brother, Saʿīd ʿAlī, became a member of the *dīwān* when it was re-established by Menou in the autumn of 1800 (A. Raymond, 1998: 227). Al-Ṭahṭāwī's accusation that Menou's conversion was insincere is, of course, not far from the truth; indeed, Menou himself never denied the political motives behind his union. As it happened, his action did not convince his friends or his foes: French troops objected to their leader's 'going native' as well as the fact that his son's name bore that of Kléber's assassin, and the Muslim population were equally unimpressed with what they clearly perceived to be a blatant (and to some extent unreligious) attempt at winning them over to the French cause. For a detailed survey of Menou's administration, see H. Laurens, 1997: 395–466; A. Raymond, 1998: 222ff.
4. Kléber was assassinated by Sulaymān al-Ḥalabī on 14 June 1800. This young (he was only 24) Aleppo-born scribe (*kātib*) had studied in Cairo for three years. However, it was in Aleppo that he was approached by two Janissary officers to kill the general. In addition

Islam in Cairo – falsely, it seems. He took the name of ʿAbd Allāh, and married the daughter of a *sharīf* from Rosetta. When the French left Egypt, he took her with him and when they arrived in France he reverted to Christianity and exchanged the turban for the European hat.[1] For a time, he remained with his wife, who had stuck to her religion, but when she bore him a son and he wanted to baptize him in accordance with Christian customs in order to make him a Christian, the wife refused and said: 'I will never let my son become a Christian and expose him to the false religion!' To this her husband retorted that all religions are true and that they all pursue the same goal, i.e. to do good things. However, she adamantly refused to accept this. Then he told her: 'The Qur'ān says this, and since you are a Muslim you must believe the book of your Prophet!' Then he sent for the Franks' most erudite Arabic scholar, the Baron de Sacy (*al-Bārūn disāsī*),[2], since he was able

to the kudos attached to ridding the Muslim community of one of its enemies, there was also a personal motive in that the conspirators offered to intercede on behalf of al-Ḥalabī's father, a butter merchant, who was involved in a dispute with the governor of Aleppo. Sulaymān was almost immediately apprehended and two days later was sentenced to death by impalement; death sentences were also passed on four Egyptian accomplices, all Azhar *shaykhs*. See ʿA. al-Jabartī, 1997: IV, 461ff.; A. Raymond, 1998: 215ff. For Kléber's policy in Egypt, see H. Laurens, 1997: 321–94; A. Raymond, 1998: 173ff.

1. *barnīṭa* (also *burnayṭa, burnīṭa*, pl. *barānīṭ*); cf. al-Sanūsī, 1976–81: I, 83, 117, 118, 120; Khayr al-Dīn, 1867: 297, 336, 409; Kazimirski, 1860: I, 118; E. Bocthor, 1882: 140; E. Gasselin, 1880–86; I, 253 (*barnīṭa*); J. Habeisch, 1896: 117; S. Spiro, 1895: 143 (*burnīṭa*); K. Vollers, 1887–97: 312; B. Ben Sedira, 1882: 28 (*barrīṭa, barnīṭa*). This statement is quite significant, inasmuch as the two types of headgear symbolize Islam and Christianity respectively; indeed, 'to don the turban' is tantamount to embracing Islam. In this respect, one may refer to the Tunisian vernacular *Bū bertella/ barṭalla* (a variant of *barnīṭa*), i.e. 'the holder of the hat', which means 'European', 'Christian'. The wearing of the Christian headdress by Muslims was a highly controversial issue in the 19th century, giving rise to fierce religious debate, the Tunisian Shaykh Sulaymān al-Ḥarāʾirī composing a treatise defending it, only to be attacked by other ʿulamāʾ (e.g. al-Sanūsī). See D. Newman, 1998: 116ff. Also see *EI1*, s.v. "turban" (W. Björkman)
2. A member of the prestigious *Académie des Inscriptions et Belles-Lettres* since 1785, Antoine-Isaac Silvestre (Baron) de Sacy (1758-1838) was also the founder of the Société Asiatique (1822). This prolific linguist and splendid Orientalist trained most of the official Arabic interpreters of his day (e.g. Desgranges, Bresnier). Apart from an edition of al-Ḥarīrī's *maqāmāt* (Paris, 1822) and the famous *Chrestomathie Arabe* (see below), he also produced what is still one of the best grammars of classical Arabic in French (see below). In addition to a political career (he became MP for the Seine district in 1808), his academic appointments included: Professor of Persian at the Collège de France (1806), rector of the Paris University (1815), administrator of the Collège de France (1823), director of the Ecole des Langues Orientales (1824), where he also held the Arabic chair, which had been created for him (1796–1838), conservator of manuscripts at the Bibliothèque Royale (February 1833), where his assistant was the equally famous J. T. Reinaud, and adviser to the Imprimerie Royale. The 19th-century Tunisian traveller Muḥammad al-Sanūsī (1891–92: 132-3) also gives some details on this scholar and refers to the comments made by al-Ṭahṭāwī. On de Sacy, see: R. Blachère in *Cent-cinquantenaire de l'Ecole des Langues*

to read the Qur'ān. Menou then told his wife: 'Ask him about this.' She did, and de Sacy answered with the following words: 'In the Qur'ān the Almighty says: *Surely they that believe, and those of Jewry, and the Christians, and those Sabaeans, whoso believes in God and the Last Day, and works righteousness – their wage awaits them with their Lord, and no fear shall be on them, neither shall they sorrow.*'[1] He convinced her with this, and she agreed to the baptism of her son. It is said that, in the end, she became a Christian, and died an infidel.

Among all the Egyptians I met in Marseilles, there was a man who also dressed like the Franks. His name was Muḥammad. He was fluent in a language other than Arabic, of which he knew very little. I asked him about his hometown in Egypt, to which he replied that he was from Asyūṭ, from a family of *sharīfs*. His father was called al-Sayyid ʿAbd al-Raḥīm, and he was one of the notables of his town. His mother was called Masʿūda, or something closely resembling that name. The French had kidnapped him when he was very young. He said that he had remained a Muslim, and that he was familiar with religious matters [such as the formulae] 'There is only one God, and Muḥammad is His Messenger', and 'God is generous'. It is strange how, listening to his words, I expected a lot of good from him. His face truly revealed the mark of the *sharīfs* of Asyūṭ. If what he told me is true then he is one of the sons of al-Sayyid Ḥurayz b. Sīdī Abī 'l-Qāsim al-Ṭahṭāwī.[2] The *sharīfs* of Ṭahṭā are descendants of Sīdī Yaḥyā b. al-Quṭb al-Rabbānī Sīdī Abū 'l-Qāsim; his third son was called Sīdī ʿAlī al-Baṣīr, whose descendants are people from the island of Shandawīl.[3] The fame of Sīdī Abū 'l-Qāsim al-Ṭahṭāwī does not escape those who know him, even though Sīdī ʿAbd al-Wahhāb al-Shaʿrānī did not mention him in his *Ṭabaqāt*.[4] Many of the *sharīfs* of the Ottoman Empire trace their lineage to the aforementioned Sīdī Ḥurayz.

Among the things I saw in Marseilles, there was a place of recreation,

---

Orientales, Paris, Imprimerie Nationale, 1948: 47-9; H. Derenbourg, 1923; H. Dehérain, 1938; H. Thieme, 1933: II, 686-8; C. Décobert, 1989; Y. Sarkīs, 1928: 901–03; L. Shaykhū, 1991: 68–9 *et passim*; E. Van Dyke, 1896: 15.

1. Qur. II:62; trans. A. Arberry, 1983: 8.
2. See Translator's Introduction.
3. Cf. al-Ṭahṭāwī, 1973–80: I, 542 (*Manāhij*). The modern town of Shandawīl is situated on the west bank of the Nile in Upper Egypt, halfway between al-Ṭahṭāwī's native Ṭahtā, and Ṣuhāj. Cf. Yāqūt, 1866–73: III, 326 (*Shandawīd*).
4. Abū 'l-Mawāhib ʿAbd al-Wahhāb b. Aḥmad al-Shaʿrānī (1491–1565) was a famous Egyptian Ṣūfī, who was a member of the Shādhiliyya brotherhood (see note no. 1, p. 153). The work mentioned here is a list of (Ṣūfī) biographies, entitled *Lawāqiḥ al-anwār fī ṭabaqāt al-sāda al-akhbār* ('Pollinating Winds of the Lights on the Categories of the Masters of Information') or *al-Ṭabaqāt al-kubrā* ('The Great Categories'). See *EI1*, s.v. "al-Shaʿrānī" (J. Schacht); Y. Sarkīs, 1928, 1129–32; G. Delanoue, 1982: 272–4.

called the *spectacles* (*al-sbiktākil*). It is a truly remarkable thing but one that must be seen with one's own eyes since it is impossible to grasp by means of a description. We shall return to this when we discuss Paris.

We stayed in this town for fifty days, after which we left for Paris.

Second Section. From our departure from Marseilles to the arrival in Paris and on the itinerary between the two cities

You should know that those who travel from Marseilles to Paris usually do so by carriage. People hire an entire carriage or a seat in one of them. Each passenger pays for his own food. Alternatively, they can pay a fixed price for the carriage and the food for the duration of the journey. The carriages drive day and night, except for mealtimes and the such.

Every town situated along the way has special places to eat and drink, which offer all kinds of meals and beverages. These places, which are extremely clean and attractive, also have beautifully furnished rooms for sleeping. In a word, they are perfectly equipped.

Each group of us boarded the carriages on the same day. As we travelled from Marseilles at a steady fast speed and since one does not undergo the influence of the wind or the like as one does at sea, we arrived in Lyons (*Liyūn*) in the morning of the third day. Lyons is 92 French leagues from Marseilles and 119 leagues from Paris, whereas Marseilles is 211 leagues from Paris. We stayed in Lyons for about 12 hours to rest. The only thing I saw of the city was when I walked through it or looked out of the window of the house where we were staying.[1]

Then we left Lyons at night for Paris, where we arrived in the morning of the seventh day after our departure from Marseilles. We traversed many villages, most of which contained shops and stores and impressive buildings and were prettified with trees.

On the whole, the villages are adjacent to another, and when one travels quickly it is as if one is forever in the same town. Travellers usually ride in the shade of trees, which line all the roads in straight rows; only rarely are there some missing at certain places.

It appears that in these villages and small towns the beauty of the women and the freshness of their bodies exceed those of the women in the capital. Nevertheless, women from the country are less made-up than those in the capital, as is common in all civilized countries.

---

1. In the second edition, the following verse was added: *He who cannot attain the summits of Raḍwā to reside on one of them has but to settle on its slopes.*

Third Essay

First Section. On the topography of Paris; its geographical location, soil, climate and surrounding area

This city is called *Pari* by the French (*al-Fransīs*), who pronounce it with the Persian *b* [*p*] – which is somewhere between the [Arabic] *f* and *b* – but it is written 'Paris' (*Bārīs*); the *s* is never pronounced, as is the custom in French, in which some letters are written but not pronounced. This is particularly the case for the letter *s* when it occurs at the end of some words. For instance, Athens (*Atīna*) – the city of the Greek philosophers – is written *Athènes* (*Atīnis*) in French, but pronounced *Atēn*. The Arabs, Turks and others write *Bārīs*, *Barīs* or *Bārīz*, and sometimes it is even pronounced *Fāris*. I believe that the most appropriate way to write it is with *s*, even though the reading of the word with *z* is widespread among non-French-speakers. This probably results from the fact that in some contexts the *s* is sometimes read as *z* in French. But while it is dropped in this case, this is not so for the *nisba*-adjective[1] derived from Paris, which is *Parisien* (*Bāriziyānī*) among the French. The reason for the deviation is that the *nisba* retraces things to their origins. However, this rule applies [only] to Arabic *nisba* adjectives, whereas here we have a foreign adjectival form. In some of the poems I wrote on this city I retained the spelling with *s*. I said, for instance:

If I were to have a final divorce from Paris[2]
it would only be to return to Cairo
Each of them is a bride to me –
however, Cairo is not the daughter of unbelief!

I also said:

All the suns of beauty have been enumerated
and it is said that they rise in Egypt

1. The Arabic *nisba* ('relation') – also referred to as *al-ism al-mansūb* ('the noun of belonging') – is formed by affixing the ending '*-ī*' (fem. '*-iyya*'; pl. '*-iyyūn/iyyīn*') to the word stem, and denotes that a person or thing is connected to or derived from something/someone; e.g. *shams* ('sun')-*shamsī* ('solar'); *Miṣr* ('Egypt'), *Miṣrī* ('Egyptian').
2. *ṭalaqtu Bārīsan thalāthan*, which literally means 'to divorce Paris thrice', is used here by the author in its sense under Islamic law, where a divorce is final if the husband utters the words, 'I divorce …' three times; *ṭalāq bi 'l-thalātha* ('divorce by three') denotes a definitive divorce.

If he had seen it shine
in Paris, it would have received a special mention

The city got its name from an old French tribe, who long ago settled along the river Seine (*al-Sīn*) and were called the *Parisii* (*al-Bārīẓīyīn*), which name meant 'dwellers of the edges or margins' in the ancient French language. So, contrary to what some people claim, this name is not related to Paris (*Bārīs*), which is the name of a famous man.

This city is one of the most populated in the world and currently one of the most magnificent cities of the Franks. It is also the capital of France and the seat of the king of France. More details on this will be given in a later chapter.

It lies at a latitude of 49 degrees, 50 minutes North, which denotes its northerly distance from the Equator. As for its longitude, this varies: if we consider the meridian in relation to which the French determine the longitude of all places – i.e. the meridian traced in their royal observatory and whose line passes through Paris and thus serves as the basis for calculations of geographical longitudes by the French – then its longitude is zero. However, if we calculate it according to the meridian used by Ptolemy (*Baṭlīmūs*)[1] for his longitudes – and which to this day remains the basis for calculating the longitudes among certain nations such as the Dutch – i.e. the meridian of the Blessed Isles[2] in the Western Sea, then Paris is at 20 degrees of longitude East.

Here, we should like to explain how to determine the degrees longitude and latitude of a certain place, and how this is used, even though this takes us away from our actual subject.

You should know that astronomers have adduced proof for the roundness of the earth, and the fact that it is not *exactly* round. They then fashioned an image true to its shape, which they called 'Picture of

1. On the geographer Claudius Ptolemy (2nd c.) and Arab scholarship, see e.g. *EI2* s.v. "Baṭlamiyūs" (M. Plessner); M. Young, 1990: 303ff. *et passim*.
2. *al-jazā'ir al-khālidāt* (lit. 'Eternal Isles' – cf. Gr. των μάκαρων νήσοι). Arabic geographers placed these islands (whose number was variously fixed at two, four or six) in the Encircling Sea (which was also home to that other mythical island, Thule). They are commonly associated with the Canary Islands, though Cádiz and the Straits of Gibraltar have also been suggested. They were also sometimes referred to as *jazā'ir al-sa'āda/al-sa'ādāt* ('Islands of Happiness'); Cf. Ibn Sa'īd, 1958: 45; Abū 'l-Fidā', 1840: 2, 6, 87; Ibn Rustah, 1892: 85; Ibn al-Faqīh, 1889: 145; al-Muqaddasī, 1906: 14; al-Mas'ūdī, 1960–79: I, 99, 137; *idem*, 1894: 68; al-Idrīsī, 1866: 2, 28; al-Dimashqī, 1866: 19, 131, 132, 133; al-Ḥajarī, 1987: 18, 43 (1997: 11/64, 44/101). Also see *EI1*, s.vv. "Baḥr al-Muḥīṭ" (Carra de Vaux), "Cádiz" (C. Seybold), "Khālidāt" (P. Schwarz); *EI2*, s.v. "Baḥr al-Muḥīṭ" (D. Dunlop), "al-Djazā'ir al-khālida" (D. Dunlop).

the earth'.[1] In order to divide the earth and more easily gain knowledge of it, they imagined meridian lines, parallels, one axis and two poles, which they drew on the artificial representation. The axis of the globe is the line parallel to the axis of the heavenly body, while its two extremities are the two poles, one of which is called the North Pole, the other the South Pole. The meridian lines are the circles that run from one pole to the other. They get their names from the fact that when the sun is at its zenith in a particular place through which this line runs, it is midday there. The centre of these circles constitutes the centre of the earth. The parallel circles, for their part, are those that run perpendicular to the meridians, and the distance between them and their centre is also the distance to the earth's axis. The largest of these circles is called the Equator. It lies at an equal distance between the two poles, and thus divides the globe into two [equal] parts, i.e. the northern and the southern hemispheres. Like all circles, the meridians and the parallels are divided into 360 degrees, each degree being subdivided into 60 minutes, every minute into 60 seconds and every second into 60 thirds and so on. The Franks have another, new system of division, by which the circle is divided into four quarters, in turn subdivided into 100 so-called centigrades, whereas each degree is broken down into 100 centesimal minutes, each minute into 100 seconds, etc. The origin of this lies in the fact that they use the decimal and metric systems,[2] the latter being the more widespread.

These circles are used to determine the longitudes and latitudes, the latter marking the distance between a [given] parallel circle and the largest parallel, i.e. the Equator. If you take this distance to the north, the northern latitude has a maximum 90 degrees, which is equally true for the southern latitude towards the south. As for the longitude, this is the distance that separates one meridian from another, which is taken as the basic, or prime, meridian. It stretches 180 degrees both to the east and to the west.

On their globes and maps the geographers have marked the distance in degrees between each parallel and the Equator. They did the same for the distance between the meridians and the prime meridian. As we have already mentioned, Ptolemy the Wise drew the prime meridian through the Blessed Isles, but when the land of America was discovered, the Franks decided that people from all regions should take their own prime meridian

1. The Arabic phrase *ṣūrat al-arḍ* is a throwback to mediaeval Arabic geographical literature, one of whose leading exponents, Ibn Ḥawqal (10th c.), even wrote a geographical encyclopaedia entitled *Ṣūrat al-Arḍ*.

2. *al-ḥisāb al-ʿushrī wa al-ḥisāb al-mitrī*; one may well wonder whether either of these would have meant anything to the author's domestic readership!

in their countries as a reference point for other places. And so, the French put their prime meridian in the city of Paris. However, other peoples, like the Dutch, for instance, have continued to calculate longitudes from the Island of Hierro,[1] which is one of the Blessed Isles.

In fact, the obvious thing to do would be to calculate longitudes from a certain point shared by all nations, which would then serve as a reference for the entire world. It should lie in a region known for its advance in civilization or in one that distinguishes itself by merit, such as Mekka, for instance. In this case, it is possible to determine the longitude by taking the time difference into consideration. Indeed, it is known that the sun – or, according to the Franks, the earth – completes its daily movement in 24 hours. So, in each hour it covers 15 degrees of the circle traced by its trajectory, which amounts to one degree every four minutes. This means that when, for instance, it is midday in Cairo, it will be midday in a place located 15 degrees west of it one hour later, and two hours later in a place that is at a distance of 30 degrees, and so on. Conversely, in an easterly direction, if it is midday in Cairo, it is already one o'clock in the afternoon in a place that is 15 degrees east from Cairo, and two o'clock in one that is 30 degrees in that direction, etc.

At this juncture, we should like to mention what time it is in Paris when it is midday in the capital cities of the countries to the west of Paris and in those to its east. In doing so, it is possible to determine its distance from these towns. It is said that when it is midday in Cairo, it will only be noon in Paris one hour and 56 minutes later. And when it is midday in Istanbul, it will only be noon in Paris after one hour and 46 minutes. In relation to Baghdad, it will only be after two hours and 40 minutes, whereas the difference with Aleppo is two hours and a quarter; with Algiers, approximately four minutes; with Tunis, 32 minutes; with Ispahan, three hours and 22 minutes; with Peking – the seat of the king of China – seven hours and 41 minutes; with Derbend,[2] one hour and 48

1. The Arabic *jazīrat al-ḥadīd* ('island of iron') is, of course, a literal translation of the name by which this island is best known, i.e. Ferro. As for the use of the Ptolemaic prime meridian of longitude by European nations, it is well established that this did not go beyond the 18th century.

2. *madīnat Bāb al-Abwāb* ('city of the gate of gates'); in classical geographical literature this term (usually *al-Bāb wa 'l-Abwāb*) denoted the town currently in Daghestan, on the western shore of the Caspian Sea. For a long time the farthest Muslim outpost, it was a major trading centre and port. See *EI1*, s.vv. "Derbend" (W. Barthold), "Daghestan" (W. Barthold). For early references to the town, see Ibn al-Faqīh, 1889: 286, 288, 291–3; Yāqūt, 1866–73: I, 437 *et passim*; al-Qazwīnī, 1848: 340–42; al-Muqaddasī, 1906: 376; al-Mas'ūdī,

minutes; and with the city of Rome,[1] 38 minutes. All these towns are to the east of Paris.

As for the cities that are to the west of Paris, it is already four minutes past midday in Paris when it is midday in Madrid – the seat of the king of al-Andalus; when it is midday in Lisbon (*Lashbūna*) – the capital of Portugal – then it was noon in Paris five and a half minutes earlier. In relation to Philadelphia (*Fīlādilfiyā*) – a town in America – it is five hours and 13 minutes earlier. If it is midday in Rio de Janeiro (*Riyūjānīrū*) – the capital of the sultanate of Brazil (*Ibrīzīlia*) – it is about three o' clock in the afternoon in Paris. When it is noon on the island of *Kunfū* [?] in Muscovite America, it is midnight in Paris, since they are on opposite sides of the earth.

The distance between Paris and Alexandria amounts to 769 French leagues, while it is 809 leagues from Cairo, 740 leagues from Mekka, 560 leagues from Istanbul, 866 leagues from Aleppo, 725 leagues from Marrakech, 370 leagues from Tunis, 100 leagues from London (the capital of the English), 546 leagues from St Petersburg (*Bitirgh*), the capital of Muscovy, 600 leagues from Moscow (the former capital of Muscovy), 325 leagues from Rome (the seat of the Pope) and from Vienna (*Baja*), the capital of Austria, and 384 leagues from Naples.[2]

The height of the city above the level of the Encircling Sea amounts to 108 feet.[3] It is known that Paris is located in a country in the Temperate Zone, as a result of which it is never extremely hot or cold, the maximum temperatures reaching 31.5 degrees. However, this is quite rare, since the average temperature is 29 degrees. The minimum temperature is generally 12 degrees, occasionally 18, the average cold temperature hovering around 7 degrees. It is known that the degree of heat is calculated from the melting point of frozen substances to the boiling of water, the degrees of coldness being calculated from the freezing point of water.

Most of the time, the weather[4] is not clear, with plenty of clouds, so that in winter the sun often does not come out for several days [running] and

---

1894: 60; *idem*, 1960–79: I, 147 (par. 295), 211–12 (par. 447); Ibn Ḥawqal, 1938: 386–9 *et passim*; V. Minorski, 1982: 145.

1. *Rūma al-kubrā* ('Rome the Great'); cf. al-Dimashqi, 1866: 208 (*Rūmiyyat al-kubrā*); al-Gharnāṭī, 1925: 193ff. (*Rūmiyya al-'uẓmā*).
2. While most of the figures are reasonably close to reality, some of them are far less so; interestingly, it is with places in the Muslim world that al-Ṭahṭāwī's orientation and measuring ability seems to have abandoned him, the distances Paris–Mekka and Paris–Marrakech being quite wide of the mark.
3. 18 *qāma*; this unit of measure originally denoted the height of a standing man and is equivalent to six feet.
4. The Arabic *al-zaman* ('time') is a literal translation of the French *le temps*.

cannot be seen. On cloudy days, the following words from the *dīwān* of al-Shihāb al-Ḥijāzī[5] are appropriate:

The sun keeps on staring at us with a mysterious,
hurt eye from behind a veil
It attempts to tear apart the resisting clouds
like an impotent man[6] *attempting to tear the hymen of a virgin*

One poet lost the sheet which had the first verse on it. Stumbling upon a sheet containing the above verses, he completed them as follows:

The clouds have kept the light of the sun from us
and so it remains hidden by its veil
as it attempts to tear apart resistent clouds
like an impotent man attempting to tear the hymen of a virgin

The eminent al-Ṣaftī incorporated this idea into one of his verses:

The face of Egypt is my beloved, but
while I wish to be reunited with her, she wishes to depart
To no avail, I attempt to penetrate what lies hidden within her
like the impotent man attempting to tear the hymen of a virgin

He also included this in a poem on ʿAkka:[7]

And ʿAkka, nonesuch of beauty
holds the pharaonic soul without dowry
Many suitors have courted her to no avail
like the impotent man attempting to tear the hymen of a virgin

Our ruler has prised open the seal, ending her virginity. It was assumed that he would be impotent before it; however, he is strong and capable of

5. Abū ʾl-Ṭayyib Shihāb al-Dīn Aḥmad b. Muḥammad al-Anṣārī Shihāb al-Dīn al-Ḥijāzī (1388–1470) was an Egyptian poet, who has left a number of works, including commentaries on Arabic literary genres like the *maqāmāt* and *muʿallaqāt*. See ʿU. Kaḥḥāla [n.d.]: I, 129–30; Y. Sarkīs, 1928: 1151; *GAL*, II, 171; *GALS*, II, 11–12.
6. The Arabic *ʿinnīn* plays on the word *ʿanān*, meaning ʻcloudsʼ, which is the more easily identifiable agnate of the verb *ʿanna*, ʻto take shapeʼ, ʻto spring upʼ.
7. The inclusion of this particular poem with the prominent mention of the city of Akka is a thinly veiled reference to Muḥammad ʿAlī's taking of the town in 1832, and thus provides an interesting clue as to the time that this particular chapter was written.

piercing the seal of all the cities of Syria and beyond. Thus, he is worthy of the following words of the poet:

O ruler of the earth
you have achieved that which you wanted
The fortress of 'Akka is indisputably yours
It is 'Akka, and much more than that!

The poets of Egypt have admirably chronicled the taking of the cities of Syria and of the *Rūm*.[1]

As for the rain, there is not a season in this city in which it stops. And when it falls, it usually does so with abundance. It is because of this that people, in order to protect themselves from harm, had to build the houses with a sloping roof, so that the water can run down the buildings. In all houses and roads, there are drains and sewers. So, when it rains, the gutters that delimit the roads of Paris resemble canals of flowing water. This is due primarily to the fact that the ground of this city is covered with stones so that the water is never absorbed [into the soil]; instead, it runs towards these gutters, and from there to the sewers.

The changing nature of the air and of the weather in Paris is a strange thing; it may vary in the course of a single day, or from one day to the next. For instance, one morning it may be so wonderfully bright and clear that nobody would expect it to change, but then, in less than half an hour, the brightness can disappear completely and give way to heavy showers. It can be 24 degrees one day, whereas the following day temperatures barely reach 12 degrees. Hence, one is seldom safe from changes in the weather in this

1. This is a reference to some of Muḥammad 'Alī's military campaigns in the first quarter of the century. The occupation of 'Rūm' territory refers to the Ottoman suppression of the Greek revolt, with Egyptian troops conquering Crete (1823) and Morea (1825). Though Egypt was ousted from mainland Greece after the destruction of the Turkish-Egyptian fleet at Navarino (October 1827) by the combined forces of France, England and Russia, Crete remained under Egyptian control until 1841. The occupation of Syria, on the other hand, was a direct result of the Greek war; indeed, when Muḥammad 'Alī was not given the governorship of 'Akkā he had been promised by the Ottoman sultan in exchange for his military assistance in Greece, Ibrāhīm Pasha in November 1831 headed an army into Syria. The Egyptian troops advanced without too much opposition, and in May 1832 'Akkā was taken. However, Ibrāhīm Pasha started marching towards Constantinople, and on the way defeated the Turkish army at Konya. It was only thanks to the intervention of the European powers – with Russia even sending military reinforcements to Constantinople – that a tragedy was averted, and an armistice signed between the liege and his vassal (April 1833), as a result of which Muḥammad 'Alī obtained the governorship of Syria and Adana (western Anatolia). See *EI1*, s.v. "Muḥammad 'Alī Pa<u>sh</u>a" (J. Kramers); M. Yapp, 1991: 69–71.

country. The temperament of the weather, in fact, is like that of its people, as will be discussed later.

Naturally, one must protect oneself against the dangers of these changes, even though the Paris air is on the whole good and salubrious. While its heat does not generally attain Cairo levels, one never gets used to it. Perhaps this is because of the transition from extreme cold to extreme heat. Although it is possible to bear the cold without much fatigue, it is not possible for people to work except if they warm themselves by fire. This is why in all coffee houses, hotels,[1] factories and shops fireplaces have been built in the ground in order to make fire. They are built in such a way that the smoke from the [burning] wood does not permeate the room. In fact, these fireplaces are connected to the outside, with the air drawing out the smoke, which is thus driven from the interior of the house. In some rooms, they have a kind of oven, which is fitted with an iron door and to which one connects a tinplated pipe. This pipe is stuck into an opening leading to the outside. People then put wood in the oven and close the door of the furnace; the smoke rises towards the pipe and from there to the outside. As the oven and pipe become hot, they heat rooms, reception halls, etc. They have another, equally strange thing, called a 'Russian chimney'.[2] Usually, the chimney or oven, which the French refer to as *poêle* (*bwāl*) – 'stove' – is beautifully decorated on the outside, and extremely clean.

A fireplace always has marble sides, the middle part being made out of iron. Because of the beautiful craftsmanship, the French consider it an object of ornamentation for their houses. In winter, people sit around it, and one of the greatest honours one can extend to a guest is to invite him to sit close by the fire in winter, which is hardly surprising. We pray God to save us from the heat of Gehenna.[3] How capable is the one who said:

1. *khān*; originally meaning 'shop', this word was used in the Levant as a synonym of caravanserai (*kārwānsarāy*), i.e. a hostelry offering accommodation for travelling merchants as well as storage room for their wares. F. al-Shidyāq, for instance, uses *khān* for village inn/pub during his stay in Britain (e.g. 1881: 73). In North Africa, *funduq* (pl. *fanādiq*) was used in preference to *khān*, though the former was known in the East as well; indeed, the Egyptian Muḥammad Amīn Fikrī, for instance, refers to European hotels as '*fanādiq*, which we call *lūkāndāt*' (1892: 13). Today, only *funduq* has survived, and it is the current MSA word for 'hotel'. See *EI1*, s.vv. "funduq" (A. Fulton), "kārwān" (C. Huart); *EI2*, s.vv. "khān" (N. Elisséeff), "funduq" (R. Le Tourneau), "kārwān" (Cengiz Orlonhu); R. Brunschvig, 1940: I, 413, 433, 435; M. Callens, 1955; al-Fīrūzābādī [n.d.]: III, 287 ('funduq'), IV, 222 ('khān'); B. Lewis, 1982: 121; A. Raymond & G. Wiet, 1979: 2-5 ('funduq'), 5-15 ('khān').
2. *madākhin Musqūbiyya*, which is, in fact, a mistranslation of the French *cheminée à la prusse* – a kind of stove (*poêle*); al-Ṭahṭāwī is confusing *prusse* with *russe*.
3. The apotropaic formula is connected to the fact that the Arabic word for fire, viz.

Fire is the fruit of winter. He who wants
to eat fruit in winter must be able to bear the heat

In short, heating is part of the everyday provisions of the French in winter as they need it to protect themselves from the cold. By way of protection against the rain they use shields, i.e. umbrellas, which we call *shamsiyyāt* ('parasols'), i.e. sun shields. The French call this thing a *parapluie*. When it is hot, women walk around with parasols, but the men can never do this.

The soil of this city is fertile, rich and productive. How can it be otherwise as none of the many houses is without a large garden with trees, vegetation, etc.? Most foreign plants are found in this city since the French take a keen interest in creating a natural environment for foreign plants and animals in their country. For instance, the palm tree grows only in hot regions; however, the French have tried numerous ways to plant at least one species of them, which, though it does not produce fruit, serves as a sample for their study of botany. It is common knowledge in our country that the palm tree can be found only in Islamic countries. Nevertheless, at the time of the discovery of America, they found palm trees, which, so it seems, could not be transplanted to our country. To this one should add the words by the learned scholar al-Qazwīnī in his book entitled *'Ajā'ib al-makhlūqāt wa gharā'ib al-mawjūdāt* ('The Wonders of Creation and the Marvels of Existing Things'): '*the palm tree is a blessed, wondrous tree; one of its wonderful properties is the fact that it grows only in Islamic countries*'.[1] The palm tree that is found in non-Islamic lands is perhaps a special species that may correspond to the name 'palm tree' used by botanists, whereas that which is restricted to Muslim lands is, because of the favourable climate in these regions, the date palm. This is something one should reflect on.

Near Paris there is a source of cold mineral water. The city is traversed by two rivers; the biggest and most famous is the Seine (*al-Sīn*); the other is that of the Gobelins (*Ghūblān*).[2] Some of the chemists among the Franks

---

nār, occurs in the Qur'ān only to denote 'hellfire'. It is also within this context that one should interpret the author's explanation of the correlation between the degree of hospitality and closeness to the fire.

1. al-Qazwīnī, 1849: 268. The two texts are slightly different, though: '*nakhl: shajara mubāraka min 'ajā'ibihā annahā lā tūjadu fī ghayr bilād al-Islām*' (al-Qazwīnī); '*nakhl shajara mubāraka 'ajība min 'ajā'ibihā innahā lā tanbutu illā fī bilād al-Islām*' (al-Ṭahṭāwī.). One should add that the date palm is attributed with a number of beneficial properties, and is often mentioned in the Qur'ān as 'an example of the beneficence of divine Providence towards humanity'; *EI2*, s.v. "nakhl" (F. Vire).
2. This is the name of the tapestry-manufacturing company (*Manufacture des Gobelins*), which started out as a dyeing works, founded in 1450 by the Dutch family of the same

have stated that the waters that are least mixed with foreign substances are those of the Nile of Egypt, the Ganges (*al-Kank*) in the Hind and the Seine in Paris. It is because of this that the medical profession claims that the water has properties that are beneficial for human health. Their water is far better than that of other rivers for the tasty preparation and cooking of vegetables, the dissolution of soap, for washing, etc.

Within Paris, there are three islands in the river Seine, one of which is called the Île de la Cité (*jazīrat al-Sīta*), which marks the location of ancient Paris. The word *cité* in fact means 'city', and so it would be like saying 'the island of the city'. How different this is from the Nile and Roda Island (al-Rawḍa),[1] and from the Nilometer; there is no comparison between a promenade there [and one in Paris] except for the fact that Cairo is traversed by *al-Khalīj*[2] and Paris by the Seine. However, the latter divides the whole of Paris into two parts. Heavily

name, on the right bank of the river Bièvre, in the Saint-Marcel district (currently in the XIIIth *arrondissement*). The company started producing tapestries in the 17th century, when the Minister Colbert established a *manufacture royale* on the site of the Gobelins tannery. Very early on, the area around the factory was known as *les Gobelins* (and it still is). The river of which al-Ṭahṭāwī speaks is the already mentioned Bièvre. Today, the river, which has since been covered over, still flows underneath the rue des Gobelins. Far more intriguing, however, is the fact that none of the other 19th-century travellers mentioned this river; the only exception was the Algerian Sulaymān Ibn Ṣiyām, who travelled to Paris in 1852, and whose description is almost identical to that of al-Ṭahṭāwī: *'yashaqquhā nahrān aḥadāhumā* (sic) *wa huwa al-a'ẓam wa 'l-ashhar yuqālu lahu nahr al-sīn wa 'l-thānī nahr ghūblān'* (Ibn Ṣiyām, 1852: 13); *'yashaqquhā nahrān aḥadahumā wa huwa al-a'ẓam wa 'l-ashhar yuqālu lahu nahr al-sīn wa 'l-ākhar nahr ghūblān'* (al-Ṭahṭāwī). The only other Arab visitor to Paris to mention the Gobelins (*Qublīn*) is the historian Aḥmad Ibn Abī 'l-Ḍiyāf, who accompanied the Tunisian Bey, Aḥmad, who visited the factory during a state visit in December 1946 (A. Ibn Abī 'l-Ḍiyāf, 1963–65: IV, 106).

1. = This is the second, smaller, island (the other being *jazīra Būlāq*, known as 'Gezira Island' in English) in the Nile in Cairo. Roda is about two square kilometres. On its southern tip there is the famous Nilometer (*miqyās, manyal*) – in effect an enclosed well with a marble column in the middle on which the scale of the height of the river is marked in ells (*dhirā'*) – the first of which was completed in 715. Today, the Manyal palace at the north end of the island houses the prestigious Cairo Méridien Hotel.
2. This word, which usually refers to a 'gulf' or ' bay', was also the name of the large canal that flowed through Cairo. Originally a silted-up branch of the Nile, it was already used in pharaonic times as a link between the Nile and the Red Sea (ending at present-day Suez), but fell into disuse in the 2nd century. It was improved and given a new lease of life by 'Amr Ibn al-'Āṣ shortly after the Arab conquest of Egypt in order to supply the Arabian Peninsula (esp. the Holy Cities!) with corn. However, the role of the *khalīj* – which was by then known as *khalīj amīr al-mu'minīn* ('Canal of the Commander of the Faithful') – as a waterway to the Red Sea ended in 762. Later on, its course was diverted to the *Birkat al-Jubb* in northern Cairo. It was drained at the end of the 19th century. See A. Raymond, 1993: *passim*; *EI1*, s.v. "Cairo" (C. Becker); 'A. Mubārak, 1888: XVIII, pp. 1–35.

laden ships sail on it, and it has nice clean quays along its banks. Nevertheless, it is not pleasant to walk along it. What a difference there is between the water of the Nile and that of the Seine in terms of taste, and other things. If the water of the Nile were filtered before usage, as is the custom with the water of the Seine, it would be one of the greatest medicines. I would also say that there is a huge difference in taste between the water of the Seine and that drawn from wells, brooks and irrigation canals in Upper Egypt.

In short, there is a big difference in soil, water, fruit – except perhaps for the peaches – and the climate between Egypt and Paris. And if it were not for the Parisians' sagacity, skill, excellent organization and their commitment to the interests of their country, their city would be worth nothing at all.[1] Take, for instance, the Seine; on warm days it is a pleasant excursion site, but in winter its temperatures drop to 8 degrees below zero[2] with the result that carriages can trundle around on it. Or look at the trees of this city; they are in leaf in the hot season, but in the cold season they are bald and ugly to look at and resemble wooden poles. However, this is the case in all cold countries. In this respect, somebody once said:

Why, so I asked the branch, are you naked in winter
while in spring you appear fully attired?
It said that spring had announced its advent
and I doffed my clothing for the bringer of this glad tiding

Also consider the weather in this city; in winter and on most warm days, the sky is always dark. If one goes for a walk, the first hour may be nice, while the next one is made miserable as the previously enjoyed pleasure is chased by thunder and lightning and torrential rains. The people there are not bothered by this. On other days, one may quote the words by somebody who described a violently cold day as '*a day on which one's wine freezes, and the embers go out; whose departure makes heavy things light, and whose onslaught makes light things heavy*'. The French frequently visit the places of entertainment on winter nights, without making any effort to protect themselves from the damaging effects of the cold night air. We pray to God the Almighty for protection against the bitter cold.[3]

1. For similar praise on the diligence of the Parisians, see, for instance, Ibn Ṣiyām, 1852: 11–12; al-Ṣaffār, 1992: 157, 159, 160; F. al-Marrāsh, 1867: 21, 69.
2. The Arabic *darajāt al-jumūd* translates literally as 'degrees of frost'.
3. The Arabic *zamharīr* has a religious connotation inasmuch as it also appears in the

If only Cairo were maintained and amply provided with the means of civilization, it would surely be the queen of cities, the pinnacle of the cities of the world, and thus live up to the widespread colloquial saying of its people that Cairo is 'the mother of the world' (*umm al-dunyā*). I praised it during my stay in Paris in a poem, which also included a eulogy of our ruler – may the glory of his rule last forever. Amen.[1]

While Cairo remains devoid of the inconveniences of the cold of Paris, it also lacks the things that are necessary in times of heat, such as means to help refresh the air. For instance, it is easy for the Parisians to sprinkle water on a vast open area in the hot season. They construct a large vat fitted with wheels, with horses pulling this vehicle. This vat has several skilfully made spouts, from which the water is expelled with great force and speed. The wheels do not cease to turn when the spouts are open, so a vast plot of land is sprinkled in about one quarter of an hour, something for which a group of men would need more than an hour. But they also have other devices at their disposal. Our Cairo should have things like this because of its overwhelming heat.

One of the strange things about the river Seine is that there are large boats on it, which contain the best-constructed baths in the whole of Paris. Each bathing establishment has at least 100 bathrooms. However, we shall have occasion to talk of this later.

Among the other laudable things is that, through accomplished engineering skill, they make subterranean ditches that transport the water from the river to the other bath houses in the centre of the city, or to reservoirs. Just imagine how much easier it would be to fill the reservoirs of Cairo this way rather than by carrying water on camels' backs. The French method is always cheaper and easier.

The banks of this river within the city are lined by formidable high walls that are about 12 feet above the water, and along which passers-by can look out on to the river. They are truly masterly built.

There are sixteen bridges across the river in Paris.[2] One of them is called 'the bridge of the botanical garden' (Pont du Jardin des Plantes), which

---

Qur'ān (LXXVI:13) in connection with the garden reserved for the believers: 'therein, they shall see neither sun nor bitter cold.' (trans. A. Arberry, 1983: 621).

1. This is followed by a 48-verse panegyric (in the *kāmil* rhyme) whose turgid language holds little or no literary – or indeed historical – interest today. As a result, it has been omitted from the translation.
2. Cf. Ibn Ṣiyām, 1852: 14. These were: Pont d'Austerlitz, Pont de la Cité, Pont d'Iéna, Pont des Arts, Pont de Marie, Pont de la Tournelle, Pont d'Alma, Pont de Bercy, Pont du Point-du-Jour, Pont-Royal, Pont-Neuf, Pont Louis-Philippe, Pont des Invalides, Pont de Billancourt, Pont de Nortre Dame and Petit Pont.

measures 400 feet in length and has a width of 30 feet. This bridge has five solid iron piers resting on blocks of freestone. It took five years to build and cost 30 million francs. Today, this bridge is called 'Pont d'Austerlitz', after the place where Napoleon defeated the kings of Austria (*Nīmsā*) and Muscovy. This is why that battle is known as 'the Battle of Austerlitz', or as the 'Battle of the Three Emperors (*salāṭīn*)', or also 'the Battle of Napoleon's Coronation [Year]'. Austerlitz is the name of a town near to where the victory took place; for the French, this victory deserves to be a beautiful memory for all time to come. It is because of this that they immortalized it with the building of this bridge, and that they named the bridge after it as a lasting monument to commemorate the event.[1]

The river Seine runs through Paris along a stretch of about two leagues. Its width in the city, however, varies: near the above-mentioned bridge, it amounts to 166 metres (*mitr*). Its water flows at an average speed of 20 *barmaq*[2] (1.2 m) per second, or 1,200 *barmaq* (660 m) per minute.

The surface of the soil of Paris is composed of two elements – gypsum and clay, which the river Seine leaves behind after high tide. The soil consists of several different layers. The first is arable, argilliferous and sandy with pebbles. The second is made up of clay, mixed in with gypsum and seashells. The third stratum is composed of siliceous clay, the fourth of calcareous shelly clay, the fifth of limestone mixed in with seashells, the sixth of salty seawater, the seventh of clay similar to the alluvial deposit of the Nile and the eighth of chalk and chalky carboniferous lime.

Rows of trees run through and surround this city. They have been planted in parallel lines, without a single tree ever being outside the line. The same can be seen along the Shubrā[3] road, in Abū Zaʿbal and in Jihādabād.[4] In the hot season, these trees are in leaf, and passers-by sit under them in search of shelter from the heat of the sun. These kinds of streets are called *boulevards* (*al-bulwār*).[5] In Paris there are exterior boulevards,

1. Cf. Ibn Ṣiyām, 1852: 15.
2. This is originally a Turkish unit of length (*parmaq*), which was approx. 5.5cm (cf. al-Ṭahṭāwī's use later on in the text). Today's *parmak* is about 3.175cm.
3. In al-Ṭahṭāwi's day, this place to the north of Cairo was still a village; today, it is a residential district sucked up by the urban sprawl of the megalopolis.
4. The site of a large army training barracks near Cairo, where there was also a military school; it was here that the famous Koenig Bey started his career in the service of Muḥammad ʿAlī as a French teacher.
5. Cf. M. Ibn al-Khūja 1900: 20 (*bulfār*); M. al-Sanūsī 1891–2: 11, 35; M. Amīn Fikrī 1892: 114–5 *et passim* (*bulwār*); F. al-Shidyāq 1881: 239 *et passim*. M. Bayram V (1884–93: III, 68) divided the roads of Paris into three categories: *āf(i)nū* ('a very wide road lined with trees on both sides, with castles behind it'), *bulfār* ('smaller than an avenue, with more beautiful shops'), and *rū* ('the name given to other roads') – cf. M. al-Sanūsī 1891–2: 11.

similar to city walls, and inner-city boulevards. The circumference of the exterior boulevards is more than five and a half leagues. There are twenty-two boulevards in Paris.

There are also vast open spaces, which are called *places* (*mawāḍi*ʿ), i.e. squares, which are similar to al-Rumayla square in Cairo,[1] though only in terms of its size, not dirtiness! In total, there are about seventy-five squares. This city also has other exterior gates, like the Bāb al-Naṣr in Cairo,[2] of which there are a total of fifty-eight. Paris has four canals, three huge wheels – similar to norias – to transport water, eighty-six cisterns and fourteen water taps [hydrants] in the streets.

One indication of the prosperity of this city is the constant increase in its population, combined with the continuing expansion of the surface and the ongoing perfection and improvement of its buildings.[3] Currently, the number of its inhabitants, by which I mean those that actually reside there, is about one and a half million. Its circumference equals seven French leagues.

The mounts of this city, like those in other French cities, are carriages. However, there is a greater number and variety of them here. Night and day, one hears the incessant trundling of the carriages. More details on this will be provided elsewhere.

Second Section. On the people of Paris

You should know that the Parisians distinguish themselves from many Christians by their keen intelligence, profound perceptiveness and depth of mind when treating recondite issues.[4] They are not like the Coptic

1. This is the name of a vast square at the foot of the Cairo Citadel. It was used as a market place, as well as a military parade and training ground. Though long gone today, it lives on in the name of the city district of al-Rumīla. See A. Raymond 1993: *passim*.
2. This Gate, whose name literally means 'Gate of Victory', is part of one of the few remaining walls delineating Fāṭimid Cairo. The original Bāb al-Naṣr was built by Jawhar al-Ṣiqillī (d. 992), the Fāṭimid general, and founder of the modern city of Cairo. Jawhar also built the original Bāb al-Futūḥ ('Gate of Conquest'). Although today there are still two gates by this name, these are, in fact, 'reconstructions', built by the Fāṭimid commander and vizier Badr al-Jamalī (d. 1094), who also built the second wall around the city and the third surviving gate, Bāb al-Zuwayla. It must be added that the two gates were not built on the sites of Jawhar's originals. See A. Raymond 1993: *passim*; *EI1*, s.vv. "Cairo" (C. Becker), " Badr al-D̲jamalī" (C. Becker).
3. In the second edition, the author added some details on the construction of houses and roads, as well as two verses of poetry.
4. One may again point to a rather close resemblance between the words of al-Ṭahṭāwī and those of the Algerian traveller Ibn Ṣiyām (1852: 11–12): *'al-Bārīziyyīn yakhtaṣṣūna min bayn kathīr min al-naṣārā bi-dhikā' al-ʿaql wa diqqat al-fahm wa ghawṣ dhuhnihim fī*

Christians, who display a natural tendency towards ignorance and stupidity. At the same time, they are in no way prisoners of tradition. Rather, they always wish to know the origin of things, while seeking proof to support it, to the extent that the common people among them can also read and write and, like others, penetrate deep matters – each according to his circumstance. So, the masses in this country are not like some herd of animals as in most barbarous countries. All the sciences, arts and crafts – even the lowly ones – are recorded in books, so it is imperative for each craftsman to know how to read and write in order to perfect his professional skills. Every craftsman wants to create something for his craft that nobody before him has thought of, or perfect that which others have invented. Apart from a desire to increase their gain, it is vanity that pushes them in this, the glory ensuing from a reputation and the desire to leave a lasting memory.[1] They indeed behave as the poet said:

Upon my life, I have seen man after his demise
become the account of what he had achieved and made
As no-one escapes remembrance after he has passed on
Being remembered for good deeds is the most sublime and exalted thing

And according to the words of Ibn Durayd:

Man is but a tale after his death
So, be a good tale for whoever should remember[2]

Someone once told Alexander: '*If you took many women, you would have many children and through them the memory of you would be good.*' He retorted: '*Lasting remembrance lies in good conduct, and it does not redound to the credit of one who has vanquished men to be vanquished by women.*'

The character traits of the French include curiosity, the passion for all things new, as well as the love of change and alternation in all things, especially when it comes to clothing. Indeed, this is never stable among

---

'al-'awīṣāt' (al-Ṭahṭāwī); *'fa-ammā ahl bārīs fa-hum yakhtaṣṣūna min bayn al-nās bi-dhikā' al-'aql wa diqqat al-fahm wa ghiyāṣ al-duhn* (sic) *fī 'umūr 'āmma'* (Ibn Ṣiyām).

1. Cf. Ibn Ṣiyām, 1852: 12.
2. The Basra-born Abū Bakr Muḥammad b. al-Ḥasan al-Azdī (d. 933) was known as a poet, grammarian and lexicographer. The verse that is quoted here is taken from his famous *Maqṣūra* (which he wrote in honour of the Mīkālid when he was chief of a *dīwān* at their court). See *EI1*, s.v. "Ibn Duraid" (J. Pedersen), *EI2* s.v. "Ibn Durayd" (J. Fück); *GAL*, I, 112; *GALS*, I, 172. This is another example where Ibn Ṣiyām was inspired by his Egyptian predecessor since the same verse is quoted in his work: Ibn Ṣiyām, 1852: 12.

them. To this day, not a single fashion has stuck with them. This does not mean they completely change their outfit, rather that they vary their wardrobe. For instance, they never give up wearing a hat (*burnayṭa*) in favour of a turban; instead, they will sometimes wear one type of hat and then, after a while, another, with a different shape, colour, etc.

Other features of their character are dexterity and agility. Indeed, one can see a respectable personage running down the street like a small child. One also finds fickleness and frivolity in their nature; people there go from happiness to sadness and vice versa, from seriousness to jesting and vice versa,[1] so that in the space of one day they can do several contradictory things. While this is true for unimportant matters, it is not the case for important issues; their political opinions do not change. Each person remains faithful to his ideology[2] and opinions and supports them for the entire duration of his life.

Despite their great attachment to their nation,[3] they love to travel. Sometimes they spend several years travelling around the world from east to west, and will actually think nothing of exposing themselves to danger if it is for the benefit of their nation. It is as if they confirm the words of al-Ḥājarī:[4]

All the residences and countries are dear to me
though none like my native land and country

Another poet said:

Move your heart as much as you can from one passion to another
Love only attaches itself to one's first love
No matter how many places on earth a young man calls home
he always yearns for his first abode

1. This is a literal translation of a passage (by the French author Raynal) in the literature manual by J.-F. Noël and P. de la Place, which al-Ṭahṭāwī studied while in France: '*Il* [the Frenchman] *s'affecte avec vivacité et promptitude (…) il passe rapidement du plaisir à la peine, et de la peine au plaisir.*' (J. Noël and P. de la Place, 1823: I, 530).
2. *madhhab* (*madhāhib*), literally means 'place where one walks (i.e. path)', and by extension 'behaviour'; in Islamic law, it denotes a religious school (of thought), particularly those associated with the teachings of the four 'orthodox' Imāms – Mālik b. Anas (see note no. 4, p. 124), al-Shāfiʿī (see note no. 1, p. 101), Abū Ḥanīfa (see note no. 5, pp. 124–5), and Ibn Ḥanbal (see note no. 1, p. 125). See *EI1*, s.v. "fiḳh" (J. Schacht); J. Schacht, 1966.
3. It is interesting to note that the original has the plural *awṭān*, i.e. 'nations', which could equally point to the traditionally strong (even to this day) feelings of *regional* affiliation or pride on the part of the French.
4. Ḥusām al-Dīn ʿĪsā b. Sanjar al-Ḥājarī (1186–1235) was a famous poet from Irbil (Iraq). See ʿU. Kaḥḥāla [n.d.]: VIII, 25; Y. Sarkīs, 1928: 731–2.

Other qualities of the French are their friendship towards strangers and a tendency to seek to be on intimate terms with them, particularly if the stranger is wearing precious clothes. In this, they are driven by their desire and longing to learn things about other countries and the customs of the people there, so that they can find out their intentions both at home and when travelling abroad. Indeed, people are accustomed to expecting things from the world that are unattainable – as the poet says:

People with their different natures
crave from the world that which they cannot attain

The French show charity only in words and deeds, not when it involves their money and possessions.[1] While they do not refuse to lend something to their friends when asked, they never give things away, except if they are certain of obtaining some form of recompense. In truth, they are avaricious rather than generous. We have explained the reason for this in our translation *Mukhtaṣar al-siyar wa 'l-'awā'id* ('Abridgement of the Conducts and Customs'),[2] in the section on hospitality. In fact, the real reason is that generosity is peculiar to the Arabs.[3]

Other qualities of theirs include the punctuality with which they mostly honour their commitments and the fact that they never neglect their work. Rich or poor, none of them tires from working. It is as if they bear out the saying that 'night and day work for you, so you have to work during them [too]'.

Firmly embedded in their nature is the love of recognition and standing, but not pride and spite. Their hearts, as they say in praise of themselves, are purer than those of sacrificial lambs,[4] even though in rage they can be more ferocious than tigers. If one of them becomes angry, he sometimes prefers death to life. It is rare to have a short period of time during which no-one has killed himself, especially for reasons of poverty or lovesickness.

One of their dominant character traits is that they keep their promises; they do not go in for treachery and seldom cheat. A wise man once said:

---

1. Similar comments were made by Fāris al-Shidyāq with regard to the English; praising their charitable nature (which he equated with the Arabic *karam*), he condemned the hypocrisy (*takalluf*) that he felt was often the underlying motive; 1881: 300; 1919: e.g. 337.
2. This is a reference to the translation of Depping's book.
3. Cf. al-Sanūsī, 1891–92:
4. This seems to be a reference to the little-used French saying, 'avoir le cœur aussi innocent que l'agneau du sacrifice', the more usual expression being, 'être aussi innocent que l'agneau qui vient de naître'.

'Promises are like the nets of the noble of heart with which they fish the virtues of free-born men.' Another one stated: *'Ingratitude springs from an ignoble nature and bad religious practice.'* Someone else put it like this: *'Gratitude is a safeguard for kindness; being grateful ensures a sound outcome.'* It is also said that *'a promise by a noble man is more binding on him than a debt is on a debtor.'* Someone else said: *'Treachery and disloyalty harm trust.'* As a result, sincerity is one of their most important features, and they set great store by chivalry.[1] Someone once said in praise of this: *'Chivalry is a collective term denoting all good qualities.'* For them, and for other nations, ingratitude is one of the ignominious human features, and they feel that gratitude is a duty. I believe that this view is common to all nations, and when this quality is lacking in certain people, it is perceived as something unnatural. In fact, gratitude is comparable to the kindness of a father and the piety of a son; although either quality may be absent from certain individuals, both are considered to be innate characteristics by all nations and religious communities.[2]

Another characteristic peculiar to the French is the money they spend on personal pleasures, [the gratification of] diabolic urges, and on entertainment and games; here, they exceed all bounds.

The men are slaves to the women here, and under their command,

1. *murū'a* (also *muruwwa*), which is derived from the word for 'man', 'human being', *mar'* (also *mur'*; pl. *mar'ān*, *marwān*), denoted (moral) qualities associated with virility and manly virtues (loyalty, generosity, courage), which make up 'ideal manhood' and may thus be equated with the traditional European concept of 'chivalry'. In the course of history, the concept, which in pre-Islamic days seems to have referred solely to a man's physical qualities, varied somewhat, and was at times extended to include such features as devoutness, zeal or diplomacy, or narrowed simply to 'virtue'. See "murū'a" *EI2* (Ed.), *EI1 Sup.*(Bichr Farès).
2. *milal*, sing. '*milla*'; in the Qur'ān (e.g. VII, 86, XIV, 16), this word always means religion – Christian Jewish (II, 114), as well as 'the True Faith' (XII, 38). Later on, it came to mean 'religious community', especially that of Islam, *ahl al-milla* denoting Muslims, in contrast with *ahl al-dhimma*, i.e. the *dhimmīs* (see note no. 4, p. 139). In the Ottoman Empire, the word *millet* was used for the recognized religious communities (e.g. the Greek and Armenian Christians, the Jews) that resided within the *umma* and were in charge of most matters of internal government, as well as for the various Christian nations of Europe. It is in this sense that *milla* is most often used by al-Ṭahṭāwī (cf. Khayr al-Dīn, 1867: *passim*), though it also occasionally means 'nation', thus becoming interchangeable with *qawm*. Indeed, in one of his later writings, al-Ṭahṭāwī explains *milla* as follows: 'in political practice, *milla* is like *race* (*jins*), i.e. the collection of people who live in one and the same country, speak one language and share the same morals and traditions' (1973–80: II, 437 [*al-Murshid al-amīn*]). It is also in this sense of 'nation' that *milla* is used by 'A. Mubārak (1882: e.g. I, 316). Also see "milla", *EI1* (F. Buhl), *EI2* (F. Buhl – [C. Bosworth]); *EI2*, s.v. "millet" (M. Ursinus); B. Lewis, 1969: 334–5.

irrespective of whether they are pretty or not.[1] One of them once said that amongst the savages women are destined to be slaughtered, in Eastern countries they are like furniture, whereas the Franks treat them like spoilt children. As the poet said:

Be disobedient to women, for this is rightly guided obedience
The man who hands women his halter will not prevail
They prevent him from developing many of his virtues
even if he were to strive towards knowledge for a thousand years!

The Franks do not have a bad opinion of their women, despite their many faults. If one among them – even a notable – is convinced of immoral behaviour by his wife, he leaves her completely, and dissociates himself from her for the remainder of his life;[2] yet, the others do not learn a lesson from this. It is indeed necessary to protect oneself against women, as the poet said:

Always think the worst of women
if you are one of the clever people
A man is never thrown into ruin
except if his thoughts were only good

And what about the following words a pure Arab directed to his wife:

One of you has betrayed a man
After you and I are gone, the world will have a deceived soul

One of the praiseworthy aspects of their nature, and one they truly have in common with the Arabs, is the fact that they do not have any propensity towards the love of boys or the celebration of its pursuit. This is a lost sentiment among them and one that is rejected by their nature and morals.[3] Among the good qualities of their language and poetry is that they refuse to extol homosexual love. Indeed, in French it is highly inappropriate for a

1. This was also commented on by the Syrian Christian Niqūlā al-Turk in his eyewitness account of the French occupation of Egypt, adding that the way French men behaved towards women was 'different from that of any other nation in the world' (1950: 31/45, 60/79).
2. In the second edition, the author expands on divorce and legal proceedings that ensue from it.
3. Cf. M. al-Ṣaffār [S. Gilson-Miller], 1992: 161.

man to say, 'I fell in love with a boy.' This would be considered repugnant and troublesome. As a result, when one of them translates one of our books, he changes the words, rendering this sentence by 'I fell in love with a girl', or 'a soul', in order to avoid this. They quite rightly consider this [kind of behaviour] immoral; indeed, each of the two sexes finds a feature that attracts him/her in the other, which may be compared to the power of magnets to attract iron or that of amber to attract things [after friction]. However, if the sex is the same, then this phenomenon disappears, and thus we depart from the natural state. The French consider homosexuality to be one of the most disgusting obscenities. As a result, they only very rarely mention it in their books and when they do, it is always in veiled terms. One will never hear people talking about this.[1]

Another of their vices is the small measure of chastity displayed by many of their women, as we have stated before, and the absence of jealousy by their men with regard to things that arouse jealousy among Muslims.[2] A French cynic stated: '*Do not be misled by the refusal of a woman whom you asked to satisfy a desire, and do not infer from this that she is chaste, but rather that she is experienced.*' How could it be otherwise, as among them adultery is part of the [human] faults and vices rather than a mortal sin, particularly in the case of unmarried people? It is as if their women bear out the following words by a wise man: '*Do not be misled by a woman, and do not trust in money, even if there is an abundance of it.*' Another one said that women are traps set by Satan. In the words of the poet:

Enjoy her for as long as she is willing, and do not worry
about whether or not she will appear – she will!
And if she has given herself to you – for sure
she will do so to the next one who asks
And if she swears that distance will not break her pledge –
with henna-dyed fingers an oath is not sworn!

In short, this city, like all the great cities of France and Europe, is filled with a great deal of immorality, heresies,[3] and human error, despite the

1. In the second edition, the author added verses on this topic by *shaykh* ʿAbbās al-Yamanī (q.v. Y. Sarkīs, 1928: 1266).
2. In the second edition, the author added that this is particularly true when it involves the different sexes frequenting and embracing each other. On Muslim travellers' views of European women, see D. Newman, 2002.
3. *bidaʿ* (sing. *bidʿa*), which, in fact, denotes practices not known in the time of the Prophet and the early disciples, and thus inherently heretical. Initially, its theological importance

fact that Paris is one of the intellectual capitals of the entire world, and a centre for foreign sciences – the 'Athens' of the French. Previously, I have already compared Paris to some extent with Athens, i.e. the city of the Greek philosophers. Then I read words to this effect by a French author, who said: '*Of all men, the Parisians are those who most resemble the inhabitants of Athens; to be more precise, they are the Athenians of our day. They have the mind of the Romans, and the character of the Greeks.*'[1]

We have already stated that the French are among those whose decision about whether something is good or bad is based solely on reason. I should like to add here that they reject anything that transcends the rational. They believe that things inexorably take their natural course; that religions appeared merely to guide man to do good things, and to eschew the opposite; that the civilization of countries, the striving of people and their progress in breeding and refinement will replace religions, after which in civilized countries political issues will take over the role of religious laws.[2]

Another of their bad customs is their claim that the intellect of their philosophers and physicists is greater and more perceptive than that of prophets. They have a great many abominable customs. Some among them even deny fate and divine decree, even though there is a maxim stating that '*the wise man is he who believes in fate and acts with resolution in all things.*' At the same time, man should not attribute all things to fate or advance it as an excuse or pretext before something has happened. According to a popular saying, '*to leave many things to fate is a sign of weakness*'. Another person once said: '*If a dispute breaks out, then silence is preferable to words; if war breaks out, then organization is better than trusting in fate.*' Others among them believe that God the Almighty created humankind, imposed a wonderful order upon it, completed it and has not ceased to observe it through one of His qualities called 'Providence', which relates to all possible things, i.e. it prevents any imbalance from disturbing the order of Creation. We shall

---

was bound up with dogmatic changes and developments considered to deviate from the Prophet's *sunna*. In modern times, it became linked to European technological inventions. See U. Heyd, 1961: 74–7; B. Lewis, 1953; V. Rispler, 1991; "bid'a" *EI1* (D. MacDonald), *EI2* (J. Robson).

1. One may well wonder whether this simile would be understood by the author's native readership, inasmuch as it is related to the perception by the European intelligentsia of the time of classical Rome and Greece as the acme of civilization. To al-Ṭahṭāwī's compatriots, however, the Greeks were simply wayward subjects of the Ottoman sultan. It is equally clear that the comparison with Rome and the connotation of rationality, scientific riguour, etc., was, if anything, an even more elusive reference.
2. Similar comments were made by 'Abd Allāh al-Sharqāwī (d. 1812), an Azharite *shaykh* who at the time of the French occupation was head of the *dīwān*; 1281/1864–65: 182.

have occasion to talk about some of their doctrines in another section of the present book.

The people of Paris have a white skin, infused with a red tint. It is rare to find a native Parisian with a brown skin. This is because they do not customarily allow marriages between a white man and a Negro woman[1] – or vice versa – in order to protect themselves against the mixing of their colour. What is more, they consider that blacks can never have any beauty at all. To them, the colour black is one of the features of ugliness. As a result, they do not have two directions in love and the following words by the poet with regard to a black youth are perceived to be indecent:

Your face is as if it were written by my finger
like a word, dictated by my hopes
Its meaning derives from the full moon – however
the night has first sprinkled its dye on it

It seems, however, that their views are better expressed by the words of another:

Truly, he who loves the brown I consider to be in error
The white beauties are far more magnificent and splendid
As for me, I love all young white maidens
with radiant faces and widely spaced teeth
But enough! I follow the true one in love
and there is no doubt that white and fair are true

It is also considered inappropriate among the French to employ a black servant girl for the cooking and other household chores of that kind as they have a deep-seated belief that black people are devoid of the necessary cleanliness.

French women are paragons of beauty and charm. They are nice and amiable company. They always make themselves pretty, and mix with the men in places of entertainment.[2] Sometimes, women – regardless of whether they are of the higher classes or not – make the acquaintance of a man in such a place, especially on Sundays, which is the Christians' feast and resting day, and Sunday night, at the balls (*bālāt*) and dance halls, which shall be dealt with later. It is appropriate to quote here what someone has said:

1. *zanjiyya*, lit. 'female of the Zanj'; see note no. 1, p. 122.
2. This was also remarked (and frowned!) upon by other travellers; see D. Newman, 2002.

The dancers with their flowing locks weaving
on hips as small as hornets' waists
their leanness covered by a gown, yet revealing
where the sashes are knotted and belts pulled taut

It has been said that Paris is a paradise for women, purgatory[1] for men and hell for horses.[2] This means that women here are endowed with material possessions or beauty. As for the men, who find themselves in between both, they are the slaves of women; they deny themselves everything, while pampering their loved ones. As for the horses, they pull carriages along the stony ground of Paris night and day, and when it is a beautiful woman who hires a carriage, the driver overworks the horses in order to take his client to her destination as quickly as possible. The horses in this city are constantly subjected to torture.

As Paris is part of France, the language of its people is, of course, French. We should like to mention a number of things about this now. You should know that the French tongue is a modern form of Frankish, the language of the Gauls (*al-Ghalwiya*), i.e. ancient French. This was subsequently perfected by Latin, with a number of elements added from Greek and Germanic (*Nimsāwiyya*) and a few from Slavonic, as well as other languages. When later the French became proficient in the sciences, they took their scientific terms from the original languages, most of the specialized terms being derived from Greek. As a result, their language became one of the richest and vastest in terms of the abundance of non-synonymous words. The converse is true, however, when it comes to word plays, expressions and the multiple usage of them, ornate rhetorical figures based on pronunciation – French is devoid of all this – or pleasant rhetorical figures based on meaning [puns]. What in Arabic is seen as embellishment, the French sometimes perceive as weakness. For instance, to the French, double entendres[3] are only very rarely considered a good stylistic device to use, and their authors will do so for comic effect only. The same is true for things

1. *al-a'rāf* (lit. 'heights'), which is also the title of the VIIth *sūra* of the Qur'ān, of which verse 46 refers to a wall that lies between paradise and hell. This wall dominates hell, and on it there are beings, the *aṣḥāb al-a'rāf* ('lords of the wall'), who distinguish between the blessed and the doomed.
2. This sentence is quoted by the Tunisian traveller Salīm al-Wardānī, who adds 'and a place of exile for priests' (!); 1888–90: no. 94.
3. *tawriya* is a literary device (related to syllepsis or zeugma) involving the use of rare acceptations of words, in which phrases and expressions (often entire poems) have an obvious 'primary' (surface) meaning and a more esoteric 'secondary' (deeper) one. See s.v. "tawrīya", *EI1* (Moh. Ben Cheneb), *EI2* (W. Heinrichs).

like full and imperfect paronomasia,[1] neither of which has any meaning to them. As a result, all the elegance of an Arabic text disappears once it has been translated.[2] This subject will be concluded later on.

On the whole, each language has its own particular conventions of usage.[3] In French, the inflexions are reduced as much as possible by conjugating a verb with another verb. For instance, if somebody wants to express that he has eaten, he will say the equivalent of 'I possess eating' [*j'ai mangé*]. So, in some cases it is not possible to conjugate the verb 'to eat' except with the verb denoting possession or involvement. It is as if you would say 'I got involved in the food (the eating)' (*talabbastu bi 'l-akl*). And if someone wanted to say that he had gone out, he would say the equivalent of 'I was one who went out' (*anā 'akūn makhrajan*, i.e. *je suis sorti*). The verb of possession ('to have') and the verb of being ('to be') they call auxiliary verbs, that is to say, they assist the conjugation of other verbs, and are thus stripped of their original meaning.[4] If they want to make a verb causative, they say 'I made him the eating' (*je le fis manger*), i.e. 'I caused him to eat' or 'I made him eat', and 'I caused him to go out', i.e. 'I made him go out', etc. As a result, they cannot conjugate verbs the way it is done in Arabic, which is why, viewed from this angle, their language is restricted.

The rules of the French language, the art of word arrangement, spelling and reading together form what the French call *grammatica* (*aghramātīqī*)

1. *al-jinās al-tāmm wa 'l-nāqiṣ*. The word *jinās* (also commonly known as *tajnīs*) denotes an extremely popular rhetorical device in classical Arabic literature based on the use of semantically different but phonetically fully ('full *jinās*') or partially identical ('imperfect *jinās*') words, usually in a pair of utterances. In the title of al-Ṭahṭāwī's book we have, in fact, an example of the imperfect variety – *takhlīṣ-talkhīṣ*; *ibrīz-bārīz*. For a full discussion, see "tadjnīs", *EI1* (Moh. Ben Cheneb), *EI2* (W. Heinrichs).
2. In order to illustrate the use of rhetorical figures in Arabic, al-Ṭahṭāwī quotes some didactic verses exemplifying figures used in the so-called 'science of tropes' (*'ilm al-badī'*) – a branch of Rhetoric – which were highly popular in classical literature. These are followed by seven verses of his own making. See "badī'", *EI 1*, *EI2* (M. Khalafallah).
3. The following exposé is the very first one in Arabic on the structure and grammar of a European language, the author coining new phrases to denote many of the foreign concepts. Another point of interest is that al-Ṭahṭāwī bases his explanations on the French approach to grammar; indeed, though later on in the century other travellers would write grammars of European languages (French, English, Italian), they nearly always did so from the the perspective of Arabic grammar. The only other traveller who grappled with the same problems as al-Ṭahṭāwī was the Tunisian al-Ḥarā'irī, when he translated Lhomond's grammar (vide post).
4. This concept of auxiliaries doubling as main verbs is alien to Arabic, which also does not have a verb to express 'to have' in its general possessive sense (instead, this is achieved by the use of prepositions such as 'by' or 'with' to which a pronoun clitic is suffixed). Similarly, it lacks a verb expressing 'being', except for the negative (namely, *laysa*, 'not to be') or the past (*kāna*).

or *grammaire* (*aghrammayr*), which, in fact, means 'the art of arranging the words in a language'. This is as if somebody used the word syntax[1] to denote everything related to language, in the same way that we speak of 'the Arabic sciences', by which we mean the twelve sciences collected in the words of our Shaykh al-ʿAṭṭār:

Syntax, inflection, prosody and then vocabulary
Then derivation, poetry and composition
Also semantics, rhetoric, calligraphy, rhyme and
history – this is how one counts the sciences of the Arabs

Somebody else added the science of tropes, while another was inclined towards the art of Qur'ānic recitation.[2] In short, everybody is free to add or omit something, and although the boundaries and divisions of the sciences are of my making, they are not to be interpreted as being restrictive. It would seem that it is appropriate for these sciences to be called 'research areas of the science of Arabic'. However, how can versification, poetry and rhyme be independent sciences, and how can inflection, conjugation and derivation be sciences in their own right? Look at what is meant by 'history' and how it came to be considered an Arab science. The early authors in this field were Greek scholars; the first books to appear in this art were those by Homer (*Ūmīrūs*) on the battle of Troy (*Trūda*). The Arabs, on the other hand, composed books only much later.[3] Calligraphy, too, is an ancient art. The Franks put these subjects together in the 'science of speech construction', which they expanded in order to include logic, composition and polemics. However, the French language, like other European languages, has its own usage, on which its syntax, inflection,

1. *fann al-naḥw* (lit. 'direction, path'). In traditional Arabic philology, *naḥw* was subdivided into *ʿilm al-ṣarf* (or *taṣrīf*, i.e. inflectional morphology), which comprises the theory on conjugation, verbal stems, noun formation, plurals, etc. – in short, changes unconnected with syntactic relations – and a more narrow *ʿilm al-naḥw* 'dealing with the relations between constituents in the sentence' (i.e. syntax). In MSA, *naḥw* is still the common word for grammar. See *EI1*, s.v. "naḥw" (Ilse Lichtenstädter); K. Versteegh, 1997: 43; *idem*, 1977: 64ff., 90ff.
2. *tajwīd* ('improvement, adornment', i.e. of Qur'ān recitation) is traditionally divided into three kinds: *tartīl* (slow recitation), *tadwīr* (medium-paced recitation) and *ḥadr* (fast recitation), etc. See "tad̲j̲wīd", *EI1* (Moh. Ben Cheneb), *EI2* (F. Denny); "ḳirā'a", *EI1* (L. Massignon), *EI2* (R. Paret).
3. In the second edition, the author added, 'except if history denotes the way in which to date annual events according to calculations based on the numerical values of letters of the alphabet (*ḥisāb al-jummal*). But even then, to call it a science would be to expand the definition of this word.'

prosody, rhyme, rhetoric, calligraphy, composition and semantics are based. And it is this that is called *grammatica* (*aghrammātiqā*). So, all languages that are governed by rules have a science in which the rules of the language are gathered, either to prevent errors in reading and writing or to beautify it. So, rather than being exclusive to Arabic, this science can be found in all languages. To be sure, Arabic is the most eloquent, greatest, most extensive and exalted language to the ear. A Latin scholar knows all that is related to this tongue, is conversant with syntax as such and other things like inflection, and so it is pure ignorance to say that he does not know anything simply because he does not know Arabic. When somebody thoroughly studies any language, he in effect becomes familiar with another language. By this I mean that if something from another language is translated and explained for him, then he is able to take it in and to compare it with his own language. Moreover, he may already have known these things before and thus he increases his existing knowledge. Then, he can study it and suppress that which reason does not accept. Why not, since knowledge is a natural disposition? And so it is possible for a man who does not understand the lengthy books written in Arabic to study them in French when they are translated for him. And so, work is done for each language, each having its own *Muṭawwal*,[1] its own *Aṭwal*[2] and its own *Sa'd*.[3] Truly, not everything that flows is water, nor is every

1. This is a reference to the famous book on Rhetoric entitled *Sharḥ al-talkhīṣ al-muṭawwal* ('Commentary of the Abridgement of Long Treatise') – usually called, simply, *al-Muṭawwal* – by the grammarian, philosopher and theologian Sa'd al-Dīn Mas'ūd b. 'Umar al-Taftāzānī (d. 1389). It was, in fact, a commentary on the abridgement (*Talkhīṣ*) written by Jalāl al-Dīn al-Khaṭīb al-Qazwīnī (1268–1337) – known as Khaṭīb Dimashq ('the Preacher of Damascus') – of *Miftāḥ al-'ulūm* ('The Key to the Sciences'), the seminal work on rhetoric by Abū Bakr b. Abī Bakr Sirāj al-Dīn al-Sakkākī (1160–1229), who is also credited with being 'the first Arabic author to set forth the influence of milieu on thought' (G. von Grünebaum, "as-Sakkâkî on Milieu and Thought", *JAOS*, 65, 1945, p. 62), some 150 years before Ibn Khaldūn. Al-Taftāzānī also wrote an abridgement-cum-commentary on his own work aptly entitled *Mukhtaṣar al-Muṭawwal*. See *EI*1, s.vv. "al-Taftāzānī" (C. Storey); "al-Sakkākī" (F. Krenkow); Y. Sarkīs, 1928: 635–38, 1033–1034, 1508–9; *GAL*, I, 294–6, II, 22; *GALS*, I, 519, II, 15ff.; 'U. Kaḥḥāla [n.d.]: X, 145–6 (al-Qazwīnī), XIII, 282 (al-Sakkākī); E. Van Dyke, 1896: 357–9.
2. This is the title of another commentary on al-Qazwīnī's *Talkhīṣ al-Miftāḥ*, by 'Iṣām al-Dīn al-Asfarā'īnī (d. 1544). Al-Ṭahṭāwī's mentor, Ḥasan al-'Aṭṭār, wrote a commentary on al-Asfarā'inī's treatise on a philological work by the theologian 'Aḍud al-Dīn al-Ijī (d. 1355), under the title *Ḥāshiyya 'alā sharḥ al-'Iṣām 'alā 'l-risāla al-waḍ'iyya al-'aḍudiyya* ('Commentary on 'Iṣām's Discussion of 'Aḍud's Treatise on Language Composition'). See Y. Sarkīs, 1928: 1330; 'U. Kaḥḥāla [n.d.]: I, 101–02; *GAL*, II, 410ff.; G. Delanoue, 1982: 614.
3. This refers to another book by al-Taftāzānī, i.e. the grammar treatise *Sharḥ al-taṣrīf al-'izzī* (often referred to as *al-Sa'dī*), which is a commentary on the *Mabādī' fī 'l-taṣrīf*

ceiling the sky, every house a house of God, or every Muḥammad the Messenger from God. As the poet said:

How wrong is it think that every breeze comes from the Ḥijāz
Nor does every light brighten East and West

Another one said:

Not every woman with dyed fingers is a Buthayna
nor everyone with an unrequited heart a Jamīl[1]

There is no doubt that the language of the Arabs is the greatest and most splendid of languages. But is it because it is pure gold that whatever imitates it is mere tinsel? How wonderful is the one who said:

The words spoken in Arabic are befitting for their people
Faithfulness leads to error, and beauty to ugliness
The distinction of the expression is that Muḥammad
brought the pure Arabic from the eloquent Arab
and that the opening chapter of the Holy Book was handed down in his language
with what was specified in the speech of divine glorification

In spite of appearances, the idea that foreigners do not understand Arabic when they do not speak it as well as the Arabs is without any foundation. Proof of this is my encounter in Paris with a distinguished French personality, famous among the Franks for his knowledge of Oriental languages, especially Arabic and Persian, whose name is Baron (*al-bārūn*) Silvestre de Sacy. He is one of the notables of Paris and a member of several scholarly societies[2] of France as well as of other countries. His translations

('Principles of conjugation') by ʿIzz al-Dīn al-Zanjānī (*floruit* 13th c.); see *GAL*, I, 283; *EI*1, s.v. "al-Zandjānī" (Ilse Lichtenstädter).

1. This is a reference to Jamīl b. ʿAbd Allāh b. Maʿmar, a famous 7th/8th-century poet, who is best known for his love poems to his beloved Buthayna (or Bathna). The tragic story of their love affair has come to symbolize unfulfilled love. Despite the opposition to Jamīl by Buthayna's father, the two lovers always continued their relationship, even after Buthayna married a kinsman. However, in the end, Jamīl had to flee and died, lovesick, after many years of wandering. See *EI*1, s.v. "Djamīl" (A. Schaade).
2. The use of the Arabic *jamʿiyya* is quite interesting since this is probably the very first occurrence of this word in the modern sense of 'society, association'. Indeed, initially used for monastic communities in Uniate churches, it was extended by the middle of

are widely distributed in Paris, whereas his proficiency at Arabic is such that he summarized a commentary of the *maqāmāt* by al-Ḥarīrī under the title *Mukhtār al-shurūḥ* ('Selection of Commentaries').[1] He learned Arabic, so it is said, by his powers of understanding, his keen intelligence and wide erudition – and without the help of a teacher, except at the beginning. He did not have instruction on, for instance, Shaykh Khālid[2] – not to mention *al-Mughnī*,[3] which he can read. Indeed, he several times taught classes on al-Bayḍāwī.[4] However, when he reads, he has a foreign accent and he cannot speak Arabic unless he has a book in his hands. If he wants to explain an expression, he uses strange words, which he is unable to pronounce properly. But let us here include the preface to his commentary of al-Ḥarīrī's *maqāmāt* in order to give an idea of his writing and his style, which is eloquent, even though it has slight weaknesses owing to his familiarity with the rules of European languages, as a result of which he tends to use expressions [from those languages] in Arabic.[5] In the French

the 19th century to cover (charitable) scientific, religious and literary societies, as well as political organizations (later to be replaced by *ḥizb*) and even economic entities (e.g. *Jam'iyyat tujjār al-ma'āsh*). In Modern Arabic, *jam'iyya* is restricted to cultural societies. Cf. *EI2*, s.v. "Djam'iyya" (A. Hourani/A. Demeerseman).

1. This is a reference to de Sacy's edition of Ḥarīrī's *maqāmāt*, *Les Séances de Hariri, publiées en arabe avec un commentaire choisi* (Paris, Imprimerie Royale, 1822, ed. H. Derenbourg and J. Toussaint, xix/660/12pp.), whose Arabic title was *Kitāb al-maqāmāt li 'l-shaykh al-Ḥarīrī, ma'a sharḥ mukhtār*. A second edition appeared in 1847–53 (2 vols, Paris, Imprimerie Royale).
2. This is a reference to the famous Egyptian grammarian Khālid b. 'Abd Allāh b. Abī Bakr al-Azharī (1434–99), whose works, the most famous of which is *al-Muqaddima al-azhariyya fī 'ilm al-'Arabiyya* ('The Azharite Introduction to the Knowledge of Arabic'), were core study materials at al-Azhar. Indeed, Ḥasan al-'Aṭṭār composed a commentary on at least two of his works, *Ḥāshiya 'alā sharḥ al-Azhariyya* (on the previously mentioned work) and *Ḥāshiya 'alā sharḥ al-Azharī li-Mūṣil al-ṭullāb ilā qawā'id al-i'rāb* (on Khālid's *Tamrīn al-ṭullāb fī ṣinā'at al-i'rāb*, 'Training Students in the Art of Declension'). See *EI1* s.v. "al-Azharī" (Brockelmann); 'U. Kaḥḥāla [n.d.]: IV, 96–7; Y. Sarkīs, 1928: 811–12; *GAL*, II, 27; *GALS*, II, 22.
3. The full title of this work is *al-Mughnī 'l-labīb 'an kutub al-a'ārīb* ('The Intelligent In-depth Guide to the Books of the Nomadic Arabs'), by the Egyptian grammarian Ibn Hishām al-Anṣārī (see above). Silvestre de Sacy translated another work by Ibn Hishām, i.e. *al-I'rāb 'an qawā'id al-i'rāb* ('Exposé on the Rules of Declensions'), which appeared in his *Anthologie grammaticale arabe, ou morceaux choisis de divers grammairiens et scholiastes arabes* (2nd edn, Paris, 1829, pp. 73–92, 155–223). See *EI1*, s.v. 'Ibn Hishām' (M. Ben Cheneb); *GAL*, II, 23ff.
4. The Persian Nāṣir al-Dīn 'Abd Allāh b. 'Umar al-Bayḍāwī (*floruit* 13th c.) is best known for his Qur'ān commentary entitled *Anwār al-tanzīl wa asrār al-ta'wīl* ('Lights of the Revelation and Secrets of Recitation'), which was based on the commentary by Abū 'l-Qāsim Maḥmūd b. 'Umar al-Zamakhsharī (d. 1144), *al-Kashshāf 'an ḥaqā'iq al-tanzīl* ('The Discoverer of the Truths of the Revelation'). See *EI1*, s.v. "al-Baiḍāwī" (C. Brockelmann).
5. al-Ṭahṭāwī includes three pages of de Sacy's Arabic introduction (1822: 3–5).

introduction to this book, he states that the *maqāmāt* by al-Badīʿ[1] are better than those by al-Ḥarīrī. In his collection entitled *Kitāb al-anīs al-mufīd li 'l-ṭālib al-mustafīd wa jāmiʿ al-shudhūr min manẓūm wa manthūr* ('The Useful Intimate Friend for Those Seeking Wisdom, and a Collection of Fragments of Poetry and Prose Works'),[2] he even translated a number of *maqāmāt* by both authors into French. In short, his knowledge, especially as regards Arabic, is famous, even though he can speak Arabic only with great difficulty. In some of his books, I have seen [proof of] his great insight, significant explanations and powerful refutations. He is highly familiar with scientific books written in all languages. All of this stems from the fact that he has a perfect command of his own language after which he devoted himself completely to the learning of [other] languages.

Among his other works, which bear out his great ability, there is a grammar book, which he called *al-Tuḥfa al-saniyya fī ʿilm al-ʿArabiyya* ('The Splendid Gift in the Science of Arabic').[3] In this book he discussed the science of grammar through a strange arrangement, which nobody had done before him. He also published an anthology entitled *al-Mukhtār min kutub aʾimmat al-tafsīr wa 'l-ʿArabiyya fī kashf al-ghiṭāʾ ʿan ghawāmiḍ al-iṣṭilāḥāt al-naḥwiyya wa 'l-lughawiyya* ('Selection of Books by the Masters of Qur'ānic Commentary and Arabic Regarding the Disclosure of Hidden Grammatical and Linguistic Usages').[4] He collected the texts and translated them from Arabic into French. He also wrote other works and translations, especially in the field of Persian, in which he is highly proficient. His fame as an eminent scholar throughout Europe cannot be denied, and numerous honours and distinctions have been bestowed upon him by the great kings of the continent.[5]

1. al-Hamadhānī.
2. This is the Arabic title of de Sacy's *Chrestomathie arabe: ou, extraits de divers écrivains arabes, tant en prose qu'en vers, avec une traduction française et des notes, à l'usage des élèves de l'Ecole Royale et Spéciale des Langues Orientales Vivantes*, the second edition ('corrigée et augmentée') of which appeared in 1826–27 (Paris, Imprimerie Royale), and of which the author offered a copy to al-Ṭahṭawī (see Fourth Essay, Sixth Section). During al-Ṭahṭāwī's stay in Paris, de Sacy published his *Anthologie Grammaticale* (see above), which was, in effect, a sequel to the *Chrestomathie*. It is also interesting to add that de Sacy's original was reprinted in Cairo and edited by Muḥammad Qāsim (Būlāq, 1879, 232pp.).
3. This is de Sacy's *Grammaire arabe à l'usage des élèves de l'Ecole Spéciale des Langues Orientales Vivantes*, 1810, Paris, Imprimerie Impérale, 2 vols (xxvi/434pp.; x/473pp.); 2nd edition, *'corrigée et augmentée, à laquelle on a joint un traité de la prosodie et de la métrique des arabes'*, 2 vols, 1831, Paris, Imprimerie Nationale. It is worth pointing out that de Sacy's grammar is still used today at French universities (the most recent publication is that by the Insitut du Monde Arabe, of 1986).
4. = *Anthologie grammaticale* (see above).
5. In the second edition, al-Ṭahṭāwī included a three-page discussion comparing de Sacy and the Muslim philosopher al-Fārābī (d. 950), based on the fact that both were

The arts in French have reached their apogee, to the extent that for each science there is a dictionary, in which the technical terms are arranged in alphabetical order. This even applies to the sciences of the common people for which there are schools, such as the school for cooking; in other words, a society for scholars and poets of cooking! And if this is somewhat whimsical, it does prove the concern in this country for the exploration of all things, including the most humble. This is equally true for men and women. In France, the women also have great literary ability. Many of them have translated books from one language into another in a style that is elegant, well crafted and faultless. Others apply themselves to composition [prose] and extraordinary correspondence. Thus, it becomes clear to the reader that the saying by someone that '*the beauty of a man is his mind, that of a woman her tongue*' is not applicable to this country, where people enquire about the mind of a woman, her talent, faculty for comprehension and learning.

French literature is not bad, but their language and poetry are based on the tradition of the Ancient Greeks, who were accustomed to deify everything they liked. For instance, they talk of the God of beauty, the God of love, the God of this and of that. Sometimes, their expressions are clearly heathen, even if they do not believe in what they are saying and if this is only by way of metaphor, etc. But on the whole, many French poems are not as bad as all that.[1]

Third Section. On the organization of the French state[2]

Let us now raise the veil on the political organization of the French, and

all-round scholars as well as formidable linguists, the latter being 'fully conversant with 70 [*sic*] languages'.

1. By way of illustration, al-Ṭahṭāwī includes some verses of an unnamed French poet he has translated. These are followed by excerpts from his own translation of *Lyre Brisée* by Joseph Agoub (see Translator's Introduction), to whom he refers as *al-khawāja* Ya'qūb al-Miṣrī. The following paragraph rounds off the quotes: '*This poem* (qaṣīda) *is like other poems translated from French; the original is of a sophisticated nature, while in the translation its eloquence vanishes and the spirit of the author barely manifests itself. This is also true for the elegant Arabic* qaṣīdas, *which are untranslatable in most European languages without their beauty being lost, whereas sometimes they also become cold. Below we shall conclude our discussion of many aspects of French literature, sciences and arts.*'
2. *tadbīr al-dawla al-Faransāwiyya*; which literally translates as 'the arrangement of the French state' (later on also *tadbīr al-mamlaka*, 'government of the kingdom'); depending on the context, it may be rendered as 'political organization', '(political) administration', as well as 'government'. From the point of view of diachronic lexicography, this is rather interesting since the MSA word for 'government', i.e. *ḥukūma*, had already 'acquired the more general sense of rule, the exercise of authority' by the end of the 18th century; *EI2*, s.v. "ḥukūma" (F. Ahmad).

discuss most of their laws, so that their wonderful government system can serve as an example to those wishing to learn from it.

We said earlier that Paris is the capital of the land of the French and the seat of the king of France, his relatives and his family, which is known as the Bourbons (*al-Burbūn*). The king of France must come from this family. France is a hereditary kingdom.[1] The king of France lives in a palace known as the Tuileries (*al-Tuwīlrī*).[2] The French usually refer to the ruling council (*dīwān*) of France as *le cabinet des Tuileries* (*kābīnat al-Tuwīlrī*), i.e. the council of the king's palace.

The fundamental power in the government of the kingdom lies with the king of France, then with the members of the Chamber of the Peers (*shambir dūbayr*), i.e. the council of Peers (*bayr*), who are the people of primary consultation,[3] then the Chamber of Deputies of the Provinces (*Chambre des députés des départements*).[4] The First Council, i.e. the Chamber of Peers (*dīwān al-bayr*), gathers in a Paris castle, called the Palais du

---

1. *mamlaka mutawārītha*. Cf. Khayr al-Dīn, 1867: 411 (*mamlaka wirāthiyya*), 238, 242 (*imbrāṭūriyya wirātha*) 321, 383 (*dawla wirāthiyya*).
2. This Palace remained the royal home until 1870. Badly damaged by fire by the Commune (May 1871), most of it was torn down, and gardens built on the site – the famous *Jardin des Tuileries*, which officially opened in 1889. See C. Courtalon, 1995: 353–4; P. Larousse, 1866–76: XV, 574–5; Berthelot, 1886–1902: XXI, 457–8.
3. *al-mashwara al-ūlā*. It would seem that al-Ṭahṭawī equates these with the so-called *ahl al-ḥall wa 'l-'aqd* ('the people who loosen and bind'). In traditional Islamic political theory these were representatives of the Muslim community who appointed and deposed a ruler. It should also be pointed out that consultation was a process already used by rulers already in pre-Islamic Arabia (especially in cases of emergency), and the need for consultation by rulers is a recurrent theme in Islamic political literature. The Islamic concept of *mashwara* (also *mashūra*) would later be used in Muslim countries to justify the introduction of the parliamentary system of government. See *EI2*, s.vv. "ahl al-ḥall wa 'l-ʿaḳd", "mas͟hwara" (B. Lewis), "mad͟jlis al-s͟hūrā" (C. Findley), "s͟hūrā" (A. Ayalon); M. Bayram V, 1898: *idem*, 184–93: III, 43–4; 22; D. Newman, 1998: 302ff.
4. *Dīwān rusul al-ʿimālāt* ('council of the envoys from the provinces'), with the variants *dīwān/majlis al-wukalā'* ('council of representatives'), and *dīwān al-mashwara* ('council of consultation'), the latter of which clearly referring to Egypt's own *dīwān al-mashwara* (set up in 1829). Later Muslim travellers would use a wide range of translations for the French parliament, ranging from the borrowing *al-Bārlamān* (M. Ibn al-Khūja, 1900: 72; M. al-Sanūsī, 1891–92: 250; Khayr al-Dīn, 1867: *passim*), *majlis al-Bārlamān* (Khayr al-Dīn, 1867: 185, 299 *et passim*), to *Dār al-nadwa* (Ibn Abī 'l-Ḍiyāf, 1963–65: IV, 106; al-Sanūsī, 1891–92: 13ff.), *Dār al-wukalā'* (Ibn Abī 'l-Ḍiyāf, 1963–65: IV, 106), *majlis al-nuwwāb* (M. al-Sanūsī, 1891–92: 13ff.; M. Bayram V, 1884–93: III, *passim*), *majlis nuwwāb al-umma* (Ibn al-Khūja, 1900: 33), *majlis shūrā al-dawla* (M. Bayram V, 1884–93: III, *passim*), *majlis wukalā' al-ʿāmma* (Khayr al-Dīn, 1867: 215 *et passim*). The first Egyptian Parliament, which was set up by the Khedive Ismā'īl, was called *majlis shūrā al-nuwwāb* (1866). Today, the various terms used in different countries still coexist happily with the direct borrowing *barlamān*. See J. Shayyāl, 1951: 214; *EI2*, s.vv. "mad͟jlis" (J. Landau), "mad͟jlis al-s͟hūrā" (C. Findley).

Luxembourg (*qaṣr Luqsumbūrgh*),[1] whereas the Second Council meets at the Palais-Bourbon[2]. After the Chamber of Deputies, there is the Council of Ministers (*Conseil des Ministres*), and the Privy Council (*Conseil Privé*). Then, there is the 'Council of the King's Secret' (*Conseil de Cabinet*), and that called the Council of State (*Conseil d'Etat*). So, the king has full authority[3] in his kingdom, provided the aforementioned councils give their approval. In addition, he enjoys other privileges, which will be discussed together with the French political system.

The function of the Chamber of Peers is to create a new law when necessary or to maintain an existing law. The French refer to secular law[4] as a *Code*,[5] and so they talk about the *Code* of such and such a king. Another role of the Chamber of Peers is to support and protect the rights of the Crown of the kingdom, and to oppose anybody who resists them. This council meets during a specified period of the year. The Chamber of Deputies, for its part, gathers by approval of the king of France. The number of members of this council [Chamber of Peers] is not fixed, but it is accessible to people above the age of twenty-five only, and one has to be at least thirty in order to be able to participate in the consultation (*shūrā*).[6]

1. This Palace had also been the seat of the Directory (1797–1800), the Consulate and the Senate. In modern times, it has been the seat of the Senate since 1958. See C. Courtalon, 1995: 357–8; P. Larousse, 1866–76: X, 811; Berthelot, 1886–1902: X, 336–49, XXII, 795–6.
2. In 1830, the old Chamber was demolished and a new one built, which was officially inaugurated in November 1832. The Chamber of Deputies had its last session there in 1940, but its successor, the Assemblée Nationale (1945), has continued to meet there until this day. See C. Courtalon, 1995: 584–7; Berthelot, 1886–1902: VII, 712–14.
3. *quwwa tāmma*, which is a calque from the French '*avoir plein pouvoir*', with the Arabic *quwwa* referring to '(physical) strength' rather than the 'power (to govern)' denoted by the French 'pouvoir'.
4. *qānūn* (pl. *qawānīn*). In traditional Islamic law, this refers to decrees issued by (local) rulers governing aspects of civil and penal law not covered by the *sharīʿa*, but that did not, however, have the binding legal authority of the latter. The underlying principle of *qānūns* was *ʿurf*, i.e. 'custom' (*lex principis*). By the middle of the 19th century, it was commonly used to denote European (secular) laws; the statesman Khayr al-Dīn stated that '*ḥukm qānūnī* ('law-based governance') is the Arabic translation of *Constitution*' (1867: 239; also see *ibid*.:10, 12, 15, 32ff., 58, 66ff. *et passim*), whereas one of the forms of government discussed by A. Ibn Abī 'l-Ḍiyāf was *al-mulk al-muqayyad bi-qānūn* ('power embedded in law'; 1963–65: I *passim*). Today, it is the common MSA term for (non-religious) 'law'. See "ḳānūn", *EI1* (Cl. Huart), *EI2* (Y. Linant de Bellefonds – C. Cahen – Halil Inalcik); M. Bayram V, 1884–93: I, 44, 46, 66 *et passim*.; A. Raymond [Ibn Abī 'l-Ḍiyāf], 1994: II, 73; M. al-Sanūsī, 1891–2: 15ff. *passim*.
5. This is another interesting example of al-Ṭahṭāwī's problem in translating European concepts, with the use of the Arabic *sharīʿa* – the divine law – to denote a collection of secular, rational laws, thus stripping it of its innate religious character. One can only guess at how this would have been interpreted by his contemporary Muslim readership!
6. Cf. article 28 of the Constitutional Charter; see below.

However, this does not apply to members of the royal household, who are members of the council by virtue of their birth, and are allowed to participate in consultations as from the age of twenty-five. The peerage (*al-bayriyya*) is hereditary and passed on to the male scions of the family, precedence being given to the first-born son, after whose death priority is accorded to the next in line, and so on.

The function of the Chamber of Deputies is not hereditary. The role of the representatives is to examine the laws, policies, decrees and regulations, to verify state revenues, income and expenses, to study them and to defend the people when it comes to duties,[1] income taxes,[2] and other levies in order to safeguard them against injustice and oppression. This council has 428 members and is composed of a number of men who have been appointed by the people of the provinces [*départements*]. In order to become a member one has to have reached the age of forty and be the owner of property on which an annual tax of 1,000 francs is levied.

As for the ministers, there are many of them. Among them, we find the Minster for Home Affairs, the Minister for War, the Minister for Foreign Affairs, the Minister for the Sea and for the Colonies,[3] the Minister for Finance, the Minister for Religious Affairs, the Minister for Education, the Arts and Employment, and the Minister for Trade.

The Minister for Home Affairs is comparable to the *Katkhūda*[4] in

1. *mukūs* (sing. *maks*), 'customs duty', 'toll', 'tithe'. The word dates back to pre-Islamic times, when it meant 'market dues'. It is primarily associated with Egypt, where it was often applied to various types of duties on a huge range of goods, services, skills, etc. See *EI1*, s.v. "maks" (W. Björkman); R. Dozy, 1967: II, 606–07.
2. *firad* (sing. *firda*; usually *farḍa* or *farīḍa*, pl. *farā'iḍ*). Strictly speaking, this tax (known in Egypt as *firde* or *firḍe*) was levied for specific purposes only; in practice, however, it was, to all intents and purposes, simply a poll tax, which Muḥammad ʿAlī set at one twelfth of the income of each subject (irrespective of rank or religion), with a maximum of 500 piastres. Ostensibly, however, it had been introduced to fund an increase in the armed forces. See E. Lane, 1923: 134–5; *EI1*, s.v. "firḍe" (M. Sobernheim); *EI2*, s.v. "furḍa" (S. Shaw).
3. Since the concept of 'colony' had not yet been transposed into Arabic, the modern Arabic term *mustaʿmara* appearing much later in the century, al-Ṭahṭāwī gives an interesting paraphrase: *al-khārijiyyīn min bilād al-Fransīs al-nāzilīn bi-bilād yaʿmurūnahā* ('French citizens living in countries settled by France'), *khārijiyyīn* being a clear calque from the French *ressortissants*.
4. This word of Persian origin ('majordomo') or its Arabicized variants *kāhiya* (Tunisia) and *kikhiyā* (Egypt) originally denoted the head of the Janissary militia. Over time, their power increased to the extent that they were, in effect, if not in name, the true rulers of Egypt (e.g. ʿAbd al-Raḥmān Katkhudā), with the creation of veritable dynasties (e.g. the House of Qazdaghlī). See E. Lane, 1923: 114; A. Raymond [Ibn Abī 'l-Ḍiyāf], 1994: II, 8–9; A. Raymond, 1995.

Egypt, whereas the Minister for Finance is similar to the *Khāzindār*,[1] the Minister for Trade to the *Nāẓir al-tijārāt* ('Overseer of commercial goods'), the Foreign Minister to the *Re'īs Efendi*[2] in the Ottoman State, the Minister for War to the *Nāẓir 'umūm al-jihādiyya* ('Overseer of military affairs'), and so on, although the last-named is not considered a minister in our country.

The Privy Council comprises a number of people chosen by the king as his personal advisers in certain matters; usually, the members of this council are relatives of the king or ministers.[3]

The Council of the King's Secret is composed of Senior Ministers,[4] as well as four ministers without portfolio,[5] and *Conseillers d'Etat*.[6]

The Council of State, for its part, comprises people appointed by the king from among his relatives, the nine Secretaries of State, the Ministers without portfolio, *Conseillers d'Etat*, and a group of *Maîtres des requêtes*[7] and one of *Auditeurs*.[8]

The above makes clear that the king of France does not have absolute power and that the French political system is a restrictive body of laws, under which governance is in the hands of the king provided that he acts in accordance with the laws approved by the members of the councils, with

1. = Treasurer (also *khaznadār, khazandār*). Traditionally, the *khāzindar* was one of the highest dignitaries in the government and one of the most trusted advisers to the rulers. A. Raymond [Ibn Abī 'l-Ḍiyāf], 1994: II, 45–6.
2. In the Ottoman Empire, the incumbent of this office (also known as *Re'īs al-kuttāb*, 'Chief of the scribes') was immediately below the Grand Vizier, and acted as the Minister for Foreign Affairs. It was officially abolished in 1836. In Tunisia, the *ra'īs al-kuttāb/al-kataba* (commonly referred to as *bāsh kātib*, 'Chief Secretary') was the head of the Beylical council of Scribes (*dīwān al-inshā'*). See *EI1*, s.vv. "Re'īs al-kuttāb" (J. Deny), "Bāsh" (C. Huart); B. Lewis 1969: 98; A. Raymond [Ibn Abī 'l-Ḍiyāf], 1994: II, 9–10.
3. In fact, all the members of this council were *Ministres d'Etat*, which may best be described as a kind of emeritus minister without portfolio.
4. *wuzarā'* (sing. *wazīr*) *al-sirr* – 'Ministers of the Secret' – is a translation of the French *Ministres d'Etat*.
5. *wuzarā' ... lahum wizāra muṭlaq*, 'ministers with an unrestricted ministry'; cf. Fr. Ministre en titre.
6. *jamā'a min arbāb al-mashwara fī 'l-dawla*, 'a group of people of consultation to the state'; these were, in fact, senior members of the Council of State.
7. *jamā'at wukalā' 'alā 'l-taqrīr* ('Group of representatives responsible for reporting'), which is a good rendition of the tasks of these members, who were magistrates, charged with reporting to the *Conseil d'Etat*.
8. *jamā'a yastami'ūna al-mashwara li-yata'allamū tadbīr al-duwal* ('Group of people attending the consultation in order to study the governance of states'). Again, the author's paraphrase gives an accurate description of these officials, whose full title was *Auditeur au Conseil d'Etat*. They were civil servants destined for high office, who were attached to the *Conseil d'Etat* (or some other *grande administration*) as a kind of training in order to acquire knowledge of the proceedings.

the Chamber of Peers protecting the king, and the Chamber of Deputies safeguarding the interests of the people.[9]

The codex followed by the French at present and the one they take as a basis for their politics is the law drawn up by their king, Louis (*Luwīz*) XVIII, which has not ceased to be followed and approved by them. It contains a number of things that no reasonable man would reject.

The book in which this codex has been enshrined is called the *Charter* (*al-sharṭ*),[10] which in Latin means 'paper' and, by extension, a document in which restricted laws are recorded. We should like to include this book – even though most of what is in it cannot be found in the Book of the Almighty God, nor in the *sunna* of the Prophet – May God bless him and grant him salvation! – so that you may see how their intellect has decided that justice (*ʿadl*) and equity (*inṣāf*) are the causes for the civilization of kingdoms,[11] the well-being of subjects, and how rulers and their subjects were led by this, to the extent that their country has prospered, their knowledge increased, their wealth accumulated and their hearts satisfied. You never hear one of them complain of injustice. Justice is indeed the basis of prosperity. But let us now cite what some scholars and wise men have said about it – and against it. So it is said for instance that

> *the oppression of orphans and widows is the key to poverty.*
> *Clemency is the veil of misfortune.*
> *The hearts of the people are the treasuries of their king – what he deposits there, he will find there.*

Someone else said:

> *There is no strength without the support of men, whereas there are no men without money, no money without civilization and no civilization without justice.*

9. *al-raʿiyya* (pl. *raʿāyā*); literally meaning 'pasturing herd of animals', it is the usual term from the Middle Ages onwards to denote a ruler's subjects, the tax-paying common people, and as such it is often used interchangeably (as indeed by al-Ṭahṭāwī) with *ʿāmma*, though the latter excluded certain classes. See *EI2*, s.v. "raʿiyya" (C. Bosworth – Suraiya Faroqhi); A. Raymond, 1998: 46ff..
10. The Arabic transliteration is interesting inasmuch as it also means 'condition, provision' (pl. *shurūṭ*), which would also have been conveyed to the reader.
11. This notion would later be subscribed to by other Muslim visitors to Europe, and would be elaborated and placed within a broader framework by people such as Khayr al-Dīn and A. Ibn Abī 'l-Ḍiyāf (see D. Newman, 1998: chap. V). For the use of the terms *ʿadl* and *inṣāf*, see note no. 2, p. 209.

In line with this it has been said that '*kings rule over the bodies – not the hearts – of their subjects*'. Another person stated the following: '*that which matters most in the government of a kingdom is to guide it with justice, and to protect it from harm*'. It is also said that '*if you want to be obeyed, only ask of people what they are able to do; the master charging his slave with something he is incapable of doing gives him an excuse to disobey him.*' As someone said in verse, pointing out that victory is dependent on justice:

Oppressive rulers covet victory over enemies
but oh, the victory was not found to be appropriate
and how can one covet victory if behind you
there are arrows invoked by stern hearts?

Another one said:

He who robs and oppresses cannot thrive
Injustice is a field with unhealthy grass
The bed of an oppressor is a bad one
and the death of the tyrant is truly a bad one
Vengeance will take place – like for like
And fate approves of successful acts

This law codex contains several objects: 1. the public rights of the French;[1] 2. the way the kingdom is governed;[2] 3. the institution of the Chamber of Peers; 4. the institution of the Chamber of Deputies, who are the proxies and representatives of the subjects; 5. the institution and position of the ministers; 6. the hierarchy and judgments of judges; 7. the rights of the subjects.[3] These are the words of the one who compiled the aforesaid *Charter*.[4]

Rights accorded to the French people

Article 1. All Frenchmen are equal before the law (*sharīʿa*).[5]

1. *al-ḥaqq al-ʿāmm li ʾl-Faransāwiya*; cf. '*Droit public des Français*'.
2. The French text says '*formes du gouvernement du roi*'.
3. *ḥuqūq al-raʿiya* cf. '*Droits particuliers garantis par l'Etat*'!
4. In the following translation of the *Charte constitutionnelle* of 4 June 1814, al-Ṭahṭāwī omitted the preamble and the *articles transitoires* (articles 75–76).
5. The French text adds '*quels que soient d'ailleurs leurs titres et leurs rangs*' ('irrespective of their title and rank').

Article 2. They all, without distinction, contribute a fixed sum to the Treasury from their property – each person according to his means.

Article 3. Each of them is eligible for any office, irrespective of its rank.[1]

Article 4. Each of them is free, and their freedom is guaranteed. No-one can be interfered with except in accordance with some rights laid down in the law, in the form prescribed by it and as requested by the ruler.[2]

Article 5. Each resident of France may practise his religion as he pleases, without interference from anyone, and can even ask assistance for this. It is forbidden to prevent anyone from performing his worship.[3]

Article 6. It is stipulated that the state belongs to the Apostolic Roman Catholic religion.[4]

Article 7. Those connected with the Catholic or other Christian churches will be paid a sum by the Christian Treasury. However, no funds will be awarded for the maintenance of places of worship of other religions.[5]

---

1. *kull wāḥid minhum muta'ahhal li 'akhdhi ayy manṣib kāna wa ayy rataba kānat*; cf. '*Ils sont tous également admissibles aux emplois civils et militaires*'.
2. '*Leur liberté individuelle est également garantie, personne ne pouvant être poursuivi ni arrêté que dans les cas prévus par la loi, et dans la forme qu'elle prescrit*'. Evidently, al-Ṭahṭāwī did not quite know how to deal with the French '*poursuivi ni arrêté*' ('neither prosecuted nor arrested'), whereas he saw fit to add a reference to the ruler (*al-ḥākim*). However, the real importance of this article lies elsewhere; it contains the first use in Arabic literature of *ḥurriyya* in the European sense of '(personal) freedom', as previously it was simply the opposite of 'enslaved'. It should be added that *ḥurriyya* would become a key component within 19th-century Arab (as well as Ottoman) political thought, such people as Khayr al-Dīn and indeed al-Ṭahṭāwī himself considering it a pillar of progress and civilization (1973–80: II, 470ff. [*al-Murshid al-amīn*]), as well as of personal well-being. In one of his later works, al-Ṭahṭāwī devotes an entire chapter to liberty (1973–80: II, 473–7 [*al-Murshid al-amīn*]), describing it as 'the faculty to perform a lawful task without any unlawful impediment or prohibited opposition', while 'the rights of all people in a civilized country are rooted in freedom'. At the same time, he also revealed a clear influence from Montesquieu as he, too, distinguished between five freedoms (1973–80: II, 473–4 [*al-Murshid al-amīn*]); cf. Montesquieu, 1979: *passim*, e.g. I, 328 [Book XXII, chap. xii]). See *EI2*, s.v. "ḥurriyya" (F. Rosenthal/B. Lewis); B. Lewis, 1969: 129ff.; A. Ayalon, 1989; A. Hourani, 1989; N. Yared, 1996: 18–23; D. Newman, 1998: 309ff.; al-Ṭahṭāwī, 1973–80: I, 346 (*Manāhij*), L. Zolondek, 1964; S. Ali, 1994: 8ff.; B. Tlili, 1972b; A. Ibn Abī 'l-Ḍiyāf, 1963–65: I, 16, 27, III, 169, IV, 99, 103; H. Rebhan 1986: 99ff.
3. '*Chacun professe sa religion avec une égale liberté, et obtient pour son culte la même protection.*'
4. *al-milla al-qāthūlīqiyya al-ḥawāriyya al-Rūmāniyya*. The French text states quite emphatically that '*la religion catholique, apostolique et romaine est* la religion de l'Etat' (my emphasis).
5. '*Les ministres de la religion catholique, apostolique et romaine, et ceux des autres cultes chrétiens, reçoivent seuls des traitements du trésor royal.*' The first point worth mentioning is the use of *ta'mīr* (*al-kanā'is*) instead of, simply, 'priests' (*qiss*), al-Ṭahṭāwī's translation referring to the expression *'ammara al-masjid* ('to withdraw from the world to a mosque for prayer'). Equally strange is his reference to the 'Christian Treasury'.

Article 8. French people may not be prevented from expressing their opinions, writing them down and printing them, provided they are not in breach of the law, which will suppress them if they are harmful.[1]

Article 9. All properties and lands are inviolable and no distinction is made between one property and another.[2]

Article 10. Only the state has the right to force a person to sell real estate property in the public interest, on condition that a commensurate price be paid prior to the takeover.[3]

Article 11. All opinions and discord prior to the present legal code must be disregarded, as must everything that happened to the courts and the people of the country.[4]

Article 12. The recruitment of soldiers is reorganized and reduced. It will thenceforth be governed by a specific law setting forth the [number of] army and navy soldiers.[5]

The way the kingdom is governed

Article 13. The king's person is inviolable, and his ministers are answerable to him for everything, i.e. they are the ones who request and judge things, but a decision can be carried out only by an executive order of the king.[6]

Article 14. The king is the highest authority of the people of the state, and it is he who commands and raises the army and navy soldiers, declares war and peace and enters into alliances and trade between his nation (*milla*)

1. '*Les Français ont le droit de publier et de faire imprimer leurs opinions, en se conformant aux lois qui doivent réprimer les abus de cette liberté.*' Interestingly, both '*abus*' (Ar. *ḍarr*, 'damage, harm') and '*liberté*' have been omitted by al-Ṭahṭāwī.
2. Al-Ṭahtāwī uses the highly religiously charged *ḥaram* for 'inviolable'.
3. Undoubtedly the most interesting point of translation here is the French '*pour cause d'intérêt public légalement constaté*', which the author renders through the calque '*li-sabab 'āmm al-naf'*', thus missing the underlying idea of 'the public interest/welfare'. This concept would have been better rendered by *maṣlaḥa*; cf. *EI2*, s.v. "maṣlaḥa" (Madjid Khadduri); Khayr al-Dīn, 1867: *passim*; al-Ṭahṭāwī, 1973–80: I, 517ff. (*Manāhij*).
4. '*Toutes recherches des opinions et votes émis jusqu'à la Restauration sont interdites. Le même oubli est commandé aux tribunaux et aux citoyens.*' Al-Ṭahṭāwī omits the '*recherches*' and bypasses the crucial reference to the 'Restoration'.
5. '*La conscription est abolie. Le mode de recrutement de l'armée de terre et de mer est determiné par une loi.*'
6. This is a rather convoluted translation of the French '*La personne du roi est inviolable et sacrée. Ses ministres sont responsables. Au roi seul appartient la puissance exécutive.*', with *kufalā'* (sing. *kafīl*), which literally means 'bondsmen', used for *responsables*. Unsurprisingly, al-Ṭahṭāwī thought it politic to omit any mention to the 'sacredness' of the king, restricting the translation to *muḥtaram* ('esteemed, respected')!

and others, makes appointments for key positions, renews some laws and policies and gives the necessary orders with a view to their execution, if this is to the benefit of the state.[1]

Article 15. The organization of issues related to human relations is carried out by the king, the Chamber of Peers and the Chamber of Deputies.[2]

Article 16. The king alone divides the laws, and determines their publication and announcement.[3]

Article 17. A law is sent by order of the king first to the Chamber of Peers, then to the Chamber of Deputies – except the law on taxes, duties, and imposts,[4] which is sent to the Chamber of Deputies first.

Article 18. The state executes laws only if they have been agreed by the majority (*jumhūr*) of both Chambers.

Article 19. Either of the Chambers may request that the king announce an Act on any matter that they deem useful for inclusion into the law.

Article 20. Such an Act can be made by either of the Chambers in a secret meeting, whereas a decision on it is expressed by the Chamber that has made it, after which it is sent to the other Chamber only after a deliberation period of ten days.

Article 21. If the other Chamber endorses the law, then it is presented to the king; if it is rejected by this Chamber, then it cannot come before this Chamber during the session of that year.

Article 22. The king alone approves laws and promulgates them to the people.

Article 23. The income of the king is fixed for him for the period of his reign in one way: it may not exceed or be smaller than the amount determined during his presidency of the Chamber of Peers, i.e. the First Consultative Council.

Article 24. The Chamber of Peers is a crucial stage in the creation of the laws of governance.[5]

---

1. The last phrase was added by al-Ṭahṭāwī.
2. This is the rather creative as well as cryptic translation of the French '*La puissance législative s'exerce collectivement par le roi, la chambre des pairs, et la chambre des députés des départements.*'
3. Another example of poetic licence on the part of the translator who elaborates freely on the French '*Le roi propose la loi*'!
4. *jabāyāt wa 'l-firda* ('imposts and poll tax'), whereas the French text simply has '*impôts*'. The mention of individual taxes (also see below) can be explained by the fact that, at the time, there was no generic word for civil taxes in Arabic (cf. MSA *ḍarība*, pl. *ḍarā'ib*). For general information on taxes and tax systems in Muslim countries, see *EI2*, s. vv. "bayt al-māl" (N. Coulson – B. Lewis), "ḍarība" (C. Cahen – J. Hopkins – Helen Rivlin).
5. It is again the '*puissance législative*' that seems to pose problems to al-Ṭahṭāwī, who this time chooses the rather circuitous '*tashrī' al-qawānīn al-tadbīriyya*'. Furthermore, none

Article 25. This Chamber convenes and its session is opened for a period of months by order of the king at the same time as that of the Chamber of Deputies. Both Chambers start and finish their sessions on the same day.

Article 26. If the Chamber of Peers were to gather before the opening of the Chamber of Deputies, or before the king of France has given his permission, all measures issued by this council during its meeting would be illegal and null and void.[1]

Article 27. The appointment[2] of somebody as a Peer of France is the sole right of the king. The number of members of the Chamber of Peers is not restricted, and the king may change the titles[3] at will; furthermore, he can make people Peers for the duration of their lifetime or make the title hereditary, whatever is his pleasure.

Article 28. The Peers may enter the Chamber at the age of twenty-five, but they cannot express their views in the consultative assembly until they have reached the age of thirty-five.

Article 29. The president of the Chamber of Peers is the Supreme Judge of France, who is proficient in the affairs of the royal household; this is, in fact, the Minister of the Seal of the king. If he is excused, a substitute is appointed by the king from among the members of the House for this purpose.

Article 30. The members of the royal household and blood relatives to the king are granted entry to the ranks of the peerage solely by virtue of their birth. During meetings of the Chamber all of them are seated behind the president. However, they may not speak or express their opinions in the council until they have reached the age of twenty-five.

Article 31. None of the members of the Chamber of Peers may enter this council when it is in session, except by permission from the king, which is sent by messenger. If they do, everything that is done in their presence is null and void.

---

of the editions of the *Takhlīṣ* mentions that this is in fact the first article of the section (articles no. 24–34) on the Chamber of Peers ('*De la chambre des pairs*'), despite the fact that it is listed in the paragraph immediately preceding the translation.

1. The French '*illicite (et nulle de plein droit)*' al-Ṭahṭāwī translates as *mamnūʿ al-imḍāʾ* (namely, 'forbidden to execute').
2. Al-Ṭahṭāwī chooses the word *tasmiya*, which, though it can mean 'appointment,' is usually used for 'nomination', instead of the more common *taʿyīn*. It is of course tempting to speculate that he was misled by this 'false friend' (which is a bane to many an English-speaker as well) by the *nom* in the French 'nomination'.
3. In an attempt to make this more understandable to his readership, al-Ṭahṭāwī opted for *laqab*, as a translation of the French *dignité* (namely, 'title'). Strictly speaking, however, *laqab* is an honorific nickname or title attached to a person's name. Examples include *ḥājj*, *Nūr al-Dīn* ('Light of the Faith').

Article 32. All the opinions expressed by the Chamber of Peers must be kept secret.

Article 33. The King's Council (*majlis al-malik*) tries acts of treason against the state [high treason] and other such offences as cause harm to the state that are set forth in laws.

Article 34. None of the members of the Chamber of Peers can be arrested, except by order of this council, nor can any of them be judged by any other authority when it involves criminal matters.

The Chamber of Deputies, who are the authorized representatives of the people

Article 35. The Chamber of Deputies is composed of all envoys elected by the voters, whom they call *électeurs* (*illiktūr*),[1] the organization being determined by special laws.

Article 36. Each province (*département*) has the same number of representatives it had prior to the introduction of this Charter.

Article 37. Henceforth, the envoys will remain [in the Chamber] for seven years, instead of five as was the case before.[2]

Article 38. A person cannot be allowed entry into the Chamber of Deputies except if he has reached the age of forty, and provided he owns property on which he pays a tax[3] to the amount of 1,000 francs.

Article 39. Each province must gather fifty people that are resident there, meet the age criterion and own the aforesaid property in order to choose the envoys from among them. If the required number of people who pay 1,000 francs [in taxes] cannot be found, then the quorum can be completed by those holding property [on which] less than 1,000 francs is paid, who can then elect the envoys from the entire group of fifty.

Article 40. The electoral college[4] that elects the envoys cannot cast their vote unless they own property on which they pay a tax of 300 francs, and if they have reached the age of thirty.

Article 41. The presidents of the electoral councils are elected by the king and are [automatically] members of the college.[5]

1. The French text refers to '*collèges électoraux*'.
2. Here, al-Ṭahṭāwī's creativity took him a bit too far from the French text – '*Les députés seront élus pour cinq ans* (sic), *et de manière que la chambre soit renouvelée chaque année par cinquième.*'
3. Cf. '... *une contribution directe*', al-Ṭahṭāwī adding the reference to property.
4. *shuraṭ illiktūrāy*, which would translate literally as 'electoral guard/troop'.
5. Cf. '*seront ... de droit membres du collège.*'

Article 42. At least half of the envoys from a province must have their permanent residence there.[1]

Article 43. The president of the Chamber of Deputies is appointed by the king and chosen from among fifty representatives presented by this council.

Article 44. The meetings of this Chamber are public, except if [at least] five of its members ask for something to be kept secret, as a result of which people who are not part of the Chamber are permitted to leave.[2]

Article 45. The Chamber is divided into small councils called *bureaux* (*al-būrū*), i.e. offices, whose members are entrusted with examining matters designated and submitted by the king.[3]

Article 46. There can be no rectification of any issues related to the form of policies of France[4] unless the king approves it, or if it has not been examined within these *bureaux*.

Article 47. The Chamber of Deputies receives reports related to requests for duties, taxes and imposts, and it is only after they have been approved by this Chamber that they can be sent to the Chamber of Peers.[5]

Article 48. No royal decree regarding the poll tax can be executed except if it has been approved by both Chambers and read by the king.

Article 49. Land and real estate property tax is fixed from one year to the next. Other taxes can be fixed for [another] fixed period.[6]

Article 50. It is incumbent upon the king to order the opening of both Chambers each year. However, the time at which this takes place is at his discretion.[7] Furthermore, only the king can dissolve the Chamber of Deputies on condition that he puts together a new Chamber of Deputies within a period that does not extend three months.

Article 51. No member of the Chamber of Deputies can be arrested when

1. Al-Ṭahṭāwī talks of 'usually being settled there' (*mustawṭan 'āda*), whereas the French text has '*leur domicile politique*'. In fact, this expression, which can still be found in French law today, means that in order to be elected in a certain district, etc., one's *principal* residence must be there. Proof of this are the electoral rolls of said electoral district.
2. Again, the author adds a little extra to the French ('*Les séances de la chambre sont publiques; mais la demande de cinq membres suffit pour qu'elle se forme en comité secret*'); the French phrase '*personnes étrangères à la chambre*' clearly shines through in the Arabic *al-nās al-ajānib min al-dīwān*.
3. Cf. '*La chambre se partage en bureaux* (*al-dīwān yanqasimu ilā dawāwīn ṣaghīra*) *pour discuter les projets qui lui ont été présentés de la part du roi.*'
4. *ādāb siyāsāt Faransā*; cf. Fr. '*aucun amendement ne peut être fait à une loi*'.
5. Cf. '*La chambre des députés reçoit toutes les propositions d'impôts; ce n'est qu'après que ces propositions ont été admises, qu'elles peuvent être portées à la chambre des pairs.*'
6. Cf. '*Les impositions indirectes peuvent l'être pour plusieurs années.*'
7. Cf. '*Le roi convoque chaque année les deux chambres.*'

it is in session, nor in the period of one month preceding the opening, and one month and a half after [the end of] it.[1]

Article 52. When the Chamber is in session, none of its members may be prosecuted[2] for a matter related to a criminal offence, except if he is caught in the act, and after permission has been granted by the Chamber to apprehend him.

Article 53. A petition presented to one of the Chambers cannot be accepted unless it has been put in writing. French political etiquette[3] does not permit a person to submit a report [in person] to the council.

The ministers

Article 54. It is allowed for ministers to be members of either Chamber, whereas they also have the right to attend either of them. When they express the wish to speak in the Chamber, they must be allowed to do so.

Article 55. The Chamber of Deputies has the right to accuse ministers, and to bring proceedings before the Chamber of Peers, in whose midst they will be judged, and who will settle the dispute between the two parties.

Article 56. A minister cannot be accused except for treason, corruption or misappropriation of funds. He will be judged in accordance with the provisions set forth in the laws governing litigation.[4]

The judges

Article 57. The administration of justice is the prerogative of the king, and it is viewed as if it came from him. The judges put in office by the king and paid by the Treasury dispense justice and pass judgments in name of the king.[5]

---

1. Again, al-Ṭahṭāwī changes the French text substantially – '*Aucune contrainte par corps ne peut être exercée contre un membre de la chambre, durant la session, et dans les six semaines qui l'auront précédée ou suivie.*'
2. The Arabic *yutbaʿu* (< *tabaʿa*','to pursue', 'to chase') is clearly a calque from the French '*être poursuivi*'.
3. *ādāb al-siyāsa al-Faransāwiyya*, 'French political practices'; (cf. '*la loi*').
4. Cf. '*Ils ne peuvent être accusés que pour fait de trahison ou de concussion. Des lois particulières spécifieront cette nature de délits, et en détermineront la poursuite.*' One may well wonder whether al-Ṭahṭāwī's addition of 'corruption' was prompted by the translator's desire for completeness, or whether it was a veiled accusation at the widespread and egregious venality of public officials in his native land.
5. It seems that here the author is putting into relief a presumption of impartiality in the French judiciary as the French text simply states '*Toute justice émane du roi. Elle s'administre en son nom par des juges qu'il nomme et institue.*'

Article 58. If the king has appointed someone judge, he must remain in office, and it is not permitted to remove him.

Article 59. The judiciary in place at the time of this Charter cannot be removed, except if another law sets out new provisions.

Article 60. The institution of judges dealing with commercial transactions can never be abolished.

Article 61. The institution of justices of the peace is also retained; however, a justice of the peace may be removed, even though they are appointed to their post by the king.

Article 62. Nothing may be relieved from the judgment of those judges.[1]

Article 63. Because of the previous, it is not permitted to set up new additional courts or councils, except for the kind of justice they call *prévotal* (*barbūtāl*),[2] if this is deemed necessary.

Article 64. Proceedings and debates between opposing parties before the judge are public in criminal matters[3] except if the fact of divulging it among the public at large is harmful or offends virtue, in which case the court notifies people that the case in question will be treated in secret [*in camera*].

Article 65. The institution of the group of arbitrators, called 'criminal *jury* (*jūriya*)' will never be abolished, except if it is necessary to change something in the judicial sphere, which can be done only through a law passed in both Chambers.[4]

Article 66. The law punishing people by appropriation of their estates is entirely abolished and can never be reintroduced.

Article 67. The king is entitled to pardon people and to reduce the punishments.

Article 68. The provisions contained in the codices of administrative law[5] in force, and which do not run counter the contents of the present Charter, will not be abrogated, except if they are changed by another law.[6]

---

1. *lā shayy' yukhriju 'an ḥukm hā'ulā'i 'l-qaḍā'*; cf. '*Nul ne pourra être distrait de ses juges naturels.*'
2. Al-Ṭahṭāwī also gives *qaḍāt al-nuqabā'* [sing. *naqīb*], i.e. 'leader of a guild, community', or 'governor, prefect' – cf. *EI2*, s.v. "naḳīb" (C. Bosworth)] for *justice prévotal*. The office of *prévot* ('provost') may be equated with that of a local magistrate. Their jurisdiction was often quite circumscribed and specialized: e.g. *prévot des maréchaux* (highway offences). Furthermore, the term was also used to denote the chief of certain guilds (e.g. *prévot des chirurgiens*).
3. Cf. '*Les débats seront publics en matière criminelle.*'
4. Cf. '*L'institution des jurés* (*'jamā'at al-muḥakkamiyyīn'*, 'group of arbiters') *est conservée. Les changements qu'une plus longue expérience ferait juger nécessaires, ne peuvent être effectués que par une loi.*'
5. *kutub qawānīn al-siyāsāt*; cf. '*le code civil*'.
6. The French text is rather more vague here – '*restent en vigueur jusqu'à ce qu'il y soit*

The rights of the subjects guaranteed by the Chamber[1]

Article 69. Every soldier in permanent service or those who have retired, and every woman who was married to a soldier who has died, retain their ranks, titles and incomes for the remainder of their lives.[2]

Article 70. The debts of the citizens to the Chamber are guaranteed in accordance with an agreement entered into between the state and the creditors.[3]

Article 71. The old nobility will not be awarded titles of honour except in name; the same applies to the new nobility. The king of France awards titles of honour to whomever he chooses, but those on whom he bestows an honour will not have their duty, etc., lifted from them, and a noble will not enjoy any privileges except that of bearing the title.[4]

Article 72. Those who have received the decoration of distinction called the title of *chevalier* (*al-shawāliya*), i.e. knight, may keep it, in accordance with the provisions that will be determined by the king of France for this title.[5]

Article 73. The tribes and settlements outside France[6] aimed at populating and settling other countries are administered in accordance with other laws and measures.

Article 74. Every ruling king of France swears that he will not deviate from this Charter.[7] This Charter has undergone a number of changes and

---

légalement dérogé.'

1. Cf. '*Droits particuliers garantis par l'Etat.*'
2. Al-Ṭahṭāwī clearly struggled a bit trying to render these social concepts, which were unknown in his native country, and he does, not, for instance, distinguish between '*retraite*' ('retirement') and '*pensionné*' ('pensioned') which are crucial in the original French: '*Les militaires en activité de service, les officiers et soldats en retraite* (*matrūkīn li-waqt al-ḥāja*, 'those who have left at the required time'!), *les veuves, les officiers et soldats pensionnés conserveront leurs grades, honneurs et pensions.*'
3. Al-Ṭahṭāwī lacks the vocabulary to explain the idea of 'public debt', choosing instead the rather awkward (and incorrect) *duyūn al-ra'īya allatī fī dhimmat al-dīwān*; cf. Fr. '*La dette publique est garantie. Toute espèce d'engagement pris par l'Etat avec ses créanciers est inviolable.*'
4. Cf. '*La noblesse ancienne reprend ses titres* (*darajāt*). *La nouvelle conserve les siens. Le roi fait des nobles à volonté; mais il ne leur accorde que des rangs et des honneurs, sans aucune exemption des charges et* des devoirs de la société' (my emphasis); al-Ṭahṭāwī completely omits the last part, replacing it with a reference to the bearing of the name (*tasmiya*).
5. Cf. '*La Légion d'honneur est maintenue. Le roi déterminera les règlements intérieurs et la décoration.*' Here al-Ṭahṭāwī confused the *rank* of *chevalier* (like *commandeur*, etc.) in the Legion of Honour with the decoration itself.
6. *qabā'il wa 'l-nazalāt al-khārija min Faransā*, which is a paraphrase of the French '*colonies*'.
7. Cf. (emphasized parts omitted in the Arabic translation) '*Le roi et* ses successeurs *jureront,* dans la solennité de leur sacre, *d'observer* fidèlement *la présente charte* constitutionnelle.'

alterations since the last revolution,[1] which took place in the year 1831 of the Christian era.[2] We will return to this in the chapter of the uprising of the French people and their call for freedom and equality.

If you think carefully about it, you will see that most of what is mentioned in this Charter is very precious. In any event, it is applicable to all French people. Let us add a few remarks here. When in the first article it is said that all French people are equal before the law, this refers to all those who live in France, from the highest to the humblest. No distinction is made between them in terms of the application of the aforesaid laws of the code to the extent that legal charges can even be brought against the king, against whom a judgment is enforceable, just as it is for other people. So, behold this first article is highly conducive to the introduction of justice; it ensures the oppressed receive assistance, whereas the souls of the poor are satisfied that they are in fact important people when it comes to the execution of the laws. This matter is almost becoming a canonical saying[3] among the French. It is also clear proof of the arrival among them of justice, and the high degree of progress in the civilized way of living. That which they call freedom and which they crave is what we call 'justice' and 'equity',[4] inasmuch as 'rule by freedom' means establishing equality in judgments and laws so that the ruler cannot oppress any human being. Indeed, in this country the laws are the ultimate court and serve as a lesson.

1. *fitna*; the choice of this word ('civil unrest', 'rebellion [within the Islamic community]') is quite interesting since it often has a religious connotation as it also used to denote the first schism in Islam. The same word was used for the French revolution by al-Shidyāq (1881: 275) and al-Jabartī (1997: IV, 103), though the latter also referred to it as 'uprising' (*qiyām*; *ibid.*: 524, in connection with the '*fête de la révolution*'), whereas he used *thawra* (the MSA term for 'revolution') for the Cairo uprising of 1798. 'Alī Mubārak, for his part, employed the less emotive *inqilāb* (1882: e.g. I, 319), and referred to the 'Urābī uprising as *fitna* and *thawra*, which are equated with 'mutiny' ('A. Mubārak, 1886–8: IX, 58). See *EI2* s.vv. "t͟hawra" (A. Ayalon), "fitna" (A. Ayalon); A. Ayalon, 1987; B. Lewis, 1985; L. Zolondek, 1965.
2. The correct date is, of course, 1830. Also see below.
3. (*min*) *jawāmi' al-kalam*, which contains a double-entendre, since the same expression – which can be literally translated as 'speech rich in meaning' – is also used to denote the Qur'ān.
4. The use of the Arabic terms *'adl* and *inṣāf* is of some significance since it relates the European concept of 'freedom' to classical Islamic notions of governance, in which the ruler is enjoined to eschew oppression (*ẓulm*), to act justly and lawfully and to ensure the welfare of his subjects. As B. Lewis rightly points out, however, '[what was] new and alien to traditional political ideas [was] the suggestion that the subject has a *right* to be treated justly' (B. Lewis, *EI2*, III, 590). See *EI2*, s.vv. "ḥurriyya" (B. Lewis), "'adl" (E. Tyan), "inṣāf" (M. Arkoun), "ra'iyya" (C. Bosworth), "siyāsa" (C. Bosworth – F. Vogel); L. Zolondek, 1964.

Freedom, in the words of the poet, occurs when:

Justice has filled its regions
and happiness and fulfilment reign there

In short, if one finds justice in a country, then this is only relative, rather than total and real, which today does not exist in any region. It is like total faith or pure lawfulnesss (*ḥalāl*), etc.

And so there is no point in restricting the impossible to the ghoul,[1] the griffon[2] and the faithful friend. As the poet said:

When I saw my contemporaries – and among them no
faithful friend could be found to share my misfortunes –
I knew for certain the impossible comes in threes:
The demon, the griffon and the faithful friend

However, this cannot be said about the griffon since it is a type of bird, a few of which can be found, and which is mentioned by botanists.[3] In his stories about the Prophet, al-Thaʿlabī[4] mentions the affair of the griffon and our lord Salomon, each of them denying fate. To be sure, there is no griffon in the sense that has gained currency among the common people of the Arabs and the Franks alike, i.e. a being whose top part is that of an eagle and its bottom half that of a lion. Nevertheless, it does exist.

As for the second article, this is of a purely political nature. One can say that if the taxes, etc., were organized in Islamic countries the way they are in this country, people would be happy, especially if the alms tax (*zakawāt*),

1. *ghūl* (pl. *ghīlān, aghwāl*), a (usu. female) variety of *jinn*, who were said to appear in a variety of guises, enticing men from their path in order to kill and devour them. See "g͟hūl" *EI1* (D. MacDonald), *EI2* (D. MacDonald-[C. Pellat]); al-Qazwīnī, 1849: 370ff.
2. *ʿanqāʾ*, a large legendary bird (cf. Biblical *ʿAnaqim*), which has variously been associated with the griffin and the phoenix. See *EI1*, s.v. "ʿanḳāʾ"; al-Qazwīnī, 1849: 419–20.
3. *arbāb ʿilm al-ḥashāʾish*, 'scholars in the science of herbs'.
4. The author of a monumental Qur'ān commentary entitled *al-Kashf wa 'l-bayān ʿan tafsīr al-Qur'ān* ('The Uncovering and Explanation of the Commentary of the Qur'ān), the 11th-century theologian and Qur'ān exegesist Aḥmad b. Muḥammad Abū Isḥāq al-Nīsābūrī al-Thaʿlabī, is best known for his history of Prophets, *ʿArāʾis al-majālis fī quṣṣaṣ al-anbiyāʾ* ('The Brides in the Councils Regarding the Stories about the Prophets'). See *EI1*, s.v. "al-Thaʿlabī" (C. Brockelmann); *GAL*, I, 350; Y. Sarkīs, 1928: 663–4.

[taxes on] collectively owned land[1] and booty of war[2] do not cover the needs of the Treasury or are completely forbidden, which probably finds its origin in the holy law (*sharīʿa*), according to claims by the school of the greatest imam [namely, the Ḥanafites].[3] According to a maxim established among the ancient philosophers, 'land tax[4] is the pillar of the kingdom'. During my stay in Paris, I have never heard anybody complain about the taxes, duties, imposts and levies. People are not bothered by it since they are levied in a way that does not harm the taxpayer and that benefits their Treasury, especially as those who own property are safe from oppression and corruption.

As for the third article, it does not contain anything that could ever be harmful. Quite the contrary, since its benefits are that it induces people to study and learn so that they can reach a higher position than the one they occupy. In doing so, their knowledge will increase and their civilization does not stagnate like that of the people of China or the Hind, where people set great store by the hereditary nature of crafts and professions, and a person always enters the same profession as that held by his father. One historian stated that '*in earlier times it was the same in Egypt. The law of the ancient Copts determined the profession of each person, who then passed it on to his children. It is said that this was because all the crafts and professions were*

1. *fay'* ('return [to the Muslim community what is rightfully theirs]'); in Islamic law this denoted all things that could be taken from unbelievers without fighting (cf. Qur. LIX: 6–7). At first, this referred to some of the land in newly occupied territories being pre-empted for the Prophet to be managed by him as communal property. Later on, the caliph ʿUmar decreed that only moveable property belonging to the infidels could be divided as booty among those who had taken part in the conquest; land would 'return' to the community as a whole for the benefit of future generations, though the native population were to continue to cultivate it, in exchange for a proportion of the yield to the Treasury – the so-called *kharāj*. See *EI1*, s.vv. "Fay'" (T. Juynboll); *EI2*, s.v. "fay'" (F. Løkkegaard).
2. *ghanīma*; derived from a root meaning 'to earn something without effort', this term denoted the moveable possessions (including prisoners of war) captured in battle from unbelievers. In the early period of Islam, four-fifths of the *ghanīma* was divided among the soldiers present, the remaining one-fifth belonging to God; in practice, it was the Prophet's to dispose of in the way that he saw fit. See *EI1*, s.v. "ghanīma" (T. Weir.).
3. As K. Al-Husry (1966: 20–21) rightly points out, the Shāfiʿī al-Ṭahṭāwī is actually recommending the introduction of a non-religious Western system of taxation on the basis of the Ḥanafī doctrine.
4. *kharāj* , a tax paid on landed property, as opposed to the poll tax (*jizya*). Originally, this was a tribute levied on land belonging to non-Muslims in newly conquered Islamic territories, the former having to pay a fixed part of their harvest of the land, which had in effect become part of *fay'*, as tribute to the Muslim Treasury, even after their conversion to Islam. In time, the *kharāj* dwindled into oblivion and rulers contented themselves with the tithe (*ʿushr*) on harvest produce. See "kharādj", *EI1* (Th. W. Juynboll), *EI2* (C. Cahen); "ʿushr", *EI1* (Grohmann), *EI2* (T. Sato).

held in great esteem among them. This custom stemmed from the requirements of the situation inasmuch as it greatly contributes to the attainment of a high degree of perfection in crafts, because the son is usually good at what he has seen his father do many times in his presence and consequently has no desire to do anything else. However, this custom eliminated ambition and caused every person to be content with his profession, without harbouring any hopes of rising above his level. Instead, each craftsman sought to invent new things useful to his craft with a view to reaching perfection in it.' One reply to this is that a person does not always have the aptitude to learn his father's profession. And while a young man may perhaps lack the ability to exercise this profession, it is possible that, if he had embarked on another profession, he would perhaps have made a success of his life and realized his hopes.

The fourth, fifth, sixth and seventh articles are useful to the people of the country as well as to foreigners. This is why the population of this country has increased, and foreigners have greatly contributed to its prosperity.

The eighth article encourages everybody freely to express his opinion, knowledge and feelings provided it does not harm others. As a result, people learn everything that goes on in the mind of their fellow man. Of special interest in this respect are the daily papers, called *journals*[1] and *gazettes*.[2] From these publications people learn all the latest news events, both from within and without, i.e. related to their kingdom or to other countries. And although there are innumerable lies in these publications, they also often contain news items that people look forward to knowing. Sometimes, they include studies of new scientific questions, useful announcements and advice, issued by both important and insignificant people, since even a lowly person may think of something that does not come to the mind of important people. As one of them said: *Do not scorn an important opinion because it is brought to you by a lowly person – the pearl is not despised, just because the diver is of a low station*. And the poet said:

1. *jurnālāt* (sing. *al-jurnāl*), whose origin can also be the Italian *giornale* (cf. e.g. K. Vollers, 1887–97: 319). Cf. M. al-Sanūsī, 1891–92: 28, 201; *idem*, 1976–81: I, 93, 94, 189, 215, 220; Khayr al-Dīn, 1867: 75, 106, 108, 124; M. Bayram V, 1884–93: II, 87; F. al-Shidyāq, 1881: 74; G. Badger, 1895: 666; J. Habeisch, 1896: 410; S. Spiro, 1895: 99 (pl. *jarānīl*); G. Gasselin, 1880–86: II, 106; J. Heyworth-Dunne, 1940–42: 408, 411.
2. *kāẓīṭāt* (sing. *kāẓīṭa*). This Italian borrowing (*gazetta*) later on in the text also appears in the pleonastic phrase *kāẓīṭāt yawmiyya* ('daily gazettes'). It first appeared in Arabic literature in the 17th-century travel account by the Moroccan al-Wazīr al-Ghassāni (1884: 151). Cf. al-Ṭahṭāwī, 1973–80: I, 517 (*ghāẓīta*) Khayr al-Dīn, 1867: (*taqrīẓ*) 39 (*ghazita*); G. Badger, 1895: 666; G. Gasselin, 1880–86: II, 106; B. Ben Sedira, 1882: 430; J. Redhouse, 1880: 205/668 (*ghazita*); J. Zenker, 1866: 648.

When I heard about him, it was of him alone
But I saw in him both humans and the jinn[1]
I found all kinds of game in the belly of the wild ass[2]
and encountered all people in one person

Another advantage of the newspapers is that when someone does something great or despicable, the journalists write about it, so that it becomes known by both the notables and the common people – to encourage the person who did something good, or to make the person who has done a despicable thing forsake his ways.[3] Similarly, if a person commits a wrong against another person, the latter publishes this in these papers. As a result, both the elite and the common people can take cognizance of it, and know the story of both the oppressed and the oppressor without any digressions from what has happened or changes. Then, the case comes before the court and is judged in accordance with the established laws. This kind of thing serves as a lesson for those who want to learn.

As for the ninth article, it is the source of justice and equity and is vital in order to restrict the oppression of the weak by the strong, and to punish the latter.

As for the provisions contained in article 10, they are clearly appropriate.

The 15th article contains a nice point, i.e. that the organization of human affairs is governed by three classes. First, the king and his ministers. Second, the peerage, which expresses its love for the king, and, third, the envoys from the provinces, who are the representatives of the citizens and enjoy their full support, to the extent that nobody complains of any of them. The envoys act in the place of the citizens, and are their spokesmen, so that, in fact, the citizens rule themselves. In any event, the citizenry protects itself against oppression, and is completely certain about this. The wisdom of the remaining articles will surely not elude the reader.

1. In Islam, *jinn* ('genie') denotes a class of airy or fiery creatures (created out of smokeless flame), in between angels and men (both created out of clay and light), the Devil (*Shayṭān, Iblīs*) generally being considered one of them (e.g. Qur. XVIII: 48). In folklore, there are both male and female, good and bad *jinns* (the latter being known as *'a/ifrīt*), and they are believed to inhabit rivers, dwellings, etc., besides appearing in their usual guises as cats, dogs, etc. See "djinn" *EI1* (D. MacDonald), *EI2* (S. Van den Bergh); "'Ifrīt", *EI1* (D. MacDonald), *EI2* (J. Chelhod); "Shayṭān", *EI1* (A. Tritton), *EI2* (A. Rippin); "Iblīs", *EI1* (A. Wensinck), *EI2* (A. Wensinck – [L. Gardet]); al-Qazwīnī, 1849: 368; C. Padwick, 1923; E. Lane, 1923: 67, 228ff.
2. *(laqaytu) kull 'l-ṣayd fī jawf al-farā'*; this saying is used for someone (or something) that combines all good qualities (thus making everything else superfluous); H. Wehr, 1976: 701.
3. It is interesting to compare these comments regarding the benefits of newspapers with those al-Ṭahṭāwī later makes about the theatre.

Abridgement of the current rights of the French since the year 1138[1] and the revision of the Charter. Rights and duties of the French. Content of the Charter after its amendment.

The French – irrespective of their importance, position, title and wealth – are equal before the laws.[2] Indeed, these are all merits that are useful only in human society and intercourse, but not in the law. Because of this, all of them have access to both military and civil positions, just as all of them help the state, each in accordance with his means.[3]

The law also provides that every person has the right to enjoy his personal freedom, to the extent that he cannot be arrested, except in accordance with the provisions mentioned in the legal codices.[4] If anybody seizes somebody in an illegal manner, he is severely punished. One of the things ensuing from freedom amongst the French is that each person who practises his chosen religion enjoys the protection of the state,[5] and anyone interfering with somebody's religious worship is punished. No endowment or donation can be given to churches except with the express permission of the state.[6]

Every Frenchman has the right to express an opinion on political or religious matters, on condition that it does not harm the order established in the legal codices.[7] Every property is absolutely inviolable, and no-one can ever be forced to surrender his property, except if it is in the common interest, on condition that compensation commensurate with the value of

1. This should, of course, be corrected to 1831, which is the date that appeared in the second edition. However, this is equally incorrect as the revision to which al-Ṭahṭāwī is referring is the Constitutional Charter of 4 September 1830. The erroneous date is also repeated afterwards.
2. Cf. Article 1: '*Les Français sont égaux devant la loi, quels que soient d'ailleurs leurs titres et leurs rangs.*'
3. Cf. Article 2: '*Ils contribuent indistinctement, dans la proportion de leur fortune, aux charges de l'Etat.*'
4. Cf. Article 4: '*Leur liberté individuelle est également garantie, personne ne pouvant être poursuivi ni arrêté que dans les cas prévus par la loi et dans la forme qu'elle prescrit.*'
5. Cf. Article 5: '*Chacun professe sa religion avec une égale liberté, et obtient pour son culte la même protection.*'
6. This is a rather strange explanation of article 6 of the renewed Constitution, which states that ministers of the recognized religions '*reçoivent des traitements du trésor public*'. Equally interesting is the author's translation of '*traitement*' as *waqf* (pl. *awqāf*), which is a term (lit. 'restraining') used in Islamic law (alongside *ḥubus*, pl. *aḥbās*) for an inalienable religious endowment (usually real estate), made out in perpetuity, for the benefit of religious and/or public institutions like mosques, schools, hospitals, etc. See *EI1*, s.v. "waḳf" (Heffening); J. Schacht, 1966: 19f., 125ff. *et passim*.
7. Cf. Article 7: '*Les Français ont le droit de publier et de faire imprimer leurs opinions en se conformant aux lois. La censure ne pourra jamais être rétablie.*'

the property has been paid prior to the expropriation. This is decided by the court.

Every person has the obligation of contributing to the military defence of the kingdom with his person, i.e. each year young men of twenty-one are called up to fulfil their conscription duty for the annual military contingent.[1] The period of military service is eight months. Every Frenchman who is eighteen years old and in possession of his civil rights[2] may voluntarily enter the armed forces. A number of people are exempt from the military:

People who are under 1.75 metres tall, i.e. under four feet and ten *barmaq*; people with disabilities; the eldest son among orphans; the eldest or only son, or the son of the eldest in the event he is no longer alive, or the only son if the mother or grandmother does not have a husband, or the father is blind or seventy years old; the elder of two brothers who are drafted at the same time; the brother of a man who has distinguished himself while performing his military service,[3] who died in the course of it or was wounded in war.

If a man wants to send someone else to do his military service for him, the mandator stands guaranty for his replacement for a year lest the latter deserts, except if the deserter is caught within one year or dies while serving the French flag. On 21 December of each year, all soldiers who have completed their military service are allowed to return to their homes.

As not every person can himself enter the state administration, the citizenry in its entirety empowers 430 representatives to act for them, and whom they send to the consultative council in Paris. These representatives are chosen by the citizens and are charged by them to protect their rights and to act in their interest. Each Frenchman who meets the necessary conditions – including the fact of being at least twenty-five years old – may participate in the election of the representative of his province.[4] Every Frenchman as from the age of thirty may be a member of the

1. In this section, al-Ṭahṭawī elaborates greatly on the French text (Article 11), which simply states: '*La circonscription est abolie. Le mode de recrutement de l'armée de terre et de mer est déterminée par une loi*'! Naturally, the recruitment of the armed forces would have been of great interest to al-Ṭahṭāwī's principal, Muḥammad ʿAlī.
2. The Arabic *ḥuqūq baladiyya* literally translates as 'national rights' and would not have meant much to the author's domestic readership, who would probably have wondered at the nature of these 'rights'.
3. *taḥt al-bayraq* ('under the banner') is, of course, a calque from the French 'sous les drapeaux', i.e. 'doing one's military service'.
4. Cf. Article 34: '*Nul n'est électeur, s'il a moins de vingt-cinq ans, et s'il ne réunit les autres conditions déterminées par la loi.*'

Chamber of Deputies, provided he meets the conditons set forth in the legal codices.[1]

In every district, there are rogatory and electoral committees, and electoral colleges for the smaller regions. The colleges of the large districts are composed of the major voters, who appoint 172 representatives. The electoral colleges of the smaller regions [together] appoint 257 representatives. The lists of voters are printed and posted along the streets one month before the opening of the electoral colleges, so that everyone can voice his opinion on it in writing. Every voter can express his view in secret on a piece of paper which he folds and gives to the president, who then puts it in the ballot box.

The entire Chamber of Deputies is renewed every five years. Members can be admitted only following a decision made by the assembly of both Chambers and ratified by the king. The people of the towns may address themselves to members of the Chambers by way of petitions to complain about certain things or to submit something useful.

Judges cannot be removed.[2] Somebody can be tried only by the judges of his town of residence. Trials are public. Capital crimes can be tried only in the presence of a group of people, known as *jurors* (*jūriyūn*). The punishment of confiscation of property is abolished.[3] The king has the right to pardon someone who has been sentenced to death or to make a sentence lighter.[4]

It is incumbent upon the king and his heirs upon their accession to the throne to swear to act in compliance with what is contained in this book of the laws of the kingdom [i.e. the Charter].[5]

It would take us too long to mention the judgments or the laws of the French. We should [just] like to say that their legal judgments are not derived from the divine books but are for the most part taken from politics. This is completely different from *sharī'a* law and is not rooted in fundamental principles. It is referred to as 'French law', which means the rights that are in force among them. There are many different legal systems among the Franks.

In Paris, there are a number of courthouses, in each of which there is a 'chief judge' [president], who may be considered the supreme judge among

1. Cf. Article 32: '*Aucun député ne peut être admis dans la chambre, s'il n'est âgé de trente ans et s'il ne réunit les autres conditions déterminées par la loi.*'
2. Cf. Article 49: '*Les juges nommés par le rois sont inamovibles.*'
3. Cf. Article 57: '*La peine de la confiscation des biens est abolie et ne pourra être rétablie.*'
4. Cf. Article 58: '*Le roi a le droit de faire grâce et celui de commuer les peines.*'
5. Cf. Article 65: '*Le roi et ses successeurs jureront à leur avènement, en présence des chambres réunies, d'observer fidèlement la charte constitutionnelle.*'

the judges. He is surrounded by fellow presiding judges and advisers, representatives from the adversaries, lawyers for both parties, substitutes for the lawyers and the recorder of the proceedings.[1]

Fourth Section. On the housing of the people of Paris and related matters

It is known that the degree of civilization of a town or city is measured by the level of learning and its distance from a state of savagery and barbary. The countries of Europe are well endowed with all types of knowledge and refinement, which, no-one will deny, are conducive to sociability and embellish civilization. It has been established that the French nation distinguishes itself among European countries through its great attachment to the arts and sciences. It is truly the greatest nation in terms of its manners and culture.

When it comes to the type and style of buildings, the provincial capitals[2] are generally superior to villages and hamlets; the large cities surpass all the provincial capitals, and the capital of the kingdom is foremost among all other cities. Therefore, it is not surprising that it is said that Paris, which is the seat of the king of the French, is one of the greatest cities of the Franks in terms of its buildings and architecture. And although its buildings are not made of good materials, the architectural design and craftsmanship with which they are constructed is excellent. By the same token, it is sometimes also said that the materials are good, even though there are flaws because of a deficiency of marble and the fact that they lack certain other things. Yet, the overall quality of construction should not surprise anyone since the foundations of their walls as well as the exterior walls are made out of freestone. The interior walls are made out of high-quality wood. The majority of the columns are made out of copper, though occasionally there are some in marble. For the ground covering they use tiles, which are made out of stone and black marble. The roads are always paved with square flagstones, as are the courtyards, while the vestibules are covered with baked bricks, wood or black marble with finely-worked tiles. The quality of the stone or wood varies according to the prosperity of the residents.

1. The Arabic *muwaqqiʿ al-waqāʾiʿ* is a translation of the French *greffier*. The choice of *muwaqqiʿ* is quite apt within the context, since it denoted an official charged with recording the decisions made by a ruler in the course of audiences or in reply to requests.
2. *banādir*, sing. *bandar*; of Persian origin, this word meant 'port, harbour' in CA, but in Egypt denotes a large town or district capital and thus neatly corresponds to the French '*chef-lieu*', i.e. the capital of a *département*, which is roughly equivalent to the British 'county town'. On the etymology of this word, see also S. Elatri, 1974: 204.

As mentioned before, the walls and the floors of rooms are made out of wood, which they cover with paint. On the walls they put nicely embossed paper, which is better than the custom of whitewashing the walls with lime since, unlike lime, the paper does not give anything off when you touch the wall. Moreover, it is cheaper, nicer to look at and easier to apply, especially in their rooms which are decorated with all kinds of furnishings that defy description. The only thing that can be said is that the French try to dim the light in rooms by fitting coloured curtains, especially green ones. The floors are covered with wood or types of red tiles. Each day, the room floors are polished with a yellow wax they call 'polishing wax'.[1] They have people who polish for a fee and make themselves available especially for this sort of thing.

Under their beds, which are covered with sackcloth, fabrics with plant designs and other coverings, there are magnificent carpets on which they put their shoes. In each room there is a chimney [with a mantelpiece] in the shape of a ledge that [we use] to place water jugs on and which is made out of fine marble. On top of it there is a pendulum clock,[2] on both sides of which there are vases out of mock white marble or crystal. They contain real or artificial flowers. At either end of the mantelpiece, there are wheel-shaped Frankish candelabra, the true appearance of which can only be imagined by one who has seen them lit. As like as not, their rooms contain a musical instrument called a *piano* (*al-biyān*).[3] If the room is a study, i.e. a place of work and reading, then it has a table with writing instruments as well as other things, like finely crafted paper knives made out of ivory, boxwood or other materials. Most of the rooms are full of pictures, especially of [the inhabitants'] relatives. The study may also contain wonderful pictures and strange things that once belonged to various ancestors. On the desk you will sometimes see different types of newspapers. In the houses of important people the rooms sometimes have beautiful chandeliers, which are lit with candles made of beeswax. And on days that they receive people, they sometimes put out the latest books, newspapers, etc. for those of the guests who take pleasure in reading such things.[4] This bears testimony to

1. *sham' al-ḥakk*, 'rubbing wax'; cf. Fr. '*cire à frotter*'.
2. *sā'a bishtakhta* (cf. Tu. *pashtakhta sā'at-i*). The latter word denoted a *canteen*, i.e. a travel case with drawers and compartments, a woman's travel toilet case being known as *bishtakhta ḥarīm*. R. Dozy, 1967: I, 88; E. Bocthor, 1882; G. Badger, 1895: 108.
3. Later on, this word most often occurred as *biyānū* (though in MSA both variants are found); cf. M. al-Sanūsī, 1891–92: 65; *idem*, 1976–81: I, 148; G. Badger, 1895: 753; J. Habeisch, 1896: 590: E. Gasselin, 1880–86: II, 390; J. Zenker, 1866: 231; J. Redhouse, 1880: 93.
4. The Arabic is more flowery and relies heavily on euphony: '*yasraḥu nāẓirahu wa yanzuhu*

the importance the French attach to reading books, which are familiar companions to them.

There is a nice aphorism which states:

'A book is like a vessel filled with knowledge.'[1]

Also:

'What else could be a flower garden which you rake over in your lap, and a vegetable garden that can be carried in the sleeve.'

How appropriate are the words in verse [written] by one of them:

My book is familiar to me, my thoughts my partner in nightly conversation
My hand is my servant, my dream my bedfellow
My sword is my tongue, my strength my poetry
My inkwell my life, my scroll my winter provisions

Another poet said:

We have table companions, whose words never bore
Intelligent, reliable – whether near or far –
They bring us the knowledge of what has passed, and
wisdom, education and sound counsel too
If you said that they were dead, you would not be mendacious
And if you said that they were alive, you would not be proved wrong

One of them once said: '*The book is indeed an excellent narrator.*' A wise man said: '*Never have I seen one who was crying who could laugh better than the pen.*'

The pleasure of all these splendid things is further enhanced by the presence of the mistress of the house, who greets the guests first, while her husband does so afterwards.[2] What a difference between these *salons* with all these fineries and our rooms, where by way of greeting a visitor receives a chibouk,[3] most often from the hands of a black slave!

---

khāṭirahu' ('[he among the guests who wants to] allow his gaze to roam and amuse his mind').

1. The author adds a pun based on the polysemy of the word *ẓarf*, which can mean both 'vessel' and 'spirit', 'mind': '[and it is] a *ẓarf* filled with *ẓarf*.
2. Cf. al-Salāwī, 1956: IX, 116.
3. *shubuq* (also *shubuk*, cf. Tu. *çubuk*); a long-stemmed tobacco pipe, generally between

As for the ceilings, they are made out of precious wood [panelling]. A house usually consists of four superimposed floors, excluding the ground floor, which is not counted as a storey. There may be up to seven floors, and there are also some beneath the earth that contain small chambers, which are also used to tie up the horses, as a kitchen or to store provisions for the house, especially wine, wood and fuel.

Their houses, like those of Cairo, contain a number of independent apartments. There are several of these on each floor of the house and each has connecting rooms. The French have the habit of classifying houses into three categories. The first is that of ordinary houses; the second, houses belonging to people of note; and third, houses belonging to the king, members of the royal family, the consultative assemblies, etc. These are respectively called 'house', 'residence',[1] and 'château' (*qaṣr*) or 'palace'.[2] It is also possible to classify the houses in a different way: first, houses that have a gatekeeper and a large gate to accommodate the passage of a carriage; second, houses with a courtyard and a doorman,[3] but that are inaccessible to carriages; and third, houses that do not have a doorman or, rather, quarters to accommodate him. The duty of a doorman in Paris is to wait for the inhabitant until midnight. If the inhabitant wants to stay out in the city until after midnight, he has to notify the doorman of this so that he can wait for him, in which case he has to be given a little something. Districts do not have doormen and there are no gates as there are in Cairo.[4]

In Paris, buildings are expensive to buy and to rent; a large residence may cost up to eight million francs, i.e. about 30 million Egyptian piastres.[5]

1.2m and 1.5m long (though some were up to two metres). This kind of pipe, which was peculiar to Egypt, is no longer used and has long since been superseded by the water pipe (*shīsha*). See E. Lane, 1923: 138ff.

1. The author uses the word *dār* (pl. *diyār, adwar, dūr, diyārāt*), which literally simply means 'house' and is thus a synonym of '*bayt*' (pl. *buyūt*), which appears throughout. Here, it clearly corresponds to the French '*Hôtel (particulier)*' (or '*maison de maître*').
2. *sarāya*, a borrowing from Turkish (*seray*) and the etymon of the English 'seraglio' ('serail') and the French '*sérail*', both of which were used in European travel literature to denote the harims of the Ottoman sultans.
3. *bawwāb* ('doorkeeper'). In modern Egypt, the duties performed by *bawwābs* are in fact those of a caretaker, or concierge.
4. Cairo, like most major Oriental and North African cities, comprised districts that could be accessed through only one gate, which was usually locked in the evening and was also guarded.
5. *qirsh*, pl. *qurūsh*. In the 1820s, the exhange rate for one pound sterling ranged between 72 and 100 piastres. In 1835, it was officially fixed at Pt.97.5=£1. As a result of inflation, the international value of the Egyptian currency was slashed by one quarter of its international value between 1805 and 1843. The piastre consisted of 40 *fiḍḍa* (or *qirsh fiḍḍī*) – which literally means 'silver' – with denominations of 5, 10 and 20. The Egyptian

The inhabitants of Paris may rent the abode either alone or with the magnificent furnishings, all the furniture and household equipment; this means all of the kitchen utensils and tableware – including the silverware – as well as the bedding, which often consists of several mattresses – one of feathers, a bed-sheet which is changed every month and blankets and counterpanes. In addition, there are attractive items of furniture for the sake of visitors. These include chairs upholstered with embroidered silk or other similar materials, sofas covered in similar fabrics, ordinary chairs, as well as impressive-looking things like large clocks which they call a *pendule* (*bandūl*), magnificent flower vases, gilt coffee pots, chandeliers with candles of purified wax or a bookcase with a glass door so that you can see which finely bound books can be found within. Everyone – both rich and poor – has a bookcase since the entire population[1] is able to write and read. In most cases, a man does not sleep in the same room as his wife if they have been married for a long time.

Another one of their habits is that they see no harm in allowing the public into the palaces and castles of the king of France and the members of the royal family when they go to the country several months each year. All the people go there to marvel at the house of the king and his family and gaze at the furniture in the palace and all the wonderful things it contains. However, none is granted access without a piece of paper on which it is printed that one, two or more persons have permission to enter. A lot of people have this piece of paper and if a person asks acquaintances for it, they give it to him. As a result, you see huge crowds agog at everything contained in the private quarters (*ḥarīm*) of the king and his family. I myself went in several times and saw many of the wondrous things that deserve to be looked at. It contains many pictures [representing people] that can be distinguished from [real] human beings only by their inability to speak. There are many pictures of the kings of France, as well as others, including all the members of the ruling family. All the objects in the royal apartments are attractive, not because of the value of the materials but

pound (*junayh*, pl. *junayhat* <Eng. *guinea*) was introduced in 1885. See E. Lane, 1923: 580–81; R. Owen, 1993: 67; M. Morsy, 1984: 114–5; K. Vollers, 1887–97: 323.

1. The choice of the Arabic '*al-ʿāmma*' is quite interesting since it is, in fact, a collective for 'commoners', which excluded tradesmen (*tujjār*) and the '*ulamā*' (though all of them formed part of the *raʿīya*, i.e. 'subjects'); in Islamic society the term is in opposition with '*al-aʿyān*', i.e. the notables (= the governing elite). Interestingly, in the *Manāhij*, al-Ṭahṭāwī divided the people of Egypt into four classes: the holders of power, the '*ulamā*' (including judges and non-Islamic religious leaders), the military and the rest of the people, *al-raʿīya* – the subjects – (see above) who include peasants, merchants and craftsmen; al-Ṭahṭāwī, 1973–80: I, 515ff. Also see A. Raymond, 1998: 52–9.

because of the overall excellent workmanship with which they have been made. For instance, all the furniture, such as the beds, chairs and even the king's throne, are magnificently covered with brocade and overlaid with gold. However, there are not many of the precious stones that you find in great supply in the houses of our princes and notables. The basic principle with the French is that everything is done for the sake of beauty and elegance, rather than for [excessive] ornamentation, the outward show of wealth or vainglory.

In winter, all the rich people of Paris live in the city itself. As we have already mentioned when talking about the climate in the Paris region, each house has fireplaces, and fires are lit in every hall and room. During periods of heat, the well-off live in the country, since the air is more wholesome in the castles in the country than in the centre of Paris. Other people go to other towns in France or to neighbouring countries in order to breathe the air of foreign lands, to discover [new] countries and to get to know the customs of the peoples. This happens especially at the time of the year they call 'the work-free period' or 'leisure period', i.e. the holidays.

Even women travel, either alone or accompanied by a man with whom they have entered into an agreement regarding the journey and whose expenses they pay for along the way. Indeed, women also have a passion for knowledge, for discovering the secrets of beings and learning more about them. Is it perhaps not so that some of them come from Europe to Egypt to see its wonders like the pyramids, the temples, etc.? They are like men in every respect. To be sure, there are even some women of wealth and high status who give themselves to a foreigner without being married. And when they become pregnant and fear a scandal, they journey to another country supposedly to travel around or for some other reason in order to give birth to the child, who is then entrusted to a nanny for a special fee and raised in a foreign land. However, this sort of thing does not happen frequently. To put it differently, not every lightning cloud sheds its rain in abundance. Among French women there are those with great virtue and others who display quite the contrary. The latter are in the majority since the hearts of most people in France, whether male or female, are in thrall to the art of love. Their amorous passion is an aim in itself since they do not believe that they serve any other purpose. At the same time, a relationship may develop between a young man and a young girl which then leads to marriage.

One must praise the French for the cleanliness of their houses, which are devoid of all dirt, even though this pales into oblivion next to the cleanliness of the houses of the Dutch, who surpass all nations in their attachment to exterior cleanliness, just as in ancient times the people of Egypt were known to be the cleanest people in the world. However, their descendants, the Copts, did not follow their example. As Paris is clean, it is also free of venomous vermin, even insects. One never hears of a person who has been stung by a scorpion. The commitment on the part of the French to keeping their houses and clothes clean is truly wondrous. Their houses are always bright because of the many windows, which are placed with such magnificent engineering skill that they allow light and air both inside and outside the houses. The window panes are always made out of glass so that even when they are closed the light is never blocked out.

Both the rich and the poor always have curtains in front of the windows. Often the people of Paris also have curtains over their beds, which resemble a kind of mosquito net.

Fifth Section. On the food of the people of Paris and their eating and drinking habits

You should know that wheat is the staple food of the people of Paris. In most cases this comes in small grains, except when it has been imported from abroad. They grind it in wind and water mills, and bake it into bread at the baker's. The bread is sold in special shops, and everyone has a daily ration which they buy from the baker. This way of doing things saves time and money, since everybody is occupied with their own activities, and to make the bread at home would add to their workload. The market supervisor[1] instructs the bakers to have enough bread for the city every day. In reality, there is never a shortage of bread in Paris, nor of any other foodstuffs for that matter. The people of this city also eat meat, legumes, vegetables, dairy produce, eggs and things of this kind. In general, their meals consist of numerous dishes, even among the poor.

The slaughterhouses are situated not in the middle of the city, but on the outskirts. There is a twofold wisdom behind this: to get rid of the filth and to prevent damage by the animals if these should escape. They have various methods for slaughtering animals. Sheep are easier to slaughter than other animals; the knife is thrust behind the animal's throat, i.e between the throat and neck, and then it is cut in the opposite direction to how we do it. Veal are also slaughtered in the same way. As for bulls,

1. *muḥtasib*; in Islamic society this denoted the market and weight inspector; see A. Raymond, 1973: 588–606; E. Lane, 1923: 125ff.

they are hit with iron clubs in the centre of the head, and as a result of the force of the blow, the animal becomes dizzy. They repeat this several times until the bull stops breathing, but is still moving. Afterwards, the animal is slaughtered in the same way as sheep are killed. One day, as is my wont, I sent an Egyptian servant of mine to the slaughterhouse to slaughter what I had bought. When he saw how badly their bulls were treated, he returned seeking protection from God and praising Him –May He be exalted – for not having made him a bull in the lands of the Franks, or he would have suffered the same torture as those he had seen. Veal and bulls are cattle, but there are no buffaloes in these lands, except as a curiosity. Fowl are slaughtered in a variety of ways; some kill them in the same way as sheep, others cut out the birds' tongues or strangle them with sewing thread. Still others slit their necks, etc. As for rabbits, they never have their throats slit. Instead, they are strangled in order to retain the blood inside their bodies. I have not seen the slaughter of pigs since this takes place at a special slaughterhouse. It appears that the procedure is the same as for veal.

Among the things intended for the comfort of the people of the city of Paris, there are eating places, called *restaurants*,[1] which are like *locandas*.[2] They have everything that a person has in his own house, only better. A person can find what he has ordered already made. In these restaurants, there are a number of nice rooms that are fitted with all kinds of household equipment. Often, they also contain sleeping rooms, with the most beautiful furniture. Besides all types of food and drink, restaurants also have both fresh and dried (candied) fruits on offer.

It is the custom of the French to eat out of plates similar to those used in Persia or China – never out of copper receptacles. On the dinner table,

1. *al-risṭurāṭūr*, which is, of course, a transcription of *restaurateur*, i.e. owner of a restaurant, or caterer. This form is not that surprising since '*restaurant*' (which first appeared in the 1835 edition of the dictionary of the *Académie française*) was still primarily the 'establishment of a *restaurateur*', i.e. one who provided food 'to restore' people. The use of the word *restaurer* ('to restore') in this sense is commonly linked to the first *restaurateur* (1765) to set up for business – a certain Boulanger (!) – who put the following notice above the doorway: 'Venite ad me omnes qui stomacho laboratis et ego restaurabo vos.' See A. Scheler, 1888: 437; P. Imbs *et al.*, 1971–94: XIV, 992.

2. *al-lūkanja* (sic) (It. *locanda*, 'guesthouse'). Cf. M. Amīn Fikrī, 1892: 13. The Moroccan al-Ṣaffār (M. al-Khaṭṭābī 1987: 21; S. Gilson Miller, 1992: 88) has both *lūkanda* and *būṣāda* (Sp./Port. *posada*), the latter offering both lodging and food, whereas al-Wardānī uses *util*, for 'hotel' and *lūkanda* and *khān* for the lower-quality *fonda, posada* and *hostería* (S. al-Wardānī, 1888–90: *passim*). The word *lūkānda* is still in use in Egypt, where it denotes a hotel of poor quality. Also see E. Gasselin, 1880–86: I, 965; G. Badger, 1895: 457 (*lūkanda*); J. Habeisch, 1896: 357; S. Spiro, 1895 (*lūkanda*): 548. In Turkish, *lūqāndah* meant 'restaurant' (cf. mod. Tu. *lokanta*); J. Zenker, 1866: 796; J. Redhouse, 1880: 152, 263, 753.

a knife, fork and spoon are always placed in front of each person. The fork and spoon are made out of silver. They consider it a sign of both hygiene and refinement if people do not touch anything with their hands. Each person has a plate in front of him; for each dish there is a different plate. Every person also has a glass in front of him in which he pours his drink from a large bottle which stands on the table. When someone wishes to drink, he does not grab the glass of the other. The drinking vessels[1] are always made out of crystal and glass. On the table there are several smaller glass vessels; one of them contains salt, another pepper, mustard, etc. In short, their table manners and layout are quite remarkable. Their meal starts with soup and ends with sweets and fruit. Most of the time, they drink wine instead of water with their food. Generally, and this applies especially to the notables, they never drink enough wine for them to get drunk, since drunkenness is considered both a weakness and a vice among them. After finishing their meal they often drink a little *'araq*.[2]

Despite the fact that they drink these alcoholic beverages,[3] they do not often eulogize it in their poetry and, unlike the Arabs, they do not have many words to refer to wine. They take pleasure in its essence and features without imagining any hidden meanings, similes or hyperbole. In truth, they have special books that deal with drunks, but those are humorous writings in praise of wine which cannot in any way be considered part of real literature. People in Paris often drink tea immediately after their meals, because they say that it is a digestant. Others drink coffee with sugar. Many people display the habit of dipping their bread in coffee with milk in the morning. If you want some [more] information on the eating and drinking habits, you should read the chapter on food and drink in my translation, entitled *Qalā'id al-mafākhir*.[4]

The total annual food and drink consumption of the people of this city is approximately as follows: they spend more than 35 million francs on bread, about 10 million francs on [cooking] fat and 5,000 francs on

1. *awānī* (sing. '*inā"*), 'vases', which refers to the vase shape of traditional wine glasses.
2. Naturally, this is al-Ṭahṭāwī's 'translation' of the French *liqueur*, though some of them do, of course, contain aniseed, which is the core ingredient of *'araq*.
3. Here, the author uses the word *khumūr*, which is the plural of *khamr* – the word exclusively used today for 'wine' – and already appeared in this meaning in early Arabic poetry. Elsewhere, al-Ṭahṭawī uses the equally classical *nabīdh* for 'wine', which originally was a collective term for a variety of intoxicating drinks. Only *khamr* is mentioned in the Qur'ān (II:219, V:90,V:91, XII:36, XII:41, XVI:69, XLVII:15). Cf. "khamr", *EI1* (A. Wensinck), *EI2* (A. Wensinck – J.Fadan); "nabīdh", *EI1* (A. Wensinck), *EI2* (P. Heine); S. Elatri, 1974: 337–8 (for the etymology of the word *khamr*).
4. See note no. 2, p. 144.

eggs. In terms of meat, they go through about 81,430 bulls, 13,000 cows, 470,000 sheep and goats and 100,000 wild boar and pigs. One of the strange things in Paris is their ingenuity when it comes to preserving perishable foodstuffs. For instance, thanks to a special technique, milk can be kept for a period of five years without its undergoing any changes. Meat remains tender for ten years, while fruit is stored so that it can be found out of season. Despite their expertise with regard to food and pastry, etc., their food lacks flavour and, with the exception of peaches, the fruit in this city has no real sweetness.

As for their wine houses, they are innumerable. There is not a single district that is not teeming with those places. It is only the lowliest of people who gather there, the riff-raff with their women. They are given to a great deal of shouting when they leave those places and say things to the effect of 'Drink, drink'. Yet, despite their state of drunkenness, they generally do not cause any real harm. One day, it happened that as I was walking along a street in Paris a drunk shouted at me, 'Hey, you Turk!', and grabbed me by my clothes. I was near a confectionery shop, so I entered with him and sat him down on a chair. I then jokingly said to the proprietor of the shop, 'Would you like to buy this man for some sweets or candied nuts?' To which the owner replied, 'Here things are not like in your country where you can dispose of the human species at your will.' My only retort to this was that I said, 'In his current state, this drunken person is not part of the human race.' All of this took place while the man was sitting down on his chair, oblivious to everything that was going on around him. I left him in that shop and went on my way.

Sixth Section. On the clothing of the French

It is known in our country that the Frankish head-dress is the hat, that their footwear generally consists of black shoes or mocassins[1] and that they usually dress in black cloth. However, the French, though they usually dress in this manner, do not have a special uniform; everyone dresses as he pleases and as he is allowed by custom.

The dominant feature about their dress is not the ornamentation but the extreme cleanliness. One of their best customs is that they wear a chemise, underpants and a vest underneath their clothes. A wealthy man

1. *tāsūmāt* (sing. *tāsūma*, pl. *tawāsīm*); often used simply to denote 'shoe' (cf. e.g. G. Badger, 1895: 962; A. Kazimirski, 1860: I, 199), these were described by E. Bocthor (1882: 565) as '*soulier en pantoufle*'; cf. R. Dozy, 1967: I, 138–9; *idem*, 1845: 104.

will change his underwear several times a week. In doing so, they attempt to prevent vermin from breeding and thus all but the very poor are free from fleas or any other such creatures.

French women's clothes are very pretty, but there is a certain immodesty about them especially when they wear their most expensive garments. However, they do not have a lot of jewellery. They wear gilded earrings, gold bracelets, which they put on their forearms and which show from under their sleeves, and a light necklace. As for anklets, these are completely unknown to them. They wear fine fabrics such as silk, calico or light cotton. When it is cold they wear a fur scarf [stole], which they put around their neck, with both ends dangling, like a *mi'zar*,[1] almost to their feet. It is also their custom to wear a thin belt on their dresses with a view to making their waists look slim and their haunches full.

Witness the words al-Ḥājarī wrote in his *Dīwān*, though they depart from propriety:

The one who wears a zunnār,[2] *if only I were his master*
so that I might win an embrace from his waist
The priest gives him to drink the rose of his cheek
and the Muslims have become his captives
To his merit, if it had not been for the nimbleness of his body
my Islam would not have digressed before his cruel heathenness

Another wonderful thing is that, once the belt has been put on, the waist is so slim that one can hold it in both hands. Women also tend to attach a tin rod to the belt, which extends from the belly to their bosom so that their posture is always straight without curves. They are indeed very wily.

One of their habits that cannot be condoned is that, contrary to the

1. This was a type of long silk veil (also *mi'zār*), which (usually older) Muslim women wrapped around their head, with the two ends left dangling on their shoulders. R. Dozy, 1967: I, 20; *idem*, 1845: 38–46. It was similar to the *'itb* (*mi'taba*), which was generally worn by younger women; see R. Dozy, 1845: 21–3.
2. Originally, this word denoted a 'girdle' in Arabic – especially the type worn by *dhimmīs* (Christians, Jews, etc.), who were often subject to dress restrictions. It was, however, primarily associated with Christians, as becomes apparent from the fact that *muzannar* ('he who wears the *zunnār*') was synonymous with 'Christian'. Later on, it would also be used for '(European) belt' (cf. MSA *ḥizām*), as well as the locks of hair worn by Jews on the sides of the head. It should, however, be pointed out that in western Islamic lands, the word also had other meanings; for instance, in al-Andalus *zunnār* denoted a coarse woollen coat, whereas in Tunisia it referred to the black and white turban of the country gentry. See *EI1*, s.v. "zunnār" (A. Tritton); R. Dozy, 1845: 196–8; *idem*, 1967: I, 606; S. Ferchiou, 1970: 18; Ibn Jubayr [n.d.]: 215 (trans. Gaudefroy-Demombynes, 361, note 2).

wont of Arab women, they do not let their hair hang freely. French women always gather their hair in the middle of their heads and put a comb in it or something like that.

On hot days they tend to uncover parts of their bodies, removing any garments between the head and their breasts – sometimes they even show a bare back. At evening dance parties the ladies' arms are bare. Yet this is not considered indecent by people of this country. However, they never show their legs and always wear stockings, especially when they go out into the street. In truth, their legs are not exceptional at all and the following words of the poet do not really apply to them:

I have not forgotten him, as he got up freely showing his
leg, as white as a shiny pearl
Do not wonder if in him I found my resurrection
Indeed the resurrection is the day of the discovery of the leg![1]

Let us now turn to the mourning attire of the French. They wear the sign of mourning for a specific period in a specific place; the men wear the mourning sign for a specific period on their hats, the women on their dresses. A son who has lost a father or mother wears the signs of mourning for six months. In the case of the loss of a grandmother, it is four months. For a woman who has lost her husband the period amounts to one year and six weeks, whereas the husband who has lost his wife displays the sign of mourning for six months. For the loss of an uncle or aunt, the period is three weeks, and for the loss of cousins, two.

Each year, one million francs' worth of cloth, three million francs' worth of silk and one million francs' worth of furs are sold in Paris. This may be explained by the fact that furs are bought as a speciality of Paris for the people of Paris.

In France, it is common for bald people or those who have bad hair to wear wigs. They even use false hair for beards and moustaches as a disguise. This was the custom in the time of the French King Louis XIV since he wore a wig which he took off only when he went to sleep. Today it has survived only among bald people and those with bad hair. The strange

1. The author of this verse with its eroticizing of the bared leg was clearly inspired by the Qur'ān, where this appears in sūra XXVII:44, but especially in LXVIII:42: 'Upon the day when the leg shall be bared, and they shall be summoned to bow themselves, but they cannot' (trans. A. Arberry, 1983: 601). The poet's 'resurrection' (*qiyāma*) – or erection – is thus in direct opposition to the Qur'ānic 'bowing' (*sujūd*, which literally translates as 'prostration' [before God]).

thing is that the wearing of wigs has become a fashion in Egypt among women in Cairo.

Seventh Section. On the entertainments of Paris

You should know that when these people finish their usual activities to ensure their livelihood, they do not get involved in matters of devotion; rather, they spend their time indulging in worldly matters, entertainments and games, in which they display a truly amazing versatility.

Among the entertainments, we find amusement gatherings in places they call *théâtre* (*al-tiyātir*)[1] and *spectacles* (*al-sibiktākil*). Here, they re-enact everything that has happened. In truth, these games deal with serious things through jest, because people learn wonderful lessons. Indeed, they see good and bad acts, whereas the former are praised and the latter condemned, so that the French say that it [the theatre] punishes and improves people's morals. Although it contains many things that are amusing, there are also many things to cry about.[2] On the screen that

1. This borrowing originally came into Arabic through the Greek θεάτρον (cf. Syriac *te'aṭron*; Heb. *teaṭron*) and was first used by the Tunisian poet Muḥriz b. Khalaf (d. 1022) in reference to the Roman theatre in Carthage (H. Ben Halima, 1974: 13). It also appears in al-Idrīsī's geographical work (R. Dozy and M. De Goeje (eds), 112/132) as *ṭiyāṭir*. For an excellent survey of references to the theatre in Arabic literature see S. Moreh, 1990. In the first half of the 19th century, the MSA *masraḥ* still had its classical meaning of 'pasture', the Lebanese playwright Mārūn al-Naqqāsh probably being the first to use in its modern sense (1869: 15). The borrowing (pl. *tiyātrāt*), with its variant *tiyātrū* (pl. *tiyātrawāt* – It. *teatro*; cf. Tu. *tiyātrō*) remained popular throughout the century: Khayr al-Dīn, 1867: 55 (*tiyāṭr*); M. Ibn al-Khūja, 1900: 22, 44 (*tiyātir*); M. al-Sanūsī, 1891–92: 177 (*tiyātir*); *idem*, 1976–81: I, 126 *et passim* (*tiyātrū*); S. al-Wardānī, 1888–91: no. 9 (p. 4), no. 30 (p. 3) (*tiyātrū*); A. Zakī, 1893: 391 (*tiyātir*); A. Ilyās, 1900: 268 *et passim* (*tiyātir*); al-Salāwī, 1956: IX, 116 (*tiyātrū*); M. Amīn Fikrī, 1892: 149, 152 *et passim* (*tiyātir*), 186 *et passim* (*tiyātrū*); M. al-Muwaylīḥī [n.d.]: 201 (*tiyātrū*); ʿA. Nadīm, 1897–1901: 40 (*tiyātir*); A. Ibn Abī 'l-Ḍiyāf, 1963–65: IV, 102 (*tiyātir*); K. Vollers, 1897: 319. It would seem that the Italian-based borrowing crowded out the French form as it is the former that tended to find its way into dictionaries: e.g. S. Spiro, 1895: 88; G. Badger, 1895: 1091; J. Zenker, 1866: 330; J. Redhouse, 1880: 333. Equally interesting is the fact that al-Ṭahṭāwī (see below) and Khayr al-Dīn (1867: 60) were the only authors to use *tiyātir* in the sense of 'play'. Very early on, the borrowing also became inflectionally active, the adjectivized form appearing, for instance, in the calque *qiṭʿa tiyātriyya* (Fr. '*pièce de théâtre*') in the title of M. ʿU. Jalāl's translation of Molière's *Tartuffe*, viz. *al-shaykh Matlūf* (Cairo, 1290/1873). It was also used by the Egyptian Yaʿqūb Ṣanūʿ for one of his comedies, *al-Qirdātī luʿba tiyātriyya ḥaṣalat fī ayyām al-Ghuzz fī 1204*.
2. These views on the theatre would be shared by many of al-Ṭahṭāwī's successors; for a discussion, see D. Newman, 2002a. The first mention of European (French) theatre in the 19th century was by ʿA. al-Jabartī (1997: IV, 536: 11 Shaʿbān, 1215/28 December 1800): 'In Azbakiyya, near a place called *Bāb al-Hawā*, they [the French] finished building a place which is called *kumidī* in their language. This word refers to a place where every

comes down at the end of the play, there is a Latin saying that may be translated as follows: '*amusement improves the morals*'.[1]

These theatres resemble large houses surmounted by a huge dome. Inside, there are several floors, each of which has rooms [boxes][2] arranged around the inside of the dome. At one side of the building, there is a large stage,[3] on which all these rooms give out, so that everything that goes on there is visible to the people that are inside the building. It is lit by magnificent chandeliers. Beneath the stage, there is a place for the musicians. Connected to it are the storerooms for the stage equipment and properties, as well as the rooms where the women and men prepare for their performance. The stage is set up in accordance with the performance; for instance, if they want to imitate a sultan and the things that happen to him, they convert the stage to make it look like a palace, create an image of the character, recite his poetry and so on and so forth. During the stage preparations, they lower the curtain so as to prevent the spectators from seeing what is going on. Then they raise it and the playing begins.

The male and female players resemble the *'awālim*[4] of Egypt. The male and female players in the city of Paris are people of great refinement and eloquence, and sometimes these people have themselves written many literary works and poetry. If you heard the verses a player knows by heart, the allusions he produces through his acting and the funny as well as exhortatory answers, you would be extremely astounded. One of the amazing things is that during their performance, they raise issues related to foreign sciences and difficult questions, which they deal with in depth at the same time. They do this so convincingly that you would think them

ten days they get together at night to watch an entertainment which lasts for four hours and is performed in their language for their recreation and amusement (*al-tasallī wa 'l-malahī*) by a group of of them. Only those who have a ticket (*waraqa*) and wear the appropriate dress are allowed entry.'

1. This is a liberal translation of the saying (attributed to both Horace and Erasmus): *ridendo castigat mores* (*lectorem delectando pariterque monendo*), i.e. 'laughter improves morals'.
2. *uwaḍ* (sing. *ōḍa*); cf. A. Ibn Abī 'l-Ḍiyāf, 1963–65: IV, 102 (*rawāshīn* – sing. *rawshan*).
3. *maq'ad* (pl. *maqā'id*), which in Egypt denoted a first-floor gallery surrounding and opening on to the central courtyard of a large house. It served as a reception room (cf. *mandara*) for important visitors. See E. Lane, 1923: 17.
4. sing. *'ālima* (lit. 'wise woman'). These were professional dancers and singers, who often figured prominently in the 19th-century Orientalist writings of Flaubert, de Nerval, etc.; Rimbaud even devoted an entire poem to one of them ('Est-elle almée?'). On the whole, these professional singers had a very bad reputation, to the extent that Muḥammad 'Alī had them banned, which, in turn, led to the emergence of a lively transvestite scene. See E. Lane, 1923: 172, 361–2, 506; D. Hopwood, 1999: 130–4; K. Van Nieuwkerk 1995; W. Buonaventura & I. Farrah 1998.

scholars. Even the small boys that play refer to important notions from the natural sciences, etc.

The performance starts with music and then the actual play begins. The title of the play that is being shown is written on posters which are stuck on the walls of the city and published in the dailies so that both the notables and the common people know what is being performed. On any given night they put on several plays. At the end of each one, the curtain is lowered. So, if, for instance, they want to impersonate the Shah of Persia, one of the players dresses up like him, after which he appears onstage and sits on a throne, etc. In these *spectacles*, they represent everything that exists, even the parting of the sea by Moses – Peace be upon him.[1] They represent the sea and create rolling waves so that it completely looks like the sea. One night, I saw that they ended the play (*tiyātir*) with a representation of a sun and its course. The light of this sun illuminated the theatre to such an extent that it outshone the chandeliers; it was as if suddenly morning had broken for people. But they do far stranger things than that. In short, with them the theatre is like a public school where both the scholar and the ignorant become educated.

The most amazing of the *spectacles* in the city of Paris is that which they call *Opéra* (*al-ūbbirā*).[2] Here you find the greatest musicians and dancers, as well as singers, accompanied by music and dances, whose gestures are like those of deaf people and make clear many wondrous things. Other types of theatre include that which they call the *Opéra-comique* (*ūbira kūmīk*),[3] where people sing wonderful verses, and the *Théâtre-italien* (*al-tiyātir al-Ṭilyāniyya*), where they have the best musicians and where verses written in Italian are recited. These are all the *grands spectacles* in Paris, which also has *petits spectacles*, which are similar, only smaller.

Then there are also other *spectacles* where horses, elephants and other animals perform shows. There is a theatre called the *Théâtre Franconi* (*Kirankūnī*), where there is a wonderfully trained elephant famous for performing extraordinary tricks.[4] Just as the Opera is the biggest theatre,

1. This is of course a reference to *Moïse en Egypte*, the famous opera by Rossini, which had its first showing in 1818, with a revised version premiering in 1827 in Paris, where the composer had settled in 1824. The opera had several seasons in Paris during al-Ṭahṭāwī's stay there.
2. Cf. M. Bayram V, 1884–93: III, 83 (*lūbirah*); M. al-Sanūsī, 1891–92: 47 (*ūbīrah*), 61 (*lūbirah*); F. al-Shidyāq, 1881: 68 (*ūrpā*), 232 (*ūbīra*); A. Ilyās, 1900: 269, 277, 278, 285 (*ūbrā*); M. Amīn Fikrī, 1892: 125, 152ff. (*ūprā*); M. al-Naqqash, 1869: 16 (*ūbirah*).
3. Founded in 1752, this theatre merged with the *Comédie italienne* in 1762. See M. Berthelot, 1886–1902: XXV: 411–12.
4. The theatre was set up by Laurent Franconi (1776–1849), who was part of a famous family

the smallest is called *Théâtre de Monsieur Comte* (*tiyātir al-Kumt*).[1] This serves to amuse children, like the *ḥāwī*[2] in Egypt. 'Comte' is the name of the manager of this *spectacle*. All the actors and actresses are young people. In this theatre, you can see sleight of hand, magic and other things like that.[3]

If there were not so many Satanic leanings in the French theatre, it would have to be considered an institution with highly beneficial virtues. Just look at the players; they do their utmost to avoid anything that is indecent or leads to temptation, which clearly sets them apart from the Egyptian *'awālim*, musicians, etc.

I do not know of an Arabic word that renders the meaning of *spectacle* or 'theatre'. The basic meaning of the word *spectacle* is 'view', 'place of recreation' or some such, whereas 'theatre' originally also meant 'game', 'entertainment', or the venue where this takes place. And so it may be compared with those actors called 'shadow players'.[4] More appropriately, shadow play is a form of theatre, as both are known by the Turks as *komedya*.[5] However, this denomination is too restrictive, except if it is used in a broader sense. There is no objection to translating 'theatre' or '*spectacle*' as *khayālī* ['imaginary'] if you enlarge the meaning of this word, as a result of which it comes close to the idea of '*spectacle*'.[6]

There are other places like that where people are shown the view of a

---

of Italian horsemen. He was particularly known for his acrobatic horse shows (*équitation acrobatique*), in which his son, Victor, also played a leading role. In 1845, they opened a Hippodrome, where there were chariot races, pantomimes, etc. The Algerian traveller Ibn Ṣiyām (1852: 16–17) attended one of their shows at the Hippodrome (*bayḍrum*), and was equally impressed with the performances on display. One should add that performing animals, circuses, etc. exerted a huge attraction on Muslim travellers, several of whom gave detailed descriptions of the shows they saw; e.g. al-Wardānī, 1888: no. 8, p. 4.

1. Louis Comte (1788–1859) was a famous prestidigator and ventriloquist. In 1815, he was given the royal imprimatur for his act by Louis XVIII. Comte travelled all over Europe to perform his tricks. The theatre mentioned here was opened in 1827, and Comte remained director until 1848.
2. Pl. *ḥuwā*; a snake-charmer, conjuror. For a good description of their acts, see E. Lane, 1923: 391ff.
3. Cf. al-Sanūsī, 1976–81: I, 160; Ibn Khaldūn [F. Rosenthal], 1986: I, 206, III, 159, 169.
4. *ahl al-la'ab al-musammā khayāliyyan* is a reference to *khayāl al-ẓill* ('shadow reflection'). On this art form in Muslim lands see 'A. Yūnus, 1994; M. al-Khozai, 1984; *EI1*, s.v. "Khayāl-i ẓill", (T. Menzel); "ḳaragöz"; *EI1* (H. Ritter), *EI2*.
5. Cf. 'A. Al-Jabartī, 1997: IV, 536 (*kumidī*); F. al-Shidyāq, 1881: 307 (*kūmīdī*); M. al-Sanūsī, 1976–81: I, 154 (*kūmīdiyā*); *idem*, 1891–92: 61 (*kūmīḍī*); Khayr al-Dīn, 1867: 57 (*kūmīdiyā*); M. Amīn Fikrī, 1892: 251 (*kūmidiyā*); M. al-Naqqāsh, 1869 (*kūmidiyā*); 16; E. Bocthor, 1882: 164; E. Gasselin, 1880–86: I, 292. The borrowing probably occurred for the first time in the *riḥla* by the 18th-century Moroccan ambassador al-Miknāsī (1965: 23 (*kūmīdiyī*)).
6. Despite the cogent argumentation, al-Ṭahṭāwī's suggestion was not followed by others, the MSA term being, as we have seen, *masraḥ* ('theatre'), which also gave rise to *masraḥiyya* ('play'), alongside '*riwāya/qiṣṣa/ḥikāya masraḥiyya* ('theatre story').

town, region, etc. These include the *Panorama* (*Bānūrama*),[1] where one can see the city they want to represent. If you look at the representation of Cairo, for instance, it is as if you were standing on the minaret of [the mosque of] Sultan Ḥasan, and below you see al-Rumayla and the rest of the city. The *Cosmorama* (*Kusmūrama*) offers the view of a town, followed by another one and so on. At the *Diorama* (*Diyūrama*)[2] one can see the view of a house, whereas the *Uranorama* (*Ūrānūrama*) provides a representation of the heavens and everything that is contained in it, in accordance with the conception of the Franks. Furthermore, the spectator can follow a course in astronomy there. Finally, there is the *Europeorama* (*Ūrūbarama*), in which views of the countries of the Franks are on display.

Among the entertainment places, there are the dance halls, called *bals* (*al-bāl*), where there is singing and dancing. It is rare to go into the house of a notable at night and not to hear music and singing there. For some time, I did not fully understand their singing as I did not know their language. How right was the one who said the following in a similar situation:

I did not understand its meaning, but
my heart was filled with love though I knew its pain
It was is if I was blind and tormented
like one who loves fair maidens but cannot see them

---

1. Patented in 1787 by the Irish painter Robert Barker, who initially called it *La Nature à Coup d'Oeil*, the panorama consisted of a circular canvas structure lined with painted scenes (often by famous artists like Loutherbourg or Thomas Gainsborough) viewed from a central platform. The views on show varied from street scenes to battle scenes, nature, etc. The powerful impact of peripheral vision and the resultant visual distortions in some cases led to hysteria among spectators. The panoramas often served as a kind of newsreel; in 1812, for instance, a panorama in Berlin presented the burning of Moscow just three months after it had taken place. The first panorama was that of the Bvd Montmartre, after which another one was built on the Blvd des Capucines. However, al-Ṭahṭāwī could have visited only the former since the latter was destroyed in 1824. The Montmartre venue was pulled down in 1831 since it had lost its public appeal. See M. Berthelot, 1886–1902: XXV, 950–51.
2. This highly popular attraction was invented by Louis Daguerre (1787–1851). Created in 1822 at the rue Sourton (later at the Boulevard Bonne-Nouvelle), it consisted of figures painted in miniature against a backdrop and viewed through a small opening, with spectacular lighting effects producing a highly realistic effect. It was closed in 1854, a military barracks (Caserne du Prince-Eugène, the current Caserne Vérines) being built on the site. See *GDU*, s.v.; M. Berthelot, 1886–1902: XIV, 617–18. Another Muslim traveller, the Moroccan al-Ṣaffār, gives a lengthy description of it in his account of his visit to Paris in 1845–46; S. Gilson Miller, 1992: 145–6. The success of Daguerre's *Diorama* was such that keen business entrepreneurs were quick to make their own versions, which came under various fantastic and enticing names such as Europeorama, Uranorama, Cosmorama, Physiorama, etc.

There are two types of balls: public balls, where everybody is allowed to enter – for instance, dances in coffee houses or parks – and private balls, where a group of people are invited to dance, sing and enjoy themselves, which is a bit like a wedding in Egypt.[1]

Balls always include men and women. The hall itself is brightly lit, with chairs so that guests can sit down. However, it is mainly the women that sit down, and no man will ever sit down before all women have found a place; if a woman joins a company and there is no seat available, then one of the men will get up and offer her his seat. Conversely, a woman does not get up to give up her seat. In social gatherings, a female is always treated with greater regard than a man. So, when somebody enters the house of his friend, he must first greet the lady of the house before the master. And regardless of his rank, he comes after his wife or the ladies of the house.

Another form of entertainment is the gathering of people, similar to the *ḍamma*[2] in Egypt, except for the fact that there is always an orchestra, as well as singing and dancing. In between each musical and singing performance, the people present are served light snacks and beverages. In short, it is primarily the music and then the light drinks that provide the pleasure at these gatherings. As the poet said:

Is life anything else but watered-down wine
sparkling in the glass with water from the clouds
and a lute plucked with the fingertips while assisted in its chant
by the dulcet tones of Zunām's[3] *flute?*

We have already mentioned that they consider dancing an art. Al-Masʿūdī already referred to it in his history entitled *Murūj al-dhahab* ('The Golden Meadows'), in which he stated that it is comparable to a wrestling match in view of the equilibrium of the participants and the mutual action of strength. Not every strong man knows about fighting; a man with a weaker build can beat him by means of tricks established among fighters. Similarly, not every dancer is able to perform the minute movements of the members.

1. Although other Muslim travellers would be equally charmed by the balls (e.g. al-Sanūsī, 1891–92: 53; S. Ibn Ṣiyam 1852: 24), some were not; ʿAlī Mubārak, for instance, called these balls ridiculous affairs where people forget who they are (1882: III, 845). Also see M. al-Muwaylīḥī [n.d]: 161ff.
2. This is a gathering of the men of a village community (or tribe) at which stories are told and poetry recited.
3. Zunām was the name of a famous flute player at the court of Hārūn al-Rashīd. He is also credited with the invention of a kind of oboe, called *zunāmī* (or *zulāmī*). E. Lane, 1863–74: I, 1259.

It appears that dancing and wrestling go back to a common origin. This is something that can be ascertained after some contemplation.

Everyone in France loves dancing, which is considered something distinguished and elegant, instead of morally depraved. By the same token, it never departs from the rules of decency, whereas in Egypt the dance is one of the specialities of women since it arouses desires. Conversely, in Paris, it is a special kind of jump, which is entirely devoid of even the slightest whiff of debauchery. Every man can invite a woman to dance with him, and when the dance is over, another one may invite her for the second one and so on, irrespective of whether the man knows the lady or not. The women are pleased if many men want to dance with them. They do not content themselves with one or two; rather, they like to be seen dancing with many men as they weary of being attached to one and the same thing. As the poet said:

You who are not satisfied with one friend
nor with two thousand friends each year
I see in you the remainder of the tribe of Moses
who were impatient to get their food

Sometimes, a special dance is performed, during which the man puts his arm around the waist of his partner, while holding her hand most of the time. In short, touching the upper part of the body of a woman, irrespective of who she is, is not considered indecent by these Christians. The more a man talks with women and praises them, the more he is considered a man of good breeding. It is also the mistress of the house who greets the people gathered.

Other entertainments are the public feasts, which take place during summer and which involve dancing, music, fireworks, and the such. These public feasts include the days known as *carnival* (*al-karnawāl*), which among the Copts of Egypt is known as *ayyām al-rifā*ʿ [Shrovetide]. During this festival, which lasts for a number of days, all people are allowed to don every kind of masquerade and disguise. Men dress up like women, and women like men, while an important personage may appear in the guise of a shepherd, etc. In short, anything that is not harmful to the calm and order of the kingdom is allowed. The French call these days 'the days of madness'. The fattest bull calf of France is taken around this city in a huge float during 'the fat days',[1] after which it is slaughtered, its owner receiving a remuneration commensurate with the slaughter expenses[2] so as to encourage other people to do the same with their calves.

Other places of entertainment in Paris are the huge public parks. There are about four large gardens in Paris where both the elite and the common folk can walk around. One of them is a park called 'Champs Elysées' (*al-Shanzalīzah*), which in Arabic means 'the gardens of paradise'.[3] This is one of the most beautiful and splendid recreation areas. This huge garden has a surface of forty *arpents* (*arbān*), which is a unit of measure approximately covering the area of a *feddan*.[4] Although the avenue is about 6,000 feet long, it has been designed in such a way that if you gaze into the distance, you can see the other end before your eyes. In this magnificent garden, there are always various types of entertainment going on, which it is impossible to enumerate. The trees of this park are lined up in parallel rows, and have been arranged in such a way that the entrance is accessible from all sides as the aisles of trees converge on it. In the centre of each group of trees there is a square. On one side, this park gives out on to the river Seine, from which it is separated by a quay. On the other side, there are houses bordering the open country. There are many cafés and restaurants (*al-risṭurāṭurāt*), i.e. eating establishments where all types of food and drink can be obtained, and which are meeting places for lovers and people of note. There are numerous riding paths, on which the notables ride around in their ornate carriages. There are several thousand chairs that can be rented and on which people sit during the daytime in spring and in the evenings in summer. It is on Sundays that you can see the biggest gathering of people in this park since Sunday is the day of rest among the French. In

1. *ayyām al-ẓafar al-thalātha*, i. e. 'Mardi gras' (*thalāthā' al-ẓafar*).
2. Interestingly enough, al-Ṭahṭāwī uses the metonym *tasmīya* for slaughter. This word, in fact, denotes the religious formula *bismillāh al-raḥmān al-raḥīm* ('In the name of God, the Merciful, the Compassionate'), which is uttered during the slaughter, as without it, meat is not *ḥalāl* (lawful) under Islamic law.
3. In the second edition, the author inserted the following sentence before this one: 'One of them is the garden of the Tuileries (*al-Tūlrī*), which is where the palace of the king is situated. This is one of the most magnificent promenades. Only the elegant people (*al-mutajammilūn*, cf. Fr. '*le beau monde*'!) may enter it, not the lower classes. It bears out the saying by one wit: 'If I had obtained the protection over these gardens, the lowly would never walk on its soil.'
4. *faddān*. Up until 1830, this Egyptian surface measure equalled 5,306.6 m^2; the feddan was divided in 24 *qīrāṭ* and consisted of 333.3 square *qaṣaba* (*c.* 3.99 m). Afterwards, the latter was reduced to 3.55m., thus bringing the feddan down to 4,200.833 m^2. One should also add that in the early 19th century, there were slight differences depending on the region, the Upper Egyptian feddan, for instance, being considerably smaller than that in use in Damietta. See E. Lane, 1923: 578; W. Hinz, 1970: 63, 65, 66; *EI1*, s.v. "faddān" (C. Huart).

short, this park is the site for public feasts, celebrations and ceremonies.[1] It is also a place where all the beautiful women stroll.

Other recreation areas are the so-called *boulevards* (*bulwār*), which are parallel rows of trees, as we have already described above. These are places where people walk every day, and where the most magnificent cafés of Paris are located. Itinerant musicians move around there with their instruments, and among them there are many that work at the theatres in the area. There are also women who stroll around there in order to make the acquaintance of men, particularly at night. Every night, especially on Sunday nights, many people can be found there, and you see lovers walking arm in arm until midnight.[2]

Finally, the market where they sell flowers is also a place of recreation. At this market, you find all types of rare and exotic bushes, plants and flowers, even out of their season, so that a person can make an entirely new garden in the space of only one day, buying everything he needs and planting it. It must be added, however, that these places of entertainment and recreation can be enjoyed only by people who are in good health.

Eighth Section. On hygiene in the city of Paris

As concern for hygiene is a requirement of wisdom and as the Franks are the wisest among nations they attach a great deal of importance to this art in terms of perfecting both the equipment and the means that promote it. Of all people they are the most committed to using everything that is beneficial to the body: hot- and cold-water baths, and sports that train the body for difficult exercises – swimming, horse riding and games that make the body nimble.

There are many different types of bathhouses in Paris. But while they are indeed cleaner than Egyptian baths, the latter are more beneficial, more perfected and generally better. Parisian bathhouses have several small rooms, each of which contains a copper bath where there is room for only one person. Although some rooms have two baths, Europeans do not use a communal bath as we do in Egypt.[3] Their way of doing things is more

1. *zīnāt*, with *yawm al-zīna* ('day of ornamentation') denoting an official celebration, with people ornamenting their houses, streets, etc.
2. This paragraph is followed by six verses (with the following metres: *basīṭ, khafīf, ṭawīl, basīṭ, rajaz* and *kāmil*), all dealing with the night theme. They have been omitted for reasons of relevancy.
3. For a description of bathing practices in Egypt at the time, see E. Lane, 1923: 343ff. Also see A. Raymond, 1969 (on the number and distribution of bathing facilities in Cairo in the early 19th century).

decent since people cannot see each other's private parts. In the bathrooms there is even a curtain between the two baths so that the person in one bath cannot see his companion in the other. When entering these small baths one does not experience the same pleasure as one gets in an Egyptian bath. People do not sweat since the heat is restricted to the bathtub, and does not fill the room. Nevertheless, it is possible to order a steam bath, which they prepare for you, and for which a special price is charged.

In the bathhouse there are two rows of cabins, one for men and one for women. In addition to the fixed baths, there are also portable baths; if somebody wants to take a bath in his house or if he is ill, etc., the bath is brought to him in a cart shaped like a barrel, half of which contains the cold water, the other half the hot water. The people from the bathhouse also bring a cauldron, which they place in the person's house and fill with hot water for the person to use to wash himself. When he is finished, the bath is taken back to the bathhouse.

There exists a type of bath in which only part of the body is submerged and which the French call a *demi-bain*.[1] It is used in the treatment of certain diseases. There are many bathhouses in Paris, of which about thirty are famous.

As for the physical exercises for the benefit of the body, there are schools where they teach the science of swimming. There are three of those on the river Seine. In other schools, people are taught to make the body agile and to enable it to perform extraordinary feats like acrobatics, wrestling, etc.

Ninth Section. On the interest in medical sciences in Paris

You should know that the city of Paris is the most important city of the Franks, and that foreigners travel there to study the sciences, especially medicine. Sick people from faraway countries often go there in search of treatment.

The medical sciences, which are also called *ʿilm al-ḥikma*,[2] comprise the science of healing, surgery, anatomy, the art of physiology (*al-fisiyūlūjiyā*) for ascertaining a man's state of health based on his condition (i.e. diagnostics), hygiene, veterinary medicine and others.

There are a great many doctors in Paris, to the extent that there are

1. *nuṣf ḥammām*, i.e. sitz bath.
2. Strictly speaking, *ḥikma* denoted the infinite wisdom of God, as well as of man, and later on 'philosophy'. Afterwards, the alchemists called their science *ḥikma* and it became associated with the profession of healing, i.e. that of the *ḥakīm*. See *EI1*, s.v. "ḥikma" (C. Huart).

several physicians in each district. What is more, the streets are so full of doctors that if a man is afflicted with an ailment in the street, he will immediately find one. The position of the sick in relation to the doctor varies. There are patients who request the doctor to visit them at home, the latter charging a specific fee for each house call. Other sick people go to see the doctor at his home, in which case the doctor has fixed hours during which he stays at home in order to receive people. Still other sick people go to a house called a 'house of health' (*maison de santé*), which is destined for people who pay a fixed sum for their food, drink, accommodation, doctor's care, service, etc.

In Paris, there are doctors' houses [clinics], which are destined for those who are afflicted with a bone disorder, such as hunchbacks. Such people go to one of these treatment centres where they redress the body by means of certain techniques. Similarly, if somebody has lost one of his limbs, they restore this by putting something made out of metal or wood in its place.

In this city there are also houses where pregnant women who are about to deliver go in order to give birth and spend their confinement. In these houses, there are midwives and everything that is needed for childbirth.

Other places that are destined for the sick and in which there are doctors are the public hospitals,[1] where patients go to get treatment and where they stay for the duration of their illness without having to pay anything.

There are two categories of doctors in Paris; the first are general practitioners for various types of illnesses, whereas the second are specialized in certain illnesses. This is because the medical science is a vast area and it is rare for someone to work in all branches and to study them. As a result, the French medical profession demands that, after having studied the various medical branches, a doctor must choose one discipline to which he will devote all his attention so as to acquire all the relevant knowledge and to penetrate and delve deeply into it until he has made a name for himself and distinguishes himself from other doctors in the study of this discipline, and to attract people who suffer from ailments that fall within this branch. Thus, in Paris, there are, for instance, doctors who specialize in lung diseases, eye diseases – these doctors are called ophthalmologists – ear diseases or nose diseases and restorations. Some of

1. Al-Ṭahṭāwī uses *māristān*, which is a variant of *bīmāristān*. This word of Persian origin was the usual term to denote hospitals-cum-medical schools in the Near East, the earliest and most famous example of which is that in Damascus. The MSA word for hospital, *mustashfā*, gained currency only in the 20th century. The word *māristān* (with its variants *maristān*, *murustān*), which al-Ṭahṭāwī also uses for the French '*hospice*', has survived in the sense of 'lunatic asylum'. Also see *EI2*, s.v. "Bīmāristān" (D. Dunlop).

these nose doctors even use techniques by which they are able to repair a broken nose.

In Paris, there are also doctors who use human magnetism (*maghnāṭīs*) for the treatment of diseases.[1] The details of this are as follows: in Paris, there is a group of natural philosophers who claim that they are in no doubt that the human body contains a fluid, i.e. human magnetism, by which is meant that this substance has the property of magnets. This effect is obtained by approaching the hand several times, as in rubbing, as a result of which the patient becomes drowsy or insensitive to sensations to the extent of not feeling anything any more. If a patient suffering from a serious illness loses consciousness, the doctors treat him by cutting or opening part of his body without his feeling the slightest thing. This was put to the test with the excision of the breast of a woman after she had been magnetized; she remained alive for several days and then she died. The magnetism scholars [the mesmerists] argued that she died because of other reasons and not because of the pain resulting from the amputation since she had remained alive afterwards. They also claim that it is useful in the treatment of nervous disorders.

In Paris, there are also doctors specializing in mental illnesses, diseases of the genitals, or gravel, whereas others specialize in repugnant skin diseases such as leprosy[2] and scabies. There are also doctors to help women give birth, because in Paris it is customary for a woman to have her child delivered by a male doctor who is a specialist in matters of childbirth. There are also doctors who treat the white that descends over the eye [cataract] and the water that blinds people [glaucoma]. Then, there are doctors for pains in the chest, and for hemiplegia, which is a paralysis of certain limbs. It is treated by means of *acupuncture* (*al-ikimbuktūr*), which involves pricking the skin by means of many fine needles, resulting in the loss of a little blood, which relieves the damaging effect of this disease. There are also doctors for the treatment of disorders of the human constitution, which is called *orthopaedics* (*al-urtūbīday*), i.e. the art of rectifying defects in the limbs of children. Finally, there are doctors who rectify deformities of the mouth or face, and others who concentrate on the restoration of missing or incomplete limbs by replacing them with other, artificial organs.

There are many branches in the medical sciences. The best known among them are: anatomy; diagnostics; the art of the chemical preparation

1. Cf. al-Sanūsī, 1891–92: 79. Also see *EI1*, s.v. "maghnaṭīs, maghnāṭīs, maghnīṭīs" (E. Wiedemann).
2. The author renders the ECA pronuncation *juzām* (classical Arabic *judhām*).

of medicines [pharmaceutics]; the art of the physiological causes of diseases [pathology]; the science of surgery, and the placing of bandages on injuries and dressing them with ointments; the art of treating bedridden, sick people suffering from external and internal disorders; the art of treating pregnant women during confinement and child delivery [obstetrics]; physics related to medicine; the science of both simple and compound medicaments and remedies [pharmacology]; and the profession of treating and following up on sick people.

The medical schools in the city of Paris and their facilities are well known. One of them is a big school called the Royal Academy (*akadima*) of Medicine, which is a council (*dīwān*) of royal doctors. It was set up to meet the needs of the kingdom of the French and to tackle illnesses that represent a public danger, such as epidemics and diseases the French think are contagious, like those causing the death of cattle. One of the functions of the scholars of the Academy of Medicine is to treat all people through things imposed by the kingdom in the interest of public. Their activities include the general vaccination against smallpox, the investigation into new and unknown remedies and the testing of mineral, natural or artificial medicines for their use in remedies. In short, the people of this royal society are the most eminent doctors of France.

The matters related to the hospital of Paris, some of which have already been mentioned in the preceding section, will be discussed in the chapter on charity. However, in order to enhance the usefulness of this travelogue, we should like to present here a treatise related to health and hygiene regulations. I translated this treatise in Paris so that it can be used by all people in Egypt, especially in view of its small size. Although it departs from our actual topic, it is of great benefit and will yield considerable profit.[1]

Tenth Section. On charity in the city of Paris

Most people in the land of the Franks and, indeed, in all countries where there are a lot of crafts and a great proficiency in them live off the fruit of

1. Here follows a translation of an unknown French medical manual, entitled 'Advice from the Doctor' (*Naṣīḥat al-Ṭabīb*), which contains an introduction followed by six sections ('articles'): 1. 'Advice to those of sound body'; 2. 'What to do when the first symptoms of the disease appear'; 3. 'What to do when the disease breaks out'; 4. 'Treatment of the convalescent'; 5. 'General recommendations on health'; 6. 'Treatments for various disorders and diseases'. In view of the general nature of the medical instructions and the absence of any literary or historical value, this translation will not be included here.

their labour. If one of them is prevented from doing so because of illness or some such thing, then he loses his livelihood and is forced to provide for himself in some other way, such as by begging, etc. So, hostels with a charitable aim have been set up so that people would not have to hold out their hands to others. The more crafts and professions there are in a town and the bigger its earnings are, the larger is the number of its inhabitants, as a result of which it requires more hospitals than another place. It is well known that Paris is among the most populous cities and the one that has the most crafts and industry and the highest degree of skills and crafts. Because of this, it has a large number of hospitals and charitable societies.[1] The hospitals and charities fill the void resulting from the tightfistedness and meanness of the individual members of this population. As has been mentioned before, the people are far removed from the generosity of the Arabs. Among them, there is no Ḥātim Ṭayy,[2] nor anybody like his son ʿAdīy, nor has their country produced someone like Maʿn Ibn Zāyid,[3] famous for his gentleness and generosity. It was about him that the poet said:

They say Maʿn does not pay the alms tax on his wealth
but how can he, he who has already given it away?
Even if a year has gone past without your finding anything of wealth in his houses
except the mention of his name and his camels,
when you go to him you will find him in an exultant mood
as if you were going to give him what you will get from him
He is the sea, irrespective of the side from which you come to him
His kindness is its depth, his charity its shore
If he passes through the valley, its hills weep
for him – if he passes a gathering, the widows weep

1. Cf. al-Sanūsī, 1891–92: 69ff.; al-Shidyāq, 1881: 229.
2. Ḥātim al-Ṭāʾī b. ʿAbd Allāh b. Saʿd was a pre-Islamic soldier and poet (*floruit* latter half of the 6th century), who was said to possess all the virtues of manhood (*murūwa*), especially generosity, which became proverbial (*ajwad min Ḥātim*, 'more generous than *Ḥātim*') and earned him the nickname of *al-Jawād* ('the open-handed one') or *al-Ajwad* ('the most open-handed'). This character trait also becomes apparent in his verses, most of which are eulogies on generosity and unselfish behaviour. See *EI1*, s.v. "Ḥātim al-Ṭāʾī" (C. Van Arendonk).
3. Maʿn b. Zāyida Abū ʾl-Walīd al-Shaybānī (d. 151/768–69) was a Muslim general and governor of the Yemen. In Arabic literature, he is remembered for his soldiering skills and extreme generosity, as well as patronage of poets. See "Maʿn b. Zāʾida", *EI1* (K. Zetterstéen), *EI2* (H. Kennedy); Yāqūt, 1866–73: I, 145, II, 548, 708, 898.

He has grown so accustomed to extending his palm that even if he
wanted to, he would not be able to close it as his fingertips would not obey him
And if his soul were the only thing left in his palm
he would grant it generously – May God protect him who asks him for it!

In their country not even the slightest thing of what is told about the ʿAbbāsids[1] and the Barmekids[2] has ever been heard about their kings and ministers. The kind Manṣūr, for instance, who is famous by the name of 'the penny-pincher',[3] would be the most generous of men in comparison with their kings. Admittedly, generosity is quite rare in civilized countries. They also believe that giving something to somebody who is capable of working induces him not to concern himself with earning a living.

In the city of Paris, there is a council for the management of the hospitals. It is composed of fifteen members who act in a general consultative capacity. There are five divisions in this council: the first is in charge of the hospitals; the second division manages the hospital facilities and equipment and the service to patients, as well as general remedies; the third division manages the estates in mortmain;[4] the fourth manages home care for the poor; the fifth division is in charge of the expenditure of the hospitals and their adjuncts.

Nobody can enter a hospital without having provided proof of his illness by means of a doctor's statement. A person who is recovering from his illness and wishes to leave before being fully recovered and having regained his strength receives a donation from the Welfare Fund[5] in order to help him recuperate so that he can return to his job.

---

1. This was the name of a dynasty of Baghdad caliphs, descended from the Prophet's uncle, al-ʿAbbās b. ʿAbd al-Muṭṭalib b. Hāshim. The dynasty (750–1258) succeeded that of the Umayyads (661–750). The ʿAbbāsid caliphate marks the golden age of Islam, with the creation of a world empire and the development of the arts, literature and science. See H. Kennedy, 1986: 124ff.; P. Holt, 1988: 104–39; P. Hitti, 1991: 288–428.
2. *Barāmika* (sing. *Barmak*), a Persian family of ministers in the ʿAbbāsid caliphate. See *EI1*, s.v. "Barmakids" (W. Barthold); *EI2*, s.v. "al-Barāmika" (D. Sourdel); H. Kennedy, 1986: 141–4 *et passim*; P. Hitti, 1991: 294–6 *et passim*.
3. *dawānqī*, which is derived from *dāni/aq* (pl. *dawāniq*), i.e. one-sixth of a dirham. The reference is to the second ʿAbbāsid caliph, Abū Jaʿfar ʿAbd Allāh b. Muḥammad al-Manṣūr (ruled 754–75), the founder of Baghdad. His reputation as a miser is based on his thrifty monetary policy and his generally austere lifestyle. See *EI1*, s.vv. "al-Manṣūr" (K. Zetterstéen), "dānaq" (C. Huart); al-Masʿūdī, 1960–79: chap. CXII.
4. *awqāf*, which is the closest the author could come to making clear the social welfare provisions (*assistance publique*) to his readership. Having said this, the religious aspect did also play a role in France, where the Catholic Church was very active in the health care sector, and owned and managed many institutions.
5. *akhdh min al-waqf*, which presumably refers to the *Caisse d'Assistance Sociale*.

The largest hospital in Paris is called the Hôtel-Dieu (*Ūtīl Diyū*), which more or less means 'the house of God'.[1] This is destined for sick and injured people. Children, patients with incurable illnesses, the mentally insane, women about to give birth, chronically ill patients and those afflicted with syphilis[2] are not admitted into this hospital since there are special facilities for each of these cases. Another famous hospital in Paris is the one they call Saint-Louis (*Sanluwīz*),[3] which is destined for people with chronic illnesses and those suffering from furunculosis, tetter, itch, scabies and other diseases of that kind.

In Paris, there is a home for foundlings, i.e. children who have been taken from the streets.[4] This is where children who have been neglected by their parents, such as illegitimate children and the like, are also taken.

In Paris, there is a also a home for orphans (*Hospice des Orphelins*), which is where children who have lost their parents enter. It can accommodate about 800 boys and girls, the boys residing in one part and the girls in another. This establishment is managed by a number of nuns, who are called *Sœurs de Charité* (*akhawāt al-iḥsān*). In this home, the little ones learn to read, write and do arithmetic. This establishment, too, is administered by a council. A child cannot be placed at the home unless authorization has been given by this council. When a child reaches the age of twenty-one, he/she leaves the home after having obtained permission from the council, and then he/she goes to live with a master craftsman, the costs relating to this being defrayed by the Welfare Fund of the home. The master craftsman may adopt the child, i.e. take him in his house as his son, provided however that he can prove to the members of the council that he has sufficient means, is of good moral conduct and is in good health.

---

1. The current Hôtel-Dieu, which is located on the north side of Notre-Dame, was built in 1866–78 on the site of the children's home (see below). The building al-Ṭahṭāwī is talking about was constructed at the time of Notre-Dame (12th c.), on the other side of the cathedral (where today is the Square Charlemagne), and straddled both banks of the river Seine. It was demolished in the course of the renovation programme of Baron Haussmann in the 1850s. Cf. al-Sanūsī, 1891–92: 76ff.; M. Amīn Fikrī, 1892: 304.
2. *al-mubtalī bi 'l-Ifranjī* [sic] literally means 'afflicted with the Frankish (disease)'. The term (with variants like *maraḍ (I)Firanjī* – 'the Frankish disease' – *balā' (I)Firanjī* – 'the Frankish affliction') goes back to the Middle Ages, the Crusaders reportedly importing the disease into the Near East. The expression was also used in Turkish as well as in Persian (*ableh Ferangī*, i.e. 'the Frankish pox'). Strangely enough, in 18th-century Europe the disease was also referred to as *morbus Gallicus* ('the French disease')!
3. Built in the early 17th century as a result of the plague epidemics at the end of the preceding century, this hospital is no longer in use.
4. This is a reference to the *Hospice des Enfants Trouvés*. Built in 1747, it was pulled down in the early 1860s to make room for the new Hôtel-Dieu.

Among the hospitals in Paris, there is also one devoted to vaccination against smallpox by the use of the cowpox virus. Then there are two homes for 'old age and senility' (*Hospice de Vieillesse*), one of which is destined for men, the other for women. There is also a hospital for people suffering from incurable diseases, which can accommodate 450 male patients and 520 female patients. Another one is the hospital for the blind of Paris and those coming from other provinces of France. Here, they get food and drink and everything they need for their education, etc. Then there is the hospital for the insane. A huge army barracks houses the so-called 'Hospital of the Invalids' (*Hôpital des Invalides*),[1] which provides care for people who have been injured in the course of wars and for those who, for instance, have had their arms or legs cut off, and so on. This is one of the cleanest and largest hospitals; it has sixteen doctors and surgeons and six pharmacists to produce the medicines.

In addition to these hospitals, there is a public council in Paris, called the 'Council of Charity' (*Bureau de Bienfaisance*), whose aim is to complete the good works that the hospitals are unable to do. For instance, if a trader's business burns down or he is bankrupt, then he receives assistance from this council, albeit on certain conditions. Every district of Paris has its own Council of Charity, providing twofold charitable aid: immediate, one-off support and long-term assistance. The former benefits the poor who have got into difficulty or who for some unexpected reason have become unemployed, whereas the latter is destined for those whose permanent state prevents them from working.

Other charitable activities can be found along the banks of the river, where there are boxes and objects containing smells to be inhaled by one who has come near drowning, who has fainted or been injured, or something like that, in order to make them regain consciousness. In these places there are also a number of men belonging to charitable organizations who administer first aid to those who have had an accident.

From all of this, it becomes apparent that while in Paris more is done for charitable works than anywhere else, it is primarily aimed at the collective [that is, society as a whole] or the kingdom. The situation is quite different when it concerns individual people. It is possible to see a man in the street who does not go to subsidized hospitals or such places and who collapses in the middle of the road because of hunger. Or you can sometimes see people brushing beggars off and sending them away empty-handed,

1. Cf. M. al-Sanūsī, 1891–92: 82–3 (*līzānfalīd*); A. Ilyās, 1900: 275–6 (*al-anfālīd*); M. Amīn Fikrī, 1892: 135, 403; A. Ibn Abī 'l-Ḍiyāf, 1963–65: IV, 104 (*al-Anfalīd*).

claiming that there is never an excuse for begging – if the beggar is able to work, he does not need to beg, and if he is not, then he belongs in a hostel or somewhere like that. It must be said that in most cases their beggars are master tricksters when it comes to obtaining money. They even go as far as to pretend to be mutilated or the like, in order to arouse people's pity.

Also part of their charitable works is the fact that they collect so much money on behalf of people in need who have been dealt an ill blow by fate that they become rich! For instance, they collected about two million francs, i.e. six million piastres, for the children of the General.[1]

Eleventh Section. On earnings in the city of Paris and the entrepreneurial skills there

You should know that the love of profit and the passionate craving for it are firmly rooted in each [Frankish] nation, as is the single-minded drive towards it, the praise of ambition, enterprise and activity and the condemnation of laziness and slowness, to the extent that 'laziness' and 'indolence' are terms of abuse among them. In their love of work they are all equal – from the noblest to the lowliest, even if it involves hardship or puts their lives at risk. It is as if they understood the words of the poet:

The love for security prevents his companion's determination
from going upwards, tempted by laziness
And if you are inclined towards it, then take a hole
in the earth, or a ladder to the sky, and isolate yourself
Leave the risk of the heights to those who have preceded in the climb
and be content with the hope of it

Until he says:

Forsooth, a man of this world is only he who
does not have to rely on anyone in this world

1. This is a reference to Michel Ney, Duke of Elchingen, Prince de la Moskowa (1769–1815), one of the most famous Napoleonic generals (marshal as from 1804). After Napoleon's abdication in 1814, Ney pledged allegiance to the restored Bourbon monarchy. When Napoleon returned one year later, Ney returned to the Bonapartist fold and commanded the Old Guard at the Battle of Waterloo. Eventually, he was charged with treason when the Bourbons were again put in place, and executed. Despite these political vagaries in later life, Ney's valour and courage became legendary.

The most important and famous business in Paris is that of banking transactions. There are two types of bankers – those of the kingdom, i.e. the government bankers, and those of Paris (private bankers). The role played by state bankers in trade is the following: people deposit what they wish there, and each year they receive an interest in accordance with their laws. This is not considered usury[1] by them as long as the rate does not exceed the limits prescribed by law. Every person can withdraw the funds deposited with the state banker whenever he wants. The bankers of Paris also deal in money at an interest. However, they give higher interests than the bankers of the Treasury. Conversely, the money deposited with state banks is more secure than at municipal banks. This is because the latter sometimes go bankrupt, whereas the money accepted by state banks constitutes a debt for the state, and the state never ceases to exist.

Another component in trade and business that is considered very important by the people of Paris is a company[2] called 'partners in liability' (*shurakā' fī 'l-ḍamāna*). For a small fixed annual sum, it insures any damage related to a domestic accident resulting from force majeure. For instance, when a person's house or shop burns down or something similar occurs, the company restores it to its original state or refunds its value.

The city of Paris has both royal and privately owned manufactories. Among them are the metallurgical factories, where they work silver and gold, making vases out of these metals. Then there are porcelain factories, wax[3] factories, soap factories, cotton factories, tanneries, factories where they work morocco leather, etc. The quality of their industries improves steadily, which is why approximately every three years, they display their work in public and show the things they have invented and perfected.[4]

1. *ribā* ('increase'); this term occurs a number of times in the Qur'ān (e.g. II, 275ff.), and in Islamic law denotes the unlawful practice of increasing capital without giving any compensation. It is particularly relevant to interest payments on loans, investments, etc. See *EI1*, s.v. "ribā" (J. Schacht).
2. *jam'iyya*. Khayr al-Dīn also employed this term for a limited company guaranteed by shares (*sharika iqtiṣādiyya/ sharika jam'iyya* – 1867: 77). The first traveller to use the modern MSA term *sharika* for a limited company was the Tunisian al-Sanūsī (1891–92: 72); some of the 19th-century dictionaries already listed *sharika* in its modern sense (e.g. Kazimirski, 1860: I, 1222; G. Badger, 1895: 157; B. Ben Sedira ,1882: 241).
3. '*al-sham' al-Iskandarānī*', ECA 'beeswax'; M. Hinds and E. Badawi, 1986: 478.
4. This is a reference to the precursors of the *Expositions universelles*, which as much as anything epitomized the industrial age. After a few early attempts in London (1756, 1757), and Prague (1791), it was in France that the then Minister for the Interior, François de Neufchâteau, introduced a national policy on displays of industrial products. The first Exposition des Produits de l'Industrie was held on the Champ de Mars in 1798, and brought together 110 exhibitors. Up until 1849, there would be 11 of these national exhibitions, which, in the first decades of their existence, were held rather irregularly,

In Paris, there are also a number of large [department] stores, which contain all types of goods, as well as lodgings for merchants,[1] shops, commercial and handicraft establishments, on whose fronts the name of the trader, his business and sometimes the name of the merchandise are written. A person is allowed to set up a business only if he has paid a sum of money, however small, to the Treasury, after which he receives a medal as proof that he has obtained permission to trade. The holder of the medal must always carry it with him and it must appear on his merchandise.

There is a special school for commerce, which is called the 'College for Commerce' (*Ecole Supérieure de Commerce*). Here, students are trained in the science of commerce and the ability to distinguish between the varieties and qualities of products, while also acquiring the necessary knowledge to fix the price and value of them. This college comprises fifteen sections (*écoles*), attended by pupils coming from several regions. Pursuant to the regulations of this institute, anyone, irrespective of nationality, is allowed to enrol here for study after paying a fixed fee.

Among the things that promote economic activity and profitability are the construction of land and water routes. This includes the making of canals and ships driven by steam,[2] the construction of bridges, the organization of stagecoach services,[3] the telegraph (*al-tīlighrāf*), which is a

---

with a gap of 13 years between the fourth one in 1806 and the fifth in 1819, after which date the intervals varied between four and five years. During al-Ṭahṭāwī's stay, there was only one, in 1827 (at the Louvre Palace). Running between 1 May and 30 June, it boasted no fewer than 1,695 exhibitors.

1. Derived from a root meaning 'to entrust', *wakkāla* (the *okel* mentioned by European travellers to the East) was the Egyptian term for *khān*. See A. Raymond & G. Wiet, 1979: 16–18. (See note no. 1, p. 170).
2. *qawārib allatī taṣīru bi 'l-dukhān*; this periphrase is the very first mention in Arabic literature of steamships (whose commercial exploitation in France had begun only a decade before al-Ṭahṭāwī's arrival). Very soon afterwards, the borrowing *fābūr* (Fr. *vapeur*, It. *vapore*), with its variants *wābūr* and *bābūr* (Sp. *babor*) would be introduced. The first to do so were the Moroccan traveller al-Ṣaffār, who visited France in 1845–46 (S. Gilson Miller, 1992: 78), and the Tunisian Ibn Abī 'l-Ḍiyāf (1963–65: IV, 96). Fāris al-Shidyāq (1881: 68, 71, 92) was the first Arabic author to use the MSA *bākhira* (pl. *bawākhir*), which would crowd out the borrowings by the end of the century. In many present-day Arabic colloquials (e.g. Syro-Lebanese, Egyptian), *wābūr* denotes a stove, as well as any motor-driven engine or machine, and in Tunisia *bābūr* is still used for 'ship' (besides denoting a small kitchen stove). Cf. Khayr al-Dīn, 1867: 64, 111, 178, 230 *et passim*; M. al-Sanūsī, 1891–92: 6, 7, 8, 11, 35 *et passim*; *idem*, 1976–81: I, 51, 85; S. al-Wardānī, 1888–90: Nos 3, 4, 5; M. Amīn Fikrī, 1892: 47 *et passim*; G. Badger, 1895: 1023; J. Habeisch, 1896: 924; J. Zenker, 1866: 936; K. Vollers, 1887–97: 321 (with the variant *bājūr*); E. Gasselin, 1880–86: II, 812–13; T. Baccouche, 1969: 30; *idem*, 1994: 464 *et passim* (see word list p. 509); J. Heyworth-Dunne, 1940–42: 408; J. Redhouse, 1880: 312.
3. *dawāwīn tasfīr al-'arabiyyāt al-kabīra*, 'councils for the dispatching of large carriages'.

signalling device,[1] the setting up of postal services by means of messengers or horses, etc. Take, for example, the city of Paris: it is surrounded by four canals on which goods arrive, and on the river Seine there are boats that are similar to carriages,[2] as well as fast steam vessels.

In Paris, there are various types of carriages, which differ in shape, name, speed and use. There are carriages destined for the transport of goods from Paris to the provinces; these are called *roulages* (*rūlāja*). There is another kind that is used for the transport of people; these are called *diligences* (*al-dāligans*). Then there are small carriages for journeys to places that are near to Paris; these are called *coucous* (*kūkū*).[3] Each person pays a fixed sum of money, like for a voyage on a ship. There are also carriages that can be hired for a specific period, such as a day, a month or a year. The usual carriages in Paris are the *fiacres* (*al-fiyāk*<*i*>*ra*), in which the passenger area consists of two opposite rows of seats, on which there is room for six people. They are pulled by two horses. The other common type of carriage is the *cabriolet* (*al-kīrwayūla*), which is a semi-*fiacre* inasmuch as it it has only one row of seats. The passengers of the *fiacres* or *cabriolets* pay by the hour or hire it to go from one place to another at a fixed fare; in other words, it is never increased or reduced. There are more carriages in the streets of Paris than there are donkeys in the streets of Cairo. Now, they have invented large carriages, called *omnibus* (*al-umnībūsa*), which means 'for all people'.[4] These are large, very spacious carriages; on the doors it is written that they go to this or that city district. Everybody who goes to the same district travels on these carriages and each person pays a fixed amount. These carriages are found in the major thoroughfares of Paris. Another type of carriage

1. Naturally, this is not a reference to the electrical telegraph, which was invented only in 1835 (by Samuel Morse), the first French line (Paris-Rouen) being established ten years later. The system to which al-Ṭahṭāwī refers is, in fact, the *télégraphe aérien* of the brothers Chappe, which was a semaphore system consisting of poles fitted on towers (or housetops) at distances of 10 to 12 kilometres from one another, the signals being relayed from one post to the next. The Chappe telegraph, though laborious, did permit a message to reach Paris from Brest (some 600 km) in eight minutes – weather permitting of course. It should also be added that it was for official use only. Also see: S. Ibn Ṣiyām, 1852: 8; al-Ṣaffār [S. Gilson Miller], 1992: 201.
2. This is a reference to the so-called *coches d'eau*, which were river barges pulled by horses.
3. Introduced in the early 19th century, these were, in fact, large *cabriolets*, i.e. two-wheel carriages seating four to eight passengers. They derived their name from their colour, i.e. yellow, which was that of the flowers of the *coucou* (cowslip). See *TLF*, VI, 289.
4. The omnibus, or *voiture omnibus*, to be more precise, was invented only one year before al-Ṭahṭāwī arrived in Paris and were thus still a novel sight. Omnibuses got their name from the low fares, which were intended to make them accessible to everyone (Lat. *omnibus*). They plied between varies city districts, along set routes with fixed stops. Also see *TLF*, XII, 492–3.

transports household furniture. Then there are the carts used by traders who load them and go around the streets with them in order to sell their wares. These carts are sometimes pulled by a horse, sometimes by a donkey and sometimes by a person alone or with his dog. There are other carts for the transport of stone, soil and other things of that kind.

As for the mail, which is called *la poste*[1] by the French, this is one of the most important and beneficial services for trading relations, etc. It facilitates the communication of information among people by means of letters, which are rapidly dispatched and to which replies also arrive quickly. This service, in its organization and operation, is one of the most magnificent things imaginable. Letters that are sent to a city or province always reach the addressee since all their houses have numbers, called *numéros* (*al-nimra*) in French, by which each house is distinguished from another. The letter that you send to someone else is put in a letter box, of which there is one in each district. Then the postman comes and takes it and the letter is delivered in another district, the reply returning the same day.

The French have the utmost respect for matters related to correspondence. Nobody can open a letter that is addressed to someone else, even if this person is suspected of something. Because of this respect for the privacy of correspondence in Paris, many letters are exchanged between friends and companions, especially between lovers, because people are certain that a letter will not be opened by someone whose name is not on it and to whom it was not sent. A declaration of love between lovers is done by post, as are the arrangements for trysts. In Paris, there is also a place where you can without any fear whatsoever send goods and personal belongings by means of a messenger.

Another useful thing in business are the newspapers (*al-jurnālāt*), in which useful or well-made goods are mentioned and praised with a view to promoting them and to informing people of them. The owner of the goods pays the newspaper a small sum for this. We shall – God willing – speak some more about the newspapers later.

Sometimes a trader who wants to promote his goods has a number of

1. *al-busṭa* (also *būsṭa*); cf. M. al-Sanūsī, 1891–92: 7, 8, 182, 185, 255; *idem*, 1976–81: I, 51, 52, 67, 85 *et passim*; M. Bayram V, 1884–93: IV, 135; Khayr al-Dīn, 1867: 61, 171, 231, 278, 331; F. al-Shidyāq, 1881: 93; M. Amīn Fikrī, 1892: 124, 424 (*būsta*); S. Spiro, 1895: 63; J. Habeisch, 1896: 622; J. Catafogo, 1858: 877; H. Salmoné, 1890: 59; E. Gasselin, 1880–86: II, 436 (*būsṭa/būshṭa*); J. Zenker, 1866: 219 (*būst*); J. Redhouse, 1880: 236 (*būsta*); H. Wehr, 1934: 54; K. Vollers, 1887–97: 319 (*busta, busṭa*); J. Heyworth-Dunne, 1940–42: 410. Although the borrowing is still used in many present-day Arabic colloquials (cf. M. Hinds and E. Badawi, 1986: 75; A. Abou-Seida, 1971: 115; A. Butros, 1973: 96), in contemporary Tunisian, the variant *būsṭ* denotes 'police station' (cf. Fr. *poste de police*); T. Baccouche, 1969: 30.

small sheets printed, which are taken to people's houses by servants and handed out to passers-by in the streets. On these leaflets he puts his name, that of his shop, what he sells and the prices of his goods.

In short, in Paris you can buy everything in the world, whether it is of great or little value. One of the most remarkable things are the pharmacies, where you can find all prepared medicines, every drug on the face of the earth of which the name and the properties are known.

Everybody in Paris, whether rich or poor, loves earnings and commerce. Even a child that can only utter a few words is happy when you give him a small coin and claps his hands while saying something that translates as 'I've earned something!'[1] If their earnings were not for the most part sullied by usury, they would surpass all other nations in terms of profitability. When the business of one of them is not going well, as so often happens in this country, his situation deteriorates and he is reduced to asking for hand-outs from people. Such a person often carries with him a letter from a notable in which it is explained that his situation is dire and that he deserves to be helped. This sort of thing is a common occurrence in this city, despite its thriving commercial life.

The alternation of rain and wind does not prevent anybody from going out to work. Their attitude is borne out by the saying: '*The idle hand rushes to evil and the idle heart rushes to sin.*' The people of Paris are very rich, so rich that the wealth of an average person exceeds that of a big trader in Cairo. They do not subscribe to the following words by the poet:

There is only glory in donation and giving
In the collecting of money there is neither renown nor glory

They strive towards acquiring wealth and embark on the road of greed, claiming that this increases their livelihoods.[2] They are not driven by the following words by the poet:

The blessings God bestows upon one who is greedy do not increase
even if he were to ride the storms in order for them to grow

It is possible to find a Parisian with a modest profession whose annual income is more than 100,000 francs. This is due to the fact that they have complete justice, on which the foundations of their political system

1. *kasabtu wa qanaytu.*; cf. Fr. '*j'ai gagné (de l'argent)*'.
2. Cf. M. al-Ṣaffār [S. Gilson Miller], 1992: 219.

rest. The reign of a tyrannical king or minister never lasts for very long with them, once it has become known that they have acted unjustly and oppressed the people. There is no doubt that the following saying of the poet is firmly embedded in their hearts:

A tyrant and one who is unapproachable
does not have anyone to lead him, to mediate on his behalf
The people of the oppressor are the meadow of war
whereas the kingdom of the just is half developed

This does not prevent them from voluntarily paying taxes since they realize that if everybody pays according to his means, the taxes constitute the pillars of the realm. Taxes support the image of kingdoms, and the best thing is to spend them on things that deserve it. As the poet says:

Wealth is the foundation of the image
and the best of it is sound consultation

And as the people thrive, the state gets a huge annual income from them; the income of the French state every year amounts to about 989 million francs.

One of the reasons for the wealth of the French is that they know how to save and manage their expenses, to the extent that they have recorded it and turned it into a science which is a branch of the administration of affairs of the kingdom. They are highly ingenious in finding ways of acquiring wealth, such as not clinging to things that entail expenditure. For instance, the [chief] minister does not have more than about fifteen servants, and if he walks in the street you would not know him from anybody else since his entourage is kept to a minimum, both inside and outside the home. I have heard that before the current king (who is one of the greatest and richest sovereigns of the French) acceded to the throne and was still Duke of Orléans (*al-dūk durliyān*), his entire entourage – which includes the private military guard, gardeners, servants, etc – amounted to no more than 400 people. Yet, the French considered even that too much for him. This shows the difference between Paris and Egypt, where a simple soldier has several servants.

Twelfth Section. On the religion of the people of Paris

We have already seen in [the discussion of] the Charter that Catholic Christianity is the state religion. However, this was removed from the aforesaid Charter after the last revolution. The French recognize the Pope, who is the king of Rome (*Rūma*), as the leader of the Christians and the head of their community. Just as the Catholic religion is the religion of the French state, so too is it the religion of the majority of its people. In Paris one also finds the Christian denomination known as 'Protestants' (*al-brūtastāniyya*) alongside others. In this city there are also many naturalized Jews. However, not a single Muslim has settled there.

As we have mentioned before, the French in general are Christians only in name. Although they are among those who have a revealed scripture, they are not concerned about what their religion forbids, imposes, etc. During the days of fasting, meat continues to be eaten in all houses, barring very few exceptions such as those of some priests, or at the residence of the former king of France. As for the rest of the people of the city of Paris, they scoff at it and never practise it. They say, 'all forms of religious worship whose wisdom we do not recognize are heresies and fanciful delusions.' Priests in this country are honoured only in the churches by people who go to see them, but who otherwise never care about them; it is as if they are considered the enemies of light and wisdom. It is said that as far as religion is concerned most of the kingdoms of the Franks resemble Paris. Upon reading this, Monsieur de Sacy made the following remark:

> *Your statement that the French do not have any religion at all and that they are Christians only in name is subject to revision. True, many French people, particularly among the Parisians, are Christians only in name and do not believe in the dogmas of their religion, nor do they fulfil the devotional services of Christianity. Instead, they focus on their actions and simply follow their desires and whims, whereas the things of this world distract them from the hereafter. You see that throughout their lives, they are only concerned with acquiring money in any way they can, and once the moment of death has arrived, they die like animals. Nevertheless, there are some who cling to the religion of their fathers, believe in God and the Day of Reckoning and perform good deeds.*[1] *In fact, they constitute an innumerable group of men and women, both common folk and notables, as well as people famous for their scientific and literary eminence. Yet, within this group one may observe various degrees of godliness and godfearingness. Some of them behave like the common people and, like them, attend places of entertainment, i.e. theatre shows, balls and musical gatherings. Others, the [so-called] ascetics, shun anything that arouses*

1. Cf. Qur. II: 62, V:69, XXII:17.

desire. The latter group is the smaller of the two. If you go into one of our churches on important feast days, the soundness of what I am saying will become clear to you.

[Here ends his commentary.]

What led him to express himself in this manner is the fact that he is one of those who are religious. However, there are so few of them that they are of no consequence.

One of the most dreadful traits in the land of the French – or indeed in all Catholic countries – is the prohibition of marriage for the clergy, irrespective of their rank or title. Celibacy increases their sinfulness and moral depravity even more. Another objectionable quality is that the priests believe that the common people have a duty to confess their sins so that they can forgive them. For this purpose, the priest remains in the church on a chair, called the confessional chair, which can be entered only through a door, with a net-like screen separating the penitent from the priest. A person wishing to have his sins pardoned sits down in it, confesses his sins before the priest and asks for his forgiveness, whereupon the priest pardons him. It is well known by them that most of those who go to church and confess are women and children. This agrees with the words of one of the Arab poets:

He who enters the church
will one day merely find wild calves and gazelles

There are various ranks in their priesthood. The first is the *cardinal* (*al-kardīnāl*), who is second to the pope in rank; only cardinals can become pope. After the cardinal comes the archbishop, then the bishop, then the priest, then the curate and then the deacon.

The French have moveable religious feasts, i.e. feasts that do not take place on the same day each year but periodically, most of the time depending on when Easter falls. One of their strange feasts is Shrovetide, which we have already discussed.[1] Another one is the 'Feast of the Appearance of the Messiah' [Epiphany], which is called 'the Feast of the Kings' (*Le Jour des Rois*) by the French. Every family makes a large cake and a broad bean is put in the dough. Then the cake is divided among the diners and the one who has the bean in his portion is 'the king'. If it is in a

1. Cf. Section 7.

man's portion, then he is called 'the king' and he is addressed by that title at the dinner table throughout the entire evening. Then he chooses one of the women and makes her 'queen'; she, too, is addressed by this title. If the bean is found in the portion of a woman, she also gets to choose someone from among the people present as her 'husband', who is then called 'king'. All honours are extended to 'the king' and 'the queen', in accordance with a special ceremony and time-honoured rules. This is the way in which it is done in every house in Paris, even in that of the king of the French.

One of the heresies of priests is their procession that is held at Corpus Christi, when they dress up in embroidered dresses and go around the city with something they call '*Le bon Dieu*' (*al-būndiyū*).[1] This word is composed of two words: the first, '*būn*', means 'good' or 'great', whereas the second, '*diyū*', means 'God'. It is as if they are saying that the deity is present in the morsel of food [the host] the priest holds in his hands. To them, the term *bon Dieu* is, in fact, synonymous with Jesus – Peace be upon Him.[2]

The French know that that this sort of thing is foolish and that it sullies their country and ridicules the intelligence of its people. The fact of the matter is that the royal family encouraged the clergy in such matters, and the people followed them in this, albeit with feelings of the utmost humiliation and repugnance. The priests practise innumerable heresies; however, the people of Paris are aware of their uselessness and scoff at them. The French have other feasts which cannot, however, be discussed in this book.

Every French person has his own feast,[3] which is the birthday of the Saint after whom he has been named. For instance, if a man is called 'Paul', then his name day is that of Saint Paul. On that day, all the men who are called Paul organize a banquet and make their name day feast public. On a person's name day, he is given all kinds of flowers.

Thirteenth Section. On progress by the people of Paris in the sciences, arts and crafts, the way these are organized, as well as an explanation of related matters

What strikes anyone who looks at the current state of sciences, literary arts and crafts in the city of Paris is that human learning is widely spread

1. It is clear that this description of the *Fête-Dieu* (also known as *Fête du Saint-Sacrement*) would have made a powerful impression on his readership, while the 'heathenness' of this feast warrants al-Ṭahṭāwī's severe rebuke.
2. For obvious reasons, the author uses '*al-ilāh*' ('deity', 'godhead'), rather than '*Allāh*'.
3. '*ayd*, cf. Fr. *la fête d'une personne* ('name day').

[there] and has reached a peak in this city. There are no Frankish scholars who can hold a candle to those of Paris, who surpass even the philosophers of Antiquity.

It is apparent to anyone endowed with a pertinent critical mind that these scholars' knowledge of all these scientific disciplines, whose effects have been proven by means of experiments, has been firmly established, nor can their proficiency in them be denied by anyone, as witness the saying of one eminent scholar, '*Things are judged by their completion, activities by their termination and crafts by their durability.*' But while they have the most in-depth knowledge of most sciences and theoretical arts, some of their philosophical beliefs depart from the laws of reason adhered to by other nations. However, they twist and defend them in such a way that they appear to be true and credible to people. The science of astronomy is a case in point; they conduct a great deal of research in this science and know more about it than anyone else, thanks to their knowledge of the secrets of the equipment already known in ancient times and that invented for this purpose. It is indeed well known that the knowledge of the secrets of instruments is the most powerful source for crafts and skills. However, in the philosophical sciences, there is a lot of misguided filling[1] that runs counter to all the holy books[2] and on which they base proofs that are hard for people to refute. We will have occasion to talk about many of their heresies and, God willing, we shall mention them whenever there is occasion to do so. May it suffice to say here that the books of philosophy are all larded with filling that contains many of these heresies. As a result most of the philosophical books are subject to 'the third rule of refutation', as mentioned by the author of *al-Sullam* in his treatment of the science of logic.[3] It is therefore necessary for anyone wishing to delve into the French

1. *ḥashawāt ḍalāliyya*', in which the latter word (*ḍalla*, 'to go astray') has a strong religious connotation, as cognates of it appear a number of times in the Qur'ān [cf. the opening sūra's reference to *al-ḍāliyyīn*, i.e. 'those who stray (from the right path)'], as well as in Ḥadīth (cf. A. Wensinck, 1992: s.v.).

2. In the original manuscript version, al-Ṭahṭāwī originally added '*ka 'l-qawl bi-dawrān al-arḍ wa naḥwahā*' ('like the statement about the turning of the earth, etc.'); cf. Caussin de Perceval, 1833: 250 (trans. 243). One may presume that this reference was taken out together with the passage on the turning of the Earth; see Sixth Essay, Seventh Section.

3. This is a reference to the Algerian philosopher 'Abd al-Raḥmān al-Akhḍarī (1513–75) and his famous didactic poem (*manẓūma*) on Logic in 94 *rajaz* verses, entitled *al-Sullam al-murawniq fī 'l-manṭiq* ('The Brilliant Staircase towards Logic'), on which al-Ṭahṭāwī's mentor, Ḥasan al-'Aṭṭār, also wrote a commentary, whereas another of al-Ṭahṭāwī's teachers, Ibrāhīm al-Bājūrī, wrote a gloss on al-Akhḍarī's commentary of his own work. It was one of the first books to be printed at the government press in Būlāq (Feb. 1826); see T. Bianchi, 1843: 34 (no. 25). The *Sullam* has also been translated into French (J. D.

language, which includes some philosophical elements, to be well versed in the Qur'ān and the *sunna*, in order to prevent him from being misled by this and his belief from weakening, and lest he should lose his footing. In one of my poems, in which I both praise and rebuke this city, I have said:

Is there another place like Paris
where the suns of knowledge never set
where the night of unbelief has no morning?
Forsooth, is this not the strangest of things![1]

Among the things that are conducive to French progress in the sciences and arts one should mention the simplicity of their language and everything that makes it perfect. Indeed, one does not need to devote a lot of time or effort in order to learn it. Anyone with a sound receptivity and aptitude is able, once he has learned the language, to read any book, since it is devoid of any obscurities and does not admit of any ambiguity. If a teacher wants to explain a book, he does not need to decipher or analyse the expressions first since the words are clear by themselves. In short, a reader of a book does not need to apply other, extraneous rules from another science in order to understand the words. The contrary is true in Arabic; a person reading a book on a particular science must apply all the tools of the language and examine the words as carefully as possible, since an expression can have meanings that are far removed from the one it has on the surface. There is none of this in the books of the French. Their books only rarely have commentaries, annotations or glosses. In some cases, one might add a few brief notes in order to complete an expression or to restrict it, etc. The texts by themselves are enough to enable one straight away to understand to what they refer. Whenever one starts reading a book on any science, one can apply one's entire mind to understanding the issues, concepts and rules of this science, without having to mull over the terms used. As a result, one is able to devote all one's attention to the study of the subject of the science in question, to the essence of what is being said, to the ideas [related to it] and to anything that may be derived from it. Anything else

Luciani, *Le Soullam, traité de logique*, Algiers, Jules Carbonel, 1922). See Y. Sarkīs, 1928: 406–07; *EI1*, *EI2* s.v. 'al-Akhḍarī' (Brockelmann); *GAL*, II, 356.

1. The idea of combining eulogy and (often fierce) criticism has its roots in classical Arabic literature (cf. e.g. the highly popular flyting genre, the *mafākhir*). The device was also used by the apostate Lebanese Christian al-Shidyāq (1804–87), who in his famous *al-Sāq 'alā 'l-Sāq* juxtaposed two poems on Paris, one praising it, the other condemning it (al-Shidyāq: 1855: 295–300; 1919: 395–400).

is a waste [of time]! For instance, if someone wants to study arithmetic, he understands the things related to the numbers, without having to look at whether the proper inflections have been used or the effect of metaphors included in it. Nor will he object to the absence of paronomasia in a phrase that was suited to it, or to the fact that the author put a certain term at the beginning when another one should have been put first, or whether an 'f' was used instead of a 'w' in cases where the contrary would have been better, etc.

One should note that the French have a natural propensity for the acquisition of learning and a craving for the knowledge of all things. This is why you see that all of them have a comprehensive knowledge of all things they have acquired. Nothing is alien to them, so that when you talk with one of them, he will talk to you in the words of a scholar, even though he is not one of them. For this reason, you can see ordinary French people examining and discussing a number of profound scientific questions. The same is true of their children; from a very early age they are extremely proficient. Any one of their children is as the poet says:

Even as an adolescent the greenhorn craved to know the meaning of things
and while still an infant he deflowered the virgin arts

You can talk to a small boy who has just left infancy about his views on this or that subject, and instead of answering, 'I don't know the origin of this thing', his reply will amount to a judgement of the thing in question according to his own lights. Their children are always prepared to learn and acquire [knowledge], and enjoy an excellent upbringing. However, this is equally true for all French people. It is customary among them not to marry their children before they have completed their studies, which is usually between the ages of twenty and twenty-five. There are only few people who by the age of twenty have not attained a degree of schooling or acquired the craft they wish to exercise.[1] Nevertheless, it may take a person

1. *ta'allum ṣan'atihi allatī yurīd ta'līmahā*, 'the learning of the craft which they wish to teach'. Naturally, this is a reference to a 'master (Fr. *maître*) craftsman', as opposed to an apprentice, as the former works independently and trains apprentices. This and other comments on the levels of education and literacy of the French were, of course, nothing short of a distortion of reality; in the early 19th century there were fewer than 800,000 pupils (out of a total population of about 29m) in fewer than 20,000 primary schools. As from the 1820s this would increase dramatically and in 1850 there were more than 3.2 million pupils (out of a total population of 35m) and more than 60,000 primary schools. Second, al-Ṭahṭāwī's comments are to some extent misleading at another level since they also imply that the opposite was true in Egypt. In fact, the English traveller Edward

a long time to reach the highest degree of proficiency in sciences and arts. It is at the above-mentioned age that most of the skills of a person and his good fortune manifest themselves. As the poet said:

If the tip of the lance misses its target[1]
what hope is there for victory for its shaft?
If a boy reaches the age of twenty
without achieving his goal, that is a shame

This age marks the end of the perfection of noble men in all nations. Behold, for instance, al-Akhḍarī, who, at the age of twenty-one, already wrote and commented on his treatise entitled *al-Sullam*. And what about the eminent scholar al-Amīr,[2] who also wrote his collection before the age of twenty, and could thus say, like al-Akhḍarī:

He who first reaches the age of twenty-one
forgiveness is easily given to him
since he wrote a book on an even harder subject before he reached that age.

As for the learned men among the Franks and their scholars, they have a different approach to things. Besides studying a number of subjects to perfection, they devote their efforts to a special branch of knowledge. They discover many things and provide unparalleled advantages, which is

Lane pointed out that most of the children (only boys though) of the higher and middle classes, and 'some of those of the lower orders' received basic instruction, whereas there were numerous schools (*kuttāb, madrasa*), each village having at least one. The main difference with French children was, of course, that their Egyptian counterparts' instruction was entirely focused on the reading (and memorizing) of the Qur'ān, their schoolmasters devoting little or no attention to developing general reading and writing skills, which were taught only to pupils destined for administrative or clerical offices or the scholarly professions (in which case they followed a regular course of study at the Azhar mosque). See E. Lane, 1923: 60ff.; N. Hanna, in M. Daly, 1998: 100ff.; F. Furet and J. Ozouf, 1977.

1. The play on words in the original '*...awwal al-khaṭiyy akhṭā*' cannot unfortunately be rendered in English.
2. The Egyptian philologist and Mālikī legal scholar Muḥammad b. Muḥammad al-Sinbāwī al-Mālikī (1741–1817) was known as *al-Amīr* ('the Prince') or *al-Amīr al-Kabīr* ('the great Prince'). Born in Upper Egypt (near the town of Manfalūṭ), al-Amīr is best known for his commentaries of classical texts in the areas of language (e.g. grammar, rhetoric) and religion. The work that is meant here is *al-Majmūʿ fī 'l-fiqh*, a collection of Mālikite law, on which he also wrote a commentary entitled *Ḍaw' al-shumūʿ ʿalā sharḥ al-Majmūʿ* ('Light of the Candles on the Commentary of the *Majmūʿ*') See Y. Sarkīs, 1928: 473–475; ʿU. Kaḥḥāla [n.d.]: IX, 68; E. Van Dyke, 1896: 499.

why they are considered scholars. They do not think that every teacher is a scholar, nor that every author is a man of intellectual distinction; rather, he must have acquired the above qualities and obtained some recognized academic degrees. The title of scholar is used only when a person possesses all these qualities and has advanced [in his profession]. Do not think that the priests in France are scholars – they are learned only in matters of religion.[1] That is not to say that there are no learned men among the priests. However, when one talks of learned men, this refers to people who have a knowledge of the rational sciences, since their scholars are not very conversant with the branches of Christian theology. If in France people say, 'that is a learned man', they do not mean by this that he is knowledgeable about his religion, rather that he has knowledge of one of the other sciences. The pre-eminence of these Christians in these sciences will become clear to you. At the same time, you will recognize that many of these sciences are absent from our countries, despite the fact that the venerable al-Azhar mosque in Cairo, the Umayyad mosque in Damascus, the Zaytūna mosque in Tunis, the Qarawiyyīn mosque in Fès, the religious schools of Bukhara, etc., all radiate through the traditional sciences as well as certain rational sciences such as Arabic philology, logic and other auxiliary sciences.[2]

The sciences in Paris progress each day and are constantly on the increase. Not a year goes past in which they have not discovered something new. Sometimes they will invent a number of new arts, skills, procedures or perfections within the space of a single year. If it pleases the Almighty God, the reader will be acquainted with some of these.

It is strange to find that among their soldiers there are men whose character is similar to that of the pure Arabs in terms of their great courage, which is a sign of strength of character, and great passion, which is apparently a sign of feeble-mindedness. And, as with the Arabs, their war chants are mixed in with love poetry. I have indeed encountered many of their sayings, which are similar to the words used by an Arab poet addressing his loved one:

I thought of you, as the clamour of war was like an overflowing sea,
the dust like the night, and the spears like stars

1. This of course implied a contrast between the Muslim *'ulamā'*, who despite their primarily religious focus, were involved in other fields (usu. language) as well, and Christian men of the faith.
2. *al-'ulūm al-āliyya*, 'the instrumental sciences', i.e. those that serve as a tool for the acquisition of other sciences, which in practice meant those related to religion, i.e. *Ḥadīth*, *fiqh* (Islamic law) and *tawḥīd* (theology).

I took it for a wedding, the two of us in its garden,
and you and I enjoying our happiness in its shade

Another poet said:

I thought of you, like my lance drinking for the first time
With my sword fashioned from the finest Indian steel dripping with my blood
I wanted to kiss the swords as
they shone as your mouth sparkles when it smiles

Or consider the words of the author of the *Lāmiyyat al-Aʿjam:*[1]

I do not feel disgust at the heavy blow accompanied
by the throw of arrows from insulting eyes
Nor do I dread the blades of swords – rather, they make me happy
When, struck by fatigue, I see you through a slit in the curtains
do not forsake the gazelles that dally about me
even if I were to be attacked by lions stalking me from their lair

We shall discuss the learned societies, famous schools and libraries[2] in order for you to become aware of the superiority of the Franks over others.

One of these libraries is the *Bibliothèque Royale*, which contains all books – both printed works and manuscripts – the French have been

1. This 'Ode in L on the non-Arabs' (or 'Persians') was composed in 505 A.H. (1111–12 A.D.) by the Persian poet al-Ṭughrāʾī (Muʾayyid al-Dīn Fakhr al-Kuttāb Abū Ismāʿīl al-Ḥusayn b. ʿAlī b. Muḥammad b. ʿAbd al-Ṣamad al-Iṣfahānī, 1061–1122). The poem – a long plainsong about the difficult times that he was living in – was translated into Latin by the Dutch Arabist Golius as early as 1629, the French translation by P. Vattier following only one year later, whereas Pococke published his edition and Latin translation of the text in 1661. As a result, it is one of the first Arabic poems to become widely known in Europe. The *Lāmiyat al-Aʿjam* was, in fact, intended to act as a foil to the equally famous 68-verse *qaṣīda*, entitled *Lāmiyyat al-ʿArab* ('Ode in *L* on the Arabs'), by the famous pre-Islamic poet al-Shanfarā (*floruit* early 6th c.), in which he eulogized the Arab virtues of manhood and bravery (later on, al-Ṭahṭāwī wrote a commentary on the latter work; Ṣ. Majdī, 1958: 26). See "al-Ṭughrāʾī" *EI1* (F. Krenkow), *EI2* (F. de Blois); "al-Shanfarā", *EI1* (F. Krenkow), *EI2* (A. Arazi); Y. Sarkīs, 1928: 1241.
2. *khazāʾin* (sing. *khizāna*) *al-kutub* ('storehouses for books'), which is also the term found in Bocthor's dictionary (1882: 92), coexisted with *kutubkhāna*. The latter was the term usually used by 19th-century Arab travellers (e.g. M. al-Sanūsī, 1891–92; M. Fikrī, 1892) alongside *dār al-kutub* (e.g. A. Ibn Abī ʾl-Ḍiyāf, 1963–65: IV, 106), the MSA *maktaba* making its début in the second half of the century (e.g. M. al-Sanūsī, *ibid.*). In fact, al-Ṭahṭāwī also used *khizānat al-kutub* for 'bookcase' (see above).

able to collect in every field of science and language.[1] The total number of printed books at this library amounts to 400,000 volumes, which also includes a great number of Arabic books that are rare in Egypt or indeed anywhere else.[2] There are a number of Qur'āns, the like of which cannot be found anywhere else.[3] These Qur'āns kept by the French in their libraries are not at all treated with disdain, but preserved with the utmost care, even though their respect for them does not have a particular purpose. However, the danger lies in the fact that they hand over these copies of the Qur'ān to anybody wishing to read it, translate it, etc.[4] In the city of Paris, Qur'āns are for sale, and one of their scholars abridged it, translating a number of selected verses, while adding a discussion of the basic principles of Islam and some of its branches.[5] In his book, the author says that it appears to

1. This library (which, depending on the regime in power, was variously known as the Bibliothèque Royale, Impériale or Nationale) was an obligatory stop for most Muslim visitors to the French capital, most of whom were quite impressed by it: e.g. M. al-Sanūsī, 1891–92: 127ff.; A. Ibn Abī 'l-Ḍiyāf, 1963–65: IV, 106; M. Fikrī, 1892: 433–6; M. Ibn al-Khūja, 1900: 24ff.
2. Al-Ṭahṭāwī's number is slightly off, as in 1822 the library already owned 450,000 printed volumes. According to Pierre Dipy's catalogue of 1677, there were 897 Arabic manuscripts, which number may be compared with the number of entries in de Slane's catalogue (1883), i.e. 4,665 (including 323 Christian Arabic MSs); in 1900 the Arabic collection comprised 10,000 books and 6,142 MSs (H. Marcel, 1907, 20, 99–100). As for the total number of books, this would increase to 800,000 in 1845 (J.-F. Foucaud, 1978).
3. al-Ṭahtāwī is probably referring to some of the showpieces of the Bibliothèque Nationale, such as the 9–10th-century miniature (40mmx75mm, 369pp.) edition (Bibliothèque Nationale, 1878: 12, no. 45; M. de Slane, 1883–95: I, 120; A. Flottès-Dubrulle, 1989), which was allegedly a gift to Charlemagne from Hārūn al-Rashīd, and the five-volume 15th-century purple Qur'ān with silver lettering (de Slane, *ibid.*: I, 119; A. Flottès-Dubrulle, 1989).
4. It is clear that the author included this comment amidst his praise for the library lest he be accused of ignoring the obvious blasphemy of the Holy Qur'ān's being held by unbelievers! Other Muslim visitors, however, were far less subdued in their criticism, the 19th-century Moroccan envoy al-Ṣaffār stating his disgust ([S. Gilson Miller], 1992: 188), which he shared with his 17th- and 18th-century predecessors (and compatriots) al-Ḥajarī (1987: 50) and al-Miknāsī (1965: 126), the former of whom was sickened to see the holy book in the hands of 'the filthy infidel'. The Tunisian al-Sanūsī, for his part, poignantly noted that most of the Arabic books and manuscripts held in European libraries were stolen from Muslim rulers (1891–92: 126–7).
5. This is a reference to Claude Savary's *Morale de Mahomet, ou recueil des plus pures maximes du Coran*, Paris/Constantinople (Lamy), 1784. It is almost certain that al-Ṭahṭāwī would have come across Savary's complete translation (*Le Coran, traduit de l'arabe, accompagné de notes, et précédé d'un Abrégé de la vie de Mahomet, tiré des écrivains orientaux les plus estimés*, 1751), which rapidly gained canonical status, as witness the author's own abridgement and the re-editions of 1783, 1786 and 1787, and completely overshadowed the earlier French version by Du Ryer (1647) and the later text (1770) based on G. Sale's English translation (1734). A revised edition of Savary's translation appeared in 1798 (Paris), with reissues in 1821–22 (Paris/Amsterdam), 1828 (Paris, Schubart & Heideloff)

him that the Islamic faith is the purest of all religions and that it includes things that cannot be found in any other.

Another library is the so-called *Bibliothèque de Monsieur*, which is actually called *Bibliothèque de l'Arsenal* (*Arsināl*)[1], whose name is derived from [the Arabic] *tarskhāna*.[2] This is the biggest library after the *Bibliothèque Royale* and contains about 200,000 printed volumes and 10,000 manuscripts. Most of these books are on history and poetry, especially Italian.

Other libraries include the *Bibliothèque Mazarine* (*māzārīna*),[3] which contains 95,000 books and 4,000 manuscripts; that of the *Institut* (*al-Insṭīṭūt*), which holds 50,000 volumes; the municipal library (*Bibliothèque de la Ville*), with approximately 16,000 books – mainly on literature – which number is constantly increasing; the library of the botanical gardens (*Bibliothèque du Jardin des Plantes*), with 10,000 books on natural sciences; the library of the Royal Observatory, which contains books on astronomy; the library of the School of Medicine; and that of the *Académie Française* (*Akadimat al-Fransīs*), with 35,000 volumes. Each of these libraries is a public foundation.[4] However, in Paris, there are also many private libraries, some of which contain 50,000 volumes. The state owns about forty libraries, each of which contains a minimum of 3,000 books, while most have 50,000 or more. There is no need to mention each of these here.

Every scholar, student or rich person has his own library in accordance with his financial means. As everybody in Paris knows how to read and

---

and 1829 (Paris, Dondey-Dupré et Fils). One may assume that al-Ṭahtāwī consulted the 1826 edition (Paris, Bureau de Courval et Cie), in which a *notice sur Mahomet* (by Collin de Plancy) had been added. Another reason why al-Ṭahtāwī would have become aware of Savary's work was the latter's *Lettres sur l'Egypte où l'on offre le parallèle des mœurs anciennes et modernes de ses habitans*, Paris: Oufroi, 1785 (+ 1786, 1798). Finally, it is worth noting that Savary's favourable comments on the Prophet Muḥammad (e.g. in the introduction to his translation of the Qur'ān) would not have escaped al-Ṭahṭāwī's attention either!

1. Founded in 1756, this library (which is still in its original home in the rue Sully) became a national and public institution in 1797, *Monsieur* being the nickname for the brother of Louis XVI, the Comte de Provence. It was affiliated to the Bibliothèque Nationale in 1935.
2. (also *tarsāna*). However, *tarskhāna* was a borrowing from Turkish (*terskhāne*) – first attested in the 16th century – which had taken it from the Italian *arsenal*, which was, in turn, a corruption of the Arabic *dār ṣināʿa* ('house of manufacture'). See H. and R. Kahane and A. Tietze, 1958: § 645.
3. Originally the private library of Cardinal Mazarin, it opened to scholars in 1643 and was thus the very first public library in France. After briefly (1923–45) being joined to the Bibliothèque Nationale, it today falls under the Institut de France, whose academies are also headquartered at the sumptuous palace on the quai Conti.
4. *khazā'in mawqūfa*, i.e. held under a *waqf*.

write, it is rare to find anyone who does not own at least a few books. In all rich people's houses there is a secluded room, which contains the library, scientific instruments, as well as strange artefacts related to the arts, such as stones used in the study of minerals, etc.

In Paris, there are numerous storehouses, called 'museums'.[5] Here, people find things desired by eminent people in order to help them increase their knowledge of the natural sciences, like minerals, stones, the preserved bodies of all kinds of land and marine animals, all stages in the history of stones, plants and many things going back to the Ancients. The benefit of these things to the sciences is that people can study what they have previously read about in books and draw comparisons. For instance, if a person reads about this stone or that animal and has that stone or animal before his eyes, he can compare them with the features mentioned in the books.

The most useful thing for the natural sciences in the city of Paris is the royal garden, which is known as the *Jardin des Plantes*.[6] This is where all the foreign exotic things known to man are kept. In its soil, they grow all domestic plants and apply themselves with great skill and wisdom to ensure they thrive in their environment. Students of pharmacology and botany study their lessons here and compare that which is in their books with the things they have before their eyes. From each genus of plants, they take a branch and place it inside something like a piece of paper, and write down its name and characteristics. There are also various species of live animals – both exotic and domestic, tame and wild. For instance, in this place you can find polar bears and black bears, lions and [other] beasts of prey, hyenas, leopards, strange cats, camels, buffaloes, Tibetan sheep, the

5. *khazā'in al-mustaghrabāt*, 'storage places of strange things', which coexisted with *dār al-tuḥaf* ('house of wonderful things'), the modern *matḥaf* being used for the first time in Europe-related travel literature by F. al-Shidyāq (1881: 70).

6. This is actually the former *Jardin Royal des Plantes Médicinales*, which was reorganized and renamed *Musée d'Histoire Naturelle* by the Convention in 1793. Founded in 1626, this natural history 'laboratory' was opened to the public in 1640. The park contains public gardens around the museum, as well as a ménagerie (added during the Revolution when the Royal Zoo was moved there from Versailles), greenhouses, a botanical garden, labyrinth, vivarium, etc. It is important to add that it was (and still is) a school as well, where subjects such as botany, anatomy, geology and chemistry have been taught since the Garden was set up. See S. Ibn Ṣiyām, 1852: 15 (*jārdān dī blānṭ*); A. al-Shidyāq, 1881: 69, 248; A. Ilyās, 1900: 282–3; M. al-Bakrī, 1906: 323ff. (*ḥadīqat al-nabāt*); A. Ibn Abī 'l-Ḍiyāf, 1963–65: IV, 106 (*dār 'ajā'ib al-ḥayawān wa 'l-nabātāt*). Cf. *GDU*, IX, 906–07; C. Courtalon, 1995: 329ff. The official documents related to this prestigious institution in the 19th century are kept in AN F17 3880–3996 (1789–1898) [F17 13558–13566 (An IV–1931)].

giraffe from Sennār,[1] Indian elephants, Berber gazelles, stags, wild cows,[2] various species of monkeys and foxes and all types of known birds. These animals, which you see alive in the garden, can also be seen dead, stuffed with straw; if you look at them, they seem alive, like the stuffed calf made by farmers in the Nile valley.[3] In this garden, there are also rooms filled with precious minerals and every kind of stone – both raw and natural. You can also see all the varieties, forms and species of the three natural kingdoms. There are many things there for which we cannot find the Arabic names, like the animals, plants and stones of America. All these things are placed in this garden as a sample or specimen of everything [that is to be found in nature]; on each item appears its name in French or in Latin. For instance, in the hall where the lions are kept the name of the [species of] lion is written in French, i.e. *lion* (*liyūn*). This is also the way it is done in the other exhibition rooms. In this garden, a famous event took place once. One of the lions was injured and its keeper entered [the cage] together with a dog, which went close to the lion and licked the latter's wound. The wound healed, and a friendship developed between the lion and the dog. The lion's heart was filled with love for the dog, who would always return to visit his friend; he fawned on him and looked at him as if they were real friends. When the dog died, the lion became ill because they were separated, and so they put another dog with him in order to examine the extent to which he had grown used to the situation. The dog consoled him for the loss [of his predecessor] and remained with him. In the *Jardin des Plantes* there is also a room called the *Salle d'Anatomie* [*comparée*], which contains a collection of mummies, i.e. embalmed cadavers, and other bodies. This room also contains part of the corpse of the late Shaykh Sulaymān al-Ḥalabī, who martyred himself by assassinating the French general Kléber (*Klaybar*) and was then himself killed by the French when they occupied Egypt – there is no power and no strength save in the Great Almighty God![4]

1. This is the giraffe sent by Muḥammad ʿAlī to Charles X in 1827; cf. Translator's Introduction.
2. *baqar waḥsh*, which Caussin de Perceval refers to as a 'little-known kind of antilope often mentioned in Arabic poetry', adding that al-Ṭahṭawī must be mistaken since there was no sample of this species in the city at the time, the first one arriving in 1832 at the *Jardins des Plantes* as a present '*envoyé, avec des autres animaux*' by the '*empereur du Maroc*' (Caussin de Perceval, 1833: 244–5.)
3. This practice (which is also used with baby camels) consisted of stuffing the calf with grass, etc., and placing it with the cow to start the milching.
4. It was the French army's chief-surgeon (and member of the Institut d'Egypte), I. Larrey (1766–1842), who had succeeded in acquiring al-Ḥalabī's corpse. In years to come, his skull would be seen by many generations of French medical students as a means of

Among the places dedicated to the science of astronomy, there is the Royal Observatory of Paris, which is one of the most amazing observatories on the face of the earth.[1] It is built of nothing but stone, without the use of iron or wood. It is built in the shape of a hexagon with parallel roofs, positioned at right angles to each other,[2] and its four sides face the four cardinal points, viz. east, west, north and south. At the south end, there are two octagonal towers; at the north end, there is a third one, which is square-shaped and serves as the entrance gate to the Observatory. In a hall on the first floor of the Observatory (*La Salle Méridienne*), the French have traced the meridian of their day. This line divides the hall into two equal parts. It is in relation to this line that the French calculate longitudes and determine the location of places that do not share the same zenith. This is something we have already explained in the First Section of the Second Essay. The roof of the Observatory building is situated at eighty-three feet from the ground. The edifice contains several rooms, all of which are especially adapted for astronomy research. Six of them have openings,[3] each with a diameter of three feet, which have been placed in such a way as to allow a view of the heavens and the observation of the necessary things. Through these observation openings you can look at the stars from the subterranean chambers.[4] It is in these halls that the [specific] weight of natural bodies and the atmospheric pressure[5] have been tested. In the Observatory there is a large room containing instruments; on the roof, there is a device for recording changes in the winds, called an 'anemometer' (*al-anīmūmitr*), which measures the force of the wind. There is also a basin, called a 'measuring vat', with which the average annual rainfall is measured. The [study] chambers of this observatory are located beneath the surface, at a depth equalling the thickness of the walls. One gains access to these chambers by descending a winding staircase, comparable to the stairs in a minaret. The total number of steps amounts to 360. These chambers

demonstrating the cranial features of the criminal and fanatical mind! See H. Laurens, 1997: 394.

1. At the time of al-Ṭahṭawī's stay in Paris, the head of the *Observatoire* was Alexis Bouvard (1767–1843), the only other astronomer (*observateur*) being the famous François Arago (1786–1853), who took over the presidency of the *Bureau des Longitudes* – the governing body of the Observatory – when Bouvard died.
2. '*'alā shakl musaddas al-asṭiḥa al-mutawāziya al-qā'ima al-zāwiyā*'. This is a rather strange description for an edifice that consists of a flat-roofed, rectangular central building flanked by two octagonal towers on the east and west sides.
3. *mamāriq maftūḥa*, 'open windows'.
4. *makhādi'* (sing. *mikhda'*), which denotes any small room. This is the translation of the French word *cabinet (d'étude)*.
5. *mīzān al-hawā'*, 'measure/equilibrium of the air'.

are used for the benefit of physicists and chemists who carry out their experiments there, turning liquids into solids and freezing bodies in order to ascertain the composition of gases.[1]

In the Observatory there is also a room called the 'whispering room', or 'the room of secrets'. It derives its name from the fact that in it one can see the strangest of occurrences related to the way sound strikes the ear and reaches it through the air. In this room, there is a column, opposite to which there is another. When a person puts his mouth against the column and whispers some words, a person standing at the other end can hear this, whereas someone standing close to the latter cannot. These are things that can be understood only by people who are acquainted with the properties of sound.

Among the scientific institutions in Paris there is a place called the *Conservatoire* (*al-kunsirwatwār*),[2] which is a French word meaning 'warehouse', 'depository' or something like that. In this place, all kinds of equipment, irrespective of size, are kept, especially those used in engineering, such as instruments of traction, and those employed in the moving of heavy objects. The French claim that this museum does not have its equal anywhere in the world. In this place, the echo returns a person's voice in an amazing fashion.

In Paris, there are also many schools devoted to various sciences, arts and crafts. The French interest in medicine has already been mentioned, and there are many schools for the study of this science.

At this juncture, we should like to talk about the places for scholars, and their ranks. I should hasten to add that in Paris scholars have important associations, which are known by various names. Some are called *académie* (*akadima*),[3] others are known as *société* (*majmaʿ*) or *conseil*

1. *ahwiya* (sing. *hawāʾ*), 'airs'.
2. = *Conservatoire des Arts et Métiers*. Founded in 1794 by the famous Abbé Grégoire, this institute, which today goes by the name of *Conservatoire National des Arts et Métiers*, serves as a teaching and training establishment. It also houses a museum – the *Musée des Arts et Métiers* – which al-Ṭahṭāwī visited.
3. *Akada/imāt*. However, for the invididual academies of the Institut de France, al-Ṭahṭāwī uses *akadamiyya* and *akadama* interchangeably, the century's first Arabic lexicographer, E. Bocthor, suggesting *dīwān/majamaʿ/jamʿiyyat ʿulamāʾ* (1882: 6). *Akadamiyya* was the preferred term of other Arab travellers; cf. M. Ibn al-Khūja, 1900: 39 (alongside *dīwān*); M. al-Sanūsī, 1891–92: 142–53; Khayr al-Dīn, 1867: 68, 262 (the St Petersburg Science Academy). Also see H. Wehr, 1934: 55; J. Heyworth-Dunne, 1940–42: 409, 410 (n. 1). Al-Ṭahṭāwī, Khayr al-Dīn and al-Sanūsī also use the MSA *jamʿiyya* (*ʿilmiyya*) alongside *majmaʿ* in the sense of a learned (or cultural) society or academy (though not for the organizations subsumed into the *Institut de France*). The Tunisian traveller Salīm al-Wardānī, for his part, referred to the *Academia Española* as *jamʿiyyat al-ʿulūm* (1888–90:

(*majlis*). As for the *Institut* (*al-Ansṭīṭūt*), this is a collective term which includes the five *académies*, i.e. the five councils. These are: the academy of the French language (*Académie Française*),[1] the academy of literary sciences and the knowledge of history and archaeology (*Académie des Inscriptions et Belles-lettres*),[2] the academy of natural and engineering sciences (*Académie des Sciences*),[3] the academy of fine arts (*Académie des Beaux-arts*)[4] and the academy of philosophy (*Académie des Sciences Morales et Politiques*).[5] What we have referred to as *akadamiyya*, *akadama* or *aqadama* is a term derived from the name of a place in the city of Athens, where Plato the Sage used to teach his pupils, and it is for this reason that a group of ancient philosophers was called 'academicians' (*akadamiyyūn*). The place itself was called *akadēmeia* (*akadamiyya*) as it was owned by a Greek man called *Akademos* (*akadamus*).[6] He bequeathed it to the people of the city of Athens, who turned it into a garden where they would stroll around and enjoy themselves. It was here that Plato taught, which is why the group of people around him were called 'academicians'. They are also called 'Platonists' (*Aflāṭūniyyūn*), and in Arabic books they are famous under the name of *ishrāqiyyūn* ('Illuminists') or *ishrāfiyyūn*,[7] though they are also known as *ilāhiyyūn* ('Theists'). Today,

no. 41). However, as we have seen (see note no. 2, p. 246), Khayr al-Dīn also used *jam'iyya* for a limited company guaranteed by shares (1867: 77), as well as for an administrative council (*ibid.*, 344). Cf. *EI2*, s.v. "djam'iyya" (A. Hourani/A. Demeerseman).

1. *akadamiyyat al-lugha al-faransāwiyya*; cf. M. al-Sanūsī, 1891–92: 145 (*akadamiyyat al-lugha al-faransawiyya*); M. Ibn al-Khūja, 1900: 39 (*al-akadamiyya al-faransawiyya*); M. Bayram V, 1884–93: III, 86 (*jam'iyyat al-lugha al-farānsāwiyya*); Khayr al-Dīn, 1867: 68 (*akadamiyyat Faransā*).
2. *akadamiyyat al-'ulūm al-adabiyya wa ma'rifat al-akhbār wa 'l-āthār* (later also *akadamat taqyīd al-funūn al-adabiyya*); cf. M. al-Sanūsī, 1891–92: 145 (*akadamiyyat al-nuqūsh wa 'l-ādāb*); M. Ibn al-Khūja, 1900: 39 (*dīwān al-nuqūsh wa 'l-adab*); M. Bayram V, 1884–93: III, 86 (*jam'iyyat 'ulūm al-adab*); Khayr al-Dīn, 1867: 68 (*akadamiyyat al-khuṭūṭ al-qadīma*).
3. *akadamiyyat al-'ulūm al-ṭabī'iyya wa al-handasiyya* (later simply *akadamat al-'ulūm al-sulṭāniyya*, 'Imperial Science Academy'); cf. M. al-Sanūsī, 1891–92: 148 (*akadamiyyat al-ṣanā'i'*); M. Ibn al-Khūja, 1900: 39 (*dīwān al-ma'ārif*); M. Bayram V, 1884–93: III, 86 (*jam'iyyat sā'ir al-'ulūm*); Khayr al-Dīn, 1867: 68 (*akadamiyyat al-'ulūm*).
4. *akadamiyyat al-ṣanā'i' al-ẓarīfa* (later on also *akadamat mustaẓrafāt al-funūn*); cf. M. al-Sanūsī, 1891–92: 146 (*akadamiyyat al-rusūmāt wa 'l-funūn al-mustaẓrafa al-adabiyya*); M. Ibn al-Khūja, 1900: 39 (*dīwān al-funūn al-mutaẓarrifa*); M. Bayram V, 1884–93: III, 86 (*jam'iyyat al-ma'ārif al-ẓarīfa*); Khayr al-Dīn, 1867: 68 (*akadamiyyat al-būẓār*).
5. *akadamiyyat al-falsafa*; cf. M. al-Sanūsī, 1891–92: 148 (*akadamiyyat al-'ulūm al-siyāsiyya*); M. Ibn al-Khūja, 1900: 39 (*dīwān al-'ulūm al-adabiyya wa 'l-siyāsiyya*); M. Bayram V, 1884–93: III, 86 (*jam'iyyat al-'ulūm al-'aqliyya*); Khayr al-Dīn, 1867: 68 (*akadamiyyat al-siyāsa wa tahdhīb al-akhlāq*).
6. Cf. M. al-Sanūsī, 1891–92: 143.
7. In contrast to the former term (*ishrāq*, 'Illuminism'), the latter has not, to my knowledge, ever been used to denote this school of thought. The only explanation for this lapsus must therefore lie in the fact that al-Ṭahṭāwī at some point consulted a North African

however, the word 'academicians' is used by the French solely to denote members of the *Académie Française* (*akadimat al-Fransīs*), who are the most eminent French scholars. Taken more narrowly, the meaning is obvious, and is similar to when one talks of the Egyptian Academy (*akadimat Miṣr*) to mean the Azhar mosque, since this refers to the association (*dīwān*) of the greatest scholars of Egypt.

The foremost scholars of Paris, indeed of France, make up the 'council of the sciences' (*dīwān al-'ulūm*), called the *Académie Française*, which counts forty scholars. Every one of these is called a *Membre*, i.e. the assembly is likened to a body, each person constituting a member of it. On the whole, the members of this council are greatly superior to other Frenchmen. Their task is to compile French dictionaries and further to examine works related to literature and history. It once occurred that a certain French scholar had attained a high degree of knowledge in the sciences and was thus qualified to replace one of the members of this Academy who had died. However, as this scholar was of the greatest impudence, they refused to admit him to this council. And so, he could not do anything except constantly mock its members. One of the anecdotes recounted about him is that one day he was walking past the Academy together with some of his friends. When the latter mentioned the merit of the scholars of the Academy, he told them: 'no-one doubts that the members of this council have a mind like four people put together'.[1] In uttering these words, he was referring to a French saying which is used to praise somebody whom one considers to have the intelligence of four people. However, he used it to imply that the intellect of ten members put together was like that of a single one. On the face of it, his words were complimentary, but the inner meaning was something completely different. Another story told about him is that before his death he had, as is customary among the French, written a poem to be inscribed on the marble headstone of his grave. The French verse may be rendered as follows:

Here lies buried someone who was nothing at all –
not even a member of the Academy!

In other words, 'this is the grave of someone who has not attained any rank, not even the miserable one of those scholars.'

---

source, as in the Maghribī script the letter *qāf* (/q/) is represented by ڢ, which in all other scripts denotes /f/.

1. '*ka 'aql arba'a*', which renders the French '*comme quatre*', meaning 'a great deal', 'excessively'.

Then, there is an Academy called the 'academy for the inscription of literary sciences' (*Académie des Inscriptions et Belles-lettres*). The council of this learned society consists of thirty people. They are entrusted with the task of studying useful languages, ancient monuments, especially foreign buildings, the literary sciences and the customs and morals of nations. Most of its activities are centred on perfecting French scientific literature by adding what is lacking from science books in such foreign languages as Latin, Arabic, Persian, Hindi, Chinese, Greek, Hebrew, Coptic, etc.

Another of these academies is called the 'Royal Academy of Sciences' (*Académie des Sciences*), whose members are subdivided into twelve sections, each of which is devoted to a special branch of science. As a result, there are twelve branches. The people in the first section devote themselves to mathematics, engineering and arithmetic. Those of the second study dynamics, which includes the science of moving heavy weights, etc. Scholars in the third section are involved in astronomy, whereas those in the fourth work on geography and experimental sciences. The fifth and sixth sections concentrate on general natural science and physics, respectively, whereas the seventh conducts research into mineralogy and petrology. The eighth section studies botany; the ninth, the management of the earth's resources; the tenth, medical care for animals; the eleventh, anatomy; and the twelfth, medicine and surgery.

And then there is also a royal academy, called the 'Academy of Fine Arts' (*Académie des Beaux-arts*), which comprises five branches. The first is that of the art of drawing; the second, sculpture; the third, architecture; the fourth, painting; and the fifth, the composition of musical notes. Affiliated to this is the 'School of Fine Arts' (*Ecole des Beaux-arts*), which focuses on the teaching of drawing and related subjects.[1] It also offers classes in drawing, painting and architecture.

Among the scholarly councils, there is a society called the *Athénée des Beaux-arts* (*athīnat al-funūn*), which is devoted to the progress of arts and crafts. This society acts as a referee in that it examines things and pronounces an opinion on them.

As for the *Athénée Royal de Paris* (*athīna Bārīs al-sulṭāniyya*), this is a place for the sciences and the arts, and where people can take classes if they pay a small contribution each year. Its teachers are men of great erudition. The *Société Philomatique* (*fīlūmāniyya*), i.e. the 'lovers of sciences', is a society that aims to further the progress of regeneration sciences, with animals,

1. Cf. Khayr al-Dīn, 1867: 67.

plants and minerals making up separate categories. There is also a society that deals with the science of composition and rhetoric; its aim is to record the literary sciences and to preserve uncommon words in order to prevent the French language from becoming corrupted. If a person invents an unusual expression, answers a rare question or creates pleasant poetry, then he is awarded a prize.

The aim of the society of 'good instruction' is to teach Catholic morals and religion. There is also a society called the 'Academy of the Sons of Apollo' (*Abūlūn*) (*Académie des Fils d'Apollon*), i.e. for authors, which is the council for those involved in the literary sciences.

The 'Asiatic Society' (*Société Asiatique*)[1] is devoted to Asian and Oriental languages, the acquisition and translation into French of rare books written in these languages or the printing of them to make them available to the public.

As for the 'Geographical Society' (*Société de Géographie*),[2] it aims to improve and perfect the science of geography. It also encourages people to travel to unknown countries; if somebody goes to one of these places and returns, he is asked about everything related to his journey. All of this is then recorded and included in geography books. This is why this science is constantly being perfected by the French. Generally speaking, this society deals with everything related to geography, such as the printing of maps, etc.

And then, there is the 'Grammar Society' (*Société Grammaticale*), which is involved with the French language. In French, 'grammar' is called *grammaire* (*al-agramīr*), but in Latin and Italian it is known as *grammatica* (*aghramātīqā*). The object of this society is to ensure the correct usage of the language and the addition of new terms or the preservation of old ones, since French is a language that does not have fixed rules of spelling or pronunciation.

The goal of the members of the 'Society of Book Lovers' (*Société des Bibliophiles [Français]*) is to encourage the printing of useful and rare books. The members of the 'Society of Calligraphers' (*Société des Calligraphes*), on the other hand, concentrate on perfecting the handwriting skills.

There is also the 'Society of Animal Magnetism' (*Société du Magnétisme Animal*), which is an association that advocates the existence of a magnetic fluid inside animals.

The 'Society for the Preservation of Vestiges of Antiquity' (*Société Archéologique*) is an organization aimed at the conservation of all splendid

---

1. *al-jam'iyya al-Āsiyātiyya*. Cf. M. Bayram V, 1884–93: III, 86; Khayr al-Dīn, 1867: 69.
2. Cf. Khayr al-Dīn, 1867: 68; M. Bayram V, 1884–93: III, 86.

remains of the Ancients, such as their buildings, mummies, clothing, etc. It also looks for such things in order to study the Ancients' customs. For instance, there are many precious objects taken from Egypt, such as the stone painted with the signs of the Zodiac from Dendera,[1] which has enabled the French to understand ancient Egyptian astronomy. They take such things without giving anything in return, despite the fact that they are well aware of their value. Instead, they keep them and draw various gains and general benefits from them.

The 'Bureau of Longitudes' (*Bureau des Longitudes*) counts twelve members – three engineers, four astronomers, four seafarers and one geographer – who busy themselves with astronomy, the compiling of almanacs, ephemerides and the establishment of the longitudes of towns.

Another association is the 'Royal Society for Agricultural Sciences and Agronomics'[2] (*Institut Royal Agronomique*). The rich people among its members award a prize to anyone who invents something new and useful. There is also a society for the improvement of wool, whose members devote themselves to everything connected with small cattle. There is also a society that has been entrusted with enhancing the French people's proficiency at the arts and crafts. It contributes to the progress of all types of skills, and if somebody proposes something useful, he receives a great gift from the members of this society, as well as notoriety.

In the city of Paris there are royal schools, called *collèges* (*kūlayj*), where people study important practical sciences. There are five of these *collèges*. It is there that students are taught composition and writing skills, as well as ancient foreign languages, sciences, mathematics, history, geography, philosophy and elementary physics (i.e. that which is contained in small books), drawing and calligraphy. The students are subdivided into classes; usually, a person completes one class each year. In each of the six years, students go from one class to a higher one, i.e. through promotion, and not because of an individual's intellectual prowess or anything else, since it is impossible for anyone to skip a year. There are two non-royal *collèges*, but they teach the same subjects as the five previously mentioned institutions.

---

1. This is, of course, the famous Dendera Zodiac – the only circular representation of the world ever found in Egypt – which was originally located in the ceiling of the Hathor temple at Dendera. It arrived in Paris in 1820 and can currently be seen at the Louvre ('Crypte d'Osiris'). The zodiac at Dendera is a plaster copy of the original. See R. Ridley 1998: 108–9; Buchwald & Josefowicz 2010.
2. '*tadbīr tawfīr al-maṣārīf al-barrāniyya wa 'l-juwwāniyya*', 'the management of the economy of exterior and interior resources'.

The most important of these schools is, however, the so-called *Collège Royal de France*.[1] Here, students study mathematics, theoretical and applied physics,[2] astronomy, practical medicine and anatomy, as well as languages like Arabic, Persian, Turkish, Hebrew, Syriac, Hindi, the language and sciences of the people of China (Sinology), the language of the Tartars (Mongolian), Greek philosophy, Latin rhetoric and eloquence and the rules of French composition and style. This *collège* boasts the most eminent teachers and counts 6,000 students.

Another famous school is the (*Ecole*) *Polytechnique* (*būliytiqniyqā*), i.e. 'the school of the totality of sciences'. At this establishment they teach mathematics and physics for the training of engineers in the fields of geography and military sciences. Geographical (civil) engineers design bridges, quays, roads, embankments and canals, as well as all traction devices and those for the lifting of heavy loads. As for military engineers, they design citadels, fortresses, towers and defences against enemy attacks, and are also responsible for the setting up of military encampments[3] and for explosions with the use of gunpowder. The teaching staff of this school is composed of scholars versed in all sciences. It indeed redounds to somebody's standing to be a student at this institute.

There is also a school called 'School of Legal Branches' (*Ecole de Droit*), where people study commercial law, criminal law, etc.

In another school, specialized in the teaching of drawing, both male and female students[4] study the art of painting. At the 'Royal School for Singing', students of both sexes study the art of vocal music and church singing. There is another school devoted to the art of drawing and mathematics as tools for other arts. Here, people study arithmetic, geometry, mensuration, stone and wood sculpture, surveying and the representation of animals, people and flowers, as well as different types of decoration and ornamentation.

The 'School for Bridges and Embankments' (*Ecole des Ponts et Chaussées*) offers classes in the engineering of roads, canals and quays. At the 'Royal School for the Study of Mineralogy' (*Ecole Royale des Mines*) one learns

1. It is likely that al-Ṭahṭāwī actually visited this institute since at the time it was run by none other than Silvestre de Sacy, who had been appointed administrator in 1823. Cf. M. al-Sanūsī, 1891–92: 119.
2. For the first variety, al-Ṭahṭāwī uses the paraphrase *'al-ṭabī'a al-makhlūṭa bi 'l-ḥisāb'*, i.e. 'physics mixed with arithmetic'.
3. *'arāḍī*, sing. *'urḍī* (Turkish *ordu*).
4. This is a significant comment since to al-Ṭahṭāwī's Muslim readership this kind of coeducation was both anathema and unknown.

about the ways and processes in which to discover and extract minerals. The 'School for Arts and Crafts' provides instruction in chemistry and engineering applicable to crafts and arts.[1] This institute possesses all the equipment known to this day for all professions. There is also the school called 'School for Living Oriental Languages',[2] where people study Persian, Malay (*al-Malābārī*), Classical and Colloquial Arabic, Turkish, Armenian and the language of the *Rūm* [Modern Greek]. At the *Ecole d'Archéologie* (*Arliyghulughī*), which means the explanation of inscriptions dating from ancient times written in old languages, people decipher the ancient writing on coins, documents and stone decorations dating back to Antiquity, and translate inscriptions on ancient temples.

There is also a royal school where they teach the history and politics, etc., of states [*Institut des Sciences Politiques*], and the 'Royal School for Music, Composition and Public Speaking' is the place of study for actors, singers and musicians[3] of both sexes. It has 400 students.

The 'school of the royal garden', i.e. that of the Botanical Garden (*Ecole du Jardin des Plantes*), provides thirteen courses related to all branches of science, such as botany, physics, chemistry, mineralogy, anatomy and comparative human and animal anatomy. Affiliated to it is the 'School of Gardening' (*Ecole d'Horticulture*),[4] where they teach the science of tree planting, the protection of trees against the cold and the acclimatization of imported exotic plants to the environments to which they have been transported. There is also a school involved in the pruning of non-fructiferous trees so as to make them bear fruit. Another school provides instruction in botany and mineralogy to people wishing to travel to other countries so as to enable them to distinguish the various plants and minerals they will encounter there.

There is also a 'School for Animal Medicine' (*Ecole Vétérinaire*), where people are taught how to treat animals. In this school, there are hospitals for sick animals, an institute for chemistry and one for physics, a pharmacy,

1. This was the *Conservatoire des Arts et Métiers* (which later became the *Musée National des Techniques*). Cf. M. al-Ṣaffār [S. Gilson Miller], 1992: 196 (*Dār al-fiziq*).
2. *maktab al-lughāt al-mashraqiyya al-musta'mala* ('school for Eastern languages that are in use'), which is, of course, the famous *Ecole des Langues Orientales Vivantes*. Cf. M. al-Sanūsī, 1891–92: 118–24.
3. *al-ālātiyya* (sing. *ālātī*), 'instrumentalists'; cf. E. Lane, 1923: 361.
4. *maktab al-bustanjiyya*, which literally translates as 'gardeners' school'. The spelling *bustanjiyya*, which should in fact be corrected to *bustānjiyya* (sing. *bustānjī*), is again an Arabic-Turkish compound from ECA, the CA term being *bustānī*/pl. *bustāniyyūn*. In this context, '*(maktab al-) bastana*' ('gardening', 'horticulture') would probably have been more appropriate.

herbal garden, a school for applied agronomy, as well as a collection of various animal species used for experiments into the differences between different animal races. For instance, they will cross one horse species with another – say, an Arab stallion with an Andalusian mare – in order to breed a new kind of horse.

The 'School for the Deaf and Dumb' (*Ecole des Sourds-muets*)[1] can accommodate 100 pupils, who attend classes here between the ages of eleven and sixteen. They learn to read and write, and study arithmetic, French,[2] history, geography, as well as practical skills. The school has a workshop where students learn cooking, painting, carpentry, turnery, sewing, shoemaking,[3] etc.

There is also a 'Royal School for the Blind' (*Ecole Royale des Aveugles*),[4] which is open only to a limited number of blind people, who learn to read here by means of a specially designed script, which they feel with their hands. They also learn geography from special maps, as well as history, languages, mathematics, singing, musical instruments and a craft such as stocking making, etc.

In addition to what we have mentioned above, there are a number of other schools in Paris. For instance, those called *pensions* (*al-bansiyyūnāt*), where small children learn to read and write and study practical sciences like arithmetic and geometry, as well as other subjects such as history and geography. There are 150 of these *pensions*. Besides accommodation and full board, the children's laundry is done there, etc. For this service, their parents pay a fixed annual fee.

In addition to these *pensions*, some learned scholars take a number of children into their homes; the students receive [full] board and instruction, either from the scholar himself or from teachers invited to his house. Furthermore, many people have a tutor for their children who comes to their houses in order to teach them at home.

Among the things that provide a great passing benefit to people are the daily memoranda, called *jūrnālāt*, which is the plural of *jurnāl* – the French plural being *journaux* (*jurnū*).[5] These are sheets that are printed each day

1. *maktab al-ṣumm wa 'l-bukm*; Cf. M. al-Sanūsī, 1891–92: 105–09.
2. *al-lisān*, i.e. a translation of the French '*la langue*', which in the French educational system is, however, an ellipsis for '*la langue française*'.
3. al-Ṭahṭāwī uses the ECA *ṣuramātī* (which is still in use today, though mostly restricted to derisory contexts).
4. Cf. M. al-Sanūsī, 1891–92: 101–03.
5. Al-Ṭahṭāwī's exposé of the press would later inspire the Moroccan Muḥammad al-Ṣaffār ([S. Gilson Miller], 1992: 150ff.).

and mention everything that has come to the attention of its publishers that day. The papers are distributed in the city and sold to all people. All the notables of Paris, as well as the *cafés*, have copies set aside for them each day.[1] In these newspapers, everyone in France may say what he feels, praise or criticize what he considers to be good or bad and voice an opinion on the running of the state. The people enjoy complete freedom, as long as they do not abuse it, in which case they are brought up before a judge and convicted. The newspapers are organized in groups, each of which follows its own school of thought and editorial policy, which it advocates, defends and supports. There is nothing more mendacious on this earth than newspapers, especially those of the French, who avoid lying merely because it is a human frailty. In general, the people who write for these newspapers are worse than poets in terms of their prejudice against or in favour of certain things.

There are different types of newspapers. One group aims to bring news related to the French kingdom or the outside world; others are specialized only in domestic news, in business and commerce, or in certain individual sciences such as medicine, etc. Each newspaper is usually printed at 25,000 copies, although the circulation may increase with public demand. Newspaper editors have news from abroad before anyone else since they have correspondents[2] in every country.[3]

The sources of knowledge in Paris also include yearbooks, modern almanacs, updated ephemerides, etc. Each year, many almanacs appear which also contain forecasts, interesting events from the world of science and art, many affairs of state, as well as the names of important people in the world, luminaries from France, including their addresses, titles and positions. And if someone requires a name or an address, he consults one of these books.

---

1. Journals were, in fact, very expensive and sold almost exclusively by subscription; the average annual rate during the Restoration was FF70–80 – at a time when average wages for manual workers were FF550 p/a (and a civil servant's *c.* FF1,000). Things would change only in 1836, when two newspapers were founded that halved the price of the subscription to FF40, i.e. *La Presse* and *Le Siècle*. This cheap press would take off immediately and gain massive popularity thanks to the introduction of the *roman-feuilleton* (serial). See D. Couty, 1988: 34.
2. This is probably the first use of the term *murāsil* (pl. *murāsilūn*) in this sense, which it still has in MSA.
3. In the 2nd edition, the author expanded more on the newspapers, and also included a passage on the role of poetry and poets among the ancient Arabs by Abū ʿAmr b. al-ʿAlā al-Māzinī (689–770), who was one of the founders of Arabic philology, one of the seven canonical readers of the Qurʾān [q.v. "Abū ʿAmr", *EI1*, s.v. (Brockelmann); *EI2* (R. Blachère)] and a compiler of pre-Islamic poetry.

In Paris, there are also reading rooms (*cabinets de lecture*), where people go and after paying a set fee read all the newspapers and other publications, as well as books, which they can borrow if they need to.[1] As for the bookstores and libraries in Paris, they truly astound the mind. Bookselling is one of the most flourishing trades, despite the great number of shops, the many printing works and the multitude of books printed each year. It is difficult even to count them. Most of them are in it for profit, not to provide any benefit. Every year, the Paris printing houses produce books the like of which cannot be found anywhere else. The interest shown by the French in knowledge is their most praiseworthy characteristic. One poet said:

If you wish to gain favour from all books
with the best of what is told, the most beautiful of what is heard
then peruse the collections of books, for they
dispel any collection of a youngster's sorrows

Another one said:

Make a book your companion – when you open it
it shows you the rulers of time, resurrected
It is your tutor of morals, a comrade in solitude
and a friend and companion in nightly entertainment when you find yourself alone

All in all, it is impossible to give a detailed overview of the sciences and arts of Paris. One can provide only a general survey as we have done here.

Fourth Essay

Introduction

On our perseverance and work in the arts required for the attainment of the goal of our ruler and on the organization of the time devoted to reading, writing and other disciplines. It also contains the great expenses on the

1. Because of the high price of books (FF3–7.50), these *cabinets de lecture* (which was an old tradition) were very popular. These places, which the *Dictionnaire de l'Académie* (6th edn, 1835, I, 242) described as '*lieu où l'on donne à lire, moyennant une rétribution, des journaux et des livres,*' were present in cities only. Some of them even offered a home service, for which people paid a flat fee *par séance* or for every quarter. See F. Parent-Lardeur, 1982.

part of our benefactor, a number of letters between myself and some of the eminent Frankish personalities with regard to learning and a mention of the arts and the books I have studied in the city of Paris.

From this essay you will understand that the study of the arts is not an easy thing and that those seeking knowledge must defy dangers in order to attain their goal in those countries. As one poet said:

Let me attain the heights that are unattainable
for its ease lies in hardship, and in ease lies hardship
You wish to attain higher things at a cheap price
but before the honey must come the bee sting!

Another one said in an epigram:

He who knows that honey brings him rest
does not fear the pain from the sting of the bee!

Another poet also said:

The virtues have a passion for dangers
so seek the virtues and make your efforts the price
And if the one who loves them shows you the insignificance, then say:
the judgement of destiny lies in the love of the friend

First Section. On the organization of instruction in reading and writing, etc., which we received at the beginning

One of the educational habits of the people of Paris is to teach a person to read by means of books with large characters so that their shapes become embedded in his mind. These books contain the letters of the alphabet in their order, followed by a number of words exemplifying nouns and verbs. It is by this method that people learn how to write; one memorizes these words and pronounces them in the way that they should be pronounced so that people learn to speak really well from a very early age. Afterwards, you find a number of sentences that are easy to understand and that are suitable for young children. Here are some sentences from the book we used: '*This is a horse with three legs; birds have only two legs, but they have wings with which they fly; as for the fish, it swims in the water*', etc. These are of course the kinds of things that are known to the speaker. This method is, in fact, similar to the [Arab] grammarians' '*the sky is over us, and the earth is below us*', which is an example of something that does not contain new information. However, this differs from the way in which they explain composition: '*Speech is the assembled expression that conveys a complete self-contained meaning through composition.*' In this book one also finds descriptions of well-known animals, particularly of the kind that children like to play with, such as birds, cats, etc., followed by a small text on how children should behave, their obedience to their parents and so on and so forth. Then there is a text on the science of arithmetic.

When this book is finished, one starts to read a more important book, one on French grammar, as well as others. The division of time devoted to classes is such that a person studies a number of different subjects each day. In the morning, you study, for instance, history, followed by a class on drawing with the arts teacher, then a lesson on French grammar, followed by one of geography,[1] and one with the writing teacher in order to learn the rules of writing, etc. This is something we have already mentioned above.

As it was the hope of our benefactor that we should learn quickly and then return to our native country, we already started in Marseilles – so before we even arrived in Paris – to learn how to write the [French] alphabet for about thirty days. When we left for Paris, we all stayed together in one house and started reading. Our activities were arranged as follows: in the morning, we would read a history book for two hours. After lunch, we had a class in writing and French conversation. In the afternoon, we had a class in drawing, followed by one on French grammar. Each week, we had three classes in arithmetic and engineering. At first, we had two hours of writing as we had to learn the French writing system. Later on, it was only one lesson per day, and when in the end we had learned to write the script our teacher did not come any more. As for arithmetic, engineering, history and geography (*jughrāfiyā*), we continued to work on them until God made easy our return [to Egypt].

For a little under a year, all of us lived in the same house and together studied the French language and the already mentioned arts. However, this did not yield any great advantage to us, except the mere learning of French grammar. Then we were divided among several schools in groups of two or three, and one of us would be put in a school together with French children or in a private house with a private teacher, against payment of a certain amount for food, drink, accommodation, tuition and care of our

1. *Taqwīm al-buldān*, i.e. 'the position of countries', which is the term that was used in mediaeval Arabic literature where it denoted geographical compendia (cf. Abū 'l-Fidā').

things – e.g. the washing of our clothes. The master of the school or the house received about 5,000 piastres[1] for this each year, and we did not want for anything in terms of food and drink. As the climate in this country is extremely cold, every one of us had 300 piastres' worth of wood for heating per year. In addition to these substantial expenses, the state also bought shirts, trousers and shoes for us, as well as all the necessary materials, tools and instruments such as books, paper, ink, drawing pens, etc. The money they paid to doctors and pharmacists for treatment when one of us was ill should also be mentioned, since the doctors in Paris – despite their huge number – demand a fee when visiting a sick person. The size of the fee depends on the extent to which they are or are not famous. It must be paid at every visit in cases where the doctor does not have a fixed annual income. We have already talked about this in the chapter dealing with the attention the French devote to medicine and health care. The least important of doctors earns three francs for each visit, which lasts for about half an hour. A doctor of medium importance gets about five francs for each visit, whereas an eminent physician commands a fee of some fifty francs for each house consultation. If there are several visits within the same day, then the fee is also multiplied. If the patient is a destitute person, the doctor may not charge him anything. However, we were counted among the well-off or even rich, because of our fine clothes, which they considered to be strange; our relation to the benefactor; the vast expenses on our education; and all other things mentioned above. The one in charge of our studies (sc. Jomard)[2] or our supervisor never ceased to remind us of this in order to encourage us to show diligence and application. You will see some examples of this in the letters which Jomard wrote to me after the general examination.

Second Section. On the supervision of our comings and goings

During the time that we were all staying together in the house of the Efendis, we did not leave it either by day or by night, except on Sundays, which is the feast day among the Franks, and then only with a permit to be shown to the doorman. The permit would be drawn up by the official whom our benefactor had appointed to supervise us. After we had been divided and put in schools called *pensions*, we went out on the days that

1. The Arabic has '10 *akyās* ('purses')'; one 'purse' (*kīs*) equalled 500 piastres; E. Lane, 1923: 580.
2. *nāẓir al-ta'līm*, which is a calque from the French *directeur d'études*.

we were free, i.e. the whole of Sunday, the Thursday after class and on the public holidays of the French. Some of us would go out every night after dinner if we did not have any more classes afterwards.

Here, we should like to mention the regulations set forth by the Efendis after our admission into the *pensions*. These rules provide a picture of the Efendis' organization of the *pensions*.

Article 1: On Sunday, when permission is granted to them to go out, the students must leave the *pensions* at nine o'clock and come directly to the main building. The first thing they need to do the moment they enter the building is to show the paper issued by their teacher to the Efendi on duty during that month so that he can note the time at which the student has entered the building. Afterwards, they may go to the designated places of recreation on condition that they get together in groups of three or four. In summer, they have to return to the *pensions* at nine o'clock, in winter at eight o'clock. This arrangement must be observed without any exceptions. It is even better for someone to return to the *pension* prior to the designated time and take his dinner there, since it must be avoided that people roam the streets at night alone. When entering the *pensions*, students must give the aforesaid slip of paper to the teacher.

Article 2: Anyone who does not comply with the aforementioned instructions will be prohibited from leaving the *pension* for one or two weeks, subject to the relevant requirements.

Article 3: Complaints against teachers will not be heard and acknowledged unless they are made in writing. Only complaints regarding the teaching or other issues resulting in harm to the complainant will be heard. However, before making the complaint in writing, the person in question must inform his teacher of this at once; it is only then that he can submit the request to the duty officer of the month.

Article 4: All the Efendis will be examined at the end of each month in order to ascertain what they have acquired of the sciences in the course of that month. They will be asked if they are in need of books and materials. Each month, their exact progress, acquired knowledge and activities will be recorded. This must be borne in mind at all times so as to achieve the goal of His Excellency the ruler.

Article 5: If the Efendis are in need of anything in terms of books and study materials in the course of the month, they should submit a written request to their teacher, who will pass it on to Monsieur Jomard. If the latter considers it appropriate, he will give his approval for the items concerned, after having informed the duty officer of this. Anyone who purchases anything without permission will have to pay for it out of his own pocket.

Article 6: If, after the exam mentioned in Article 4, one of the Efendis deserves a prize for his excellence, he will be given books, study materials and money.

Article 7: In places of recreation or in the street, none of them may do anything that may detract from his dignity. This instruction is the most important of all and trangressions are strictly forbidden.

Article 8: The Efendis residing in the *pension* may enter the mission house premises only once every fifteen days,[1] and then only on Sunday.

Article 9: On the Sunday on which they do not come to the mission house they are expected to go out with French children or with their teachers to places of entertainment or sports venues and to visit the sites they are supposed to visit. Similarly, on Thursdays or public holidays, provided they do not have any work to do, they will go with the aforesaid people and to the above-mentioned places.

Article 10: The students will abide by the regulations of their *pension* with the same meticulousness and attention as French children, at least for those matters not related to religion.

Article 11: Anyone who breaks this regulation will be punished in accordance with the offence. If he shows a lack of obedience, he will be completely confined to quarters. If someone persists in inappropriate acts and unsatisfactory behaviour, or his teacher's report attests to his bad behaviour and bears out his refractoriness, we shall, in compliance with the instructions received from His esteemed Excellency, the beneficent ruler, consult with the friends of our esteemed Efendi among the people of this city and send the one who has been guilty of shameful conduct and insubordinacy back to Egypt, without any doubt or hesitation whatsoever.

Article 12: All the Efendis are equal when it comes to the regulations to be upheld in the *pensions*. In the event that the *pensions* have a separate table for teachers and another for the students, then our Efendis will eat with their teachers.

Article 13: All the regulations mentioned are without distinction binding on the above-mentioned Efendis. For this reason, we have given each of them a copy of said regulations.

Article 14: All the preceding articles constitute an abridgement of our thoughts and the result of our reflection and that of the personages

1. This is, of course, again a literal translation from the French expression for 'fortnightly', i.e.– *tous les quinze jours*.

to whom our esteemed Efendi (sc. Muḥammad ʿAlī) has entrusted us. Consequently, everyone is bound to follow them with care in order to gain the favour of our esteemed Efendi, the beneficent ruler. Anybody who does not comply with it or seeks any kind of excuse will be subject to the law of our esteemed Efendi, the beneficent ruler – may God protect him!

Third Section. On how our ruler exhorted us to work and show diligence

From the time of our departure from Egypt, our ruler usually deigned to send us a *firmān*[1] every couple of months in which he exhorted us to acquire the necessary arts and crafts. Some of these firmans were similar to those the Ottomans call *iḥyāʾ al-qulūb* ('revitalization of the hearts'), an example of which is included below. Others belonged to the category of rebuke of what had reached him about us and what he was told about us by people – whether it was true or not. An example of such a firman was the last one we got prior to our return to Cairo. Here, we should like to give an example of the first type of firman, i.e. one 'to revive the hearts' – even though it also contains some censure, so that you can see how he – May God protect him – exhorted us to study. This is a copy of the text, which I have translated:[2]

To the most noble and valued Efendis residing in Paris with a view to acquiring the sciences and arts – may God increase their strength.

You are hereby informed that we have received your monthly bulletins and the schedules of your study activities. However, these schedules, which included information on your activites in the course of one trimester, are obscure and one cannot understand from them what you have achieved in that period; in fact, we have not learned anything from them. Yet, you are in the city of Paris, which is the source of the sciences and the arts! In view of your paltry activities in this period, we have understood that you lack zeal and a thirst for learning, which pains us greatly. My dear Efendis, what are our hopes of you? Each one of you should send us something of the fruit of his labours and proof of his skill. If you do not exchange this idleness with hard work, diligence and zeal, and if you return to Egypt merely after having read a couple of books, thinking that you have studied the [European] sciences and arts, then you are deceiving yourselves! Here, with us – praise and thank God – your educated comrades are working and are gaining a reputation for themselves.

1. Originally a Persian word (*framān*), it passed into Arabic via Turkish (*fermān*) and denotes a written order. See *EI1*, s.v. "fermān" (C. Huart).
2. Translated from (Ottoman) Turkish, which was the only administrative language during Muḥammad ʿAlī's reign.

So, how will you face them if you return in this state? How will you show them the perfection of the sciences and arts? People should always look at the implications of things; an intelligent person must not let an opportunity slip by if he is to reap the fruit of his efforts. So, you have neglected to take advantage of this opportunity; you have conducted yourselves foolishly, without paying heed to the hardships and punishment that you will incur as a result of it. You did not exert yourselves in order to obtain our attention, despite the fact that we have favoured you so that you might distinguish yourselves from your peers. If you wish to gain our approval, each one of you must not let a single minute go by without studying the sciences and arts. Henceforth, each of you will communicate the progress he has made between the beginning and end of each month. Furthermore, you must also include your level in geometry, arithmetic and drawing, as well as the amount of time required to finish these sciences. Every month, you must record the progress in your studies in relation to the preceding month. If you lack perseverance and zeal, you must inform us of the reason and whether it is a lack of interest on your part or due to illness and, if it is the latter, the nature of the illness and whether it is due to natural causes or the result of an accident. In short, you must describe your actual condition so that we can understand how you are doing. This is what we require of you. Read this order all together, and apply yourselves to understanding the aim of this decree.

This order was written in the Dīwān *of Egypt during our council meeting in Alexandria, thanks to the Exalted one. When our order reaches you, you must act accordingly and avoid any breach of it. On this, the fifth of the month of* Rabīʿ al-awwal, *1245 of the Hijra.*[1]

(This marks the end of the text.)

Since receiving this missive, we have each month written about everything we read and learned in the course of the month in question. The teachers signed these letters and sent them on to our benefactor. When one of us was neglectful in doing this, Monsieur Jomard wrote a letter to all of us, ordering those who were assiduous in writing these monthly letters to persevere and rebuking those who were neglectful. This is a copy of a translation of a letter on this subject, which he sent to me and which we quote in its entirety:

Paris, 15 June – 25 Muḥarram,

My dear Shaykh Rifāʿa,

You are no doubt familiar with the order from your benefactor regarding the monthly letters containing the reports on what you have studied. Continue to show

1. = 4 October 1829 A.D.

perseverance and submit these letters on the 30th day of each month to Monsieur *Muhrdār Efendi and also ask him for blank sheets for the next report. Everyone knows that it only takes half an hour to write this monthly letter since it is only intended to record the number and nature of the lessons you have studied, so that the head of your school can write his name under yours in each monthly report. Your diligence has not escaped me, and I appreciate the value of your work. I should therefore like to ask you to continue to apply yourself assiduously to the duties with which you have been charged.*

With my sincere friendship,
*Jomard, member of the Institut (*al-Ansṭīṭūt)[1]

Fourth Section. On some of the letters between myself and some of the leading French scholars, other than Monsieur Jomard

Among those who wrote to me several times, there was Monsieur de Sacy. We shall cite several of his letters, some of which he wrote in Arabic, others in French.

Here is one of them:

From one who is humbled before the mercy of his Lord – Glory be to Him the Sublime – to his highly esteemed friend, honoured and respected brother, the eminent Shaykh Rifā'a al-Ṭahṭāwī – may the Great and Almighty God keep him from adversity and evil and bless him with good health, happiness and goodness.

I am returning to you by hand of your servant the extract of your precious book on the events of your stay in Paris, which I have finished reading. Enclosed you will find my remarks regarding the things you stated in the chapter on the verb inflexion in our French language.[2] *If you study them carefully, it will become clear to you that our use of the past tense is correct.*

You should write a book on the grammar of the French language, which is used by all peoples of Europe and in all its kingdoms, in order to lead the people of Egypt to the sources of our works on sciences and skills, as well as their methods. This would indeed give you great fame in your country and make people remember you for centuries to come. May you always stay healthy.

Yours in friendship,
Silvestre de Sacy

---

1. Namely, the Institut de France. The rather periphrastic Arabic *aḥad arbāb dīwān al-ansṭīṭūt* ('one of the members of the council of the Institut') is a translation of the French '*membre de l'Institut*'.
2. See Third Essay, Second Section.

This is a copy of another letter:

To our dear friend Shaykh Rifāʿa al-Ṭahṭāwī, may God protect and preserve him.

Enclosed please find the certificate you have requested and which states that I have read the account of your journey. Everything you have examined in terms of the traditions of the French, their customs, politics, religious prescriptions, sciences, literature, we have found pleasant and useful. It pleases those who look at it and strikes wonder in those who apply themselves to it.

There is no harm in your submitting my manuscript to Monsieur Jomard. God willing, this work will grant you favour with His Excellency the Pasha, who will bestow upon you a fitting reward.

With best wishes.
Your friend,
Silvestre de Sacy al-Bārīzī

Together with this letter, he also sent me a page of text written in the French language, which I submitted to Monsieur Jomard. This, in fact, amounted to something of a eulogy, a translation of which follows now:

As Monsieur Rifāʿa wanted me to peruse his travel book written in Arabic, I have read all but a small part of this treatise.[1] *I am right in saying that the structure of the work seems to be excellent and that it will enable his compatriots to gain a full understanding of our customs, our religious and political practices and our sciences. However, it also contains some Islamic prejudices.*[2] *One also gains knowledge of cosmography from this book. The work shows that the author has a good critical sense and sound intelligence. At the same time, he sometimes expresses judgements on all Frenchmen despite the fact that these apply for the most part only to the inhabitants of Paris and other large cities. However, this may be the result of his own specific situation as he himself never knew anything except Paris and a few other cities. In the chapter on the sciences,*[3] *he strove towards discussing known things as an introduction to those that are unknown, especially in the part related to arithmetic and cosmography. The language of the book is for the most part clear,*

1. The Arabic word used by Rifāʿa is *tārīkh*, which literally means 'history'. It is more than likely that the explanation for this peculiar choice of words lies in the author's mistranslation of de Sacy's '*histoire*', which, in addition to history, also means 'story', 'narrative', etc.
2. Caussin de Perceval (see below) perhaps expressed fundamentally the same view more aptly, stating that the author judged European institutions, customs, etc., '*avec l'esprit oriental et les idées musulmanes*' (*Journal Asiatique*, XI, 1833, 222).
3. See Sixth Essay.

and devoid of affected elaborate embellishments, as befits the issues treated in the book. However, it does not always comply with the rules of Arabic grammar. This may be due to the fact that the author wrote things down in a hurry, and he will probably correct the mistakes in the fair copy. When treating the art of poetry, he digresses and cites a number of Arabic poems, which, to my mind, are alien to the subject of this book, but perhaps this pleases his compatriots. When talking about the virtues of round shapes over others, he says few useful things and so this passage should be removed.[1]

I have mentioned these things and explained them solely to show that I have carefully read the book. All in all, it has become apparent to me that Monsieur Rifāʿa has spent his time in France well and that he has acquired formidable knowledge, which he has perfected. As a result, he is qualified to be of use to his country. I am only too happy to certify to this and to express my great esteem and friendship for him.

Baron Silvestre de Sacy, Paris, in the month of February 1831 – 19 Shaʿbān 1246.

This is the translation of a letter he sent me a short time prior to my departure from Paris:

Salutations to Monsieur Rifāʿa,

I should find great pleasure if he were to come and visit me at home this coming Monday, at three o'clock, and, if possible, give me the pleasure of seeing him for a few agreeable moments. I should also be most happy if he were to send me news about himself after his arrival in Cairo. In the event that I should be unable to see him again, I should like to wish him a safe journey. I shall always remember his works and always with joy look forward to hearing news from him.

Baron Silvestre de Sacy

This is a reproduction of a letter sent to my by Monsieur Caussin de Perceval,[2] lecturer of spoken, i.e. vernacular, Arabic at the Bibliothèque

1. In the final version of the book, Rifāʿa indeed removed this part. Unfortunately, it is impossible to judge the content (or size) of the passage since it does not seem to have survived.
2. Armand Pierre Caussin de Perceval (1795–1871) was the son of the Arabist Jean-Baptiste Jacques Antoine Caussin de Perceval (1759–1835), the conservator of Arabic manuscripts at the Royal Library, the incumbent of the chair of Arabic (*arabe classique*) at the prestigious *Collège de France* between 1783 and 1833 (!), as well as the translator of the *1001 Nights* and editor of al-Ḥarīrī's *Maqāmāt* and a collection of pre-Islamic poetry (*al-muʿallaqāt*). From an early age Armand Caussin de Perceval received training in Oriental languages (Arabic, Persian, Turkish) at the *Ecole de Jeunes de Langues* in Paris,

Royale[1] in Paris. I had written to him to ask him for his opinion on this *riḥla*, and this is what he wrote back to me:

To the dear, beloved and esteemed friend, eloquent in speech and writing, the honourable Shaykh Rifāʿa – may God protect him – Amen.

Accept our abundant salutations, greetings and esteem.

After receiving your letter yesterday, I without any delay sought to accede to your request. Enclosed you will find a document[2] *containing my opinion about the book recounting the events of your journey, which you have generously allowed me to read. I have stated truthfully what I believe. I have set forth the good qualities I have found in it; as far as flaws are concerned, I have not found any. As you have decided to leave at the end of this month, I hope in friendship that you will not forget me after your arrival – may it be a safe one! – in your country and that you will continue to keep me informed of your health. I should also like to ask you to send me a copy of your book when it has been printed. I should be very grateful for this. May God the Almighty protect you. Salutations.*

Your friend Caussin de Perceval, 24 February of the year 1831.

The enclosed document referred to a certificate testifying that he had read this book and gave his opinion on it. Here is a translation of this

where his teachers included the famous Pierre Ruffin (d. 1824), who was also the King's Interpreter. Caussin de Perceval started his professional career (as an apprentice interpreter) at the French embassy in Constantinople in 1814. Three years later, he was the official dragoman at the French consulate in Aleppo, where he stayed until his return to France in 1821, when he succeeded the Asyūṭ-born Copt Ellious Bocthor (Ilyās Buqṭur) as professor of Vernacular Arabic (*arabe vulgaire*) at the *Ecole des Langues Orientales*, which chair he would occupy for the next 50 years. In 1824, he published one of the first grammars of colloquial Arabic (*Grammaire Arabe Vulgaire suivie de dialogues, lettres actes, etc., à l'usage des élèves de l'Ecole Royale et Spéciale des Langues Orientales Vivantes*, Paris, Dondey-Dupré, with subsequent editions in 1833, 1843, 1858), preceded only by C. Savary's posthumous *Grammaire de Langue Arabe Vulgaire et Littérale. Grammatica linguae arabicae vulgaris necnon litteralis, dialogos complectens* (ed. L. Langlès with the cooperation of S. de Sacy, Dom Raphaël and Mīkhā'īl Ṣabbāgh, Paris, Imprimerie Impériale, 1813, 536pp.). In 1828, Caussin de Perceval published his edition of Bocthor's *Dictionnaire Français-arabe* (2nd edn, 1848), which the author had not been able to complete before his death. In April 1833, he succeeded his father as Arabic professor at the Collège de France. See J. Balteau, 1933-: VII, 1475–76; G. Colin, in *Cent-cinquantenaire de l'Ecole des Langues Orientales*, 106–7; Y. Sarkīs, 1928: 1579–80; L. Shaykhū, 1991: 69–70, 183–4.

1. Ar. *kutubkhāna sulṭāniyya*. This is slightly misleading since it would imply that the school itself was called *Bibliothèque Royale*. In fact, for a number of years, students of the *Ecole des Langues Orientales* had classes at the Royal Library.
2. The Arabic reads *'fa wāṣala lakum ṭayya taḥrīr'*, the latter word denoting a 'fold' or 'pleat'; again, this is a calque from the French (this time committed by de Perceval) *'pli'*, viz. letter, as in *sous ce pli* ('enclosed'). At the end of the letter, al-Ṭahṭāwī corrects de Perceval's grammar to *'ṭayyat al-taḥrīr'*.

document, which he wrote in French for Monsieur Jomard in order to give him his views on this *riḥla*.

I have read the work by Shaykh Rifāʿa, entitled Takhlīs al-ibrīz fī talkhīṣ Bārīz, *and I found that it was a short story dealing with the journey undertaken by the Egyptians who were sent to France by the vizier of Egypt, Ḥājj Muḥammad ʿAlī Pasha. It contains a description of the city of Paris, as well as details on all the branches of the sciences these students are expected to study. It appears to me that this work deserves great praise. It is written in such a way that it will provide great benefit to the author's compatriots. He offers them reliable accounts of the arts of France, the customs, the character of its people and the administration of the state. And when he observed that his native country was inferior to the lands of Europe when it comes to human sciences and the useful arts, he also expressed his regret over this and his desire to awaken Muslims*[3] *with this book of his and to instil in them the wish for useful knowledge, to stimulate in them a love for learning about European civilization and progress in the practical skills of life. When he speaks about the royal institutions, education and other such things, he wants to remind his compatriots of the fact that they must emulate all of that. The remarks he makes in certain passages are for the most part indicative of good sense and devoid of arbitrariness and prejudice. The language of the book is simple, i.e. without any convoluted embellishments, yet very pleasant to read. At the time that I had a copy of this book, the part on the sciences and arts had not yet been finished, and I saw only [some] passages on mathematics, cosmography and the principles of engineering and natural geography. These extracts, though short, were quite satisfying. I hope that the author will continue to write the remaining ones in the same fashion. If these extracts were to be collected in one book, this would constitute an independent science book that would serve as a key for other sciences and be of use to the Arabic-speaking peoples. Once the book has been completed in this manner, it will attest to the great intellect of its author and the breadth of his knowledge.*

Caussin de Perceval

If one puts this letter next to the previous one, one will see that Monsieur de Sacy and Monsieur Caussin agree on the fact that the present book is good, on its simple language, i.e. free from stylistic embellishments, and on its use for the people of Egypt. However, Monsieur de Sacy considered that it had three faults: first, that it includes certain issues which he viewed as Islamic prejudice; second, that we have generalized things that hold only for Paris and major cities to the whole of France; and third, the lack of interest in

3. In Arabic, the author used the rather strange '*ahl al-Islām*', i.e. 'people of Islam', where one would have expected the more common (and appropriate) '*ummat al-Islām*'.

some of the things we said with regard to our preference of round shapes over others. Monsieur Caussin, for his part, did not go into what Monsieur de Sacy considered to be prejudices. When I spoke about this to him he replied that he did not see any harm in it and that I had written in accordance with my conviction. He added that if I had followed what Europeans say and agreed with their views simply out of shame or other motives, this would have been nothing short of duplicity. When Monsieur de Sacy said that the style of the book is simple, he meant that no attempt had been made in its constructions to take the road of rhetoric. According to French scholars, simple style is on a par with eloquent style.

Next, we should like to quote a letter from a person who was a close friend of mine. We met when I entered a library to read the Gazettes (*kāẓīṭāt*), that is the events of the day. I got to know this person, who is an accountant with the Treasury, while his brother is the prefect[1] of a *département* (*dibarṭmān*), i.e. one of the provinces of France. He is the offspring of a great family, called 'the Saladins' (cf. *les Saladins*), whose name goes back to Ṣalāḥ al-Dīn. Indeed, they believe that they can trace their origins to Ṣalāḥ al-Dīn al-Ayyūbī, claiming that it is likely that during his battles with the Franks he had a French concubine who became pregnant with his child, after which she returned to her country, and the name remained with her children and her descendants to the present day. As I became acquainted with this man, I also got to know his entire family, with whom I had close ties during my stay in Paris. And when I left, he was with his brother, the Prefect of the *département* of Tarn, in a city called Albi, and he sent me the following letter. Here is a translation, albeit with some acceptable omissions:

My dear Shaykh Rifāʿa,

I have given that which you have entrusted to me to the son of the governor of the district so that he may return it to you. You can expect it shortly after receiving this letter. My brother has instructed me to express his appreciation for the kindness

1. *maʾmūr* ('one who is ordered'); originally an Ottoman term (*meʾmūr*) meaning 'civil official', in Egypt it denoted 'official' and, from the 1820s, the chief officer of a local district (*maʾmūriyya*). At the time of writing, Egypt was divided into seven provinces (*mudīriyya*), each governed by a *muḥāfiẓ* (or *mudīr*). A province was subdivided into a number of *maʾmūriyyas* (64 in total nationwide), each of which was, in turn, divided into a number of subdistricts (*qism*, pl. *aqsām*), headed by a *nāẓir* (pl. *nuẓẓār*). See E. Lane, 1923: 129; "maʾmūr", *EI2* (C. Findley); M. Morsy, 1984: 115–16. The brother in question is Jean-François Léon Saladin (1795–1873), who was Prefect of the Tarn département (28.08–10.09.1830) and later went on to occupy the same post in the Saône-et-Loire (22.01–9.12.1831), Hautes-Alpes (17.01–3.03.1834), Drôme (1.07–1.08.1835), Aude (5–19.06.1840) and Yonne (23.11–26.12.1841). See R. Bargeton *et al.*, 1981: 272.

you have extended to him in lending him the thing in question, and to congratulate you on attaining the aspired goal. Will you be leaving us soon in order to see your native country again? If it pleases God, you will again meet all your relatives and friends and find your country in a good state. I have heard that your departure is near and I do not think that I shall be able to meet you in Paris. However, shortly before the appointed time, we shall meet each other in Marseilles, which will allow me to say goodbye to you in the last French city that you will cross on your journey. If only your departure had been postponed for a short while, we would have seen each other in Paris, in the place where we first met. I do not know whether our meeting is destined or not. The many vicissitudes of fate are such, particularly for Europeans, that I am unable to ascertain whether we might never have met. But then, there is no doubt that you will leave in France a friend who thinks of you, who feels with you the good and bad things that happen to you and who will be overjoyed to hear that you will enjoy the fruit of your merit and qualities in your country.

If only I knew the view of the nature of the French that you take with you to your country! You have seen this nation at what was surely one of the most extraordinary times in its entire history. I think that in your country you will often be asked about this big revolution and the victory by the French people in their call for freedom. If your departure should be postponed for a couple of days, I hope that I shall be able to see you in Paris. If not, I beg of you not to leave without saying goodbye with your pen.

With all my friendship.

Jules Saladin

Here is another letter, after which you will understand the extent to which the French wish to obtain strange books and to encourage authors and translators to write and translate books. This is the translation of the letter:

To Monsieur Shaykh Rifāʿa,

Monsieur Depping has asked me to enquire about your translation of the short science book which deals with the character, customs and morals of nations, of which Monsieur Depping is the author.[1] *If your translation is printed in Egypt, can the author of the original reserve a number of copies of that book for purchase?*

We should also like to bring to your attention our request to notify us of your progress in the translation of the first volume of Malte-Brun's Geography,[2] *as this*

1. See note no. 2, p. 144.
2. The Danish-born geographer Conrad Malte-Brun (1775–1826), founder of the first modern geographic society, the *Société de Géographie de Paris* (1821), is best known for his monumental *Précis de Géographie Universelle ou description de toutes les parties du monde, sur un plan nouveau, d'après les grandes divisions naturelles du globe, précédée de l'histoire*

is currently being printed in a revised edition with additions to the first one. We should like to bring to your attention the fact that the printing will be finished in the course of this month.

With kind regards.

Your friend,

Reinaud,[1]

Bibliothèque Royale, Paris

Fifth Section. On the books I read in the city of Paris; the nature of the exams; what Monsieur Jomard wrote to me; reports of the final exam in scholarly journals

I am going to mention here what I have read, even though this means repeating things I have mentioned before.

---

de la géographie chez les peuples anciens et modernes et d'une théorie générale de la géographie mathématique, physique, et politique, et accompagnée de cartes, de tableaux analytiques, synoptiques et élémentaires (8 vols, Paris, Buisson, 1810–26; 2nd edn 1812–29; rev. edn by J. J. Huot, Paris, A. André, 1832–37, 12 vols). Al-Ṭahṭāwī published his translation of the first volume in 1254/1838–39 (Būlāq, 32/205pp.) under the title *al-Jughrāfiyā al-ʿumūmiyya* ('General Geography'). Several bibliographies also mention a *Jughrāfiyya ṣaghīra* ('Small Geography'), which, according to T. Bianchi (1843: 43), was published at Būlāq in 1250/1834, although others suggested 1246/1830 (J. Heyworth-Dunne, 1940–42: 400; Y. Sarkīs, 1928: 944). E. Van Dyke (1896: 409), for his part, gave the wholly fanciful 1230 (= 1815 ad!), which ʿĀ. Nuṣayr corrected to 1830 (Ā. Nuṣayr, 1990: 239 no. 9/37). Besides the date, there is also the problem that the work in question is conspicuous by its absence from most modern bibliographies. Despite the fact that Bianchi was a contemporary of al-Ṭahṭāwī's, his catalogue should be approached circumspectly for a number of reasons. First, the titles in his list are, at best, approximate (the *Takhlīṣ*, for instance, appears as *Riḥlat al-shaykh Rifāʿa yaʿnī akhbār bilād Ūrūbā*, which translates as 'Shaykh Rifāʿa's travelogue, that is, news about the countries of Europe'!). Second, he does not mention the *Jughrāfiyya ʿumūmiyya* (though Y. Sarkīs and Van Dyke do). As no additional information is available about this book, other than that it was a translation from French into Arabic, it would seem logical to assume that it refers to the translation of the first volume of Malte-Brun's book, which al-Ṭahṭāwī completed in 1834 during his stay in his native Ṭahṭā when Cairo was hit by a plague epidemic. Alternatively, it may be a reference to *al-taʿrībāt al-shāfiyya li murīd al-jughrāfiyya* (see Translator's Introduction), which Y. Sarkīs (1928: 944) incorrectly identifies as a translation of Malte-Brun's geography.

1. A former pupil of S. De Sacy, Joseph-Toussaint Reinaud (1795–1867) succeeded his master to the Arabic chair at the Ecole des Langues Orientales Vivantes, which position he combined with that of curator at the Bibliothèque Nationale. Among his many publications, there was a re-edition of de Sacy's edition of al-Ḥarīrī's *Maqāmāt*, as well as the editio princeps (with M. de Slane) of the geographical encyclopaedia *Taqwīm al-Buldān* ('Survey of Countries') by the Syrian prince-scholar Abū 'l-Fidā' in 1840, and the first part of the translation (1848), which also includes an exhaustive survey of classical Arabic geographical literature (*Introduction Générale à la Géographie des Orientaux*). See Y. Sarkīs, 1928: 960; L. Shaykhū, 1991: 116.

Study of the principles of French grammar

We were released from quarantine on the 27th day of the month of Shawwāl of the year [12]41.[1] After spending a few days in Marseilles, we started our instruction in spelling and reading, and after about forty days we had learned the letters of the French alphabet and spelling. We arrived in Paris in the month of Muḥarram[2] and again started learning the basics of the alphabet. This kept us busy for about one month, after which we all started reading Lhomond's grammar of the French language.[3] Whenever necessary, the teacher would add things from another grammar book. After leaving the house of the Efendis, I read another grammar book with Monsieur Chevalier (*Shawālīh*) and studied two others with a teacher called Laumonier (*Lumūnrī?*). In each of the houses, i.e. that of the Efendis and that of the teacher, I worked on grammatical parsing[4] and the rules of pronunciation; in other words, on the application in the spoken language of the grammar and pronunciation rules. I also worked on dictation, composition and reading. This I did over a period of three years.

History

When we all still lived together at the house of the Efendis we started studying the *Lives of Greek Philosophers*,[5] a book which we read from beginning to end. Afterwards, we went on to a work that offered an

1. 4 June 1826.
2. <of the year 1242> = August 1826.
3. The author uses the Arabic *ājurrūmiyya* (also *ājrūmiyya*), which is in fact the title of a well-known treatise of Arabic grammar written by the Fès-born Ibn Ājurrūm (d. 1323). See *EI1* s.vv. "Ibn Ādjurrūm" (M. Ben Cheneb), *EI2* (G. Troupeau). The Egyptian students studied from the revised 1825 edition of Charles-François Lhomond's *Eléments de la grammaire française*. This book was also the very first grammar of a European language to be translated into Arabic under the title *Naḥw Faransāwī. Grammaire française de Lhomond traduite en arabe* (1857) by the Tunisian emigré Sulaymān al-Ḥarīrī (d. 1877).
4. *al-iʿrāb al-naḥwī*, which strictly speaking refers to the rules of the so-called *nunation* (*tanwīn*, sc. declensions) in Arabic.
5. = P. C. Levesque (comp./trans.), *Vie et Apophtegmes des Philosophes Grecs*, Paris (Debure l'Aîné), 1795, 192pp. The author uses the Arabic *al-jāhiliyya*, which normally denotes '[the age of] ignorance', i.e. the period before the advent of Islam. Parts of this book would also end up in the compilation *Bidāyat al-qudamā' wa hidāyat al-ḥukamā'* (see Translator's Introduction), which al-Ṭahṭāwī revised and introduced (1838). In his catalogue of works printed by the Būlāq press, T. Bianchi (1843: 47) also mentions a *Tārīkh qudamā' al-falāsifa* ('History of the Ancient Philosophers'), translated by al-Ṭahṭāwī and published in 1252/1837. However, I have not been able to trace this work (listed by E. Van Dyke as *Qudamā' al-falāsifa*). Presumably, this is the already mentioned (see Translator's Introduction) *Tārīkh al-falāsifa al-Yūnāniyyīn* ('History of Greek Philosophy'), which was *revised* by al-Ṭahṭāwī, but translated by ʿAbd Allāh Ḥusayn al-Miṣrī.

abridgement of general history and included details on the life of people in ancient Egypt, Iraq, Syria, Greece, Persia, Rome, India, etc. At the end of it, there was a short treatment on the science of mythology (*mīthūlūjiyā*), by which is meant the science of prehistoric Greece and its legends. Afterwards, Monsieur Chevalier introduced me to a book entitled *The Niceties of History* (*Les Agréments de l'Histoire*), which comprises stories, tales and anecdotes. Then I read a book called *The Morals of Nations, and their Habits*,[1] another entitled *The History of the Reason of the Greatness and Decline of the Roman Empire*[2] and the book of the journey to Greece by the young Anacharsis.[3] I also read a book by Ségur on general history,[4] a biography of Napoleon,[5] a book on historiography and genealogy, one entitled *Panorama* (*Pānūramā*) *of the World*, i.e. the mirror of the world, and a travelogue on the Ottoman state and another one set in Algeria.

Arithmetic and geometry

For arithmetic I studied the book by Bezout,[6] and in geometry the first four fascicles of the manual by Legendre.[7]

1. = G. Depping's *Aperçu Historique sur les Mœurs et Coutumes des Nations.*
2. = *Considérations sur les Causes de la Grandeur des Romains et de leur Décadence* by Montesquieu. Some 50 years later, one of al-Ṭahṭāwī's pupils, Ḥasan al-Jubaylī, translated this work (presumably at the instigation of the master), which was published under the title *Burhān al-bayān al-burhān fī istikmāl wa ikhtilāl dawlat al-Rūmān* (Būlāq, 1293/1876, 48pp.). Y. Sarkīs, 1928: 757; J. Shayyāl, 1951: 146; ʿĀ. Nuṣayr, 1990: 252 (no. 9/459).
3. = '*Voyage du Jeune Anacharsis en Grèce, dans le milieu du IVe siècle avant l'ère vulgaire*' by Abbé Barthelémy (Paris, 1788, 4 vols). During al-Ṭahṭāwī's time in Paris, this immensely popular book was reprinted several times, whereas abridged (school) versions started appearing as from 1821.
4. = *Histoire Universelle Ancienne et Moderne* (Paris, A. Eymery, 1821–22, 10 vols) by Comte Louis-Philippe de Ségur (1753–1810).
5. This is probably a reference to the highly popular (hagiographical) biography by Paul-Philippe de Ségur (1780–1873) – Louis-Philippe's son – entitled *Histoire de Napoléon et de la grande armée pendant l'année 1812* (Paris, Baudouin Frères, 1824, 2 vols), of which no fewer than ten editions appeared between 1825 and 1834.
6. = *Traité d'Arithmétique à l'usage de la marine et de l'artillerie, ..., avec des notes et detables de logarithmes*, 7th edn (by A. A. L. Reynaud), Paris, 1813 (1816, 1821, 1826, 1828), by Etienne Bezout (1730–83).
7. = Book 3 of *Eléments de Géométrie, 2ème édition, augmentée de trigonométrie* (12th edn, Paris, F. Didot, 1823, 431pp.) by the famous mathematician Adrien-Marie Legendre (1752–1833), best known for his work on the theory of numbers and the method of least squares. Al-Ṭahṭāwī also translated this work into Arabic; *Mabādiʾ al-handasa* ('Principles of Geometry'), Cairo (al-Maṭbaʿa al-amīriyya), 1257/1842, 16/125pp. (1843, Būlāq, 13/6/125pp.; 1270/1853, Būlāq, 13/4/4/130pp.; 1291/1874, Būlāq, 130pp.). The whole of Legendre's manual was translated by Muḥammad ʿIṣmat Efendi (1255/1839, Cairo, Būlāq, 4/284pp.), based on a Turkish translation by Edhem Bey (cf. *Bibliothèque Nationale*, XCIII, 19), whereas an abridged translation, entitled *Nukhbat al-ʿizziyya fī*

Geography and its various disciplines

With Monsieur Chevalier I studied a geography textbook which comprised historical geography, physical geography, mathematical geography and political geography. Afterwards, I read another treatise on natural geography in the form of an introduction to a geographical dictionary,[1] after the fashion of the *Dictionary of Countries*.[2] Then I studied the first book with another teacher. With Monsieur Chevalier I also read large extracts from Malte-Brun's *Geography*, as well as a *mawwāl*[3] which he had written to teach his daughter astronomy. I also read many works on this art on my own.

The art of translation

During my stay in France I translated twelve books or parts of books, which will be mentioned at the end of this book.[4] In other words, twelve translations, some of which were full-length books, others short abridgements.

Books on various arts

I studied a work on French logic with Monsieur Chevalier and Monsieur Laumonerie,[5] as well as several parts from the 'Port-Royal' (*Burt Rūyāl*) book,[6]

---

tahdhīb al-uṣūl al-handasiyya (Būlāq, 234pp.), by ʿAlī ʿIzzat Badawī, followed in 1272/1858 (1276/1859, Būlāq, 234pp.). Cf. ʿĀ. Nuṣayr, 1990: 168 (Nos 5/147–52).

1. This is another of Conrad Malte-Brun's works, *Dictionnaire Géographique Portatif, contenant la description générale et particulière des cinq parties du monde connu, revu ...et précédé d'un vocabulaire de mots génériques ... par M. Malte-Brun, augmenté de plus de 20.000 articles qui ne se trouvent dans aucune édition des dictionnaires dits de Vosgien, par M. le Dr Friéville et M. Félix Lallement*, Paris (C. Gosselin), 1827, xxviii/940pp. (1828, Froment & Lequien, 2 vols).
2. This is a reference to the famous *Muʿjam al-Buldān*, a geographical encyclopaedia, by the Byzantine-born freed slave Yāqūt al-Ḥamawī al-Rūmī (d. 1229).
3. Pl. *mawāwīl*. This refers to a popular genre of sung folk poetry, relying heavily on improvisation on the part of the performer. See "mawālīya", *EI1* (M. Ben Cheneb), *EI2* (Ed.); P. Cachia, 1977; Ibn Khaldūn [F. Rosenthal], 1986: III, 475ff.
4. In fact, the list appears in the next section (Six).
5. = C. Dumarsais' *La Logique*, which was later translated by one of al-Ṭahṭāwī's pupils at the language school, Khalīfa Maḥmūd, under the title *Tanwīr al-mashriq bi-ʿilm al-manṭiq*; see Translator's Introduction.
6. This is a reference to the famous *La Logique ou l'art de penser contenant, outre les règles communes, plusieurs observations nouvelles, propres à former le jugement* (Paris, 1662), which was written by Antoine Arnauld (1612–94) and Pierre Nicole (1625–95) for the instruction of the Duke de Chevreux. The two most recent editions of the book prior to al-Ṭahṭāwī's arrival in Paris were those of 1816 (Paris, A. Delalain) and 1824 (*ibid.*). The book is also known as *La Logique du Port-Royal*, which was the name of the main Jansenist communities, *viz.* *Port-Royal de Paris* and *Port-Royal des Champs*. Its leader and most eloquent theologian was Arnauld, and his sister ('*Mère Angélique*') was the abbess of the Port-Royal community. Nicole was one of Arnauld's collaborators and an ally in the latter's relentless anti-Jesuit

which includes the categories.[1] I also read another book on logic called the *Book of Condillac* (*Qundilyāq*),[2] except for the parts dealing with Aristotelian logic.

With Monsieur Chevalier I studied a booklet on minerals, which I also translated.[3]

As far as literature is concerned, I read the collection by Noël,[4] many extracts from the works of Voltaire, Racine and Rousseau – especially his *Persian Correspondence*,[5] which reveals the difference between European and Persian morals. In fact, it strikes a balance between Western and Eastern morals.

I also studied English letters written by Count (*qūnt*) Chesterfield for the education and instruction of his son,[6] as well as many French narratives (*maqāmāt*). In short, I read many famous works of French literature.

Together with my teacher of natural law, I studied Burlamaqui's book on the subject, which I translated and understood very well.[7] This

---

campaigns. Any subsequent references to *La Logique* ... are to the critical edition (based on the text of the *editio princeps* of 1662) by P. Clair and F. Girbal.

1. I.e. the Categories of Aristotle. In fact this was only a small chapter in the book and takes up a mere three pages. For al-Ṭahṭāwī's translation, see below.
2. = *La Logique* by Etienne Bonnot de Condillac (d. 1780).
3. = Cyprien-Prosper Brard's *Minéralogie Populaire, ou avis aux cultivateurs et aux artisans, sur les terres, les pierres, les sables, les métaux et les sels qu'ils emploient journellement, le charbon de terre, la tourbe, la recherche des mines, etc.* (Paris, L. Colas, 1826, 102pp.), an immensely popular work, which was reprinted in 1828 and 1830, with a second edition appearing in 1832. Al-Ṭahṭāwī's (abridged) translation, which appeared in 1248/1833 (Būlāq, al-Maṭbaʿa al-amīriyya, 48pp.), was entitled *al-maʿādin al-nāfiʿa li-tadbīr maʿāyish al-khalāʾiq* ('The Beneficial Minerals for the Arrangement of Creation').
4. The grammarian François Joseph Michel Noël (1755–1841) wrote a number of standard schoolbooks for French children, the most popular among which was the *Nouvelle Grammaire française* (Paris, 1823, iv/211pp.), of which there appeared no fewer than 21 editions in its first decade (and which remained in use well into the 20th century). The reference here, however, is to *Leçons de Littérature et de Morale, ou recueil en prose et en vers des plus beaux morceaux de notre langue dans la littérature des deux derniers siècles*, 2 vols, Paris, Le Normant, 1804 (the 15th edn appearing in 1826), which Noël wrote with Pierre de La Place.
5. This is, of course, a reference to Montesquieu's *Lettres Persanes*; the howler about authorship is surprising for two reasons. First of all, it is certain that al-Ṭahṭāwī read the book. Second, in his translation of G. Depping's work, which appeared in 1833 – one year before the *Takhlīṣ* – he correctly ascribes it to Montesquieu (al-Ṭahṭāwī, 1833: 91).
6. = *Letters Written by the Late Philip Dormer Stanhope, Earl of Chesterfield, to his Son Philip Stanhope, Published by Mrs Eugenia Stanhope* (London, 1774), by Philip Dormer Stanhope, 4th Earl of Chesterfield (d. 1773). The French translation is *Lettres du Comte de Chesterfield à son fils Philip Stanhope ... avec quelques autres pièces sur divers sujets*, 4 vols, Paris (Volland Aîné et Jeune, Ferra Aîné, H. Verdier), 1779.
7. This is a reference to the *Elémens du Droit Naturel et devoirs de l'homme et du citoyen tels qu'ils lui sont prescrits par la loi naturelle* by the Swiss naturalist-philosopher Jean-Jacques

art involves the explanation of things that, in accordance with reason, are considered good and those that are considered reprehensible. The Europeans have made it the basis of their political judgements, which they call 'laws'.[1] Together with Monsieur Chevalier I also studied two volumes of the book entitled *The Spirit of the Laws*, which was written by an author who is famous among the French and who is called Montesquieu.[2] The work can best be compared to a balance between the legal and political schools (*madhhab*); it is based on commending the good and censuring the bad in accordance with reason. Among the French, Montesquieu is nicknamed the European Ibn Khaldūn,[3] whereas the latter is known as the Eastern Montesquieu or the Montesquieu of Islam.

On the same topic I also read a book called *The Social Contract*,[4] by an author called Rousseau, who says things of great import.

On philosophy I read the above-mentioned *History of Ancient Philosophy*,[5]

Burlamaqui (1694–1748), which first appeared in his home town of Geneva in 1746. The most recent editions at the time of al-Ṭahṭāwī's writing were those of 1820 (Paris, Janet et Cotelle, xvi/428pp.) and 1821 (Paris, Delestre-Roulage, 339pp.). The Arabic translation was never published. It is hardly surprising that al-Ṭahṭāwī was attracted to Burlamaqui (whose ideas were first outlined in the 1741 'bible' of natural philosophy, *Principes du Droit Naturel*) and to his *Elémens...*, in which the philosopher states: '*La loi naturelle est une loi divine que Dieu a donné à tous les hommes et qu'ils peuvent connaître par les seules lumières de leur raision, en considérant attentivement leur nature et leur état*'. (1821 edn, 24).

1. *[aḥkām] shar'iyya*, which, in principle, can be used in reference to Islamic law only, i.e. the *sharī'a*.
2. = Montesquieu's *Esprit des Lois*. This would later be translated into Arabic by Yūsuf Afandī b. Hammām Āṣāf under the title *Uṣūl al-nawāmīs wa 'l-sharā'i'* (Cairo, al-Maṭba'a al-'Umūmiyya, 1310/1892, 252pp.); 'Ā. Nuṣayr, 1990: 108 (Nos 107–09); Y. Sarkīs, 1928: 2.
3. The Tunis-born historian 'Abd al-Raḥmān Ibn Khaldūn (1332–1406) is the author of a history of the world, entitled *Kitāb al-'Ibar wa Dīwān al-mubtada' wa 'l-khabar fī ayyām al-'Arab wa 'l-'Ajam wa 'l-Barbar* ('The Book of Admonitions, and the Account of the Beginning and News Related to the History of the Arabs, Persians and Berbers'). Although this monumental survey is still a major source for the history of the Berbers, its author owes his fame to the first volume, i.e. the *Muqaddima* ('Introduction'), which offers an encyclopaedic survey of all branches of Arab sciences and culture. It is Ibn Khaldūn's discussion of the rise (and decline) of civilization and culture and the links with human society and the environment that have rightly earned him the title of 'father of modern sociology'. See F. Rosenthal [Ibn Khaldūn], 1984: I, xxix-cxv (the definitive account of Ibn Khaldūn's life and work); "Ibn Khaldūn", *EI1* (Alfred Bel), *EI2* (F. Rosenthal); *GAL*, II, 242–5.
4. = Rousseau's *Le Contrat Social*. It is clear that al-Ṭahṭāwī had great difficulty in translating the word 'social' as the title in Arabic reads '*'aqd al-ta'annus wa 'l-ijtimā' al-insānī*', which literally means 'the contract of incarnation and human gatherings.' The present-day word for 'society' – *mujtama'* – would be coined only later.
5. Strangely enough, the author gives two different titles to the same work; above, it is called '*siyar falāsifat al-Yūnān*' ('Lives of Greek Philosophers'); here, it is simply '*tārīkh al-falsafa al-mutaqaddam*'.

which contains information on the philosopher schools, their beliefs, wisdoms and exhortations. I read a number of valuable passages from the *Dictionary of Philosophy*[1] by Voltaire,[2] as well as several extracts from the books on philosophy by Condillac.[3]

In physics I read a small treatise with Monsieur Chevalier, without, however, doing any experiments.

On the art of warfare, I studied the book entitled *Operations by Senior Officers* with Monsieur Chevalier and translated 100 pages from it.[4]

I spent a great deal of time reading daily and monthly scientific journals (*kāẓīṭ*), which each day deal with news events from at home and abroad and which are called '*political*' (*būlītīqiyya*). I was extremely fond of reading them and used them to gain a better understanding of the French language. Occasionally, I would translate scientific and political articles, particularly at the time of the war between the Ottoman empire and the state of Muscovy.[5]

At this juncture I should like to propose my translation of an imaginary letter from a French volunteer in the Muscovite army to a brigadier in Paris. The letter was sent from the town of Shumlā[6] and is dated 22 July[7] 1828.

1. *mu'jam al-falsafa*. This is, in fact, *Questions sur l'Encyclopédie* (1764), which was commonly known as '*Le Dictionnaire Philosophique*'.
2. Rather than using *Monsieur* (his customary title of address for French scholars and luminaries), al-Ṭahṭāwī calls him '*al-khawāja* Voltaire'. Originally derived from the Turkish and Persian words for teacher (*khōja*), this word was – and in Egypt still is – the common term of address for any European male (although on rare occasions it may also be used in reference to a European woman). At the same time, one must not exclude the possibility that al-Ṭahṭāwī used the term in its old-fashioned, i.e. etymological, meaning as an honorific in the sense of 'Master Voltaire'.
3. It is worth adding that Khayr al-Dīn was the only other 19th-century Muslim traveller who also mentioned European philosophers; 1867: 30, 58, 59, 88.
4. The book in question is J.-P.-A. Léorier's *Théorie de l'Officier Supérieur, ou essai contenant des détails sur l'art militaire, les positions, les affaires, les marches, etc.*, Paris, Leblanc, 1820, xvi/367pp. (a Turkish translation entitled *Tuḥfat ül-ẓābitān* by Kiyānī Bey would appear in 1251/1836). It is worth pointing out that this is the only reference to a science that was highest on the list of priorities of the Egyptian ruler Muḥammad 'Alī.
5. This conflict took place in 1828–29. It is interesting to draw a parallel with the 17th-century Moroccan traveller al-Wazīr al-Ghassānī, who also reported on accounts in Spanish newspapers on the advancing Ottoman armies (al-Ghassānī, 1884: 179). Further, the Morisco al-Ḥajarī proudly recounted that 'all Christian kings tremble with fear before the Ottoman sultans' (1987: 96).
6. = the Romanian town of Şimla Silvaniei.
7. *yūlīh al-Ifranjiyya*, 'the Frankish July'.

Know, dear friend, that this is the first time since my enlistment in the Russian[1] *army that we have engaged the Muslim forces in battle. The events I have seen would confound the intelligent and confuse the wise. Hence, I will curtail my account of them. How could this not be a strange thing for someone like myself? If, like your eminence, I had been a soldier experienced in war, one who had participated in the Egyptian campaign and seen the battle of Abukir and the siege of the city of Akka, then I should not have been so confused at seeing something new as to be unable to describe it.*

But consider, my friend, that, since my command, which I served in our King's Guard after graduating from the School of Saint-Cyr (Sansīr), *I had not been involved in any battles, except that of al-Andalus! Then, all of a sudden, after having crossed open country and deserts and having endured hardships, I found myself facing the Balkan mountains with a population that threatened us, eluded us and astounded our troops. Behold my surprise and shock when the Turkish cavalry rode forth from above Shumlā with their troops arranged in those strange rows in which Muslim armies wage war. Your eminence has undoubtedly already heard the details of this battle from the Russian army report; the slaughter of many of our soldiers and the news that the battle had been lost. However, I have seen with my own eyes the vicious way in which the Russian Colonel Barady (?) was killed as he was split in two by a Turkish cannonball. Only then did the difficulty of this war become clear, whereas I realized that it would probably last for a long time.*

In spite of the courage and strength of our soldiers in battle, the Muslim troops possess a formidable power of assault in which there is no room for flight. It is this power of assault that makes them despise danger and break through obstacles in order to achieve the desired goal. This yields two advantages: the first is that it confuses the minds of [our] men. The second is that it always strikes terror in the hearts of their enemies, however heroic they may be. If your eyes had seen what I have witnessed – the way the Ottoman cavalry cause terror merely by their frightening exterior, the speed of their astounding and admirable incursions, the way in which they march to the sounds of savage music, the whinnying of their Kurdish stallions and their lightning descent upon the Russian infantry – then you would, like me, come to the conclusion that this war will last for a long time and that its rage will abate only slightly, if at all.

The Ottoman State has a magnificent cavalry, arranged in a strange fashion, with great determination and unusual organization. Surely nobody can deny the

1. *Mūsqūbī* (namely, Muscovite), which is the only one to appear to denote the Russian soldiers, except at the very end of the text, where al-Ṭahṭāwī uses '*al-Rūs*'. It would seem that this choice was motivated by a desire to underscore the political entity, rather than the nation, since *al-Rūs* as a people are already mentioned by the earliest Arab geographers; cf. "Rūs", *EI1* (V. Minorsky), *EI2* (P. Golden).

fact that their soldiers are trained horsemen and that their horses with a naturally savage disposition obey their masters both in attack and in retreat, carrying them to the desired goal in battle. Woe unto the soldiers whose ranks are in close contact with these horses ridden by those masterful horsemen who, aside from their fighting strength, are supported by their Islamic and patriotic fervour. This is a virtue that is not at all found in Russian soldiers. The piling up of people in times of war is proof of sound organization, but in this battle everyone, even a Cossack (al-Quzāq), will know that the glory goes to the soldiers of Islam.

This report may seem strange to you, particularly as it comes from someone like me, who volunteered in the Russian army in order to join them in defying dangers and to share in the glory with them. However, when I arrived here, it seemed to me that my hopes were dashed and that I had made a mistake. I saw that our enemies, whom we had accused of being inferior and wicked, are in actual fact lions who are not in the least bit inferior. What is more, they are more receptive to good manners and elegance than Europeans. I should like you to know, my dear friend, that my passion for the liberation of the Greeks from the Ottomans has not waned even in the slightest. Yet, I wish I knew whether the attack on Istanbul is necessary for their liberation or whether this is not something that will be regretted. The soldiers we lost during the taking of the city of Brăila[1] *alone would be sufficient to free the Greeks and to lessen the shedding of our blood by the Muslim soldiers.*

Recently, we captured a Turkish army officer. He was a marvellous-looking young man who had sustained many injuries. Our soldiers spared him – a fate that did not befall the other prisoners of war – and took pity on him because of his looks and injuries. I spoke to him in Italian and he understood what I was saying. He answered my questions and told me that his father was now 80 years old and that he had brothers who were in the service of Ḥusayn Pasha.[2] *He does not doubt the victory of the Ottoman State; indeed, he says that the Turks will push on until they reach Moscow. You should know, my friend, that in Shumlā there are about 200,000 [Muslim] troops, with reinforcements arriving each day, and their sultan is without doubt their greatest hero.*

At this point, I shall close my letter to you in order to put my foot in the stirrup. Presently, the enemy soldiers are waging battle with our advance guard, while I

---

1. This port, which is currently in south-eastern Romania, was the scene of violent fighting during the Russo-Turkish war and was all but destroyed by the end of it.
2. A one-time governor of Brussa and Izmir, Agha Ḥusayn Pasha (1776–1849) was the Turkish commander-in-chief during the 1828–29 war against Russia, until replaced by the Grand Vizier Reshid Mehemmed. After the war, he was appointed Governor of the *vilayet* of Adrianople, and later led the Turkish forces against Muḥammad ʿAlī's invasion of Syria in 1832 but suffered a crushing defeat at the hands of Ibrāhīm Pasha in July of that year. See *EI1*, s.v. "Ḥusain Pasha" (J. Mordtmann); *EI2*, s.v. "Ḥusayn Pasha" (H. Reed).

am being drowned by the noise of the Turkish music and the din of the voices of the Russians. If you look at it closely, this war is truly dreadful!

Sixth Section. On the exams I took in the city of Paris, especially the final exam before my return to Egypt

You should know that in the field of science the French do not content themselves with someone's fame as a person of knowledge or zeal or with the praise a teacher bestows upon a student. Rather, they must have clear and tangible proof that bears out the strength of the person concerned and his distinction among his peers to those present at the exam. For this reason, there are public examinations, which people from all stations can attend following an invitation – very much like an invitation to some function or other. There are also private examinations, during which a teacher examines his students each week or month with a view to evaluating their progress during that period, and after which the results are communicated to their parents.

This was the course of things when we were living at the *pensions*. In addition, every year we took a public exam in the presence of French notables.[1] Our first interrogation was almost entirely related to the French language. In accordance with their custom, they offer a gift to those who display particular skill in their answers and distinguish themselves from the others. After the first exam, Monsieur Jomard sent me a book entitled *The Voyage to Greece by the Young Anacharsis*,[2] in seven well-bound volumes, whose covers were embossed with gold. The books were accompanied by the letter below, which I have translated:

1 August 1827

You have earned the prize for French for the progress you have made in it and the result you have obtained at the last public examination. I find great pleasure in being able to send you this gift on behalf of the supervising Efendis as proof of your commitment to your studies.

There is no doubt that your Benefactor will be pleased when he is told that your zeal and the fruit of your studies were worth the considerable expense he has disbursed for your education and instruction.

With kind regards.

1. The first of these exams took place in July 1827; see Translator's Introduction.
2. See Translator's Introduction.

His mention of the last exam in fact refers to the fact that it was the last in regard to those that preceded it. In fact, the exam gift resembles a prize, such as a prize awarded to poets.

After the second public exam,[1] he sent me the book written by Monsieur de Sacy, entitled *al-Anīs al-mufīd li 'l-ṭālib al-mustafīd wa jāmiʿ al-shudhūr min manẓūm*,[2] which was accompanied by the following letter, which I have translated:

Paris, 15 March 1828

You have earned the prize for French grammar for the progress you have made in this language and for the result you have obtained at the last public exam. I am delighted to be able to send you this token of my appreciation of your endeavours. It will undoubtedly instil new courage in you. I will send a report of your exam to your Benefactor with comments about your diligence and success. There is no doubt that he, too, will be pleased with the fact that your work has borne fruit and that you deserve his protection, and the great attention he bestows on your education and instruction.

Yours sincerely.

I thus obtained the prize for both these exams. As for the last exam, after which I returned to Egypt, it happened that Monsieur Jomard convened a jury[3] composed of a number of famous people, among them the Muscovite Minister for Education, who presided over the proceedings.[4] The purpose of this gathering was to ascertain the strength of my humble person in the art of translation, which had been my chosen field during my stay in France. The results of the exam were published in a scientific journal.[5] The text ran as follows:[6]

1. This took place on 28 February and 1 March 1828; see Translator's Introduction.
2. See Translator's Introduction.
3. *majlis*, 'council'.
4. This was Nikolai Turgenev (1789–1871), brother of the Russian historian Alexander Turgenev (1783–1845). A keen champion of peasants' rights, he was sentenced to death in absentia in his home country (1825), after which he briefly stayed in England before taking up permanent residence in France.
5. The Arabic term *'waqāʾiʿ al-ʿulūm'* literally means 'events regarding the sciences', and seems to be a clear reference to the Egyptian government *Gazette*, *'al-Waqāʾiʿ al-Miṣriyya*, which had only shortly before been founded (1828) with al-Ṭahṭāwī's mentor, the Shaykh al-ʿAṭṭār, as the editor.
6. This is a literal translation of the account that appeared in the *Revue Encyclopédique*, XLVIII, (Nov.) 1831, 521–3. The only omission is the beginning: *'M. le cheykh Refâh, l'un des élèves distingués de la Mission égyptienne en France, et qui est sur le point de retourner en Egypte, après avoir achevé le cours de ses travaux, a été examiné, le 19 du mois d'octobre, chez*

The examination of the student Rifāʿa was conducted in the following manner: two lists were read out at the meeting. The first list contained 12 translations from French into Arabic which the aforesaid person had translated in the course of the year:

1. *an extract dealing with the history of Alexander the Great from the book on ancient history;*
2. *a book on mineralogy;*[1]
3. *the Almanac of the year 1244 compiled by Monsieur Jomard for use in Egypt and Syria and containing a variety of scientific and practical information;*
4. *Encyclopaedia of the Morals and Customs of Nations;*[2]
5. *Introduction to Natural Geography in the edition by Monsieur Humboldt;*[3]
6. *an extract from the book by Maltebrun on geography;*
7. *three chapters from Legendre's book on geometry;*
8. *a passage on cosmography;*
9. *an extract from 'The Operations of Military Officers';*[4]
10. *'The Principles of Natural Law' adhered to by the Europeans;*[5]
11. *a passage dealing with mythology, i.e. on ancient Greece and its legends;*
12. *a treatise on hygiene.*[6]

The second list comprises the student's travelogue in which he describes his journey.[7] *Afterwards the student was presented with several works printed in*

M. Jomard. MM. Reinaud, orientaliste, attaché au cabinet des manuscrits de la Bibliothèque du roi; Muller, secrétaire-interprète pour la langue arabe; Habaïby père syrien; M. le Muhurdar Abdi Efendi, chef de l'école; M. le professeur Delile; M. Allou, ingénieur des mines; M. le comte de Tourguéneff, ancien ministre de l'instruction publique en Russie, etc., étaient présents à la réunion. L'objet de la séance était de soumettre l'élève Refâh à quelques épreuves, pour constater son aptitude comme traducteur, profession qu'il a embrassée.'

1. The French original 'Eléments de Minéralogie Populaire par Brard' is, to say the least, misleading, as Brard never wrote a book with this title, which seems a strange mix of the above-mentioned *Minéralogie Populaire* and *Nouveaux Eléments de Minéralogie, ou manuel du minéraliste voyageur* (2nd edn, Paris, 1824).
2. For the word 'encyclopaedia', the author coined '*dāʾirat al-ʿulūm*' ('Circle of Sciences'), thus observing the etymology of the French word. As it happens, the very first modern Arabic encyclopaedia, which was started by the Syrian Maronite scholar Buṭrus al-Bustānī (1819–83) in 1875 and completed by, among others, his sons Salīm and Sulaymān, was entitled *Dāʾirat al-Maʿārif* ('Circle of Knowledge').
3. This seems to be a reference to *al-Taʿrībāt al-shāfiyya li-murīd al-jughrāfiyya* ; see note no. 3, p. 45.
4. See note no. 4, p. 297.
5. The French text has '*Eléments du Droit Naturel de Burlamaqui*'.
6. This is the medical booklet whose Arabic translation the author included in the *Takhlīṣ*.
7. French: '*Du sommaire d'un écrit très étendu, composé par le cheykh Refâh, sur son Voyage en France.*'

Būlāq[1] *from which he translated passages with great ease. Then he also translated on sight French articles of various length from the* Gazette *of Egypt* (al-Kaẓīṭa al-Miṣriyya)*, which is also printed in Būlāq. This was followed by a discussion with the student of his translation of the work on 'The Operations of Military Officers'. At this stage, one of the people present had the French original in hand, while the Shaykh was holding the translation. The latter then gave a quick oral translation of the Arabic into French with a view to comparing the phrasing of the translation against that of the original. He passed this test with flying colours; he faithfully rendered the expressions, without modifying the meaning of the translated original. The nature of the Arabic language occasionally forced him to render one metaphor by another, without, however, corrupting the intended meaning. For instance, in translating the comparison of the basis of the military science to a rich mine from which this or that is extracted, he changed the words by saying that the military science is a vast sea from which pearls are won.*[2] *During the exam, he was, however, told that sometimes his translation did not tally fully with the original; there were occasional repetitions, and sometimes he translated a sentence by several sentences or one word by means of an entire sentence. However, this did not lead to confusion as his version was at all times in keeping with the spirit of the original. The Shaykh indeed realizes now that if he wishes to translate science books, he must eschew any text fragmentation* [i.e. paraphrases] *and, if need be, must invent changes that are appropriate to the intended meaning.*

He was also examined on another book, i.e. the introduction to the General Dictionary *pertaining to physical geography, a book that he himself translated into Arabic.*[3] *But at the time he translated this book,*[4] *he had not reached his current level of knowledge of the French language, and his translation was inferior to that of the book that had previously been discussed with him. His mistake was that he had not always preserved all aspects of the expressions contained in the*

1. This suburb north-east of Cairo was, for centuries, the city's port, and it played a crucial role in Muḥammad 'Alī's modernization programme, with the construction of factories and a printing works (1822). See *EI2*, s.v. "Būlāḳ" (J. Jomier); A. Raymond, 1993: *passim*.
2. The French original leaves out any mention of the subject, and simply has: '*Le génie de l'arabe le forçait quelquefois à substituer une métaphore à une autre, mais sans dénaturer le sens; ainsi, par exemple, au lieu de dire (au sens moral) "une mine riche qu'on exploite", il tournait par ces mots: "Une mer d'où l'on tire des perles".*'
3. The French is far less ambiguous than the Arabic (*muqaddimat al-qāmūs al-'āmm al-muta'allaqa bi 'l-jughrāfiyā al-ṭabī'iyya, wa hādhā 'l-kitāb tarjamahu huwa ilā al-'Arabiyya...*'), since al-Ṭahṭāwī had translated the introduction (and not the entire book) previously: '*Monsieur Refâh a été soumis à une épreuve semblable sur un autre ouvrage, le* Dictionnaire Universel de Géographie*, dont il a traduit l'introduction portant sur la géographie physique*'.
4. Cf. Fr. '*Ce morceau a été traduit, il y a un an*'.

original, even though he had not changed the meaning in any way and thus his translation method was entirely appropriate.

The assembly rose, firmly convinced of the progress of the aforesaid student and unanimous in their belief that he would be able to make himself useful to his country in translating important books that are necessary for the spread of the sciences and whose proliferation is desirable in civilized countries.[1]

There is no doubt that several of these books will contain illustrations, for which purpose al-ʿAṭṭār, a compatriot of his, is studying lithography. He [al-ʿAṭṭār] *was present at the exam, and presented to the board of examiners a number of trials of lithographic prints he had made of pictures, and Arabic and French writing. He had already started learning the use of the engraving style, writing pen and brushes. Among his pictures, there are animals, architectural subjects, as well as other things, made with lines without any shading. Unfortunately, he was already very old when he came to France and he is no longer capable of drawing correctly without making mistakes. Nevertheless, he is perfectly able to learn all there is to know about the process of lithography, both in theory and practice, and to make copies of samples of illustrations that he is given, and to print them himself, if need be. He is also able to open and manage a printing house. He has also translated a treatise on the art of lithography, which he wrote on stone, and printed with his own hands. A copy of it was lying on Monsieur Jomard's desk.'*

Thus ends the account that appeared in the journal (*kāzīṭa*) *La Revue Encyclopédique* (*dā'irat al-ʿulūm*).

He [Jomard] wrote a letter to me, congratulating me on my return to Egypt after I had attained the desired result. However, this letter has been lost by me. It would have been a good idea to include it here.

Now follows a translation of a letter written to me by Monsieur Chevalier, which is similar to a study certificate,[2] as well as a testimonial for me:

---

1. Again, the Arabic deviations from the French original are quite interesting: '*L'assemblée s'est séparée, satisfaite des progrès du cheykh Refāh et persuadée qu'il est en mesure de rendre des services à son gouvernement; il sera capable de traduire les ouvrages qu'il importe de répandre pour propager l'instruction et la civilisation.*'
2. *ijāza*; literally meaning 'permission', this is originally a term used in Ḥadīth science, where it denoted the permission granted by a competent carrier of a text, to pass it on further. In practice, an *ijāza* was a sort of teaching certificate in that it constituted an endorsement given by a famous *faqīh* to teach his text(s), and both parties gained kudos from the arrangement. Indeed, the number of *ijāzas* acquired would redound to an individual's prestige, both intellectual and social, while a scholar's fame and recognition were measured by the number of 'permissions' sought from him. See "idjāza" *EI1* (I. Goldziher); *EI2* (G. Vajda – I. Goldziher – [S. Bonebakker]).

The Ministry for War

I, the undersigned, Chevalier, former student at the school of sciences, called the Polytechnique (bulūtiknīqā),[1] *officer in the engineering corps, registered with the Ministry for War, charged by Monsieur Jomard and the Efendis with the supervision of the studies of Monsieur Shaykh Rifā'a, hereby testify that for the approximately three and a half years that the above-mentioned student was with me I have not seen anything in him that has given me cause for dissatisfaction; this is true for his studies, his general behaviour – which is full of wisdom and caution – his good nature, as well as his pleasant disposition.*

In the first year, he studied French and cosmography (qusmughrāfiyā) *with me, followed by geography, history, arithmetic, as well as other subjects. As he was devoid of the required inclination and agility to study drawing with success, he worked at it only once every week, merely to comply with the orders of his benefactor. However, he exerted himself with the utmost zeal in translation, which is his chosen trade. His activities in it are expounded in my special monthly bulletins, especially in the first reports* (jurnālāt) *I submitted to Monsieur Jomard. The contents of these bulletins and reports sufficiently provide a profile of this student.*

Mention should also be made of Monsieur Shaykh Rifā'a's zeal, which went so far that it made him work for long periods during the night. This even caused a weakening in the left eye, to the extent that he needed to consult a doctor, who forbade him to read at night; however, he did not comply with this instruction for fear it would hamper his progress. And when he saw that in order for his studies to progress faster he required other books than those provided for him by the state, and that he should also have another teacher in addition to his official one, he spent a large part of his stipend on the purchase of books and on a teacher, who stayed with him for most of the year and provided classes for him[2] *during study periods that he was not working with me. I thought it my duty upon his departure to give him this report, which truly corresponds to reality, and to add to it my conviction of his merit and friendship.*

Monsieur Chevalier, 18th of the month of February of the year 1831.

Fifth Essay

[*On the revolution in France and the removal of the king prior to my return to Egypt. I include this essay only because the French consider these events to be*

1. = 'Ecole polytechnique'.
2. The Arabic *yu'ṭīhu al-durūs* is again a calque from French – *'donner des leçons'*.

among the best and most famous of their history, while they may indeed have marked a milestone in history for them.]

First Section. Being an introduction in order to understand the reason why the French no longer obeyed their king

You should know that this people[1] is divided in terms of their opinion into two major parts: the Royalists and the Liberals. The former term refers to those who follow the king and who claim that the power must be handed over to the person in charge[2] without opposition from the people. The other group have a predilection for freedom, i.e. they hold that only the laws need to be taken into account, and that the king is only the executor of decisions and judgments in accordance with the laws – in other words, he should merely be considered a tool. There is no doubt that the two views are divergent, which is why there is no unity among the people of France since there is no unanimity of opinion.

The majority of the Royalists are priests and their followers, whereas most of the Liberals are philosophers, scholars, doctors and the majority of the population. The first party[3] attempts to support the king, whereas the other supports the weak and wishes to help the people. The second party contains a large group who want all the power to be in the hands of the people, as a result of which there is no need whatsoever for a king. However, as the people cannot simultaneously govern and be governed, there must be people who represent them and are chosen by them to rule; this is 'republican government',[4] and the leading members are called

1. *ṭā'ifa* (pl. *ṭawā'if*); derived from a root meaning 'to turn around' (something, esp. the Ka'aba), the word denoted a group of people (cf. *qawm*) and later also 'a trade corporation'. In later mediaeval and modern usage, the meaning of the word is limited to a 'religious or sectarian group', the derivative *ṭā'ifiyya* denoting 'sectarianism'. In Ṣūfī terminology it means 'community', 'sect', and is thus synonymous with *ṭarīqa*. *Ṭā'ifa* was also consistently used for the French by al-Ṭahṭāwī's compatriot al-Jabartī (1997: IV, *passim*). See *EI2*, s.vv. "ṭā'ifa' (E. Geoffroy), "ṭā'ifiyya" (A. Rieck).
2. In the Arabic text the author underscores this idea through his choice of words: *taslīm al-amr li-walī al-amr*.
3. *firqa* ('division', 'group'). The modern term denoting a political party, i.e. *ḥizb* (whose basic meaning is 'a group of supporters of a man who share his ideas and are ready to defend them', but also 'a confederation of idolatrous Arabs united to wage war on the Prophet', 'hard soil', and, generally, 'a body of men'), would only appear later. The first author to use *ḥizb* in the modern sense was the reformer and champion of Pan-Islamism, Jamāl al-Dīn al-Afghānī (d. 1897) at the end of the century. See *EI2*, s.v. "d̲jam'iyya" (A. Demeerseman), "ḥizb" (E. Kedouri – D. Rustow); E. Lane, 1863–74: 559; Ibn Manẓūr, 1881–90/1: I, 299–300.
4. *ḥukm al-jumhūriya*, 'government by the masses'.

'senators'.[1] This is similar to what happened in Egypt during the Hammām regime, when Upper Egypt was governed through *iltizām*-based majority rule.[2] From this it becomes clear that some Frenchmen want an absolute monarchy, whereas others want a monarchy limited by the provisions embedded in the laws, or a republic.[3]

The French already rebelled in 1790 [sic], and sentenced their king and queen to death. Then they instituted a republic and expelled the ruling family called the 'Bourbons' (*al-Barbūn*) from the city of Paris, and proclaimed them enemies [of the state]. The effects of the revolution continued until the year 1810 [sic], after which Bonaparte (*Būnābārtah*), who was known as Napoleon (*Nābulyūn*), became ruler and took the title

1. The Arabic original *mashāyikh wa jumhūr* ('Elders and the people') should be corrected to *mashāyikh al-jumhūr* ('the Elders of the people'). The word *mashyakha* (sing. of *mashāyikh*) could also mean the abstract '*shaykh*hood', i.e. the office of *shaykh*. In the Muslim West, however, it denoted the group of urban elders and notables. See *EI2*, s.v. "ma<u>sh</u>yakha" (A. Ayalon).

2. *jumhūriyya iltizāmiyya*. The reference is to the power struggle between the *shaykh al-'Arab* (Sharaf al-dawla) Hammām b. Yūsuf al-Ḥawārī, who had taken control of Upper Egypt, and 'Alī Bey (d. 1773), the chief Mamlūk of Cairo (*shaykh al-balad*). In 1769, after being betrayed by chiefs of the Ḥawārī tribes who had constituted the mainstay of his power, Hammām was defeated by 'Alī, who thus effectively gained control of the whole of Egypt. Hammām fled his capital Farshūṭ (east of Nag' Ḥammādī) and went to Esna, where he died on 7 December of that year. His remains were buried in Qamūla, a village near Luxor. See 'A. al-Jabartī, 1997: II, 646–8.

3. *jumhūriyya*. This is the first time ever that this word is used in Arabic literature to denote a 'republic'. However, the Ottomans had already coined *jümhūriyyet* (mod. Tu. *cumhuriyet*) at the end of the 18th century, based on the Arabic *jumhūr*, which basically means 'group of people' (for other classical meanings, see E. Lane, 1863–74: I, 461–2; G. Freytag, 1830–37: I; 308; Ibn Manẓūr, 1299/1881–1308/1890–91) [1300/1883]: V, 219–20). At the turn of the preceding century, two eyewitnesses of the French invasion of Egypt, 'Abd al-Raḥmān al-Jabartī and Niqūlā al-Turk, used *al-jumhūr al-Faransāwī* and *jumhūr Faransawiyya*, respectively, for the French republican government. Conversely, the earliest French-Arabic dictionary of the century, by the military interpreter J.-F. Ruphy (1802: 185), lists *mashyakha*, which was the term subsequently used in official communiqués of the French occupation army in Egypt. It is also suggested by E. Bocthor (1882: 707) – alongside *jumhūr* – who also used the latter word in his translation of 'democracy', i.e. '*qiyām al-jumhūr bi 'l-ḥukm*' (E. Bocthor, 1882: 242). The new coining seems to have caught on very quickly, and is found, almost to the exclusion of all others, as from the middle of the 19th century; cf. Khayr al-Dīn, 1867: 121, 321, 335; M. Bayram V, 1884–93: III, 83 *et passim*; M. al-Sanūsī, 1891–92: 13 *et passim*. The Tunisian statesman Khayr al-Dīn, who is the only one to have the borrowing *rībūblīk*, also used *jumhūr* in its adjectival form in compounds like *dawla jumhūriyya* ('republican state'; Khayr al-Dīn, 1867: 87, 124, 325 *et passim*), *ḥukm jumhūrī* ('republican rule'; *ibid.*, e.g. 327 *et passim*), while Ibn Abī 'l-Ḍiyāf talks of *al-mulk al-jumhūrī* (1963:5: I *passim*). See *EI2*, s.vv. "<u>d</u>jumhūriyya" (B. Lewis), "ḥurrīya" (B. Lewis); A. Ayalon, 1989; H. Rebban, 1986: 65–9; H. Wehr, 1934: 40–41; V. Monteil, 1960: 191.

of 'emperor'.[1] Later on, when he became involved in an increasing number of wars, and conquered so many countries that his strength and might began to be feared, the kings of the Franks entered into an alliance against him in order to drive him out of his kingdom. They succeeded in doing so, in spite of the love the French people had for him. Then they reinstated the Bourbons, albeit against the wishes of the French nation.

The first of the Bourbons whom they made ruler of France was Louis XVIII. In order to make his regime popular among the people and to consolidate his authority, he created a law that governed both him and all French people, after consulting the latter and obtaining their approval. He forced himself to follow it and not to depart from it. This law was the Charter (*al-Sharṭa*), which we have already quoted in translation in the chapter on the political system of the French. There is no doubt that the word of a noble man is more binding than the debt of a debtor. And he [Louis XVIII] made this law both for him and his successors who would inherit [the throne of] the kingdom of France. Nothing can be added or taken away from it, except with the approval of the king, the Chamber of Peers and the Chamber of Deputies. As a result, both councils and the king are absolutely necessary. It is said that he did all of this against the will of his family and entourage, who would have liked to him to have absolute power over the people. It is also said that they conspired against him and that his brother, Charles X (*Sharl*), was the leader of the group. However, the king found out what he was secretly plotting and foiled his plans. It is said that when Louis XVIII had grown old Charles X wanted to rescind this law and return to absolutist reign, but was unable to do so.

After the death of his brother, Charles reverted to a ruse, suppressed

1. The Arabic *sulṭān al-salāṭīn*, though translating literally as 'ruler of rulers', seems to be al-Ṭahṭāwī's way of rendering the French '*empereur*', even though the Latin borrowing *imbarā(a)ṭur* already appears in mediaeval Arabic geographical literature: al-Dimashqī, 1866: 342 (*Inbarāṭūr, Inbarūr*); Ibn Sa'īd, 1958: 126 (*Inbaraṭūr*); Abū 'l-Fidā', 1840: 202; Ibn Khaldūn [n.d.]: 238 (*Inbaradhūr*). Furthermore, in the 17th and 18th centuries, *imperador/imperaṭorı* was the customary title used in official Ottoman correspondence with the Roman emperor (cf. M. Köhbach, 1992). The borrowing also appears regularly in the works of other Muslim visitors to Europe: Khayr al-Dīn, 1867: *passim* (*Imbarāṭūr*); S. al-Wardānī, 1888–90: no. 11 (*inbaraṭūr*); F. al-Shidyāq, 1881: 256 (*imbarāṭūr*); M. al-Sanūsī, 1891–92: 16, 138 (*imbarāṭūr*); A. Ilyās, 1900: 4, 5, 15 *et passim*. Very early on, the word also became inflectionally active, with *imbarāṭūrī* for 'imperial' (e.g. F. al-Shidyāq, 1881: 228; Khayr al-Dīn, 1867: e.g. 325), Khayr al-Dīn even using it to denote 'Empire' in connection with France (*ibid..*, 125, 132) and Austria (*ibid..*, 241, 242). Also see E. Gasselin, 1880–86: I, 627 (*anbarūr*); J. Redhouse, 1880: 108; J. Zenker, 1866: 153 (who adds the Turkish feminine form, though adding '*nur von der Kaiserin Maria Theresia*'!). Far more enigmatic, however, is the date 1810, as Napoleon was proclaimed emperor in May 1804!

his intention and pretended that he had never wanted such a thing. He allowed everyone to express their opinon in the newspapers, without requiring revision prior to printing and publication. People believed his words and were convinced that he would not renege on his promise. What is more, the entire population rejoiced at his government and the way in which he complied with the laws. But, in the end, he shamed the laws in which the rights of the French people were enshrined.[1] An indication of this even before the law was broken was the fact that he entrusted the prime ministership to the Minister Polignac (*Bulinyāq*),[2] whose ideas and policies are well known; he is in favour of putting all the decision-making power in the hands of the king. It is said that this minister is the offspring of an adulterous relationship his mother had with this king, so that he is, in fact, the king's son. He is famous for being unjust and oppressive. According to a highly common adage, the injustice by the followers falls back onto the ruler. In a *ḥadīth* we find the following: '*He who pulls out the sword of injustice, against him the sword of defeat is drawn, and sorrow will stay with him for ever.*' A poet said:

He who is just to people, yet does not demand
recompense from them in exchange, is truly a prince
As for him who wants justice in the same measure
he has given it, he is truly unique
But he who wants justice, while he himself
does not show it, is truly a despicable wretch

When this aforesaid minister had been sent to the land of the English, i.e. as a messenger acting in the interests of both countries, the French used to attribute to him everything that ran counter to freedom. Each time there was a rumour going around that he was coming back to France, all people thought that he had come back only to take up the post of Prime Minister and to change the laws. Because of this, all of the Liberals and most of the population hated him. The French knew in advance that his appointment as Chief Minister was something that was in store for them. And this is indeed what happened approximately one year after the king's accession to power.

1. The Arabic clearly shows the difficulty al-Ṭahṭāwī had in explaining the concept of non-religious laws, rights of the people, etc.: '*hataka al-qawānīn allatī hiya sharā'iʿ al-Faransāwiya*'.
2. Appointed Minister for Foreign Affairs in August 1829, Auguste-Jules-Armand-Marie, Prince de Polignac (1780–1847) was made Prime Minister only three months later. In December of the following year, he was imprisoned and then banished.

As we have already said, the Chamber of Deputies, who are the representatives of the people, gather each year for a general consultation. And when this Chamber met, they submitted a petition to the king requesting that he should dismiss this Minister [Polignac] as well as all six other ministers. However, he did not pay any heed to their words. It is customary in this consultative council that all matters are decided by a majority of its members. When the matter of the minister was presented before the assembly in this consultative council, 300 of the 430 people present voted against retaining the ministers, whereas 130 were in favour of retaining them. So, the majority was against them and a minority was in favour of them. As a result, it was certain that they were going to be deposed. However, the king wanted them to stay on as he sought their help in order to carry out his secret plans, and so he kept them on. Then, he broke the law [the Charter] through a number of royal decrees, which resulted in the removal from office of these ministers and their banishment from the country. This is how the poet put it:

He did not know the harm the word would bring him
nor to what things it would eventually lead him
holding forth in the way he had always spoken
without clearly thinking about the consequences of his words
Such is the way of careless speech
and the consorting with evil and fools
A fool humiliates you when he extols you
and harms you when he claims to be useful to you

Second Section. On the changes that were introduced and on the revolution that ensued from them

When discussing the laws in the course of our exposé of the rights of the French we have shown that pursuant to Article 8 no-one in France may be prevented from making his opinion public, writing it or printing it, on condition that it does not violate the provisions contained in the laws. If it does, then a stop is put to it.

However, in 1830 the king suddenly issued a number of ordinances, one of which prohibited people from expressing their opinions, writing them or printing them under certain conditions, especially if it involved the newspapers. Henceforth, they had to submit what they wanted to print to a state official, who then examined it and decided whether or not it could be published. Yet, this right did not belong to the king alone; he could take such action only through a law, and a law can be made only following an agreement by the king and the members of the consultative councils, i.e. the Chamber of the Peers and the Chamber of Deputies. As a result, he had decreed something that can be carried out only if it is approved by the two other authorities.

Through these ordinances, he also introduced certain changes to the electoral colleges for the representatives of the provinces, i.e. the bodies that select the delegates who are sent to Paris, and opened the Chamber of Deputies before they had gathered, although he can only rightfully do this after they have assembled – as he did the last time. All of this was in breach of the laws. And when these ordinances were promulgated, as if he suspected protests, he appointed leading personalities to military posts. These were all known enemies of freedom, which is after all the goal of the French people. These ordinances appeared so suddenly that the French seemed to be caught totally unawares. They had barely been published when most of the people who are familiar with politics said that the city would be hit by severe tribulations and that the consequences would be incalculable. As the poet said:

Amidst the ashes I saw the glowing of the embers
and it was on the verge of becoming a blaze
Then the fire in the palm trees flared up
And oft it is words that start wars

On the eve of the day on which these ordinances would be published in the newspapers, a crowd of people started to move towards a place called the *Palais Royal* (*Bāliruwāyāl*), i.e. the royal palace. This is the home of the family and relatives of the king, known as the Orléans (*Urliyān*) family, from which springs the current king. There was sadness on people's faces. The date was the twenty-sixth of July. And on the twenty-seventh, most of the Liberal newspapers did not appear since they did not accept the conditions [imposed by the ordinances]. And so the news reached all the people, and the movement gained momentum as a result of the non-publication of the newspapers, which usually appear except in cases of very important events. Workshops, plants, factories[1] and schools were shut. Some Liberal newspapers did appear, ordering disobedience to the king

1. *fabrīqāt* (sing. *fabrīqa*); cf. Khayr al-Dīn, 1867: 61, 65, 246 *et passim*; M. al-Sanūsī 1891–92, (*fābrīka*). It seems that, in practice, the spelling *fābrīqa* was the most popular: E. Gasselin,

and listing his dastardly actions. They were distributed to the people free of charge.

In this country, as indeed in others, words may reach farther than arrows, especially when it concerns speeches; they are very powerful, while the rhetorical composition, in particular, is highly exhortatory. As someone once said: '*if divine revelation comes to a people after the Prophets, then it comes to those of eloquent writing.*' This is especially true if what these dailies write is accepted by ordinary people, and deemed worthy by the elite; the very essence of eloquence is indeed that it is understood by the common folk and accepted by the notables.[1]

When the police prefects heard about the events that were taking place, they appeared in public places and forbade people to read these newspapers. They also raided the printing works where they were printed and began to break the printing presses. They smashed several of them and imprisoned and charged the printers; they also maltreated many of those among the people who had in any way expressed their opposition to the king's government. This, in turn, exacerbated the anger of the French.

Those in charge of these newspapers, i.e. the leading personalities among the French who write their opinions in them, drew up a letter of protest, which they made public, copied and put up on the walls of the city. In it, they called on the population to go to war, and fixed a place for this. The meeting place was in an alley near the Palais Royal. It was there and in the surrounding districts that a huge crowd of people from many different walks of life gathered. The king's soldiers attempted to disperse the crowds. The roar of the crowds swelled, more and more voices were raised and the people's wrath resounded through all the streets and districts. Then, the soldiers charged the crowd and a fight broke out between the two parties.

Initially, the people fought with stones while the soldiers retaliated with swords and 'machines of war' [guns]. The battle became ever more widespread, and each party chased the other with increasing violence. Then people went in search of firearms and soon the sound of gunpowder rang out from both sides in the city of Paris. The actions of the French truly bore out the following words: '*spears have been raised among your cousins!*'.

The battle raged with increasing intensity, and most of the casualties

---

1880–86: I, 768; T. Zenker, 1860: 653; S. Spiro, 1895: 438 (with plurals *fābrīqat, fāwrīqāt, fawārīq*!).

1. One is tempted, of course, to interpret this passage as a veiled reference to the situation in the author's native land and, indirectly, to the fact that Muḥammad 'Alī's modernization plans could succeed only if their use and purpose were fully understood by all sections of society.

were among the people, which only increased their wrath further. They put the dead bodies on display in public squares in order to incite people to participate in the battle and to show the ignominy of the soldiers. The people's anger rose against their king because they were convinced that he had ordered the killing. At that time, it was impossible to cross a district without hearing shouts of '*To arms! To arms! Long live the Charter! Death to the king!*' From that moment onwards, the bloodshed increased. The people got hold of weapons from the armourers, either by buying them or by taking them by force. Most of the workers and the craftsmen, but especially the printers, attacked police stations and army barracks, seized the weapons and gunpowder that were kept there and killed the soldiers present. The people also removed the royal insignia from stores and public places. The emblem of the French king is a picture of a lily, just as the emblem of a Muslim king is the crescent and that of the Muscovite king an eagle. The people shattered the street lanterns, prised the paving stones from the city streets and piled them up in the main thoroughfares in order to block the way for the cavalry. They also looted the royal ammunition depots.

When matters reached a head and the king, who was at that moment out of town, found out what was going on, he ordered the siege of the city, and appointed as the commander in chief of the army a prince from among the enemies of the French people, one who was famous for his treachery of the ideas of the liberal movement – in spite of the fact that this decision went against all common sense, political acumen and good leadership. This action clearly proved that the king was ill-guided, since otherwise he would have made some gesture of leniency or forgiveness – for a king's ability to pardon lengthens his rule – and he would have given the command of his soldiers to a group of reasonable men, loved by him and by the people, and not to people who are hated or who are known enemies. Instead, [it is clear] he wanted the ruin of his subjects in that he treated them as if they were his enemies. Yet, '*it is more clever to be conciliatory towards an enemy than to seek his destruction.*' In this respect, it is apt to remember the following words of a poet:

Be clement and bashful,
and show gentleness and forbearance towards him who has sinned
If you cannot steady one who has stumbled
then you will nigh be afflicted by fools

And so, contrary to his wishes, the king's action turned against him as a result of his intentions regarding his adversaries. If only he had graciously granted freedom to a party worthy of this quality, then he would not have found himself in such a predicament, and he would not have lost his throne in the course of these last tribulations. Indeed, the French had grown so accustomed to the quality of freedom that it became one of their natural features. How fitting are the words of the poet:

The people have customs to which they have become used
and habits and duties[1] *they abide by*
And whoever lives with them without paying heed to their custom
Is a burden for them, and hateful

On the 28th day [of July] the people captured a place called the Hôtel de Ville[2] from the soldiers. This place is the residence of the mayor (*shaykh*) of the city of Paris.[3] It was at that moment that the National Guard[4] – 'the protectors of the people' – appeared; these are soldiers who previously protected the population, just as the king had his own soldiers who protected him. King Charles X disbanded the National Guard, but with the outbreak of the revolution, it was again set up in order to safeguard the

1. The Arabic uses the religiously loaded *sunan wa furūḍ*.
2. *dār al-madīna*. The reason why al-Ṭahṭāwī needed a calque is that the concept of 'town hall' as the seat of local government was unknown in Arab countries at the time. One should add, however, that the Hôtel de Ville al-Ṭahṭāwī saw no longer exists as the building would be completely destroyed by fire in 1871. The modern town hall was built on the same site in 1882. See C. Courtalon, 1995: 414–16; M. Berthelot, 1886–1902: XX, 296–7; P. Larousse, 1866–76: XII, 247–9.
3. Technically, Paris did not have a 'mayor' as such. It was governed by the *Préfet de la Seine*, which corresponded to the earlier *maire central*. The residence of the Prefect was the *Hôtel de Ville*. Paris was administered by three officials: the Prefect, the Police Commissioner-in-Chief (*Préfet de police*) and the President of the Municipal Council. Before 1789, Paris had been divided into 21 *quartiers* and 60 *districts*, with a *maire central* at its head. The Constitution of 1794 introduced the division into 12 *arrondissements* (each, like today, headed by a mayor), the office of *maire central* being replaced by that of a President of the Municipal Council; the office of Prefect was created some time later (1800). Normally, the Prefect was in charge of a *département*, but as Paris was (and still is) a special case, its Prefect (i.e. the *Préfet de la Seine*) combined the office of department prefect and that of mayor. See M. Berthelot, 1886–1902: XVII, 560ff.; P. Larousse, 1866–76: IV, 748–9 ('Commune de Paris'), XIII, 57–61 ('Préfecture'), X, 961–2 ('Maire').
4. *al-khafar al-jinsī*; this is the only time the latter word is used to denote *national*, as elsewhere the term *waṭanī* appears. At the time of writing *jinsī* (MSA *jinsiyya* is the usual term for 'nationality', 'citizenship') was related to the basic meaning of *jins*, i.e. 'family', 'lineage' or 'race'.

people.[1] Brandishing their weapons, they drove all the soldiers from their positions, burning many of them down. At that time, courts were set up, with the people acting as judge. The State could not do anything any more. It applied all its might in order to quell the uprising and to restore calm, but was unable to do so. All the *gendarmes*[2] were mobilized, and the artillery provided support to the 12,000 Royal Guardsmen and 6,000 infantrymen.[3] So, the total strength of the royal troops amounted to 18,000 men, without counting the artillery and the gendarmes. There were fewer citizens who had weapons, but the others fought with stones or assisted their armed comrades. When the revolutionaries took the Hôtel de Ville, and captured a cannon, the defeat of the royalist troops became evident in the city. They withdrew towards a place called the Louvre (*Lūfr*) and to the palace of the Tuileries (*al-Tūlrī*), which is the king's palace, and the battle between the soldiers and the people of the town continued in both these places. While they were fighting there, the Tricolour – the symbol of the Freedom Party[4] – was hoisted atop of churches and public edifices. The large bells tolled in order to call on all people both inside and outside of Paris to take up arms and to help in the fight against the soldiers. When the soldiers saw that the people were going to win and that using their arms on the people of their country and on their kinsmen was shameful, most of them refused to fight, and many of their commanding officers even resigned from their posts.

On the morning of the twenty-ninth day [of July], the people had taken control of three quarters of the town. The palace of the Tuileries and the Louvre also fell into their hands; they were occupied, and the flag of the

1. The *Garde Nationale* (1789–1871) was a kind of bourgeois militia, though it had its own grenadiers, artillery and elite corps, in which those who paid taxes had to serve at one time or another. The National Guard would gain huge importance during the July Monarchy, Louis-Philippe using them as his Praetorian Guard; indeed, when he eventually lost their support in 1848, his regime collapsed. Charles X had dissolved the National Guard in April 1827, though they had never been asked to hand in their weapons. A. Malet, 1908: 336–7; M. Berthelot, 1886–1902: XVIII, 512–1, 519; P. Larousse, 1866–76: VIII, 1023ff.
2. *qawwāṣa* (Sg. *qawwāṣ*); cf. E. Bocthor, 1882: 370 (*qawwās*). This is a Turkish word (cf. mod. Tu. *kavas*), which denoted 'a kind of policeman' (J. Redhouse, 1880: 706).
3. The rather peculiar *'asākir al-ṣiffa* is a calque from the French '*soldats*' (usu. *Infanterie*) *de ligne*'.
4. The Arabic *ḥurriya* is rather ambiguous here, since it may refer either to the Liberal party or to liberty. However, in view of the fact that *ḥurriya* occurs most often as the collective term for 'Liberals', and that throughout his account al-Ṭahṭāwī clearly identifies both parties involved in the conflict, it seems likely that the flag (*bayraq*) represents the people or the movement, rather than the abstract concept of 'freedom'. It is also worth pointing out that the Tricolour at the time also had the image of a cockerel ('*le coq gaulois*') on it.

Freedom Party was raised on both of them. When the military commander-in-chief,[1] who was in charge of making the people of Paris obey their king again, heard about this, he withdrew. This marked the total victory of the people of the town, to the extent that the troops joined them under the banner of the citizens.

Immediately afterwards, a provisional government and a provisional council were set up in order to govern the country until a decision was made regarding the appointment of a permanent ruler. The head of this provisional government was a general called Lafayette (*Lafayītah*), who had also fought in the first revolution for freedom. This man is famous for the fact that he loves freedom and is a great defender of it. Because of this quality, and because of the fact that in politics (*al-būlītīqa*)[2] he is faithful to one principle and doctrine, he is honoured like a king. And although he is not a man of genius who creates sciences out of nothing – as is the case for most Frenchmen and their famous personalities, especially in the area of military sciences – he is the greatest among men because of his personal standing. Not because of his genius or his knowledge. This is not to detract from his knowledge or to denigrate the fact that the leadership eventually fell to him. In all countries of the world one can observe that the pre-eminence of an office is not always commensurate with the incumbent's degree of learning, even though it should be so both from a legal and a natural point of view. The strange thing is that something like this can also occur in countries that have attained a high degree of civilization. I, for one, think that all of this only confirms the *Ḥadīth* according to which the intelligence of a person is not always credited to the one who holds it. As the poet said:

If one of virtue sees you in poverty
do not wonder about the paucity of his possessions

1. This was Auguste-Frédéric Viesse de Marmont (1774–1852), a former Napoleonic general who had also taken part in the battle of the Pyramids (1798). After the revolution, he accompanied Charles X in exile to England.
2. Cf. S. Spiro, 1895: 63 (*būlīṭīka*, *būlītīka*, 'diplomacy', 'compliments'). In the *Manāhij*, al-Ṭahṭāwī defined this concept as 'the art of royal management (*siyāsa malakiyya*), the art of administration (*idāra*), the science of the governance of the kingdom, etc., research into this science, the talking about it, the fact of discussing it at councils and assemblies, the examination of it in newspapers – all of this is called *būlītīqa* or *siyāsa*' (al-Ṭahṭāwī, 1973–80: I, 517). Very early on, *būlītīk(a/ā)* gained the dialectal meaning (ECA) of 'smooth talking', 'chit-chat'. In this respect, one may also draw a parallel with the way the word was used by Shakespeare in his plays. See O. Jespersen, 1912: 155–6; S. Somekh, 1984: 183; M. Hinds and E. Badawi, 1986: 96.

The Prophet spoke true words when he said:
Intellect is something entrusted to a man

And how apt are the words of another poet:

If the rain poured forth from the clouds by intellect
then it would not rain on the palm tree and tragacanth at the same time
And if it gave rain measured by height
Then it would water hills and skirt valleys

Third Section. On the actions of the king in this period and what happened after he agreed to a conciliation when it was too late, and his abdication in favour of his son

The ordinances of the king were promulgated when he was in the town of Saint-Cloud (*Sanklū*), near Paris.[1] So, the revolution took place in Paris when the king was not there. The people of the city sent word to him to change the Cabinet and to withdraw and repeal the ordinances. In other words, they called on him to issue a decree by which he would take back what he had ordered. But he refused to do so, and so the people sent him a number of representatives in order to attempt to change his mind on this and to plead with him. However, their words were to no avail or, to be more precise, they were wasted, like tears shed in the sea. They told him that the people would not in any way accept this and that it might even exacerbate the misery, to which he retorted that his words were not subject to change.

When it became clear to him that his country was on the verge of destruction as a result of his refusal to accept the peace offering, he himself asked the people for peace. But they told him that there was no more room for peace, that the time for conciliation had passed, that he had not paid heed to the consequences – and misfortune befalls one who is not mindful of the consequences of something – and that he had not been careful enough, since otherwise all of this would not have happened to him.

1. Acquired by the Orléans family in 1658, the palace of Saint-Cloud (some 7 km north-east of Versailles) was later bought by Marie-Antoinette. It was here that the revolution of 18 Brumaire (10 November 1799) started (which overthrew the first Republic) and Napoleon proclaimed the Empire (18 May 1804). It was nearly destroyed by the Prussians in 1815. After Napoleon, the palace was the main residence to Louis XVIII, Charles X and Louis-Philippe. See M. Berthelot, 1886–1902: XXIX, 113–14; P. Larousse, 1866–76: IV, 475–6.

On the thirtieth day of the month of July, the members of the Chamber of Deputies agreed to send word to the Duke of Orléans (*al-dūq durliyān*) – a relative of the king in the second degree – to request him to assume the leadership of the kingdom until such time as another consultation assembly decided who should take over the ruling of their kingdom. The duke was not in Paris, but as soon as he learned of what was required of him as a result of this consultation, he arrived in the city; this was on the thirty-first of the month. The duke took up quarters at the Hôtel de Ville, where he expressed his agreement with what the members of the Chamber had proposed. After his arrival he delivered an impressive speech on the reasons that had caused him to accept the proposal. The gist of his peroration was as follows: '*I greatly regret the events that have plunged Paris in this situation, which was caused by the violation of the laws or a vile interpretation of the meaning contained therein. I have obeyed [the call of the people] and I have come amongst you in order to protect the country from disaster. It is incumbent upon me to wear – with you – the Tricolour, which I so often donned in my childhood.*' He concluded his speech by saying, '*Henceforth, the Charter will be a right!*' – i.e. he would act in accordance with the laws of the kingdom and he would not deviate from them since they constituted the Law. This sentence has become a saying among the French and arouses great enthusiasm and fervour.

Charles X thought he could avoid the collapse of his regime by abdicating in favour of his son and by the latter's accession to the throne. However, as the poet said:

He wished he could return to the days of protection
However, it is only seldom that one sees the return of something that has gone

And so, one day at Saint-Cloud, his son, the dauphin (*al-dufīn*), appeared in a courtyard where the soldiers had gathered and declared that his father had appointed him king. This message was received by the soldiers with disdain and indifference. After handing the throne over to his son, the king left with his Cabinet and courtiers in the night of the twenty-ninth. The dauphin, for his part, remained alone to await the consequences of his accession to power. He convened all the soldiers and let them march before him in order to ascertain their disposition. And when he found out that they did not wish to fight with him, he decided to depart and to leave Saint-Cloud. A few hours after his departure, the Tricolour was hoisted all over the château of Saint-Cloud, which is the royal residence in this town.

The king and his entourage arrived in Rambouillet (*Ranbūliyā*) on the first of the month of August.[1] On the second day of this month, Charles X and his son, the dauphin, sent a message to the Duke of Orléans (who is one of their relatives), in which they stated that they had relinquished the kingdom to the Duke of Bordeaux (*al-dūq diburd*)[2] – the king's grandson and the dauphin's nephew – and that they had appointed the Duke of Orléans as regent until the new king came of age. In this statement, they also requested him to send them an escort to ensure their safety on their journey out of France. The Duke of Orléans submitted this to the People's Representatives, who disagreed with the relinquishment of the kingdom, but consented to send to the king a number of representatives from among the eminent personalities in order to ensure his safety during his departure from France. Then the news reached Paris that the king did not agree to leave immediately, and so a detachment of soldiers was dispatched to force him to do so. As soon as he heard about this, he set off for England. The following lines seem appropriate here:

Destiny sometimes lies in power
that commands; at other times it lies in disgrace

During this time, his cousin, the deputy commander[3] of the kingdom, was in Paris. All the power lay in his hands and those of the consultative councils. The first decision he took was to retain the Tricolour, which symbolizes the freedom of the French nation (*milla*). Then he opened the Chamber of Deputies and the Chamber of the Peers. It is customary that the king is present at the opening of the Chamber of Deputies and delivers an eloquent speech from the dais (*minbar*) in which he mentions

1. It is perhaps symbolic that Charles X should spend his darkest moment at this château, which had been his favourite hunting residence.
2. This was Henri Dieudonné d'Artois, Count de Chambord, Duke of Bordeaux (1820–83), the posthumous son of Charles X's son, Charles-Ferdinand, the Duke of Berry, who had been assassinated in February 1819, and Marie-Caroline de Bourbon-Sicile. His birth gave rise to considerable controversy, and he was very early on referred to as '*l'Enfant de Miracle*' as the princess was said to have delivered him without witnesses. There were even calls that this was some veiled kind of coup d'état, the legitimacy of the child being openly questioned in newspapers. The last heir of the elder branch of the Bourbon family, Chambord never renounced his claim to the throne, taking on the title of Henri V.
3. The Arabic *qā'im maqām* – which al-Ṭahṭāwī uses here to translate the French *lieutenant-général* (*du royaume*) – was a rank used in Turkey, and denoted the deputy Grand Vizier who ruled in the latter's absence. In Egypt, it meant 'lieutenant' in the sense of 'second in command' and, later on, 'lieutenant-colonel'. See "ḳā'im-maḳām", *EI1* (J. Mordtmann), *EI2* (P. Holt).

the improvements he has carried out for his country and what he intends to do over the coming year. However, as this duke replaced the king at this time, it was he who ascended the platform and made a short declaration, in which he expressed his regret over the danger to which Paris had been exposed as a result of the breach of the laws of the kingdom. After he had finished, he showed the Assembly the document that Charles X and his son, the dauphin, had sent to him, and in which they stated that they had relinquished the kingdom to the Duke of Bordeaux (*al-dūq Burdū*), whom they named Henry (*Hanrī*) V, because France had previously had four kings who had been called Henry. Then, the deputy commander of the kingdom left the Assembly, which would thenceforth be open to conduct its day-to-day activities.

Fourth Section. On the decision made by the Chamber of Deputies and how as a result of this revolution the Duke of Orléans was appointed king of the French

You should know that it was the consultative Chamber that organized the future state of France. We have already stated that the wide differences in [political] opinions among the French are even reflected in the seating arrangements within the Chamber: the Royalists sit on the right, the Liberals on the left, whereas the government supporters sit in the middle. Each of them may express his opinion without any opposition, since it is the number of votes that matters. This state of affairs has continued until this day; the revolution did not change it in any way.

The adherents of the various ideologies were divided into two parties: a party that wanted a monarchy (*mamlaka*) and one that was in favour of a republic (*jumhūriyya*). Among the members of the former there were those who wanted to put the Duke of Bordeaux, the grandson of the former king, on the throne, while others wanted to appoint the son of Napoleon (Bonaparte) as ruler. Still another group wanted the Duke of Orléans, the deputy commander of the kingdom, as king. The house of Orléans was the second in line and would inherit the monarchy after the extinction of the first branch, i.e. that of the house of Bourbon (*al-Būrbun*).

Then a printed document appeared, which was posted in districts and at public crossroads, and which included the following: '*Experience has taught that the republic is not suited to the country of France. As for the Duke of Bordeaux* (al-dūq dābīrdū), *his appointment as ruler would bring the French under the regime of the Bourbons and they would end up in the same situation as that from which they had escaped. The son of Napoleon, on the other hand, was raised by priests and they are the enemies of liberty. As a result, the Duke of Orléans has been appointed.*'[1]

However, the consultative Assembly put forth several articles on which they expressed an opinion:[2]

The first was the fact that the throne was vacant, both literally and figuratively, and no-one was entitled to it, but that, on the other hand, it had to be occupied by someone.[3] Second, it is one of the objectives of the French people and in their interest[4] to delete any expressions referring to an elevation [of the king] from the Charter, i.e. the book containing the laws of the kingdom, since to retain them [the expressions] in their present form reduces the position of the French people. As a result, some articles in the Charter must be removed and replaced by others that correspond to what is required in the present situation. After this has been done, the Chamber of Deputies will in the public interest of all Frenchmen demand that his Highness the Duke of Orléans, Louis Philippe (*Luwīz Filīb*), deputy commander of the kingdom, be requested to take over as king, and that his monarchy, after him, be inherited by his male offspring, passing to the eldest of his own sons and so on. In other words, when the king dies, his throne will pass to his eldest son and, when the latter dies or is prevented [from succeeding his father], to his eldest son, etc. Upon the acceptance of the rule of the kingdom, the incumbent must accept the conditions as well as the form of the pledge of allegiance[5] determined by the members

1. Interestingly, al-Ṭahṭāwī omits any mention of the fact that only 219 Deputies – barely half of the Chamber – voted in favour of his investiture.
2. What follows is a loose translation of the declaration by the Chamber of Deputies published in the *Moniteur universel* on 10 August 1830.
3. The original states: '[...] *le trône est vacant en fait et en droit, et qu'il est indispensable d'y pourvoir*'.
4. *min maṣāliḥihim*; the singular *maṣlaḥa* literally means that which is for the benefit of the Islamic community; here, however, it is stripped of its religious meaning, and is used as a synonym of the 'neutral' *naf'* (pl. *nufū'*) or *manfa'* (pl. *manāfi'*), both meaning 'benefit', 'advantage'. It appears as a leitmotiv in other works on Europe with new coinings like *maṣāliḥ khuṣūṣiyya* ('personal benefits') and *maṣāliḥ waṭaniyya 'umūmiyya* ('general national interest'), both of which were first used by Khayr al-Din (1867: 40, 89 *et passim*), whereas 'Alī Mubārak considered it a binding agent for society (1882: 1, 179). In modern times, *maṣlaḥa* has remained the basis of legislation in many Muslim countries, and the single most important guiding principle for Arab statesmen in the independence movements of the 20th century.
5. *mubāya'a*; derived from a root meaning 'to enter into an agreement (to sell something)', this word is related to *bay'a* (lit. 'the sealing of a contract by shaking hands'), which denoted the oath of allegiance to the caliph on his accession to the throne. The etymology of the word was borne out by the official ceremony which involved the placing of the hand into the open hand of the ruler. It should be added that, later on,

of the consultative Chamber (*ahl al-mashwara*), and will assume the title of 'King of the French' ('*roi des Français*'), and not 'King of France ('*roi de France*').[1] The difference between the two titles is that 'King of the French' holds great psychological meaning to individuals inasmuch as it is they who make him king, as opposed to 'King of France', which means that, as long as France exists, the country remains his dominion over which he holds sway as its lord and king without any contest or opposition from the people of his country. The reason for this is that the previous kings bore the title 'King of France'. When one of them drew up a document, he would write the following: '*I, such and such, by the grace of God, King of France and Navarra (*Nawār*) – to all who will see the present orders, greetings! We have ordered and we order what follows.*'[2] The expression 'King of France' is self-evident. However, as far as 'King of Navarra' is concerned, this is a conventional title, which was purely an honorific. The reason for this was that the ancestors of the king of France ruled the kingdom of Navarra, which later went to the kings of Spain, and became a part of Spain, whereas the kings of France retained the title. As for the king of the French, he uses the following formula: '*I, such and such, King of the French. To all those present and future, greetings. We have ordered and we order.*'[3] There is a difference between the formulas in that by the former someone makes himself king of France and Navarra by the grace of God – Praise be to Him. In the second formula, the ruler is King of the French without saying 'by the grace of

this practice of investiture (albeit with some permutations) was also adopted in some Ottoman Regencies; for instance, in Tunisia the coming to power of a new Bey was marked by two *bay'as*, a 'private' one (*bay'a khāṣṣa*) – by the elite and religious leaders – and a 'public' ceremony (*bay'a 'āmma*) – by the population at large. See *EI1*, s.v. "bai'a" (C. Huart), A. Raymond [Ibn Abī 'l-Ḍiyāf], 1994: II, 3–4 *et passim*.

1. Cf. '*La Chambre des pairs* [sic] *déclare secondement que selon le voeu et dans l'intérêt du peuple français, le préambule de la Charte constitutionnelle est supprimé comme blessant la dignité nationale, en paraissant octroyer aux Français des droits qui leur appartiennent essentiellement et que les articles suivants de la même Charte doivent être supprimés ou modifiés de la manière qui va être indiquée. Moyennant l'acceptation de ces dispositions et propositions, la Chambre des pairs déclare enfin que l'intérêt universel et pressant du peuple français appelle au trône SAR Louis-Philippe d'Orléans, duc d'Orléans, lieutenant-général du royaume et ses descendants à perpétuité de mâle en mâle par ordre de primogéniture, et à l'exclusion perpétuelle des femmes et de leur descendance. En conséquence, SAR Louis-Philippe d'Orléans, duc d'Orléans, lieutenant-général du royaume, sera invité à accepter et à jurer les clauses et engagements ci-dessus énoncés, l'observation de la Charte constitutionnelle et des modifications indiquées, et après l'avoir fait devant les Chambres assemblées, à prendre le titre de Roi des Français.*'
2. This is a translation of the French '*X, par la grâce de Dieu, roi de France et de Navarre, à tous ceux qui ces présentes verront, salut.*' (e.g. the Charter of 1814).
3. In the new version of the Charter (9 August 1830), the preamble ran as follows: '*Louis-Philippe, roi des Français, à tous présents et à venir, salut. Nous avons ordonnés et ordonnons ...*'.

God'. He avoids saying this in order to satisfy the French people, because they say that he is king of the French as a result of the will of the nation, and because they made him king – not because of some special privilege bestowed by God the Almighty – Praise be to Him – on his family, without his people having any say in the matter. It will become apparent from this that to them the expression 'by the grace of God' means that the king has a right to be on the throne because of his birth or lineage, just as 'King of France' means that the king is the owner of the land and has absolute power over it. In our country, these two expressions would be synonymous, since the fact of being the king by choice of the people is not incompatible with the fact that this is given by God the Almighty – Praise be to Him – as a favour or beneficence. For instance, to us, there is no difference between 'King of the Persians' or 'King of the land of Persia'.[1]

After the consultations had been completed, the members of the Chamber sent a number of envoys to Louis-Philippe and the president of the Chamber read out what had been agreed by the members of the consultative Chamber. He replied immediately, saying: '*I have heard, with a moved heart, what you have told me of the decision taken by the consultative council regarding my election as king. It is certain to me that what you have expressed also represents the voice of all the people. It is also clear to me that what you have done with the laws agrees with my political convictions which I have pursued in the course of my life. I am greatly distraught since I will never forget the terrible things I have endured in the past, and which even made me decide never to strive towards becoming sovereign but rather to seek an anonymous and peaceful existence among my children. However, my love for the prosperity of my country was stronger, and it is only proper this is more important, particularly since I am convinced that necessity makes it so.*' Then he set the day for his coronation in the Chamber of Deputies. When the appointed day came, he arrived at the agreed hour, in a grand procession, but without royal guard and courtiers, both of which usually adorned the progress of former French kings. And whenever he took a step, all the people would greet him from all sides with the words 'God save the Duke of Orléans! God save the King!' After he had entered the Chamber, he ascended a dais near to the throne and greeted the entire assembly three times. Then he sat down on a bench in front of the throne, with his eldest son to his right, the second to his left, while behind him there stood four military leaders, called *maréchaux* (*mārishālāt*)

1. It is clear that al-Ṭahṭāwī felt obliged to include this, since otherwise he might well have been accused of challenging the very idea of the caliphate! Indeed, was not the Ottoman sultan 'the shadow of God on Earth'?

– the plural of *maréchal* (*mārishāl*).[1] This is the highest military rank that exists in the French state, and is always found in an *iḍāfa* (*status constructus*) with 'France', and so people refer to [someone as] '*maréchal de France*' (*mār<i>shāl diFarānsā*), the *de* marking the annexation of the genitive head and the governed noun; this is like the determining [letter] *lām* in [the Arabic] genitive construction. The French, however, make the annexation [namely, genitive construction] visible.

After having sat down, he bade the members of the Chamber of the Peers and that of the Deputies sit down, and requested the president of the Chamber to read the decision by the members of both Chambers regarding the transfer of the kingdom to him. When the president had finished reading, the Duke answered by saying: '*Gentlemen, it is with great attention that I have heard the statement by both Chambers, and I have weighed and carefully pondered the words contained therein. I hereby say to you that I unconditionally and unreservedly accept all the provisions in it as well as the title of "King of the French", which you have granted me. And I am here, ready to swear the oath that I shall protect them.*'[2] Then, the king got up, bare-headed, held up his right hand and, with solemnity and a steady unfaltering voice, pronounced the formula, which translates as follows: '*I swear by Almighty God faithfully to protect the Charter containing the laws of the kingdom as well as the revisions made to it mentioned in the declaration; to govern only by and in compliance with the written laws; to give everybody the rights to which they are entitled under the laws; and to always act in the best interest of the French people and in furtherance of their happiness and glory.*'[3] Then he mounted the throne of the kingdom, and delivered the following speech: '*Gentlemen, I have just sworn a momentous oath. I am fully aware of the considerable and*

1. Cf. Khayr al-Dīn, 1867: 155, 162, 176, 257, 308, 361 (*mārīshāl*); M. al-Sanūsī, 1891–92: 16 (*marīshāl*); A. Ibn Abī ʾl-Ḍiyāf, 1963–65: III, 176, IV, 100, 101, 104 (*marshāl*). Khayr al-Dīn is the only one to use this title for various countries, which would lead one to assume that in many cases he was in fact talking about the rank of *maréchal de camp* (today's *général de brigade*). Cf. E. Gasselin, 1880–86: II, 386 (*mārishāl*); G. Badger, 1895: 610 (*marīshāl*); H. Wehr, 1934: 54; A. Butros, 1973: 99.
2. This is al-Ṭahtāwī's translation of part of the official proceedings which appeared in the *Moniteur Universel* of 10 August 1830 (*Procès verbal de la séance de la Chambre des Pairs et de la Chambre des Députés réunies, le 9 août 1830*). The French text reads as follows: '*Messieurs les pairs, Messieurs les députés, J'ai lu avec une grande attention la déclaration de la Chambre des Députés, et l'acte d'adhésion de la Chambre des Pairs; j'en ai pesé et médité toutes les expressions. J'accepte sans restriction ni réserve les clauses et engagements que renferme cette déclaration et le titre de "roi des Français" qu'elle me confère, et je suis prêt à en jurer l'observation.*'
3. Cf. Fr. '*En présence de Dieu, je jure d'observer fidèlement la Charte constitutionnelle avec les modifications exprimées dans la déclaration, de ne gouverner que par les lois et selon les lois; de faire rendre bonne et exacte justice à chacun selon son droit, et d'agir en toute chose dans la seule vue de l'intérêt, du bonheur et de la gloire du peuple français.*'

extensive duties imposed on me by it, and my inner voice tells me that I will fulfil them. I have wholeheartedly accepted the pledge of allegiance. I had decided never to climb the throne which the French nation has given to me, but when I saw that the liberty of France was wounded, that the general order in the land was disturbed, and that the violation of the laws of the kingdom had brought it to the edge of destruction, it was necessary to restore the laws. This was the task of the Chamber of the Peers and that of the Deputies, and I have entrusted them with this. The revisions we have carried out to the Charter will require peace and security in the future, and I hope that with this France will experience calm and tranquillity at home and respect abroad, and that peace will increasingly be rooted in the countries of Europe.'[1] When he finished his speech, there were shouts of 'God save the King Louis-Philippe I!'. Then the king greeted the assembly and left, shaking hands with some of the members of the council as well as other people present. Afterwards, he mounted his horse and rode off, shaking hands with the people that had crowded on his right and left. He also embraced a great many of the people that had gathered. His escort consisted of both people of the town and the 'Guard of the Nation' (*khafar al-milla*) – the so-called 'People's Guard' [the National Guard]. When night fell, Paris was illuminated by a huge bonfire. His accession to the throne took place on 7 August of 1830 A.D.

Fifth Section. On what happened to the Ministers who signed the royal ordinances that caused the end of the reign of the first king, and who committed this act without thinking of the consequences and desired that which cannot be attained. As the poet says: 'People, though their natures may differ, covet from the world that which they have not obtained'

You should know that after this revolution the French went to great lengths to find the ministers who had been the cause of it. Indeed, ministers are by law answerable for the harm that befalls the kingdom, and it is they – not the king – who are held accountable since the ruler does not have any

1. Cf. Fr. '*Messieurs les pairs et Messieurs les députés, Je viens de consommer un grand acte* (ḥafaltu fī hādha ʾl-waqt yamīnan ʿaẓīman), *je sens profondément toute l'étendue des devoirs qu'il m'impose, j'ai la conscience que je les remplirai. C'est avec pleine conviction que j'ai accepté le pacte d'alliance qui m'était proposé. J'aurais vivement désiré ne jamais occuper le trône auquel le voeu national vient de m'appeler, mais la France, attaquée dans ses libertés, voyait l'ordre public en péril* (takaddarat al-rāḥa al-ʿāmma), *la violation de la Charte avait tout ébranlé; il fallait rétablir l'action des lois, et c'était aux Chambres qu'il appartenait d'y pourvoir. Vous l'avez fait, Messieurs; les sages modifications que nous venons de faire à la Charte garantissent la sécurité de l'avenir* (yastalzimu al-amn fi 'l-mustaqbal) *et la France, je l'espère, sera heureuse au-dedans, respectée au-dehors et la paix de l'Europe de plus en plus affermie.*'

obligations whatsoever. And so, their burden is heavy, and their task is a difficult one since the responsibility for everything that happens rests on their shoulders. A poet said:

People pass power alternately between themselves
I should want to share in this, but I cannot
entrust others with the heavy burden; indeed
those that are affected by it are the subordinates and never the leaders
The underlings shoulder the heavy burden of what is thrown on them
while the leader's obligation merely consists of the stamp and the signature

In all streets of the land, orders were posted to apprehend them if they should pass there. We have already said that the Prime Minister was Polignac (*Būlinyāq*). Four of the ministers were seized, and among them there was this Prince.[1] He was caught while attempting to leave France dressed up as a servant to an important lady.[2] He was recognized and arrested, but the Guardsmen who were present in the street protected him from the people. The Chamber in Paris was then advised of this. Polignac himself wrote a letter to the Chamber of the Peers, stating that his arrest was unlawful since he was a member of the Chamber; he invoked Article 34 of the Charter according to which a peer can be imprisoned only by other peers, who are also the only ones that can judge him in criminal matters. Consequently, the members of the Chamber gathered to read his letter and deliberated on its contents. The result of this consultation was that permission was granted to arrest and imprison him until such time as he would be judged. He was subsequently brought to the town of Vincennes (*Wansīnah*) in the vicinity of Paris, and imprisoned in its castle.[3] Then the other three were arrested and gaoled together, although none of them was subjected to any form of maltreatment during the term of their imprisonment.

During the time the men were in custody, a large enclosure was built for them in the Chamber of the Peers in order to try them. The construction

1. The other three were: Charles-Ignace Comte de Peyronnet (1778–1854), Minister for the Interior; Jean-Claude de Chantelauze (1787–1859), the Keeper of the Seal; and Count Martial-Côme de Guernon-Ranville (1787–1866), the Minister for Education. Although all three were also sentenced to life imprisonment, none actually served the full term. Peyronnet and de Guernon-Ranville were released in 1836, de Chantelauze in 1837.
2. The arrest took place in the port of Granville (north-western France).
3. Built in the 14th century, the Château de Vincennes ceased to be a royal residence in the 16th century, instead becoming a prison, initially reserved for convicts 'of note'. Among its famous inmates we find people like the encyclopaedist Diderot and the Marquis de Sade. See C. Courtalon, 1995: 698–705.

was made extremely solid and secure in order to prevent the people from attacking the accused and harming them and the latter's friends from liberating them from gaol. All of this cost a fortune. Then the prisoners were taken to this place and locked in a separate room from which they were brought in each day. Their trial was one of the most impressive that a person is ever likely to hear and constituted clear proof of the civilization of the French and the justice of their state.[1]

By way of explaining some of the things related to this, it should be said that as soon as the new king of the French came to power, he expressed the wish to dismiss seventy members of the Chamber of the Peers who had been appointed by Charles X, the previous king. He then appointed new members from among those who shared his goals. If these seventy peers had stayed, they would have rallied to the defence of the [convicted] ministers. Most of the members of the Chamber of the Peers were hostile to them, but their strict adherence to the laws, general good nature and natural disinclination towards injustice were the reasons that the aforementioned ministers were saved. The most remarkable thing about this was the fact that during his arrest Minister Polignac wanted only one legal scholar to defend him, and chose Martignac (*Martinyāq*)[2] – a minister who had been deposed before him – despite the fact that there was no friendship between them. Even more astounding than this was the fact that Martignac fulfilled his task with the utmost faithfulness, applying all his expertise in order to defend his client against all the charges that were brought against him. Each of the other ministers arrested also appointed his own lawyers. When the trial proceedings began, each of these ministers was asked questions regarding his person with the utmost kindness and gentleness. The first thing that was asked was something like, 'What is your name? What are your personal features? What is your position? What is your rank or title?' Each of them replied to these questions, even though the answers were known in advance. Then they asked each of them the following question:

'Do you admit signing the king's ordinances?' 'Yes,' the people in question replied.

1. This aspect of French society also impressed the historian al-Jabartī, who gave a very detailed description of the way Kléber's assassin, Sulaymān al-Ḥalabī was tried (1997: IV, 461ff.). European justice was also one of the few things that found favour with the otherwise vehemently European-hating 12th-century chronicler of the Crusades, Usāma Ibn. Munqidh (1886: 97ff.; trans. P. Hitti, 1987: 161ff.).
2. A former royalist, Jean-Baptiste Gaye, Viscount of Martignac (1776–1832) had been appointed Minister for the Interior after the 1827 elections and subsequently joined the Liberal camp, which, of course, led to his losing his post in the Polignac ministry.

'Why did you do that?' The answer was, 'Because the king wanted me to.'

'Why did the king want this to be done? Did he decide it a long time ago or only at the end?'

Each of them replied to questions such as these by saying, 'I will never reveal the secret of the Privy Council of his Majesty the king.' This revealed the high degree of esteem in which the deposed king was held by the members of the council. And so none of them ever revealed anything of the secrets of the [king's] council, nor did anybody force them to do so. After the questioning had finished and the proceedings had been recorded, the lawyers arrived. They also stayed a number of days in order to show that the ministers were innocent of any wrongdoing, that they had acted in good faith, etc. Afterwards, the assembly examined the entire trial and then handed down the following judgment: '*As the ministers placed their signature under the ordinances that ran counter to the laws of the kingdom, and as they violated the sanctity of the laws, the assembly sentences them to life imprisonment and the loss of their honorary privileges and titles.*' Polignac was, in addition, sentenced to 'judicial death' (*al-mawt al-ḥukmī*), which is similar to someone of whom there is no news and whom a judge – following his own interpretation[1] – declares to be dead when a certain period of time has elapsed after which the individual in question is probably no longer alive. This 'judicial death', which is called '*mort civile*' by the French,[2] means that a living person is treated like a dead person. Someone who is sentenced to such a punishment loses all his possessions, which pass unto his heirs, as if he had really died. He is no longer able to inherit from anybody else, nor can he bequeath any possessions which he may require afterwards. He may not dispose of his possessions either in part or in their totality whether it be by gift or by legacy. He may not receive any gifts or bequests, except in food, and he is not permitted to be a guardian, legator or witness before the

1. *ijtihād* ('the fact of exerting oneself'); in classical Islamic legal theory, this concept denotes the use of individual reasoning (*ra'y*) by a qualified jurist (*mujtahid*) with regard to matters of religion, such as the interpretation of legal texts or the authenticity of traditions (*ḥadīth*). A particular type of *ijtihād* is that which involves deducing legal prescriptions from the Qur'ān and the *sunna*; this 'deduction by analogy' is known as *qiyās*. Originally, the underlying reasons for this process were, of course, highly practical. After the death of the Prophet, the changes in Muslim society – not least the expansion of Islam – meant that increasingly believers were confronted with issues that were not addressed directly in the Qur'ān or *sunna*. As a result, the only way out of the dilemma was to address the issue by sound reasoning through interpretation. See N. Coulson, 1978: 59–60, 76–7; "id̲j̲tihād", *EI1* (D. MacDonald), *EI2* (J. Schacht); *EI1*, s.v. "ḳiyās" (A. Wensinck); J. Schacht, 1966: 37, 69ff.
2. This phrase, which the dictionary of the Académie Française of 1835 (II: 232) explains as '*[une] cessation de toute participation aux droits civils*' quickly gained currency in its figurative meaning of being ostracized.

law. Any complaints from him are inadmissible in law, and he cannot enter into matrimony – indeed, the contract of his first marriage is annulled and any legal obligations ensuing therefrom are thus rendered null and void. As for his wife and his children, they have free disposal of his property and may act in all other ways as if he were actually dead. In other words, he is a dead man among the living. However, as people who are sentenced to this kind of punishment are part of the elite, and as their offspring are well brought up, they usually retain the position they had prior to the conviction as their families are convinced that this kind of ruling is a flagrant infringement [of their rights] and that he is saved before God. The wife of the convicted person will on no account leave him since she firmly believes that she is married to him in the deep sense of the word. And if afterwards she bears him a son, his brothers will make him an heir together with them, even though this runs counter to the prescriptions embedded in a *mort civile.*

When the population heard this, they rose and demanded that a real death sentence be pronounced against the person in question. The members of the government informed them that this would contradict that which they had been requesting, i.e. freedom, justice and equity, and that the codex did not set forth the type of punishment for ministers guilty of treason, but that the assembly [the Chamber of Peers] decided on a sentence that would serve as a deterrent to others.[1]

On the evening of the day on which the judgment was passed, and before the convicted men were informed of the decision by the Chamber, they were taken from the prison that had been built especially for them and escorted to the castle of Vincennes, where they were incarcerated. From there, they were transported to another castle, where they have been held to this day.[2] Their manner of conviction is proof of the good morals of the French state.

Sixth Section. On how after the revolution Charles X was scorned by the French and how it did not stop there

You should know that shortly before this revolution, the French learned that Algeria had fallen into their hands.[3] They received this news without

1. In the second edition, this sentence was followed by two verses.
2. This was the Château of Ham in northern France, which was famous for its political prisoners; it was here, for instance, that Napoleon III would be held for six years (1840–46).
3. Polignac had declared war on Algeria on 31 January 1830, with the troops headed by the Minister for War, Bourmont, himself, landing on the territory (at Sidi Ferruch) on 14 June. The reference here is only to the capture of the capital Algiers on 5 July, since it would take many more years before the entire country was under French control.

any enthusiasm, even though they did display some happiness and joy. As soon as this news reached the Prime Minister, M. Polignac, he ordered a celebratory gun salute. How right was the one who said the following:

How many joys are accompanied by sadness
This is why time was created

He then began to strut around town as if to display his self-admiration, as his will had been executed and the French had vanquished Algeria during his ministry. However, only a few days later, the French gained an even greater victory over him and their king, with the result that the Algerian question was completely forgotten as people spoke only of their latest triumph. And while the ruler of Algiers left the city under certain conditions and took his possessions with him, the king of the French left his kingdom, repenting what had happened because of his actions. The vicissitudes of time follow one another, and events run their course. This resulted in his raid on Algeria, which was based on specious motives that did not justify this but only served to gratify a personal whim, and when fancy prevails, reason ceases.

There was something else that happened: when the archbishop heard of the capture of Algiers and the former king entered the church to thank God the Almighty – Praise be to Him – the archbishop congratulated him on this victory. In his speech, among other things, he praised God the Almighty for granting the Christian nation a huge victory over the Muslim nation and [expressed the wish] that it might continue.[1] However, the war between the French and the Algerians was purely a question of politics and of quarrels related to trade, money and disputes springing from arrogance and pride.[2] There is a maxim that says that *'if a quarrel were a tree, then its only fruit would be distress.'*[3] At the outbreak of the revolution, the French destroyed the house of the archbishop after the latter had fled and demolished all of its contents. He was forced to go into hiding, and for a

1. The archbishop in question was Mgr Hyacinthe-Louis de Quelen (1778–1839), who held this office between 1821 and 1839. It must be added that the church was very much in favour of the Algerian campaign, seeing it as an opportunity to win over new souls. Cf. A. Julien, 1986 : 62.
2. Al-Ṭahṭāwī refers here to the origins of the French attack on Algeria and the Bakrī affair (see Translator's Introduction). The arrogance and pride, on the other hand, would seem to refer to the direct cause of hostilities, i.e. the argument in April 1827 between dey Husayn and the French consul, Pierre Deval.
3. The Arabic hinges on the *jinās* of *mushājara* ('quarrel', 'dispute') and *shajar* ('tree'): *law kānat al-mushājara shajaran lam tathammara ilā ḍajran.*

while no trace of him was found. Then, he reappeared, only to disappear for a second time, and his house was again attacked. He is still decried and shunned.[1] As the poet said:

Do not be surprised, and tread carefully:
The turns of fortune in this world go from one people to the next

When the French saw that Charles X had, like the Pasha of Algiers, been driven from his kingdom, they began to poke fun at him, representing him and the Pasha together, and satirical papers published odd insinuations and witty jokes. For instance, in one of these pictures he and the aforesaid Pasha were represented, with the caption underneath the latter asking, '*Has your turn also come?*' – as if the Pasha were mockingly asking the king the question, '*Have you, too, been deposed?*'

Say to those who are rejoicing in our misfortune; beware –
misfortunes and misery are before you!

Another poet said:

Fate ravishes men; so do not be
one of those whose head is confused by positions and titles
Many a blessing vanishes through the slightest lapse
but each thing holds a reason for its reversal

In the satirical press, they also wrote that the aforesaid Pasha had said to Charles X, '*Let us play a game for a specific stake. If you do not have anything on you, we should be pleased to collect some alms from the people for you!*' This alluded to the fact that the Pasha of Algiers had left his country with all his wealth, whereas Charles X had left his a poor man. They also represented the king as a blind man, begging and asking people, '*Give a little something to a poor blind man.*' This referred to the fact that he had not seen the consequences of the ordinances. He was also pictured leaving church together with his Prime Minister, Polignac, implying that they were only good for this kind

1. The reason behind the attack on the prelate (1831) – whose palace was ransacked, with the library and much of the furniture thrown into the Seine – was of course not his support of the Algerian campaign but his unwavering loyalty to the Bourbons and his outspoken opposition to the revolution. Afterwards, he was also accused of having embezzled one million francs from the poverty fund. See P. Larousse, 1866–76: XIII, 513; M. Berthelot, 1886–1902: XXVII, 1127.

of futile worship, and that they were priests rather than princes. There were claims that on a number of occasions the king had donned the priest's habit and read mass to people in the chapel of his palace.

After the revolutions, criers sold pamphlets containing details about the love affairs of this king and his debauchery during his youth, the moral depravity of the archbishop and other such things, as well as the fact that his grandson was not his son's real son, but an impostor. The surprising thing about all of this was that these pamphlets were sold by criers on the square of the residence of the new king, who is, after all, one of his predecessor's relatives. Even more astounding is the fact that this pamphlet mentioned that the new king was the one who had previously revealed these things in English newspapers after the birth of the former king's grandson. All of this is shouted out loud, and nobody objects to it since this is in accordance with the freedom to express one's opinion both orally and in writing.

After the coming to power of this [new] king, several powerful groups emerged. Their members included people who wanted to depose him and establish a republic (*jumhūriyya*) as they were not satisfied with freedom and demanded more. Others had joined together with a view to re-establishing the old regime[1] and putting the former king's grandson on the throne. The consequences of this revolution continue to live on to this day, and in some cases its effects were also felt in other countries. For instance, the [French] revolution led to the secession of Belgium (*Baljīk*) from the kingdom of Holland, of which it had been a part, as well as to calls for freedom and independence from peoples under Russian rule; it also inspired the revolution that took place in Italy.

Seventh Section. On the reaction by Frank states upon hearing of the ousting of the first king and the assignment of the kingdom to the second and on their acceptance of this

It is well known that the former royal family[2] returned to the throne after the states of Europe had entered into a confederacy against Emperor (*sulṭān*) Napoleon. He was subsequently driven out and banished to the island of Saint Helena (*Sint Hilīna*), after which this family, which had been living abroad, was returned to the country. So, this family was returned to power

1. The Arabic *al-ḥukm al-qadīm* is, of course, a literal translation of the French '*ancien régime*'.
2. *al-ʿīla al-sulṭāniyya*, the first word being the ECA variant of CA *ʿāyila* (or *ʿāʾila*), *ʿiyāl*.

solely through the alliance between the kings of the states of Europe. If truth be told, this was imposed on France against the will of the majority of the French people. When the revolution broke out, the French were afraid that the aforementioned kings would come with their armies to their country in order to return this family to the throne. They were saved from this by transferring power to another family, that of the Orléans, but the people did not know whether the kings would agree to this. If the latter did not, the people were determined, come what may, to engage them in battle, as witnessed by the preparations they took.

At this juncture, we should like to compare the attitudes of Frankish kings in relation to this issue. One should know that in his policies and behaviour the king of Spain agreed with the former king of France, who was also one of his relatives since the family that rules Spain is part of that which rules France. As a result, it is favourably inclined towards it, both in public and in private. The same tendency exists in Portugal. So, the old dynasty has nothing to fear from these two countries. As for Italy, the policies of the states of Naples, Rome and Sardinia also agree with that of the Bourbons, the former French ruling family. At the time, the kings of these states were very moved by the events that took place in France. Muscovy, Austria, Prussia and England, for their part, formed an alliance in order to bring the Bourbons to power. Their kings, too, had been touched by the revolution to a certain extent, especially Muscovy. As for the smaller states of Europe, they follow the big states. And so, only a few small territories who wanted freedom themselves remained on the side of the new French state. However, the people of England expressed their approval of what was happening, and so their king was the first to recognize the new king of France. It is customary that when a king takes power, his accession to the throne must be recognized and approved by other kings, which is usually done in accordance with established etiquette. It is said that our Most Gracious Majesty, the Sultan, after having been apprised of the situation and informed by his ambassadors, replied that he would not undertake anything until he had seen what the kings of Europe would do. If they acknowledged him, then he would, too. The intervention by the Ottoman state in the interest sphere of Frankish states is very limited. The king of Muscovy was one of those who withheld approval for a long time. But, in the end, he too endorsed it, on condition, however, that it would not change anything in the balance of power among European countries, and that they should stay as they were, without there being any state(s) gaining political ascendancy to the detriment of other(s). In other words, the kingdom of France, for example, cannot become bigger than it was before the revolution.

It seems that most of the kings who acknowledged the new king of France did so only on this basis and approved of what had happened only provisionally. The French felt this, and said so in public, as if they did not trust this peace, which, as one can see, is like a truce and a state of limbo. When I left France, all the people expected a declaration of war and an outbreak of hostilities with the Austrians and Muscovites or the Spanish (*al-Isbanyūl*) and Prussians. But God the Almighty – may He be praised – alone knows best what has been and what will be! At present, the French and English enjoy better relations than ever before! For the account of my return, the reader is referred to the epilogue of this travelogue.

Sixth Essay

Containing extracts from the sciences and arts already dealt with in the second chapter of the introduction. It comprises several books. The first section deals with the division of the sciences and arts as such, as well as with all the arts and sciences that are important to all students.

First Section. On the division of the sciences and arts according to the Franks

The Franks have divided human knowledge into two parts: the sciences and the arts. The former are achievements that have been empirically proven. Art, on the other hand, denotes skills, i.e. knowledge of the techniques for certain things in accordance with specified rules.

The sciences are subdivided into mathematical branches and non-mathematical branches. The latter are, in turn, split into natural and theological sciences. The mathematical sciences are made up of arithmetic, geometry and algebra.[1] The natural sciences are composed of natural history, physics and chemistry. Natural history is taken to refer to botany,[2]

1. The Arabic text refers to *al-jabr wa 'l-muqābala*; the former concept denoting 'to make something complete' (i.e. to restore fractions to a complete number), and the latter 'to be in opposition' (i.e. two sides of an equation). The combined expression is used in old mathematical works for 'the method of solution of equations of the first and second degree'; *EI1*, s.v. "al-d̲jabr" (H. Suter).
2. The Arabic *'ilm al-ḥashā'ish wa 'l-a'shāb* literally translates as 'sciences of grasses and plants'. The modern term '*'ilm al-nabāt*' ('the science of plants') would be introduced some time later.

mineralogy,[1] and zoology. These three branches are called 'the classes of production': i.e. the botanical class, the mineral class and the animal class.

As for theology, it is also referred to as 'metaphysics'.[2]

The arts are subdivided into intellectual arts[3] and applied arts. The former are closest to the sciences and include, for instance, the science of eloquence and rhetoric,[4] grammar, logic, poetry, drawing, sculpture and music. All of these are intellectual arts because they require scientific rules. Conversely, the applied arts are the crafts.

Such is the division drawn up by Frankish scholars. However, in our country there is very often no difference between sciences and arts; a distinction is made based only on whether an art is an independent science or serves as a tool for another.

The sciences that are obligatory for all pupils are arithmetic, geography, history and drawing. The knowledge of all these subjects comes after the knowledge of the French language and matters related to it. For this purpose, we should discuss it briefly here.

Second Section. On the classification of the languages as such, and the use of the French language

Know that language in the sense of a precondition for comprehension on the part of the listener is something about which it is best not to say any more; rather, as it is necessary to make something understood both in speeches and dialogues, it is vital for students in all nations that they should start with it, and make it the means with which to acquire other things.

Language as such consists of specific expressions that denote specific meanings. It is conveyed through the various speech and writing systems used by various nations. There are two types of languages; those that are used and those that have fallen into disuse. The former category comprises those that are currently spoken, such as those of the Arabs, Persians, Turks, Indians, French, Italians, English, Spaniards, Austrians and Muscovites. The second category contains languages whose peoples have perished and whose speakers have died out, and which do not exist except in books.

---

1. *ʿilm al-maʿādin wa ʾl-aḥjār*: 'the science of minerals and stones'.
2. *ʿilm mā wara' al-ṭabīʿāt*: 'the science of what lies beyond the natural occurrences'. This is synonymous with the more traditional *falsafa mā wara' al-ṭabīʿa*.
3. *funūn ʿaqliyya*, which can also be translated as 'theoretical arts' (cf. theoretical/pure vs. applied science).
4. The Arabic terms *al-faṣīḥ wa ʾl-balāgha* denote eloquence in both senses: fluency of speech and the science of rhetoric in the classical sense of the use of stylistic devices. Also see *EI1*, s.v. "balāg̲h̲a" (A. Schaade).

These include Coptic, Latin and ancient Greek.[1] A knowledge of languages that are no longer spoken is useful for anybody wishing to read the books of the Ancients and, in Frankish lands, there are special schools dedicated to the learning of these languages since people there recognize their use. Each language must have rules governing the way in which it should be written and read [spoken]. These rules are called *grammatica* (*aghramātīqā*) in Italian and *grammaire* (*Aghrammayr*) in French; this means 'the construction of speech', i.e. the science of fixing language through its syntax. There is indeed no objection to using 'syntax' to denote the rules of a language as such. It is in this sense that it is used here, i.e. a science providing the correct use in speech and writing in accordance with the conventions of a given language. What is meant by 'speech', on the other hand, is the communication of a meaning to a listener, but this is something that we had better not talk about here. Speech is composed of the word, which Arabic philologists divide into three parts: the noun (*ism*), the verb (*fi'l*) and the particle (*ḥarf*). A noun may appear variously as a substantive,[2] e.g. *Zayd*; a personal pronoun (*muḍmar*), e.g. *huwa* ('he'); or a demonstrative pronoun (*mubham*), e.g. *hādhā* ('this'). The verb may be in the preterite (*māḍin*), as in *ḍaraba* ('he hit'); in the imperfect (*muḍāri'*), e.g. *yaḍribu* ('he hits'); or in the imperative (*amr*), e.g. *iḍrib* ('hit!'). The particle, on the other hand, relates to one of the other two categories (*qasīm*) – e.g. *min* (with nouns) or *qad* (with verbs) – or it can be attached to both, as with *hal* (interrogative particle) and *bal* ('nay', 'however').

We have included this division here because we shall see in the following that among the French the pronoun (*ḍamīr*) and the demonstrative (*ism al-ishāra*) are two separate categories like the noun and are not considered to be part of it in any respect. The French divide the word (i.e. speech) into ten independent parts, each of which has its own mark. The French parts of speech are: the noun, the pronoun, the article (*ism al-ta'rīf*), the epithet (*na't*), the active participle (*ism al-fā'il*), the passive participle (*ism al-maf'ūl*), the verb, the adverb (*ẓarf*) – which they call 'verb modifier' (*mukayyif al-fi'l*) – the preposition (*ḥarf al-jarr*), the conjunction (*ḥarf al-rabṭ*) and the interjection

1. *al-Yūnāniyya al-qadīma al-musammā bi 'l-Ighrīqiyya*, where al-Ṭahtāwī of course makes a clear distinction between the language of the modern Greeks (*al-Yūnān*) and that of their ancestors, *al-Ighrīqiyyūn*.
2. *al-muẓhar* (or *al-ẓāhir*) literally translates as 'that which is apparent'; in Arabic grammar, it denotes the noun that replaces the pronoun (*al-ḍamīr*), with which it is perceived to be in opposition. Arab grammarians in fact distinguish between six types of 'nouns': the *ism* (or *al-mawṣūf, al-man'ūt*); the adjective (*ṣifa, waṣf, na't*); the numeral (*ism al-'adad*); the demonstrative (*ism al-ishāra*); the (relative) pronoun (*ism al-mawṣūl, al-mawṣūl al-ismī*); and the (personal) pronoun (*ḍamīr, muḍmar*).

(*ḥarf al-nidā'*). They define the noun as a word that refers to a person or a thing – i.e. something endowed with intelligence or not – such as 'Zayd', 'horse' or 'stone'. The pronoun is defined as being 'that which stands in place of a noun'. Their definite article is, as in Arabic, *l*, except for the fact that it varies with the noun to which it refers; the masculine form is with *u* (in fact, '*le*') and the feminine '*la'*. The plural for both of them is '*les*', but the *s* is not pronounced here. They define the adjective as a word that denotes a particular characteristic or quality, such as 'good' or 'beautiful'; as such, it is similar to [the Arabic] qualifying adjectives (*ṣifa mushabbaha*).[1] As for the active and passive participles, they are like *ḍārib* ('hitting') and *maḍrūb* ('hit'). In French, the adverb is like that in Arabic. The prepositions are like the Arabic adverbs and prepositions. For instance, if a person says in French, '*I came before Zayd and after him*', then '*before*' and '*after*' are considered the prepositions. And if you say 'Zayd came *first*' or '*afterwards*' or something of that kind, then these are adverbs. As for the conjunctions, they are defined as being that which is between two words or two sentences and may thus be compared to the [Arabic] '*wāw* ('and') of attachment ('*atf*)', as in '*Jā' Zayd wa 'Amr*' ('Zayd and 'Amr came'), or with 'that', if you say, 'I hope *that* I will live a long time'. This category also includes *idhan* ('therefore') and *ḥīna'idhin* ('then'), as when you say, 'You are intelligent; *therefore* you are able to learn' or '*then* you are able…'. As for the interjections and other such particles, they are well known [and thus do not require any explanation].

This division, which is necessary according to the rules of their language, bears out the statement by one of their scholars that the word (*kalima*) or speech (*kalām*) consists of three parts in all languages and that this is due to an intellectual restriction since the parts of speech are insufficiently or not at all independent of meaning, and the expression of what is semantically independent is based on time [indications] or absent altogether.

Every person expresses what he means through speech or writing. The oral expression of it is called [in Arabic] *'ibāra* (expression) or *manṭiq* (pronunciation). Its written expression is called *nafas* (style), *musaṭṭara* (recording) or *qalam* (style). The [written] style (*qalam*) of a person may be more eloquent than his oral expression; for instance, a stammerer may write very elegantly. And if someone expresses himself in a pure and flawless language, using only accepted forms, then his expression is said to be 'high'; if it conveys his meaning adequately, then it is 'suitable'; if, however, it contains something that the listener rejects, then his speech

1. This is short for *ṣifa mushabbaha bi-asmā' al-fā'il wa 'l-maf'ūl*, i.e. 'adjective similar to active and passive participles', and is an adjective derived from the first form of the verb. It usually denotes a quality inherent in people or things.

is 'weak' or 'bad'. In any case, the expression is either verbose or terse or conveys a fundamental meaning.

An author, on the other hand, expresses himself either in poetry (*naẓm*) or in prose (*nathr*). In any event, his speech or his work will be in the language used in conversation, i.e. the so-called vernacular (*al-dārija*), or in a 'received' language. The rules of prose constitute the underlying basis for speech and writing. Prose does not require metre or rhyme, except in *saj*ʿ (rhyming prose).[1] Prose is the language used in the sciences, history, trade, correspondence, speeches and so on. As a result of the vastness of the Arabic language, there are many scientific books that have been written in verse; in French, on the other hand, scientific books are never written in verse.

Poetry is the expression of a person's meaning through well-considered rhymed speech (*al-kalām al-muqaffā*). Besides metre (*wazn*), poetry requires delicate expressions and powerful motives that induce it. I am charmed by one of our poet's words, which are full of double meaning.

Poetry is fashioned to suit various men
Many a poem is a pebble, and a precious jewel
And if you wish to win its pearls
that are strung, then go to al-Jawharī's Ṣiḥāḥ[2]

Another one said:

You who make unpolished poetry
thus forcing the burden of refining it on me -
If creation assisted me in this

1. This literary device involves the intermittent use of rhyming words; it is distinguished from poetry (*shiʿr*) in that it is not governed by the stringent rules of rhythm and metre. It is interesting to see that, a bit further on, al-Ṭahṭāwī also uses the rather circuitous *taqfiyyat al-nathr* ('rhyming of prose'). See "sadj<u>j</u>ʿ", *EI1* (F. Krenkow), *EI2* (T. Fahd/W. Heinrichs/Afif Ben Abdesselem).
2. The poem is indeed a wonderful example of *tawriya*. In the last line, the pun is on the literary reference in *fa-khudhhu min ṣiḥāḥi 'l-jawharī*. On the face of it, this refers to the dictionary *Tāj al-lugha wa ṣiḥāḥ al-ʿArabiyya* ('The Crown of the Language and Correct Usage of Arabic') by the Persian lexicographer Abū Naṣr Ismāʿīl b. Ḥammād al-Jawharī (d. 1003?). Yet, the phrase can also be read 'and take from it the authentic pieces of the jeweller'. Furthermore, *al-Jawharī* is made to rhyme with *jawhar*, which denotes 'jewel', but also 'substance', i.e. something that exists by itself. The theme of gold and goldsmithing is already present at the start of the verse with the use of the verb *ṣāgha* ('*ṣuwigha al-qarīḍ*'), which usually denotes 'shaping, moulding (gold, silver)', but also 'to coin a word', or 'fabricate' (e.g. verse). Finally, in *durrihi naẓman* ('arranged, strung pearls'), the latter word means 'order' or 'arrangement', but also 'poetry'!

You would be amazed at how your ravings would hurry away[1]

Another poet said the following about the loss of motives:[2]

They said, 'Have you left poetry?' I replied, 'Out of necessity' –
The door of reasons and motives is closed!
The land is empty, devoid of a generous one from whom a benefit can be expected and of a pretty one to love

Still another one said:

The state of poetry does not hold a secret to any of you
It does not sell and has scattered, after having been much prized
So have pity on the poets, for they
are like the dead among the living because of impoverishment

Poetry is not peculiar to the Arabic language; each language allows the making of verse in accordance with the rules that govern its poetic art. Indeed, the special quality of the art of versemaking as it is codified in the Arabic language and its limitation of the number of metres used to fifteen are peculiar to Arabic.[3] In French there is no rhymed prose, and its poets do not have the required knowledge of the art of poetry in order actually to compose it. To be sure, a poet must have a natural disposition and inborn instinct for poetry, without which his style is cold and his poetry would not be accepted.[4]

Third Section. On the art of writing

This is an art by which one expresses what one means through special drawings, called the 'letters of the alphabet (*ḥurūf al-hijā'*)' or the 'letters

1. These two verses rely on the meanings of *hadhdhaba* ('to hurry', 'to trim', 'to purify', 'to polish', 'to improve', 'to correct', 'to bring up', 'to educate').
2. *faqd al-asbāb* plays on *asbāb* (sing. *sabab*) meaning 'nouns', or part of a metrical foot made up of two consonants, as well as the more usual 'reasons'.
3. In fact, it is generally accepted that classical Arabic poetry has 16 metres; see "'arūḍ", *EI1* (Weil.), *EI2* (Gotthold Weil/G. Meredith-Owens); W. Wright, 1981: 359–68.
4. Here follow a number of verses which the author introduces as 'a small selection of the finest and best *qaṣīdas* and poems', all of which are intended to show the lexical cornucopia of Arabic. Among the authors, all of whom are famous experts in *badī'*, we find the satyrist Jarīr b. 'Aṭiya b. al-Khaṭafā (d. *c.* 730), Muslim Ibn al-Walīd (d. 818), Ibn Sahl al-Isrā'ilī (see note no. 1, p. 158), Amīn Efendi al-Zalalī, al-Shihāb al-Ḥijāzī (see note no. 1, p. 168) and Muḥammad b. Aḥmad al-Ghassānī al-Wa'wā' al-Dimashqī (d. 990). Each citation is prefaced by praises such as '*And how beautiful are the words of…*', '*I find the words of … highly pleasing*'.

of the dictionary (*ḥurūf al-mu'jam*)'. Most of the letters of the alphabet are common to all languages, *alif* (*a*) being the first one, except among the Ethiopians, where *alif* is the 13th letter.

The craft of writing is of the greatest use among all nations as it is the soul of all social intercourse, the present manifestation of the past and the organization of the future; it is the messenger of the will and constitutes half of what has been witnessed.

The Arabs, the Hebrews and the Aramaeans (*al-Siryāniyyūn*) write from right to left, the Chinese from top to bottom and the Franks from left to right. Is it more natural to write from right to left – the way it is done by the Arabs and the other peoples we have just mentioned – or in the opposite direction, the way the Franks write? Proof supporting the first thesis is the arrangement of the numbers such that they follow a natural order; they start from the right and go to the left, whereas the units, which are part of the tens, stand to the right of the latter. The same is true for [the position of] the tens in relation to the hundreds and for the hundreds in relation to the thousands. If the numerals constitute the basis for other things, i.e. if they are elementary things on which all people, regardless of their nature, agree, then this is an indication that to go against this runs counter the principle, which proves the contradiction, as we intended [to show]. The Franks devoted a great deal of attention to this, and by reducing reading and writing solely to the reading and writing of numerals, they have demonstrated that their method is the most natural. As a result, there is all the more reason for stating that writing from top to bottom goes against nature.

It is said that the Arabs already knew writing in the days of Job – Peace be upon him. A disagreement has arisen about whether the letters of the alphabet are a divine creation or the work of man and, if it is the latter, by which nation (*milla*)? Some have stated that they were invented by the Aramaeans, whereas others held that the alphabet was a creation of the ancient Egyptians. The former hypothesis has gained the upper hand and so the Aramaic alphabet is said to have been transmitted to the Greeks[1] – as witness the fact that the Greek letters are the same as the Aramaic ones, except that the Greek alphabet is the reverse (with the letters running from left to right). The Romans (*al-Rūmāniyyūn*), in turn, took their letters from the Greeks.

Although fine handwriting is not an indication of culture and refinement, the fact of not paying the necessary attention to writing is proof of ignorance.

1. Despite his own earlier distinction, al-Ṭahṭāwī uses *al-Yūnān* here for what must clearly denote the Ancient Greeks, i.e. *Ighrīqiyyūn*.

Poets have fought over whether to prefer the sword or the pen, and then over whether it is the pen used in literary composition or in that for accountancy that deserves precedence. Al-Mutannabī[1] stated his preference for the sword, when he said:

The word of the sword is truer than that of books
Its cutting edge marking the boundary between what is serious and play –
Long-bladed sabres, not scribbled sheets –
As their blades clear up all doubt![2]

In his book entitled *al-Awā'il*, al-Suyūṭī,[3] for his part, expressed a preference for the pen over the sword, with the following words:

Books are the refuge of fugitive words[4]
And writing is the thread for the pearls of wisdom
By writing you can bring order to everything that is strewn
And separate everything that is ordered
As you know, it is the sword that
imposed the duty to worship the pen

---

1. al-Mutanabbī ('he who professes to be a prophet') was the nickname (*laqab*) of the famous Kufa-born poet Abū 'l-Ṭayyib Aḥmad b. al-Ḥusayn al-Ju'fī (915–55), who is best known for his extremely ornate panegyrics (*madīḥ*). See *EI1*, s.v. "al-Mutanabbī" (R. Blachère); J. Ashtiany *et al.*, 1990: 300–14 *et passim*.
2. *al-sayf 'aṣdaq inbā' min al-kutub fī ḥaddihi al-ḥadd bayna al-jidd wa 'l-la'b; bīḍ al-ṣafā'iḥ lā sawwad al-ṣaḥā'if fī mutūnihā jalā' al-shakk wa 'l-rayb.* The complex sound and word plays in the verses are, unfortunately, completely lost in translation. For instance, the poet contrasts *bīḍ* (white', but also 'blank [e.g. sheet of paper] and, rarely, 'swords') and *sawwada* ('to cover with writing' but also 'to blacken' and graphemically identical to *sūd*, 'black'). In addition, there is implied opposition between *bayyaḍa* ('to make a fair copy of') and *sawwada* ('to make a rough draft'). The contrast is further heightened by *ṣafā'iḥ* ('sheet [of metal]' but also 'a sabre with a long blade') and *ṣaḥā'if* ('sheet [of paper]') and continued by *mutūn* ('texts' but also, rarely, 'blade of a sword', by analogy with 'shaft of an arrow below the feathers'), *jalā'* ('departure, emigration' but also 'clarity' and 'appearance [of a shining object]') and *shakk* ('doubt' but also 'coat of mail with tightly-knit mail', with the homographemic *shikk* and *shakka* respectively denoting coverings of the extremities of a bow to protect it from humidity, and 'to be armed from head to toe'). Finally, *sayf* ('sword') in the first line is also a direct reference to the poet's patron, the Ḥamdānid prince of Aleppo, Sayf al-Dawla ('Sword of Religion'), at whose court al-Mutanabbī stayed for nine years (948–57).
3. This is a reference to *al-Wasā'il ilā ma'rifat al-awā'il* ('The Means towards Knowing the Primary Elements') by the famous Egyptian historian and polymath Abū 'l-Faḍl 'Abd al-Raḥmān b. Abī Bakr Jalāl al-Dīn al-Suyūṭī (1445–1505). See "al-Suyūṭī", *EI1* (Brockelmann).
4. The poet plays on the double meanings of *'aql* ('intellect, wisdom' but also, rarely, 'refuge, fortress') and *shawārid* ('fugitives' but also 'something that is on everybody's tongue [especially poetry]').

The controversy was once and for all laid to rest in the *Tārīkh al-duwal* ('History of Nations') by Ibn al-Kardabūsī,[1] who said that '*power rests on two things; the sword, and the pen, the latter having priority over the former*', and adduced evidence to prove this. It appears that one may conclude this issue by referring to what has been said about the two types of writing, i.e. that while the craft of composition is nobler, that of accountancy is more useful. Similarly, the sword is higher than the pen, but the latter is more useful.

Fourth Section. On the science of rhetoric, which includes eloquence, the hidden meanings of words and stylistic embellishments[2]

This is the science of elegant expressions, or the science of making the expression appropriate to what is required by the circumstances. Its general aim is to enable a person to enunciate his inner thoughts in pure and eloquent speech. Viewed from this angle, this science is not peculiar to the Arabic tongue, but can be found in any other language. In European languages, it is referred to as 'rhetoric' (*'ilm al-rīthūrīqī*). But as this science is more complete and more perfected in Arabic than in other languages, especially the art of style ornaments and tropes (*badī'*), and as it is poorly developed in European languages, it may seem that it is one of the specialities of Arabic. The eloquence of the style of the Qur'ān, which was sent down to man as an inimitable creation, is exclusive to Arabic.

1. In fact, the reference here is to the history of the caliphate running from the life of the Prophet up until the beginning of the Almohad period, the last caliph included being Yūsuf b. 'Abd al-Mu'min, known as Yūsuf I (1163–84). The book is entitled *al-Iktifā' fī akhbār al-khulafā'* ('Satisfaction Regarding the News about the Caliphs') and was written by the 12th-century Tunisian historian Abū Marwān 'Abd al-Malik b. al-Kardabūs (al-Ṭahṭāwī corrupted the name to 'al-Kardabūsī') al-Tawzarī. This work (part of which has been edited by A. al-'Abbādī, 1971) should not be confused with the similarly entitled *Kitāb al-Iktifā' fī maghāzī al-muṣṭafī wa 'l-thalātha al-khulafā'* by Abū al-Rabī' Sālim al-Kalā'ī al-Balansī. On al-Kardabūs, see, for instance, A. al-'Abbādī, 1971: 8ff.; *GAL*, I, 421; *GALS*, I, 587.
2. The Arabic title *Fī 'ilm al-balāgha al-mushtamal 'alā al-bayān wa 'l-ma'ānī wa 'l-badī'* refers to the three parts of rhetoric (*'ilm al-balāgha/al-ma'ānī*) traditionally identified by Arab philologists: *ma'ānī* ('the ideas', 'notions'), *bayān* ('representations') and *badī'* ('the ornaments', i.e. tropes). It should be added that *balāgha* technically denotes the correct use of language (esp. Arabic), and as such is often equated with *faṣāḥa*, i.e. purity of language. As for *al-ma'ānī wa 'l-bayān*, this may be said to denote the 'semantics of syntax', i.e. finding the appropriate expression to suit a given context'. See *EI2*, s.vv. "badī'" (M. Khalafallah), "balāgha" (A. Schaade – [G. von Grunebaum]), "bayān" (G. von Grunebaum); "al-Ma'ānī wa 'l-bayān" (B. Reinert). It is likely that among the Arabic sources used by the author *al-Jawhar al-Maknūn fī 'l-thalātha funūn* ('The Hidden Jewel in the Three Arts') by the already mentioned 'Abd al-Raḥmān al-Akhḍarī figured prominently, as he would have studied this text during his time at al-Azhar.

Something that is considered to be eloquent in one language may in another be wholly devoid of elegance, or even repulsive. Conversely, an expression may be eloquent in two or more languages. For instance, if you wish to express the fact that a man is courageous by comparing him to a lion, as in '*Zayd is a lion*', then this is acceptable in languages other than Arabic. However, if you wish to express the beauty of a person by comparing him to the sun or [by referring to] the redness of his cheeks by saying that they are ablaze, this is considered beautiful in Arabic but not at all so in the language of the Franks. The same is true when you talk about saliva or things like that, as, for instance, in the following words by the poet:

'Oh, my loved one,' Buthayna said, 'why has he come to us
without appointment?' She was told, 'He is distracted and engrossed with his own affairs –
he who night after night gazes at the stars becomes absent-minded.'
In the morning, Buthayna takes some of the shine away from the rising sun
When she emerges, then not a day of radiance remains with her
Her eye is wide open and naturally kohled
as if her father were a gazelle and her mother a wild cow
She struck me with deadly love, which was my ruin,
How many of the ones who loved her has she killed with this love
She walked with a proud gait, gracefully gyrating her sides
and I beheld the branch of the willow as it was moved by her shaking
and as I rushed in pursuit of her in order to cut off her way and prevent her from continuing,
I said, 'The choicest wine of my saliva has matured and been purified
and he who does not drink himself to death with it is a weakling
In the red lips lie the cure for all those who are seriously ill
and if you wish to sip from them, here they are!'[1]

Most of the similes contained in these verses are unacceptable to the French since they say that one is not naturally drawn to saliva, for instance, because it is basically spit. If you compare the vulva of a virgin before she has been deflowered to a rose that has not yet blossomed and afterwards to a rose in bloom, that is considered gruesome by the French. They believe

1. The main feature of the original Arabic is the rhyme in the second hemistichs: *lahā lahā; al-suhā sahā; bihā bahā; ummahā mahā; wadddihā dahā; hazz hāzzahā; mahāmahā; ṣafwihā wa hiya; rashfihā fahā.*

that eloquence is based on that which is accepted by a person's natural disposition.

It is said that the relation between rhetoric and eloquence is similar to that between prosody and poetry. And thus it is possible to find eloquence with someone who is not versed in the science of rhetoric, just as one can find an expert in rhetoric who is not eloquent.

Eloquence yields most benefit in poetry, speeches, etc., in the composition of works of literature and history. The biggest benefit of this science is that through it one attains the knowledge to unlock the secrets of divine revelation and its inimitability. The mission of the Prophet – may God bless him and grant him salvation! – took place at a time of poetry, verse and prophecies, and in order to support him, God the Almighty – Praise be upon Him – gave him the Qur'ān, which '*if men and jinn banded together to produce the like of this Qur'ān, they would never produce its like, not though they backed each other.*'[1] It appeared to people endowed with common sense that there is a Word that has power and above which there is no power, and which is unlike the words of mortal people, and so they believed in it and followed it, except those who deserved [divine] punishment. And so the Holy Qur'ān was sent down in accordance with the requirements of the circumstances, and the words and meanings of its expressions are suited to these circumstances. If you wish further explanation on the three sciences and knowledge about their rules, you should consult the books of *ma'ānī, bayān* and *badī'*.

Fifth Section. On logic

This is a science in which representative concepts and assertions are investigated through their links with other concepts.[2] It is well known that its creator was the sage *Arisṭū*, who is also known as Aristotle (*Arisṭāṭālīs*). In French books it is stated that it was he who perfected this art, that Plato (*Aflāṭūn*) also refined it and that Zeno (*Zanūn*)[3] put it down in writing. This science is to the heart what syntax is to language, prosody to verse, etc.

This science has *principles* and *intentions*. The principles are the *concepts* and *assertions*, whereas its intentions are the *definitions* and *syllogisms*. The

1. Cf. Qur. XVII:89; trans. A. Arberry, 1983: 284.
2. Al-Ṭahṭāwī refers here to the role of logic as a tool (όργανον), Aristotle's logic writings commonly being known as *Organon*.
3. The philosopher Zeno of Elea (*floruit* 5th c. bc) is best known for the rhetorical method of ή εις το αδυνατον απαγωγη (Lat. *reductio ad absurdum*), which he used to great effect in defence of his tutor Parmenides.

concept (*taṣawwur*) is an awareness without a judgement, and its opposite is the assertion (*taṣdīq*). If we imagine the being of a man without attaching an affirmative or negative judgement to it, then this is a concept. On the other hand, if one judges him to be learned, for instance, then that is an assertion. There are two types of concepts – *simple* (*basīṭ*) and *composite* (*murakkab*). The simple concept is the perception of something devoid of its features. The composite variety is the perception of a thing with some of its characteristics. An example of the first type is when you imagine man without thinking about him as a moving being. An example of the second type is when you imagine him as distinguishing himself from inanimate beings through his movement.

Concepts exist only as isolated terms, just as the assertion exists only in the form of *propositions*. A proposition (*qaḍiyya*) is a judgement that is produced by the affirmation or negation of one concept in relation to another. The concept to which the affirmation or negation is attributed is called the *subject* (*mawḍūʿ*), whereas the concept to which the said subject is ascribed is called the *predicate* (*maḥmūl*). The subject and the predicate are called *the two parts* (terms) *of the proposition*. These two parts are joined by a third, called the *copula* (*rābi-ṭa*). For example, when you say '*Zayd faṣīḥ*' ('Zayd [is] eloquent'), *Zayd* is the subject, *faṣīḥ* is the predicate, and the copula is implicit [in Arabic], and is equivalent to '*Zayd huwa al-faṣīḥ*' ('Zayd is the eloquent one')[1] or '*Zayd yakūnu faṣīḥan*' ('Zayd will be an eloquent one'). If you say '*Zayd huwa al-faṣīḥ*', then the copula is visible. A proposition is either *universal* (*kulliyya*), which means that it encompasses all individuals, as when you say 'every human being is the creation of God the Almighty', or *particular* (*juz'iyya*), as when you say 'some animals are human beings'. Every proposition – whether universal or particular – is restricted. Propositions can also be *individual* (*shakhṣiyya*) or *indefinite* (*muhmala*). The former is true in, for instance, '*Zayd qā'im*' ('Zayd is standing'), the latter in, for instance, '*al-insān kātib*' ('a human being is someone who writes'), irrespective of whether it is universal or particular. A proposition can also be *natural* (*ṭabīʿī*) as in, for instance, '*al-ẓulm radī* [sic]' ('injustice is bad'), as well as *simple* and *composite*. The simple proposition is one that does not have multiple subjects and predicates, as when you say 'virtue is praiseworthy and vice is blameworthy'. By contrast, the composite proposition is one in which only the subject or predicate, or both, consist

1. The pronoun *huwa* (3rd person sing. m.) inserted in the nominal sentence is called *ḍamīr al-faṣl* ('the pronoun of separation'), *ḍamīr al-ʿimād* ('the pronoun of support') or *al-diʿāma* ('the support') by Arab grammarians.

of several parts, as when you say 'virtue and vice are opposites', 'virtue is desirable and wanted' or 'virtue and vice are irreconcilable opposites', etc. If the proposition is composite, it is made up of several simple propositions and, in order to refute it, it is sufficient to refute one of its terms.

As for the *definitions* (*ta'rīf*), these are the intentions of the concepts and 'rectifiers' (*muṣaḥḥiḥāt*) of the propositions. They can be *limitative* (*ta'rīf bi 'l-ḥadd*), *formal* (*ta'rīf bi 'l-rasm*) or *verbal* (*lafẓī*). An example of a limitative definition is when you say '*al-insān ḥayawān nāṭiq*' ('man is a rational animal'). An example of a formal definition is when you say '*al-insān ḥayawān kātib*' ('man is a writing animal'). An example of a verbal definition is when you say '*al-insān huwa al-Ādamī*' ('man is the human being'), if we assume that the term *Ādamī* (namely, human beings as the children of Adam) is more famous or better known than the expression *insān* ('human being'). Both the limitative and formal definitions are subdivided into *complete* (*tāmm*) and *incomplete* (*nāqiṣ*) categories, depending on whether they are made up of the near or far category (or class), a specific characteristic or a general accident (or attribute) applicable to each separately or all together. All of this is explained in the books on Logic.

The *syllogism* (*qiyās*) constitutes the basic goal of the science of Logic. It is something that, by itself, requires another assertion. An example of this is when we say that 'God the Almighty – praise be to Him – will definitely wreak vengeance on the oppressor on behalf of the oppressed', and you reply that 'God the Almighty – praise be to Him – is a righteous judge, and everyone who is righteous wreaks vengeance on the oppressor on behalf of the oppressed'. The result [conclusion] is then the following: 'God the Almighty – praise be to Him – wreaks vengeance on the oppressor on behalf of the oppressed'. If we accept the first two propositions, then we must also accept the third. The first two propositions are called *premises* (*muqaddama*), one of them being the 'smaller' (or minor), the other being the 'greater' (or major). The *conclusion* (*natīja*) constitutes the quintessence of the syllogism. The syllogism is *valid* (*ṣaḥīḥ*) when the substance and the form are true, and *invalid* (*fāsid*) when only one of them is. The soundness of the substance denotes that all its propositions are true, whereas the soundness of the form refers to the fact that it is arranged in such a way that its conclusion is inevitable. A valid syllogism is called an *argument* (*ḥujja*) or *proof* (*burhān*), whereas an invalid syllogism or proof is known as a *sophism* (*sufisṭa*); this resembles a valid syllogism, but is not, since its apparent conclusion does not hold fast to the valid premises. In French books, the basis on which the true syllogism rests and distinguishes itself from sophistry is that it is rooted in two principles: one is built on soundness, the other on wrongness. These entail that what is required for the requirement of one thing is required for that thing [specifically], whereas that which negates one thing and negates another is identical to that which negates another thing, or both of them together. This is how this is applied to the syllogism: if you are asked whether wrath is blameworthy and you wish to prove that it is, then you search for the core of the proposition, which is the subject. From the whole of the definition of wrath you will see that it is a flaw. This means that the word 'wrath' includes the meaning of flaw. You then compose a premise as follows: 'wrath is a flaw'. Then you oppose 'flaw' and 'censure', which makes up the predicate of the proposition, and you will find that the flaw requires censure, and you say 'the flaw is blameworthy'. And when you see that 'wrath' requires 'flaw', and 'flaw' requires 'censure', you conclude from this that wrath is blameworthy. Any syllogism to which you cannot apply this rule is a sophism; for instance, 'Aristotle is a philosopher', 'some philosophers are virtuous' and so 'Aristotle is virtuous'. This conclusion is invalid. The propositions do not require a conclusion since the fact that Aristotle is a philosopher and that some philosophers are virtuous does not require that Aristotle is virtuous. Some parts of the syllogism may be omitted because they are known, as when you say, for instance, 'virtue is praiseworthy, and it is desirable that you should acquire it.'

A syllogism can also be *categorial* (*ḥamalī*) or *conditional* (*sharṭī*). All of the above is an example of the categorial syllogism. An example of the conditional type would be: 'if the sun rose, it would be day, but the sun does not come up', the conclusion being that it is not day. This can all be found in books on Logic.

In the same way that the Franks apply words to the rules of the French language and call this 'grammatical analysis',[1] so, too, do they apply them to the rules of Logic and call it 'logical analysis'. For instance, if one wishes to analyse 'Zayd is outstanding' grammatically, one says that *Zayd* is the *mubtada'* (grammatical subject), and *outstanding* its *khabar* (grammatical predicate),[2] or something of this sort, which is in accordance with the rules of their syntax. If you wish to conduct

1. al-Ṭahṭāwī's translation *i'rāb naḥwī* aptly extrapolates the original to an Arabic context with its reference to (desinential) inflections (*i'rāb*) and syntactic features (*naḥw*).
2. The Arabic *mubtada'* ('that with which a start is made') and *khabar* ('announcement') are used in relation to *nominal* sentences (*jumla ismiyya*). For a verbal sentence (*jumla fi'liyya*), the corresponding terms are *fā'il* ('agent') and *fi'l* ('action', 'verb'). At the proposition level, the terms used for 'predicate' and 'subject' are, respectively, *musnad*

a logical analysis, then you would say that *Zayd* is the *mawḍū'* and *outstanding* the *mahmūl*, which is an individual proposition. This they do for all sentences.

Sixth Section. On the ten categories that are attributed to Aristotle[1]

It is well known that Aristotle limited intelligible things to ten ranks, which are called *categories* (*maqūlāt*); he put matter in the first category and all of the accidents in the nine others.[2]

The first category is that of *substance* (*al-jawhar*), which is corporeal and spiritual.

The second [category] is that of *quantity* (*al-kamm*); this is said to be *discrete* (*munfaṣal*) if the parts are dispersed as is the case, for instance, with numbers, or *continuous* if the parts are clustered. It can be either *consecutive*, like the movement of the heavenly bodies, or *static*. It is what is called the size and extent of bodies in terms of length, width and depth. Of the length it is also the lines that are intelligible, of the width, the planes, whereas both together with the depth make up the instructional volumes (*jism ta'līmī*).[3]

The third [category] is that of *quality* (*al-kayf*), which Aristotle subdivided into four parts:

the *dispositions*, i.e. aptitudes of the mind or the body that are acquired through repeated actions, such as sciences, virtues, vices, the ability to write, draw and dance;

natural strength, such as the strength of the soul and of the body – e.g. perception, volition, the power to memorize things, the five senses and the ability to walk;

('that which leans upon [the subject]') and *al-musnad ilayhi* ('that on which [the attribute] leans'). See W. Wright, 1981: 250ff.

1. This chapter is a translation of two pages of the already mentioned *La Logique ou l'Art de Penser...* (Book I, chap. III, 'Des dix catégories d'Aristote') by A. Arnauld and P. Nicole [1965: 49–51 (1824: 48–50)].
2. Cf. Fr. '*On peut rapporter à cette considération des idées, selon leurs objets, les dix catégories d'Aristote, puisque ce ne sont que diverses classes auxquelles ce philosophe a voulu réduire tous les objets de nos pensées, en comprenant toutes les substances sous la première, et tous les accidens sous les neuf autres. Les voici.*' (A. Arnauld, 1965: 49–50).
3. Cf. Fr. '*La Quantité, qui s'appelle discrète quand les parties n'en sont point liées, comme le nombre. Continue quand elles sont liées, et alors elle est ou successive, comme le temps, le mouvement. Ou permanente, qui est ce qu'on appelle autrement l'espace, ou l'étendue en longueur, largeur, profondeur; la longueur seule faisant les lignes, la longueur et la largeur les surfaces, et les trois ensemble les solides.*' (A. Arnauld, 1965: 50).

the *powers of perception*: e.g. hardness, softness, density, coldness, heat, the colours, sounds, smells and flavours;
the *forms* and *shapes* through which quantity manifests itself, such as roundness, squareness, sphericalness and cubicalness.[1]

The fourth category is that of *apposition* (*al-iḍāfa*), i.e. the relation between two things, such as between father and son, master and servant, a king and [his] subjects, or the relation between the ability and the will of those who are concerned by them, between sight and that which is virtually visible, or like the relation that requires participation, such as the similar, the equal, the dissimilar, the smaller and the larger.[2]

The fifth category is that of *doing* (*al-fiʿl*), whether it be within the actor – such as walking, standing, dancing, knowing or loving – or directed towards someone else, such as hitting, killing, etc.[3]

The sixth category is *the state of being acted upon* (*al-infiʿāl*), such as being broken or bent.[4]

The seventh category is that of the *where* (*al-ayna*), i.e. the answer to the question related to place, such as when you say 'in Egypt', 'in the harim' or 'in bed'.[5]

The eighth category is that of the *when* (*al-matā*), which provides an anwer to questions related to time, such as when you say 'When did so and so live?' and someone replies, 'One hundred years ago'; or 'When did this happen?' 'Yesterday'.

The ninth category is that of *situation* (*al-waḍʿ*), such as the state of sitting down or standing, or the fact that something is before or after, opposite or to the right or the left.[6]

---

1. Cf. Fr. '*La Qualité, dont Aristote fait quatre espèces. La 1. Comprend* les habitudes, *c'est-à-dire, les dispositions d'esprit ou de corps, qui s'acquièrent par des actes réiterés, comme les sciences, les vertus, les vices; l'adresse de peindre, d'écrire, de danser. La 2.* Les puissances naturelles, *telles que sont les facultés de l'âme ou du corps, l'entendement, la volonté, la memoire, les cinq sens, la puissance de marcher. La 3.* Les qualités sensibles, *comme la dureté, la mollesse, la pesanteur, le froid, le chaud, les couleurs, les sons, les odeurs, les divers goûts. La 4. La forme et la figure, qui est la détermination extérieure de la quantité, comme être rond, carré, sphérique, cubique.*' (A. Arnauld, 1965: 50).
2. Cf. Fr. '*La Relation, ou le rapport d'une chose à une autre, comme de père, de fils, de maître, de valet, de roi, de sujet; de la puissance à son objet, de la vue à ce qui est visible; et tout ce qui marque comparaison, comme semblable, égal, plus grand, plus petit.*' (A. Arnauld, 1965: 50).
3. Cf. Fr. '*L'agir, ou en soi-même, comme marcher, danser, connoître, aimer; ou hors de soi; comme battre, couper, rompre, éclairer, échauffer.*' (A. Arnauld, 1965: 50).
4. Cf. Fr. '*Pâtir, être battu, être rompu, être éclairé, être échauffé.*' (A. Arnauld, 1965: 50).
5. Cf. Fr. '*Comme, être à Rome, à Paris, dans son cabinet, dans son lit, dans sa chaise.*' (A. Arnauld, 1965: 50).
6. Cf. Fr. '*La Situation, être assis, debout, couché, devant, derrière, à droit, à gauche.*' (A. Arnauld,

The tenth category is that of *possession* (*al-mulk*), i.e. the fact that something exists with a person or is attributed to him, such as clothes, fineries, weapons – this category is that of belonging and possession.[1]

So, these are the ten categories mentioned by Aristotle, and which are counted among the hidden things (or mysteries). The Franks say that the knowledge of these categories does not have a great use and that it may even be harmful for two reasons.[2] The first is that people think that [these categories] are based on rational judgement and that they are subject to deduction-based limitation. However, they are merely conventional and artificial, and their limitation is that one person put forth this division to show his ascendancy over others, despite the fact that among them there may be someone who has another, new classification. Indeed, another person actually limited the categories to seven, calling them 'intelligible matter' (*mawādd 'aqliyya*).[3]

The first fundamental constituent is the *mind*, or the thinking substance;
the *body*, or the extended substance;
the *size*, or smallness of each particle of matter (atom);
the *situation* of the atoms in relation to each other;
the *shape* of things;
movement;
rest.[4]

The second reason is that someone who has learned the categories

---

1965: 51).

1. Cf. Fr. '*Avoir, c'est-à-dire avoir quelque chose autour de soi pour servir de vêtemens, ou d'ornement, ou d'armure, comme être habillé, être couronné, être chaussé, être armé.*' (A. Arnauld, 1965: 51).
2. Cf. Fr. '*Voilà les X. Catégories d'Aristote dont on fait tant de mystères, quoiqu'à dire le vrai ce soit une chose de soi très peu utile, et qui non seulement ne sert guères à former le jugement, ce qui est le but de la vraie logique, mais qui souvent y nuit beaucoup pour deux raisons qu'il est important de remarquer.*' (A. Arnauld, 1965: 51).
3. Cf. Fr. '*La première est, qu'on regarde ces Catégories comme une chose établie sur la raison et sur la vérité, au-lieu que c'est une chose toute arbitraire, et qui n'a de fondement que l'imagination d'un homme qui n'a eu aucune autorité de prescrire une loi aux autres, qui ont autant de droit que lui d'arranger autrement les objets de leurs pensées, chacun selon sa manière de philosopher. Et, en effet, il y en a qui ont compris en ce distique tout ce que l'on considère selon une nouvelle philosophie en toutes les choses du monde.* Mens, mensura, quies, motus, positura, figura – sunt cum materia cunctarum exordia rerum.' (A. Arnauld, 1965: 51). One should point out that this was not a new or another philosophy, as al-Ṭahṭāwī seems to indicate, but simply a mnemomic representation of Aristotle's Categories by Aegedius Regius (Gilles de Coninck, 1571–1633).
4. Cf. Fr. '*C'est-à-dire que ces gens-là se persuadent que l'on peut rendre raison de toute la nature en n'y considérant que ces sept choses ou modes. 1.* Mens, *l'esprit ou la substance qui pense.* 2. Materia, *le corps ou la substance étendue.* 3. Mensura, *la grandeur ou la petitesse de chaque partie de la matière.* 4. Postura, *leur situation à l'égard les unes des autres.* 5. Figura, *leur figure.*

contents himself with hypothetical expressions, thinking that he knows something about things of which he is entirely ignorant and that in reality have a clear and distinct meaning.[1]

Seventh Section. On the science of arithmetic, which is called arithmétique in the language of the Franks

You should know that the science of arithmetic (*al-artīmāṭīqī*) is one of the pure mathematical sciences. This is because Frankish scholars divided mathematics into a *pure* and an *impure*, or *mixed*, type. The pure mathematical sciences include arithmetic,[2] algebra, geometry, etc. As for mixed mathematics, these are the mechanical sciences, the art of moving weights (kinetics) and so on. Pure mathematical sciences are those in which quantities and things that may increase or decrease are studied. Mixed mathematics are those in which external elements – from physics or other sciences – come into play. Arithmetic is the most important of the mathematical sciences. Historians have shown that the founders of this science were the Byzantines (*Rūm*) of Syria, i.e. the Phoenicians,[3] and the ancient Egyptians. These two peoples were the first to put together the numerals and arithmetic, and to arrange them in a particular order. Indeed, the scholar Pythagoras (*Fīthāghūras)* travelled from Greece to Egypt and studied this science there. It was well known among the ancients that the science of arithmetic was a Phoenician invention. It is said that they were also the first to use lists and ledgers.

It seems that the fingers were the first method used by people for counting, which is why the first series of numerals are the tens; the second, the tens of tens, i.e. the hundreds; the third, the tens of hundreds, i.e. the

6. Motus, *leur mouvement.* 7. Quies, *leur repos ou moindre mouvement.*' (A. Arnauld, 1965: 51)

1. Cf. Fr. '*La seconde raison qui rend l'étude des Catégories dangereuse est qu'elle accoutume les hommes à se payer de mots, et à s'imaginer qu'ils savent toutes choses, lorsqu'ils n'en connoissent que des noms arbitraires qui n'en forment dans l'esprit aucune idée claire & distincte …*' (A. Arnauld, 1965: 51).
2. The Arabic text has *'ilm al-ḥisāb al-ghubārī wa 'l-hawā'ī* – 'the science of arithmetic on the ground (*ghubār*: 'dust')', i.e. in the sand (or on a board spread with dust), 'and in the air' (*hawā'*). Cf. *EI2*, s.v.v. "ḥisāb", "ḥisāb al-ghubār" (M. Souissi). The importance of arithmetic to the modern European sciences was recognized very early on in Egypt, as witness the fact that one of the first books to be printed at the government press in Būlāq was Shihāb al-Dīn Aḥmad b. Muḥammad b. 'Imād's *Lam' yasīra fī 'ilm al-ḥisāb* (1826).
3. *al-Ṣūriyyūn*, i.e. the ancient Tyrians, in reference to the most famous Phoenician city-state of Tyre (Ṣūr), in north-west Lebanon.

thousands; and so on and so forth, because there are ten fingers, and one goes from one series to another by going from ten to ten.[1] As the fingers can be used to distinguish ten things only, there was a need for another method and other marks, and so they took small stones, grains of sand, wheat, etc., and used them to determine the exact quantity of what they wanted to count, just as this is still done today among certain savages in America (*Amrīka*) and in some other parts of the world. Some of the ancient nations did not have a language in which they could express numbers above tens; so, for instance, in order to say 127, they would say seven and two times ten, and ten times ten. This was because the ancients mentioned the smaller number before the large one, starting with the units, then the tens, followed by the hundreds, etc. Some authors said that Hebrew and Greek books provided proof of this, and the same method is found in the Arabic language for amounts below 100.[2] However, nations have acquired an in-depth knowledge and mastery of the complexities of the science of arithmetic and have perfected it.

The science of arithmetic is defined as the science involving the study of numbers in terms of the [various] operations to which they are subject. The number is a collection of units, and is divided into two types, *viz.* integers and fractions, to which someone else has added a third, i.e. a composite of both, which is called *a number including fractions*. Related to these numbers are four operations, which are: addition, subtraction, multiplication and division. All of these are known in the books dealing with this art.

As for the science of geometry, its object is the measuring of the three expanses [dimensions], i.e. *length, width* and *depth*, as indicated in our [mnemonic] poem on the science of geometry:[3]

Its object is the measuring of the extension
Its discovery lies in the three dimensions
Length, width and depth too
but this requires no explanation

As for geography, an abridgement of it has been included in the

1. Cf. J. Lemoine, 1932.
2. In fact, the more classical counting method in Arabic, whether below or above 100, is to put the units first, followed by the tens, hundreds and thousands. In MSA, only the 'European' method is used for numerals above 100. Linguistically, al-Ṭahṭāwī's comment is therefore of some interest since it proves that the traditional order had already fallen into desuetude.
3. See Translator's Introduction.

introduction to this book. However, we need to mention its divisions here. When one looks at Earth in terms of its shape, immobility or movement, and its relation to other celestial bodies, then we talk of *mathematical geography* or *the science of the physiognomy of the world* [cosmography]. If you consider it from the point of view of its material in terms of soil or water and the manifestations related to it on the surface, such as mountains, then it is called *natural geography*, since it is related to the naure of the planet. If you look at it from the point of view of the differences between the peoples in terms of religion or race, then it is called *religious geography*. If you view it from the point of view of the differences between peoples in terms of administration, political structures, rules, regulations and laws then this is called *administrative* or *political geography*. One may also consider it from the point of view of the religious, political, etc., changes and upheavals that take place during the various eras on Earth and in various parts of the world; this science is known as *historical geography*.

These are the principles, but the division is not exhaustive; those wishing to know more about this should consult our treatise entitled *al-Ta'rībāt al-shāfiyya li murīd al-jughrāfiya* ('Healing Translations for the Pupil of Geography'), in which this is clearly explained. At this point, we should however discuss one of the issues related to mathematical geography, i.e. astronomy. We have said that the Franks divided the heavenly stars into those that are fixed,[1] planets, satellites, and comets.[2] They counted the sun among the fixed stars, and considered Earth a planet, and the moon a satellite inasmuch as it follows the path of the planets. This school of thought (*madhhab*) they call the *Copernican system*.[3] Recent Frankish scholars have discovered a number of planets, which remained unknown to the ancients because they lacked the instruments that [modern] Franks have at their disposal. As a result, the number of known planets among them has reached eleven, without counting the sun and the moon since, as we have seen, the former is considered a fixed star and the latter a satellite. At this juncture, we should like to mention these planets, ranked according to their proximity from the sun. They are: Mercury; Venus; Earth; Mars; Vesta (*Wistah*), i.e. the fiery planet; Juno (*Yūnūn*), which is called Jupiter's wife, and the daughter of Saturn; Ceres (*Siriys*), which is also referred to as *Qirīs*, i.e. the 'spike (of grain)

1. *thawābit* (sing. *thābit*). The idea of 'fixed stars' emerged in Antiquity and had its origins in the fact that certain celestial bodies did not seem to move in relation to one another.
2. The last two are *sayyārat al-sayyāra* ('planet of a planet') and *dhawāt al-dhanb* ('those with a tail'), respectively.
3. *madhhab Kubarnīq al-nimsāwī*, 'the school of Copernicus the Austrian'.

planet'; Pallas (*Ballās*), which means the father of Aurora;[1] Jupiter; Saturn; and Uranus (*Ūrānūs*), which means the highest star. The circular movement of these new stars cannot be easily observed with the naked eye because of the small size of some of them and the distance of others. With the exception of Uranus, they can be observed only through telescopes, which is why they are called *telescopic planets*[2] by the Franks. The Franks hope to discover other planets.[3]

As for history, this is also something that needs to be studied by people,

1. *falaq*, 'daybreak'.
2. *al-sayyārāt al-naẓẓāriyya*; it is highly implausible that al-Ṭahṭāwī's readers would have understood the latter word, which is an adjective derived from the neologism *naẓẓāra* (or *naẓẓārāt*), i.e. 'glasses'; cf. E. Bocthor, 1882: 799 ('télescope, lunette d'approche'). On the other hand, it may be a misprint for '*naẓariyya*' ('visible').
3. It is here that al-Ṭahṭāwī's manuscript originally had a passage on the turning of planet earth: '*wa qāla ba'ḍ 'ulamā' al-Ifranj inna al-qawl bi-dawrān al-arḍ wa istidāratihā lā yukhālifu mā waradat bihā 'l-kutub al-samāwiya, wa dhālika li-anna al-kutub al-samāwiyya qad dhakirat hādhihi 'l-ashyā* (sic) *fī ma'raḍ wa'ẓ wa naḥwahu jarīyan 'alā mā yuẓhiru 'l-'āmma lā tadqīqan falsafiyyan mathalan warada fī 'l-sharḥ anna Allāh ta'ālā waqafa al-shams fa 'l-murād bi-wuqūf al-shams ta'khīran ghiyābuhā 'an al-a'yun wa hādhā yaḥṣulu bi-tawqīf al-arḍ wa innamā awqa'a Allāh al-wuqūf 'alā 'l-shams li-annahā hiya allatī yaẓharu fī ra'y al-'ayn siyaruha intahā fa ẓāhir kalāmihi annahu irtakaba ghāyat al-ta'wīl*' ('A Frankish scholar has said that the statement regarding the circular movement of earth and its roundness does not run counter to what appears on this subject in the holy books. This is because the holy books, when they mentioned these things, did so in the form of moral admonitions, etc., in accordance with the way things appeared to the people, without scientific accuracy. For instance, in the divine scripture it is stated that God the Almighty stopped the sun, which means that he delayed the time during which it disappears from the eye, while, in fact, this is caused by the stagnation of the earth. The claim that God causes the stopping of the sun is due to the fact that the sun seems to have a movement to the eye. End quote. It appears that the statement by this scholar is the result of excessive interpretation' (Caussin de Perceval, 1833: 251; trans. 245–6). Despite his censure at the end of the citation, al-Ṭahṭāwī obviously deemed this passage too dangerous for inclusion, fearing severe criticism from the *'ulamā'*. However, the decision may also have been taken in consultation with Jomard; indeed, in his translation of Depping's *Aperçu Historique*, al-Ṭahṭāwī reports that his French mentor emphasized that any statements derogatory or defamatory of Islamic customs should be left out (al-Ṭahṭāwī, 1833: 3). It is worth noting that if these lines had not been chosen by Caussin de Perceval in his article, they would probably have been lost for ever. In fact, the French scholar included them for his own reasons, as witness his comment: '*Cette interprétation paraît bien hardie au cheikh Réfaa; mais, comme il sent la supériorité de nos connaissances astronomiques sur celles des Arabes, et l'impossibilité de les répandre parmi ses compatriotes, sans adopter notre système, il se résigne à marcher dans cette voix …*' (*ibid.*, 246). Al-Ṭahṭāwī himself returned to the issue in later works, albeit with great caution and circumspection, stating emphatically that one may *report* these European views, which are wholly unreligious; indeed, he peremptorily dismissed the rotation of the earth, adding that, in any case, Europeans would eventually renounce the Copernican system and readopt Ptolemy's; al-Ṭahṭāwī, 1838: I, 6; *idem*, 1898: 230–1(= 1973: III, 202–3). Finally, it is worth noting that some 50 years later, another *'ālim*, the Tunisian Bayram V would include a very similar passage in his geographical encyclopaedia: 1884–93: I, 6–7.

especially statesmen. Here, we shall include a nice fragment of what one Frankish author wrote in this regard:

History is like a public school that attracts every nation that seeks instruction. It is also the repository of experiences of past events that are helpful to the present situation. Through the inclusion of lessons learned from former times, it helps man to think about that which seems to be coming. Indeed, history can teach lessons to everybody who wishes to learn, irrespective of their rank or standing. It shows everyone the evil consequences ensuing from strife and discord between people, and this presents such a gruesome picture that they are driven towards adopting praiseworthy moral traits such as forbearance and justice. It is from history that kings learn that during the rule of a wisely governing king, power and his throne constitute shelter and protection.

Bossuet (Busūh)[1] *said that 'if one were to assume that history is useful only to princes, then it must be read to princes'. However, history opens its treasures more for the wise in order for him to gain an understanding of its secrets and symbols, so that, during his study, his mind will be diverted from the vicissitudes of the trivialities of human existence, after which it transports it [the mind] to more serious matters, revealing the many chains of time, the last link of which is attached to the creation of the world. And are these chains not like a huge field where people can at once observe all nations, states and times? Behold this overwhelming assembly that contains both happiness and misfortunes. How many cities have been destroyed, dynasties died out, kingdoms perished and forgotten, places ruined and tombs built? Everything eventually ends up in the grave, and it is the graves alone that extend above the field of the earth. How miserable and insignificant seems the beauty of worldly life when you look at it from the height of history. How unimportant and insignificant seems the human society of our time when it is put next to those of peoples of past centuries and ages. What a difference there is between the kings of our time, whose tangible stature can be measured by the onlooker, from the rulers of these past ages who appear to the eye as if they were tall mountains on the horizon of times past. What are our momentary wars and our love for ephemeral greatness and honour next to the wonders of the struggle waged by the ancients since the beginning of the world over one place or another,*

1. This is a quote from *Discours sur l'Histoire Universelle*, written by the famous bishop Jacques-Bénigne Bossuet 1627–1704) for his pupil, the dauphin, i.e. the eldest son of Louis XIV. This work remained very popular and there were innumerable editions/ reprints in the 19th century. The Tunisian statesman Khayr al-Dīn also mentions Bossuet (*Būssuwī*) whom he praises for the clarity of exposition in his general history essay (*ḥusn al-tabyīn fī khuṭbatihi 'alā al-tārīkh al-'āmm*), which became a model among all Europeans (1867: 57).

or over an inch of land? Anyone who takes a truthful look at the wonders of history will be attired in the dress of seriousness, doff the clothes of jest, climb the peak of observation and will see the world in its entirety at his feet, like an ocean on which ships laden with human hopes and aspirations float aimlessly; exposed to storms,[1] *they end up crashing into reefs, the shreds of former times being the only port where they can dock. And if you look [down] from this place with eyes devoid of greed you will see the wreckage of the transitory world and the futile praise avidly pursued by so many people but which amounts to nothing. And is it not so that fate brings with it misfortunes and vicissitudes in everything that it bestows and grants? Is there any kingdom of which we can be sure that its throne will not fall, or one for which there is no hope that its throne may be elevated? Indeed, have we not seen that in one temple's prayer niche* (qibla) *a number of differing religions alternated with each other? How many depravities have been committed in places where the virtues once resided? How often have the foundations of glory and wealth been followed by poverty and misery? How often have we seen barbarity and civilization descend upon the surface of this globe with hurried pace, and then exchanged their parts without any interval? What has become of you, o Ctesiphon*[2] *– you who once prospered in Asia and ruled all nations? O Nineveh of Jonah, Babylon of the Magians, Persepolis of the Persians and Solomon's Palmyra, how come your cities lie in ruins, while they were once the seats of states of science? Nothing has remained of your ancient glory and blinding brilliance except your names and a few stone engravings! However, none of the countries of the world has been struck by so many astounding calamities and strange scourges as the unfortunate land of Egypt, whose horses once overtook all those of other kingdoms in speed in the arenas of glory, science and wisdom. It is as if fate wanted to smite this country with everything at once, whether it be the greatest beneficence or torments of vengeance, even though there was not a single ancient nation that exerted themselves as did the [ancient] Egyptians, who through the lofty and impressive edifices of their temples sought to achieve eternal life. However, all of them have disappeared, perished, so that today's Egyptians do not constitute a race of a nation, but an amalgamation of heterogeneous elements, whose lineage goes back to a number of different races from Asia and Africa. They are like a mixture in which there is no common measure, and their features do not*

1. The Arabic continues the metaphor through a pun involving *'urḍa* ('exposed to') [*li 'l-riyāḥ*] and *'urḍ* as in *fī 'urḍ 'l-baḥr* ('at sea').
2. *al-Madā'in*. Although this is also the plural of *madīna* ('city'), alongside the more common *mudun*, there is little doubt that in this context it refers to the city of Ctesiphon (Seleucia on the Tigris), which was also known as *Madā'in Kisrā* (some 32km south of modern Baghdad) and served as capital to both the Parthian and Sasanian empires. For more details on this city, see *EI1*, s.v. 'al-Madā'in' (M. Streck).

make up a distinct shape by which it is possible to tell whether a person is Egyptian simply by looking at his face. Truly, it is as if all the nations of the world helped populate the land of the Nile.

[This passage is] a translation of the introduction by Mr Agoub (*Ākūb*) on the history of Egypt.[1] At the end of it, he praises our ruler, he who resurrected Egypt from nothingness. He also praised him in a French poem (*qaṣīda*), which he called *Naẓm al-ʿuqūd fī kasr al-ʿūd*, and which I have translated. I have included a few passages of it in the Second Section of the Third Essay [of this book].

The science of history is a vast discipline, and with the will of God and the help of our ruler, all of the different areas of history will be translated from French into our language.[2] In short, we have, in accordance with God's will and with the eager support from our ruler who is a great lover of the sciences and the arts, undertaken to translate the two sciences of history and geography in our felicitous Egypt, so that his rule will count as an era that is used to mark the beginning of sciences and learning that are being regenerated in Egypt, just as they were in the time of the caliphs in Baghdad.[3]

1. J. Agoub, *Discours Historique sur l'Egypte*, Paris, 1823. Even though Agoub was himself Egyptian, al-Ṭahṭāwī refers to him at the beginning of the quote as 'a Frankish scholar', and again uses *al-khawāja* as the term of address (see above).
2. Unfortunately, the author's high hopes would be dashed as fewer than ten European history books were translated during the whole of Muḥammad ʿAlī's time; this also includes those that were rendered only into Turkish. See T. Bianchi, 1843.
3. This is, of course, a reference to the Golden Age of the ʿAbbāsid caliphate (750–1258), which succeeded the Omayyads and arguably became the most celebrated dynasty of Islam. The ʿAbbāsid caliphate (which included rulers such as Hārūn al-Rashīd and al-Ma'mūn) was a time of territorial expansion and empire-building but also of unparalleled intellectual activity. To this day, this period is considered the acme of both Muslim and Arab achievement.

Epilogue

On Our Return from Paris to Egypt and a Number of Other Matters

The reader of this *riḥla* no doubt wishes to know the end of this voyage, on which our ruler has spent more money than any other king before him, and the like of which has never been heard in the chronicles of any known nation. The fact that the travelogue is written in the Khedivial reign proves that his Eminence, the high-aspiring one, has pondered the effects of things and achieved the objective in everything he has prescribed, and all of this will be remembered in the course of time. There is no doubt that this is equal to the ambition of a Caesar, whereas even the force of Alexander the Great (*Iskander al-akbar*) would grow weary in the attainment of similar things. Not even somebody like Napoleon would be able to surpass him with his magnificence, while a Frederick (*Afrīdrīzūs*) [the Great] would not [even] be able to direct his attention or hopes towards it. All the more so since the decision by our ruler to send the Efendis to Paris has yielded the utmost results and has borne fruit since the majority of them have acquired the favour of the Benefactor by rushing towards what was required with both seriousness and zeal. And in doing so, he – may God the Almighty protect him – has suckled infants in all countries at the breast of sciences so that they became men of perfect learning. Indeed, some of them achieved the ranks of prominent personalities among the Franks, whether it be as administrator for royal affairs for one who has reached perfection in civil administration, like his highness ʿAbdī Efendi[1] – the master of proficiency, the pen and good fortune, he of noble descent and sound judgement[2]; as a fully accomplished master in the administration of military affairs; as an expert in marine affairs or medicine; as a specialist in the natural sciences; or as an adept in

1. On ʿAbdī Efendi Shukrī, see above.
2. This construction, while convoluted in English, pandered to a predilection for *ijnās* on the part of the readership: '*ṣāḥib al-barāʿa wa 'l-yarāʿa rabb al-ṭāliʿ al-saʿīd wa dhū al-najāba wa 'l-ra'y al-sadīd.*'

agriculture and botany. Others surpass their peers in the arts and crafts and are capable of opening factories, indisputably gaining a name for themselves through their expertise. If I were not afraid of expanding too much, I would mention all the Efendis that have attained their aim, in accordance with the high ranks they achieved, but, my word, this is not possible because of the number of individuals involved. However, I cannot omit mention, albeit briefly, of some of them whose eminence resulted in their achieving the highest distinction. How can I not talk of the honourable Muṣṭafā Mukhtār Bey Efendi,[1] who attained the same degree as leading French scholars in the science of military organization, after reaching a high level in the sciences and expertise in both its form and concepts? There can be no doubt of his eminence in the administrative sciences and that he has acquired all the knowledge [that exists about this science] in Frankish nations. May God expand knowledge in the kingdom of Egypt and Syria through him, make him find favour with our great ruler and general and have lions as offspring. It is not from one who has acquired learning that good deeds ensue, as the poet says:

It is customary for the sword to pride itself on its substance
but it does not work except in the hands of a hero

As for the honourable Ḥasan Bey Efendi[2] and the marine Efendis, their merits and the perfection of their sciences have been established by their distinction among their peers. The reputation of Iṣṭifān Efendi[3] does not require further proof either; he has successfully acquired the necessary sciences and arts. The understanding of Alṭīn Efendi[4] in all

1. See above.
2. See above.
3. Born in Sivas, in Central Turkey, the Armenian Iṣṭifān (Eṣṭefān) Efendi al-Armanī was 22 when he arrived in Paris to study civil administration. After his return to Egypt in 1831, he was put in charge of equipment at the Ministry of Public Education, after which he joined the Administration College (*madrasat al-idāra*). He was the only one to return to Paris as he headed the Egyptian military school between 1844 and 1849, and also acted as tutor to Muḥammad ʿAlī's grandsons, Aḥmad and Ismāʿīl (the future Khedive). Iṣṭifān Bey even married into the French aristocracy, and was involved in the creation of an Egyptian information (or propaganda) agency in Paris in 1851. See J. Heyworth-Dunne, 1939: 160, 243ff.; A. Louca, 1970: *passim*; J. Tagher, 1949; E. Jomard, 1828.
4. This is, of course, the famous Artin Bey, though at the time he was still simply Artīn Sikyās. Born in Constantinople in 1804, of Armenian extraction, he studied civil administration in Paris. It is worth noting that Artin's brother Khusrū was also a member of the student mission. After Artin's return to Egypt, he would play a major role in the modernization of the country's educational system, his first important post being that of head of the newly founded engineering college (*al-muhandiskhāna*)

areas of knowledge cannot be gainsaid and neither can that of Khalīl Efendi Maḥmūd,[1] whereas the learning of Aḥmad Efendi Yūsuf[2] has been irrefutably ascertained. In short, most of the Efendis have achieved the desired objective and have returned in order to spread [their knowledge] among the nations of Islam.

---

in Būlāq in 1834. One year later, he became head of the *madrasat al-Idāra,* as well as member of the High Council (*al-majlis al-ʿalī*), with his appointment as head of the Schools Council following in 1836. In 1839, he became secretary to Muḥammad ʿAlī. In 1844, he succeeded his coreligionist patron, Boghos Bey, as Minister for Foreign Affairs after the latter's demise in 1844. It was in this capacity that he met the French authors Maxime du Camp and G. Flaubert (who transcribed his name as Hartim-Bey or Artim-Bey). The former gave the following description: '*un Arménien à cheveux blancs, très fin, peu véridique, dont le regard ne se fixait pas volontiers et dont le nez énorme ressemblait à un bec inachevé.*' Artin Bey's political career met with an untimely and dramatic end when, after his appointment as Prime Minister by the Khedive ʿAbbās Pasha (1848–54), he was accused of embezzlement. In order to escape prosecution, he fled to Constantinople. It was on his way there, during a stopover in Beirut, that he again met up with Flaubert and du Camp, and all three travelled to Rhodes on the same ship. He died in 1859. One of Artin's sons, Yaʿqūb, followed in his father's footsteps and became Minister for Education in Egypt (cf. his *L'Instruction Publique en Egypte*, Paris, E. Leroux, 1890). See G. Flaubert, 1991: 103, 173; J. Heyworth-Dunne, 1939: 142–4, 159; A. Louca, 1970: *passim*; A. Naaman, 1965: lxiv, 122; M. du Camp, 1882: I, 526.

1. Born in Cairo in 1806, Khalīl Efendi studied agriculture in Paris and subsequently went on to get some hands-on experience at an experimental farm in Roville, near Nancy. He returned to Egypt in early 1832. Despite his excellent results, he was one of several returnees whose qualities and achievements were not recognized by the ruler. Khalīl at one stage even offered his services as a tourist guide, in which capacity he met Gustave Flaubert and Maxime du Camp when they visited the country, Flaubert referring to him as an '*ingénieur arabe*'. He was of great assistance to them and also acted as their tutor in all matters Egyptian. According to M. du Camp, Khalīl had attended classes at the Ecole Polytechnique and Ecole de Droit, after which he went to Lyons to study commerce and silk weaving. Unfortunately, there are no records to substantiate the claims made by du Camp, who also adds that 'Khalill-efendi' had been offered the position of binder at al-Azhar by Muḥammad ʿAlī. His refusal to accept had led to his falling out of favour with the ruler. Still according to du Camp, Khalīl subsequently converted to protestantism and received an allowance from the British consulate! E. Jomard translated one of Khalīl's works under the title *Mémoire sur le Calendrier Arabe avant l'Islamisme et sur la Naissance et l'âge du Prophète Mohammad* (Paris, 1858). Khalīl Maḥmūd also published a translation of a French manual under the title *Kanz al-barāʿa fī mabādīʾ fann al-zirāʿa* ('The Treasure of Proficiency Regarding the Principles of the Art of Agriculture', Būlāq, 1243/1838) See G. Flaubert, 1991: 245–6, 316; M. du Camp, 1882: I, 545–6, II, 472–3; A. Naaman, 1965: 200–03; A. Silvera, 1980: 14; A. Louca, 1970: 50, 115; E. Jomard, 1828: 99, 100; Ā. Nuṣayr, 189 (6/356).
2. Born in Cairo in 1806, Aḥmad Efendi Yūsuf studied chemistry in Paris and, after his return to Egypt in 1832, he worked at the Cairo Mint and was sent to the Sudan on a gold-finding mission by Muḥammad ʿAlī, on whose orders he is said to have visited goldmines in Mexico. ʿU. Ṭūsūn, 1934: 43. According to J. Heyworth-Dunne, it was Aḥmad Efendi Yūsuf (and not Khalīl) who studied agriculture and went to Roville, where he developed a tangerine variant, which today still bears his name (ECA *Yūsif Afandī*, 'tangerine'); J. Heyworth-Dunne, 1939: 151; A. Silvera, 1980: 15.

At this stage, by way of completing this *riḥla*, we should like to talk about the humble servant's return to Egypt.

We left Paris in the month of Ramaḍān of the year 1246,[1] and travelled to Marseilles in order to take to the sea there and return to Alexandria. We passed by the city of Fontainebleau (*Funtanblū*), near Paris, where there is a royal palace that is famous since it is there that in 1815 [sic] of the Christian era Napoleon renounced his throne and abdicated as emperor of France.[2] At this palace you can see a stone column built in the shape of a pyramid, which serves as a reminder of the return of the Bourbons to France. Their names, dates of birth and other such things are engraved upon it. During the last revolution the people struck out these names so that nothing but the traces of them can be seen today. Such is the custom of time that it takes on all colours, betraying and annihilating some people while bestowing its favour upon others, even within the space of a single day. As the poet said:

Brave men I have killed, not a single enemy left untouched
Respite I have granted none to their army of men
I emptied capitals after the departure of their kings
and drove them away into exile, dispersing them in the east
And when my might had reached high up to the stars
and the necks of all people had bent for me as slaves
an arrow was violently thrust towards me, appeasing the fire that raged within me
And now here I am, lying in my pit, unarmed, discarded

It is customary among the Franks to write such inscriptions, after the fashion of the ancient Egyptians and other peoples. Look at how the Egyptians built the temples and pyramids of Giza. They built them as monuments that would be seen by those who would come after them. Let us now mention the views of the Franks on this and what they have discovered after careful research so that you may compare it with the fanciful yarns spun by [Arab] historians on this subject.[3] The gist of the

1. = 13 February–14 March 1831.
2. This should, of course, read 1814 (5 April). Built in the 16th century, the castle of Fonainebleau was originally the autumn residence of Louis XIV. It was Napoleon who made it his imperial seat, whereas Louis XVIII and Charles X rarely went there. See M. Berthelot, 1886–1902: XVII, 737–42; P. Larousse, 1866–76: VIII, 569–70.
3. The inclusion of a section on Egyptology should come as no surprise since Champollion had only shortly before deciphered the hieroglyphics, which discovery heightened

theory is that the kings of Egypt built the pyramids, although there is disagreement regarding the date of construction. Some say that they were built by a king called Qūf[1] three thousand years ago; others claim that it was a king called *Khamīs*[2] or Cheops (*Khayūbs*) who built them. It seems that the stones were cut in Upper Egypt and not in Lower Egypt. Some European scholars claim that it took no more than twenty-three years to build them and that the number of workers amounted to 360,000. The cost was also huge since according to Pliny (*Bāniyās*) the expenses for onions and leeks for the workers alone amounted to 20 million Egyptian piastres. These pyramids are traced to one of the kings of the Pharaohs,[3] who is said to have erected the Great Pyramid in order to house his remains, the others being destined to serve as a tomb for his wife and daughter. However, he himself was not buried in the first pyramid, which has remained open to this day. His wife and daughter, on the other hand, were buried in the other two pyramids, which were then hermetically sealed. This is what the Franks say about the pyramids. These are some of the words that were inspired by the magnificent construction of the two great pyramids:

My loved ones, there are no buildings under the sky
like those of the two pyramids of Egypt
These buildings are feared by time just as
on earth there is always a fear of the assault of time

In his *Muntahā al-ʿuqūl*, al-Suyūṭī[4] states that he was surprised at scholars

---

the 'Egypt-mania' that had gripped France in the wake of Napoleon's expedition. It is also interesting to note that Champollion was appointed as curator of the Egyptian antiquities at the Louvre in the year of al-Ṭahṭāwī's arrival in France, and died only a few months after the latter's return to Egypt.

1. There is little doubt that this is in fact a corrupted transliteration of *Khūfū*, who is better known by his Greek name Cheops.
2. It seems al-Ṭahṭāwī confused Cheops with Khaemuas – the son of Ramesses II – who is indeed associated with the pyramids inasmuch as he is said to have restored a number of momuments, as witness inscriptions found on pyramids at both Saqqara (e.g. Unas) and Giza (e.g. Mycerinus). See I. Edwards, 1985: 171ff.
3. *al-farāʿina* (sing. *firʿawn*). This in fact refers to the *firʿawns* of Muslim tradition. In the Qur'ān (e.g. II: 49–50; VII: 127ff.), this figure is the enemy of Mūsā and Hārūn, whereas in commentaries it often occurs as the nickname of the Amalakite kings. In *Ḥadīth* literature, a number of other *firʿawns* are mentioned, though there does not seem to have been a consensus on their number. See *EI1*, s.vv. "firʿawn" (A. Wensinck), "Mūsā" (Bernhard Heller).
4. The actual title of the work is *Mushtahā al-ʿuqūl fī muntahā 'l-nuqūl* ('The Object of Desire of the Mind Regarding the Highest Degree of Transmission'). See GAL, II, 150; Y. Sarkīs, 1928: 1084.

claiming that the most wondrous things in Egypt were the pyramids, even though the *barābī* ('ancient temples') of Upper Egypt are more extraordinary. It is the *barābī* that are known among the common people as obelisks.[1] Because of their strangeness, the Franks transported two of them to their countries; one was shipped to Rome in ancient times, whereas the other was taken to Paris not that long ago, marking the abundant beneficence of our ruler.[2] I should like to say that as Egypt has started to emulate the civilization and instruction of European countries (*bilād Ūrūbā*), it is more entitled to that which has been left by its ancestors in terms of artistic ornaments and craftsmanship. The fact of stripping [this heritage] away piece by piece is considered by intelligent people to be like taking away the jewels and fineries of others in order to adorn oneself with them. It is, in fact, tantamount to robbery! This assertion does not require any proof since it is self-evident.[3]

1. *barābī*, sing. *birba*, is only used for ancient Egyptian temples (others being simply *ma'bad*/pl. *ma'ābid*). The word is a Coptic borrowing, *p* (masculine definite article) + *rpe* ('temple'), which, in turn, goes back to the Ancient Egyptian *rpy* (also *r-pr*); see J. Černy, 1976: 138; W. Crum, 1939: 298b; R. Faulkner, 1976: 146.
2. In fact, there are no fewer than five obelisks in Rome, the first one having been erected in 1585, opposite St Peter's. The Paris obelisk (at the Place de la Concorde) came from the Ramesses II temple at Luxor, and was a gift from Muḥammad 'Alī to Louis-Philippe on the occasion of his accession to the throne. A special vessel (aptly called *Le Luxor*) was constructed to ship the monument, which arrived in Paris only in 1835. As a result of problems with the site, it took another year and a half for it to be raised completely (25 October 1836).
3. Historically, this is a hugely important passage and one that would not have gone unnoticed in Cairo. Muḥammad 'Alī did not set great store by the legacy of Ancient Egypt except in so far as it could help him secure alliances or to bestow favours on European treasure hunters like the Italian Belzoni or the French consul Drovetti, whose collection formed the core of the Egyptian Antiquities Department of the Louvre. At the same time, Muḥammad 'Alī was keen to be seen to be a patron of the arts like European rulers and in 1835 (15 August/20 Rabī' 1251) he issued a decree forbidding all exports of antiquities. The task of preserving ancient Egyptian artefacts found was entrusted to al-Ṭahṭāwī, who was to store the items in the Language School until such time as a museum would be built! In light of his views, there is little doubt that he played a key role in the creation of the legislation and may even have had a hand in the actual writing of the decree. Again, there is an interesting connection with Champollion, who in December 1829, at the end of his only journey to Egypt, submitted a report to Muḥammad 'Alī in which he, too, underscored the necessity for the conservation of all the monuments testifying to the greatness and glory of ancient Egypt (Champollion's report was later published as an annex to his *Lettres Ecrites d'Egypte et de Nubie*, Paris, Firmin Didot, 1833). Finally, it is worth adding that the theme of Ancient Egypt and its civilization appears in several of al-Ṭahṭāwī's writings, most notably, of course, in what was to become a monumental history of Egypt, *Anwār Tawfīq al-jalīl fī akhbār Miṣr wa tawthīq banī Ismā'īl* (1868), as well as in *Manāhij al-albāb al-Miṣriyya fī mabāhij al-ādāb al-'aṣriyya* (ed. M. 'Imāra, 1973–80: I, 383–91); *al-Murshid al-Amīn li 'l-banāt wa 'l-banīn* (ed. M. 'Imāra, 1973–80: II, 455–57 *et passim*).

Napoleon used the guns that he had captured from the Russians (*al-Mūsqū*) and the Austrians (*a-Nimsā*) to make a hollow column, which was erected in Paris. The Russians tried to pull it down when they were in Paris. The fact that there were unable to do so only proved their weakness.

After we had passed Fontainebleau, we saw the city of Nemours (*Nīmūr*) after travelling for four hours. The town lies twenty hours from Paris. Then we passed the city of Cosne (*Kūna*), which is located on the banks of the river Loire (*al-wāra*). This is where they manufacture the anchors for the imperial vessels. We then went on to the city of Melun (*Mūlin*), where there are many offspring of Arabs who accompanied the French troops after their withdrawal from Egypt to France.[4] We continued our journey until we arrived at the city of Roanne (*Ruwāna*), which is seventy-seven French leagues to the south of Paris and thirteen leagues from Lyons.

Roanne counts 7,000 inhabitants. It has a Council of Industry (*majlis li 'l-fabrīqāt*), a Council for Agriculture, a library and a museum for natural science and mechanical devices. The town also has a nice bridge across the river Loire (*Luwār*) and a famous quay. It is the main harbour for trade from Lyons and other towns [in the area] and from it all types of goods are shipped out. In the surrounding area, there are marble quarries. The Loire (*Luwāra*) is navigable when it is close to this city, which should not be confused with Rouen (*Ruwān*), which is thirty leagues to the north of Paris, on the river Seine, in the region of Normandy (*Nūmandiyā*).

Then, we arrived in the city of Lyons, of which mention has already been made. From there, we travelled to Orgon (*Ūrghūn*), which is 178 leagues to the south of Paris. It is situated at the foot of a mountain and is famous for the fact that when Napoleon passed through it he hid himself out of fear of the population. We continued to pass one town after another until we finally arrived at Marseilles, which has already been sufficiently discussed before. Here, we boarded a trading ship and sailed to Alexandria. However, there is no need either to mention what we saw on this journey since it is the same as the outward voyage, which was described at the beginning of the *riḥla*. Nevertheless, I should add that all of my French acquaintances requested that upon my return I should mention everything that struck me as I had been far away from Egypt for such a long time, seen things that were totally different from those I had known, and grown accustomed to seeing other things that appeared strange to me when I saw them for the very first time upon my arrival in France. I made a promise and kept it.

4. See above.

And so we have reached the end [of this *riḥla*], which I have abridged as much as possible.[1] All that remains for me now is to provide a summary of this journey and the observations and ideas that I have carefully scrutinized and examined.

I should like to say that after having investigated the morals of the French and their political system it appears to me that they more closely resemble the Arabs than the Turks or other races. Their affinity manifests itself most strongly in things like honour, freedom and pride. The word they use for 'honour', i.e. personal dignity, is the same as that for 'honour' in the sense of nobility and high rank.[2] It is on this 'honour' of theirs that they swear in important matters, and if they enter into a covenant, they commit themselves to keeping their promise and they live up to it. There is no doubt that the honour that exists among the pure Arabs is the most important human feature, as shown in their poetry and borne out by their history. As one poet said:

Forsooth, I am sweet for my friends but
bitter towards the rancorous, to whom I show my hatred
I want for nothing, and am not haughty because of wealth
Freely I give to anyone desiring a loan from me
Sometimes I am impoverished, only to see my fortunes reversed
It is with ease that I obtain wealth for with me there is always my honour![3]

They consider any breach of honour to be shameful and a disgrace.

You rebuke me for being small in number
I said to this: truly, there are few generous ones
There is no harm in the fact that we are few when our neighbour
is strong as he is despised by the majority
The yearning for death approaches our era
and their time, as it lingers on, gives rise to disgust
We are a people who do not think of killing as a disgrace

1. The Arabic text is slightly corrupted here as it reads: '*hādhā ḥāṣil mā kāna lakhkhaṣtu ḥasaba 'l-imkān.*' This may be corrected to: '*hādhā ḥāṣil ma kāna min hādhihi 'l-riḥla lakhkhaṣtuhā ḥasaba 'l-imkān.*'

2. The Arabic text contrasts *'irḍ* with *sharaf*; the former denotes honour related to one's reputation and that of one's kith and kin, whereas the latter refers to high social rank or greatness (cf. *sharīf*).

3. The last two verses of this poem were originally written by the Iraqi satirical poet al-Ḥakam (d. 718); cf. Abū ʿAlī Ismāʾīl b. al-Qāsim al-Qālī, 1950: II, 261. Also see A. Beeston [S. Jayyusi], 1983: 409ff.

even if this is the view of the ʿĀmir and the Salūl[1]
If one of our lords passes away, another one rises
who speaks with the eloquence of nobles
If you do not know people, ask for us and for others –
One who knows is not equal to one who is ignorant[2]

One should not assume that because they are not jealous about their women, they do not have any honour in this regard, since it is in this area that it is most visible. Although they are devoid of jealousy, when their women misbehave, they are the most malicious of men against themselves and against those who have betrayed them with their women. At the most, they make the mistake of handing power over to their women, although there is nothing to fear from those of unblemished reputation.[3] As the poet said:

If her husband is not with her, she will not reveal his secret
and is content to have him home, whenever he returns

When commenting on the account by the Almighty of the words of Potiphar[4] – '*thou, woman, ask forgiveness of thy crime; surely thou art one of the sinful*' – al-Zamakhsharī[5] stated that Potiphar showed nothing but clemency, whereas others said that he had little jealousy. When commenting on this verse, Shaykh Athīr al-Dīn Abū Ḥayān[6] said the following: '*the soil of Egypt requires this* [the small measure of jealousy]. *What is this compared with that*

1. These are the names of South Arabian tribes; see *EI1*, s.vv. "ʿĀmir b. Ṣaʿṣaʿa" (Reckendorf), "Salūl" (F. Krenkow).
2. The first four verses are extracted from an ode written by the Jewish poet al-Samaw'al Ibn Gharīḍ b. ʿĀdiyā' al-Awsī al-Ghassānī (d. 560), the last two verses belonging to ʿAmr b. Sha's (d. *c.* 640), a fellow tribesman and contemporary of the Prophet Muḥammad. Cf. al-Qālī, 1950: I, 269, 270. On al-Samaw'al, see Y. Sarkīs, 1924: I, 1053–4.
3. The Arabic *muḥsina* is a term used in Islamic law to denote a woman of pure morals.
4. *al-ʿazīz* ('the mighty one'), which is also one of the 99 'beautiful names' of God. See *EI1*, s.vv. "ʿAzīz", "5iṭfīr" (B. Heller), 'Yūsuf b. Yaʿqūb' (B. Heller). The Qur'ānic verse in question is XII:29 (trans. A. Arberry, 1983: 229).
5. The Persian-born Abū 'l-Qāsim Maḥmūd b. ʿUmar al-Zamaksharī (1075–1144) was a famous philologist, grammarian and Qur'ān commentator. See *EI1*, s.v. 'al-Zamakhsharī' (C. Brockelmann).
6. Of Berber extraction, the grammarian and Ḥadīth and Qur'ān commentator Athīr al-Dīn Muḥammad b. Yūsuf Abū Ḥayyān al-Gharnāṭī (1256–1344) was born in Granada, but spent much of his life in Egypt, after having travelled extensively through North Africa. A formidable linguist, he wrote not only on Arabic but also on Ethiopic, Persian and Turkish, for which he wrote grammars. See *EI1*, s.v. "Abū Ḥaiyān" (M. Houtsma); *GALS*, II, 146.

which befell one of the kings of our country? He was sitting with intimate friends in a friendly gathering while a female slave sang behind a curtain. One of his companions asked the girl to repeat two verses. She had barely sung them when her severed head was brought on a platter. The king said [to the one who made the request to the slave girl], 'Ask this head to repeat the two verses!' Then he fainted, and remained ill for as long as he was king.' So, what is the jealousy of this king compared with that of ʿAbd al-Muḥsin al-Ṣūrī[1] with regard to his loved one, when he says:

I clung to her, drunk from the wine of her youthfulness
so that she would ignore my lovesickness and wailing
I shared her love with many others
She shared a part of my very being
So do not impose jealousy on me to which I am not accustomed
Truly, my friend is he who loves the way I love my loved one

This ends the *Sukkardān* of Ibn Ḥajala, the author of the *Dīwān al-ṣabāba* ('Collection of Love Poems').[2] In short, all nations complain about women, even the Arabs. As one poet said:[3]

That Umm Awfā departed from home pained me
But Umm Awfā does not care

Another one said:

If you want to ask me about women, then you should know that I am
an expert doctor for your women trouble
If the head of the man is confused, or if he has little money
then he cannot partake of their passion
When they find out, they want plenty of money
whereas the prime of youth rarely comes out in them

1. This is the Tyre-born poet ʿAbd al-Muḥsin b. Muḥammad b. Aḥmad b. Ghālib b. Ghulbān al-Ṣūrī (950–1028). See 'U. Kaḥḥāla [n.d.]: VI, 173, XIII, 402; Yāqūt, 1866–73: I, 869.
2. This is a reference to the Tlemcen-born mystical poet Shihāb al-Dīn Abū 'l-ʿAbbās Aḥmad b. Yaḥyā b. Abī Bakr b.ʿAbd al-Wāḥid Ibn Abī Ḥajala (1325–75). The work that is mentioned here is a collection of poems entitled *Sukkardān al-sultān al-malik al-nāṣir* ('The Sugar Pot of Sultan al-Malik al-Nāṣir'). 'U. Kaḥḥāla [n.d.]: II, 201; *GAL*, II, 12–13, *GALS*, II, 5; M. de Slane, 1883–95: 586–7.
3. The following lines are from the pre-Islamic poet Zuhayr b. Abī Sulmā (d. 609), many of whose poems centre on his beloved Umm ʿAwf, who was his first wife (but whom he divorced). See *EI1*, s.v. "Zuhair b. Abī Sulmā" (F. Krenkow).

As everybody is often asked about the condition of women among the Franks, we have lifted the veil that hangs over their situation. In summary, we can again say that the confusion with regard to the chastity of women does not arise from whether they wear the veil or not. Rather, it is linked to whether a woman has a good or bad education, whether she is accustomed to loving only one man rather than sharing her love among others and whether there is peace and harmony within the couple. Experience has shown that in France chastity dominates the hearts of women belonging to the middle classes, while this is not the case for those of the upper classes or the riffraff. The latter two classes often give occasion for suspicion and concern. The French often levelled accusations at the women of the family of the Bourbons, and their words only gained more credence as a result of what happened to the daughter-in-law of the deposed king of France. She was the mother of the Duke of Bordeaux (*al-dūk dūburdū*), for whom his grandfather gave up his throne, something that the French did not accept. They said that this boy was an illegitimate child and that his mother had delivered yet another illegitimate child, while claiming she had got married in secret. As a result, her honour and good reputation were shattered. After having claimed the kingdom of France for her first son and using tricks in order to get him invested, people were afraid that she would do something to the kingdom, and so she lost all credibility. When she fell into the hands of the French [authorities], people assumed that her end had come, but she was allowed to continue her way, [her captors] saying that she had become of little importance. She returned to the bosom of her family with her younger son.

One of the strangest things that happened in the lands of the Franks in this respect is the fact that George IV (*Jirjis*), the king of England, accused his wife of adultery, after he had witnessed this from her on numerous occasions. In fact, everyone knew that she had been travelling around Europe with anyone she pleased and had a lover in every place.[1] Her case was tried according to their laws and the charge was made accordingly. The king filed for a divorce on the grounds of her proven adultery so that he could marry another woman. However, as it turned out, there was not enough evidence to grant a divorce, and the judge ruled that the king had

1. This is a reference to Princess Caroline of Brunswick-Lüneburg (1768–1821), the daughter of George III's sister, and thus George IV's cousin. The couple separated after a mere eight months of marriage. When her estranged husband became Regent (1811–20) Caroline was not allowed at court. She spent a number of years in exile in Italy and was the subject of great controversy because of her alleged adultery (especially with her Italian courtier, Bartolomeo Pergami).

to remain married to her. From that time onwards, they lived separated, but the king could not marry any other woman. Their tribulations became common knowledge everywhere. However, in truth, though people believed everything about her, this was based merely on indirect evidence and not on any eyewitness accounts, otherwise her honour would have been discredited.

The issue of personal honour, which makes the French and the Arabs similar to each other, consists of the perception of the ideal of manhood, the fact of telling the truth and other qualities of [moral integrity and] perfection. Honour also includes decency and probity. It is rare to find a meanness of spirit among them. This is also one of the features that is found among the Arabs and is rooted in their noble character. However, these days it has waned and melted away as they have suffered the hardships of oppression and the calamities of time, and their situation has driven them to humbling themselves and begging. In spite of this, there are some who remain faithful to their original Arab nature, and reveal decency and high-mindedness. As the poet said:

Leave me my dignity and decency, for to me
decency was a habit in my life
And for a man the severing of his hands is more difficult
than a good deed bestowed upon him by the hands of the wicked

As for freedom, which the French are forever requesting, this was also part of the character of the Arabs in past times, as illustrated by the following *mufākhara*[1] that took place between al-Nuʿmān Ibn al-Mundhir,[2] king of the Arabs, and Khosrow,[3] king of the Persians. This is a copy of it:[4]

1. This word (lit. 'boasting', 'vainglory') denotes a literary genre that has continued to this day, and consists of a 'war of words', often involving famous personages and a fictional account of their exchanges. See A. Beeston [R. Serjeant], 1983: 118.
2. Abū Qābūs al-Nuʿmān b. Al-Mundhir was the last Lakhmid ruler of al-Ḥīra (*c.* 580–602), to the south of Mekka. His name often appears in classical Arabic poetry, though not always in a favourable light. See *EI1*, s.v. 'al-Nuʿmān b. Al-Mundhir' (A. Moberg); 'Lakhm' (H. Lammens).
3. The Arabic *kisrā* was in fact an Arabicization of the Persian *Khosrow* (Ar. *Khusraw*), which was the name of only two Sasanian kings – Khosrow (I) Anūshirwān (531–79) and Khosrow (II) Parvīz (590–628) – but was afterwards used as a title for all Persian kings. See *EI1*, s.v. 'Kisrā' (Cl. Huart).
4. This *mufākhara* appears, with some minor omissions, in the famous anthology by the Cordoba-born Aḥmad b. Muḥammad Abū ʿUmar Ibn ʿAbd al-Rabbīh (860–940), entitled *al-ʿIqd al-farā'id* (see e.g. A. Amīn, A. Al-Zayn, I. Al-Abyārī (eds), *Lajnat al-ta'līf*

Al-Nuʿmān went to see Khosrow, in whose presence delegations from al-Rūm, *the Hind, China, the Persians, Turks, as well as from other nations had gathered. They all talked about their kings and their countries. Al-Nuʿmān boasted of the Arabs, whom he put above all other nations, without making an exception for the Persians, or anyone else for that matter. However, overcome by jealousy, Khosrow retorted, 'O Nuʿmān, I have thought much about the Arabs, as well as about other nations, and I have observed the condition of the delegations that have come before me. I have found that the Rūm are fortunate as they form a tightly knit community, possess a mighty sultan, many cities and a trustworthy religion. I have seen that the Hind is famous for its wise men, while boasting appreciable wealth, a multitude of rivers, regions, resources, amazing craftsmanship, radiantly beautiful women and a large population. China, too, is remarkable because of its social organization, the multitude of manual crafts, their fighting zeal, their iron-working skill and the fact that they have a king who unites them. As for the Turks, despite their bad conditions of living, the lack of fertile agricultural land, of fortresses and the absence of things that lie at the root of worldly civilization, like habitation and clothing – even they have kings who keep their remote regions together and administer their affairs. However, among the Arabs I have not seen any laudable qualities in religious or worldly matters such as respect [for things], strength, determination, cohesion or wisdom. Conversely, there is ample proof of their vileness, baseness and inherent weakness, which is reminiscent of fleeing animals and confused birds. Out of poverty, they kill their children, while they eat each other out of need. They are deprived of the food, drink, clothing and entertainments and pleasures of this world. The best they have to eat is camel meat, which deters many birds and wild animals because of its indigestibility, foul taste and the fear of [contracting] illness. If one of them receives a guest, he considers it a generous deed, and if he receives a morsel of food, he treats it as if it were booty. Their poetry talks about this, while their men boast about it, except in the Ṭanūkh tribe, whose society was founded by my grandfather, who strengthened their kingdom and protected it from its enemies, to the extent that he is talked about until this day. In spite of the above, they have monuments and fortresses and riches that are similar to those of other people. And yet, rather than keeping quiet about your lowliness, dearth, poverty and misery, I see you boasting about it, wishing to put yourselves above the ranks of other people.'*

Al-Nuʿmān replied, 'God has rightly guided the king. You have spoken the truth; truly, this nation distinguished itself through its merit, power, and high rank. However, I have a reply to everything the king has said, without refuting or

---

wa 'l-tarjama wa 'l-nashr, Cairo, 1940, II, 4–9). On Ibn ʿAbd al-Rabbīh, see *EI1*, s.v. 'Ibn ʿAbd Rabbihi' (C. Brockelmann); *GAL*, I, 154.

denying anything. If you guarantee that you will not be angry at what I have to say, I will proceed.'

Khosrow said, 'You may rest assured!'

To which al-Nu'mān said, 'As for your nation, no-one will gainsay its excellent position in terms of the minds and morals of its people, the expanse of its territory, its awesome might and the honour that the Almighty God has bestowed upon it by your reign, that of your father and that of your grandfather. However, as for the nations that you have just mentioned, none of them surpasses the Arabs in excellence.'

Khosrow said, 'Why is that?'

Al-Nu'mān replied, 'Because of their strength, sturdiness, beautiful physique, their attachment to their word, their courage, leadership, generosity, the wisdom of their tongues, their mental strength and acuity and their loyalty.

'As for their strength and sturdiness, they remained neighbours to your father and grandfather who conquered the land, and imposed their will, established the kingdom and led their armies forth. Nobody challenged them, and they [the Arabs] remained respected among them, whereas none of them granted them any favours; their fortresses are the backs of their horses, the earth is their bed, the sky their roof. Their swords at their sides, their equipment consists of the roofs over their heads. Other nations, for their part, draw their power from stones and clay, islands, seas, castles and fortresses.

'As for the Arabs' physical beauty and colour, one must surely recognize their superiority over the burnt Indians, the hairless Chinese, the deformed Turks and the Rūm with their niggardly faces.

'Let us now turn to their lineage and noble descent. There are nations who do not know anything about their ancestors, roots or history, to the extent that if you asked one of them who came before his father, he would not be able to trace his lineage or even give the name of his grandfather. However, there is not a single Arab who is not able to name all of his ancestors, one after the other. This way, they have protected their noble descent, and preserved their lineage. There is not a single man [among them] who wants to enter any tribe but his own, to trace his lineage to any ancestry but his own or to be known by a name other than that of his father.

'As for their bravery and generosity, if the most wicked man among them has a young camel or a very old one that carries the bare necessities, his burden, his food and water rations, he will nevertheless slaughter his camel for a wanderer who knocks on his door and who contents himself with a morsel of food and a gulp of water. He will be happy to part with all his wordly possessions since this will yield him praise and acclaim and result in his being remembered favourably.

'As for the wisdom of their tongues, the Almighty God has given them poetry,

the splendour of their speech, the beauty of its metre and rhymes, together with their knowledge of allusions, the creation of proverbs and their eloquence in descriptions. None of this exists in the languages of [other] races. And then, there are their horses, which are the best horses; their women, who are the most chaste of women; their clothing, which is the most beautiful to be found. Their metals are gold and silver, the stones of their mountains are onyx, and it is only with mounts like theirs that travellers can reach their destination and cross deserts.

'As for their religion and their laws, they are attached to them in the highest degree. They have holy months, a holy town and a house of pilgrimage, where they perform their rituals and slaughter their sacrificial animals. If a man should meet the murderer of his father or his brother there, his nobleheartedness and religion, as well as the respect and high esteem for this shrine, will prevent him from doing harm to this man, even though he would be able to take blood revenge and vent his anger.

'As for their loyalty, if one of them does so much as throw a glance, then this constitutes a bond with regard to the parties involved, and he will not go back on what he has pledged in his mind until he has fulfilled his obligation. If one of them picks up a twig from the ground, this becomes security for his debt and he will not release his collateral or renege on his debt, out of fear for God the Almighty. If one of them – even when he is far away from home – learns that someone is in need of his assistance, he will protect and defend him from his enemy, even if this means the annihilation of his own tribe or that against which his protection was asked, merely in order to protect his bond. And if a deprived man or someone about whom someone else has spoken – even if he is not known to them or is no relative – seeks refuge among them, they welcome him in their midst and protect his possessions with their lives and property.

'When you, O King – may God protect you – say that they kill their children because they have to, [know that] any one of them who does this, does so in spite of himself, to prevent shame and out of fear of the jealousy of husbands.

'As for your statement, O King, that camel's meat is the best food they have to eat, as you have described it, [know then] that they have left all the rest out of contempt, since they are interested only in the most splendid and excellent. Their camels are both their mounts and sources of food. Furthermore, of all animals, the camel has the most meat, the best fat and the finest milk, and in addition they are the least harmful and their meat the most pleasant to chew. Indeed, there is no other meat that surpasses the meat of the camel, whose merit is clearly noticeable.

'As for the Arabs' internecine strife, their mutual attrition and their refusal to follow the leadership of one man to rule them and manage their affairs, it is only nations that are aware of their inherent weakness and live in fear of an advance

of their enemies that need a king to govern their affairs. This is one of their most important and most powerful men, whose honour they recognize above that of all other men, whom they will follow in times of crisis and to whose orders they submit themselves. As for the Arabs, O King, because of their great noblemindedness, their loyalty, their religion, the wisdom of their tongues and the generosity of their souls, many of them say that they are all kings in their elevation and that no man submits himself to another, since both are of noble blood.

'As for the Yemen, which the king has just described, your father and grandfather know its ruler better than anyone. When, after the king of Abyssinia attacked him with an army of 200,000 men and conquered his kingdom, he came to your door, crying for help – humbled, miserable and dispossessed – none of your ancestors or fathers came to his aid. But when he sought help from the Arabs, they gave it to him.[1] *If it had not been for the Arabs, he would probably have been lost and never been able to return to his homeland again. If he had not had men who together with him killed free men, scattered the ranks of the unbelievers and slaughtered the wicked black slaves, then he would never have been able to return to the Yemen.'*

Khosrow was astonished by what al-Nuʿmān had told him, and said, 'Forsooth, you are worthy of your place as a leader among your people, as a leader of the inhabitants of your region and of things even better than that.' Then he dressed him, bestowed favours upon him, as well as an abundance of gifts, and sent him home to al-Ḥīra.

Afterwards, however, he sent somebody to kill him. The Tanūkh are a south Arabian tribe.[2] The following is said about Anas b. Mālik[3] – may God be pleased with him:

An Egyptian came to see ʿUmar b. al-Khaṭṭāb and started complaining about ʿAmr b. al-ʿĀṣ. 'O Lord of the Faithful,[4]*' he said, 'I have come here to seek refuge.' ʿUmar replied, 'You may be assured of it. What is your business?' The man said, 'I raced with my horse against the son of ʿAmr b. al-ʿĀṣ, and I beat him. Afterwards,*

---

1. This is, of course, the famous story of Ṣayf Ibn Dhī Yazan, who liberated the Yemen from Abyssinian rule and who succeeded thanks to the Arab king of al-Ḥīra. The king introduced him to the Persian (Sasanian) ruler, Khusraw Anūshirwān (Khosrow I), who sent soldiers to help the Yemenites. Soon after, the Yemen became a Sasanian province (satrapy). See P. Hitti, 1991: 65–6.
2. Now follows a poem by al-Mutanabbī, introduced by al-Ṭahtāwī as follows: 'al-Mutanabbī said about the tongue of one of them [namely, members of the tribe]'.
3. A servant to the Prophet Muḥammad as from the age of ten, Anas b. Mālik Abū Ḥamza was one of the most prolific transmitters of *ḥadīths*. He is said to have died at a very advanced age (the dates given vary between 97 and 107) in Basra. See *EI1*, s.v. 'Anas b. Mālik Abū Ḥamza' (A. Wensinck).
4. *amīr al-mūʾminīn* ('Prince of the Faithful'), which title continued to be used by caliphs (and those that claimed the caliphate). See *EI1*, s.v. (A. Wensinck).

he attacked me with a whip in his hands, and started to beat me with it, saying, "I am the son of the most noble ones." When this reached the ears of 'Amr b. al-'Āṣ, he imprisoned me as he feared that I might come to you and complain about his son. However, I escaped from the prison and here I am before you.' Thereupon, 'Umar b. al-Khaṭṭāb wrote a letter to 'Amr b. al-'Āṣ, stating, 'Upon receipt of this letter, you and your son must perform the Ḥajj.' Then, he turned to the Egyptian, and said, 'Get up, and wait until your adversary comes.'

When 'Amr b. al-'Āṣ and his son had performed the Ḥajj, they came and sat before 'Umar b. al-Khaṭṭāb. Again, the Egyptian complained as he had done the first time. 'Umar b. al-Khaṭṭāb signalled to the Egyptian [to come forward] and said, 'Take the cosh[1] *and beat him with it.' Upon this, the Egyptian approached the son of 'Amr b. al-'Āṣ and beat him with it.'*

And Anas continued by saying:

By God, he beat him and we also had a desire to beat him. But he continued to beat him with such ferocity, with strike following after strike, that we wanted him to stop. 'Umar – may God be pleased with him – egged him on by saying, 'Hit him! Hit the son of the most noble ones!'

Then 'Amr b. al-'Āṣ said, 'O Lord of the Faithful, now you have your vengeance!' But 'Umar b. al-Khaṭṭāb said to the Egyptian, 'Take off his turban and apply the whip to his bald pate.' However, the Egyptian was afraid to do this, and said, 'O Lord of the Faithful, I have struck the one who had struck me! Why should I strike somebody who did not strike me?' To this, 'Umar – may God be pleased with him – replied, 'If you had done it, no-one would have tried to prevent you from it.' Then, he turned to 'Amr b. al-'Āṣ and said to him, 'Since when do you turn people whose mothers caused them to be born free men (aḥrār) *into slaves?'*

From this, it becomes clear that the love for freedom has also been part of the Arab character from ancient times.

We cannot end this *riḥla* without expressing thanks for the munificences of a man who has helped our ruler successfully achieve his goal by organizing the affairs of the students and their instruction in the city of Paris – a friend of Egypt and its people, *Maître* Jomard (*al-khawāja Jūmār*). Through his zeal and commitment he endeavours to achieve the goal of our Efendi, our benefactor. He has thrown himself into this, without any hesitation, as if he himself were a faithful and devoted son of Egypt. Indeed, he deserves to be put among the ranks of the friends of the Khedive himself. The most eloquent proof of this is provided by what he mentions

---

1. *dirrat* (rarely *darra*), whereas previously *sawṭ* ('whip') is used. Technically, however, the former denotes any object used for striking, ranging from a rolled-up cloth to a cosh.

in his *Almanac*,[1] which he wrote in 1244 A.H. for Egypt and Syria. In this book, he states that, as a result of a supreme decree (*irāda*) and Khedival edicts received by him, he will publish a similar *Almanac* every year with a view to contributing to the improvement in civilization of the Egyptian provinces (*iyāla*). In the preface to the *Almanac*, he states, among other things, that he will discuss a range of issues:

A description of the priority of crafts and skills necessary for Egypt, from beginning to end;

The commerce of the peoples of Europe (Ūrūbā), Asia and Africa, such as the caravans of the Berbers, Darfur, Sennar and the Ḥijāz, as well as a comparison of the various weights and measures used in the various countries;

Details about issues related to agriculture, which was the main reason for the wealth of the people of Egypt in former times, and which should therefore be the first to which the state of the kingdom of Egypt, with its high-quality soil, should devote itself. Agriculture consists of many important branches, among them the science of the management of land resources available (agronomy) *and that which falls under it in terms of the improvement of plantations, and of newly administered lands; the perfection of the cultivation of cotton, indigo, grapes, olives and mulberries; the extraction of indigo flour and of the many types of oils; knowledge of the growing of palm trees, the breeding of silkworms and of cochineals; the keeping of domestic animals; improved breeding of native animals such as horses, goats and wool-producing animals by isolating them from others and by importing animals from abroad; the knowledge of veterinarian medicine and the treatment of diseases such as epidemics; the protection of grains from worms; the planting of trees and their arrangement on the sides of roads; the exploitation of vegetable gardens and of all available buildings that are suited for agriculture. In terms of agriculture, we shall also deal with canals and feeders for the irrigation and drainage of lands, as well as with roads, dams and aqueducts for the supply of water to plains and mountains. All of these will be discussed together with farming.*

We shall talk about various issues related to natural science, the science of the three kingdoms of nature, about mathematics, the magnetic substance (al-mādda al-maghnāṭīsiyya) *that is used by doctors in the treatment of paralysis and other such ailments, as well as about magnetism, the earth's temperature, meteorological phenomena, the moisture and rain that occur between turnings of the earth. We shall also talk about meteorites, fire-spewing mountains called* volcanoes

1. See above.

(burkāniya) *and about natural science instruments such as devices to measure time, heat, humidity, as well as about the protection against lightning, glasses that magnify minute things that cannot be seen with the naked eye. We shall also discuss the science of minerals and metals and their extraction, the breaking and dividing of stones, the science of medicinal herbs, the plants that are used in arts and crafts, useful animals and, finally, algebra and geometry.*

The fifth topic includes all the branches of the science of the economy (tawfīr al-maṣārīf), *the governance and administration of the state, as well as details on the science of the conditions of kingdoms and states, the reasons for their wealth and prosperity of its peoples, the present and future living conditions and the birth rates of males and females in every town of the country, the civil service; the general principles on which the political systems of the Franks are based, i.e. the secular rights, rights guaranteed by laws* (ḥuqūq qānūniyya) *and human rights* (ḥuqūq bashariyya), *that is to say, the rights extended by individual states to each other.*

The organization of public and private health care. In this regard, we shall also speak of vaccination against smallpox, of the plague and treatments for it, of diseases and general disorders, while providing some details of anatomy.

In this section, we shall mention various instructions regarding literary and philosophical questions, languages and certain sciences like the science of elocution. We shall also talk about the schools and educational establishments in various countries, while providing extracts from the history of countries, especially Egypt, with stories, anecdotes on strange phenomena in Frankish and Eastern literature and rhetoric. In addition, we shall also touch upon the science of Logic, pointing out the means by which to facilitate and shorten the learning of reading, writing, arithmetic, as well as ways of teaching these things to the general public in the shortest possible time.

In the final chapter, we shall investigate a number of miscellaneous things; we shall discuss events related to trade, shipping, the establishment of public carriages, the improvement of roads, irrigation canals and suspension bridges, the signalling system called the telegraph *(tīlighrāf), i.e. the signalling of messages, as well as all new inventions that exist among the Franks. In order to complete the benefit [of this book], plates and illustrations are included, and we have also drawn geographical maps and pictures of plants and animals, which will be imported from other countries and bred in Egypt. We shall also mention many things that have been revived in the course of time. In short, we shall provide small treatises in connection with important matters and which are taken from the mouths of trustworthy people in an accessible form in order to facilitate their understanding by all people. It should be added that none of these things is borrowed from books.*

This marks the end of his exposé.

However, he did not carry out what he had promised as he made it contingent upon a supreme decree, and such an order has not hitherto been issued. In short, he is an ardent friend of Egypt, in both his words and deeds, as well as in his heart. He is one of those who wish to serve our ruler out of love for him and his state.

This marks the end of what I have been able to write with the help of the Almighty God – praise be to Him – about the events of the journey in this region of the world, whose know-how can be denied only by one who lacks justness or knowledge. As the poet said:

The eye, when inflamed, may deny the brightness of the sun
while the mouth may deny the flavour of water because of sickness
But virtue like the sun is not hidden from anyone
except from one who has been born blind

As the value of an act lies in the intention and depends on a proper inclination, one cannot rely on those who lack clear guidance and manifest astuteness. Hence, I shall pay heed not only to one who has reached high office in officialdom or the law, or who is attached to the *sharīʿa*, in which he occupies a leading position, and who is aware of the object [of this book].[1] Rather, it is a question of urging the people of our lands to import that which will yield them strength and fortitude, and enable them to dictate judgements. In short, things are today with us the way they were in the days of the [ʿAbbāsid] caliphs. As the poet said:

The blue of the morning appears before the white
Before the rain comes a drop, and then it pours down

In any case, I should like to ask anybody who looks at this book to read it carefully in its entirety so as to gain an insight into the things it contains. He who peruses the book will more clearly see where its failings lie. I, for my part, can only quote the words of the poet:

Here you have something embroidered
on paper, by a man with little talent

---

1. This is, of course, a thinly veiled reference to the author's mentor, Ḥasan al-ʿAṭṭār, who, as appears earlier on, encouraged his student to acquaint himself with all things European and write the present account.

Try to hide the defect when it appears –
as God forgives many sins!

Let us conclude by calling on the divine protection for the Khedive and his offspring, and may God increase his prestige among the kingdoms of the East and the West. May God make Egypt and its provinces enjoy the high civilization and justice that have been showered on them by our ruler, and extend the days of his reign through the glory of the seal of the Prophet who has guided his master. God bless him and his family, his companions, his friends and his tribe. Amen!

Bibliography

A. Archives

AN: Archives Nationales in Paris at the Centre d'Acceuil et de Recherche des Archives Nationales (CARAN)

B. Works in Arabic

al-ʿAbbādī, A. M. (ed.) (1971): *Tārīkh al-Andalus li Ibn al-Kardabūs, wa waṣfuhu li Ibn al-Shabbāṭ. Naṣṣān jadīdān*, Madrid: Instituto de Estudios Islámicos.

ʿAbd al-Karīm, Aḥmad ʿIzzat (ed.) (1976): *ʿAbd al-Raḥmān al-Jabartī*, Cairo: al-Hay'a al ʿĀmma li 'l-Kitāb.

ʿAbd al-Karīm, A. ʿI. (1945): *Tārīkh al-taʿlīm fī ʿMiṣr*, 3 vols, Cairo: Maṭbaʿat al-Naṣr.

ʿAbd al-Karīm, A. ʿI. (1938): *Tārīkh al-taʿlīm fī ʿaṣr Muḥammad ʿAlī*, Cairo: Maṭbaʿat al- Nahḍa al-Miṣriyya.

ʿAbd al-Karīm, Muḥammad [n.d.]: *ʿAlī Mubārak (Ḥayātuhu wa ma'āthiruhu)*, Cairo: Maṭbaʿat al-Risāla.

'Abd al-Mawlay, Maḥmūd (1977): *Madrasat Bārdū al-ḥarbiyya,* Tunis: MTE.

ʿAbduh, Ibrāhīm (1983): *Tārīkh al-Waqā'iʿ al-Miṣriyya, 1828–1942*, Cairo: Maktabat al-Ādāb li 'l-Ṭibāʿa wa 'l-Nashr wa 'l-Tawzīʿ.

ʿAbduh, I. (1951): *Taṭawwur al-ṣiḥāfa al-Miṣriyya*, 3rd edn, Cairo: Maṭbaʿat al-Namūdhajiyya.

ʿAbduh, I. (1948): *Aʿlām al-ṣaḥāfa al-ʿArabiyya*, Cairo: Maṭbaʿat al-Namūdhajiyya.

Abū 'l-Fidā' (1840): *Taqwīm al-buldān*, ed. J. T. Reinaud and Mac Guckin de Slane, Paris: Imprimerie Royale; trans. (part I) J. Reinaud, Paris: Imprimerie Nationale (1848); trans. (part II), S. Guyard, Paris: Imprimerie Nationale (1883).

Abū ʿAlī al-Qālī (1950): *Kitāb al-amālī wa 'l-dhayl wa 'l-nawādir*, 2 vols, ed. M. ʿAbd al-Jawwād al-Aṣmāʿī, Cairo: Dār al-Kutub.

Abū Ḥamdān, Samīr (1993): *ʿAlī Mubārak al-mufakkir wa 'l-mu'ammir*, Beirut: Sharika al-ʿĀlamiyya li 'l-Kitab.

'Allām, Mahdī, 'Abd al-Ḥamīd Ḥasan, Muḥammad Khalaf Allāh Aḥmad, Aḥmad Badawī and Anwar Lūqā (eds) (1958): *Mukhtārāt kutub Rifā' Rāfi' al-Ṭahṭāwī*, Cairo: Wizārat al-Tarbiyya wa 'l-Ta'līm.

Amīn, Aḥmad (1949): *Zu'amā' al-iṣlāḥ fī 'l-'aṣr al- hadīth*, Cairo: al-Nahḍa al-Miṣriyya.

'Awaḍ, Luwīs (1962–66): *al-Mu'aththirāt al-ajnabiyya fī 'l-adab al-'Arabī al-ḥadīth,* 2 vols, Cairo: Dār al-Ma'rifa.

Badawī, Aḥmad Aḥmad (1959): *Rifā'a Rāfi' al-Ṭahṭāwī*, 2nd edn, Cairo: Lajnat al-Bayān al-'Arabī.

Badawī, Aḥmad A., Anwar Lūqā, Jamāl al-Dīn al-Shayyāl and Muḥammad A. Ḥusayn (1958): *Nashra 'an kutub Rifā'a Rāfi' al-Ṭahṭāwī*, Cairo: Dār al-Kutub al-Miṣriyya.

Badr, 'Abd al-Muḥsin Ṭaha (1963): *Taṭawwur al-riwāya al-'Arabiyya al-ḥadītha fī Miṣr, 1870–1938*, Cairo: Dār al-Ma'ārif.

al-Bakrī, Abū 'Ubayd (1968): *Jughrāfiyā al-Andalus wa Urūbā min al-Kitāb al- Masālik wa 'l-Mamālik*, ed. 'A. al-Ḥājjī, Beirut: Dār al-Irshād.

Bayram V, Muḥammad (1898): *Mulāḥaẓāt siyāsiyya 'an al-tanẓīmāt al-lāzima li 'l-dawla al-'aliyya*, Cairo: al-Maṭba'a al-I'lāmiyya.

Bayram V, M. (1884–93): *Ṣafwat al-i'tibār bi-mustawda' al-amṣār wa 'l- aqṭār*, 5 vols, Cairo: al-Maṭba'a al-I'lāmiyya.

Binbilghīth, al-Shībānī (1995): *al-Jaysh al-Tūnisī fī 'ahd Muḥammad al-Ṣādiq Bey (1859- 1882). L'Armée Tunisienne à l'Epoque de Mohamed Sadok Bey*, Zaghwān/Ṣfāqs: FTERSI/Faculté des Lettres et Sciences Humaines Université de Sfax.

Dāghir, Yūsuf (1972–83): *Maṣādir al-dirāsa al-'Arabiyya*, 4 vols, Beirut: Manshūrāt al-Jāmi'a al-Lubnāniyya (Qism al-Dirāsāt al-Adabiyya).

al-Dimashqī, Shams al-Dīn (1866): [*Nukhbat al-dahr fī 'ajā'ib al-barr wa 'l-baḥr*] *Cosmographie de Chems-ed-Din Abou Abdallah Mohammed ed-Dimichqui. Texte arabe, publié d'après l'édition commencé par M. Fraehn d'après les manuscrits de St- Pétersbourg, de Paris, de Leyde et de Copenhague*, ed. A. F. Mehren, Saint Petersburg; trans. A. F. Mehren, *Manuel de la cosmographie du Moyen Age traduit de l'arabe 'Nokhbet ed-Dahr fi 'adjaib-il-birr w al-bah'r de Shems ed-Dîn Abou-'Abdallah Moh'ammed de Damas et accompagné d'éclaircissements*, 1874, Copenhagen: C. A. Reitzel.

Dī Ṭarrāzī, Philippe (1913–14): *Tārīkh al-ṣiḥāfa al-'arabiyya*, 4 vols, Beirut: al- Maṭba'a al-adabiyya.

Durrī, Muḥammad Bey al-Ḥakīm (1894): *Tārīkh ḥayāt al-maghfūr lahu 'Alī Mubārak Bāshā*, Cairo: al-Maba'a al-Ṭibbiyya al-Durriyya.

Fikrī, Muḥammad Amīn (1892): *Irshād al-alibbā' ilā maḥāsin Ūrubbā'*, Cairo: Maṭba'at al-Muqtaṭaf.

al-Fīrūzābādī, Muḥammad b. Ya'qūb [n.d.]: *al-Qāmūs al-muḥīṭ*, 4 vols, ed. M. M. b.al-Talamīd al-Turkuzī al-Shinqīṭī, Cairo: al-Maṭba'a al-Yamaniyya.

al-Gharnāṭī, Abū Ḥāmid (1925): 'Le Tuḥfat al-albāb de Abū Ḥāmid al-Andalusī al-Garnāṭī édité d'après les Mss 21267, 2168, 2170 de la Bibliothèque Nationale et le MS d'Alger', *Journal Asiatique*, 207, pp. 1–148, 195–303.

al-Ghassānī, Muḥammad b. ʿAbd al-Wahhāb, al-Wazīr (1884): *Voyage en Espagne d'un Ambassadeur Marocain (1690–1691)*, trans. H. Sauvaire, Paris: Ernest Leroux.

al-Ghazzāl, Aḥmad (1941): *Natījat al-ijtihād fī 'l-muhādana wa 'l-jihād*, ed. A. Bustānī, Larache: Instituto General Franco para la investigación Hispano Arabe.

Ghurbāl, Shafīq (1932): *al-Jinrāl Yaʿqūb wa 'l-fāris Laskārīs wa mashrūʿ istiqlāl Miṣr fī sanat 1801*, Cairo: Maktabat al-Maʿārif.

al-Ḥajarī, Aḥmad Qāsim (1987): *Nāṣir al-dīn ʿalā 'l-qawm al-kāfirīn*, ed. Muḥammad Razīq, Casablanca: Kulliyyat al-ādāb wa 'l-ʿulūm al-insāniyya; ed./trans. P. Van Koningsveld, Q. al-Sāmarrā'ī & G. Wiegers, Madrid: Consejo Superior de Investigaciones Cientificias (1997).

al-Hamdānī (1968): [*Ṣifat Jazīrat al-ʿArab*] *al-Hamdānī's Geographie der arabischen Halbinsel nach den Handschriften von Berlin, Constantinopel, London, Paris und Strassburg*, ed. David Hezinrich Müller, Leiden: E. J. Brill.

Ḥamīda, ʿAbd al-Raḥmān (1984): *Aʿlām al-jughrāfiyyīn al-ʿArab*, Damascus: Dār al-Fikr.

Ḥamza, ʿAbd al-Laṭīf (1950): *Adab al-maqāla al-ṣuḥufiyya fī Miṣr*, vol. I, Cairo: Dār al-Fikr al-ʿArabī.

al-Ḥarā'irī, Sulaymān (1861): *Guide de l'Afrique du Nord et de l'Orient (Conseils adressés aux Musulmans)*, Paris.

al-Ḥarā'irī, S. (1860): *Risāla fī 'l-qahwa sammāhā al-qawl al-muḥaqqaq fī taḥrīm al-bunn al- muḥarraq aw tanbīh al-ghāfilīn ʿammā irtakabūhu min tanāwul al-bunn al-muḥarraq fī hādhihi 'l-sinīn*, Paris: G.-A.Picard.

Hasan, Muḥammad ʿAbd al-Ghanī and ʿAbd alm-ʿAzīz al-Dasūqī (1968): *Rawḍat al-madāris*, Cairo: al-Hay'a al-Miṣriyya li 'l-Kitāb.

Ḥasan, M. ʿA. (1968): *Ḥasan al-ʿAṭṭār*, Cairo: Dār al-Maʿārif.

Ḥasan, M. ʿA. (1949): *Aʿlām min al-sharq wa 'l-gharb*, Cairo: Dār al-Fikr.

al-Ḥijāzī, Maḥmūd Fahmī (1975): *Uṣūl al-fikr al-ʿArabī al-ḥadīth ʿinda 'l-Ṭahṭāwī*, Cairo: al-Hay'a al-Miṣriyya li 'l-Kitāb.

al-Ḥimyarī, Ibn ʿAbd al-Munʿim (1938): [*Kitāb al-Rawḍa al-Miʿṭār fī Khabar al- Aqṭār*] *La Péninsule Ibérique au Moyen-âge d'après le Kitāb al-Rawd al-miʿtar fī khabar al-aqtār d'Ibn ʿAbd al-Munʿim al-Himyārī. Texte arabe des notices relatives à l'Espagne, au Portugal et au sud-ouest de la France, publié avec une introduction, un repertoire analytique, une traduction annotée, un glossaire et une carte*, ed./trans. E. Lévy-Provençal, Leiden: E. J. Brill.

Ibn Abī 'l-Ḍiyāf, Aḥmad (1963–65), *Itḥāf ahl al-zamān bi akhbār mulūk Tūnis wa ʿahd al-amān*, 8 vols, Tunis (Wizarat al-Thaqafa); partial ed. A.

Raymond, *Présent aux Hommes de notre Temps. Chronique des rois de Tunis et du Pacte fondamental. Chapitres IV et V*, 2 vols, Tunis (IRMC/ISHMN/ALIF), 1994; A. Abdesselem, *Chapître VI (Chronique du règne d'Aḥmad bey). Edition critique, d'après 5 manuscrits, et résumé analytique annoté*, Tunis (Université de Tunis), 1971.

Ibn ʿĀshūr, Muḥammad al-Fāḍil (1972): *al-Ḥaraka al-adabiyya fī Tūnis*, Tunis.

Ibn Faḍlān, Aḥmad b. Ḥammād (1939): [*Risāla*] ed./trans. A. Zeki Validi Togan, *Ibn Fadlān's Reisebericht*, Leipzig: Kommissionsverlag F. A. Brockhaus.

Ibn al-Faqīh al-Hamadhānī, Abū Bakr (1885): *Kitāb al-buldān*, ed. M. J. de Goeje, Leiden: E. J. Brill.

Ibn Ḥawqal, Abū ʾl-Qāsim (1938): [*Kitāb ṣūrat al-arḍ*] *Opus geographicum auctore Ibn Ḥauqal. Secundus textum et imagines codicis Constantinopolitani conservati in Bibliotheca Antiqui Palati No 3346 cui titulus est "Liber Imaginis Terrae", (Bibliotheca Geographorum Arabicorum*, II), 2 vols, ed. J. H. Kramers, Leiden: E. J. Brill; trans. J. G. Kramers and G. Wiet: *Configuration de la Terre*, 2 vols, Paris: G.-P. Maisonneuve & Larose (1964).

Ibn Jubayr al-Kinānī, Abū ʾl-Ḥusayn [n.d.], *Riḥla*, Cairo: n.p.; French trans. M. Gaudefroy-Demombynes: *Ibn Jobair: Voyages*, 4 vols, Paris: Paul Geuthner, 1949–56.

Ibn Khaldūn (n.d.): *al-Muqaddima*, Cairo: n. p.; trans. Franz Rosenthal, *The Muqaddimah. An introduction to history*, 3 vols, London: Routledge & Kegan Paul (1986).

Ibn al-Khaṭīb (1956): *Kitāb Aʿmāl al-aʿlām*, 2nd ed., 2 vols, ed. E. Lévi-Provençal, Beirut: Dār al'Makshūf.

Ibn al-Khūja, M. (1331/1913): *al-Riḥla al-Nāṣiriyya bi-diyār al-Faransāwiyya*, Tunis: al-Maṭbaʿa al-rasmiyya al-Tūnisiyya.

Ibn al-Khūja, Muḥammad (1900): *Sulūk al-ibrīz fī masālik Bārīz*, Tunis: al-Maṭbaʿa al-Rasmiyya al-Tūnisiyya.

Ibn Kur(ra)dādhbih, ʿUbayd Allāh b. al-Qāsim (1889): [*Kitāb al-masālik wa ʾl- mamālik*] *Kitāb al-Masālik wa ʾl-Mamālik auctore Abu'l-Kāsim Obaidallah ibn Abdallah Ibn Khordādhbeh*, ed. M. J. de Goeje (*Bibliotheca Geographorum Arabicorum*, VI), Leiden: E. J. Brill.

Ibn Manẓūr, Jamāl al-Dīn (1299/1881–1308/1890–91): *Lisān al-ʿArab*, 20 vols, Būlāq.

Ibn Munqidh, ʿUsāma (1886): *Kitāb al-iʿtibār*, ed. Hartwig Derenbourg, Paris: Ernest Leroux; trans. Philip Hitti, *An Arab-Syrian gentleman and warrior in the period of the Crusades; Memoirs of Usāma Ibn-Munqidh*, London: I. B. Taurus (1987).

Ibn al-Nadīm (1871–72): *Kitāb al-fihrist*, 2 vols, ed. Gustav Flügel, Leipzig: F. C. W. Vogel.

Ibn Rustah, Abū ʿAlī Aḥmad b. ʿUmar (1892): [*al-Aʿlāq al-nafīsa*] *Ibn Rosteh.*

Kitāb al-aʿlāk an-nafîsa VII auctore Abû Ali Ahmed ibn Omar Ibn Rosteh (*Bibliotheca Geographorum Arabicorum*, VII:2), 2nd edn, ed. M. J. Goeje, Leiden: E. J. Brill.

Ibn Saʿīd, Abū al-Ḥasan ʿAlī b. Mūsā (1958): *Kitāb basṭ al-arḍ fī 'l-ṭūl wa 'l- arḍ*, ed. Juan V. Gines, Tetuan: Maṭbaʿat Mawlāy al-Ḥasan.

Ibn Sālim, ʿUmar (1975): *Qābādū. Ḥayātuhu, āthāruhu wa tafkīruhu al-Iṣlāḥī*, Tunis: al-Jāmiʿa al-Tūnisiyya.

Ibn Ṣiyām, Sulaymān (1852): *Kitāb al-Riḥla ilā bilād Faransā. Relation du voyage en France de Si Sliman-Ben-Siam*, Algiers: Imprimerie du Gouvernement.

Ibn Sudā, ʿAbd al-Salīm (1950): *Dalīl mu'arrikh al-Maghrib al-Aqṣā*, Tetuan.

al-Idrīsī (1970–84): *Nuzhat al-mushtaq fī ikhtirāq al-āfāq*, 9 fasc., ed. E. Cerruli *et al.*, Naples/Rome; partial ed./trans. R. Dozy and M. J. de Goeje, 1866, Leiden: E. J. Brill (1866).

Ilyās, Adwār (1900): *Kitāb mashāhid 'Urubbā wa 'Amrīkā*, Cairo: Maṭbaʿat al- Muqtaṭaf.

ʿImāra, Muḥammad (1988): *ʿAlī Mubārak, mu'arrikh wa muhandis al-ʿumrān*, Cairo: Dār al-Shurūq.

al-Iṣṭakhrī, Ibrāhīm b. Muḥammad (1927): [*Kitāb al-Masālik wa 'l-mamālik*] *Viae regnorum: descriptio ditionis moslemicae auctore Abu Isḥák al-Fárisí al-Istakhrí* (*Bibliotheca Geographorum Arabicorum* I), ed. M. J. de Goeje, Leiden: E. J. Brill.

al-Jabartī, ʿAbd al-Raḥmān (1997): *ʿAjā'ib al-āthār fī 'l-tarājim wa 'l-akhbār*, 4 vols, ed. ʿAbd al-ʿAzīz Jamāl al-Dīn, Cairo: Maktabat Madbūlī; ed. Ḥasan Muḥammad Jawhar, ʿAbd al-Fattāḥ al-Sarnajāwī, ʿUmar al-Dasūqī and Ibrāhīm Sālim, Cairo: Lajnat al-Bayān al-ʿArabī, 7 vols (1958–67); English trans. Thomas Philipp, Moshe Perlmann *et al.*, Stuttgart: Franz Steiner (1994).

al-Jabartī, ʿA. (1975): [*Tārīkh muddat al-Faransīs*] *Al-Jabartī's chronicle of the first seven months of the French occupation of Egypt, Muḥarram-Rajab 1213/15 June- December 1798*, ed./trans. S. Moreh, Leiden: E. J. Brill.

al-Jabartī, ʿA. (1969): *Maẓhar al-taqdīs bi-dhahāb dawlat al-Faransīs*, ed. Ḥasan Muḥammad Jawhar and ʿUmar al-Dasūqī, Cairo: Lajnat al-Bayān al-ʿArabī.

Jayyid, Ramzī Mīkhā'īl (1985): *Taṭawwur al-khabar fī 'l-ṣiḥāfa al-Miṣriyya*, Cairo: GEBO.

al-Jurjānī, al-Sharīf (1983): *Kitāb al-taʿrīfāt*, ed. Ibrāhīm al-Abyārī, Cairo: Dār al-Kutub al-ʿIlmiyya.

Kaḥḥāla, ʿUmar Riḍā [n.d.]: *Muʿjam al-mu'allifīn. Tarājim muṣannifīn al-kutub al-ʿArabiyya*, 15 vols, Beirut: Dār al-Aḥyā' al-Turāth al-ʿArabī.

al-Kardūdī, Abū 'l-ʿAbbās (1885): *al-Tuḥfa al-saniyya li 'l-ḥaḍrat al-sharīfa al-Ḥasaniyya bi 'l-mamlaka al-Isbanyūliyya*, Mss no. 1282, Rabat Royal Library.

Khalaf Allāh, Muḥammad Aḥmad (1957): *'Alī Mubārak wa āthāruhu*, Cairo: Anglo-Egyptian Library.

al-Khaṭṭābī, Muḥammad al-ʿArabī (1987): 'Mushāhadāt dīblūmāsī Maghribī fī Firansā ʿām 1845/1846 fī ʿahd al-Mawlā ʿAbd al-Raḥmān b. Hishām', *Daʿwat al-Ḥaqq*, no. 263 (March), pp. 19–29, no. 264 (April), pp. 36–48.

Khayr al-Dīn al-Tūnisī (1284/1867–68): *Aqwam al-masālik fī maʿrifat aḥwāl al-mamālik*, Tunis: al-Maṭbaʿa al-Rasmiyya.

al-Khūrī, Y. (1967): 'al-ʿArab wa Urūba', *al-Abḥāth*, 20, pp. 352–92.

al-Khwārizmī, Muḥammad, b. Mūsā (1926): *[Kitāb ṣurat al-arḍ]*, ed. Hans von Mzik, *Das Kitāb ḥurat al-Arḍ des Abū Ja'far Muḥammad Ibn Mūsā al-Ḫuwārizmī: Herausgegeben nach dem handschriftlichen Unicum der Bibliothèque de l'Université et Régionale in Strassburg/Cod. 4247*, Leipzig: Otto Harrassowitz.

Krachkovskij, I. I. (1963): *Tārīkh al-adab al-jughrāfī al-'Arabī*, 2 vols, trans. Ṣalāḥ al-Dīn ʿUthmān Hāshim, Cairo.

Lūqā, Anwar (1958): 'Thawrat al-nathr al-ʿArabi yaqūduhā Rifāʿa min Bārīz', *al-Risāla al-Jadīda*, October, pp. 44–5.

Majdī, Ṣāliḥ (1958): *Ḥilyat al-zamān fī manāqib khādim al-waṭan*, ed. Jamāl al-Dīn al-Shayyāl, Cairo: Maṭbaʿat Muṣṭafā al-Bābī al-Ḥalabī.

Marrāsh, Fransīs (1867): *Riḥla ilā Bārīs*, Beirut: al-Maṭbaʿa al-Sharqiyya.

al-Masʿūdī, ʿAlī b. Ḥusayn (1960–79): *Murūj al-dhahab wa ma'ādin al-jawhar*, ed. B. de Meynard and Pavet de Courteille (rev. C. Pellat), 7 vols, Beirut: Université Libanaise de Beirut; trans. C. Pellat: *Les Prairies d'Or*, 5 vols, Paris: Paul Geuthner (1962-97).

al-Masʿūdī, ʿA. (1894): *Kitāb al-tanbīh wa 'l-ishrāf* (*Bibliotheca Geographorum Arabicorum*, III), ed. M. J. de Goeje, Leiden: E. J. Brill

al-Miknāsī, Muḥammad (1965): *Iksīr fī fikāk al-asīr*, ed. M. al-Fāsī, Rabat: al-Markaz al-Jāmiʿī li 'l-Baḥth al-ʿIlmī.

Mubārak, ʿAlī (1979–80): *al-A'māl al-kāmila*, 3 vols, ed. Muḥammad ʿImāra, Beirut: al-Mu'assasa al-ʿArabiyya li 'l-Dirāsāt wa 'l-Nashr.

Mubārak, ʿAlī (1305–6/1886–88): *al-Khiṭaṭ al-Tawfīqiyya al-jadīda li-Miṣr al-qāhira wa mudunihā wa bilādihā al-qadīma wa 'l-shahī*ra, 20 vols in four, Būlāq: al-Maṭbaʿa al-Amīriyya.

Mubārak, ʿA. (1882): *'Alam al-Dīn*, 4 vols, Alexandria: Maṭbaʿat Jarīdat al-Maḥrūsa.

al-Muqaddasī (1906): *Aḥsan al-taqāsīm fī ma'rifat al-aqālīm*, ed. M. J. de Goeje, Leiden: E. J. Brill.

Muruwwah, Adīb (1961): *al-Ṣiḥāfa al-'Arabiyya. Nash'atuhā wa taṭawwuruhā*, Beirut: Dār Maktabat al-Ḥayāt.

Nadīm, ʿAbd Allāh (1897–1901): *Sulafāt al-nadīm fī muntakhabāt al-Sayyid 'Abd Allāh Nadīm*, 2 vols, Cairo: Maṭbaʿat al-Hindiyya.

al-Najjār, Ḥusayn Fawzī (1967): *'Alī Mubārak, Abū 'l-ta'līm* (Aʿlām al-ʿArab, no. 71), Cairo: Dār al-Kātib al-ʿArabī.

al-Najjār, Ḥusayn Fawzī [n.d.]: *Rifāʿa al-Ṭahṭāwī* (Aʿlām al-ʿArab, no. 53), Cairo: al-Dār al-Miṣriyya li ʾl-Taʾlīf wa ʾl-Tarjama.

al-Naqqāsh, Mārūn (1869): *Arzat Lubnān*, Beirut: al-Maṭbaʿa al-ʿUmūmiyya.

Nuṣayr, ʿAida Ibrahim. (1990): *al-Kutub al-ʿarabiyya allatī nushirat fī Miṣr fī ʾl-qarn al-tāsiʿ ʿashar. Arabic Books Published in Egypt in the Nineteenth Century*, Cairo: The American University in Cairo Press.

Qābādū, Maḥmūd (1984): *Dīwān*, ed. ʿUmar b. Sālim, Tunis: al-Maṭbaʿa al-ʿAṣriyya li 'l- Ṭibāʿa wa 'l-Nashr.

al-Qazwīnī, Zakariyyāʾ b. Muḥammad (1849): [*ʿAjāʾib al-makhlūqāt wa āthār al- bilād*] ed. Ferdinand Wüstenfeld, *Zakarija Ben Muhammed Ben Mahmud el-Cazwini's Kosmographie. Erster Theil. ʿAjāʾib al-makhlūqāt. Die Wunder der Schöpfung. Aus den Handschriften der Bibliotheken zu Berlin, Gotha, Dresden und Hamburg*, Göttingen: Dieterischen Buchhandlung.

al-Qazwīnī, Z. (1848): [*thār al-bilād wa ʾl-akhbār al-ʿibād*], ed. Ferdinand Wüstenfeld, *Zakarija Ben Muhammed Ben Mahmud el-Cazwini's Kosmographie. Zweiter Theil. ʿAthār al-bilād. Die Denkmäler der Länder. Aus den Handschriften des Hn. Dr. Lee und der Bibliotheken zu Berlin, Gotha und Leyden*, Göttingen: Dieterischen Buchhandlung.

al-Rāfiʿī, ʿAbd al-Raḥmān (1987): *ʿAṣr Ismāʿīl*, 2 vols, Cairo: Dār al-Maʿārif.

al-Rāfiʿī, ʿA. (1954): *Shuʿarāʾ al-waṭaniyya fī Miṣr*, Cairo: Maktabat al-Nahḍa al-Miṣriyya.

al-Rāfiʿī, ʿA. (1930): *ʿAṣr Muḥammad ʿAlī*, Cairo: Maṭba ʿat al-Fikra.

Ramaḍān, ʿAbd al-Jawād (1367/1948): "Bayna ʾl-Khashshāb wa ʾl-ʿAṭṭār", *Majallat al-Azhar*, XIX, pp. 32–5, 139–44, 220–25.

Riḍwān, A. (1953): *Tārīkh maṭbaʿat Būlāq wa lamḥa ʿan tārīkh al-ṭibāʿa fī buldān al-sharq al-awsaṭ*, Cairo.

Ṣābāṭ, Khalīl (1958): *Tārīkh al-ṭibāʿa fī ʾl-sharq al-ʿArabī*, Cairo: Dār al-Maʿārif.

Sāʿid Ibn Aḥmad, Abū ʾl-Qāsim (1967): *Ṭabaqāt al-umam*, ed. Muḥammad Baḥr al-ʿUlūm, Najaf: al-Maktaba al-Ḥaydariyya.

al-Salāwī, A. (1956): *Kitāb al-istiqṣā li-akhbār duwal al-Maghrib al-aqṣā*, 9 vols, Casablanca: Dār al-Kitāb.

al-Sanūsī, Muḥammad (1976–81): *al-Riḥla al-Ḥijāziyya*, 3 vols, ed. ʿA. al-Shannūfī, Tunis: MTE.

al-Sanūsī, M. (1309/1891–92): *al-Istiṭlāʿāt al-Bārīsiyya fī maʿaraḍ sanat 1889*, Tunis: al- Maṭbaʿa al-Rasmiyya.

Sarkīs, Yūsuf Ilyās (1928): *Muʿjam al-maṭbūʿāt al-ʿarabiyya wa 'l-muʿarabba, wa huwa shāmil li-asmāʾ al-kutub al-maṭbūʿa fī ʾl-aqṭār al-sharqiyya wa ʾl-gharbiyya maʿa dhikr asmāʾ muʾallifīhā wa lamʿa min tarjamtihim wa dhālika min yawm ẓuhūr al-ṭibāʿa ilā nihāyat al-sana al-hijriyya 1339 al-muwāfiqa li sanat 1919 mīlādiyya*, 2 vols, Cairo: Maktabat al-Thaqāfa al-Dīniyya.

Sawāʿī, Muḥammad (1999): *Azmat al-muṣṭalaḥ al-ʿArabī fī 'l-qarn al-tāsiʿ*

ʿashar: muqaddima tārīkhiyya ʿāmma, Damascus: Institut Francais de Damas/Beirut: Dār al-Gharb al-Islāmī.

Sayyid Aḥmad, Aḥmad (1973): *Rifāʿa Rāfiʿ al-Ṭahṭāwī fī 'l-Sūdān*, Cairo: Lajnat al-Ta'līf wa 'l-Tarjama wa 'l-Nashr.

al-Sharqāwī, ʿAbd Allāh (1281/1864–65): *Tuḥfat al-nāẓirīn fī-man waliya Miṣr min al-wulāt wa 'l-salāṭīn*, Cairo: Maṭbaʿat Muṣṭafā Wahbī.

al-Sharqāwī, Maḥmūd (1962): *ʿAlī Mubārak, ḥayātuhu wa daʿwatuhu wa āthāruhu*, Cairo: Anglo-Egyptian Library.

al-Sharqāwī, Maḥmūd (1955–56): *Dirāsāt fī tārīkh al-Jabartī. Miṣr fī 'l-qarn al-thāmin ʿashar*, Cairo: Anglo-Egyptian Library, 2nd edn (1957).

Shaybub, Khalil (1948): *ʿAbd al-Raḥmān al-Jabartī* (Iqra', no. 70), Cairo.

Shaykhū, Luwīs (1991): *Tárīkh al-ādāb al-ʿarabiyya 1800–1925*, Beirut: Dār al-Mashriq.

al-Shayyāl, Jamāl al-Dīn (1958): *al-Tārīkh wa 'l-mu'arrikhūn fī Miṣr fī 'l-qarn al-tāsiʿ ʿashar*, Cairo: Dār al-Nahḍa.

al-Shayyāl, Jamāl al-Dīn (1958b): *Rifāʿa Rāfiʿ al-Ṭahṭāwī*, Cairo: Dār al-Maʿārif.

al-Shayyāl, Jamāl al-Dīn (1951): *Tārīkh al-tarjama wa 'l-ḥaraka al-thaqāfiyya fī ʿaṣr Muḥammad ʿAlī*, Cairo: Dār al-Fikr al-ʿArabī.

al-Shidyāq, Aḥmad Fāris (1881): *al-Wāsiṭa fī maʿrifat aḥwāl Mālṭa/Kashf al-mukhabba' fī funūn Ūrubbā*, Istanbul: al-Jawā'ib.

al-Shidyāq, A. F. (1855): *al-Sāq ʿalā 'l-sāq fīmā huwa al-Fāryāq aw ayyām wa shuhūr wa aʿwām fī ʿajam al-ʿArab wa 'l-Aʿjam. La Vie et les Aventures de Fariac*, Paris: Benjamin Duprat (Cairo: Maktabat al-ʿArab, 1919).

al-Ṭahṭāwī, Rifāʿa Rāfiʿ (1973–80): *al-Aʿmāl al-kāmila li-Rifāʿa Rāfiʿ al-Ṭahṭāwī*, 4 vols, ed. Muḥammad ʿImāra, Beirut: al-Mu'assasa al-ʿArabiyya li 'l-Dirāsāt wa 'l-Nashr.

al-Ṭahṭāwī, R. R. (1285/1898): *Anwār tawfīq al-jalīl fī akhbār Miṣr wa tawthīq banī Ismāʿīl*, 2nd edn, Būlāq.

al-Ṭahṭāwī, R. R. (1287/1871): *al-Qawl al-sadīd fī 'l-ijtihād wa 'l-tajdīd*, Cairo: Wādī 'l-Nīl.

al-Ṭahṭāwī, R. R. (1279/1872–73): *al-Murshid al-amīn li'l-banāt wa 'l-banīn*, Cairo: Maṭbaʿat al-Madāris al-Malakiyya.

al-Ṭahṭāwī, R. R. (1254/1838): *al-Jughrāfiyā al-ʿumūmiyya*, 4 vols, Būlāq.

al-Ṭahṭāwī, R. R. (1249/1833): *Qalā'id al-mafākhir fī gharā'ib ʿawā'id al-awā'il wa 'l-awākhir*, Būlāq.

Tājir, Jāk [n.d.]: *Ḥarakat al-tarjama bi Miṣr khilāl al-qarn al-tāsiʿ ʿashar*, Cairo: Dār al-Maʿārif.

Taymūr, Aḥmad (1967): *Aʿlām al-fikr al-Islāmī fī 'l-ʿaṣr al-ḥadīth*, Cairo: Lajnat Nashr al-Mu'allafāt al-Taymūriyya.

al-Turk, Niqūlā (1950): *Chronique d'Egypte (1798–1804)*, ed./trans. Gaston Wiet, Cairo: IFAO.

Ṭūsūn, ʿUmar (1934): *al-Baʿthāt al-ʿilmiyya fī ʿahd Muḥammad ʿAlī thumma fī ʿahday ʿAbbās I wa Saʿīd*, Alexandria: Maṭbaʿat Ṣalāḥ al-Dīn.

Van Dyke, Edward Cornelius (1897): *Iktifāʾ al-qanūʿ fīmā huwa maṭbūʿ*, rev. by Muḥammad ʿAlī al-Babalāwī, Cairo: Maṭbaʿat al-Hilāl.

al-Wardānī Salīm (1888–90): ʻal-Riḥla al-Andalusiyyaʼ, *al-Hāḍira*, Nos 3–9, 11, 26–8, 30, 33–4, 37, 40–43, 53, 61–2, 76, 90–91, 94.

al-Yaʿqūbī, Aḥmad Ibn Abī Yaʿqūb (1892): [*Kitāb al-buldān*] *Kitāb al-boldān auctore Ahmed ibn abî Jakûb ibn Wādhih al-Kātib al-Jakûbî* (*Bibliotheca Geographorum Arabicorum*, VII:1), 2nd edn, ed. M. J. Goeje, Leiden: E. J. Brill.

Yāqūt al-Ḥamawī (1355/1936–1357/1938): *Muʿjam al-udabāʾ: Irshād al-arīb ilā maʿrifat al-adīb*, 20 vols, ed. A. F. Rifāʿī, Cairo: Maṭbaʿat al-Maʾmūn.

Yāqūt al-Ḥamawī (1866–73): *Muʿjam al-buldān*, 6 vols, ed. Ferdinand Wüstenfeld, Leipzig: F. A. Brockhaus.

Yūnus, ʿAbd al-Ḥamīd (1994): *Khiyāl al-ẓill*, Cairo: al-Dār al-Miṣriyya li ʻl-Taʼlīf wa ʻl-Tarjama wa ʻl-Nashr.

al-Zabīdī, Abū ʾl-Fayḍ Muḥammad Murtaḍā (1306–07/1888–90): *Tāj al-ʿarūs min sharḥ jawāhir al-qāmūs*, 10 vols, Cairo: al- Maṭbaʿa al-Khayriyya.

Zaydān, Jurjī (1957): *Tārīkh ādāb al-lugha al-ʿArabiyya*, new ed. rev. by Shawqī Ḍayf, 4 vols, Cairo: Dār al-Hilāl.

Zaydān, J. (1910): *Tarājim mashāhīr al-sharq fī ʾl-qarn al-tāsiʿ ʿashar*, 2 vols, Cairo: Dār al-Hilāl.

Zaydān, Yūsuf (1996–98): *Fihris makhṭūṭāt Rifāʿa Rāfiʿ al-Ṭahṭāwī*, 3 vols, Cairo: Maʿhad al-Makhṭūṭāt al-ʿArabiyya.

Zāyid, Saʿīd (1958): *ʿAlī Mubārak wa aʿmāluhu*, Cairo: n.p.

Zaytūnī, Laṭīf (1994): *Ḥarakat al-tarjama fī ʿaṣr al-nahḍa*, Beirut: Dār al-Nahār li ʻl-Nashr.

C. Works in European Languages

ʿAbd al-Raziq, M. H. (1922): ʻArabic literature since the beginning of the nineteenth centuryʼ, *Bulletin of the School of Oriental Studies*, II, 249–65, 755–62.

Abdel Moula, Mahmoud (1971): *L'Université Zaytounienne et la Société Tunisienne*, Tunis: Centre National de la Recherche Scientifique.

Abdesselam, Ahmed and Nebil Ben Khelil (1975): *Sadiki et les Sadikiens (1875–1975)*, Tunis: Cérès productions.

Abdesselem, Ahmed (1973): *Les Historiens Tunisiens des XVIIe, XVIIIe, et XIXe siècles. Essai d'histoire culturelle*, Paris: C. Klincksieck.

Abou-Seida, A. (1971): *Diglossia in Egyptian Arabic: Prolegomena to a pan-Arabic sociolinguistic study*, Unpublished PhD thesis, University of Texas at Austin.

Académie Française (1835): *Dictionnaire de l'Académie Française*, 2 vols, 6th edn, Paris: Firmin Didot Frères.

Agoub, Joseph (1824): *La Lyre Brisée*, Paris: Dondey-Duprey, père et fils.
Ahmed, Leila (1978): *Edward Lane*, London.
Ahmed M., 1968, *Muslim Education and the Scholars' Social Status*, Zurich.
Al-Husry, Khaldun S. (1966): *Origins of Modern Arab Political Thought*, Delmar, NY: Caravan Books.
Ali, Saïd Ismaïl (1994): 'Rifa'a al-Tahtawi (1801–1874)', *Perspectives*, XXIV, vol. XXIV, Nos 3–4, pp. 649–76.
Alleaume, G. (1982): 'L'orientaliste dans le miroir de la littérature arabe', *British Society for Middle Eastern Studies Bulletin*, 9:i, pp. 5–13.
Al-Qadi, Wadad (1981): "East and West in ʿAlī Mubārak's *Alamudddin*", in ed. Marwan Buheiry, *Intellectual Life in the Arab East, 1890-1930,* Beirut: AUB Press, pp. 21–37.
Altman, Israel (1976): *The Political Thought of Rifāʿa Rāfiʿ aṭ-Ṭahṭāwī, a Nineteenth Century Egyptian Reformer*, Unpublished PhD dissertation, University of California.
Amor, Abdelfattah (1983): 'La notion d' "*umma*" dans les constitutions des états arabes', *Arabica*, XXX, pp. 267–89.
Ampère, Jean-Jacques (1881): *Voyage en Egypte et en Nubie*, Paris: Calmann-Lévy.
Arberry, Arthur J. (1983): *The Koran Interpreted*, Oxford: Oxford University Press.
Arnauld, Antoine and Pierre Nicole (1965): *La Logique ou l'Art de Penser contenant, outre les règles communes, plusieurs observations nouvelles, propres à former le jugement*, ed. Pierre Clair and François Girbal, Paris: Presses Universitaires de France.
Arnoulet, François (1994): 'L'enseignement congrégationiste en Tunisie aux XIXe et XXe siècles', *Revue du Monde Musulman et de la Méditerranée*, 72, pp. 26–36.
Arnoulet, F. (1954): 'La pénétration intellectuelle en Tunisie avant le Protectorat', *Revue Africaine*, 98, pp. 140–82.
Artin, Yacoub (1890): *L'Instruction Publique en Egypte*, Paris: Leroux.
Ashtiany, Julia, T. M. Johnstone, J. D. Latham, R. B. Serjeant and G. Rex Smith (eds) (1990): *The Cambridge History of Arabic Literature. 'Abbasid belles-lettres*, Cambridge: Cambridge University Press.
Ashtor, Eliyahu (1969): 'Che cose sapevano i geografi Arabi dell'Europa occidentale?', *Rivista di Storia Italiana*, 81, pp. 453–79.
Aumer, Joseph (1866): *Die arabische Handschriften der K. Hof- und Staatsbibliothek in Muenchen* (Catalogus codicum manu scriptorum Bibliotheca Regiae Monacensis, I/2), Munich: Palm'schen Hofbuchhandlung.
Auriant (1933): *Aventuriers et Originaux*, Paris: Gallimard.
Auriant (1923): 'Un précurseur du Docteur J.-C. Madrus', *Le Monde Nouveau*, 1–15 Sep., pp. 176–81.

Ayalon, Ami (1995): *The Press in the Middle East. A History*, Oxford: Oxford University Press.

Ayalon, A. (1989): 'Dimuqraṭiyya, ḥurriyya, jumhūriyya: the modernization of the Arabic political vocabulary', *Asian and African Studies*, 23:2, pp. 23–42.

Ayalon, A. (1987): 'From Fitna to Thawra', *Studia Islamica*, pp. 149–74.

Ayalon, A. (1984): 'The Arab discovery of America in the nineteenth century', *Middle Eastern Studies*, 20, pp. 5–17.

Ayalon, David (1960): 'The historian al-Jabartī and his background', *Bulletin of the School of Oriental and African Studies*, XXIII:2, pp. 217–49.

Ayalon, D. (1949): 'The Circassians in the Mamlūk kingdom', *Journal of the American Oriental Society*, 69, pp. 135–47.

Baccouche, T. (1994): *L'emprunt en arabe moderne*, Tunis: Beït Al-Hikma.

Baccouche, T. (1969): 'Description phonologique du parler arabe de Djemmal', in *Travaux de phonologie. Parlers de: Djemmal, Gabès, Mahdia (Tunisie), Tréviso (Italie)*, Tunis (C.E.R.E.S.), pp. 23–82.

Bachtaly C. (1934–35): 'Un membre oriental de l'Institut d'Egypte: Don Raphaël (1759-1831)', *Bulletin de l'Institut Français d'Egypte*, XVII, pp. 237–60.

Badawi, M. M. (1993): *A Short History of Modern Arabic Literature*, Oxford: Clarendon Press.

Badawi, M. M. (ed.) (1992): *The Cambridge History of Arabic Literature. Modern Arabic Literature*, Cambridge: Cambridge University Press.

Badawi, M. M. (1988): *Early Arabic Drama*, Cambridge: Cambridge University Press.

Badger, George Percy (1895): *An English-Arabic Lexicon, in which the equivalents for English words and idiomatic sentences are rendered into literary and colloquial Arabic*, London: C. Kegan Paul & Co.

Baer, Gabriel (1962): *A History of Land Ownership in Modern Egypt, 1800–1950*, Oxford: Oxford University Press.

Bahgat, Ali (1900): 'La famille musulmane du général Abdallah Menou', *Bulletin de l'Institut Egyptien*, 4th series, 1:2, pp. 37–43.

Bahgat, A. (1898): 'Acte de mariage du général Abdallah Menou avec la dame Zobaïdah', *Bulletin de l'Institut Egyptien*, 3rd series, 9:2, pp.221–35.

Balayé, Simone (1988): *La Bibliothèque Nationale des Origines à 1800*, Geneva.

Balteau, J. *et al.* (eds) (1933-): *Dictionnaire de Biographie Française*, Paris: Letouzey et Ané.

Bannerth, Ernst (1964–66): 'La Khalwatiyya en Egypte. Quelques aspects de la vie d'une confrérie', *Mélanges de l'Institut Dominicain d'Etudes Orientales du Caire*, VIII, pp. 1- 74.

Bargeton, René *et al.* (1981): *Les préfets du 11 ventôse du VIII au 4 septembre 1870. Répertoire nominatif et territorial*, Paris: Archives Nationales.

Barthélemy, A.-M. and Méry (1827): *La Bacriade ou la guerre d'Alger, poème héroï-comique en cinq chants*, Paris: A. Dupont.

Barthes, Roland (1972): *Le Degré Zéro de l'Ecriture suivi de nouveaux essai critiques*, Paris: Editions du Seuil.

Beeston, A. F. L., T. M. Johnstone, R. B. Serjeant and G. R. Smith (eds) (1982): *The Cambridge History of Arabic Literature. Arabic literature to the end of the Umayyad period*, Cambridge: Cambridge University Press.

Ben Halima, H. (1974): *Un Demi-siècle de Théâtre Arabe en Tunisie (1907–1957)*, Tunis: Publications de l'Université de Tunis, Faculté des lettres et sciences humaines de Tunis.

Ben Sedira, Belkassem (1882): *Dictionnaire Arabe-Français*, Algiers: A. Jourdan.

Berthelot, M. *et al.* (eds) (1886–1902): *La Grande Encyclopédie. Inventaire raisonné des sciences, des lettres et des arts*, 31 vols, Paris: Lamirault.

Bianchi T. X. (1843): 'Catalogue général des livres arabes, persans et turcs, imprimés à Boulac en Egypte depuis l'introduction de l'imprimerie dans ce pays', *Journal Asiatique*, série iv:2 (July-August), pp. 24–61.

Bibliothèque Nationale (1897–1981): *Catalogue Général des Livres Imprimés de la Bibliothèque Nationale*, 231 vols, Paris.

Bibliothèque Nationale (1878): *Notice des Objets Exposés*, Paris.

Bilici, Faruk (1989): 'Révolution française, révolution turque et fait religieux', *Revue du Monde Musulman et de la Méditerranée*, vol. 52–3:2/3, pp.173–85.

Bittar, André (1992): 'La dynamique commerciale des Grecs-catholiques en Egypte aux XVIIIe siècle', *Annales Islamologiques*, 26, pp. 181–96.

Blachère, Régis and Henri Darmaun (1957): *Extraits des Principaux Géographes Arabes du Moyen Age*, 2nd edn, Paris: C. Klincksieck.

Bocthor, Ellious (1882): *Dictionnaire Français-Arabe*, 2nd edn (rev. Caussin de Perceval), Paris: Firmin Didot.

Bozarslan, Hamit (1989): 'Révolution française et jeunes Turcs (1908–1914)', *Revue du Monde Musulman et de la Méditerranée*, vol. 52–3:2/3, pp.160–72.

Braune, Walther (1933): 'Beiträge zur Geschichte der neuarabischen Schrifttums', *Mitteilungen des Seminars für Orientalische Sprachen*, XXXVI:2.

Brocchi, Giovanni Batista (1841): *Giornale delle osservazioni fatte nei viaggi in Egitto, nella Siria e nella Nubia*, Bassano.

Brockelmann Carl (1937–49): *Geschichte der arabischen Literatur*, 2 vols, 3 Suppl. vols, Leiden: E. J. Brill.

Brown, Leon Carl (1974): *The Tunisia of Ahmad Bey, 1837–1855*, Princeton: Princeton University Press.

Brugman, J. (1984): *An Introduction to the History of Modern Arabic Literature in Egypt*, Leiden: E. J. Brill.

Brunschvig, Robert (1965): 'Justice religieuse et justice laïque dans la Tunisie des deys et des beys jusqu'au milieu du XIXe siècle', *Studia Islamica*, 23, pp. 27–70.

Brunschvig, R. (1940–47): *La Berbérie Orientale sous les Hafsides: des origines à la fin du XVe siècle*, 2 vols, Paris: Adrien-Maisonneuve.

Buchwald, Jed Z. & Diane Greco Josefowicz (2010): *The Zodiac of Paris: How an Improbable Controversy over an Ancient Egyptian Artefact Provoked a Modern Debate between Religion and Science*, Princeton NJ: Princeton University Press.

Buonaventura, Wendy & Ibrahim Farrah (1998): *Serpent of the Nile: Women and Dance in the Arab World*, London: Saqi.

Butler, A. J. (1978): *The Arab Conquest of Egypt*, ed. P. M. Fraser, Oxford: Oxford University Press.

Butros, Albert (1973): 'Turkish, Italian and French loanwords in the colloquial Arabic of Palestine and Jordan', *Studies in Linguistics*, 23, pp. 87–104.

Cachia, Pierre (1990): *An Overview of Modern Arabic Literature*, Edinburgh: Edinburgh University Press.

Cachia, P. (1977): 'The Egyptian *mawwāl*', *Journal of Arabic Literature*, VIII, pp. 66–103.

Callens, M. (1955): 'L'hébergement à Tunisie. Fondouks et oukalas', *IBLA*, pp. 257–71.

Carré, Jean-Marie (1956): *Voyageurs et Ecrivains Français en Egypte*, 2nd edn, 2 vols, Cairo: Institut Français d'Archéologie Orientale du Caire.

Catafogo, Joseph (1858): *An English and Arab Dictionary in Two Parts, Arabic and English, and English and Arabic, in which the Arabic words are represented in the Oriental character, as well as their correct pronunciation and accentuation shewn in English letters*, 2 vols, London: Bernard Quaritch.

Caussin de Perceval, A. (1833): 'Relation d'un voyage en France par le Cheikh Réfaa', *Journal Asiatique*, 2ème série, XI, pp. 222–51.

Černy, Jaroslav (1976): *Coptic Etymological Dictionary*, Cambridge: Cambridge University Press.

Charles-Roux, François (1955): *Edme-François Jomard et la Réforme de l'Egypte en 1839*, Cairo: IFAO.

Chater, Khelifa (1984): *Dépendance et Mutation Précoloniales. La Régence de Tunis de 1815 à 1857*, Tunis: Université de Tunis.

Cheddadi, Abdessalam (1980): 'Le système de pouvoir en Islam d'après Ibn Khaldûn', *Annales ESC*, vol. 35:3–4, pp. 534–51.

Chenoufi, Ali (1976): 'Un rapport inédit en langue arabe sur l'Ecole de Guerre du Bardo', *Cahiers de Tunisie*, 24, pp. 45–118.

Chenoufi, Moncef (1974): *Le Problème des Origines de l'Imprimerie et de la Presse Arabes en Tunisie dans sa Relation avec la Renaissance 'Nahda' (1847–1887)*, 2 vols, Lille: Université de Lille.

Choueiri, Youssef M. (1989): *Arab History and the Nation-state: a study in modern Arab historiography 1820–1980*, London: Routledge.

Clot-Bey, Antoine-Barthélemy (1943): *Mémoires*, ed. Jacques Tagher, Cairo: IFAO.

Clot-Bey, A. (1840): *Aperçu Général sur l'Egypte*, 2 vols, Paris: Fortin et Masson.

Clot-Bey, A. (1833): *Compte-rendu des Travaux de l'Ecole de Médécine*, Paris.
Cole, Juan R. (1980): 'Rifāʿa al-Ṭahṭāwī and the revival of practical philosophy', *Muslim World*, 70, pp. 29–46.
Colin, G. S. (1948): 'Histoire, organisation et enseignement de l'Ecole des Langues Orientales', *Cent-Cinquantenaire de l'Ecole des Langues Orientales*, París: Imprimerie Nationale de France, pp. 95–112.
Cook, Michael (2000): *Commanding the Right and Forbidding the Wrong in Islamic Thought*, Cambridge: Cambridge University Press.
Courtalon, Corinne (ed.) (1995): *Guide Bleu. Paris*, Paris: Hachette.
Couty, Daniel (1988): *Histoire de la Littérature Française. XIXe siècle. Tome I: 1800–1851*, Paris: Bordas.
Crabbs, Jack A. Jr (1984): *The Writing of History in Nineteenth-century Egypt. A study in national transformation*, Cairo: The American University in Cairo Press/Detroit: Wayne State University Press.
Crum, W. E. (1929–39): *A Coptic Dictionary*, Oxford: Oxford University Press.
Cuoq, Joseph M. (1979): *Journal d'un Notable du Caire*, Paris: Albin Michel.
Cuoq, J. M. (1975): *Recueil des Sources Arabes concernant l'Afrique Occidentale du VIIIe au XVIe Siècle (Bilād al-Sūdān)*, Paris: CNRS.
Daly, M. W. (ed.) (1998): *The Cambridge History of Egypt. Volume 2. Modern Egypt, from 1517 to the end of the twentieth century*, Cambridge: Cambridge University Press.
Davison, Roderic H. (1985): 'Vienna as a major Ottoman diplomatic post in the nineteenth century', in A. Tietze (ed.): *Habsburgisch-osmanische Beziehungen*, Vienna: Verlag des Verbandes der wissenschaftlichen Gesellschaften Österreichs, pp. 251–80.
de la Brière, L. (1897): *Champollion Inconnu: lettres inédites*, Paris.
Décobert, Christian (1989): 'L'orientalisme, des lumières à la Révolution, selon Silvestre de Sacy', *Revue du Monde Musulman et de la Méditerranée*, Nos 52-3:2–3, pp. 49-62.
de Goeje, M. J. (1879): *Bibliotheca geographorum arabicorum. IV. Indices, glossarium et addenda et emendanda ad part. I-III*, Leiden: E. J. Brill.
Dehérain, Henri (1939): 'Etablissements d'enseignement et de recherche de l'Orientalisme à Paris', *Revue Internationale de l'Enseignement*, pp.125–48.
Dehérain, H. (1938): *Silvestre de Sacy, ses Contemporains et ses Disciples*, Paris: P. Geuthner.
Derenbourg, Hartwig (1923): *Bibliothèque des Arabisants Français: Silvestre de Sacy*, 2 vols, Cairo: IFAO.
De Jong, F. (1983): 'The itinerary of Ḥasan al-ʿAṭṭār (1766–1835): a reconsideration and its implication', *Journal of Semitic Studies*, XXVIII:1, pp. 99–128.
Delanoue, Gilbert (1982): *Moralistes et Politiques Musulmans dans l'Egypte du XIXe Siècle (1798-1882)*, 2 vols, Cairo: IFAO.

Demeerseman, André (1978): 'La fonction de Cheikh al-Islam en Tunisie, de la fin du XVIIIème au début du XXème siècle', *IBLA,* 142, pp. 215–70.

Demeerseman, A. (1956): 'Un grand témoin des premières idées modernisantes en Tunisie', *IBLA*, pp. 343–73.

de Slane, Mac Guckin (1883–95): *Catalogue des Manuscrits Arabes de la Bibliothèque Nationale*, 2 vols, Paris: Imprimerie Nationale.

de Tott, François (1784): *Mémoire sur les Turcs et les Tartares,* 4 vols, Amsterdam.

Didier, Charles (1856): *Cinq Cents Lieues sur le Nil,* Paris: Hachette.

Donini, Pier Giovanni (1991): *Arab Travellers and Geographers,* London: IMMEL.

Dor, Edouard (1872): *L'Instruction Publique en Egypte*, Paris: Lacroix.

Douin, Georges (1926): *Les Premières Frégates de Mohammed Aly (1824–1827)*, Cairo: IFAO.

Douin, G. (1924): *L'Egypte Indépendante. Projet de 1801*, Cairo: IFAO.

Douin, G. (1923): *Une Mission Militaire Française auprès de Mohamed Ali*, Cairo: Société Royale de Géographie d'Egypte.

Dozy, Reinhard Pieter (1967): *Supplément aux Dictionnaires Arabes,* 2 vols, 3rd edn, Leiden: E. J. Brill/Paris: G. P. Maisonneuve-Larose.

Dozy, R. P. (1845): *Dictionnaire Détaillé des Noms des Vêtements chez les Arabes*, Amsterdam: Jean Muller.

Drevet, R. (Commandant) (1922): *L'Armée Tunisienne*, Tunis: Impr. Ch. Weber et Cie.

Du Bres, Charles (1931): 'Edme-François Jomard et les origines du Cabinet des cartes, *Bulletin de la Section de Géographie du Comité des Travaux Historiques et Scientifiques*, XLVI, pp. 1–133.

Du Camp, Maxime (1882–83): *Souvenirs Littéraires,* 2 vols, Paris: Hachette.

Dunant, J. Henri (1858): *Notice sur la Régence de Tunis,* Geneva: Imprimerie de Jules-G^{me} Fick.

Dunlop, D. M. (1957): 'The British Isles according to medieval Arabic authors', *Islamic Quarterly*, IV, pp. 11–28.

Dupont-Ferrier, G. (1921–25): *Du Collège de Clermont au Lycée Louis-le-Grand (1563–1920)*, 3 vols, Paris: De Boccard.

Edwards, I. E. S. (1985): *The Pyramids of Egypt*, rev. edn, Harmondsworth: Penguin.

EI1, EI2: see *Encyclopaedia of Islam*

Eisenstein, H. (1994): 'Die Darstellung Europas an mittelalterlichen arabischen Weltkarten', in W. Scharfe (ed.): *Geschichte der Kartographie*, Berlin: Deutschen Gesellschaft für Kartographie, pp. 119–27.

Elatri, Salah (1974): *Les Rapports Etymologiques et Sémantiques des Langues Classiques et de la Langue Arabe*, Lille: Université de Lille.

El-Hajji, A. A. (1970): *Andalusian Diplomatic Relations with Western Europe during the Umayyad period (138–666 ah/755–976 ad)*, Beirut: Dar al-Irshad.

Encyclopaedia of Islam, 1st edn, 4 vols, Leiden/London (1913-34; Supplement, 1938) [= *EI1*]; 2nd edn, 12 vols, Leiden/London: E. J. Brill (1960-2005) [= *EI2*].

Enani, M. M. (2000): *On Translating Arabic: A Cultural Approach*, Cairo: General Egyptian Book Organization.

Erlich, Haggai and Israel Gershoni (eds) (2000): *The Nile: Histories, Cultures, Myths*, Boulder, CO: Lynne Reiner Publishers.

Fahmy, M. (1954): *La Révolution de l'Industrie en Egypte et ses Conséquences Sociales au 19è Siècle*, Leiden: E. J. Brill.

Faroqhi, S. (1986): 'Coffee and spices: official Ottoman reactions to Egyptian trade in the later 16th century', *Wiener Zeitschrift für die Kunde des Morgenlandes*, 76, pp. 87–93.

Faulkner, Raymond O. (1976): *A Concise Dictionary of Middle Egyptian*, Oxford: Oxford University Press.

Fénelon, François de Salignac de la Mothe- (1995): *Les Aventures de Télémaque*, ed. Jacques Le Brun, Paris: Gallimard.

Ferchiou, Sophie (1970): *Techniques et Sociétés. Exemple de la fabrication de chéchias en Tunisie*, Paris.

Findley, Carter Vaughn (1989): *Ottoman Civil Officialdom. A social history*, Princeton: Princeton University Press.

Flaubert, Gustave (1991): *Voyage en Egypte*, ed. Pierre-Marc de Biasi, Paris: Grasset.

Fliedner, Stephan (1990): *'Alī Mubārak und seine Hiṭaṭ. Kommentierte Übersetzung der Autobiographie und Werkbesprechung*, Berlin: Klaus Schwarz Verlag.

Flottès-Dubrulle, A. (1989): *Trésors. Bibiliothèque Nationale*, Paris.

Foucaud, Jean-François (1978): *La Bibliothèque Royale sous la Monarchie de Juillet (1830–1848)*, Paris: Bibliothèque Nationale.

Frémaux, Jacques (1989): 'La France, la Révolution et l'Orient: aspects diplomatiques", *Revue du Monde Musulman et de la Méditerranée*, 52–3, pp.18–28.

Freytag, Georg Wilhelm (1830–1837): *Lexicon Arabico-Latinum praesertim ex Djeuhari Firuzabadique et aliorum arabum operibus adhibitis golii quoque et aliorum libris confectum accedit index vocum Latinarum Locupletissimus*, 4 vols, Halle: C.A. Schwetschke et Filium.

Fück, J. (1955): *Die arabischen Studien in Europa bis den Anfang des 20. Jahrhunderts*, Leipzig: O. Harrassowitz.

Furet, F. and J. Ozouf (1977): *Lire et Ecrire. L'alphabétisation des Français de Calvin à Jules Ferry*, Paris: Ed. de Minuit.

Gallagher, Nancy E. (1983): *Medicine and Power in Tunisia, 1780–1900*, Cambridge: Cambridge University Press.

Gallagher, N. E. (1977): *Epidemics in the Regency of Tunis, 1780–1880: a study in the social history of medicine*, Unpublished PhD thesis, UCLA.

Ganiage, Jean (1959): *Les Origines du Protectorat Français en Tunisie (1861–1881)*, Paris: P.U.F.

Gardet, Louis (1973): 'Quelques réflexions sur un problème de théologie et philosophie musulmanes: toute-puissance divine et liberté humaine', *Revue de l'Occident Musulman et de la Méditerranée (Mélanges Le Tourneau, I)*, 13–14, pp. 381- 94.

Gasselin, Eduard (1880–86): *Dictionnaire Français-Arabe (arabe vulgaire - arabe grammatical)*, 2 vols, Paris: Leroux.

Gellens, Simeon (1990): 'The search for knowledge in medieval Muslim societies: a comparative approach', in D. Eickelman and J. Piscatori (eds): *Muslim Travellers: Pilgrimage, Migration, and the Religious Imagination*, Berkeley/Los Angeles: Routledge, pp. 50–65.

Gilson Miller, Susan (1992): *Disorienting Encounters. Travels of a Moroccan scholar in France in 1845–1846*, Oxford: Oxford University Press.

Goby, J.-E (1953): 'Où vécurent les savants de Bonaparte en Egypte?', *Cahiers d'Histoire Egyptienne*, 5, pp. 290–301.

Göcek, M. F. (1986): *East Encounters West. France and the Ottoman Empire in the 18th century*, Istanbul.

Goldziher, Ign. (1890): 'Alî Bāschā Mubārak: *al-khiṭaṭ al-Tawfīqiyya al-jadīda li-Miṣr al-Qāhira wa mudunihā al-qadīma wa 'l-shahīra*', *Wiener Zeitschrift für die Kunde des Morgenlandes*, 4, pp. 347–52.

Goodwin, Godfrey (1992): *The Janissaries*, London.

Gorceix, Septime (1953): *Bonneval Pacha, pacha à trois queues, une vie d'aventures au XVIIIe siècle*, Paris: Plon.

Graf, Georg (1944–53): *Geschichte der christlichen arabischen Literatur*, 5 vols, Vatican.

Gran, Peter (1979): *The Islamic Roots of Capitalism: Egypt 1760–1840*, Austin, TX: University of Texas Press.

Guémard, Georges (1927): 'Les auxiliaires de l'armée de Bonaparte en Egypte (1798–1801)', *Bulletin de l'Institut d'Egypte*, 9, pp. 1–17.

Guidi, Ignazio (1909) : 'L'Europa occidentale negli antichi geografi arabi', *Florilegium ou Recueil de Travaux d'Erudition dédiés à Monsieur le Marquis Melchior de Vogüe à l'occasion du 84ème anniversaire de sa naissance*, Paris, pp. 263-69.

Guidi, I. (1877): 'La descrizione di Roma nei geografi arabi', *Archivio della Società di Storia Patria*, I, pp. 173–218.

Gunny, Ahmad (1978): 'Montesquieu's view of Islam in the *Lettres Persanes*', in Haydn Mason (ed.), *Studies on Voltaire and the Eighteenth Century*, CLXXIV, Oxford: Oxford University Press.

Haarmann, Ulrich (1988): 'Arabic in speech, Turkish in lineage: Mamluks and their sons in the intellectual life of fourteenth-century Egypt and Syria', *Journal of Semitic Studies*, XXXIII:1, pp. 81–114.

Habeisch, Joseph [and J. C. Lagoudakis] (1896): *Dictionnaire Français-Arabe*, 2nd edn, Paris: Boyveau et Chevillet.

Haddad, Geogre (1970): 'A project for the independence of Egypt, 1801',

Journal of the American Oriental Society, pp. 169–83.
Hadj-Sadok (1948): 'Le genre "rihla"', *Bulletin d'Etudes Arabes*, VIII:40, pp. 195–206.
Hamilton, Alistair (1994): 'An Egyptian Traveller in the Republic of Letters: Josephus Barbatus or Abudacnus the Copt', *Journal of the Warburg and Courtauld Institutes*, 57, pp. 123–50.
Hamont, P. N. (1943): *L'Egypte sous Méhémet Ali*, 3 vols, Paris: Léautey et Lecointe.
Hattox, Ralph S. (1996): *Coffee and Coffeehouses. The origins of a social beverage in the medieval Near East*, Seattle.
Haywood, John (1971): *Modern Arabic Literature, 1800–1970. An introduction with extracts in translation*, London: Lund Humphries.
Heyd, Uriel (ed.) (1961): *Islamic History and Civilization*, Jerusalem: The Hebrew University.
Heyworth-Dunne, James (1940): 'Printing and translation under Muhammad ʿAlî: The foundation of modern Arabic', *Journal of the Royal Asiatic Society*, pp. 325- 49.
Heyworth-Dunne, J. (1938): *An Introduction to the History of Education in Modern Egypt*, London: Luzac and Co.
Heyworth-Dunne, J. (1937–42): 'Rifāʿa Badawī Rāfiʿ aṭ-Ṭāhṭāwī: the Egyptian revivalist', *Bulletin of the School of Oriental and African Studies*, IX (1937–39), pp. 961–7; X (1940–42), pp. 399–415.
Hinds, Martin and El-Said Badawi (1986): *A Dictionary of Egyptian Arabic. Arabic-English*, Beirut: Librarie du Liban.
Hinz, Walther (1970): *Islamische Masse und Gewichte umgerechnet ins metrische System*, Leiden: E. J. Brill.
Hitti, Philip K. (1991): *History of the Arabs*, 10th edn, Basingstoke: Macmillan.
Hoeffer, Ferdinand (ed.) (1862–77): *Nouvelle Biographie Générale depuis les Temps les plus Reculés jusqu'à nos Jours*, 46 vols, Paris: Didot.
Holt, P. M. and M. W. Daly (1994): *A History of the Sudan: from the coming of Islam to the present day*, 4th edn, London: Longman.
Holt, P. M., Ann K. S. Lambton and Bernard Lewis (1990): *The Cambridge History of Islam. 2B. Islamic society and civilization*, Cambridge: Cambridge University Press.
Holt, P. M., Ann K. S. Lambton & Bernard Lewis (1988): *The Cambridge History of Islam. IA. The Central Islamic lands from the pre-Islamic times to the First World War*, Cambridge: Cambridge University Press.
Holt, P. M. (ed.) (1968): *Political and Social Change in Modern Egypt. Historical studies from the Ottoman conquest to the United Arab Republic*, Oxford: Oxford University Press.
Homsy, Gaston (1921): *Le Général Jacob et l'Expédition de Bonaparte en Egypte (1798–1801)*, Marseilles: J. Castanot.
Hopwood, Derek (1999): *Sexual Encounters in the Middle East: The British, the*

French and the Arabs, Reading: Ithaca Press.

Hourani, Albert (1991): *A History of the Arab peoples*, London: Faber and Faber.

Hourani, A. (1989): *Arabic Thought in the Liberal Age 1798–1830*, Cambridge: Cambridge University Press.

Houtsma, M. (1888): *Uit de Oostersche correspondentie van Th. Erpenius, Jac. Golius en Lev. Warner. Eene bijdrage tot de geschiedenis van de beoefening der Oostersche letteren in Nederland*, Amsterdam: J. Müller.

Hugon, Henri (1913): *Les Emblèmes des Beys de Tunis*, Paris: Ernest Leroux.

Humbert, Jean Pierre Louis (1819): *Anthologie Arabe, ou choix de poésies arabes inédites, traduites en français, avec le texte en regard, et accompagnées d'une version latine littérale*, Paris: Treuttel et Würtz.

Imbs, Paul *et al.* (1971–94): *Trésor de la Langue Française: dictionnaire de la langue du XIXe et du XXe siècle (1789–1960)*, 16 vols, Paris: Gallimard.

Jabre Mouawad, Ray 92001): *Lettres au Mont-Liban d'Ibn al-Qilāʿī (XVème siècle), publiées, traduites, commentées, précédées d'un aperçu historique du Mont-Liban aux XIVème–XVème siècles*, Paris: Paul Geuthner.

Jal, Auguste (1848): *Glossaire Nautique: repertoire polyglotte de termes de marine anciens et modernes*, 2 vols, Paris.

Jespersen, Otto (1912): *Growth and Structure of the English Language*, 2nd edn, Leipzig: B. G. Treubner.

[Jomard, Edme-François] (1831): 'Extrait d'une lettre adressée par le cheykh Refah, ancien élève de la mission égyptienne en France, à M. Jomard, Membre de l'Institut, etc. Kaire, 15 août 1831)', *Nouveau Journal Asiatique*, VIII (November), pp. 534–5.

Jomard, E.-F. (1828): 'L'école égyptienne de Paris', *Journal Asiatique*, 2, pp. 96–116.

Jomard, E-F. *et al.* (eds) (1821–30): *Description de l'Egypte ou Recueil des observations et des recherches qui ont été faites en Egypte pendant l'expédition de l'armée française*, 24 vols, Paris: Impr. C. L. F. Panckoucke.

Julien, Charles-André (1986): *Histoire de l'Algérie Contemporaine. I. La conquête et les débuts de la colonisation (1827–1871)*, Paris: Presses Universitaires de France.

Kahane, Henry and Renée, Andreas Tietze (1958): *The Lingua Franca in the Levant. Turkish nautical terms of Italian and Greek origin*, Urbana, IL: University of Illinois Press.

Kazimirski, A. de Biberstein (1860): *Dictionnaire Arabe-Français contenant toutes les racines de la langue arabe, leurs dérivés, tant dans l'idiome vulgaire que dans l'idiome littéral, ainsi que les dialectes d'Alger et de Maroc*, 2 vols, Paris: Maisonneuve et Cie.

Keddie, Nikki R. (ed.) (1972): *Scholars, Saints, and Sufis. Muslim religious institutions in the Middle East since 1500*, Berkeley: University of California Press.

Kennedy, Hugh (1986): *The Prophet and the Age of the Caliphates. The Islamic Near East from the sixth to the eleventh century*, London: Longman.

Kenny, Lorne M. (1967): "Alī Mubārak: Nineteenth century Egyptian

educator and administrator', *Middle East Journal*, 21, pp. 35–51.
Kenny, L. M. (1965): 'The Khedive Ismāʿīl's dream of civilization and progress', *Muslim World*, vol. LV, pp.143–55, 211–21.
Khoury, René (1978): 'Le mariage musulman du général Abdallah Menou', *Egyptian Historical Review*, XXV, pp. 65–93.
Al-Khozai, Mohamed A. (1984): *The Development of Early Arabic drama (1847–1900)*, London: Longman.
Köhbach, Manfred (1992): 'Çasar oder imperaṭor? – Zur Titulatur der römischen Kaiser durch die Osmanen nach dem Vertrag von Zsitvatorok (1606)', *Wiener Zeitschrift für die Kunde des Morgenlandes*, 82, pp. 223–34.
Kraïem, Mustafa (1973): *La Tunisie Précoloniale*, 2 vols, Tunis: Société Tunisienne de Diffusion.
Kreiser, Klaus (1995): 'Etudiants ottomans en France et en Suisse (1909–1912)', in D. Panzac (ed.), *Histoire Economique et Sociale de l'Empire Ottoman et de la Turquie (1326–1960)*, (Collection Turcica, vol. VIII), Paris: Peeters, pp. 843–54.
Laissus, Yves (2004): *Jomard, le dernier Egyptien*, Paris: Fayard.
Laissus, Y. (1998): *L'Egypte, une aventure savant 1798–1801*, Paris: Fayard.
Lane, William Edward (1923): *The Manners and Customs of the Modern Egyptians* (Everyman's Library, no. 315), London: J. M. Dent & Sons/ New York: E. P. Dutton & Co.
Lane, W. E. (1863–74): *Arabic-English Lexicon derived from the best and the most copious Eastern sources; comprising a very large number of words and significations omitted in the Kāmoos, with supplements to its abridged and defective explanations, ample grammatical and critical comments, and examples in prose and verse*, 5 vols, London, (vol 6-8, ed. Stanley Lane Poole, London, 1877-93).
Lane-Poole, Stanley (1877): *Life of Edward William Lane*, London: Williams and Norgate.
Laqueur, Walter Z. (ed.) (1958): *The Middle East in Transition: Studies in Contemporary History*, New York: Frederick A. Praeger.
Larousse, Pierre (ed.) (1866–76): *Grand Dictionnaire Universel du XIXe Siècle*, 15 vols (2 Sup., 1878–90), Paris: Larousse.
Laurens, Henri (1997): *L'Expédition d'Egypte, 1798–1801*, Paris: Editions du Seuil.
Lemoine, Jean-Gustave (1932): 'Les anciens procédés de calcul sur les doigts en Orient et en Occident', *Revue des Etudes Islamiques*, pp. 1–58.
Lévi-Provençal, E. (1953): *Histoire de l'Espagne Musulmane*, Paris: Maisonneuve.
Lewis, Bernard (1994): *The Muslim Discovery of Europe*, London: Phoenix.
Lewis, B. (1985), 'Les concepts islamiques de Révolution', *Le Retour de l'Islam*, Paris, pp. 51–67.
Lewis, B. (1971): *Race and Color in Islam*, New York: Harper and Row.
Lewis, B. (1969): *The Emergence of Modern Turkey*, 2nd edn, Oxford: Oxford University Press.

Lewis, B. (1964): *The Middle East and the West*, London: Weidenfeld and Nicolson.

Lewis, B. and P. M. Holt (eds) (1962): *Historians of the Middle East*, London: Oxford University Press.

Lewis B. (1953): 'Some observations on the significance of heresy in the history of Islam', *Studia Islamica*, I, pp. 43–63.

Livingston, John W. (1996): 'Western science and educational reform in the thought of Shaykh Rifaʿa al-Tahtawi', *International Journal of Middle East Studies*, 28, pp. 543–64.

Louca, Anouar (1989): 'Yaqub et les lumières', *REMMM*, no. 52/53, pp. 63–76.

Louca, A. (1970): *Voyageurs et Ecrivains Egyptiens en France au XIXème Siècle*, Paris: Didier.

Louca A. (1958): 'Joseph Agoub', *Cahiers d'Histoire Egyptienne*, IX:5–6, pp.187–201.

Louca A. (1953): 'Ellious Bocthor, sa vie et son œuvre', *Cahiers d'Histoire Egyptienne*, V:5–6, pp. 309–20.

Malet, Albert (1908): *Histoire Contemporaine, 1789–1900*, Paris: Hachette.

Marcel, H *et al.* (1907): *La Bibliothèque Nationale*, Paris.

Marsot, Afaf Lutfi al-Sayyid (1977): 'The wealth of the Ulama in late eighteenth century Cairo', in T. Naff and R. Owen (eds), *Studies in Eighteenth Century Islamic History*, Carbondale, pp. 205–16.

Marty, Paul (1935): 'Historique de la mission militaire française en Tunisie', *Revue Tunisienne*, pp. 171–207, 309–46.

Massé, André (1933): 'Les études arabes en Algérie (1830–1930)', *Revue Africaine*, 74, pp. 208–48.

Masson, Frédéric (1897–1919): *Napoléon et sa Famille*, 13 vols, Paris: P. Ollendorff.

Masson, F. (1881): 'Les Jeunes de Langues. Notes sur l'éducation dans un établissement des Jésuites au XVIIIe siècle', *Le Correspondant*, Nouvelle série, LXXXVIII.

McCarthy, Justin A. (1976): 'Nineteenth-century Egyptian population', *Middle Eastern Studies*, 12, pp. 1–39.

Messaoudi, Alain (2008): *Savants, conseillers, médiateurs : les arabisants et la France coloniale (vers 1830–vers 1930)*, Unpubl. PhD diss., Paris I Sorbonne.

Meyerhof, E. (1935): 'Esquisse d'histoire de la pharmacologie et de la botanique chez les Musulmans d'Espagne', *al-Andalus*, III, pp. 3–13.

Michaud (1854): *Biographie Universelle Ancienne et Moderne, ou Histoire par ordre alphabétique, de la vie publique et privée de tous les hommes qui se sont fait remarquer par leurs écrits, leurs actions, leurs talents, leurs vertus ou leurs crimes. Nouvelle édition, revue, corrigée et considérablement augmentée d'articles omis ou nouveaux*, 43 vols, Paris: C. Desplaces/Leipzig: G. A. Brockhaus.

Miquel, André (1967–80): *La Géographie Humaine du Monde Musulman jusqu'au milieu du 11ème siècle. I. Géographie et géographie humaine dans la littérature arabe des origines à 1050. II. Géographie arabe et représentation du monde: la terre et l'étranger. Le milieu naturel*, 3 vols, Paris/New York/The Hague: Mouton.

Miquel, A. (1975): 'Rome chez les géographes arabes', *Comptes rendus des séances de l'Académie des Belles-Lettres*, pp. 281–91.

Miquel, A. (1966): 'L'Europe occidentale dans la relation arabe de Ibrāhîm b. Ya'qûb', *Annales ESC*, vol. 21, pp. 1048-66.

Mollat, M. (1966): 'Ibn Batoutah et la mer', *Travaux et Jours*,18, pp. 53-70.

Monchicour, Charles (1929): *Documents Historiques sur la Tunisie: Relations inédites de Nyssen, Filippi et Calligaris (1788, 1829, 1834)*, Paris.

Monteil, Vincent (1960): *L'Arabe Moderne* (Etudes Arabes et Islamiques. Etudes et Documents, III), Paris: Klincksieck.

Moosa, Matti I. (1970): 'Early 19th-century printing and translation', *Islamic Quarterly*, XIV:4 (Oct.-Dec.), pp. 207–15.

Moreh, Shmuel (1990): 'The background of the mediaeval Arabic theatre: Hellenistic-Roman and Persan influences', *Jerusalem Studies in Arabic and Islam*, 13, pp. 295–329.

Morsy, Magali (1984): *North Africa 1800–1900. A survey from the Nile Valley to the Atlantic*, London: Longman.

Motzki, Harald (1979): *Dimma und Egalité. Die nichtmuslimischen Minderheiten Ägyptens in der zweiten Hälfte des 18. Jahrhunderts und die Expedition Bonapartes (1798–1801)*, Bonn: Selbstverlag des orientalischen Seminars.

Mzali, M. and J. Pignon (1934–40): 'Documents sur Khéreddine', *Revue Tunisienne*, 18 (1934:2), pp. 177–226; 19–20 (1934), pp. 347–96; 21 (1935:1), pp. 50–80; 22 (1935:2), pp. 209–33; 23–4 (1935:3–4), pp. 289–307; 26 (1936:2), pp. 223–54, 1937, pp.209–52, 409–32; 1938, pp. 79–153; 1940, pp. 71–107, 251–302.

Naaman, Antoine Y. (1965): *Les Lettres d'Egypte de Gustave Flaubert d'après les manuscrits autographes*, Paris: Nizet.

Nallino, C. A. (1944): *Raccolta di scritti editi e inediti. V. Astrologia – Astronomia-Geografia*, Rome: Istituto per l'Oriente.

Nallino, Maria (1966): '"Mirabilia" di Roma negli antichi geografi arabi', in *Studi in onore di Italo Siciliano*, Florence: Olschki, pp. 875–93.

Nallino, M. (1964): 'Un'ineditta descrizione araba di Roma', *Annali Istituto Orientale di Napoli*, vol.14, pp. 193–7.

Nasrallah, Joseph (1958): *L'Imprimerie au Liban*, Beirut: Harissa (Imprimerie de Saint Paul).

Netton, Ian Richard (1996): *Seek Knowledge. Thought and travel in the House of Islam*, Richmond: Curzon Press.

Netton, I. R. (ed.) (1993): *Golden Roads. Migration, pilgrimage and travel in mediaeval and modern Islam*, Richmond: Curzon Press.

Netton, I. R. (1984): *Muslim Neoplatonists: an introduction to the thought of the Brethren of Purity (Ikhwan al-Safa')*, London: Routledge.

Newman, D. L. (2002a): 'Myths and realities in Muslim Alterist discourse: Arab travellers in Europe in the age of the *Nahda* (19th c.)', *Chronos*, 5, pp. 7–76.

Newman, D. L. (2002b): 'The European influence on Arabic during the *Nahḍa*: lexical borrowing from European languages (*taʿrīb*) in 19th-century literature', *Arabic Language & Literature*, Vol. 5, no. 2, pp. 1–32.

Newman, D. L. (2001): 'Arab travellers to Europe until the end of the 18th century and their accounts: historical overview and themes', *Chronos*, 4, pp. 7–61.

Newman, D. L. (1998): *19th-Century Tunisian Travel Literature on Europe: vistas of a new world*, Unpublished PhD dissertation, London: School of Oriental and African Studies.

Nicolle, David (1978): 'Nizam. Egypt's army in the 19th century', *Army Quarterly*, 108, pp. 69–78.

Noël, Jean-François and Pierre de la Place (1823): *Leçons Françaises de Littératures et de Morale, ou Recueil, en prose et en vers, des plus beaux morceaux de notre langue dans la littérature des derniers siècles: avec des Préceptes de genres, et des Modèles d'exercices*, 2 vols, Paris: Le Normand Père.

Orani E. (1983): '"Nation", "patrie", "citoyen" chez Rifāʿa al-Tahtāwî et Khayr-al-Dīn al-Tounsi', *Mélanges de l'Institut Dominicain d'Etudes Orientales du Caire*, 156, pp. 169–90.

L'Orient des Provençaux dans l'Histoire, Marseilles: Archives Départementales, 1984.

Owen, Roger (1993): *The Middle East in the World Economy, 1800–1914*, London; I. B. Tauris.

Padwick, Constance E. (1923–25): 'Notes on the *jinn* and the *ghoul* in the peasant mind of Lower Egypt. Illustrated by transcripts of peasant tales taken from the lips of the fellāḥīn of the Menûfia Province, Lower Egypt', *Bulletin of the School of Oriental Studies*, III, pp. 421–46.

Panzac, Daniel (1989): 'Médecine révolutionnaire et révolution de la médecine dans l'Egypte de Muhammad Ali: le Dr. Clot-Bey', *REMMM*, no. 52–3, pp. 95–110.

Panzac, D. (1986): *Quarantaines et Lazarets: l'Europe et la peste de l'Orient*, Aix-en-Provence: Edisud.

Panzac, D. (1985): *La Peste dans l'Empire Ottoman*, Louvain: Peeters.

Parent-Lardeur, F. (1982), *Cabinets de Lecture. La lecture publique à Paris sous la Restauration*, Paris: Payot.

Paton, Archibald Andrew (1863): *A History of the Egyptian Revolution from the Period of the Mamelukes to the Death of Mohamed Ali: from Arab and European memoires, oral tradition and research*, 2 vols, London: Trübner.

Peled, M. (1979): 'Creative translation: towards the study of Arabic translations of Western literature since the 19th century', *Journal of Arabic Literature*, X, pp. 128–50.

Pérès, Henri (1957): 'L'Institut d'Egypte et l'œuvre de Bonaparte jugés par deux historiens arabes contemporains', *Arabica*, IV, pp. 113–30.

Pérès, H. (1937): *L'Espagne Vue par les Voyageurs Musulmans de 1610 à 1930*, Paris: Librairie d'Amérique et de l'Orient Adrien-Maisonneuve.

Pérès, H. (1935–1940): 'Voyageurs musulmans en Europe aux XIXe et XXe siècles', *Mémoires de l'Institut d'Archéologie Orientale du Caire*, LVXIII (*Mélanges Maspero*), III, pp.185–95.

Philipp, Thomas and Guido Schwald (1994): *A Guide to 'Abd al-Raḥmān al-Jabartī's History of Egypt*, Stuttgart: Franz Steiner (= first volume of *'Abd al-Raḥmān al-Jabartī*'s *History of Egypt*).

Philipp, Thomas (1985): *The Syrians in Egypt*, Stuttgart: Steiner-Verlag.

Plantet, Eugène (1930): *Les Consuls de France à Alger avant la Conquête, 1579–1830*, Paris: Hachette.

Polk, W. and R. L. Chambers (eds) (1968): *Beginnings of Modernization in the Middle East*, Chicago: Chicago University Press.

Pouillon, François, Jean Ferreux (Auteur), Lucette Valensi (eds) (2008): *Dictionnaire des orientalistes de langue française*, Paris: Karthala.

Quémeneur, Jean (1968): 'La Ruzname de M'hamed Belkhodja', *IBLA*, XXXI, pp. 17–44.

Quémeneur, J. (1967): 'Almanachs tunisiens', *IBLA*, no. 117, pp. 67–74.

Raphael, P. (1950): *Le Rôle du Collège Maronite Romain dans l'Orientalisme aux XVIIe et XVIIIe Siècles*, Beirut: Université Saint Joseph.

Raymond, André (1998): *Egyptiens et Français au Caire 1798–1801*, Cairo: IFAO.

Raymond, A. (1995): *Le Caire des Janissaires. L'apogée de la ville ottomane sous 'Abd al- Raḥmān Kathkudā*, Paris: CNRS.

Raymond, A. (1993): *Le Caire*, Paris: Fayard.

Raymond, A. & Gaston Wiet (1979): *Les marchés du Caire. Traduction annotée du texte de Maqrīzī*, Cairo: IFAO.

Raymond, A. (1973): *Artisans et Commerçants au Caire au XVIIIe Siècle*, 2 vols, Beirut: Imprimerie Catholique/IFAO.

Raymond, A. (1969): 'Les bains publics au Caire à la fin du XVIIIe siècle', *Annales Islamologiques*, 8, pp. 129–50.

Rebhan, Helga (1986): *Geschichte und Funktion einiger politischer Termini im Arabischen des 19. Jahrhunderts (1798–1882)*, Wiesbaden: Otto Harrassowitz.

Redhouse, James W. (1880): *Redhouse's Turkish Dictionary in Two Parts, English and Turkish, and Turkish and English, in which the Turkish words are represented in the Oriental character, as well as their correct pronunciation and accentuation shown in English letters*, 2nd ed. rev. Charles Wells, London.

Régnier, P. & A. F. Abdelnour (1989): *Les Saints-Simoniens en Egypte*, 1833–1851, Cairo: IFAO.

Reid, Donald Malcom (2002): *Whose Pharaohs? Archaeology, Museums and Egyptian National Identity from Napoleon to World War I*, Berkeley: University of California Press.

Reimer, Michael J. (1997): 'Contradiction and consciousness in 'Alī Mubarak's description of al-Azhar', *International Journal of Middle East Studies*, 29, pp. 53–69.

Reinaud, Joseph-Toussaint (1831): 'Notice des ouvrages arabes, persans et turcs imprimés en Egypte', *Journal Asiatique*, 8, 2 sér., pp. 333–41.

Renan, Ernest (1947–1952): *Œuvres Complètes*, 5 vols, ed. Henriette Psichari, Paris: Calmann-Lévy.

Ridley, Ronald T. (1998): *Napoleon's Proconsul in Egypt. The Life and Times of Bernardino Drovetti*, London: The Rubicon Press.

Rispler, V. (1991): 'Towards a new understanding of the term *bid'a*', *Der Islam*, 68, pp. 320-28.

Rivlin, Helen Anne B. (1961): 'The railway question in the Ottoman-Egyptian crisis of 1850–1852', *Middle East Journal*, 15:4, pp. 365–88.

Ruphy, Jean-François (1802): *Dictionnaire Abrégé François-Arabe, à l'usage de ceux qui se destinent au commerce du Levant*, Paris: Imprimerie de la République.

Salem, Elie (1965): 'Arab reformers and the reinterpretation of Islam', *The Muslim World*, LV, pp. 311–20.

Salmoné, Anthony H. (1890): *An Arabic-English Dictionary on a New System*, 2 vols, London: Trübner.

Sawaie, Mohammed (2000): 'Rifa^{c}a Rafi^c al-Tahtawi and His Contribution to the Lexical Development of Modern Literary Arabic', *International Journal of Middle East Studies*, 32: 3, pp. 395–410.

Sayili, A. (1960): *The Observatory in Islam*, Ankara: Turkish Historical Society.

Sauvaget, Jean (1948): *'Ahbār aṣ-ḥīn wa 'l-Hind. Relation de la Chine et de l'Inde*, Paris: Les Belles Lettres.

Savant, Jean (1949): *Les Mamelouks de Napoléon*, Paris: Calmann-Lévy.

Schacht, Joseph (1975): *The Origins of Muhammadan Jurisprudence*, Oxford: Oxford University Press.

Schacht, J. (1966): *An Introduction to Islamic Law*, Oxford: Oxford University Press.

Scheler, Auguste (1888): *Dictionnaire d'Etymologie Française d'après les résultats de la science moderne*, 3rd edn, Brussels: Th. Falk.

Schurchardt, H. (1909): 'Die Lingua Franca', *Zeitschrift für Romanische Philologie*, XXXIII:4, pp.441–61.

Sédillot, Louis-Amélie (1854): *Histoire des Arabes*, Paris: L. Hachette.

Sharabi, Hisham (1970): *Arab Intellectuals and the West: the formative years, 1875–1914*, Baltimore/London: Johns Hopkins Press.

Al-Sharqāwī, Maḥmūd (1960): 'Alī Moubarak et la civilisation européenne', *Revue du Caire*, XXIII:239–40, pp. 1–14.

Shaw, Stanford J. (1971): *Between Old and New: the Ottoman Empire under Sultan Selim III (1789–1807)*, Cambridge, MA: Harvard University Press.

Shboul, Ahmed (1979): *Al-Mas'ūdī and his World. A Muslim humanist and his interest in non-Muslims*, London: Ithaca.

Silvera, Alain (1980): 'The first Egyptian student mission to France under Muhammad Ali', *Middle East Studies*, XVI:2, pp. 1-22.

Silvera, A. (1971): 'Edme-François Jomard and Egyptian reforms in 1839', *Middle Eastern Studies*, VII:ii.

Smida, Mongi (1970): *Khéreddine. Ministre Réformateur, 1873–1877*, Tunis: Maison Tunisienne de l'Edition.

Somekh, S. (1984): 'Colloquialized fuṣḥā in modern Arabic prose fiction', *Jerusalem Studies in Arabic and Islam*, 16, pp. 176–94.

Spiro, Socrates (1895): *An Arabic-English Vocabulary of the Colloquial Arabic of Egypt, containing the vernacular idioms and expressions, slang phrases, etc. etc., used by the native Egyptians*, Cairo.

Sraïeb, Noureddine (1995): *Le Collège Sadiki de Tunis, 1875–1956. Enseignement et nationalisme*, Paris: CNRS.

Starkey, Paul and Janet (eds) (1998): *Travellers in Egypt*, London: I. B. Tauris.

Stephen, Leslie and Sidney Lee (1937–38): *The Dictionary of National Biography from the Earliest Times to 1900*, 21 vols/1 Sup., Oxford: Oxford University Press.

Stetkevych, Jaroslav (1970): *The Modern Arabic Literary Language. Lexical and stylistic developments* (Publication of the Center for Middle Eastern Studies, Number 6), Chicago: The University of Chicago Press.

Storey, Charles Ambrose (1939–97): *Persian Literature: a bio-bibliographical survey*, London: Luzac.

Sublet, Jacqueline (1971): 'La peste prise aux rêts de la jurisprudence. Le traité d'Ibn Ḥajar al- 'Asqalānī sur la peste', *Studia Islamica*, XXXIII, 141–49.

Tagher, Jacques (1951): 'Un agent de rapprochement entre l'Orient et l'Occident: Osman Noureddin Pacha', *Cahiers d'Histoire Egyptienne*, 3, pp. 392–405.

Tagher, J. (1950): 'Les locaux qui abritrèrent la mission scolaire à Paris existent toujours', *Cahiers d'Histoire Egyptienne*, II, pp. 333–36.

Tagher, J. (1949): 'Jacques de Valserre et la création du premier bureau égyptien d'information à Paris', *Cahiers d'Histoire Egyptienne*, I:3, pp. 221–29.

Thieme, Hugo P. (1933): *Bibliographie de la Littérature Française de 1800 à 1930*, 3 vols, Paris: Droz.

Tlili, Béchir (1974): *Les Rapports Culturels et Idéologiques entre l'Orient et l'Occident, en Tunisie, au XIXe siècle (1830–1880)*, Tunis: Université de Tunis.

Tlili, B. (1972a): 'La notion de *'umrān* dans la pensée tunisienne précoloniale', *Revue de l'Occident Musulman et de la Méditerranée*, 12, pp. 30–56.

Tlili, B. (1972b): 'Autour du réformisime tunisien du XIXe siècle. La notion de liberté dans la pensée de Hayr ad-Dīn (1810–1889)', 77/78, pp. 59–85.

Toledano, Ehud R. (1990): *State and Society in Mid-nineteenth-century Egypt* (Cambridge Middle East Library: 22), Cambridge: Cambridge University Press.

Van Krieken, Gerardus (1976): *Khayr al-Din et la Tunisie (1850–1881)*, Leiden: E. J. Brill.

Van Nieuwkerk, Karin (1995): *A Trade Like Any Other: Female Singers and Dancers in Egypt*, Austin: University of Texas.

Vaperau, Gustave (1893): *Dictionnaire Universel des Contemporains, contenant toutes les personnes notables de la France et des pays étrangers, avec leurs noms, prénoms, surnoms et pseudonymes, le lieu et la date de leur naissance, leur famille, leurs débuts, leur profession*, 6th edn, Paris: Hachette (Sup. Paris, 1895).

Vatikiotis, Peter (1991): *The History of Modern Egypt from Muhammad Ali to Mubarak*, 4th edn, London: Weidenfeld and Nicolson.

Versteegh, Kees (1997): *Landmarks in Linguistic Thought. III. The Arabic linguistic tradition*, London: Routledge.

Versteegh, K. (1977): *Greek Elements in Arabic Linguistic Thinking*, Leiden: E. J. Brill.

Von Grünebaum, G.E. (1945): 'As-Sakkaki on Milieu and Thought', in *Journal of the American Oriental Society*, 65, p. 62. American Oriental Society.

Vollers, Karl (1887–97): 'Beiträge zur Kenntnis der lebenden arabischen Sprache in Ägypten', *Zeitschrift der Deutschen Morgenländischen Gesellschaft*, 41 (1887), pp. 365–402; 50 (1896), pp. 607–57; 51 (1897), pp. 291–326, 343–64.

Vollers, K. (1893): 'Alī Pasha Mubārak', *Zeitschrift der Deutschen Morgenländischen Gesellschaft*, 47, pp. 720–22.

Wahrmund, Adolf (1870): *Handwörterbuch der arabischen und deutschen Sprachen*, 2 vols, Giessen: Ricker.

Wallis Budge, E. A. (1895): *The Nile. Notes for travellers in Egypt*, 4th edn, London: Thos. Cook & Son (Egypt) Ltd.

Wassef, Amin Sami (1975): *L'Information et la Presse Officielle en Egypte jusqu'à la fin de l'occupation française*, Cairo: IFAO.

Wehr, Hans (1976): *A Dictionary of Modern Written Arabic*, ed. J. Milton Cowan, 3rd edn, Ithaca N.Y.: Spoken Language Services.

Wehr H. (1943): "Entwicklung und traditionelle Pflege der arabischen Schriftsprache in der Gegenwart", *Zeitschrift der Deutschen Morgenländischen Gesellschaft*, 97, pp. 16–46.

Wehr, H. (1934): *Die Besonderheiten des heutigen Hocharabischen mit Berücksichtigung der Einwirkung der europäischen Sprachen*, Berlin: Reichsdruckerei.

Wensinck, Arent Jan *et al.* (1992): *Concordance et Indices de la Tradition*

Musulmane. Les six livres, le Musnad d'al-Dārimī, le Muwaṭṭa' de Mālik, le Musnad de Aḥmad b. Ḥanbal, 2nd edn, 4 vols, Leiden: E. J. Brill.

Wielandt, Rotraud (1980): *Das Bild der Europäer in der modernen arabischen Erzähl- und Theaterliteratur*, Beirut/Wiesbaden: Deutsche Morgenländische Gesellschaft.

Wiet, Gaston (1948): 'Le voyage d'Ibrahim Pacha en France et en Angleterre, d'après les archives européennes du Palais d'Abdine', *Cahiers d'Histoire Egyptienne*, I:1, pp. 78- 126.

Wright, W. (1981): *A Grammar of the Arabic Language. Translated from the German of Caspari and edited with numerous additions and corrections*, 3rd edn (rev. by W. Robertson Smith and M. J. de Goeje), Cambridge: Cambridge University Press.

Yapp, M. E. (1991): *A History of the Near East. The making of the modern Near East, 1792-1923*, Harlow: Longman.

Yared, Nazek Saba (1996): *Arab Travellers and Western Civilization*, London: Saqi.

Young, M. J. L., J. D. Latham and R. B. Serjeant (eds) (1990): *The Cambridge History of Arabic Literature. Religion, learning and science in the 'Abbasid period*, Cambridge: Cambridge University Press.

Zeki Validi Togan, A. (1937–8): 'Bīrūnī's picture of the world', *Memoirs of the Archaeological Survey of India*, No. 53, pp. 90–104.

Zenker, Julius Theodor (1866): *Türkish-Arabisch-Persisches Handwörterbuch. Dictionnaire Turc-arabe-persan*, 2 vols, Leipzig: Wilhelm Engelmann.

Zolondek, L. (1965): 'French revolution in Arabic literature', *The Muslim World*, 57, pp. 202–11.

Zolondek L. (1964): 'al-Tahtāwī and political freedom', *Muslim World*, 54, pp. 90–97.

Index